The Open
Housing
Question

The Open Housing Question

Race and Housing in Chicago, 1966-1976

Brian J.L. Berry
Harvard University

Ballinger Publishing Company ● Cambridge, Massachusetts
A Subsidiary of Harper & Row, Publishers, Inc.

International Standard Book Number: 0-88410-429-X

Library of Congress Catalog Card Number: 79-14912

Printed in the United States of America

Library of Congress Cataloging in Publication Data

Berry, Brian Joe Lobley, 1934–
    The open housing question.

    Includes bibliographical references.
    1. Discrimination in housing—Illinois—Chicago—History. I. Title.
HD7304.C4B47   301.5'4   79-14912
ISBN 0-88410-429-X

A house is a concrete symbol
of what the person is worth.

Kenneth B. Clark, *Dark Ghetto*

Contents

List of Tables

List of Figures

Preface

During the summer of 1966, Chicago's racial problems exploded into headlines across the country. The conflict centered on racial segregation in housing, as attempts were made to eliminate constraints on the housing choice of Chicago's black population. The Rev. Dr. Martin Luther King, Jr., of the Southern Christian Leadership Conference, joined with the Chicago Freedom Movement in a series of marches and demonstrations in and around Chicago. At a July 10 mass rally Dr. King said, "For our primary target we have chosen housing . . . we shall cease to be accomplices to a housing system of discrimination, segregation and degradation. We shall begin to act as if Chicago were an open city."[1] Rioting broke our on the city's west side later in July, and 3,000 National Guardsmen were called out to restore order. But hostility mounted and violence continued as the marchers pressed on. Faced by an impending crisis of even greater scale than the July riots, The Chicago Conference on Religion and Race convened what since has become known as the "summit meeting," to which came persons representing government, religion, labor, civil rights, business, and other sections of the community. The agenda for the gathering contained only one item: to find the means to ensure equality of housing opportunity in the Chicago metropolitan area.

The late August product of this meeting was the Summit Agreement, which listed the specific commitments made by the participating groups to contribute to programs of education and action to

1. *Chicago Sun-Times,* July 11, 1966.

end the dual housing market in the metropolitan area. To help implement these commitments, the document also provided for the creation of an organization to be called The Leadership Council for
Metropolitan Open Communities. This new organization was, in the
words of the Summit Agreement:

> To accept responsibility for the education and action programs necessary
> to achieve fair housing.
> To be headed by a board consisting of recognized leaders from govern-
> ment, commerce, industry, finance, religion, real estate, labor, the civil
> rights movement, and the communications media, with sufficient
> stature to formulate a strong and effective program and to provide
> adequate financing and staff to carry out that program.
> To make a major effort to educate citizens of the metropolitan area in the
> fundamental principle that freedom of choice in housing is the right of
> every citizen and in their obligations to abide by the law and recognize
> the rights of others regardless of race, religion, or nationality.
> To assist in the drafting of fair-housing laws and ordinances.
> To make clear the stake that commerce, industry, banking, real estate, and
> labor have in the peaceful achievement of fair housing.
> To emphasize that the metropolitan housing market is a single market.
> To promote the development of fair-housing centers.
> To set up specific goals for achievement of fair housing in the Chicago
> metropolitan area.
> To regularly review the performance of the program undertaken by gov-
> ernmental and nongovernmental groups, take appropriate action
> thereon, and provide for public reports.

The Leadership Council was formally established on December 6,
1966. The year that followed was spent organizing, appointing a
director (Edward M. Holmgren) and staff, finding quarters, and
charting program initiatives. Then, in April 1968, the Leadership
Council submitted "A Proposal to Test the Effectiveness of a Market
System Fair Housing Service for Metropolitan Chicago" to the
United States Department of Housing and Urban Development. Under the terms of this proposal, tests would be made to determine if:
"(a) the existing real estate market system could be modified so as
to serve nonwhite persons who are actively seeking housing in a
metropolitan area: and (b) through the use of proposed techniques,
including assistance to nonwhite persons in acquiring housing on a
nondiscriminatory basis, the market system might be so altered that,
after termination of the fair housing service the system would operate more effectively with markedly reduced racial restrictions."[2]

2. *Leadership Council for Metropolitan Open Communities Newsletter* no. 7
(August 1968): 2.

In its proposal, the Leadership Council emphasized that "Because the most influential civic leadership in the metropolitan area, including representatives of the real estate, home-building and mortgage-lending industry created the Leadership Council and is part of it, the Council is in a unique position to obtain cooperation from the real estate industry."[3] The council proposed to provide a free, centralized source of all nondiscriminatory sale and rental housing in the Chicago metropolitan area. To develop housing listings, the housing service would use newspaper advertising; work with fair housing contacts in the metropolitan area; ask real estate boards, brokers, and management agents to provide listings on a regular basis; monitor housing units covered by local fair housing ordinances; and undertake promotional campaigns beamed at owners and landlords whose property was not covered by such fair housing ordinances. Special efforts were to be made to work with brokers and management agents whose clientele was mainly black and to enlist the aid of black brokers to work with suburban employers of blacks to aid those persons interested in living near their work. In addition, the service was to maintain complete and current information on all available nondiscriminatory housing in the Chicago area and to provide a biweekly listing of selected housing units to cooperating brokers, agents, groups, and individuals.

Based upon the proposal, a contract was granted the council by the Department of Housing and Urban Development (HUD) to begin work in the summer of 1968. The initial grant covered a one year period, but was subject to renewal that ultimately extended it for an additional five years.

The Center for Urban Studies at the University of Chicago received a contract at the same time to enable me to evaluate the effectiveness of the Leadership Council's activities and to provide feedback to the council's staff on whether this was a useful social experiment. Evaluation began with the receipt of the HUD financing by the Leadership Council on August 1, 1968, and continued for six years thereafter.

In this book, I draw together the evaluation reports and the results of related research conducted simultaneously with the evaluation and, from the perspective of a later time and a more distant place, attempt to assess why the Leadership Council's efforts were unable to achieve their principal objectives. The materials in Part I draw upon my reports to HUD and to the Leadership Council. The com-

3. "A Proposal to Test the Effectiveness of a Market System Fair Housing Service for Metropolitan Chicago," Leadership Council for Metropolitan Open Communities, April 5, 1968.

munity studies and basic research that were undertaken and that enabled Parts 2 and 3 to be written were supported by The National Science Foundation.

As in all such efforts, many others contributed to the work, and to each and all I am indebted. Special words of thanks have to go to Katherine Barry Smith, who kept the evaluation on target, as well as to Darrel J. Vorwaller, Robert Koenig, Carole A. Goodwin, Carol Corden, Steven Golant, Robert Lake, Jack Meltzer, Lee Margerum, Judith Favia, and Robert Bednarz, each of whom made important contributions to different phases of the work. Edward Holmgren, Kale Williams, William Caruso, David Schucker, and many other staff members of the Leadership Council were both generous of their time and gracious about the evaluation. For what appears here, however, I take full responsibility.

May 1979   Brian J.L. Berry
Cambridge, Mass.

✳ *Part I*

The Leadership Council's Programs
—An Appraisal

※　*Chapter 1*

Baseline Conditions in 1968

Chicago's black population had not always lived in segregated residential neighborhoods. In 1898, only a quarter of the city's 30,000 blacks resided in areas that were more than 50 percent black and over 30 percent lived in areas that were at least 95 percent white.[1] As late as 1910, blacks were less highly segregated from native whites than were Italian immigrants.[2]

It was not until the early twentieth century that segregation was forced on the black population of Chicago. Increased residential separation of the city's black and white populations accompanied mass movement of blacks to the North during World War I as blacks not only became more visible but also offered more competition in the job market. In 1910, Chicago's black population had been 44,000, whereas by 1920 it had risen to 110,000. In the same period, there was a 21 percent increase of the white population, including foreign immigrants. Most of the increase occurred in eighteen months in 1917-1918, when an estimated 50,000 blacks arrived in Chicago.[3]

These blacks had left the South in search of increased opportunity in wartime industry and in the face of worsening race relations in that region—recall that the Ku Klux Klan had been reestablished in

1. Paul Cressy, "Succession of Cultural Groups in the City of Chicago" (Ph.D. dissertation, University of Chicago, 1930), p. 93.
2. Stanley Lieberson, "Comparative Segregation and Assimilation of Ethnic Groups" (Ph.D. dissertation, University of Chicago, 1960), pp. 176-79.
3. Chicago Commission on Race Relations, *The Negro in Chicago. A Study of Race Relations and a Race Riot in 1919* (New York: Arno Press and the New York Times, 1968).

1915—but, arriving in Chicago, they were forced to live in increasingly segregated neighborhoods as racial fears increased among the white population. Many methods were used to achieve racial separation: violence; activities of neighborhood organizations such as the Hyde Park Improvement Protective Club, which "induced" real estate agents to develop dual listings to confine blacks to designated Negro Districts and even proposed that the city enact a Residential Segregation Ordinance; and the general acquiescence or active support of the majority of the white community.[4] A major race riot occurred in 1919, and then, to cement the racial fears of Chicago's white community, in 1919 and 1920 the city's *Property Owners' Journal* forcefully advanced the idea that Negroes destroy property values.[5] One result was that much of the housing that was built was protected by racially restrictive covenants. As a consequence, after World War I, Chicago's growing black population became progressively more highly segregated and the housing market lapsed into duality. White hostility, boycotts, violence, and the institutionalization of white attitudes in the practices of the real estate industry, effectively limited the housing choice of the city's blacks, forcing them to live in a limited "black belt." In response, the growing Negro community turned inward and created a "black metropolis."[6] In 1920, 11.3 percent of Chicago's black population lived in tracts with less than a 10 percent black population. By 1950 only 2.8 percent and by 1960 only 1.5 percent of the city's blacks were in this position. Conversely, in 1920 none of Chicago's blacks lived in tracts that were more than 90 percent black; in 1950 66.9 percent did so.[7] Of the eleven metropolitan areas in the United States with black communities of over 200,000, Chicago in 1960 manifested the greatest degree of racial segregation.[8]

4. Allan H. Spear, *Black Chicago. The Making of a Negro Ghetto 1890-1920* (Chicago: University of Chicago Press, 1967).

5. Chicago Commission on Race Relations, pp. 120-22.

6. St. Clair Drake and Horace Cayton, *Black Metropolis* (New York: Harper & Row, 1962). Also see Talcott Parsons and Kenneth B. Clark, eds., *The Negro American* (Boston: Beacon Press, 1966), p. 43.

7. Pierre de Vise, *Chicago Widening Color Gap* (Chicago: Inter-university Social Research Committee, 1967), p. 84.

8. Kenneth B. Clark, *Dark Ghetto* (New York: Harper & Row, 1965), p. 23. Also Karl E. Taeuber and Alma F. Taeuber, *Negroes in Cities* (Chicago: Aldine Publishing Company, 1965). "Case Studies of 12 local [public housing] programs were included in the report. Each city was given a fictitious name, but 'Babylon' clearly referred to Chicago. . . . According to the report, 'the entire program represents an accommodation with the extreme pattern of racial segregation in Babylon. The index of racial segregation in Babylon is one of the highest in the nation.'" *Chicago Sun-Times*, November 26, 1968.

SPREAD OF THE GHETTO, 1920-1960

In the intervening years the city's black population grew and along with it the physical limits of the ghetto, but the dual housing market permitted the Negro housing supply to expand only by outright transfer of property from the white housing market to the black housing market, incrementally, on a block-by-block basis involving "invasion" and "succession" at the ghetto margins.

Figure 1-1 shows the sequence of expansion between 1920 and 1960. Note how limited the black belt was until 1950. Table 1-1 portrays the result in 1960, but understates the segregation of blacks by using the census "nonwhite" category of that year, since other nonwhites tended to have greater flexibility than blacks in their housing choice. Even with that, only 3 percent of the city's white population, but 93 percent of the nonwhite population, lived in areas 50 percent or more black in 1960, thus emphasizing the sharpness of separation of black and white in the city.

RACIAL DISTRIBUTION IN 1960 IF
CHICAGO'S HOUSING MARKET
HAD BEEN COLORBLIND

One might reasonably ask what the residential distribution of blacks and whites might have been in 1960 if Chicago's housing market had been colorblind rather than lapsing into duality after World War I. Let us suppose that the geography of household incomes remained the same and that there were no changes in the income distribution of blacks and whites. The question might then be asked: What would the residential distribution of blacks have been if the proportion of blacks in a particular income group living in a particular census tract were the same as the proportion of blacks in that income group in the metropolitan area as a whole? The answer may be derived by obtaining the income-standardized geographic distribution of the black population, as follows:

To repeat, the distribution of households by income class (e.g., $5,000-$5,999, $6,000-$6,999, etc.) within each census tract regardless of race is taken as given. Likewise, the proportion of blacks and whites in each of these income classes in the metropolitan area as a whole is taken as given. The intermixture potential of a tract is computed by assuming that in a colorblind housing market the proportional black-white split of families in any income category in any census tract is the same as the proportional black-white split of all families in that category in the entire metropolitan area.

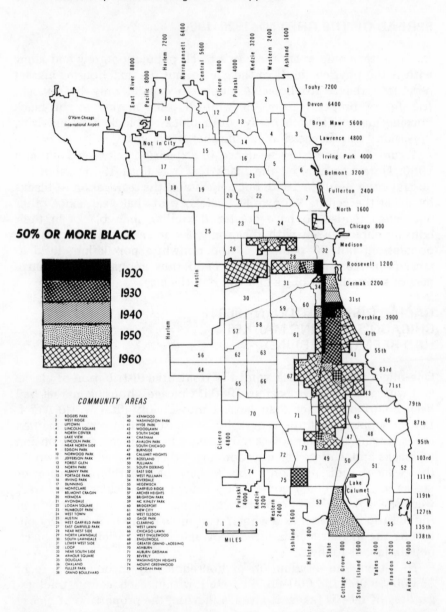

Figure 1-1.   Growth of Black Residential Areas in the City of Chicago, 1920–1960.

Table 1-1.   Racial Intermixture in Chicago, 1960.

Percentage of Census Tract Population Nonwhite	Percentage of the White Population	Percentage of the Nonwhite Population
Under 1.0	85.8	0.6
1 - 9.9	6.8	0.9
10 - 29.9	3.9	3.2
30 - 49.9	1.0	2.3
50 - 74.9	1.5	8.6
75 - 89.9	1.0	19.1
90 - 97.4	0.4	27.7
97.5-100.0	0.1	37.9

Symbolically, if there are m census tracts and n income categories and h_{ij} represents the number of families of tract i in income category j, the tractwise distribution of families by income can be arrayed in a matrix as follows:

$$h_{11}\ h_{12}\ h_{13}\ \ldots h_{1n} \qquad \Sigma_n h_{1n} = H_{1.}$$

$$h_{21}\ h_{22}\ h_{23}\ \ldots h_{1n}$$

$$\vdots \qquad\qquad \vdots$$

$$h_{m1}\ h_{m2}\ h_{m3}\ \ldots h_{mn}$$

$$H_{.1}$$

A row sum indicates the number of families in a tract (e.g., $\Sigma_m h_{m1} = H_{.1}$ in tract 1), whereas a column sum indicates the total number of families in an income category (e.g., $\Sigma_m h_{m1} = H_{.1}$ in category 1). The latter, for the metropolitan area, is composed of white and black parts ($H_1 = W_{.1} + B_{.1}$), and therefore the mix coefficient $\mu_1 = B_{.1}/H_{.1}$ is the metropolitanwide proportion of families in income category 1 who are black. Thence $\mu_1 h_{11}$ is the expected number of black families of income category 1 in tract 1, $\mu_2 h_{12}$ of category 2 in tract 1, and so forth. Therefore $\Sigma \mu_n h_{1n} = \hat{B}_1$ is the expected number of black families in tract 1, and $100\hat{B}_{1.}/H_{1.}$ is the expected black percentage, $\hat{P}_{1.}$. The difference between the actual black percentage $P_{1.}$ and the expected $P_{1.}$ is a measure of the extent of segregation in the housing market.

Figure 1-2 shows the distribution of the black population in

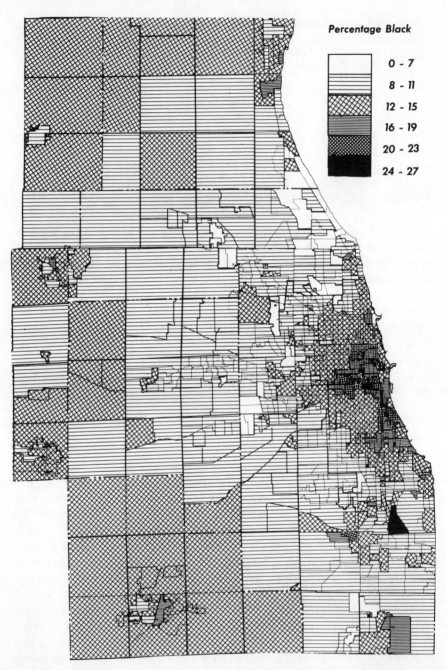

Figure 1-2. Distribution of the Black Population in a Colorblind Housing Market.

metropolitan Chicago as it might have been in 1960 if the above conditions obtained. The greatest black concentrations would have been only 27 percent of any tract population, and the least would have been around 10 percent. Figure 1-3 portrays the changes that would have been required in the actual spatial distribution of the black population in 1960 to achieve income-standardized equality. Ghetto concentrations would have had to be reduced by 60 to 80 percent, and the black population of the suburban areas would have had to be increased to 10 percent of the total population. This serves to refute one commonly heard argument, that it was income differences that were in the main responsible for the pattern of ghettoization. The reasons, instead, reside in some interacting mixture of prejudicial discrimination against blacks by homesellers, apartment owners, and their agents and the preference of many black families for residential exclusivity.

Such reasons are not hard to find. Certainly, through the 1950's there was deeply embedded institutional racism that both stemmed from and supported individual prejudice. Before World War II, the duality was built into federal practice in the concept of neighborhood homogeneity when the Federal Housing Administration (FHA) issued its 1938 *Underwriting Manual* that emphasized both the presumed importance of stability and the perils of change:

> Areas surrounding a location are investigated to determine whether incompatible racial and social groups are present, for the purpose of making a prediction regarding the probability of the location being invaded by such groups. If a neighborhood is to retain stability, it is necessary that properties shall continue to be occupied by the same social and racial classes. A change in social or racial occupancy generally contributes to instability and a decline in values.[9]

Clearly, the federal government was saying that we should accept the conclusions of the leading real estate analysts of the time, for example Homer Hoyt, who wrote:

> If the entrance of a colored family into a white neighborhood causes a general exodus of the white people it is reflected in property values. Except in the case of Negroes and Mexicans, however, these racial and national barriers disappear when the individuals in the foreign nationality groups rise in the economic scale or conform to the American standards of living. . . . While the ranking given below may be scientifically wrong

9. United States Federal Housing Administration, *Underwriting Manual* (Washington, D.C.: United States Government Printing Office, 1938), Par. 937.

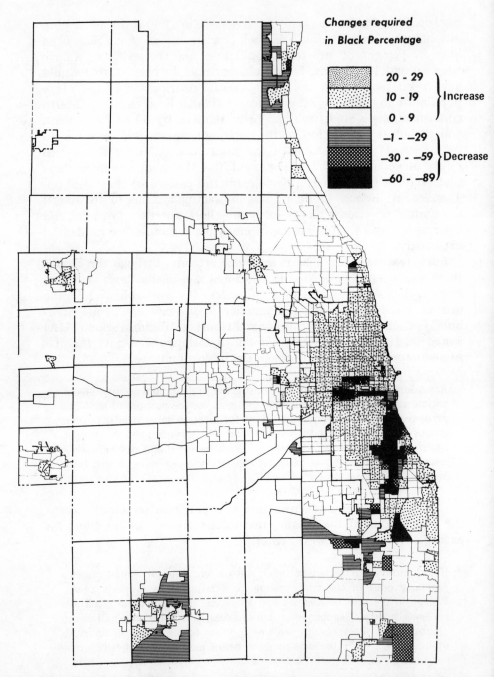

Figure 1-3. Redistribution of the Black Population Required to Achieve Income-Standardized Equality.

from the standpoint of inherent racial characteristics, it registers an opinion or prejudice that is reflected in land values; it is the ranking of races and nationalities with respect to their beneficial effect upon land values. Those having the most favorable effect come first in the list and those exerting the most detrimental effect appear last. . . .

1. English, Germans, Scotch, Irish, Scandinavians
2. North Italians
3. Bohemians or Czechoslovakians
4. Poles
5. Lithuanians
6. Greeks
7. Russian Jews of the lower class
8. South Italians
9. Negroes
10. Mexicans[10]

The revised (1947) FHA *Underwriting Manual* did little to alleviate the pressures inevitably placed upon the black community by such authoritative conclusions: "The tendency of user groups to seek compatible conditions can sustain and enhance, diminish, or destroy neighborhood desirability. Neighborhoods constituted of families that are congenial . . . generally exhibit strong appeal and stability.[11] And to ensure that there should be no doubt about what was being said, the manual went on to say:

If a mixture of user groups is found to exist it must be determined whether the mixture will render the neighborhood less desirable to present and prospective occupants. If the occupancy of the neighborhood is changing from one user group to another, or if the areas adjacent to the immediate neighborhood are occupied by a user group dissimilar to the typical occupants of the subject neighborhood or a change in occupancy is imminent or probable any degree of risk is reflected in the rating.[12]

and later:

Protective convenants are essential to the sound development of proposed residential areas since they regulate the use of the land and provide a basis for the development of harmonious, attractive neighborhoods suitable and desirable to the user groups forming the potential markets.[13]

10. Homer Hoyt, *One Hundred Years of Land Values in Chicago* (Chicago: University of Chicago Press, 1933), pp. 315–316.
11. United States Federal Housing Administration, *Underwriting Manual* (Washington, D.C.: United States Government Printing Office, 1947), par. 1320 (1).
12. Ibid., par. 1320(2).
13. Ibid., par. 1354(1).

In 1948, the United States Supreme Court handed down a decision that restrictive covenants used for discrimination on the basis of race were unconstitutional.[14] However, segregationist practices continued in many areas of housing. For example, it was not until July 1, 1969, that "the Chicago Housing Authority was ordered [by U.S. District Court Judge Richard B. Austin] to build 75 percent of all new public housing in white areas of the city and suburbs in order to remedy its past practices of racial segregation."[15]

GHETTO SPREAD, 1960-1968

The block-by-block process of ghetto expansion continued after 1960 and can be traced in shifting racial head counts in the city's public schools. Figure 1-4 identifies the principal zones of neighborhood transition between 1963 and 1968, and Figure 1-5, the resulting racial composition of the schools in 1968. The gradient of racial mix in schools lying between the ghetto and the city's white communities, to be seen in Figure 1-5 and the wavelike pattern of neighborhood change suggested by Figure 1-4 bespeak of a ghetto expansion process involving at least the first three of the four stages that together comprise the classical cycle of succession described by Chicago's urban ecologists:[16]

1. *Penetration*—the stage of initial entry of Negroes.
2. *Invasion*—takes place when substantial numbers of Negroes move in.
3. *Consolidation*—continued increase in numbers and in the proportion of Negroes.
4. *Piling up*—increasing numbers after virtually complete Negro occupancy has been achieved.[17]

Because the incoming black population tends to be younger, with more school children, than the outgoing white population, racial

---

14. Shelley v. Kramer, 334 U.S. 1, 1948.

15. *Chicago Sun-Times*, (July 2, 1969. Prior to Judge Austin's ruling, the program of the Chicago Housing Authority fostered de facto segregation because public housing projects were of two kinds—low income housing in black communities serving only black families and a limited number of projects serving the elderly in all white areas. The effect of the Austin decision was to pave the way for integration in public housing projects.

16. See Otis Dudley Duncan and Beverly Duncan, *The Negro Population of Chicago. A Study of Residential Succession* (Chicago: University of Chicago Press, 1957).

17. Ibid., p. 115. See pp. 118-119 of that work for a classification of census tracts (in lieu of neighborhoods) by these stages.

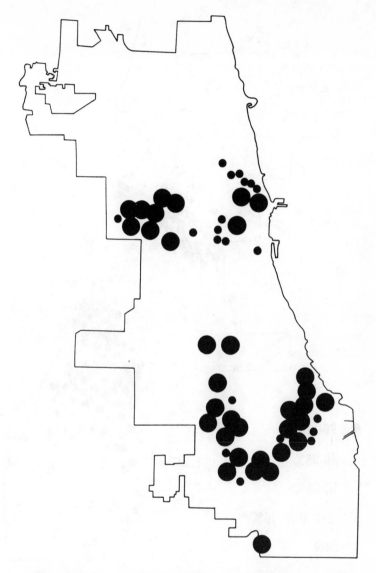

● **More than 20% increase in the percentage figure**

• **School headcount increased by 10-20%**

Figure 1-4. Chicago Public Schools with Major Increases in Black Racial Percentage, 1963–1968.

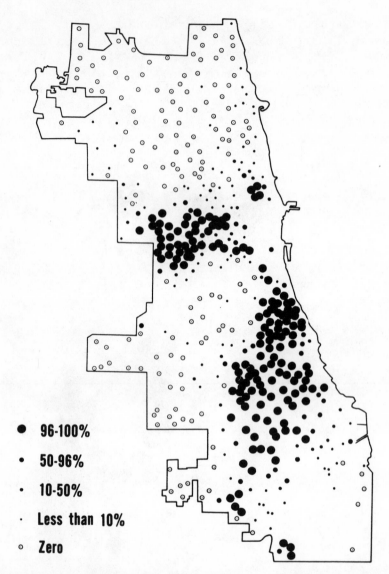

96-100%

50-96%

10-50%

Less than 10%

Zero

Figure 1-5. Percentage of the Enrollment of Each of Chicago's Public Elementary Schools that was Black in 1968.

head counts in the schools tend to overstate the actual pace of population transition somewhat, but the relationship between the two is simple.[18] Thus, a neighborhood map of racial head counts in the

18. The equation $B = -0.04 + 0.90E$, where B is the proportion of the population black and E is the proportion of public elementary school enrollment that is black, yielded the best fit in 1970 ($R^2 = 0.93$).

public elementary schools produced from data made available by the Chicago Board of Education each fall (Figure 1-6) can be translated immediately into a map of ghetto expansion (Figure 1-7). This map represents the 1968 baseline against which the evaluation proceeded.

Yet a baseline is but a snapshot of a continuing tide, and it is the tide that is the active process. In 1950 there had been only 114,000 housing units available to the 500,000 blacks living in Chicago's black belt. Over half of these were in poor physical condition, and

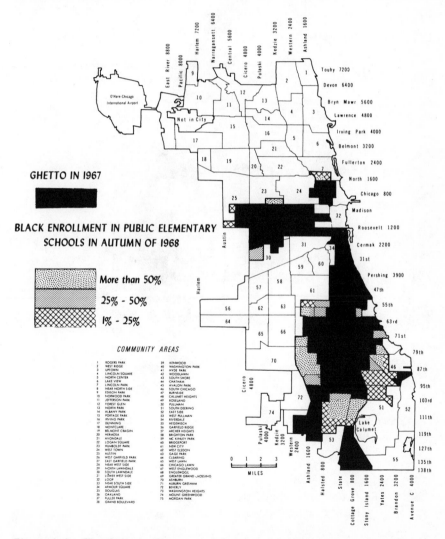

Figure 1-6. The Chicago Ghetto, and Communities Experiencing Black Expansion, in 1968.

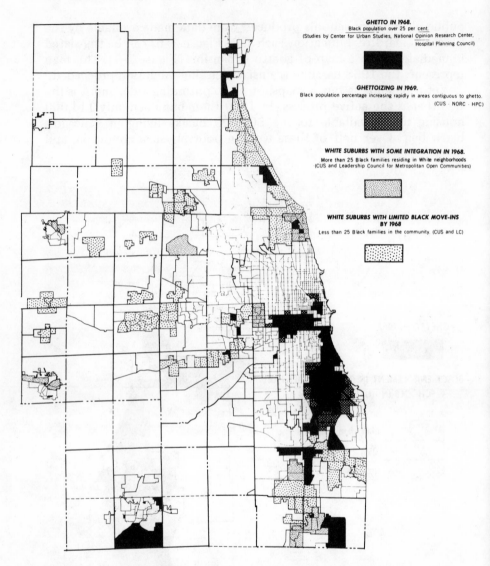

GHETTO IN 1968.
Black population over 25 per cent.
(Studies by Center for Urban Studies, National Opinion Research Center,
Hospital Planning Council)

GHETTOIZING IN 1969.
Black population percentage increasing rapidly in areas contiguous to ghetto.
(CUS · NORC · HPC)

WHITE SUBURBS WITH SOME INTEGRATION IN 1968.
More than 25 Black families residing in White neighborhoods
(CUS and Leadership Council for Metropolitan Open Communities)

**WHITE SUBURBS WITH LIMITED BLACK MOVE-INS
BY 1968**
Less than 25 Black families in the community. (CUS and LC)

Figure 1-7. The Assessment Baseline: Racial Status and Trends in Metropolitan
Chicago in 1968.

barely 13,000 were owner occupied. Crowding was severe, and the vacancy rate was only 1 percent. By 1960, close to 20,000 of the worst units had been demolished, but physical expansion of the ghetto had doubled the black housing supply to 233,000 units (34, 600 owner occupied), while the black population had increased only to 800,000. As a consequence, the vacancy rate in the ghetto had risen to 4.6 percent, the average number of persons per dwelling unit had fallen from 4.4 to 3.4, and the proportion of units in poor physical condition had dropped to a quarter of the total supply.

This march continued after 1960. Within the 1964 ghetto limits, 330,000 housing units were available for black occupancy, while within the 1967 ghetto limits, the number had grown to 360,000, with an additional 120,000 within the transitional areas of that time, for a total of 480,000 units theoretically available to black residents at a time when the black population was estimated to be approximately one million. A similar although much more modest increase in the ghetto housing stock took place in suburbia. In two decades, Chicago's black population approximately doubled, but ghetto expansion had increased black housing opportunities almost four-fold! This is an important fact to keep in mind in what follows. We shall return to it later when we ask why it was that so many of the Leadership Council's programs failed to change the essential pattern of residential separation that emerged after World War I and find it to be because there were apparently so few black families interested in moving into white suburbia, basically there were no black brokers willing to move their base of operation from the areas of active ghetto expansion, and because there were so many suburban alternatives available to whites.

✱ *Chapter 2*

An Equal Opportunity Housing Service

Things were changing in the 1960s, but not fast enough for
the city's civil rights advocates. The acceleration of ghetto
spread did nothing to ameliorate the profound dualism
that existed in the city's housing market, leading some to react with
despair:

in many significant ways, remarkably little has changed since 1920. Increased numbers had vastly expanded the ghetto, but had not changed its
basic structure. Negroes were still unable to obtain housing beyond the
confines of the ghetto, and within the black belt the complex of separate
institutions and organizations that had first developed between 1890 and
1920 continued to serve an isolated Negro populace. . . . The same restrictions that had limited Negro opportunities in the early twentieth century
still operated. In fact, four civil rights bills, dozens of court decisions, and
thousands of brave words about Negro rights had barely touched the life
of Chicago's Negroes. It remained as constricted as it had been two generations earlier. And the bitter hostility of the residents of Gage Park,
Belmont-Cragin, and Cicero toward Dr. King's marches demonstrated
that thousands of white Chicagoans were still determined to preserve the
status quo. . . . No other ethnic enclave in Chicago had changed so little
over the past fifty years. While the city's Irish, Polish, Jewish, and Italian
sections had broken down or developed new forms in the suburbs, the Negro ghetto remained much as it had been—cohesive, restrictive, and largely
impoverished. . . . From its inception, the Negro ghetto was unique among
the city's ethnic enclaves. It grew in response to an implacable white hostility that has not basically changed. In this sense it has been Chicago's

only true ghetto, less the product of voluntary development within than of external pressures from without.[1]

It was in this context that the Leadership Council proposed to conduct its experimental program. The council contended that it was possible to develop an equal opportunity housing service that would utilize and at the same time alter the marketing system so as to eliminate its racial restrictions. They further believed that reforming the system instead of creating a competing one would be more effective in expanding housing opportunities for nonwhites in the long run.

Therefore, the Leadership Council proposed to operate, for three years, a program that they believed would effect these desired changes. The service would provide an interim means of assisting Negro homeseekers to secure access to nondiscriminatory housing in the Chicago metropolitan area. They believed that the program would reform the then existing real estate system as to make the interim service unnecessary at the end of the three year period.

At the same time, the council entered into a contract with the Center for Urban Studies of the University of Chicago to provide an independent evaluation of the effectiveness of the service. Periodic feedback was to be provided to the council on whether its activities were making a difference to black homeseekers, and at the end of the three year period, the center was to report on whether the principal objectives of the council's program (reforming the existing real estate system by eliminating its racial restrictions; expanding nondiscriminatory housing opportunities for black homeseekers) had been achieved.

THE APPROACH

Previously, fair housing programs in Chicago and elsewhere had worked outside the existing real estate marketing system and had created a substitute, artificial apparatus for placing individual black families in predominantly white communities. Bypassing the real estate industry, these efforts usually focused on bringing together willing white homesellers and black homeseekers and inevitably, through their preoccupation with community education and individual contact, they reached many blacks who were not seeking housing at the time of initial contact. Experience with these fair housing programs demonstrated that an appeal to blacks to move out of the ghetto based on the value of integration would not, of itself, be successful.

1. Allan H. Spear, *Black Chicago. The Making of a Negro Ghetto 1890–1920* (Chicago: University of Chicago Press, 1967), p. 224.

Neither were such extramarket changes capable of correcting the fundamental dualism of the market itself.

The Leadership Council therefore proposed to operate an Equal Opportunity Housing Service that would serve as a centralized source of all nondiscriminatory housing in the Chicago metropolitan area and would communicate its availability to black homeseekers. The service was to be available without fee to home brokers, management agents, homeseekers, homesellers, and public agencies. All usual brokerage fees, however, would be paid as applicable. Details of the proposal were as follows:

Organization. The Service was to be a distinct unit within the Leadership Council, linked to the council through the council's executive director and its housing information committee. Policies were to be defined by the board of directors of the Leadership Council and its staff under the supervision of the council's executive director. The central office of the service was to be in the offices of the Leadership Council in Chicago's Loop, and it was proposed to locate neighborhood offices in South Shore, Austin, and the near southwest side.

Advisory Committee. The council's existing housing information committee was to be enlarged to include academic, real estate, and other representatives, advising on policy and operations and providing service whenever possible. In addition, it was planned to develop with the Center for Urban Studies of the University of Chicago a means of providing continuing guidance, consultation, and evaluation to the staff in the establishment and operation of the program.

Functions: 1. Development of housing supply. The service was to use newspaper advertising and a system of fair housing contacts throughout the metropolitan area to obtain listings of homes and apartments that were available on a nondiscriminatory basis. The service was to work with the real estate industry to obtain maximum voluntary cooperation. To get this cooperation the service was to use examples of successful integration, community acceptance, and the potential loss of profit to the broker when nondiscriminatory sales or rentals are arranged outside normal real estate channels. Real estate boards and individual brokers and management agents were to be asked to cooperate by providing the service with nondiscriminatory listings on a regular basis. Because the most influential civic leadership in the metropolitan area, including representatives of the real estate, homebuilding, and mortgage lending industry, created the Leadership Council and was part of it, the council felt that it was in a unique position to obtain cooperation from the real estate industry. For example, the president of the Chicago Real Estate Board and the past president of the Evanston-North Real Estate Board were members of the Leadership Council Board of Directors, and a past president of the Illinois Association of Real Estate Boards was a member of the council. An additional source of listings was to be housing units covered by local fair housing ordinances. A promotional campaign to secure nondiscriminatory listings from homeowners and landlords also was to be undertaken in areas where the ordinance did not cover the owner of the property. The service was to utilize all housing units covered by federal nondiscrimination provisions.

The service was to provide the housing industry and available housing with a link to clients not previously served. Special efforts were to be made to promote a single, nondiscriminatory housing market system that would continue payment of broker and management fees so that the normal processes of real estate transaction could be developed to serve a racially inclusive market on a profitable basis, without the stimulation of the service, which would terminate in three years.

The service was to use the financial resources of Home Investments, Inc., a Chicago group formed to help blacks buy homes in predominantly white suburbs. This organization makes secured loans to financially qualified blacks to help meet down payment requirements and guarantees the resale value of the house. The service also was to utilize the resources of fair housing and human relations groups that were being developed by the Leadership Council and the Chicago Conference on Religion and Race and that were working to obtain house and apartment listings in their own communities from local brokers and individuals. Approximately sixty fair housing groups and thirty-five human relations commissions and councils were operating in the metropolitan area when the Leadership Council began its fair housing service.

Functions: 2. Consumer Development. Special emphasis also was to be placed on working with real estate brokers and management agents whose clientele was predominantly black and to develop contact with black brokers who might promote and market the listings obtained by the service. Efforts were made to get black real estate brokers into multiple listing services. The service's three neighborhood offices were to be located in communities where a large number of black families were looking for housing and were to provide information and assistance to those persons willing to consider living in predominantly white neighborhoods elsewhere in the metropolitan area. The service was to publicize its listings and to attempt to reach customers in much the same way that the existing real estate system does.

The proposed housing service also was to work with suburban employers of blacks, to maximize the opportunity for those persons interested in living near their place of employment to do so. Creating housing opportunities for blacks in the suburbs was also to be a stimulus to other suburban employers to recruit and hire blacks.

The service also was to locate and refer blacks who were transferred to the Chicago area from other parts of the nation in an effort to direct their housing choice to the total housing market, as well as to develop and maintain contact with groups and individuals whose constituency includes potential black homeseekers, such as community organizations, churches, social and civic clubs, civil rights groups, employers, and government.

Functions: 3. Data Processing. The service was to maintain complete and current information on all available nondiscriminatory housing in the Chicago metropolitan area. A biweekly listing of selected housing units was to be prepared for mail distribution to cooperating brokers, agents, groups, and individuals, and current lists of black homeseekers and the relevant information about the type, price, and location of the desired units were to be maintained. Fees were not to be charged for these services in order to encourage their utilization by real estate brokers.

THE HOUSING SERVICE

The housing service, when finally organized, was under the control of the director of housing information, who reported directly to the deputy director of the Leadership Council, whose responsibility was to coordinate the four principal functional offices of the council (development, community relations, housing information, and public agency liaison). The deputy director reported to the executive director (Edward L. Holmgren), who reported to the board of directors. The housing information unit had, in addition to its director, three other "core" specialists (two housing industry liaison specialists and one listing specialist) who reported directly to the housing information director and two neighborhood field offices (EOH centers, one on the west side, one on the south side, each staffed by a director and a secretary). Thus, as the organization chart in Figure 2-1 shows, communication of board decisions to staff and of staff discussion

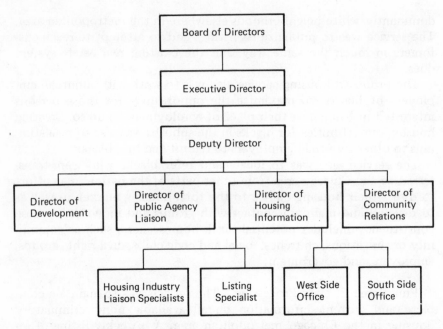

Figure 2-1. Leadership Council Organization Chart.

and debate to the executive director and the board depended upon flows of information through the director of housing information and the deputy director, an arrangement that was to lead to difficulties later.

The Neighborhood Offices

At the beginning of the contract, the council, with headquarters in Chicago's downtown area, had two neighborhood housing referral offices—one at 1940 East 71st Street in South Shore, the other at 5028 West Madison Street in Austin. An office proposed for the south west side of Chicago never opened, and no reason for this was ever given. The office on West Madison Street was closed on May 1, 1969, and was incorporated in the downtown office. The Organization for a Better Austin (OBA), a local community organization, had originally encouraged the Leadership Council to open this office. As the office developed its program, however, and as white resistance to fair housing increased in the city, OBA accused the Leadership Council of blockbusting and demanded that the office be closed. The offices were open from 9:00 A.M. to 5:00 P.M., five days a week. During the spring renting season they were open some evenings and on weekends.

In all, during the period August 1, 1968, to June 30, 1969, the west side office (operating out of the main office as of May 1) processed 297 applicants and placed 30 families, the south side office processed 253 applicants and placed 16 families.

From the beginning, the operations of these centers were affected by a continuing questioning of council decisions and policy by staff members and by bottlenecks in communication among different levels of the council's organization. For example, a sign outside of each office identified it as an "Equal Opportunity Housing Center," and the same phrase was used in answering the phones. Some of the staff of the Leadership Council felt that its name should be used at the neighborhood centers to make clear to the public who they were and to take advantage of any publicity given the council. Passersby, they said, sometimes thought they were either an employment agency or a traditional real estate office and often stopped in to inquire about fees. The feeling seemed to be that a name similar to "Leadership Council Free Housing Service" should be prominently displayed. When interviewed, one black staff member said, for example, that "equal opportunity housing just makes black people fall out laughing because they know there isn't any such thing."

This attitude was indicative of a more profound uncertainty that plagued staff members throughout the year. Many felt that they were powerless to affect materially the historic constraints imposed by the real estate industry on black homeseekers, and this affected their attitudes to work and to the housing center idea.

Publicity

On October 1, 1968, it was announced that "The Leadership Council for Metropolitan Open Communities is preparing full-page newspaper ads reading, 'The Supreme Court has reminded us that we have had an open-housing law since 1866. How long will it be before we make it work?',"[2] but these ads never appeared, for several reasons. The council claimed their main concern was that the 1968 political campaign then in progress would detract from and be confused with material contained in their advertisements.

Thus, a typical ad that ran throughout the year in the black press publicizing the HUD service read: "Tired of Paying the Color Tax? Upgrade your housing at the Equal Opportunity Housing Center nearest you: 5028 W. Madison, 261-6597; 1950 E. 71st St., 324-7509."[3] Spot radio announcements on WVON, WBEE, and other stations catering to the black community also were used. One such announcement, it was felt by the staff, was misleading because it said, in part, "We will place you in the neighborhood of *your* choice"

2. *Chicago Sun Times,* October 1, 1968.
3. *Daily Defender,* October 24, 1968.

(italics added). It was never clear to the prospective applicants that the housing service staff were providing help primarily to move into five selected all white target areas. Part of the problem was that at about the same time as the HUD contract project began, the Leadership Council inaugurated a campaign to open up housing opportunities for black people in five predominantly white target areas. The five areas were Oak Park, Lake View, Albany Park, Rogers Park, and Niles Township. These areas were chosen by the council because of the active volunteer fair housing groups then operating in them. The council intended otherwise, but a resulting confusion of the goals of the fair housing campaign and the HUD service meant that the staff perceived their task as steering black applicants toward the target areas.

Goals of the Service

By the fall of 1968 it finally became apparent to the staff that there was some flexibility in selecting areas in which to work. The rule of thumb seemed to be that the area chosen must be predominantly white, not on the fringe of the ghetto, and not in danger of becoming resegregated within five years. The council thus committed itself to the idea of integration per se, excluding any attempt to help black people merely upgrade their housing situations,[4] because

> we believe that there are large numbers of black families in the Chicago area willing to seek housing in integrated neighborhoods, even in view of recent highly publicized trends of black nationalism which tend to imply the contrary. We feel that if and when black families are really given the opportunity to rent and purchase in any neighborhood of the metropolitan area, many will avail themselves of the opportunity.[5]

4. That there is a diversity of possible goals is illustrated by the following: The Fair Housing Center's theory. . . is that people . . . can gain a degree of control over their own destiny if they can have some freedom of choice in where they will live. The Center, thus, when a family expresses an interest in moving, seeks to suggest several options. One might be a home outside of a racially or ethnically restricted area that rents for less money than the family is now paying, or that has better amenities or more rooms than the present house or apartment. Another choice might be one closer to work or potential work. Another choice might be in a less crowded school district. Even another possibility might be the Housing Authority dwellings at considerably reduced rent. In each case, desegregation is the goal, but some of the options do not always afford desegregation along with other improvements. Also, we always try to help people move from substandard to standard quality housing.
"Narrative Report on Center," Metro Denver Fair Housing Center, Inc., December 31, 1967, p. 13. Mimeographed.
5. "Housing Referral Service," Leadership Council for Metropolitan Open Communities, February 1, 1969.

Many of the black applicants to the housing centers were not interested in moving to all white neighborhoods, and many did not have the resources. Of the applicants who did make application for housing in the target areas, it was believed that a sizeable number had no real intention of seeking housing in such areas. The black staff of the council felt that it was very difficult to uproot people from their neighborhoods, and it was on this issue that latent black-white conflicts began to surface. Said one staff member: "How would *you* [whites] like it if you were told to pick up and move out of town?" It was mentioned among the staff that some blacks felt that the Leadership Council was just a front organization for the white power structure whose scheme was to disperse blacks throughout the city and thus weaken the black community as a cohesive political force. Indeed, the black staff said that the black community did not have a high opinion of the Leadership Council; in fact, it was often referred to as the Followship Council. However, the directors of the neighborhood housing centers were encouraged to be "persistent and aggressive" in attempting to persuade black people to move to all white areas.

Screening of Applicants
Another problem facing the council was how to "screen" applicants. Some in the council strenuously objected to screening of any kind, but it soon became obvious that large, low income families were going to be extremely difficult, if not impossible, to place.

A memorandum was issued by the council which said, in part:

We must stress, however, that there is little we can do as a housing referral service for large families with low incomes. In those neighborhoods into which we are attempting to place minority families, three bedroom apartments begin at $150 a month with the average around $200. Normally, landlords require that tenants come up with two months' rent before they move in; the first month's rent in advance and one month's rent as security deposit. We are rarely able to assist housing applicants who cannot meet these standard market requirements.[6]

This issue of incomes versus rental rates haunted the council the entire first year, for there was a continuing mismatch between the characteristics of applicants and the characteristics of the five areas into which the staff was trying to place the applicants.

It was decided then, that the only valid criteria for screening should

6. Undated memorandum signed by Edward L. Holmgren, executive director of the Leadership Council.

be the size of the unit available and the family income.[7] Staff criticism was leveled at many volunteer fair housing groups, who, it was alleged, were doing additional screening of the council's applicants to find the "right kind" of people to integrate their neighborhoods. A similar screening was evident in those organizations that had professional staffs engaged in placement and supporting activities. [8] "Since white people aren't screened in this manner, why should black renters all have to be 'Ralph Bunche types?'" said one black critic on the council's staff who, understandably, asked that his name not be given. At this point, the council was trying hard not to antagonize volunteer groups, but questioned whether it was worth using them if they continued to operate in this manner. The same black staff member felt that it should cut loose from them and "let them get their own show-piece spades." The majority, however, felt that volunteer groups were essential to the council's operation and that through meetings and educational programs these problems could be resolved.

Development of Housing Supply

On this basis, the housing service continued its operations. Daily listings of apartments for rent were clipped from all Chicago daily papers. Apartments considered too expensive and those in undesirable locations were eliminated. Telephone calls were then made to elicit additional information on individual apartments and to try to determine if they were still available. No mention, initially, was made that the applicant would be a black person. After this process, the daily list was compiled and mailed to the neighborhood offices.

No listings were furnished to the council by the real estate industry at first, and few individuals called in offering apartments on a nondiscriminatory basis. Some people did offer homes for sale on such a basis, but it was felt, generally, that they fell into four categories: people who were "running" from a changing neighborhood,[9]

7. "Two criteria must be met by the minority applicants for our service: 1) They must be willing to move into nonghetto or nonchanging neighborhoods, and 2) they must have the financial ability to pay the going rental or price level commensurate with their family size and the available housing. These criteria appreciably affect the number of applicants that can be served. For example, during the week of January 20 to 24, 1969, the two Centers reported 57 inquiries from people whose location requirements or economic circumstances precluded their becoming applicants. During the same period the Centers took a total of 5 applications from people meeting the criteria." "Housing Referral Service," Leadership Council for Metropolitan Open Communities, February 1, 1969.

8. One such group was the Chicago Conference on Religion and Race, whose Home Investment Fund was initiated in August 1968 to help minority families purchase homes in suburban communities.

9. "It was Cousins [Alderman William Cousins] who asked Fitzpatrick [Peter Fitzpatrick, chairman of the Chicago Human Relations Commission]

people who wanted to avoid a broker's commission, people who hated their neighbors and wanted to leave them a "legacy" when they moved, and some suburbanites who, with a degree of altruism, offered overpriced houses to blacks.

The Leadership Council's liaison specialists made "direct contact with real-estate brokers, seeking to elicit listings and general cooperation from them," but this was "ill-conceived [since] brokers in white areas do not seek to serve Negroes, while brokers with Negro clientele do not wish to give them up and thereby lose a commission to white brokers."[10]

Throughout the year, then, the council had to rely mainly on newspaper ads, although listings of buildings constructed under FHA's 221(d)(3) program gave them access to apartments for low and moderate income families. In fact, of the forty-six placements during the period August 1, 1968–June 30, 1969, eighteen were made in three 221(d)(3) buildings located in Chicago's Uptown area. Six other placements, twenty-four applicants in all, were placed in Uptown, which was rapidly becoming a polyglot haven for many new immigrant groups to the city. The council also had available to it monthly lists of FHA-VA-FSLIC repossessions provided by the regional offices of the respective agencies, but the generally low quality of these housing units made them unacceptable to the council's applicants.

Two real estate companies eventually did furnish regular listings to the council. Both lists contained mostly studio and one bedroom apartments. Of the two bedroom ápartments available, the average rental was $165 to $175. It was noticed from the listings that there were many apartments offered in various large buildings, and it was suspected by the council's staff that the buildings were "turning" or being made available for black occupancy for one reason or another. In addition, one list was of almost no value because it referred the council staff back to the local real estate office for information, and the three or four days spent trying to make contact with the person responsible for the building often meant that the apartment was rented by then.

As the techniques for development of adequate nondiscriminatory listings seemed to be trial and error, criticisms were leveled at them. Comments were made by the council staff that most black

---

whether the commission had made any progress in promoting housing integration in their city. 'I don't think so,' Fitzpatrick replied. 'When the first Negro moves in [to an all white neighborhood], in five or six years it will be all-Negro. We deplore that, [but] there are only a few islands [of whites in Negro areas] here or there." *Chicago Sun-Times*, November 21, 1968.

10. "Summary and Outline of First Year's Activity and Revised Work Program, 1969-1970," Leadership Council for Metropolitan Open Communities, June 27, 1969.

people will check the *Daily Defender, Daily News,* and *Sun-Times*
for apartment ads, so, in effect, all the council was doing was adding
ads from the *Chicago Tribune,* which "represents the white power
structure to black people, who wouldn't think of following up any
lily-white apartment rentals listed there." (The council, of course,
used the *Tribune* because it contained more apartment for rent ads
than the other papers combined.) In addition, the policy of not in-
quiring whether or not an apartment was available on a nondiscriminatory basis was a disservice to the black applicants. "What service is
the council providing them?" it was asked in a staff meeting. "Applicants are told to go with a white volunteer to look at an apartment
that you have no certainty they will get. They get insulted and pushed
around . . . . they can get that kind of treatment by themselves."[11]

Fair housing groups did serve as "checkers" in attempting to identify discriminatory landlords by

> sending a white applicant to a building which has advertised a vacant apart-
> ment. If the white applicant is offered and refuses the apartment, a Negro
> is immediately afterwards sent to look at the same apartment. If the Negro
> applicant is told there are no vacancies, a presumption of discrimination
> appears reasonable. This device has helped to provide apartments for Ne-
> gro applicants in previously segregated buildings. But most of the applicants
> are single people or young couples who are free from the responsibilities
> of raising children in an unfriendly neighborhood . . . . But the appeals to
> Negro families to settle in white areas involve a permanent commitment in
> which the comfort and safety of one's children are risked.[12]

And, although complaints could be filed with the city in cases of
discrimination, the slowness of settling them was a discouraging factor. The Chicago Fair Housing Ordinance had no provision for an injunction to prevent the offender from renting or selling while the case
is being investigated and prosecuted by the Chicago Commission on
Human Relations. The commission received 150 complaints during
the first nine months of 1969. Resolution of the problem was

11. "'Time and again I got the run-around about a place already being rented
or sold when I inquired about it . . . . I called one agency which told me to come
and pick up the key to look at the home I was interested in. I drove to the agency
with a Jewish friend. Since I was driving, he ran in to pick up the key. We looked
at the place, and altho it wasn't exactly what I wanted, I needed a house, so I
went into the real estate office to talk about it. When the woman [the real estate agent] saw me, she about fell off her chair. She was really angry and insisted
I had tricked her.' The man was informed by the agency a few days later that the
house had been listed 'by mistake' and was already rented." *Chicago Tribune,*
January 23, 1969.

12. Roger Starr, *The Living End: The City and Its Critics* (New York: Coward-
McCann, Inc. 1966), pp. 125–26

achieved in sixty-eight cases, while sixty-two cases were dismissed for lack of evidence, one was dismissed as not being under the commission's jurisdiction, and three were withdrawn.[13] Until the Leadership Council began using its most effective legal tool—the Civil Rights Act of 1866—it thus was virtually hamstrung in handling complaints. This century-old law enables the person discriminated against to obtain an injunction prohibiting sale or rental of the property in question until the case is settled.

Conflict with Fair Housing Groups

High levels of frustration were exhibited by the fair housing groups and the staff of the Leadership Council because of the council's inability to secure the cooperation of real estate brokers. This, in turn, led to friction between the council and many fair housing groups.

Carl Van Kast, director of the Metropolitan Fair Housing Alliance, a coalition of eleven city and suburban groups, said that the council was ineffective because it was dominated by real estate interests.[14] His opinion echoed Clark's that:

> In many all-white suburbs, human relations committees and fair housing committees have now been organized by liberals to break down the housing

13. *Chicago Sun-Times*, November 12, 1969.

14. "In the fall of 1968, many volunteer fair-housing groups offered to work with the Leadership Council. After a conference held at Northeastern Illinois State College, several organizations with mutual interests in fair housing held follow-up meetings. The concensus of opinion from these organizations was that none of their suggestions to the Leadership Council for better and more aggressive operation was ever taken seriously, much less implemented. Thus, in January, 1969, the Metropolitan Fair Housing Alliance (MFHA) was formed.

MFHA visited Leadership Council board meetings and repeatedly tried to suggest methods for improving the operation. When these suggestions were ignored, they turned into demands. MFHA split with the Council when it became apparent that its efforts were going to be totally rejected.

In lobbying to bring about changes, MFHA representatives found apathy on the part of the Council's board members, a desire to see the Council fold up, and a basic ignorance of their own Council's structure and function. It became obvious to MFHA that the Leadership Council was run by a few persons or interests.

The February 1, 1969 "Comparison and Contrast" seminar held at the Center for Continuing Education proved to us that the Council was the poorest operation of its kind in the United States but it had the most substantial funds and power.

Communication with the Council has always been a one-way street: we at MFHA tried to work with them; they ignored our overtures. We have offered to cooperate under a subcontract several times (to do the work and let the Leadership Council get credit). This proposal, too, was refused. We are still willing to work with the Council on a subcontract basis, and on September 2, 1969 submitted such a proposal," "A Project to Provide Equal Opportunity Housing in the Chicago Metropolitan Area," to the Department of Housing and Urban Development. Memorandum from Carl Van Kast, September 15, 1969.

barriers. Such campaigns are a fascinating illustration of the fact that the Negro is forced to consider himself special—otherwise, why would campaigns be needed to permit him to exercise the rights which the law assures him?

White liberals have been having a frustrating time finding Negroes who will offer themselves as test cases. For one thing, it is not particularly comfortable to be a test case. For another, middle-class Negroes who break out of the ghetto are often themselves convinced that they are already accepted by whites—to be a test case would be to allow race to become salient again in one's life, to bring the ghetto nightmare along when all one has sought is effective escape.[15]

Staff Unrest and Internal Communication Problems

A prevalent feeling among the staff was that black people were being exploited through the service and that the heads of the council and its board ("which has some big real-estate people on it") should come to grips with the problem and get complete listings of available housing from all Chicago metropolitan area real estate brokers. "As long as the real-estate industry can hide behind ruses and deceptive practices in renting," said one staff member, "we are just beating our heads against a stone wall. And when people find out what service you are actually offering your prospects will dry up."

While some of the staff pressed for a confrontation with the board, others urged caution in order to avoid alienating board members. It was pointed out several times that board members served as "individuals, not as representatives of their firms," and so, therefore, could not be responsible for their companies' actions, which, as one staff member observed when interviewed:

> gives them a nice cop-out. They can use us by being on the board and mouthing open housing, but we can't use them. They know what the score is but won't admit it. How can we sit around and call ourselves the Leadership Council if we don't do anything. Black people get the message clearly: there is still the same hard-core resistance no matter what you say. Confront the board and if everything collapses, that's just too bad.

One continuing problem was that while the thrust of much of this staff dissent and debate was clear to the director of housing informa-

15. Kenneth B. Clark, *Dark Ghetto: Dilemmas of Social Power* (New York, Harper and Row, 1965), p. 235. Cited in Marcie L. Setlow, "Metropolitan Open Housing Ordinances in Illinois. Their Effectiveness as a Deterrent to Segregated Housing" (M.A. Thesis, University of Chicago, 1968).

tion, the transmission and receipt of messages upward in the organization from that level was increasingly befogged.

Meanwhile, the staff conscientiously continued to try to carry out the program, despite their concerns about the appropriateness and effectiveness of the tactics. Staff concerns were that the program was not powerful enough to achieve the stated goals. In addition, some disagreement was expressed by staff members with the goals of the project (integration per se). They felt that upgrading the quality of housing regardless of location should have a higher priority than integration. The staff was disappointed that their firsthand experience in black housing and that their points of view were not used to develop policy and program. They were unhappy that their administration was not more aggressive with public agencies and the like. They felt that little was happening, while their idealistic activism led them to ask the board, staff, and others to "change things" now, to make an immediate breakthrough. This may have been unrealistic, but these were their feelings.

Thus, staff and volunteer attitudes often seemed to mirror the truth of Aaron Wildavsky's remarks:

> Disheartened by the magnitude of the change required in racial behavior, unwilling to recognize the full extent of the resources required to improve economic conditions, we are tempted to try a lot of small programs that create an illusion of activity, ferment, and change. But nothing much happens. Confusion is rampant because it looks to some (mostly white) like so much is being done, and to others (mostly black) that nothing is happening. Hence the rival accusations of black ingratitude and white indifference. It is apparent that we should abandon symbolic policies that anger whites and do not help blacks and should concentrate instead on programs that will materially increase the well-being of poor people in the United States. Programs should be large rather than small, and provide tangible benefits to many citizens, not symbolic rewards for a few.[16]

Change in Program;
Continuing Bottlenecks

At the urging of the staff, a policy change in mid-August of 1968 permitted the question—Would you rent to a black person?—to be asked when calling individuals who listed apartments for rent. This time-consuming process produced answers running the gamut from deception to obscenity, and appropriate notations were made on the daily listing sheets. Letters were sent to those individuals and agencies

16. Aaron Wildavsky, "The Empty-head Blues: Black Rebellion and White Reaction," *The Public Interest* 11 (Spring 1968): p 5.

who openly refused to rent to Negroes informing them that they were in violation of the Chicago Fair Housing Ordinance, which forbids discrimination by homeowners, apartment owners, and brokers, and asking them to reconsider their positions. Copies of the letters were sent to the director of housing of the Chicago Commission on Human Relations. However, enforcement was difficult because a family must actually have applied for housing and been refused in order to file a complaint. Telephone refusals were not enough. Of one hundred and four calls made during a three week period, only twenty-nine said they would be willing to rent to Negroes.

Attempts by a black listing specialist for the Leadership Council to check out ten apartments supposedly available on a nondiscriminatory basis resulted in a revealing memorandum:

> On Tuesday, November 26, I made or attempted to make appointments to see 10 of the apartments listed as available on a nondiscriminatory basis, as a prospective lessee. I was unsuccessful in making an appointment to see an apartment at _____ W. Farragut (Lincoln Square). This was a blind ad, the address was given during our telephone inquiry. On phoning for an appointment, the request was made to see the apartment at _____ W. Farragut. The party answering said the apartment could not be seen today (Tuesday), tomorrow (Wednesday) or Friday. No, they didn't know when you could see the apartment. In 2 other instances—apartments at _____ W. Lawrence and _____ W. Leland (both in the Lincoln Square area)— the respondents asked "What nationality are you." Appointments were given to see the apartments the following day, neither of which was kept by the agents and/or owners. An apartment on West Surf that *was going to be available in 2 or 3 weeks* was rented, according to the agent, by the time I arrived the following day. An appointment with a janitor for a Lakewood apartment was not kept. Attempts to reach him by phone were unsuccessful. He was not in, his wife stated, and she knew nothing of the appointment nor when he would be in. Of the 10 apartments, I was shown only 3, and in all 3 cases the janitors showing the apartments could not give me applications but could only refer me back to the real estate firm in 2 instances and to the owner in the third instance.[17]

Early in 1969, the practice of asking if the accommodation was available to members of minority groups was discontinued. Its use was sharply criticized by some of the fair housing groups who felt it was "capitulation to segregationist tactics. Consequently, some groups discontinued full cooperation with the Leadership Council."[18]

17. Memorandum from Barbara J. Birthwright, listing specialist for the Leadership Council, January 9, 1968.

18. "Summary and Outline of First Year's Activity and Revised Work Program, 1969-1970," Leadership Council for Metropolitan Open Communities, June 27, 1969.

Intractability of the Real
Estate Industry

Meetings were held, beginning in April 1968, with the Chicago Real Estate Board, in the hope of getting their cooperation in persuading their members to furnish the council with lists of available apartments. The board refused and suggested, instead, that they be furnished lists of "applicant profiles" by the Leadership Council to see what they could do with them. Many of the council staff strongly felt that this was going at the problem backward, that this information should not be furnished the realtors, and that this proposal was in no sense a breakthrough. Nevertheless, to the dismay of many, this program was adopted for a five month period. As the Leadership Council itself related:

> The Board assured us that its member firms would provide us with appropriate listings to meet specific requirements related to apartment size, rent level and location. The suggestion was complied with by sending such profiles on a biweekly basis from October, 1968 to February, 1969, but no listings were forthcoming. Often the scant listings received included units located only in ghetto or ghetto fringe areas.[19]

The real estate industry's sincerity in espousing good race relations seemed questionable as *"it became increasingly clear that despite the commitments made during the 1966 Summit Agreement, the realestate industry had no real commitment or intention to accommodate its practices to the needs of minority homeseekers,"*[20] because

> "As far as the small apartment building owner or the estate man is concerned," said Mrs. Helen Jost, the committee's [Metropolitan Housing Committee] co-chairman, "there's too much profit in controlling an area—in keeping it all-white, making it change or keeping it black.
> "They [the real estate interests] have control," she added. "Where it comes from I don't know. It just filters through."[21]

The real estate industry refuted such charges, reiterating their classical stance that the problem is economic, not their own practices: "Newly passed open housing laws aren't making any dent in the housing problems of Negroes . . . . The problem is economics . . . . Until these people have money . . . laws are not going to help them any."[22]

19. Ibid.
20. Ibid.
21. *Chicago Daily News*, September 28, 1968.
22. *Chicago Daily News*, October 9, 1968 (but refer back to the analysis in Chapter 1).

Edwin C. Berry, executive director of the Chicago Urban League and member of the board of the Leadership Council, recognized the continuing immensity of the difficulties under which the service labored:

> A year after the Kerner Report warned that America is heading toward "two societies—one black, one white," the picture in Chicago appears largely unchanged.
>
> "There has been a flurry of activity in the area of jobs, with some obvious upgradings, . . . but the problems are as bad as ever in such other areas as housing, education and welfare."[23]

A conference held by the American Medical Association at the same time termed "racism one of the major mental health problems in the United States,"[24] and attitudes encountered by the Leadership Council in attempting to introduce black families into white neighborhoods would seem to confirm this.[25] There was hostility, of course, but deception seemed to have become the more popular course of action in order to avoid the possibility of being caught breaking the law.

Probably the most common, overt method of discrimination against black people was the "no children allowed" prohibition. Most of the people looking for two and three bedroom apartments have children. By using this device, the owner or agent felt he was on safe ground, since, obviously, this refusal does not involve the individual's color. Apparently few owners or agents, and even fewer apartment seekers, were aware of the 1909 Illinois Revised Statute that made it unlawful

> to require as a condition precedent to the leasing of any dwelling house, flat or apartment, that the person or persons desiring so to lease such dwelling house, flat or apartment shall have at the time such application is made for the leasing or renting of such dwelling house, flat, or apartment no children under the age of 14 years residing in their families, and it shall be

23. *Chicago Daily News,* February 27, 1969.
24. *Chicago's American,* March 16, 1969.
25. *Chicago Daily News,* April 30, 1969, contained the following:

> A black psychiatrist and author has warned white America against destroying themselves through greed and racism. The warning was made Tuesday night by Dr. William H. Grier, co-author of *Black Rage,* a book dealing with racial injustices in America. Dr. Grier [said] that "white racism is institutionalized as well as individualized." He rejects the belief that racism is confined only to a few bigots. "The extent of this type of hatred is of such proportion that most of us don't even want to know its full dimensions," Dr. Grier said . . . .

deemed unlawful and opposed to public policy to insert in any lease or agreement for the letting or renting of any dwelling house, flat or apartment, a condition terminating said lease if there are or shall be any such children in the family of any person holding such lease . . . .[26]

Despite this law, newspapers continued to print ads for apartments to rent that specified "no children." When asked not to accept advertising using this phrase, the papers said that they could not dictate what appeared in ads and seemed indifferent to the appeal. Attempts were made by the Leadership Council, in cooperation with the Community Legal Counsel, to get the state's attorney to follow through on complaints of discrimination against children, but several attempts proved futile, and these efforts were discontinued.

Some ruses for excluding black people were old: "This apartment has just been rented," but newer, subtle ones also were prevalent: a "six month employment clause" restriction; the insistence that a family needs more bedrooms than are available or than they can afford. But the "bedroom ploy" also was reversed: two sisters, thirty-nine and forty-five years of age, were denied a two bedroom apartment in a federally subsidized 221 (d)(3) building managed by a private firm unless they could supply a written statement from their doctor stating that they could not sleep in the same bedroom together! They asked, "Would you consider this a sound reason for two sisters not being able to occupy a two-bedroom apartment? We feel that two grown women of our ages should not have to share the same bedroom."[27] One landlord who had a five room, two bedroom apartment available (for adults only) at $175 a month insisted that the head of the household earn five times the rent or $875 a month.

Another of the Leadership Council's applicants reported his apartment-hunting experiences in Chicago's western suburbs. During the period from May 31 to September 23, 1968, he repeatedly contacted twenty real estate firms and owner-agents in attempts to rent a two bedroom apartment in the rental range of $155 to $170. Nine contacts were made in Addison, two in Glen Ellyn, four in Villa Park, one in Summit, two in Wheaton, one in Bellwood, and one in Broadview. Employed by Commonwealth Edison Company in Lombard for two years at a salary of $650 a month, he had a wife and infant twin sons. He had been commuting to the Lombard location from the South Shore area in Chicago and, quite naturally, wanted to move closer to work.

26. Illinois Revised Statutes, Chapter 80, p. 656, pp. 37, 38 (Filed June 16, 1909, L. 1909, p. 272).
27. Letter from applicant to Leadership Council, April 4, 1969.

Several firms took his application and told him nothing was available; some firms told him to telephone a specific person, but this individual was never available to talk to him. He viewed apartments listed as "available now" and then was told that no apartment would be available until March of 1969. He was told by a realtor that he would not rent a two bedroom apartment to a family with two children. In attempting to see the manager of one building, he was told repeatedly that the manager was on vacation. One real estate agency said that they had no two bedroom apartment available anywhere. One individual said that the apartment was only suitable for two adults. Many companies never returned any of his calls. This family was ultimately settled in Elgin, twenty minutes driving time from Lombard, through the efforts of the Leadership Council, after which Commonwealth Edison reassigned him to work in Elgin.

The Attempt to Reduce Separation
of Homes and Jobs

Many of the applicants to the Leadership Council traveled long distances to their places of employment. In a large number of cases where the husband and wife both worked, their places of employment were in different sections of the city. Therefore, for them, good public transportation was a must, and they often preferred a central location to one near either job location.

The Chicago Alliance of Businessmen, a voluntary group seeking jobs for hard core unemployed, claimed

that practically all of Chicago's suburban areas can be defined as "hard to reach" by public transportation.

Travel to the suburbs requires numerous transfers, additional costs and excessive time. It would not be unusual to spend more than hour and a dollar each way in transit from the urban ghetto to a suburban job location.

There are other barriers to solving this problem.

Housing in the suburban industrial-residential communities, like Elk Grove Village, Arlington Heights and Des Plaines is neither racially nor economically integrated. In spite of open housing laws, many blacks are reluctant to be the first to integrate.[28]

To get more applicants and to help black people live nearer their jobs, the Leadership Council did some work with large industrial concerns and union officials in western and northwestern suburbs.

Twelve companies have been contacted to date, first by letter and then by a personal visit. Seven have responded with strong public statements, and

28. *Chicago Today*, May 11, 1969.

the remaining five have failed to respond yet. There have been no refusals.

. . . Each company was also asked to inform their local real estate board of their policy statement . . . 106 industries in the western suburbs are being sent a letter . . . asking them to cooperate with the housing referral program of the Council.

. . . Some [of the companies] go out of their way to help, such as sending special correspondence to employees, others permit the Council to put notices on bulletin boards or stuff them in envelopes for employees.[29]

It would seem from the above statement that progress was being made in dealing with industry; however, notes made at a seminar sponsored by the Leadership Council indicate that one of their staff said, "Although there is about a 75 percent positive response from corporations, they are not really cooperating. These people are the 'maintenance men' of the status quo."[30]

Several hundred letters were sent to black employees of various west suburban companies saying, "your employer has referred your name to our organization in the event you are interested in renting an apartment or purchasing a home *outside the ghetto* (italics added)." The letter itself shocked some of the black employees of the council who had been stressing the fact that the word "ghetto" should never be used in dealing with the council's black applicants. One of the staff members said "white people just don't understand black people and can't communicate with them. Maybe some of these people live in a ghetto and maybe they don't, and if they do, maybe they never even thought it was a ghetto. How would you like to get a letter like that?" Also, the neighborhood offices were not aware that these mailings had gone out and were surprised when they received calls, mostly from black laborers making from $80 to $90 a week, asking for housing in the western suburbs. It became necessary to explain to each one that because of his income it would be impossible for the Leadership Council to help him. Several calls were received also from black workers who said a rumor was circulating at Automatic Electric Company that if black workers made application for such housing, they would be fired. The council assured callers that this, obviously, was not true, but it was decided, after discussion, not to call it to the attention of Automatic Electric Company. The reasoning seemed to be that since it clearly was a "scare tactic" and not company policy, what could the company do about it anyway? Again, some of the staff disagreed and thought it should be brought

29. *The Leadership Council for Metropolitan Open Communities Newsletter* 2, 2 (March, 1969): 1, 2.

30. Notes from "Comparison and Contrast Seminar," held at the Center for Continuing Education, February 1, 1969.

to the attention of company officials for whatever action they might want to take on the matter. This considerably dampened the enthusiasm of prospective applicants and detracted from the Leadership Council's "image."

Problems of Image

Meetings were held through the year to try to change this image.[31] Those with volunteer groups appeared to be more an outlet for frustrations than meaningful interchanges of ideas. Meetings with business and civic leaders gave all a chance to reaffirm their support of fair housing without committing themselves or their companies to positive action. Conferences with local FHA and Public Aid officials degenerated, perhaps justifiably, into "don't pass the buck here, that's not our responsibility" sessions. Time spent bringing together white volunteers and black applicants produced scant turnouts. Other conferences produced well-intentioned resolutions and allowed the Leadership Council and other organizations to state their positions and talk about what they could do.[32] Meetings with community and

31. Opposition to the council was occasionally in evidence. A leaflet was distributed at the Leadership Council's luncheon meeting held November 1, 1968, at the Oak Park Arms, Oak Park, Illinois, saying:

This meeting is being held under the sponsorship of the Leadership Council for Metropolitan Open Communities.

Its purpose is to promote the socialization and the control of the housing market by using tax monies obtained from the State Housing Development Authority to provide low and middle income housing in Oak Park and River Forest.

For which of the following reasons were you selected to attend this meeting?

1. You agree with their purposes?
2. You are a community leader whose name can be used to promote their cause?
3. You will profit financially from the creation of a tax-supported community action organization that will build or secure housing which is to be used for the redistribution of our population in order to implement the social goals of the Comprehensive "master" Plan of the Northeastern Illinois Plan Commission;

(Signed)   Concerned Taxpayers of
Oak Park–River Forest

32. *Chicago Sun-Times*, April 1, 1969:

Everyone seemed to have a good time at the fair-housing confrontation in a West Side church basement Monday night . . . . The villains were supposed to be S. Thomas Sutton, head of anti-integrated Operation Crescent; Steve Telow of the Polish Homeowners Assn. and Jack Gorham of Operation 8 Ball. The heroes were supposed to be Henry Burwell of the Commission on Human Relations; John Dwyer, an Oak Park realtor; Wayne Lewis of the

church groups designed to produce more applicants were unsuccessful, since, as one staff member said, "no pastor wants to lose his best-paying people." It is to be noted that the question, "How did you hear of this housing service?" on the council's application form was seldom, if ever, answered. Most applicants were "walk-ins"—people who lived or worked in the south and west side areas where the council's neighborhood offices were located (see Figure 2-2), and their economic and other characteristics precluded effective council assistance.

THE APPLICANTS

Two-thirds of the applicants for Equal Opportunity Housing during the first year of operation of the council's housing service were households supported by two wage earners. Over two-thirds of the applicants were employed in service and lower manual occupations. The median monthly gross family income was $620, providing $220 gross income per member of the household. Ninety-three percent of the applicants were seeking rental apartments. The median rent they wished to pay for an apartment was $140 per month. An average application remained in the open files of Equal Opportunity Housing for seven weeks. It took about five weeks to place an applicant. Of the first three hundred sixty-six applications, forty-one (11.2 percent) were placed by EOH, ninety-six (26.2 percent) found housing through their own or other resources,

---

Proviso Open Housing group; and Edward L. Holmgren, executive director of the Leadership Council of Metropolitan Open Communities. Oddly enough, it turned out that the [integrated] audience enjoyed the villains more than the heroes. . . . Gorham . . . got up and said that if only one percent of the Negroes are bad people, why don't the good 99 percent take care of them. *The heroes talked for the most part about the rights of men and the morality of fair housing* (italics added) . . . . The villains became the stars . . . . At one point, he [Sutton] raised his fist and said whites would win in any confrontation, any struggle. But when the confrontation finally was over and the sated audience drifted out into the streets, the question of who won the evening was moot. The show was over. The reality remained.

Chicago's American, April 1, 1969:

Edward Holmgren, director of the Leadership Council for Metropolitan Open Communities, said attitudes have improved along with fair housing laws, federal, state and local. He called for massive programs of construction for low income families.

"We are quite a distance from the achievement of our 2 goals—to secure opportunity for all to obtain open housing, and to correct the economic imbalance in the housing market," he said.

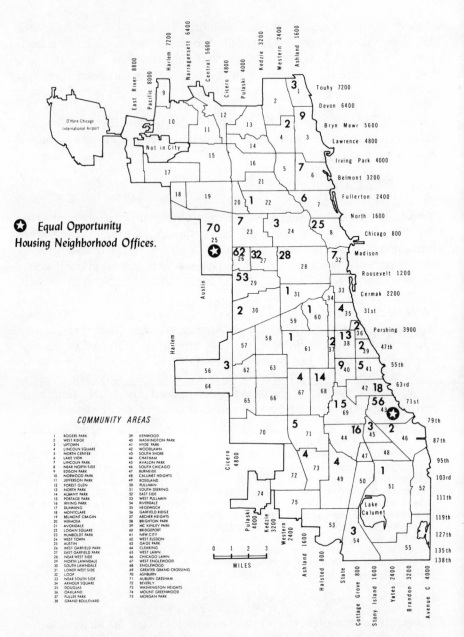

Figure 2-2. Communities in Which the First 505 Applicants to the Leadership Council's Equal Opportunity Housing Centers Lived.

and one hundred ninety-six, or over half, could not be assisted (sixty-three percent).

Applicants who registered at the south side office were employed in somewhat higher status occupations and reported a higher gross monthly household income than did the applicants at the west side office. The greater affluence of the southsiders was reflected by their requests for costlier housing. Data contrasting south with west side applicants is represented in Table 2-1.

Motivations for Movement
Over four-fifths of the applicants resided in neighborhoods that had changed from white to black since 1960. On the surface it appeared that the applicants were seeking better residential circumstances for themselves once again. Some moved into transitional neighborhoods possibly thinking that they could find a reasonable solution to their housing needs, but eventually were disappointed that conditions failed to meet their expectations. Others had obtained resources in their current neighborhood that now permitted them to

Table 2-1. Characteristics of Applicants.

	South Percent^a N = 183	West Percent^a N = 183	Chi Square	Df	P
Occupational Status					
White Collar	33.9	15.3			
Manual	63.4	84.2	24.432	4	<0.000
Annual Household Income					
Under $7,000	48.2	56.4			
Over $8,000	51.8	43.6	3.158	3	<0.368
Number in Household					
3 or under	62.9	63.4			
4 or more	36.0	36.6	4.766	8	NS
Head of Household					
Male	68.9	74.3			
Female	31.1	25.7	1.343	2	NS
Preferred Rent					
Under $150	51.9	62.6			
$150–$200	40.1	34.4			
Over $200	8.0	3.1	5.364	2	<0.051
Type Dwelling Sought					
Rent an Apartment	91.2	95.6			
Buy a House	7.7	3.3	7.483	4	<0.113

^{a}Percentage does not include not applicable, no response categories, and, therefore, may not total 100 percent.

Table 2-2. Applicants and the Racial Composition of Neighborhood (percent).

	Greater than 30 Percent Black in Indicator Years					
	1950	*1960*	*1964*	*1967*	*1968*	*Total*
West Office	12.9	35.5	21.3	23.9	6.5	N = 155
South Office	19.6	47.8	11.6	6.5	14.5	N = 138

Chi Square = 27.423   5df   P = <0.000

move into better quality housing elsewhere. It is noted in Table 2-2 that significantly more of the southside applicants came from neighborhoods that had been populated by 30 percent or more black residents since 1960 than was the case for the westside applicants. But this may be an artifact of the location of the EOH centers (Figure 2-3). Both offices were located in communities that had only recently become accessible to black people. The services of EOH were therefore geographically more accessible to residents living in areas that had become black only since 1960, which increased the likelihood that residents in the immediate neighborhood would use them (Table 2-3).

Application data were searched with little success for clues that would shed some light on the applicant characteristics affecting movement into white neighborhoods. The search was limited to the application data recorded at the time EOH took the applicants into their services. Only occupation and family income of the applicants differentiated those placed from the nonplaced and then at low confidence levels. Among the placed, applicants with higher white collar and higher manual occupations were somewhat overrepresented, as were applicants with low family incomes. At first sight this finding appears contradictory; however, when the volume of lower manual applicants who were placed is considered, the apparent

Table 2-3.   Applicants and Ghettoization of Neighborhood (percent).

	High Ghetto	*Low Ghetto*	*High Transitional*	*Low Transitional*	*High Integrated*	*White Suburb*	*NA*	*Total*
West Office	72.1	7.8	1.1	2.2	11.2	—	5.6	N = 179
South Office	60.8	14.0	1.2	4.7	10.2	1.2	7.6	N = 171

Chi = 8.966   7df   P = 0.256

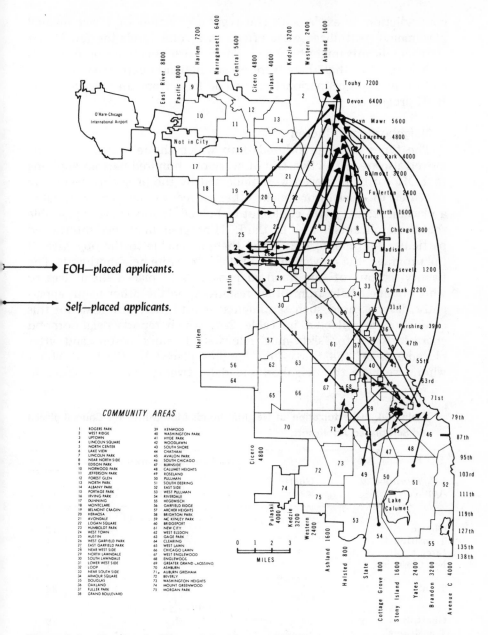

Figure 2-3. Changes in Place of Residence of EOH-placed and of Self-placed Applicants to the EOH Centers.

contradiction is explained. The high proportion of lower manual placements neutralizes what effect on income levels the few higher status applicants might have had. The important conclusion from this data is the fact that there were no strong biases expressed in the exclusion of any occupational or income level from the services of the EOH program.

Neighborhoods Chosen

The types of neighborhoods into which the relocated applicants moved also are instructive. Out of every one hundred persons applying to EOH for help, eleven were relocated by the program; twenty-six relocated themselves or sought other sources of help that eventuated a placement; sixty-two could not be helped. It appears very plausible that the applicants helped by the EOH program may have entertained particular sentiments that made them amenable to the objective of the program—the movement of blacks into white neighborhoods. The twenty-six out of one hundred persons who placed themselves or who obtained help from other resources, on the other hand, apparently did not hold such sentiments or attitudes. The basis for this conjecture is reflected in Table 2–4, which reports neighborhood characteristics for sixty-nine relocated families before and after placement. Of the thirty-four families placed by EOH and about whom we have the neighborhood data, twenty-one were placed in

Table 2–4.   Ghettoization of Neighborhoods Moved into for Council-placed and Self-placed Applicants.

| Neighborhood at Application | Neighborhood Moved Into | | | | |
	Ghetto-ized	Transi-tional	Inte-grated	White	Total
	Placed by Council				
Ghettoized	—	14	—	5	19
Transitional	—	1	—	—	1
Integrated	—	4	—	4	8
Not Classified	1	2	—	3	6
Total	1	21	—	12	34
	Placed by Self				
Ghettoized	22	1	3	3	29
Transitional	—	1	—	—	1
Integrated	3	—	—	—	3
Not Classified	—	1	—	1	2
Total	25	3	3	4	35

transitional neighborhoods—that is, neighborhoods undergoing racial change—and only twelve, or about one-third, were placed in white neighborhoods. In contrast, of those families who relocated through their own or other resources, twenty-five, or nearly 70 percent, remained in ghetto neighborhoods. Only four families found their way into white neighborhoods.

The black applicant requesting help from EOH in finding housing was confronted with the proposal that he move into a white neighborhood. The family had to decide whether it was amenable to such a proposal and whether to extend its relationship with the program further. In the event that the goals of the family did not coincide with those of the council, there was no alternative except to go elsewhere for assistance. On the other hand, the family that agreed with the goals of the program continued and was helped.

To carry this to its logical conclusion, what is suggested is that the frequency with which sentiments congenial to the goals of the EOH occurred in the total population was critical in limiting the Leadership Council's ability to reach its goals. EOH had to contend with at least two major probabilities—the probability that a family wished to move and the probability that a family was amenable to moving into a white neighborhood. If we assume that this probability is represented in the twelve families that moved into white neighborhoods, we deduce that the probability of such an event occurring is approximately three out of one hundred chances. EOH set a goal of placing 1,000 families in the first year of operation. From the probability of 0.03 above, persons representing 34,000 families seeking housing would have to be screened to produce the needed 1,000 integration moves, clearly far beyond the EOH centers' capabilities. And by extension, if the same sentiments persisted throughout Chicago's 300,000 black households in 1968–1969, there would have been barely 9,000 interested in integrated living!

The Applicants' Attitudes

This, however, is to speculate about the applicants' attitudes. To learn more, seventy black applicants to the Equal Opportunity Housing (EOH) offices were interviewed to determine the impact of EOH services on their efforts to find housing. Interviews with the seventy included questions directed at identifying the forces affecting their entrance into the housing market and their eventual selection of dwellings.

The sample of seventy was obtained from the three hundred sixty-six people who sought assistance from EOH between August 1968 and June 1969, using a conventional random sampling technique. In obtaining the seventy interviews, it was necessary to expand the sample to one hundred thirty-six applicants, however. The 48.6 percent attrition rate warrants attention, since the incompleted interviews obviously did not occur in a random chance fashion. The final seventy applicants who were interviewed differed form the total of all applicants in the following ways:

- Their average income was higher than the 366 base population, although not significantly so.
- Skilled craftsmen and professional workers were somewhat underrepresented in the sample, although not significantly so. The 7.5 index of dissimilarity on occupational status indicates a favorable, although not perfect, correlation between the population of applicants making the original contact with EOH and those interviewed in the follow-up study.
- Persons residing in neighborhoods that had been ghettoized for a long period of time were likely to be excluded.

The interviewees may be broadly described as middle class black people in search of housing. The application of the findings to lower working class blacks may be appropriate for representing racial effects, but their absence from the sample tends to exclude lower social class influences from within the racial context of the data.

The excessive rate of attrition from the sample is indicative of the transient nature of these applicants in the housing market. At the time of their contact with EOH, they had entered the housing market or were on the verge of doing so. Although EOH had placed 11.2 percent of those people seeking housing through their channels, an additional 26.2 percent in the total had found housing through other means, bringing the total up to 37.3 percent. The interviews provided confirmation of residential changes from an additional 10 percent for a total of 47 percent who had moved since the initial contact with EOH. Forty-three percent of the interviewees still wanted to move. Allowing for the sampling bias, this would bring the rate of residential changes up to 90 percent for those who had set a goal of moving.

The implication of the low rate of applicants placed in target neighborhoods for the tactical effectiveness of the EOH approach is evident: The black homeseekers who contacted the EOH offices were not predisposed to a move into white neighborhoods. The large majority of black homeseekers decided to locate in black or integrated neighborhoods, which apparently were viewed as being compatible, secure places to reside.

As noted earlier, EOH offices primarily attracted people residing in the immediate neighborhoods (see Figure 2–2). The resourcefulness of the homeseeker indicated by his contact with EOH probably was not typical of all people hunting for housing. The seventy people interviewed were described by the following characteristics:

- Three out of five applicants had high school educations or more. Two out of five had pursued education beyond the twelfth grade.
- Three-quarters of the applicants were employed in low manual jobs. Corresponding with occupational makeup of the black population, the applicants were underrepresented in the skilled labor occupations. One out of five was employed in a low white collar job.
- The mean family income of the applicant was $8,530. Virtually one-third had combined family incomes of more than $10,000. On the other hand, the annual family income of two-thirds of the applicants was less than $10,000, which placed severe limitations on the quality and location of housing they could afford. Family income is recapped as follows:

Less than $7,000 per year   42.9 percent
$7,000 to $10,000 per year   25.7 percent
More than $10,000 per year   31.4 percent

- Two out of five homeseekers were without children. Nearly two out of five had one or two children, and one out of five had three or more children.

No children   41.4 percent
One or two children   37.1 percent
Three to seven children   21.5 percent

- One-half of the interviewees had lived in Chicago for twenty years or more. One-half (47.9 percent) gave Illinois as their state of birth. nearly two out of five had immigrated to Chicago from the southern states:

Born in Illinois   47.9 percent
Born in southern states   38.0 percent
Born in northeastern states   2.8 percent
Born in midwestern-western states   9.8 percent

- The applicants moved, for the most part, into transitional neighborhoods or neighborhoods that had changed racial composition as recently as 1960. Three-fourths of the interviewees resided in neighborhoods that were integrated, transitional, or recently ghettoized. The movement reflected in the change of residence by the applicants shows a preference for the transitional or recently changed neighborhoods, which indicates a search for improved quality of housing. Only one out of seven (14.3 percent) of the interviewees resided in neighborhoods in which the proportion of blacks exceeded 30 percent by 1950 or earlier. On the opposite end of the ghettoization continuum, roughly one out of eight families (12.5 percent) resided in integrated or white communities. Thus, successful efforts to acquire quality housing or housing in integrated areas were very limited. The racial composition of the residence of respondents at the time of interviews is detailed below:

Greater than 30 percent black in 1950[a]	16.3 percent
Ghettoized prior to or by 1968[a]	44.8 percent
Ghettoized in 1969	17.9 percent
Ghettoization projected by 1975	7.5 percent
Ghettoization projected for 1975	14.9 percent
Integrated	10.4 percent
White, suburban	4.5 percent

Other identifying characteristics of the sample are:

- Intentions to move were serious.
- The preferred residential location was the nieghborhood that had changed in racial composition recently, a correlate to the quality of housing acquired.
- The black homeseeker was representative occupationally of the black population. He was employed and relatively well educated.
- At the most, the applicant who contacted EOH could afford only moderately priced housing.

Questions regarding satisfaction with services received from EOH pointed dramatically to the lack of sympathy and understanding present in the guiding objectives of the EOH program. The things the dwelling seekers did not like about EOH were the parts of the program related to the target objective of aiding black families to move into white neighborhoods. Suggestions for improving EOH services, if adopted, would have transformed EOH into a conventional rental agency. Respondents wanted EOH to gear listings to the needs of the applicant (62 percent) or to give financial help for getting housing (4.2 percent). Interviewees disliked the limitation of listings of housing to the north side of Chicago (29.6 percent). One out of three

[a]Percentage of black by 1950 is repeated in the 1968 figure.

applicants resented EOH's apparent lack of concern for the problem that brought them to EOH, indicating that the services of EOH were not clearly understood. Only one person volunteered that EOH should devote more of its resources to improving the chances for eventual integration, although nine persons interviewed (12.7 percent) supported EOH efforts at integrating housing.

When asked about their response to the suggestion of moving into a white neighborhood, two out of five persons said that they thought it was a good idea. The remaining three out of five were either undecided about how they felt or did not favor the suggestion. Seventy percent of those interviewed preferred a mixed black and white neighborhood, 30 percent a predominately black one. The preference for such racial composition pointed to a basic flaw in the keystone tactic of EOH, that of attempting to interest blacks in moving into white neighborhoods.

In spite of the confusion regarding the purpose of EOH, three out of five applicants were satisfied with their contact and the help received, while two out of five were disgruntled about their experiences.

The applicants' reports of help received from EOH reflect a consistency between the operational program of EOH and what EOH was providing, although the program failed to serve the self-perceived needs of the applicants. Of the seven out of ten applicants who reported that EOH had helped them,

- 60.6 percent were given listings of housing.
- 7 percent were given guide service to inspect housing in target neighborhoods.
- Two people (2.8 percent) were referred to other agencies for help.
- One person received help in dealing with a complaint.

The major asset of EOH in the applicants' view was the helpfulness of the staff. Virtually all persons interviewed were satisfied with the treatment they received. Nearly half (46.5 percent) of those interviewed give unsolicited compliments about the helpfulness of the staff.

All housing applicants at EOH were asked whether they would be interested in moving into a white neighborhood. In the follow-up interview, respondents were queried about their reactions to the proposition. As it turned out, applicants were split almost evenly on the issue, 51.4 percent approving the aggressive approach to integration and 48.6 percent disapproving it. Such verbal approval, however, was insufficient to support positive action on the part of 90 percent of the people who contacted EOH. It appears that while there was concern for integrating neighborhoods, the underlying objective was to open access to a greater volume of better quality housing and the accoutrements that accompany it.

Analysis of the approval of the aggressive approach on several dimensions—including the effects of satisfaction with neighborhood and the effect of income, occupation, geographic origin, and racial composition of neighborhood—did not show any noticeable influence, which explains the split obtained. The actual preference in racial composition of the neighborhood showed 70 percent favoring residence in an integrated neighborhood and 30 percent preferring an essentially black neighborhood. The presence of children in the family increased the likelihood of preference for a racially mixed neighborhood by twenty points (78 percent versus only 58.6 percent in families with no children; see Table 2-5). The conjecture here is that quality of living conditions desired by families with children affected the preference for racial composition, if we assume that mixed neighborhoods generally were perceived as offering safety, better quality housing, and improved education.

What factors affected the decision of these black people to move? Following the investigations of Peter Rossi[33] and Lewis Watts,[34] the role of the applicant's satisfaction with neighborhood conditions, the quality of social life in the neighborhood, and family space needs in making a decision to move were probed. It was expected that a satisfaction quotient would be directly related to the decision to move.

Whether there was a relationship between the racial composition of the neighborhood and the level of dissatisfaction with physical and social conditions of the neighborhood also was of interest. The existence of a direct relation between neighborhood quality, satisfaction, and the decision to move would suggest the existence of a disproportionately high rate of movement in racially homogeneous neighborhoods occupied by residents who are dissatisfied with neighborhood conditions. Such moves should be in the direction of better quality housing and living conditions, toward the transitional periph-

33. Peter H. Rossi, *Why Families Move* (Glencoe, Ill.: The Free Press, 1955).

34. Lewis G. Watts et al., *The Middle Income Negro Family Faces Urban Renewal* (Waltham, Mass.: Research Center of the Florence Heller Graduate School for Advanced Studies in Social Welfare, 1964). Other authors concerned about consumer decisions in the housing market include Nelson Foote et al., *Housing Choices and Housing Constraints* (New York: McGraw-Hill Co., 1960); Sam H. Leaman, "A Study of Housing Decisions by Negro House Owners and Negro Renters" (Master's thesis, University of North Carolina, Chapel Hill, North Carolina 1960); Shirley F. Weiss, Kenneth B. Kenny, and Roger C. Steffens, "Consumer Preferences in Residential Location: A Preliminary Investigation of the Home Purchase Decision," *Research Previews* 13 (1966): 1–32.

Table 2-5. Preference in Racial Composition of the Neighborhood (percent).

Position	No Children in Family	Children in Family	Total
(Number of Cases)	(29)	(41)	(70)
Approve Suggestion to Move into White Neighborhood	48.2	53.7	51.4
Disapprove Suggestion	51.7	46.3	48.6
	Chi Square = 0.04	Not Significant	
Prefer a Mixed Neighborhood	58.6	78.0	70.0
Prefer a Primarily Black Neighborhood	41.4	22.0	30.0
	Chi Square = 2.197	$P = <0.25$	

eries of the solid black communities, or to so-called integrated communities.

Four scales were designed to probe these questions. They served as indications of factors affecting decisions to move and were examined for their relationship to applicant characteristics that would explain factors related to the search for housing (details of scale design appear at the end of the chapter):

1. *Satisfaction with Neighborhood* measured the contentment of the applicant with condition of his neighborhood.
2. *Satisfaction with Dwelling* measured the contentment of the applicant with the physical condition of his dwelling.
3. *Sense of Power* measured the applicant's sense of influence over the conditions of his immediate environment.
4. *Self-disparagement* measured the applicant's self-esteem.

The self-disparagement scale failed to provide any variance that was helpful in understanding the dynamics affecting the search for housing. Self-disparagement thus did not affect an applicant's satisfaction, dissatisfaction, or sense of control over his environment. The correlations presented in Table 2-6 indicate a strong interplay among satisfaction factors and sense of power, where a high score on any one of the three measures predicts a high score on the other three, however. Thus an applicant who was satisfied with his neighborhood

Table 2-6. Intercorrelations of Four Scales: Self-Disparagement, Satisfaction with Neighborhood, Satisfaction with Dwelling, and Sense of Power.

	1	2	3	4
Self-disparagement				
Satisfaction with Neighborhood	0.125			
Satisfaction with Dwelling	0.032	0.683*		
Sense of Power	0.109	0.583*	0.634*	

*Significant at 0.05 level.

tended also to be satisfied with his dwelling and to possess a sense of influence over conditions in his neighborhood. The same direct relation held for the opposite situation. Where the applicant was dissatisfied with his neighborhood and housing, he was likely to express a feeling that he was unable to exert as much control over his circumstances as he would prefer. This provides clear support for the relationship between satisfaction and power. Does this in turn affect participation of black homeseekers in the housing market, as Peter Rossi asserted in his study of white dwelling seekers?

The single most important effect on the level of satisfaction with neighborhood conditions was the event of moving from one dwelling to another. The change of neighborhood residence served as a lever for satisfaction. As shown in Table 2-7, those families that changed their residence expressed significantly greater satisfaction with all aspects of neighborhood conditions than those that did not move. It appears, then, that dissatisfaction mounted until it precipitated an actual search and eventual change of residence. At that point, conditions generating dissatisfaction were removed, and the ex-homeseeker began to express satisfaction with his circumstances. This same dynamic held for satisfaction with dwelling and sense of power.

The sense of power is particularly interesting since it showed a direct relation to the two measures of satisfaction. The data do not permit us to specify whether it has the sense of power that facilitated the successful search for housing or whether the consummated move served to reinforce the sense of control over life conditions. Theory supports the former dynamic, although the latter could also be true, particularly in the case where the housing market and economic condition mitigated against immediate fulfillment of the desire to move. The frustrated efforts to upgrade housing accommodations nourished the belief that one indeed lacks power over such environmental conditions.

Table 2-7. The Effect of Moving on Satisfaction (percent).

Satisfaction Factor	Moved Since First Contact	Not Moved	Total
(Number of Cases)	(33)	(37)	(70)
Satisfied with Surroundings of Neighborhood	78.8	35.1	55.7
Dissatisfied	21.2	64.9	44.3
	Chi Square = 11.760	P < 0.001	
Satisfied with People in Neighborhood	63.6	43.2	52.9
Dissatisfied	36.4	56.8	47.1
	Chi Square = 2.150	P < 0.25	
Satisfied with Grocery in Neighborhood	75.8	56.8	52.9
Dissatisfied	24.2	43.2	27.1
	Chi Square = 2.015	P < 0.25	
Neighborhood Good Place for Rearing Children	71.9	48.6	59.4
Neighborhood Poor Place	28.1	51.4	40.6
	Chi Square = 2.936	P < 0.10	
Neighborhood a Safe Place to Live	66.7	35.1	50.0
Neighborhood Not Safe	33.3	64.9	50.0
	Chi Square = 5.733	P < 0.02	
Condition Same or Getting Better	54.4	32.4	42.9
Condition Getting Worse	45.6	67.6	57.1
	Chi Square = 2.638	P < 0.25	

Factors influencing the level of satisfaction with neighborhood and dwelling, the sense of power, and the self-disparagement also were investigated. The analysis included preference for racial mix of neighborhood, geographical region of birth, presence of children, family income, educational attainment, and whether the respondent had changed residence.

Only the event of changing residence proved to be a significant factor in accounting for significant patterning of the responses shown

Table 2-8. The Impact of Moving on Self-disparagement, Satisfaction with Dwelling, Satisfaction with Neighborhood, and Sense of Power.

Variable	Mean		Differ-ence	t-Test	Signifi-cance
	Moved Since Termination (N = 33)	Not Moved (N = 37)			
Self-disparagement	11.42[a]	10.60	0.83	1.445	(P = 0.15)
Satisfaction with Neighborhood	19.12[b]	24.95	−5.83	−4.976	(P = 0.001)
Satisfaction with Dwelling	8.82[b]	12.97	−4.16	−3.963	(P = 0.001)
Sense of Power	6.46[b]	7.95	−1.49	−2.995	(P = 0.004)

[a] Higher score represents high self-esteem.
[b] Lower scores represent greater satisfaction or sense of power.

in Table 2-8. The factors examined did not produce significant differences in levels of satisfaction, senses of power, and self-disparagement. Those homeseekers who had succeeded in locating and moving into new residences were significantly more satisfied with both the neighborhood conditions and their dwellings. They expressed greater confidence in their ability to effect change, and they held themselves as persons in higher regard than those who had not moved. It made no difference what the financial status, educational background, family status, preference for racial mix of neighborhood, or region or birth were; the fact of moving was the significant event influencing the four factors. It should be stressed that a unique group of people was analyzed here—people in search of housing. The multitude of factors represented in a compressed fashion in the fact of moving significantly altered their sense of satisfaction and power and increased their self-esteem.

From these findings, it would appear that the search for housing was a search for suitable environment in which to transact the business of living. The expectations and aspirations for the good life served as measuring devices against which to assess the suitability of the environment for contributing to the good life. When conditions were perceived as being adverse, the individual sought to alter his circumstances by moving to a neighborhood more compatible with his living needs. When the move was consummated, the compatibility between living needs and environment increased and resulted in increased satisfaction and sense of power.

The residents of a neighborhood collectively create a social milieu that influences the attitudes and beliefs held regarding various aspects of community life. The intensity and frequency of information communication occurring in the neighborhood should therefore influence the degree to which common sentiments are held. How did racial composition of the neighborhood affect choices and sentiments?

The contextual effects of neighborhood were operationalized for our purposes as the degree and length of time of ghettoization. A neighborhood was said to be ghettoized when people moving into it were predominately black.

The ghettoization hypothesis contends that satisfaction and sense of power are inversely associated with the degree of ghettoization. Where the racial composition is predominately black, the physical condition of the neighborhood is altered adversely, and the level of dissatisfaction increases. In terms of the dynamics of the black housing market, the ghettoization hypothesis holds that residential movement generally is out of ghettoized neighborhoods.

Contrary to this hypothesis, the data did not produce significant differences in numbers of dissatisfied homeseekers according to the ghettoization factor, as shown in Table 2-9. A closer examination of the patterning of responses according to the three types of racial composition—ghettoized, transitional, and integrated—shows that the percentage differences were in the direction predicted by the hypothesis however. The sample size, in this case sixty-seven people, was too small to produce significant levels of confidence in the data. However the following tendencies should be noted:

- More respondents were satisfied than dissatisfied with neighborhood conditions, regardless of racial composition.
- There was close to an even split on satisfaction with people in the neighborhood, assessment of the safety of the neighborhood, and concern that neighborhood conditions were worsening. In the ghettoized neighborhoods, concerns about safety and worsening of conditions were slightly higher, but not significantly so.
- Satisfaction was usually higher in the integrated neighborhood, with the exceptions of satisfaction with buildings and concern that conditions were worsening. Apparently the interviewees were uncertain about the stability of the neighborhood, although this cannot be conclusively confirmed because of insufficient evidence.

The decisions that a homeseeker must make about type of neighborhood, condition of dwelling, consumer facilities, and nearness to work and associates lead to the ultimate event of the move into the

Table 2-9. Satisfaction According to Racial Status of Neighborhood.

Variable	Ghetto-ized Neighbor-hood	Neighbor-hood Tran-sitional 1975+	Inte-grated Neighbor-hood	Total
	(N = 42)	(N = 15)	(N = 10)	(N = 67)
Satisfied with Buildings	64.2	73.3	60.0	65.7
Dissatisfied with Buildings	35.7	26.7	40.0	34.3
Chi Square = 0.469			Not Significant	
Satisfied with Neighborhood	50.0	67.7	50.0	
Dissatisfied with Neighbor-hood	50.0	33.3	50.0	
Chi Square = 0.8			Not Significant	
Prefer Mixed Neighborhood	61.9	80.0	70.0	67.2
Prefer Black Neighborhood	38.1	20.0	30.0	32.8
Chi Square = 1.564			Not Significant	
Satisfied with People	61.9	40.0	40.0	53.7
Dissatisfied with People	38.1	60.0	60.0	46.3
Chi Square = 2.948			$P < 0.25$	
Satisfied with Grocery	59.5	73.3	80.0	65.7
Dissatisfied with Grocery	40.5	26.7	20.0	34.3
Chi Square = 1.826			Not Significant	
Neighborhood Good for Rearing Children	53.7	73.3	70.0	60.6
Neighborhood Not Good for Rearing Children	46.3	26.7	30.0	39.4
Chi Square = 2.178			Not Significant	
Neighborhood Safe	45.2	60.0	50.0	49.3
Neighborhood Unsafe	54.7	40.0	50.0	50.7
Chi Square = 0.871			Not Significant	
Conditions Staying Same	40.4	53.3	30.0	418
Conditions Worsening	59.6	46.7	70.0	58.2
Chi Square = 1.340			Not Significant	

desired housing. The importance of the decision and the unique preference for a given type of neighborhood, dwelling, and related conditions may complicate the search for housing if the total package desired is scarce. If the combination of things desired in a residence is relatively accessible, the complications are reduced.

We were interested in two aspects of factors requiring decisions in the selection of housing: (1) what was the dominant priority of decisions affecting the selection of housing; and (2) what was the extent of agreement about priority among black homeseekers on conditions requiring decisions.

Two approaches were taken to establish the dominant way in which black homeseekers ranked housing factors. Each interviewee was asked to rank the ten items listed in Table 2-10. The mean rank score was taken to represent the overall importance of a given item. The ranking obtained in this fashion was then checked against the rank being chosen the greatest number of times by all interviewees. The ranking thus obtained was contrasted for congruity with that obtained by the averaging method. While some disparities did occur, the clustering of items was congruent enough to justify the claim that there does appear to be a dominant pattern for ranking choices involved in the selection of housing.

In the dominant priority approach, the quality and cost of housing were given highest priority. Neighborhood conditions and quality of consumer facilities were given second consideration. Nearness to work, relatives, and friends were given last consideration.

Table 2-10. Priorities for Selecting a Dwelling.

Decision Item	Rank by Average of All Choices	Rank by Highest Frequency of Choice
Housing Factors		
High 1 Condition of the Dwelling	3.4	1
2 Cost of the Dwelling	3.5	4
Neighborhood Factors		
3 Appearance of the Neighborhood	3.7	2
4 Safety of the Neighborhood	3.8	3
5.5 Shopping Places	5.2	4
5.5 Schools and Education	5.2	1,10 split
8 People in the Neighborhood	5.7	8
Propinquity Factors		
7 Nearness to Work	5.6	6, 10 split
9 Nearness to Relatives	7.3	9
Low 10 Nearness to Friends	7.5	10

Two interesting departures occurred. There was a near even split on the importance of schools and quality of education. Nearly one-fifth of the interviewees placed schools at the top of their priority lists, while about the same proportion put schools at the bottom. For those families with children, school programs and facilities were a major factor involved in the search for housing. Since quality housing is usually available in neighborhoods where quality schools are located, these two priorities were highly compatible.

The second question was the degree to which interviewees were in agreement about the importance of factors represented in the selection of a dwelling. A rank order statistic was employed for this purpose. The closer the statistic approaches unity, the greater the agreement among the individual rankings.

Several subgroupings of respondents were examined to establish common characteristics that produced greater agreement regarding importance of housing factors. Rank order correlations ranged from 0.415 to 0.245, all of which were statistically significant at conventional levels. (Table 2-11).

Interviewees without children in the home showed the highest level of agreement (0.415), although this was far from being perfect agreement. The subgroup among which the lowest level of agreement obtained was people who had not yet moved. It appears that there was considerable disparity among them as to what they wanted in housing. The complement of conditions and qualities sought in housing was difficult to locate in a specific dwelling. It also could be that the family was not sure enough of its preferences to make a decision or that the family's preferences were out of line with what the market offered, and it therefore was unable to find a dwelling to

Table 2-11. Preference for Racial Mix, Geographic Origin, Family Status, Residential Stability, and Rank Correlation of Factors Affecting the Selection of Dwelling.

| Subgrouping | Rank Order Coefficients | | | | | |
	Group 1	(N)	Significance	Group 2	(N)	Significance
Prefer Mixed Black Neighborhood	0.355	(45)	<0.001	0.273	(22)	<0.001
Born North Born South	0.328	(40)	<0.001	0.310	(26)	<0.001
Children —None —Some	0.415	(28)	<0.001	0.342	(39)	<0.001
Moved—Not Moved	0.345	(33)	<0.001	0.245	(37)	<0.001

match its desires. One could speculate that such people may go through a process of preference altering until it becomes possible to match their desires to a specific dwelling.

Thus, among the black homeseekers who went to the EOH center, social and demographic differences had little influence on whether they were satisfied or dissatisfied with housing and neighborhood conditions. Change of dwelling produced a major effect on satisfaction with dwelling, satisfaction with the neighborhood, and sense of power over the immediate environment. Satisfaction is an indication of the needs felt by a family given the opportunity for fulfillment in the particular housing and neighborhood chosen. Where housing and neighborhood mitigate against such fulfillment, the dynamics that culminate in a move are set in motion. Further, degree of ghettoization of the neighborhood did not affect the collective level of satisfaction with housing and neighborhood. People managed to be satisfied or dissatisfied regardless of the type of neighborhood. And in the search for housing, the dominant mode for making a selection was to consider the quality of the dwelling first, then the neighborhood, and finally the nearness to work and associates. For those families with children, quality of schools was a high priority. Very few of the applicants were in sympathy with the goals of Equal Opportunity Housing per se.

DISCUSSION

What, then, might be said of the Leadership Council's attempt to initiate Equal Opportunity Housing? During its first year, virtually no progress at all was made in having real estate boards, individual brokers, or management agents provide the service with nondiscriminatory listings. No brokers or agents used the listings obtained by the service. The listings did not improve significantly on the newspaper advertisements widely available to all; indeed, in the main they were such advertisements. There were 537 applications for the council's service, and 46 placements were made. The majority of applicants neither understood nor were in sympathy with the goals of EOH. Perhaps more might have been, had housing choices been as constrained as they were in the 1950s, for housing objectives dominated the desire to move. But such was not the case at the end of the 1960s. As we shall see later, it was probably the dramatic change in access to the central city's housing that was occurring as white flight accelerated that was as instrumental as any factors in the future of the EOH program.

The crux of any evaluation is an assessment of whether goals have been achieved. In January of 1969, the staff of the Leadership Council assessed their first year on the job, commenting, "Calm, painstaking, behind-the-scenes efforts at persuasion and counseling are and will continue to be valuable and productive, but there is every indication that we must have forceful, dramatic and above all immediately visible action and progress in fair housing." The report concluded:

> There are many in the metropolitan community who feel that much of the initiative gained at the conference table in August 1966 has been dissipated and that little tangible progress can be shown. Despite this belief by some, the fact is the Summit Agreement remains an important document in the achievement of an open housing market. Moreover, the Leadership Council as the primary instrument in the implementation of that agreement has demonstrated both the willingness and ability to secure the promises spelled out in the Summit Agreement. No one can say that the job is done, but the past twelve months have pointed the metropolitan area toward the ultimate realization of a democratic housing market.[35]

This was entirely too sanguine. The Leadership Council's Equal Opportunity Housing centers were a dismal failure. Perhaps the only glimmer of program success during the first year of their operation was that the rate of move ins of black homeseekers to Chicago's suburbs had increased. This was not the result of the EOH programs, however, even though the majority of moves were into suburbs with open housing ordinances that the Leadership Council had helped promote.

In the suburbs, too, racial separation had been the rule. Of a 1960 total suburban nonwhite population of 82,000, over 15,000 lived in four all Negro communities (Dixmoor, East Chicago Heights, Phoenix, and Robbins[36]) and over 50,000 of the rest lived in segregated

35. *The Leadership Council for Metropolitan Open Communities Newsletter* 1, no. 3 (January 1969): 3.

36. In 1922 Robbins was described as "the only exclusively Negro community near Chicago . . . . Robbins is not attractive physically . . . . There is no pretense of paved streets . . . . The houses are homemade, in most cases . . . . There are 380 people all told, men, women, and children, living in something more than seventy houses . . . . " The Chicago Commission on Race Relations, *The Negro in Chicago. A Study of Race Relations and a Race Riot in 1919*, (New York: Arno Press and the New York Times, 1968), p. 138.

A half century later: "'Robbins welcomes you: we learn to do by doing. Schools, Water, Sewers, Sights, Pop. 7,511,' the sign said. The sign—like the schools, water, sewers, sights, and population figure in the all-black suburb—was rundown and 10 years outdated . . . . Housewives and homeowners talked about sewers that overflowed and schools with no money, about 'fixed' elections and no place for kids to play, about 500 people without running water . . . . There

black districts in eighteen other suburban towns. Very few of the remaining 17,000 nonwhite suburbanites were black. For example, the community of Hinsdale was reported as having a nonwhite population of ninety-six in 1960, but its first black family entered in 1966 and remained the only one in that suburb until 1968, when two others entered.

The first reasonably accurate actual counts of the black population of suburban Chicago were developed through 1966 by the Commission on Religion and Race of the Presbytery of Chicago, in cooperation with the Illinois Commission on Human Relations and Home Opportunities Made Equal, Inc., an affiliate of the American Friends Service Committee. In 1967 the Leadership Council took over the job of estimation. The counts (not a census) were made by contacting several reliable sources (both public and private) in each community in the metropolitan area to obtain and verify the information. They refer to black moveins into predominantly white suburban neighborhoods, and they exclude peripheral expansion of the suburban ghettos as well as the city of Chicago.

The counts (of black family units, not population) are shown in Table 2-12. Table 2-13 shows the distribution by suburb. The numbers were extremely small and show much tokenism. It was, of course, undoubtedly significant that the 1968 moveins were almost double those of 1967, a sign that racial constraints were easing a little and that all but 19 of the 353 black families moving into pre-

Table 2-12.   Movement of Black Families into Chicago's Suburbs.

Year	Number of Move Ins
1945–1960	5
1961–1962	4
1963	26
1964	45
1965	75
1966	165
1967	191
1968	353

are 19 taverns and 23 churches in Robbins, and four paved streets . . . . Robbins ranked last among 250 Cook County communities (including Chicago) in education, income and employment. 'The problem is massive poverty and ignorance. It's a town that should never have happened,' said broadcaster Vince Sanders . . . . 'People came up to Chicago in 1900, but they wanted their own plot of land. So they got locked in here worse than they would have on the South Side.'" *Chicago Daily News*, February 16, 1969.

Table 2-13.   Black Residents of Chicago's Suburbs.[a]

Suburban Community	1959–1965	1966	1967	1967 Total[c]	1968	1968 Total
Addison	1	2	2	4[b]	0	4
Arlington Heights	0	1	2	3	1	4
Aurora	0	1	4	5	36	41
Barrington[c]	1	0	0	1	0	1
Batavia	2	0	3	5	6	11
Bellwood	1	0	2	3	4	7
Brookfield	1	0	0	1	0	1
Butterfield West	0	0	2	2	1	3
Calumet City	2	0	0	2	0	2
Calumet Park	1	0	0	1	0	1
Carol Stream	0	1	1	2	2	4
Chicago Heights	8	16	20	44	20	64
Country Club Hills	1	0	0	1	0	1
Deerfield	1[c]	0	2	3	1	4
Des Plaines	0	0	0	0	2	2
Dolton	7	0	0	7	0	7
Downers Grove	6	0	5	11	4	15
Elgin	10	9	6	25	16	41
Elk Grove	4	1	1	5[b]	0	5
Elmhurst	0	0	0	0	1	1
Evanston	0	7	10	17	15	32
Flossmoor	1	0	0	1	1	2
Glencoe	1	4	4	9	4	13
Glendale Heights	0	2	1	2[d]	2	4
Glen Ellyn[c]	0	0	4	4	4	8
Glenview	2	0	0	2	0	2
Hazelcrest	1	0	0	1	1	2
Highland Park	4	11	5	20	20	40
Hinsdale	0	1	0	1[d]	0	1
Hoffman Estates	1	0	2	2	1	3
Homewood	1	0	0	1	0	1
Kenilworth	1	0	0	1	0	1
LaGrange	1	1	0	2	1	3
Lake Bluff	0	4	0	4	0	4
Lake Forest	3	1	0	4	0	4
Lisle	0	0	0	0	3	3
Lombard	0	2	2	2[f]	0	2
Maywood	3	8	17	28	38	66
Naperville[g]	1	0	0	1	2	3
Niles	0	0	0	0	1	1
Northbrook	0	0	1	1	1	2
North Chicago	25	10	15	50	25	75
Oak Park	8	2	2	12	12	24
Olympia Fields	0	0	1	1	1	2
Olympia Gardens	1	0	1	2	0	2

Table 2-13. continued

Suburban Community	1959–1965	1966	1967	1967 Total[c]	1968	1968 Total
Palatine	1	2	1	4[h]	0	4
Park Forest	39	42	33	100[h]	80	180
Riverdale	1	0	0	1	1	2
River Forest	0	0	1	1	0	1
Rolling Meadows	1	0	1	1[d]	1	2
St. Charles	2	2	0	4	0	4
Schaumberg	1	0	0	1	0	1
Skokie	11	3	3	16[d]	6	22
South Holland	0	0	1	1	0	1
Waukegan	15	15	20	50[f]	15	65
Western Springs	2	1	0	3	0	3
Westmont	0	1	0	1	1	2
Wheeling	0	2	2[g]	4	1	5
Wheaton[g]	12	4	4	20	14	34
Wilmette	1	2	0	3	2	5
Winnetka	1	0	1	1[d]	0	1
Woodridge	0	1	3	4	1	5
York Center	18	2	1	21	0	21
Zion	12	3	5	20[f]	5	25
			191	549 (64 suburbs)	353	902

[a]Excludes black families moving into all black neighborhoods in such towns as Aurora, Chicago Heights, Elgin, Evanston, Glencoe, Maywood, North Chicago, Waukegan, Wheaton, and Zion.
[b]1 move out occurred in 1967.
[c]Includes unincorporated area near this suburb.
[d]1 family has moved out.
[e]Total Negro families living in predominantly white areas as of January 1, 1968.
[f]Approximation.
[g]Includes nearby unincorporated area near this suburb.
[h]14 families moved out between 1959–1967.

dominantly white neighborhoods had moved into municipalities that had passed open housing ordinances. As noted, the Leadership Council had played an important role in the passage of these ordinances. In Illinois as a whole, seven ordinances were passed in 1963–1966, eighteen in 1967, fifty-four in 1968, and three in the first nine months of 1969, with fifty-four of these eighty-two in metropolitan Chicago. The decline in new local ordinances thereafter is attributable to the Federal Civil Rights Acts of 1968, Title VIII of which provided a national fair housing law, and the June 17, 1968, decision of the U.S. Supreme Court in the case of *Jones v. Mayer*, discussed in the chapter that follows, reaffirming the constitutionality of the Civil Rights Act of 1866 that "bars all racial discrimination, private as well as public, in the sale or rental of property." The strong correlation of suburban moveins with communities passing local ordinances served, on the other hand, to emphasize the profound importance of local attitudes and the relative ineffectiveness of federal provisions until or unless supported by a substantial legal assault.[37] It is to this assault that we now turn.

APPENDIX: PROFILE OF SCALES USED IN ATTITUDINAL ANALYSIS

TITLE: *Satisfaction with Neighborhood*

DEFINITION: This scale measures the contentment of the respondent with environmental conditions of the neighborhood in which he resides

TYPE: A Likent scaling procedure was used in which the numerical categories of a set of scale items are summed to obtain the scale value

SCALE COMPOSITION:

1. How satisfied are you with how the buildings in the neighborhood look?
2. How satisfied are you with the surroundings of the neighborhood?
3. How satisfied are you with the people in the neighborhood?
4. How satisfied are you with the grocery stores in the neighborhood?
5. How safe do you feel it is to live in this neighborhood?
6. Do you feel conditions in this neighborhood are getting better or worse?

RANGE OF SCORE:

6 to 29

High score indicates dissatisfaction
Low score indicates satisfaction

TITLE: *Satisfaction with Dwelling*

DEFINITION: This scale measures the respondent's contentment with the physical condition of his dwelling

---

37. See Setlow, "Metropolitan Open Housing Ordinances in Illinois."

TYPE: A Likent scaling procedure was used in which the numerical categories of a set of scale items are summed to obtain a scale value

SCALE COMPOSITION:

1. How do you feel about the amount of living space you have?
2. How do you feel about the amount of privacy you have?
3. How do you feel about the condition of this dwelling?
4. How comfortable and pleasant do you feel in this dwelling?
5. In general, how satisfied are you with this dwelling?

RANGE OF SCORE:

5 to 24

High score indicates dissatisfaction
Low score indicates satisfaction

TITLE: *Sense of Power*

DEFINITION: This scale measures the respondent's sense of influence over the condition of his immediate environment

TYPE: A Likent scaling procedure was used in which the numerical categories of a set of scale items are summed to obtain a scale value

SCALE COMPOSITION:

1. How much do you feel you as an individual can do to make this neighborhood a nice place to live?
2. How much influence do you have for improving the condition of your dwelling or getting someone to do it?

RANGE OF SCORE

2 to 10

Low score indicates high sense of power over environment
High score indicates high sense of powerlessness over environment

TITLE: *Self-disparagement*

DEFINITION: This scale measures the respondent's self-esteem relative to his racial identity

TYPE: A Likent scaling procedure was used in which the numerical categories of a set of scale items are summed to obtain the scale role

SCALE COMPOSITION:

1. I don't worry about the race problem because I can't do anything about it.

2. I sometimes get the feeling that it is just not worth fighting for justice and equal treatment of Negroes in this city.
3. Negroes shouldn't go in business establishments where they think they're not wanted.
4. Negroes blame white people for their position, but it's really their own fault.
5. Negroes are always shouting about their rights but have nothing to offer.
6. Generally speaking, Negroes are lazy and ignorant.

RANGE OF SCORE

6 to 12

Low score indicates low self-esteem
High score indicates high self-esteem

※ *Chapter 3*

Legal Action: Building a Body of Law

By mid-1969 the conclusion was clear. Few blacks were being placed in integrated residential settings by the Leadership Council's fair housing service, and the other activities of the council had little effect on the dual housing market. During the period August 1, 1968–June 30, 1969, 550 applications for housing were taken by the Leadership Council, but the council succeeded in placing only 46 of these applicants. A conference called by the Leadership Council on February 1, 1969, to discuss the programs and experiences in other metropolitan areas (New York, Seattle, Los Angeles, and Denver)

came to similar conclusions about the obstacles to the traditional approaches of the fair housing movement: intransigence of the real estate industry, unavailability at that time of effective legal tools, etc. Each of the other groups reported that they were making substantial changes in program directions, with the two routes most favored either (a) abandoning the effort to achieve a nondiscriminatory housing market and placing emphasis upon creating a supply of low-income housing, or (b) developing new legal techniques to achieve the overall objective of integration through non-discrimination.[1]

Four papers were presented by fair housing groups from the cities mentioned above; the Leadership Council, representing Chicago's

1. "Summary and Outline of First Year's Activity and Revised Work Program, 1969–1970," Leadership Council for Metropolitan Open Communities, June 27, 1969.

fair housing efforts, also made a presentation. Notes taken at the conference revealed a consensus among the participants that:

Substantial changes of emphasis have taken place in several programs. The white liberal do-goodism of the fair-housing movement is now faced by the dilemmas of black activism and more importantly, the articulation of housing goals by the black community that reflect that community's problems rather than white liberals' perceptions of these problems. Generally, the white definition is "integration," whereas the black community is concerned with freedom of access to more and better housing. Integration may be a way to achieving a better housing supply but not the only way open today. Hence, New York focuses on the immediate goal of providing shelter. Seattle has switched from an integration orientation to one of developing a low-income housing supply. Chicago, on the other hand, still has a suburban, integration, fair-housing orientation.[2]

Strategies being pursued were quite diverse. Traditionally, they had involved placing single qualified families in homes on an individual basis, perhaps with checking. But there were calls for replacement of the client-realtor approach by a broad attack on the system creating segregation, using the Civil Rights Act of 1866.

There were, however, a series of continuing dilemmas:

1. Stable integration apparently was only being achieved in high status communities. At lower levels, black entry led unremitingly to resegregation.
2. Fair housing, by emphasizing movement of middle class blacks out of the ghetto, was producing an intensification of the ills of the ghetto, removing educated leadership and leading to concentration of the low end of the economic spectrum.
3. Institutional constraints still remained as formidable barriers to achievement of freely available options in housing at all income levels.
4. Emerging conflicts of black and white perceptions of the problem and differences in their statements of goals constituted real dangers for the older fair housing groups.

Two weeks after the seminar was held in Chicago, Howard Cayton, director of Urban Renewal Demonstration Program in the Department of Housing and Urban Development, Washington, D.C., wrote

2. Notes from "Comparison and Contrast Seminar," held at the University of Chicago, February 1, 1969.

Edward Holmgren, executive director of the Leadership Council, saying, in part:

> the meager results of the services rendered by the two referral centers (18 families placed in three months) make it clear that a reexamination of the Council's approach is in order. Our meetings indicated that no one was directly placed as a result of the Council's contacts with the Chicago Real Estate Board. In fact, Mr. Schucker [housing information director for the Leadership Council] told us that the single most important factor preventing progress is the combined unwillingness of the management firms and the owners to change their discriminatory practices. If in fact the goal of this program is to alter the real estate market system so that the options available to whites are available to minority groups on an equal basis, it seems clear that a different and more vigorous approach must be adopted. Thus far, the housing center supplies the Board with lists of families seeking housing; it has also asked some larger firms to earmark a certain percentage of vacancies for Council use (an "active affirmation" of the firm's good intentions). However, this approach seems to touch the issue of system-changing only minimally. What is needed is a more direct and intensive approach which does not rely so much on the expressed general intentions of the industry . . . . In addition, in order to encourage the industry to act in compliance with the laws, it may be necessary to prosecute: thus the role of the staff attorney needs review.[3]

In June of 1969, the Leadership Council submitted a revised work program to HUD. Since the council had earlier disavowed abandoning the effort to achieve a nondiscriminatory housing market by placing emphasis upon creating a supply of low income housing, it therefore, . . . sparked by the HUD directive, began a concerted legal attack on the discriminatory practices constraining housing choices of Negro homeseekers. In its self-evaluation at the end of the first contract year of operations, the council wrote:

> Previous efforts by volunteer housing organizations attempted to link nondiscriminatory home sellers and apartment renters directly to interested minority group homeseekers. These well-intentioned efforts were designed to circumvent the existing real estate market system, rather than to directly deal with it. The Leadership Council's experimental program was designed to stimulate and supplement the existing real estate market, so as to make it equally accessible to everyone . . . . We envisioned the focus of our efforts to be a drive to enlist the active *cooperation* of real estate interests in our work. This approach, based upon what we perceived to be a new

3. Letter from Howard Cayton to Edward Holmgren, February 13, 1969.

spirit of good will among professional real estate dealers, proved essentially fruitless.

. . .

Experimental efforts conducted cooperatively with the Leadership Council and the Chicago Conference on Religion and Race prior to this program's funding had resulted in a small and infrequent supply of listing of available homes and apartments from certain real estate dealers. To increase the flow of such listings after the program obtained federal funding, two staff members were assigned to meet with real estate brokers on a continuing basis and to obtain a greater number of listings. Visits by staff to real estate professionals met generally with either of two alternative responses:

1. Hostility—Leadership Council staff was told that the firm did not intend to cooperate.
2. Many firms responded with the bland assertion that their practices were free of racial discrimination and that there was no point in their providing listings to us. Staff was instructed by these firms, "Send your applicants around to the office."

. . .

It became increasingly clear that despite the commitments made during the 1966 Summit Agreement the real estate industry had no real commitment or intention to accommodate its practices to the needs of minority home seekers.

. . .

Subsequently, a series of meetings was held with attorneys to examine the applicability of the 1968 law and the Supreme Court decision (*Jones v. Mayer*). It was learned that three law suits had been filed invoking the 1866 Civil Rights Act in state or federal courts, and that two of these complaints had been successful in obtaining the housing sought by this means. The third obtained a $200 cash settlement, as the housing unit had been rented before the suit was filed.

An experimental relationship was established between the Leadership Council and staff attorneys of the Community Legal Counsel, a local OEO funded agency . . . . Staff began referring cases of discrimination to CLC lawyers who promptly filed suit in federal court on behalf of Leadership Council applicants. Again, the overwhelming majority of these resulted in an offer of appropriate housing to the plantiff . . . . A decision was made following these early experiments to supplement the cooperative approach with the real estate industry with this new, effective legal device . . . . At the end of May, 1969, a total of 24 law suits citing the 1866 Civil Rights Act had been filed by Leadership Council attorneys.

. . .

The main departure [of the revised work program] from the original proposal is that instead of an attempt to place minority families in non-ghetto housing by *any* means, the focus will now be on working with the minority homeseeker from the point of application through placement with the aim of filing legal action in the Federal District Court and complaints with HUD in instances where discrimination is found. Therefore, the service will 1) seek out bona fide minority homeseekers who will also be willing to follow through with legal action, if necessary; 2) work closely with all applicants in their housing search, and in some cases escorting them to various available housing accommodations; 3) where necessary, utilizing a white witness, promptly verifying that discrimination took place; 4) file complaints of discrimination with HUD and in Federal District Court, where applicable; 5) consulting with real estate boards and brokers in order to develop and promote positive programs of equal opportunity housing; and 6) provide extensive publicity throughout the metropolitan area regarding the outcome of court cases and the existence of latest developments in this program.[4]

The change in program strategy would not have been possible had it not been for two Civil Rights Acts and the United States Supreme Court ruling in *Jones v. Mayer* reaffirming and reinterpreting the 1866 Civil Rights Act. Together, the 1866 and 1968 Civil Rights Acts guaranteed equal rights to any person seeking housing. There were exceptions in the 1968 legislation. The act did not apply to most single family homes sold or rented by a private individual owner without the use of a broker of advertisement nor to certain properties owned by religious and private organizations. But the 1866 Civil Rights Act covered even these circumstances. In *Jones v. Mayer*,[5] Justice Stewart, speaking for the Court, ruled that "42 U.S.C. 1982 bars all racial discrimination, private as well as public, in the sale or rental of property."[6]

As noted, to test the effectiveness of the new federal law in the United States District Court, the council established relationships with attorneys employed by legal assistance organizations and Chicago-based law firms. Early results were encouraging. Clients represented by volunteer lawyers working with the Leadership Council were generally able to obtain, after a speedy hearing in court, either the housing units initially denied them or cash settlements, or both. Attorneys, at the time they filed complaints, would include a motion

---

4. "Summary and Outline of First Year's Activity and Revised Work Program, 1969-1970," Leadership Council for Metropolitan Open Communities, June 27, 1969.
5. 392 U.S. 409, 88 S.Ct. 2186, 20 L. Ed. 2nd 1189 (1968).
6. Id.

for a temporary restraining order, designed to keep the housing in question from being rented or sold pending a full examination of the evidence. This entitled them to an early hearing before a judge—usually one or two days after the initial filing. The courts tended to grant restraining orders where a strong presumption of discrimination was suggested by accompanying affidavits of complainants and witnesses. This—the court-ordered removal of a dwelling unit from the open market—brought many defendants to a willingness to resolve complainants' grievances quickly and without further litigation.

When these early results were reviewed, two weaknesses regarding the use of volunteer attorneys became apparent:

1. While cooperating attorneys were adept at quick resolutions of litigation in most cases, the limitations on their time made pursuit of difficult or complex lawsuits very hard.
2. The use of volunteers made the legal approach a piecemeal affair. Individual homeseekers got quick settlements, but the ultimate cost to defendants was so minimal that the propensity for repeated discrimination was still high. Offending real estate professionals and property owners could escape court orders and large damage awards by settling quickly and inexpensively with the plaintiffs. Thus no real change in the real-estate-marketing system was likely to result.

Activities were, therefore, redesigned to provide the Leadership Council with the kinds of resources it would need to meet the immediate housing needs of plaintiffs, while at the same time building a body of law around the federal statutes with an ultimate objective of eliminating descrimination in the real estate industry throughout the Chicago metropolitan area.

Four attorneys were hired on a full-time basis under the new program, one of whom was made available through VISTA. Other staff assignments were restructured to give attorneys investigative and supportive personnel, thus enabling them to prepare carefully for the presentation of cases before the courts. A subcontract with the Dearborn Real Estate Board, a predominantly black real estate board operating in the Chicago metropolitan area, was designed to increase the awareness among black homeseekers of integrated housing opportunities and to create channels within the real estate industry whereby homeseekers could be linked with housing supplies previously reserved for whites by facilitating black brokers' applications for membership in suburban real estate boards (see Chapter 4).

GOALS

In formulating its new legal strategy, the Leadership Council set forth the following goals:

1. The development of the law with regard to cases involving housing discrimination;
2. The development of forms and procedures to be used in such cases so that private attorneys and other organizations may take these cases and handle them promptly and competently;
3. Obtaining judgments including money damages and legal fees so that private attorneys will be assured that prosecuting such cases can be worthwhile from a monetary standpoint;
4. The analysis of new ways to effect change in the real estate market, including class action suits;
5. Investigation of problems relating to the exclusion of minority group brokers from certain real estate boards; and
6. Study of the legal implications of exclusionary zoning and discriminatory mortgage lending.

THE INITIAL PROGRAM YEAR

The legal program soon expanded to a pace of over one hundred cases per year. Through January of 1970, for example, lawyers for the Leadership Council filed one hundred eighteen cases. Litigation was terminated in ninety-three, and twenty-five were pending. The large number of pending cases was partially due to the long wait (about a year) between the time cases were filed and finally heard in federal court. Since cases could be settled at any time before the actual trial began, most were resolved by the attorneys before trial. Only fourteen cases actually came to trial. Of these, eight received judgements for the plaintiffs, six for the defendants. Of the seventy-nine cases settled out of court, thirty-nine had settlements that included agreed orders and damages, thirty-four were voluntary dismissals, and three were miscellaneous judgments for the plaintiffs, while only three cases were withdrawn by Leadership Council lawyers and their clients.

These outcomes must be interpreted with caution, because of changing council policies. From 1969 until May 1, 1970, the council considered it a "victory" to acquire disputed housing on any terms. This then changed, and thereafter adequate damages were also sought. Thus the early development of the program reflects a higher percentage of voluntary dismissals than occurred in succeeding years. Two groups of judgments, involving agreed orders and awarded damages, reveal that even in the first year of activity, progressive development of the law in fact did take place.

Attitudes of the Real Estate Industry

Evidence selected from a few of these suits gives some flavor of both the nature of the discriminatory practices of real estate brokers toward black homeseekers, and the accompanying attitudes of white residents of the areas in which the homes are sought. For instance, the voice of the industry, *Chicagoland's Real Estate Advertiser*, editorialized

> Ethnic neighborhoods, which contribute to segregated housing patterns, are generally the agglomerations of groups with economic and social likenesses. They are not placed together by Realtors or real estate boards. Black neighborhoods like Italian, Irish, Polish and Jewish are for the most part the result of rent or price capabilities and social interests of the tenants. We challenge the assertion that any real estate board ever set out to form a segregated neighborhood, black or Bohemian. Real estate brokers are subject to supply and demand . . . .[7]

On the other hand, one finds the following story concerning Rise Construction Co. of Lansing, Illinois, in the *Chicago Sun-Times:*

> A temporary restraining order against a south suburban construction company was won Friday by two black Chicago couples who said the concern's salesmen "ran away" when the couples tried to inspect model homes.
>
> U.S. District Court Judge Abraham L. Marovitz issued the order preventing the Rise Construction Co., 18208 Torrence, Lansing, from selling any of 21 lots or four model homes at 167th and Prince Dr. in South Holland during the next 10 days.
>
> The black couples told Marovitz every time they came to see the model homes, the salesmen ran to their autos and drove off, sometimes leaving other customers behind.
>
> The home-seekers are Mr. and Mrs. Allen Doiger, and Mr. and Mrs. Wayne Brown. Doiger, a former Chicago policeman, is a gasoline station owner, and Brown is a biology teacher at Farragut High School.
>
> Larry W. Peters, president of the construction company, told Marovitz that couples were shown model homes Thursday in accordance with a court order. He said the homes were quoted at $38,900 and $49,000 "without extras," such as fireplaces and carpeting.
>
> But lawyers for the Leadership council for Metropolitan Open Commun-

7. *Chicagoland's Real Estate Advertiser*, October 9, 1970.

ities, which brought the suit on behalf of the couples, said the "extras" included such things as kitchen sinks and the number of 2-by-4 boards supporting the houses.

In issuing the restraining order, Marovitz said of the couples, "These are fine American citizens and not second-class citizens. Let's do something in this crazy, mixed-up world, and the place to start is in court."[8]

Association with the Justice Department

In another case, the council enabled the first black family to move into the all white western suburb of Westchester (population 23,000) when Mr. and Mrs. Ralph R. Moore won a suit against Golz Realty of Westchester in May of 1970. Houses in Westchester range in price from $24,000 to $65,000; the Moores bought their home for $53,000. After the court decision was handed down, the Leadership Council and the Moores began receiving threatening calls and letters, and a Westchester village board meeting became a discussion of housing rights on April 23, 1970, highlighting white suburban attitudes toward black homeseekers. More than one hundred village residents demanded the board "do something" about the Moores' imminent move in. Frederick Wedinger, village president responded "the Board understands and sympathizes with the homeowners of the village, but this is something we will have to accept gracefully." One resident said he "had always felt no prejudice against them, having Negro maids and mechanics doing work for him, but that his attitude had changed since recent Black Power developments . . . . They don't want to live with whites." A harassment hearing was held in U.S. District Court on May 11, and, although dismissing the suit, Judge Hubert Will warned the leaders of the Westchester resistance, saying, "I will do anything to enforce the law . . . requiring no discrimination in the sale of real estate."

Violent reaction to black attempts to secure housing in white suburbs surfaced in July when the offices of the Tri-City Human Relations Council in Chicago, a voluntary community action group, were bombed. A Molotov cocktail was thrown into the building a week after the organization, which serves Riverdale, Dolton, South Holland, Phoenix, and the Chicago neighborhoods of Altgeld Gardens, North Riverdale, Golden Gate, and Eden Green, was cited by the Leadership Council for its efforts in helping prepare suits against seven real estate brokers and a land developer operating in the south suburban area. The legal actions were filed on behalf of four families who visited the firms in May and June and were turned away because

8. *Chicago Sun-Times*, November 7, 1970.

they were black. An additional action was filed alleging that the eight defendants together "conspired . . . to deprive plaintiffs of rights to purchase and enter into negotiations upon property, secured by the Constitution and laws of the United States of America."

Subsequent testimony before Judge Julius Hoffman by Mrs. Paula Bennett, former saleswoman with Homestead Realty, one of the defendants, illustrates one of the techniques by which brokers discriminate against black homebuyers. Mrs. Bennett said the company used a "double X" system. If a home listed for sale was in a black or integrated neighborhood, a double X would be used to identify the home on the salesman's listing. In that case, prospective black buyers would be shown the property. If, however, a home was in a white neighborhood, the firm would try to avoid showing it to blacks. Blacks would be told an offer was being made to buy the building and therefore it couldn't be shown. Sometimes, she added, no offer was pending. Her description belied that of Richard Nelson, co-owner of Homestead Realty, when he was asked to comment on the charges against him: "we have five offices, and one-third of the homes are sold to colored, which is approximately equal to their percentage of the population." He neglected to mention the influence of segregationist policies on the offerings made to blacks.

The Moore-Golz case was one of two that involved the West Suburban Board of Realtors. The first was the specific action on behalf of the Moores against Golz Realty, which was handled by Leadership Council lawyers. The second was an action against the members of the West Suburban Board of Realtors as a group prosecuted by the Justice Department with information supplied by the Leadership Council.

In this second suit, Judge Hubert Will issued a consent decree ordering the board and its members not to discriminate against anyone because of race, creed, or color in the sale or rental of housing. Under the decree, the board and ten of its member companies, including Golz, were ordered to post notices in their offices stating that it is against federal law to discriminate in the sale or rental of real estate. The order also granted the U.S. government the right to examine board and realty company records at six month intervals for two years to ensure compliance. The brokers were ordered to record the race of prospective buyers and to set up a conciliation service within the board to review any complaints of discrimination. The decree also permanently prohibited the board from denying real estate brokers membership in the board or participation in its multiple listing service because of race, creed, or national origin, a provision that was prompted by the experience of Mrs. Penny Guice, a black broker from Maywood.

Consent Decree in Tri-City Case

The Tri-City case was the second case in which the Leadership Council was involved where conspiracy was charged against several members of a particular real estate board. By decision of U.S. District Judge Bernard Decker, the individual cases were reassigned to be heard by separate federal judges. Judge Decker subsequently dismissed the conspiracy charge on the grounds that in civil rights conspiracy cases the burden of proving such conspiracy is greater than in other cases. The individual cases, however, had more successful results. The evidence that the Justice Department used in prosecuting these cases was largely supplied by the Leadership Council. In one of the individual cases, that of Homestead Realty Co., the consent decree issued by Judge Julius Hoffman followed the pattern set in the suit against the West Suburban Board of Realtors but was more stringent and explicit. We quote at length, because the provisions indicate the variety of ways in which realtors can and do discriminate.

The order permanently enjoined Homestead Realty from:

(1) Making unavailable or denying any dwelling to any person because of race or color.

(2) Discriminating against any person in the terms, conditions, or privileges of sale of a dwelling, or in the provision of services in connection therewith, including services relating to the financing of such dwelling, because of race or color of persons occupying dwellings in the neighborhood of such homes.

(3) Refusing or failing to show or sell homes to any person because of the race or color of persons occupying dwellings in the neighborhood of such homes.

(4) Making, printing, or publishing, or causing to be made, printed or published, any notice, statement or advertisement, with respect to the sale of a dwelling that indicates any preference, limitation or discrimination based on race or color, or an intention to make such preference, limitation, or discrimination, with the exception of the affirmative action required of the defendant by paragraph B. (3.) (b.) below.

(5) Representing to any person, because of race or color, that any dwelling is not available for inspection or sale when such dwelling is in fact available.

It (was) further ordered that the defendant shall forthwith adopt and implement an affirmative action program, including, but not limited to, the following steps:

(1) The defendant shall, within 30 days of the entry of this order, conduct an educational program for its sales personnel and other agents and employees to inform them of the provisions of this decree and

their duties under the Fair Housing Act. Such program shall include the following:

(a) A copy of this decree shall be furnished to each agent and employee.

(b) By general meeting or individual conference, the owners of Homestead Realty, Inc., shall inform each agent and employee of the provisions of this decree and of the duties of the company and its agents and employees under the Fair Housing Act. Each agent and employee shall also be informed that his failure to comply with the provisions of this decree shall subject him to dismissal or other disciplinary actions by Homestead Realty.

(c) Each agent and employee shall sign a statement that he has read this decree and received the instructions described in the preceding paragraph.

(2) The defendant shall inform the public generally and its customers or clients specifically of the defendant's non-discriminatory policy by the following action:

(a) Each of the defendants' listing contracts, exclusive or non-exclusive, shall contain the printed statement, in conspicuous type size at least as large as that used herein, that "homes and other dwellings will be shown and made available for sale to all persons without regard to race or color in compliance with the 1968 Fair Housing Act, 42 U.S.C. 3604." In addition, at the time of listing, sellers are to be orally informed of this provision.

(b) The defendant shall post and maintain a sign, of conspicuous location, in each of its offices, containing the language set forth in the preceding paragraph.

(c) The defendant shall periodically (at least once per month for the first two years following the entry of this Order and once per quarter thereafter) place conspicuous advertisments in public media which are directed primarily at a black audience, such as the *Chicago Daily Defender* or the *Chicago South Suburban News*, stating that Homestead Realty, Inc., has listings of homes available for inspection and sale throughout the South Suburbs of Chicago or any other locality in which the company has such listings.

(d) In all its advertising, the defendant shall avoid the use of words or phrases which indicate, by common usage or understanding, a preference that the homes advertised be shown or sold to persons of a particular race or color.

(e) Current listings of the defendant are to be made available by locality but not by address, to all interested civic groups, upon request.

(3) The defendant shall develop and implement procedures to insure that all black prospective purchasers are provided with an informed choice of homes for inspection and sale throughout the localities in which

the company has listings, including, but not limited to the following:

(a) Homestead Realty shall adopt a uniform procedure for informing all prospective purchasers of the financial requirements necessary or desirable for the purchase of a home, including the amount of family income and down payment required and the sources of mortgage loans for home purchases.

(b) The defendant shall instruct each of its agents and employees that when a black prospective purchaser inquires either (1) with respect to a specific home listed with Homestead Realty and located in or near an area known by the company or its personnel to be a predominantly black or rapidly integrating area or (2) with respect to homes in or near such an area generally, the prospective purchaser is to be informed of homes in his price range, if any exist, listed by Homestead Realty and located outside such areas. However, after being so informed, no prospective purchaser is to be denied the opportunity to inspect or buy such homes inquired about.

(4) The defendant shall recruit and hire black agents and employees on the same basis as white agents and employees are recruited and hired. Black agents and employees hired by the defendant prior to the entry of this decree and black agents and employees here after hired by the defendant shall be assigned duties and responsibilities, including those involving the general public, without regard to race or color and on the same basis as white agents and employees are assigned.

It (was) further ordered that ninety days after the entry of this decree, and at three month intervals thereafter following the entry of this decree for a period of four years, the defendants should file with this court, and serve on counsel for the plaintiff, a report containing the following information:

(1) The listing of each home secured by the defendant including the date, address, price, and the available means of financing (i.e., conventional, FHA or VA).

(2) The number of white prospects who inquire in person about the purchase of a home, the number who are shown homes, and the date (of firm commitment), address, and price of each home sold to a white person.

(3) For each non-white prospect who inquires about the purchase of a home:

(a) his name, race, and address.

(b) the location of the defendant's office where inquiry is made.

(c) the dates of contact.

(d) the sales agent(s) serving the prospect.

(e) the type of home desired by size (number of bedrooms) and price range.

(f) the income of the prospect including that of his wife; the amount of money he is able to make on a down payment; the maximum price home he is able to purchase, as evaluated by the defendant, and whether he is able to purchase a home under conventional financing.

(g) whether the prospect requests a specific home or area, and if so, the address of the home or area.

(h) the address of each home recommended by the defendant for showing, and the address of each home shown.

(i) the reasons for the rejection of each home by the prospect or the reasons for his inability to purchase any specific home.

(j) the address and price of the home purchased (if any) by the prospect and whether the financing is conventional or guaranteed by either (FHA or VA).

(4) Violations of the Fair Housing Act of 1968 which come to the attention of the defendant, including, but not limited to:

(a) The name and address of each seller who refuses to give the defendant an exclusive listing on account of the defendant's duty to show that house to any prospect regardless of race or color; and, in addition, the name of the real estate company (if any) which subsequently receives the exclusive listing from the seller.

(b) The name of any financial institution which refuses to give a mortgage to a non-white buyer seeking to purchase a home in a predominantly white area, the name of the buyer, and the reasons for such refusal offered by the institution.

(c) Any other interference with the rights secured by the Fair Housing Act of 1968.

(5) Copies of all real estate advertisements placed by the defendant (if the same advertisement is placed in more than one newspaper, one copy plus a notation of where else the advertisement was placed will be sufficient).

(6) The name, race, date of employment and office assignment of each sales agent or other employee hired by the defendant.

It (was) further ordered, that forty-five days after the entry of this decree, the defendant should file with the court, and serve on counsel for the United States, a report enumerating the preliminary steps it had taken to implement the provisions of this decree. This report was to indicate whether new exclusive listing forms had been printed and were in use pursuant to paragraph B(2)(a) and to include a copy of such form. The report was to include a copy of the form signed by each employee pursuant to paragraph B(1)(c), indicate whether training sessions for all agents and employees had been conducted pursuant to paragraph B(1) to inform them of the contents of this decree and the means of carrying it out, and include a copy of the sign posted in defendant's offices pursuant to paragraph B(2)(b) above.

It (was) further ordered that:

(1) The defendant's keeping of racial records for the purpose of complying with this decree shall not be considered discriminatory.

(2) In the event that a complaint is filed with the United States, alleging a violation of this decree, the United States will, in writing, inform the defendant of the nature of the allegation. The defendant shall have 15 days after such notification to investigate the matter and advise the United States of the corrective steps, if any, to be taken. After the expiration of the 15 day period, the United States may initiate any appropriate proceeding to insure compliance with this decree. Where it appears that a lapse of 15 days would effectively preclude corrective action by the Court, the United States may apply for supplemental relief at any time after advising the defendant, either orally or in writing of the alleged violation.

(3) Representatives of the United States shall be permitted to inspect and copy all pertinent records of the defendant at any and all reasonable times, provided, however, that the United States shall endeavor to minimize any inconvenience to defendant caused by the inspection of such records.

(4) No costs shall be assessed against either party with respect to any matter predating the entry of the decree.

(5) This Order in no way determines the validity of any claims that have existed or may exist in the future between the defendant and any other person or organization other than the United States.

(6) All reports provided to the United States pursuant to this decree shall be kept in confidence and not communicated to business competitors of the defendant or any other person not authorized to see such reports pursuant to this decree or other Order of this Court.

Cases Involving Discriminatory Practices in the Media and by Home Builders

Discriminatory advertising, or unwillingness of major metropolitan newspapers to indicate that housing is available to all homeseekers, regardless of race, was another continuing problem addressed by the legal program. Much behind the scenes work by council members and staff persuaded at least some advertising executives that their practices should cease, and an increasing number of "equal opportunity" listings in real estate advertisements began to be seen in 1970. In other cases legal action had to be taken.

One judgment for the plaintiff was the result of a suit against three west side community newspapers charging bias in the publication of advertising. According to the lawsuit, the newspapers each had published classified ads on a regular basis that listed ethnic or racial preferences in the sale or rental of housing. An injunction prohibiting the defendants from subsequent publication of such advertisements was received. This was the council's first action against a publisher under federal statutes.

In another distinctive case, action was taken against a suburban land developer, Pasquinelli Development Corporation of Dolton, for refusal to build a house sought by the Leadership Council's client. The judge awarded a $2,000 settlement to the plaintiff, $1,000 in attorney's fees, and ordered the house to be constructed per a contract to be executed. This case indicated the ability to exert pressure in areas of new construction and development to ensure that the practice of building vast new suburban areas restricted to all white occupancy slowly comes to an end.

BUILDING A BODY OF LAW

In carrying out the task of fighting discriminatory practices in housing, the Leadership Council's use of the similar but not identical language of the 1866 and 1968 acts showed that federal law effectively covered virtually all cases where discrimination occurs. Some of the ways of using these two laws in conjunction most effectively were outlined in detail in the *Guide to Practice Open Housing Under Law*, the principal components of which will be summarized below to provide some sense of the prosecution of a case.

Developing A Case: A Sample Situation
Typically, the case of discrimination involves a minority person who is told either (1) that he or she cannot have a home, apartment, or piece of property; (2) that the home, apartment, or property is already rented or sold; or (3) that the home, apartment, or property is available, but at a different price or under different terms. In cases such as these, the best and easiest way to prove the fact of discrimination is to send a cooperating white person (the "tester") to the location where discrimination has been experienced or is expected.

In some cases the white tester is preceded by the minority individual. However, in some situations—such as a sophisticated broker who may be alert to a test—the tester may go in first, well acquainted with the financial and family situation and the exact housing requirements of the bona fide buyer or renter.

The tester makes an appearance and inquires about the apartment or house sought. He inspects it as though he were looking for an opportunity to rent or purchase. His application specifies as closely as possible the same facts as those concerning the would-be buyer. He indicates simply that the application is tentative, that he has more property to look at and does not yet wish to take the unit. He ascertains that he could have it if he wished.

The tester has now established the availability of the housing in question. As soon as possible after the tester leaves, the buyer goes to the unit. This brief lapse of time prevents the defendant from stating that another person showed up in between. The buyer makes his credentials known. If the buyer is told, for example, that the property in question is not available, he makes note of all the facts. The white tester then calls back to say that he no longer desires the unit. The buyer calls again and asks for the property and again is told it is not available.

At this point, the party injured and the tester both swear out affidavits relating all pertinent facts to support a motion for a temporary restraining order. If accomplished within twenty-four hours, this maintains the status quo, and the property will not be lost.

A temporary restraining order is usually allowed in these matters because of the historically recognized specific and irreplaceable nature of real estate. Such an order is further justified by the fact that the unit could be lost. The 1968 act protects a good faith, bona fide person with no knowledge of the discriminatory act who, subsequent to that act, seeks and obtains the housing. For these reasons, an injunction barring disposal of the property in question is vital.

At this point, the papers for the case are prepared and filed. A complaint and motion for a temporary restraining order are filed pursuant to the civil rights acts noted above and the federal, state, or local rules.

Since service by the marshal may take several days, in seeking a temporary restraining order, all that is necessary is notice of the hearing on the motion to the defendant. In most jurisdictions this can be done by personal delivery of a copy of the complaint and motion or, if necessary, by a telephone call. If no one is available to receive notice, an affidavit of the efforts made to secure notice must be presented to the court with the motion.[9]

The Court Stage

Typically, an appearance is made by either the defendant, *pro se*, or by his attorney. If *pro se*, the defendant will usually be able to get a continuance for up to forty-eight hours in which to secure counsel.

9. Rule 65 of the Federal Rules of Civil Procedure and refer to applicable state or local rules.

If he is already represented by counsel, the continuance gives the attorney time to familiarize himself with the facts. If the continuance is granted, the plaintiff has to be certain to extract assurance from the defendant or his counsel that the housing is still available and will remain so—that is, the status quo must be maintained until the court decides on the motion for a temporary restraining order. At this point, a defendant may offer the disputed property to a plaintiff. The plaintiff may accept the offer if he wishes.

The suit can be put on the regular calendar in an action for damages even if the housing in question is accepted. If the defendant is adamant and will make no offer, a hearing will be held on the motion for a temporary restraining order, at which time the court will first hear the case.

In presenting the case, it must be assumed that the court has not read the supporting affidavits, so the opening statement has to detail the facts of the discrimination. Then the witnesses and the plaintiff present again the facts set forth in the opening argument and affidavits.

The court rules immediately on its decision. The courts have shown a great tendency to decide that a case is over if the plaintiff is shown the property that he previously was told was not available. Similarly, if the property is actually obtained, the same feeling is held.

In these cases, the Leadership Council's position soon became one that an act of discrimination is a compensable act and is not more excused by subsequent proper behavior than a bank robber's act would be forgiven if he returns the money he has stolen. Even if the court's pressure to dismiss is considerable, especially if an apartment is tendered or a home is shown, the council recommended that the pressure be resisted. The council also argued that $2,500 should be a minimum amount to be apportioned as attorney's fees and damages.

Trial Preparation
Interrogatories and depositions under the federal rules help to obtain both information and settlements. In each instance a complete trial outline is prepared. In some cases a trial brief or memorandum is also drafted to help both in the trial of the case and in arguments on appeal or rehearing.

One of the guidelines in preparation of the trial of these lawsuits is a simple presentation that is easily understood and will eliminate the number of defenses that may be presented.

In the case of a full hearing on the motion for a temporary restraining order and at a subsequent trial, special care has to be taken to prepare the white tester for cross-examination. It will be charged that he has been "lying," that he did not actually want the housing, and that he probably falsified a number of facts about himself or signed a false rental application. The witness should be prepared for this attack, and it should be carefully explained to him that there is no penalty for his admission of these practices, but rather that there is a fine tradition of this behavior in the civil rights field.

LEGAL PRECEDENTS

The relevant legal precedents fall into five major categories: (1) jurisdiction and applicability of the federal acts; (2) damages—punitive and actual; (3) the use of testers; (4) jury trial; and (5) attorneys' fees.

Cases Relating to the Jurisdiction of the Court and Applicability of Federal Acts

The best known case relating to the interpretation of the 1866 act[10] and its relation to the 1968 Act is *Jones v. Mayer*,[11] The case was decided on June 17, 1968, and holds that all racial discrimination, private as well as public, in the sale and rental of property is prohibited by the 1866 act.

Joseph L. Jones, a Negro, and Barbara Jo Jones, his white wife, were seeking a home in Paddock Woods, a residential development constructed by Alfred H. Mayer near St. Louis, Missouri. The case was dismissed in the district court, and the circuit court of appeals of the 8th circuit affirmed the dismissal. The United States Supreme Court reviewed the case and found the 1866 act to be a valid exercise of power under the Thirteenth Amendment.

The case was decided after the passage of Title VIII of the 1968 Fair Housing Law. It was noted that the coverage of the 1866 act is different from that of the 1968 act[12] and that the 1866 statute would stand independently.

In the case of *David Brown v. Guy S. LoDuca*,[13] an action for injunctive relief and punitive damages under the 1866 act,[14] the court concurrently considered the motion for preliminary injunction and the motion to dismiss.

10. 42 U.S.C. 1982 (1866).
11. 392 U.S. 409 (1968).
12. Compare 42 U.S.C. at 1982 with 3604 of the 1968 act.
13. 307 F. Supp. 102 (1969).
14. 42 U.S.C. 3601 et seq.

The court considered the difference between Section 3610 (d) of Title VIII and Section 3612 (a) below:

> Provided, that no such civil action may be brought in the United States District Court if the person aggrieved has a judicial remedy under a State or local fair housing law which provides rights and remedies for alleged discriminatory housing practices which are substantially equivalent to the rights and remedies provided in this subchapter . . . .[15]
>
> The rights granted by Sections 3603, 3604, 3605 and 3606 of this Title may be enforced by civil actions in appropriate United States District Courts without regard to the amount in controversy and in appropriate State or local courts of general jurisdiction . . . .[16]

In the event a defendant should argue that there is available a substantially equivalent state remedy, the following language of the case would be instructive:

> I believe that § 3612 provides an alternative to § 3610 and is not limited by the language of § 3610. Section 3610 sets forth the procedure that HUD is to follow on the receipt of complaints from individuals. If there is a state law, then HUD is required to refer the complaint to the appropriate local agency. If the local agency does not act within thirty days, then HUD may take over and attempt a conciliation . . . .[17]

And further:

> Of course, by the time the complainant has gone the 3610 route, the housing unit involved would in all likelihood have been rented or sold. Congress, recognizing the § 3610 might not be an effective remedy, then set up an alternative procedure for one who claims to have been discriminated against in the sale or rental of housing. The alternative remedy was provided for in § 3612.
>
> Section 3612 contains no statement that the procedures outlined in § 3610 must be followed before one can go to Federal court under § 3612.[18]

This case also contains references to legislative history that might be of assistance in arguing the question of applicability of the 1968 Civil Rights action. The court in the *Brown* case said that Mr. Brown had been discriminated against because of his race with respect to the

15. Id. at 3610(d).
16. Id. at 3612(a).
17. Brown v. LoDuca, 307 F. Supp. 102.
18. Id.

rental of the apartments in question in at least the following respects:

1. The availability of the apartments,
2. The amount of rent, and
3. The necessity of making a security deposit.[19]

The plaintiff was also found to have shown that the course of conduct of the defendants was directed against the plaintiff for foreclosing an opportunity to negotiate the terms of rental.

In the case of *Cheryl Walker, et al. v. G.M. Pointer,*[20] the application of the 1866 act was considered in the context of an eviction from an apartment. The plaintiffs, a brother and sister, were white and both had black friends who visited their apartment. The court decided that there was jurisdiction because they were victims of the effects of racial discrimination against blacks.

A second ground for jurisdiction was found in the deprivation of rights of Negroes as a result of defendant's acts in accepting white tenants with white friends. The court cited *Barrows v. Jackson,*[21] a restrictive covenant case where the Negro purchasers were not parties to the suit. The court said "in light of the decision of the Court in the Jones case, it is reasonable to characterize the frequency of Negro persons to come and go at the invitation of one lawfully in contract of the premises as sufficiently pertaining to a condition of property to be a right to 'hold' under Section 1982."[22]

> Since the breadth of § 1982 is sufficient to encompass all cognizable property interests, "real and personal," it is perforce broad enough to protect prospective black visitors to the Walker apartment from a racially motivated disability to receive and hold such interests. It is broad enough to protect "unidentified but identifiable" Negro persons from the chilling effect of such action gone unremedied on the attitudes of other non-Negro hosts.[23]

There is also good language in this case relating to the handling of damages.

There has been a question as to whether the acceptance of an apartment or closing a deal on a contract to purchase property at

19. Id.
20. 304 F. Supp. 56 (1969).
21. 346 U.S. 249 (1953).
22. Walker v. Pointer, 304 F. Supp 56.
23. Id. at

issue in a civil rights case under Section 360 et seq. of the 1866 act makes moot a suit for damages in relation to that property or apartment. A court of appeals held that taking the apartment does not make moot the damages issue.[24]

Cases Relating to Damages—Punitive and Actual

Damages under Section 1982 of the 1866 act are discussed in both *Jones v. Mayer*[25] and *Sullivan v. Little Hunting Park, Inc.*.[26] Congress created federal jurisdiction for damages, equitable, or other relief under Section 1343 (4) of the 1968 act, and therefore, damages are available for violations under Section 1982 of the 1866 act.

Under the 1968 act, punitive damages are limited to $1,000.[27] However, the 1866 act allows damages without specifying the type,[28] so it appears that actual damages are unlimited.

Bell v. Hood[29] contains a statement of policy of the federal court:

[W]here federally protected rights have been invaded, it has been the rule from the beginning that courts will be alert to adjust their remedies so as to grant the necessary relief. And it is also well settled that where legal rights have been invaded, and a federal statute provides for a general right to sue for such invasion, federal courts may use any available remedy to make good the wrong done.[30]

The federal policy of fashioning a remedy is contained in *Texas and Pacific Railway v. Rigsby*:[31] "A disregard of the command of the statute is a wrongful act, and where it results in damage to one of the class for whose especial benefit the statute was enacted, the right to recover the damages from the party in default is implied . . . ."[32]

In *Wright v. Chicago Burlington & Quincy R.R.*,[33] 223 F. Supp.

24. Cash v. Swifton Rental Corp. 434 F. 2d 569 (1970). Examples of other rights that have been found to be productive under § 1982 of the 1866 act can be found in Sullivan v. Little Hunting Park, 396 U.S. 221 (1969) (refusal to allow lessor to transfer interest in a recreational facility in a development. This case also emphasizes that the 1866 and 1968 Civil Rights Acts operate independently of one another); and in Contract Buyers League v. F. & F. Investment, 300 F. Supp. 210 (1969) (higher prices and different terms than used in selling to whites).
   25. 392 U.S. 409 (1968).
   26. 396 U.S. 221 (1969).
   27. See 42 U.S.C. 3604 for discussion.
   28. Section 1343.
   29. 327 U.S. 678 (1946).
   30. Id. at 648.
   31. 241 U.S. 33 (19 6).
   32. Id. at 39.
   33. 223 F. Supp. 660 (N. Dist. Ill., E. Div. 1963).

660 (N. Dist. Ill., E. Div. 1963) an action relating to interstate commerce and common carriers, was brought under[34] which statute provides for liability" for the full amount of damages sustained in consequence of any such violation of the provisions of this Chapter."[35] When acts of discrimination were established, Judge Perry allowed actual compensatory and punitive damages to the plaintiffs under the preceding statutory language.[36]

The Use of Testers to Prove Discrimination

In an action brought under the 1866 act, *Bush v. Kaim*,[37] the United States District Court for the Northern District of Ohio commented favorably regarding the use of testers. Mr. and Mrs. Bush contacted "Operation Equality" in their search for a home in Cleveland and later sought a house that was listed in the paper as being for rent. A white couple rented the home for the Bush family and the defendant argued that they were not entitled to injunctive relief because of their tactics. The court said:

> The defendants urge that injunctive relief should be denied because of the methods used by the plaintiffs in obtaining a lease. Such tactics are, indeed, not to be favored. Nevertheless, had the plaintiffs not utilized such tactics to acquire possession of the premises, they would have found themselves without a remedy once the home had become occupied by another tenant who was without knowledge of the prior discrimination.[38]

On March 30, 1971, in the unreported case of *Mitchell et al. v. Charles Quain* D/B/A Quain Realty et al.,[39] Judge Austin, of the northern district of Illinois, eastern division, entered as one of his conclusions of law the finding "2. That the efforts of Mrs. Marjorie A. Bridges, Mrs. Ruth Rosenthal, Mrs. Linda Edwards (the three women who tested therein) and Mrs. Bernice Klosterman to assist the MITCHELLS in their search for housing was a good faith effort by civic-minded women to assist a homeseeker in obtaining housing."[40]

In the case of *Newbern v. Lake Lorelei, Inc.*,[41] the United States

34. 49 U.S.C. 1.
35. Id.
36. Other cases supporting the theory of damages are: Lee v. Southern Home Sites Corp., 429 F. 2nd 290 (1970), Equal Opportunity in Housing Reporter 2.2, (1972); Pina v. Homsi 1 Race Relations Law Survey 183 (1969); and Smith v. Sol D. Adler Realty Co., 436 F. 2d 344 (1971).
37. 297 F. Supp. 151 (1969).
38. Id.
39. 70 C 1640.
40. Id.
41. 308 F. Supp. 407 (1968).

District Court of Ohio, Northern Division, noted that a statement of discriminatory practices had been

made to a white person who "masqueraded" as a buyer for purposes of testing the situation and giving testimony. The defendants liken that to an informer in a criminal case. However, even in a criminal case—let alone in a civil case—the testimony of an informer is competent (although it should be considered with caution), *On Lee v. United States*, 343 U.S. 747, 72 S. Ct. 967, 96 L. Ed. 1270; and there is no entrapment if the informer merely furnishes "a favorable opportunity," *Lopez v. United States*, 373 U.S. 427, 83 S. Ct. 1381, 10 L.Ed. 462.

It is well settled that, in cases involving racial discrimination, the motives of the victims are immaterial to the issue of whether or not the defendants violated the law. In *Evers v. Dwyer*, 358 U.S. 202 (1958), reversing 3 Race Relations Law Reporter 743 (W.D. Tenn., 1958, 3-Judge Court), a Negro from Chicago came to Memphis and "tested" the bus line. He was directed to the rear of the bus and sued to enjoin segregated operation of the bus system. The District Court found that he had never ridden a Memphis bus before, that he owned a car and that "he was not a regular or even an occasional user of bus transportation; and that in reality he boarded the bus for the purpose of investigating this litigation." 3 Race Relations Law Reporter 746. On the basis of these facts, the District Court dismissed the action. The Supreme Court [3580 U.S. at 204] in a *per curiam* opinion summarily reversed, saying: That the appellant may have boarded this particular bus for the purpose of instituting this litigation is not significant.[42]

As is carefully pointed out, it is not entrapment to provide an opportunity.

The Illinois Court of Appeals very recently held that in a proceeding under the Chicago Fair Housing Ordinance, it was no defense that one of the applicants for housing (a black person) was testing and was not attempting to obtain housing for himself.[43]

We conclude that, where a person who was denied a listing of apartments admits that he was testing for compliance to the ordinance, such an admission does not preclude a finding that he was denied a listing because of his race, and that therefore the real estate broker was in violation of the ordinance. The fact that a person was testing is an evidentiary fact. The evidence in the instant case supports the conclusion that the broker was not aware that Hamilton was testing, and the further conclusion that Hamilton was denied a listing solely because of his race.[44]

42. Id.
43. Bell Realty and Insurance Agency v. Chicago Commission on Human Relations, 266 N.E. 2d 769, 774 (1971).
44. Id. Other cases have approved testing, for example: Harris v. Jones, 296 F. Supp. 1082 (1969); and Newbern v. Lake Lorelei, et al. 308 F. Supp. 407 (1968).

Jury Trial

In *Rogers v. Loether*,[45] 312 F. Supp. 1008 (1970), the court holds there is no right to jury in a 1968 civil rights housing case as follows:

An action under Title VIII is not an action at common law. The statute does not expressly provide for trial by jury of any issues in the action. In the absence of a clear mandate from Congress requiring a jury trial, I find that the similarities between the remedial provisions of the Civil Rights Acts of 1964 and 1968, in light of the undivided authority holding that the issue of money damages for back pay under Title VII of the 1964 Act is not an issue for the jury, compel the conclusion that the issue of compensatory and punitive money damages in an action under Title VIII of the 1968 Act is likewise an issue for the Court. Accordingly, defendants' request for a jury trial must be denied.

Therefore, it is ordered that defendants' request for a jury trial be and it hereby is denied.[46]

Attorneys' Fees

The 1968 act specifically provides for granting attorneys' fees. In applying for attorneys' fees under Title VIII, the council has relied on general authority for granting attorneys' fees and the provisions of the 1968 act. It is suggested that careful time sheets be maintained in accordance with a set procedure for all cases. Cases under Title VII are helpful in regard to attorneys' fees in Title VIII actions.[47]

DEVELOPMENT OF NEW PROCEDURES

From the base of law laid out in the foregoing, the Leadership Council attempted to develop new procedures and to extend the relevant body of law so as to:

1. increase efficiency,
2. assure favorable judgments, and
3. make legal action financially remunerative to private lawyers, to enable the Leadership Council to withdraw and leave the legal profession a profitable new task.

One area of progress was the standardization of the rules of evidence, as discussed in the section on case development above. Another was to affirm the principle of money damages and legal fees from the

45. 312 F. Supp. 1088 (1970).
46. Id.
47. Examples of cases dealing with attorneys fees include: Alex Clark v. America Marine Corporation, 320 F. Supp. 709 (1970) (awarding $20,000); and Newman v. Piggie Park Enterprises, Inc., 390 U.S. 400 (1968).

defendant. In the first year, thirty-nine cases resulted in damages and agreed orders from the defendant. The council took the position that $2,500 should be a minimum amount to be apportioned as attorney's fees and damages.

The amount awarded by the court in fact increased steadily. In one case the council's lawyers had sought $1,000 in actual damages and $10,000 in punitive damages on behalf of a black dentist who tried to buy a home for $125,000 in Flossmoor. The agreed order that was entered included $2,500. In two cases, U.S. District Court Judge Napoli set precedents in motions and briefs that damages in civil rights suits were not limited to $1,000 as set forth in the 1968 Civil Rights Act if the plaintiff also charged violation of the 1866 act. The older legislation makes no reference to damages and was not overridden by the more recent act.

In another case, the U.S. Court of Appeals reversed the decision of the U.S. District Court dismissing a complaint against Adler Realty Co. The plaintiff was awarded $1,000 damages for "mental anguish" and $2,000 for attorney's fees. In addition the defendant was ordered to pay court costs totaling $931. Total costs to the defendant, then, for one act of discrimination, approached $4,000. Such cases were positive signs that the council's goal of making discrimination too costly to practice was being reached. Reaction by the real estate industry was not far behind.

ACCUMULATING SENSITIVITIES OF THE REAL ESTATE INDUSTRY

As the legal action program moved into its second year, there was an attempted counterattack by representatives of the real estate industry. This came on February 25, 1971, when the Northwest Real Estate Board filed a suit in federal district court charging the Leadership Council with deliberately contriving discrimination incidents and threatening more harassment if brokers did not contribute money to its program. The suit asked $500,000 in damages and that the court enjoin the council from deliberately and maliciously fomenting litigation for the Council's personal gain. This suit was filed after the council had entered suits against several members of the Northwest Real Estate Board on behalf of Mrs. Gladys Seaton, who complained that she was unable to buy or rent property in the area served by the board.

Subsequently, attorneys for the Northwest Board asked for and received a voluntary dismissal of their complaint without prejudice, which enabled them to reinstitute the suit on June 16, 1971, with the additional allegation that the council was practicing law without a license. This allegation involved an assertion that the council's board of directors, unqualified in the law, controlled the activities of its legal staff. The motion was denied in this case. What is instructive is that the Northwest Real Estate Board had thought the council's activities so important that it spent several thousand dollars to try to restrain the council from acting against its members in open housing cases. The tenacity with which the concerns were expressed is revealing, since it reflected a sore and none too well considered response by the real estate fraternity to a newly perceived threat to its normal mode of doing business. What was significant about the real estate board suit was that in spite of the expenditures and tenacity with which it was pursued, it failed to limit or damage the Leadership Council programs.

Copeland v. Rubloff and Jefferson v. Kramer

Issues of the relations between the Leadership Council's board of directors, the executive director, and the legal staff were raised by the Northwest Real Estate Board at a time in 1971 when two other cases began to question the nature of board influence on the legal program. The legal work of the council's attorneys proceeded relatively smoothly through 1970 until the filing of *Copeland v. Rubloff.* Arthur Rubloff, one of Chicago's leading real estate developers, managed the University Apartments in Chicago, where the alleged discrimination against Mrs. Copeland, a black, occurred. While most Chicago papers published straightforward accounts of the suit, *Chicagoland's Real Estate Advertiser* carried a rather strange account:

> Officials at Rubloff are puzzled by the suit because the apartment complex . . . is a well-known integrated project. . . "I don't know why the suit was filed", says Harry Bennett, vice president of the Management Department of Rubloff. "This firm has never practiced discrimination of any kind in any of our facilities."
>
> F. Willis Caruso—who . . . is handling the suit for the Leadership Council —also seemed baffled by the case. He acknowledged that the complex is integrated and said he was told by a Rubloff attorney that it is 20 per cent black.
>
> "There could be several reasons as there are different isolated causes in these cases", he said.[48]

What had actually happened was fairly obvious: Mrs. Copeland had

---

48. *Chicagoland's Real Estate Advertiser,* August 14, 1970.

fallen victim to a quota system.[49] Those who laud such a system say that it is the only way to keep buildings integrated; those who oppose it say that it is an illegal means of keeping out blacks—"rent to whites, lie to blacks." Mrs. Copeland arrived on the scene when the University Apartments' black quota was filled, and she was denied an apartment.

It was at this time that pressures were allegedly brought to bear in the attempt to persuade the Leadership Council to drop the case against Rubloff. It was reported by several respondents that Mr. Rubloff individually approached members of the Leadership Council's board of directors to discuss the case with them. Board members were then said to have questioned the legal staff about whether or not it was wise to proceed in this case, whether all the facts were known, and so forth. Significant factors in the minds of several of the board members involved were the issues of whether it was appropriate for the Leadership Council to prosecute cases in integrated or transition areas and whether suits should be taken in cases where the discrimination apparently resulted from the application of a quota system. To others involved there was a much stronger feeling, a threat to the independent operation of the legal action program.

The legal staff did bring the case to court, and it was settled by an agreed order, without damages. The settlement "called for nondiscriminatory advertising in newspapers and on radio by the Rubloff Company, the posting of Civil Rights Acts, and monthly delivery to the Leadership Council of 'all of its classified residential advertisements that appear in any newspaper and radio. . . .'"[50] After this relatively quiet decision, in which Mrs. Copeland received the apartment she sought, board pressures apparently subsided.

49. The council believed that companies that managed developments such as Lake Meadows, South Commons, and Sandburg Village were alerted to the fact that it was aware of their use of the quota system by the Rubloff suit.

50. Report for the Six Months Ended May 31, 1971 of the Leadership Council for Metropolitan Open Communities under its Prime Contract Number H-961 with the Department of Housing and Urban Development, June 15, 1971.

Arthur Rubloff's and Co.'s compliance with court orders was not satisfactory. The Leadership Council received from them monthly copies of their ads in the *Chicago Tribune*, but no copies of their advertising in other media. Monitoring of Rubloff's radio advertising indicated that the phrase "equal opportunity broker" was absent, particularly in Sandburg Village ads. Sandburg Village, a large near-north development, was believed to operate on the quota system.

Enforcing compliance is not simple. Not only is monitoring difficult, but because of the adversary system of justice it would have been necessary for the plaintiff, Mrs. Copeland, to press suit against Rubloff & Co. for non-compliance with court orders.

March of 1971 saw the beginnings of what has sometimes been referred to as the "famous Draper and Kramer case." Draper and Kramer is one of Chicago's largest real estate management firms, and the Leadership Council's offices were in one of the buildings it manages. Mr. Ferd Kramer was a former member of the council's board of directors. Basically, the case involved Mr. and Mrs. Carl F. Jefferson, a mixed couple, who tried to rent an apartment in a building containing 450 apartments and managed by Draper and Kramer. At the time they made application for this apartment they were renting in a Lake Meadows building managed by Draper and Kramer.

On March 10, 1971, we mailed the [deposit] check in the amount of $50 to 2626 North Lakeview.

On Monday, March 15, 1971, I called to inquire about the length of time necessary to decide upon our application. I spoke to Mr. Dunn. [He] said that it takes about 10-14 days to complete a credit check.

I told Mr. Dunn that we presently rented at Lake Meadows [in] a building managed by Draper and Kramer. Mr. Dunn then asked, "what was that name again?" I repeated my name.

Mr. Dunn replied, "I'm sure that application was rejected." He said he would call me back in a day or so to confirm that rejection.

I insisted that he pull my file immediately. He examined the file and confirmed the rejection. [He] stated that he was only the middle man and did not know the reason for the rejection.

I then asked, how did they make a decision so quickly, as I had only mailed the check on Wednesday, March 10, 1971? Mr. Dunn stated that the check arrived on Thursday, March 11, and that he carried all pending applications to the rental board immediately. [He] stated that our refund check had been put in the mail earlier.

On Tuesday, March 16, 1971, we received the refund check. The letter enclosed with the check refund was dated March 12, 1971. Mr. Dunn referred me to Mr. Hamilton of the 30 West Monroe office about the reasons for rejection.

. . . .

Mr. Hamilton informed me that he did not know why the lease was rejected. He stated, however, that he would ask the leasing board for the reason. . . , also he stated he would ask the leasing board to reconsider the application and to call him back in one week. I requested Mr. Hamilton to send me a letter to that effect.

I informed Mr. Hamilton that Mr. Dunn had told my wife that he was the person who knew the necessary information about acceptance and rejection of lease applications.

I again repeated my request for a reason for rejection. Mr. Hamilton said nothing in reply, but added that he would write me in one week.

On Tuesday, March 16, 1971, my wife and I received a cancelled check for $50 and a letter stating that Draper and Kramer could be of no service to us.[51]

In this case, it was alleged by a council staff member that Mr. Kramer "approached the [Leadership Council] Board president and screamed bloody murder about being stabbed." In addition, it also was asserted by a staff member of the council that a "powerful political figure" in Chicago told some of the Leadership Council board members that "Ferd Kramer is doing a lot for the community, and since you are community leaders you should think about this." The board became very apprehensive about following through on *Jefferson v. Kramer*. However, the case went to trial and was dismissed by Judge Napoli after the Jeffersons were offered an apartment in another Draper and Kramer building, a result that was satisfactory to the plaintiffs.

The Moratorium

In May, when *Jefferson v. Kramer* was in discovery, the Leadership Council's board of directors issued a moratorium on the filing of new law suits and directed that any new suits being filed receive prior approval.

An internal split emerged between the legal staff on the one hand and the executive director on the other about the nature of board control. There was a strong undercurrent of feeling that for the Leadership Council's legal action program to be successful, it was necessary to bring to court anyone involved in discriminatory practices. To the extent that the board was to be involved in the legal action program, it was agreed that it should be in a manner consistent with Formal Opinion 324 of the Standing Committee on Ethics and Professional Responsibility of the American Bar Association—namely, that the board of directors should establish guidelines to determine which kinds of cases can be taken. (The full opinion is included as the appendix to this chapter.)

In an atmosphere of confrontation, a meeting was held on June 28, 1971, between Messrs. Michael Schneider and Irving Horwitz, representatives of the Department of Housing and Urban Development; Edward L. Holmgren, executive director, and F. Willis Caruso, general counsel and director of the Legal Action Program, Leadership Council. I attended this meeting.

Schneider stated that the current issue was the position of Leader-

51. From signed affidavits of Mr. and Mrs. Jefferson.

ship Council's board that it should advise its attorneys on cases; that such a posture could cause the board to be cited for practicing law without a licence, as it had been in the Northwest Suburban Board suit filed on June 11, 1971.

Holmgren disagreed, saying:

> That is not the nature of the problem. The board is trying to establish guidelines in relation to the Leadership Council's basic position. We should reject suits in changing areas where we are not proving anything, or where, de facto, some degree of integration has been achieved, like Hyde Park. [It should be noted that both the Draper and Kramer and Rubloff suits would not have come to pass had this in fact been a guideline of the council]. In addition, the board will not make decisions on the suits. The interpretation of whether or not a particular suit fits the guidelines will be left to me.[52]

When Schneider asked for the history of the conflict, Caruso commented that it began with the Draper and Kramer case and was exacerbated by the Rubloff suit.

The question was then raised as to who should make the decision of whether or not a particular suit fell within the guidelines to be established. Schneider asserted HUD's position that this should be a matter of the lawyers' judgement. Holmgren, however, felt that "What is important is who is running the program. It is my responsibility to decide which cases to take. The guidelines are to be established by the board and interpreted by me. Once it has been determined that a case will be accepted by the Leadership Council, then all legal procedures are the concern of the lawyers."[53] Caruso then asked for the specifics of the guidelines:

> They have to be worked out ahead. We can't wait for specific cases and decide on each case. We must have no range of uncertainty as to what guidelines the council is operating under. The major emphasis seems to be on cases in new areas of opportunity especially predominantly white areas, but if an interesting case came up in a racially changing area we should take it.[54]

Holmgren then reaffirmed his position that such cases should not be taken by the council.

The heart of the issue, said Caruso, is whether or not the "big

52. Notes of the June 28, 1971, meeting.
53. Ibid.
54. Ibid.

boys" are going to be squeezed. Schneider followed this up by saying:

> There is a real credibility problem. The community knows right now that if a low income family is involved, the Leadership Council won't help because of the questions of ability to pay the rent. Now, if guidelines are made public, and essentially they must be what would be the effect? Are you then telling the big boys that, okay, you can have a quota system in South Commons and dual listings in Hyde Park and we won't touch you there. What would the effects be?[55]

"Our objective," Holmgren said, "is to create a single residential market. The Leadership Council will accept cases (a) that open white residential areas to minority residents, (b) that expand or clarify open housing law, (c) that increase minority residents in predominantly white communities."[56]

Caruso then took the position that since these criteria were very broad, it would give Mr. Holmgren a tremendous degree of discretion in determining whether a particular case would fit the guidelines. Indeed, Mr. Holmgren and the board could easily be put in an untenable legal position—namely, that it could be said that they were practicing law without a license.

Holmgren felt, however, that there was no suit until a complaint was launched, and the guidelines would only enable him to determine whether the council should join in lodging a complaint in a particular case. "Since until a complaint is filed you are not in legal process, this would not violate the American Bar Association statement."[57]

Schneider again stated that the selection of cases must be the attorney's decision. I then commented that I felt the guidelines must be explicit enough to, in effect, protect the board members from intimidation or pressure; that flexible guidelines would not be workable. Caruso followed this by saying that this was:

> particularly true because what you don't see is how Kramer put on the heat. Generally what is visible is not explicit pressure but the workings of the "Chicago style" friendship network . . . until clear guidelines are established the situation is going to be slimy. . . . [Guidelines] must be written so that no one is exempt, so that they cannot use political clout to get around them.[58]

Concluding the meeting, Schneider requested that guidelines be

55. Ibid.
56. Ibid.
57. Ibid.
58. Ibid.

formulated within which the legal program could work. These guidelines were to be submitted to HUD before presentation to the council's board of directors. He also said that HUD had to be represented or given the opportunity to be present at any Leadership Council board meeting where any issues relating to the HUD contract might be discussed. To the last request, Holmgren responded that "This kind of thing isn't discussed at board meetings. Berry, Jaicks, Ayres, and O'Connor present faits accomplis to the board . . . most organizations operate this way."[59]

During the period July through December 1971, when the guidelines were being formulated, an informal arrangement prevailed in legal program operations. Complaints of discrimination were given to Holmgren. He gave his approval to the filing of all suits. The final set of guidelines was formulated on January 11, 1972, as follows:

The Legal Action Program will accept only the following categories of cases unless otherwise approved by the Board of Directors or officers:

1. Cases that tend to expand or clarify Fair Housing Law, including the Fair Housing Act of 1968, the Civil Rights Act of 1866 as defined in *Jones v. Mayer*, 392 U.S. 409, 20 L. Ed. § 1189, 88 S. Ct. 2186, constitutional provision, both federal and state, state and local government laws, rules and regulations.
2. Cases that tend to eliminate artificial barriers that restrict housing.
3. Cases that tend to eliminate the practice of panic peddling.
4. Cases that tend to encourage minority residence in predominantly non-minority communities.
5. Cases that tend to expand the relief available to victims of discrimination based on race, religion, national origin or sex.

The initial report of complaints shall be given immediately to the Executive Director and Legal Action staff attorney. A third copy shall be maintained in the files. Such complaint is confidential and information therein shall not be revealed to anyone outside the Leadership Council staff and officers. It is recognized that there is a duty to the client to protect the confidentiality of facts of and incident of discrimination. Action by the Leadership Council staff and officers shall be consistent with this confidence.

The Executive Director shall review initial complaints of discrimination to determine the applicability of the guidelines and he shall approve action thereon.

The Board of Directors will review the subject matter on the cases undertaken by the legal staff on a continuing basis.

59. Ibid.

HOW THE LEGAL STAFF VIEWED
ITS PROGRAM

How, after the experience of the moratorium, did the legal staff view its program at the end of 1971?

The philosophy behind the legal program of the Leadership Council at the outset was to take individual cases of discrimination into court and through these suits to "educate" courts, lawyers, judges, the power structure, and brokers as to what the law is and how it operates, as well as to develop precedents, and therefore the law.

By the end of 1971, the legal staff felt that the judges in the Chicago district were alert to the types of cases they were filing. Judges had become aware through the stance and appeals of the council that they could not summarily dismiss a case or procedurally interrupt progress, as they had in the past. Four suits in 1971 were dismissed by judges on the grounds that they were "bad suits" on which no time should be wasted. Council attorneys ordered transcripts in two of these suits; the judges then reversed themselves and set trial dates.

Attorneys also had begun to feel the impact of the council's strategy, and a lot of them admitted that they didn't know much about this type of law: the Leadership Council had the expertise. This led to the preparation of the *Guide to Practice Open Housing Under Law*, discussed earlier.

It was the view of the legal staff that the larger and more sophisticated real estate firms were feeling an impact of its strategy by the end of 1971. As a result of the suits, it was believed that many were changing their practices to avoid litigation. They were taking time to educate their sales people and clerks. Several firms put out confidential memos stating procedures to be followed; other included in contracts provisions that indicate that if an owner discriminates or desires to do so he or she is obliged to pay costs of court action. Other firms shied away from written instructions, however, because they could imply corrections of past discriminatory practices.

The staff felt it had gotten tougher. Once, getting an apartment alone was sufficient; then came money damages. Some firms were required to publish that they are "equal opportunity brokers." Some were required to report to the Leadership Council. The council used this as basis for a drive to be directed eventually to every realtor and board in the city, with the aim that all have affirmative programs. Only then did the council feel that it could serve the locked in, lower income black.

The legal staff felt that it had generated public confidence in a way that the EOH centers never did. An increasing number of calls indicated that the public now relied on them to produce.

THE ROLE OF PUBLICITY

Part of this change was due to more and better publicity. In 1970 the council began focusing attention on efforts to publicize its successes with the newly formulated Legal Action Program. Staff member David Karraker, who had administered the legal project prior to its expansion, was appointed director of public information in May 1970. The post had been vacant since 1967. A number of efforts were launched to attract the attention of the press to the council's new efforts, resulting in 163 references to the council in 1970 in local newspapers serving the Chicago area. Council staff appeared on radio and television on a number of occasions, and a newsletter entitled "Housing Action Report" was published periodically and sent to the council's mailing list.

These efforts were continued during 1971. Th council's mailing list of 5,400 names was brought up to date and expanded to a year end total of 7,500. Responsibility for introducing a systematic approach to new fund-raising efforts was given to the public information department. A new year end campaign aimed at attracting contributions from individuals produced seventy new gifts totaling $2,200, and research had begun on sources of new corporate support for council programs. The council received 232 mentions in news stories appearing in a variety of newspapers during 1971, and staff made fifteen appearances on radio and television. Issues of "Housing Action Report" widened their scope to examine broader issues, such as a report of Edward L. Holmgren's speech dealing with suburban response to moderate income housing programs and an analysis of black attitudes toward housing dispersal.

CASE EXPERIENCE IN 1972

By the end of December 1972, the Leadership Council had filed some 202 cases and had at that time over 40 cases pending. Table 3-1 shows the dispositions of litigations from the beginning of the legal program in 1969 through 1972.

Sampling of Routine Cases

The majority of the cases handled by the attorneys during 1972 were those seeking relief for individual plaintiffs who had been victims of discriminatory practices in the sale of homes or rental of

Table 3-1. Report of the Leadership Council for Metropolitan Open Communities Legal Action Program Case Analysis.

	1969– December 31, 1971[a]	*January 1, 1972–December 31, 1972*	*Total thru 1972*
CASES FILED	156	46	202
LITIGATION TERMINATED	133	27	160
Judgments for Plaintiff	13	7	20
Agreed Orders and Damages	58	13	71
Voluntary Dismissals	25	1	26
Cases Withdrawn by Plaintiff	5	0	5
Miscellaneous Judgments for Plaintiff	4	0	4
Other[b]	28	5	33

[a]Estimated figures for the period 1969–January 1970.
[b]Includes judgments for defendants, involuntary dismissals, and a small number of miscellaneous actions, e.g., consolidation with another case.

apartments. A sampling of these "routine" cases shows the range of tactics that were still being used to deny housing to blacks and other minority group members, from flat assertions that no blacks wanted to more subtle deceptions.

In *Melton v. Fleece*, the plaintiff had called the landlord of an apartment advertised for rent in south suburban Harvey, was asked his race, and when he replied that he was black, he was told that the apartment was in an all white area and would not be rented to blacks. The suit was settled with the defendant agreeing to pay the plaintiff $300. The Meltons did not move into the contested apartment.

Antoine v. Revay, which resulted in a default judgment against the defendant amounting to $1,365.68 in damages, attorney's fees, and court costs, involved a similar situation. Antoine was told by Revay, the landlord, that he could not rent to "colored" because his white tenants would move. Antoine alleged that Revay also told him that he would rent him an apartment in the same building at a later date, when the building "goes black." The building was located in a Chicago changing neighborhood. Mr. and Mrs. Antoine did move into the apartment.

In *Thompson v. Shevchuk* a more typical ploy was used by the owner of an apartment building on Chicago's north side. The owner showed the plaintiff, a black woman, the apartment but refused to accept a deposit. When Ms. Thompson called the owner the following day, she was told that the unit was no longer available because the present tenant was not sure he wanted to move. Testing proved this to be false; the tester overheard the owner tell another tenant that a Negro woman had applied for the apartment and looked like a nice person, but that she had turned her down because "you never can tell about those people."

The plaintiff in *Simpson v. Diamond* made an appointment with the landlord to see an apartment in an all white area on Chicago's northeast side, but was told when he arrived that it had just been rented. When the Leadership Council tester went out to see the apartment, the plaintiff went along but waited some distance from the building, pretending not to know the tester. According to the affidavit by the tester, the landlord said: "Did you see him before we went in? I thought I saw him listening to us by the door. I don't rent to them. You rent to one and they all move in. They tear up your building. He tried to rent the apartment from me the other day, and I told him that it was already rented."

Tharbs v. Supera Property Management, et al. involved denial of an apartment to a black couple whose income was $17,000 a year for alleged "credit reasons." However, testing by the Leadership Council substantiated the client's complaint that race and not credit was the real reason for the refusal. The case was dismissed without prejudice when the couple was given a lease on the apartment.

The plaintiffs in *Dodson v. Hudland Corp.* were a black salesman and his blind white wife who tried to buy a new $35,000 townhouse in Chicago's Lincoln Park area. They were repeatedly stalled by the agents and finally were told that the unit had been sold to someone else and that no more were immediately available. The case was settled by agreement, with the plaintiffs being allowed to purchase the unit.

The plaintiff in *Sanders v. 1310 Ritchie Court Condominium, et al.*, a black woman stockbroker whose income was $30,000 a year executed a contract for the purchase of a condominium subject to financing within thirty days. The contract was returned to her with the thirty day clause altered to read three days, and it was rejected on the grounds that she had not met the financing requirement. The case was settled with the defendants to pay $10 and to allow the plaintiff to purchase the unit.

Three cases involving evictions or threatened evictions were handled in 1972. *Manning v. Anderson* was a sex discrimination case in which the owner of a townhouse complex decided to rent only to men and gave notice of eviction to a white female tenant. A permanent injunction was issued against the owner. In *Sherling v. Hinz*, the white plaintiff charged that the landlord of her west suburban Broadview apartment was harrassing her and threatening eviction because she entertained her black finance and other black friends in her apartment. The case was voluntarily dismissed by the plaintiff. *Kondic v. Townsend* found the Leadership Council's attorneys on the defense side of an eviction suit filed by the landlord in the Chicago municipal branch of the circuit court. The Townsends received notice of eviction after Ms. Townsend, a Mexican, reconciled with her black husband, from whom she had been separated when she rented the apartment, and he moved in with her. The judge found for the plaintiffs, refusing to admit the defendant's counterclaim of discrimination and ruling that discrimination was not an allowable defense in eviction cases.

The Evolution of Precedents

In some of its 1972 cases, the Leadership Council was successful in obtaining damages for its clients that were substantially greater than judges had been willing to award previously, suggesting that the courts were beginning to perceive loss of civil rights as a serious injury.

The first of the large damage awards came in January 1972, in the case of *Seaton v. Sky Realty, et al.* when the judge finally ordered the defendants—Sky Realty, its manager, a salesman, and the owner of the disputed house—jointly to pay $500 in actual damages, and in addition assessed $1,000 each in punitive damages against all defendants except the owner of the house. The total damage award was $3,500. The Seatons, a black couple, had gone to Sky Realty seeking a home that they specified should be west of 5000 west and north of Division Street, an area of Chicago that is notorious for its exclusion of blacks. In particular, they wished to see a home at 5035 Crystal, which the salesman agreed to show them only after the Seatons complained to the Chicago Commission on Human Relations. When the Seatons visited the home, the salesman refused to turn on lights in darkened rooms, answer questions, or show them the back yard or exterior of the house. The owner of the home is reported to have told the Leadership Council investigator that she would "rather go to jail than sell to colored" and that she was worried that damage would be done to the house if she did sell to blacks. In the investigator's opinion, "The neighborhood is of Polish and Irish ethnicity and tough. There would definitely be a violent aftermath to a black move in." Sky Realty's prospect sheets, which were entered into evidence in the trial, showed a detailed system of coding by race and ethnicity, serving to maintain the sharp distinction between white and black neighborhoods that exists in this part of Chicago.

The case of *Williamson, et al. v. Hampton Management Co., et al.,* where the manager of the 3130 North Lake Shore Drive building refused to allow a white tenant to sublet her apartment to two single black women, resulted in a finding in favor of the Leadership Council's clients and damages of $1,000 and $750 in attorney's fees. With the precedent for large damages established in court, the Leadership Council was able to obtain higher damage settlements out of court as well. In 1972, such settlements included *White v. Santeforte*, $2,000; *Kimbrough v. Meister-Neiberg*, $4,250; *Brown v. Town and Country*, $5,000; and *McAllister v. Eich*, $1,250.

The Leadership Council's largest settlement through the end of 1972 was in *Lhotka v. National Homes, et al.*, an interesting case that raised the issue of whether an employee is protected by law if he refuses, contrary to company policy or direct orders from superiors, to discriminate. Richard Lhotka, a salesman for National Homes Corporation's Bel Aire subdivision in south suburban Sauk Village, charged in June 1972 that the was fired for selling a home to a black family. He alleged that office policy regarding black applicants was that their applications were to be written up and then given to the manager without being processed in a normal manner. Lhotka had dealt with black applicants in three separate cases, and in two of them he adhered strictly to company policy. In one of the cases, the applicant, a public aid recipient, was told by the manager that there were no Section 235 funds available, although Lhotka claimed that this was not true and that he had, in fact, sold homes to several white public aid recipients. In another instance, the black applicants were stalled until they lost interest in buying the home, although they apparently complained of their difficulties to FHA, for Lhotka received a letter from FHA accusing him of discriminating. Becoming worried, Lhotka contacted the Chicago FHA office and was told that he was responsible and could be sued for discrimination even though he was following orders. When he broached the subject to his superiors, they allegedly told him that everything would be all right as long as he followed orders—that is, continued to turn the applications of blacks over to the sales office manager rather than process them. Not satisfied, Lhotka decided that he would process the next black application exactly as he did applications from whites. The opportunity came on April 30, 1972, when Lhotka sold the first home, of the 450 already sold, to a black family. He sent the finished papers to the manager on May 1. On May 3, the manager called him into the office, told him he was "through" and gave "lack of work" as the reason, although a new man was working in Lhotka's position by May 6. The suit was settled in April 1973, when National Homes agreed to pay Lhotka $12,000 plus $2,000 in attorney's fees. Thus the legal question remained unresolved, but the amount of the settlement and the publicity it received had sufficient impact to cause discriminatory real estate concerns to reevaluate their policies.

Another important case from the point of view of development and extension of the law was *Residents of West Pullman v. Miller.* The court enjoined Lee Miller, a white real estate broker, from panic peddling, the first panic-peddling injunction obtained by the Leadership Council. Miller sold a home in the West Pullman community on Chicago's far south side to Noah Robinson, black leader in SCLC's Breadbasket Commercial and half-brother of Jesse Jackson, Chicago's wellknown civil rights activist. Then Miller allegedly visited the neighbors, informing them of Robinson's purchase and asking if they would like to sell their homes. One of these neighbors testified in a sworn affidavit that Miller said, "Well, you're going to have to sell. Everyone is selling around you. If you sell now, I can give you cash. Right now you can get a good price for your home, but if you wait you will have to give it away. Jesse Jackson's brother wants these four houses for his bodyguards." Another neighbor testified that she was told basically the same thing by Miller. *West Pullman v. Miller* was a class action suit, the last such filed by the Leadership Council. The council's policy thereafter was to refrain from class actions, particularly in ordinary discrimination suits, because: (1) they required substantial time and effort to prepare; (2) judges tended to look upon them unfavorably; and (3) a judgment for an individual plaintiff in itself provided relief for the class—that is, affirmed their right to equal opportunity in housing.

There were other cases with great potential impact on the structure of the housing market. One example is *Morales v. Haines, et al.*, a suit against the city of Harvey, its mayor, and its planning commissioner challenging the legality of the city's resolution to deny further permits for the construction of federally subsidized homes. In a decision entered September 22, 1972, Federal Court Judge Philip Tone declared the Harvey resolution void, stating:

> The refusal of building permits for Section 235 houses violates the Equal Protection Clause of the Fourteenth Amendment. . . . The fact that the Federal Government subsidizes part of the interest on the mortgage indebtedness on Section 235 houses is not a reasonable basis for classifying them differently from other houses. To hold otherwise would be to countenance a basis for classification which is clearly impermissible under the Fourteenth Amendment, viz., the financial means of the prospective owner.

He enjoined the defendants from refusing a permit for the construction of the plaintiff's home. However, he did not find that racial discrimination was involved, and he did not award damages, although he ruled that the plaintiff was entitled to costs.

THE CASES AND THE CLIENTS

By the end of 1972 enough cases had been brought to a conclusion to make it possible to make some first generalizations about the kinds of cases that were most and least likely to be successfully prosecuted. An analysis was therefore undertaken to determine whether there were any specific characteristics of the clients, of the relationships between the clients and the legal action program, or of the manner of disposition of cases in the courts that might provide insights leading to revision of legal action practices or procedures.

Nature of the Data

According to Leadership Council statistics, 156 cases were filed from 1969 through December 31, 1971. During 1972, the Council filed 46 additional cases, a total of 202 law suits in all; 160 suits had been concluded as of the end of 1972.

The analysis that follows deals with one hundred one of these cases. The fifty-nine cases not studied were either unavailable in Leadership Council legal files because they were in Leadership Council office use, or they were cases handled by volunteer attorneys who kept the files, or they were cases dating from 1969 that lacked pertinent information because recordkeeping was not routinized at that time. Not all records were complete in all cases; hence, in the summaries that follow, not every table refers to all one hundred one cases.

Client Characteristics

Significant characteristics of the clients appear to be the following:

Seventy-eight percent of the applicants were black, with slightly more black couples than black singles requesting legal aid:

Black Couples/families	43
Mixed or non-black Couples/families	18
Black Singles	35
Nonblack Singles	5
	101 total

In cases where the household had a male family head, incomes tended to be in the middle or upper middle income range:

< 6,000	3
6,000–9,999	12
10,000–14,999	12
> 15,000	12
	39 total

On the other hand, female-headed households tended to be at best of lower middle income:

< 6,000	7
6,000–9,999	14
10,000–14,999	0
> 15,000	1
	22 total

Cross-classifying family type and family income (Table 3–2), the majority of clients in the lowest income categories were either families with a female head or single individuals. On the other hand, the greatest percentage of families in the highest income range were those with male heads.

The majority of the lower income applicants were seeking central city residences, while the higher income families were seeking suburban locations. The majority of the nonblack singles and mixed marriage couples were also seeking central city rather than suburban homes (Table 3–3).

While many of the applicants lived in black or changing neighborhoods from which they wanted to move, a significant number of the council's clients did live in white areas already:

Unknown	56
Black	41
White	28
Integrated/Changing	6
Out of town	5

The majority of the clients did move into white areas:

White	56
Black	2
Integrated/Changing	3

Table 3-2. Clients' Income Levels and Family Types.

	<6,000	*6-9,999*	*10-14,999*	*>15,000*	*Total*
Male family head	1 (3.6%)	6 (21.2%)	8 (28.6%)	13 (46.6%)	28
Wife of head	3 (23%)	7 (57.9%)	2 (15.4%)	1 (7.7%)	13
Male unrelated	1 (10%)	6 (60%)	2 (20%)	1 (10%)	10
Female unrelated	1 (10%)	8 (80%)	0%	1 (10%)	10
Female family head	2 (66.7%)	1 (33.3%)	0%	0%	3

Table 3-3. Client Characteristics by Location.

	Less than 10,000	*10- 15,000*	*15,000+*	*Unknown*	*Totals*
Oak Park	1	0	1	1	3
South Suburb	0	3	10	4	17
Chicago North Side	5	8	6	3	22
Waukegan	2	0	2	1	5
					47

	Married	*Single*	*Totals*
Oak Park	2	3	5
South Suburb	20	6	26
Chicago North Side	14	13	27
Waukegan	4	1	5
			63

	Black Singles and Couples	*Nonblack Singles/ Couples Mixed*	*Totals*
Oak Park	5	0	5
South Suburb	25	2	27
Chicago North Side	19	13	32
Waukegan	4	1	5

Most clients received very quick service from the legal staff. More that one-half of all suits were filed within one week of the client's complaint to the Leadership Council:

Less than one week	30
One to two weeks	20
Two weeks–one month	20
More than one month	13

However, as shown in Table 3-4 there were statistically significant relationships between race and filing time—that is, filing time by the Leadership Council was much more rapid for blacks than for non-blacks and mixed couples. Further, filing time was much more rapid for low rather than high income families and for singles rather than couples.

Therefore, as shown in Table 3-5, when filing time is cross-classified by type of family and income level a definite trend can be seen in which the low income single, particularly the low income black single, received a very quick hearing whereas the high income couples waited a much longer time before their case went into the courts:

Once in the courts, more than one-half of all cases took longer than three months for final disposition after the initial filing of the suit by the Leadership Council:

Less than one month	23
1–3 months	17
3–7 months	23
More than seven months	27

Apparently a much larger number of black applicants received more rapid disposition than did nonblack applicants. However, as shown in Table 3-6, cross-classifying race against time elapsed between filing and disposition is not statistically significant.

Table 3-4. Filing Time and Race.

	Less than 1 Week– 2 Weeks	*Two Weeks– 1 Month*	*Greater than 1 Month*
Black	41	16	7
Nonblack, mixed	8	6	6
Degrees of freedom = 2			
Chi square = 5.2			
Significant at 0.1 level			
Low Income (less than 10,000)	15	2	1
Medium Income (10–15,000)	10	1	1
High Income (greater than 15,000)	9	4	7
Single	26	9	2
Couple	24	12	11
Degrees of freedom = 2			
Chi Square = 5.63			
Significant at 0.1 level			

Table 3-5. Hearing Times and Client Characteristics.

	Less than 1 Week- 2 Weeks	2 Weeks- 1 Month	Greater than 1 Month
Single			
Low	11	2	1
Medium	3	1	0
High	2	1	0
Couples			
Low	4	2	0
Medium	7	0	1
High	7	3	7

An important feature of the relationship between disposition time and client characteristics involved client income. The lower the income, the more rapid disposition of the case in court. The higher income families, in general, were also those families for whom the disposition time was greatest (Table 3-6). Further, while the overall relationship between family status and disposition time was not sta-

Table 3-6. Time Between Filing and Disposition by Race.

	Less than 1 Month	1-7 Months	More than 7 Months
Nonblack	3	13	7
Black	20	26	19
Degrees of freedom = 2			
Chi Square = 3.1			
Not significant at 0.1 level			
10,000	10	8	1
10-15,000	5	7	3
15,000	3	6	11
Not known	5	18	11
Single	12	15	7
Couple	11	22	19
Degrees of freedom = 2			
Chi Square = 3.28			
Not significant at 0.1 level			
Single			
Low	8	7	1
Medium	1	3	0
High	1	0	0
Couples			
Low	2	1	0
Medium	4	4	3
High	2	6	11

tistically significant, the principal difference that did arise was in the three to one ratio of couples to singles in the longest disposition category.

The combination cross-classification of family status and income confirms the preceding results. Quite clearly, low income singles received rapid redress in the courts. On the other hand, high income couples became involved in very lengthy court proceedings.

Of the final decisions, the plaintiff was successful in 75 percent of the cases:

For Plaintiff	56
For Defendant, or	
dismissed	19

Ultimate success in the courts did not depend upon race, however, as Table 3-7 shows.

Table 3-7.   Disposition, by Client Characteristics.

	Finding for Defendant/ Dismissed	For Plaintiff
Black	14	51
Nonblack; mixed	5	14
Degrees of freedom = 1		
Chi Square = 0.19		
Not significant at 0.1 level		
Low	2	17
Medium	3	11
High	7	13
Degrees of freedom = 2		
Chi Square = 3.35		
Not significant at 0.1 level		
Single	6	26
Couple	12	35
Degrees of freedom = 1		
Chi Square = 0.498		
Not significant at 0.1 level		
Singles		
Low	2	14
Medium	0	4
High	0	0
Couples		
Low	0	3
Medium	3	7
High	7	13
Chi Square = 4.68		
Not significant at 0.1 level		

Similarly there was no significant simple relationship between level of income and decisions for the plaintiffs, nor apparently were there simple correlations with family status. However, when family status and income were cross-classified with the nature of the decision, an important difference did emerge for the highest income couples. Whereas in all other cases there was a significant degree of success by the plaintiffs, a much higher share of cases involving higher income couples (one of every three) was decided for the defendant.

Several interesting patterns are thus revealed. On the one hand, the clients tended to be on the upper end of the central city income scale, but on the other hand, there was an inverse relationship between income, family status, disposition time in the courts, and degree of success. The lower income singles seeking apartments on the north side of the central city received rapid and successful disposition. Higher income couples seeking homes in white suburbs became involved in much more prolonged cases with much higher probability that the final decision would be for the defendants. One possible interpretation relates to filing time; those cases taking longest to file were least likely to be successful. Another relates to the perceived self-interest of the defendant. On the part of both the real estate dealer and the white home owner in the suburbs, there remained a much greater feeling that it would be more profitable to contest a fair housing suit rather than acquiesce to a decision for the client, whereas central city apartment owners generally cut their losses by entering into an agreement for the plaintiff.

SUMMARY COMMENTS

The effectiveness of the Leadership Council's legal action program in obtaining relief for individual clients increased steadily through 1972. Of the cases terminated in 1972, 74.1 percent resulted in judgments for the plaintiffs or agreed orders and damages, as compared with 62.5 percent for the period February 1970 through December 1971 and 51.6 percent for 1969 through January 1970. There were fragmentary signs, too, that changes in attitudes and practices of members of the real estate industry were occurring as a result.

To cite one example, a meeting was held in the Park Forest Village Hall on April 11, 1973, attended by some residents of the village's Lincolnwood area, who called the meeting to discuss clustering of blacks in their neighborhood. A number of area real estate men participated. The residents pressured the brokers not to sell houses in proximity to one another to blacks, and the real estate people protested that because of the multiple listing service, it was impossible for any one firm to know what the other firms were doing. The Park Foresters then asked if it would not be possible for the companies to exchange information as to where blacks were seeking houses. The brokers comments were of interest:

> We can't keep track of where people live by race. We could be accused of violation if blacks asked to buy a specific house and we did not show it.
>
> Every Relator is being tested by blacks. We have no choice. There are law suits against brokers who have refused to show properties to certain people. Some have settled out of court, some are in the process.
>
> I am not going to lose my license over this. I can't call anybody up or contact them in any way legally and ask them where they are selling to colored.

Perhaps another indicator is the fact that the Chicago Real Estate Board ordered several hundred copies of the Leadership Council's *Guide to Practice Open Housing Under Law* in 1972 and distributed them to its members.

APPENDIX:
EXCERPTS FROM FORMAL OPINION 324, STANDING COMMITTEE ON ETHICS AND PROFESSIONAL RESPONSIBILITY, AMERICAN BAR ASSOCIATION

"We believe that the foregoing quotation from the Code of Professional Responsibility militate against any interference with the lawyer-client relationship by the directors of a legal aid society *after a case has been assigned to a staff attorney* (emphasis added) . . . .

We believe that under EC-24 of the Code of Professional Responsibility, the governing board of a legal aid society has a moral and ethical obligation to the community to determine such broad policy matters as the financial and similar criteria of persons eligible to participate in the Legal Aid Program, *selection of the various services which the society will make available to such persons, setting priorities in the allocation of available resources and manpower, and determining the type or kinds of cases staff attorneys may undertake to handle and the type of clients they may represent* (emphasis added) . . . .

The composition of the board of directors may be important in determining the propriety of board-imposed limitations or restrictions upon the types of cases a legal aid society permits its staff attorneys to undertake or the type of clients it permits them to represent . . . . Furthermore, just as an individual attorney should not decline representation of an unpopular client or cause, an attorney member of a legal aid society's board of directors is under a similar obligation not to reject certain types of clients or particular kinds of cases merely because of their controversial nature, anticipated adverse community reaction, or because of a desire to avoid alignment against public officials, governmental agencies, or influential members of the community . . . .

We believe that it is more desirable for the board of directors of a legal aid society, in determining which clients its attorneys may undertake to represent and the cases its attorneys may prosecute, to set broad guidelines respecting the categories or kinds of clients and cases rather than to act on a case-by-case, client-by-client basis. There is in a case-by-case consideration the very real danger that the more controversial causes—those which often provide opportunities for law reforms aiding the poor—will be subject to board veto solely because of a fear of criticism from certain influential segments of the community. A broader policy approach, we believe, is not only mandated by the Code of Professional Responsibility, specifically EC 5-24 and DR 5-107 (B), but is also a reasonable accommodation of the sometimes conflicting responsibilities that a legal aid board and its staff attorneys feel towards the community.

In addition to establishing broad policy, the board has the concomitant obligation to insure that its policies are being faithfully carried out by the society's executive director (who, of course, has no more latitude than the Board he represents) and staff attorneys. To this end, the board may employ reasonable procedures to periodically review the actions of society personnel to determine whether the board's policy directives have been adhered to . . . .

After the attorney has accepted a client or case of the nature and type sanctioned by board policy, the board must take special precautions not to interfere with its attorney's independent professional judgment in the handling of the matter. The staff attorney must similarly prevent his actions in handling particular cases from being directly or indirectly influenced by the board or by individual board members, thus impairing his primary obligation of loyalty to his client.

Chapter 4

Building Bridges into Suburbia

To complement its emerging legal action program and to help replace the ill-fated Equal Opportunity Housing centers, the Leadership Council began in 1969 to experiment with alternative mechanisms that might aid and stimulate black houseseekers to move into suburbia. First, an alliance was sought with an organization having roots in Chicago's black community, to serve as the means through which black houseseekers might be channeled toward suburban houses. Second, an attempt was made to have black real estate brokers appointed to white suburban real estate boards so as to gain access to suburban housing supplies. Like the EOH activities beforehand, this experiment was difficult, always frustrating, and quite unsuccessful.

AN ALLIANCE WITH BLACK REALTORS: THE DEARBORN REAL ESTATE BOARD CONTRACT

A number of groups were considered as possible sources of black homeseekers, including Operation Breadbasket (the Chicago arm of the Southern Christian Leadership Council), the Contract Buyers' League, and the Urban League. The final choice was the Dearborn Real Estate Board (DREB), which was organized in 1940 and chartered in 1941. This predominantly black trade organization was formed in response to the exclusionary practices of the National Association of Real Estate Boards, which, in the forties, had no black members.

DREB's past history was rather impressive: it had initiated a court battle against restrictive covenants in 1948, sponsored the first black convention to be held in a major Chicago hotel (the National Association of Real Estate Brokers meeting in the early 1950s), struggled to get mortgage money for the black community, fought to prevent insurance companies from revoking insurance in the midsouth area of Chicago and, in 1962, confronted the Chicago Real Estate Board with the issue of discrimination in membership. However, in 1969, it seemed a weak reed to grasp in a storm: its membership was small (there were only thirty active members); its organization was weak and riddled with internal conflict. Because of the nature of the dual housing market, DREB was, as one of its members later explained to the staff of the Center for Urban Studies, dedicated to integrationist rhetoric and segregationist tactics.

It is doubtful that the Leadership Council initially realized the Dearborn board's limitations or the effect that changes in external market conditions would have on the willingness of both black homeseekers and black brokers to explore the suburban alternative. Prospects for business totally in black communities had always been poor, because of the relative lack of resources compared with large real estate firms, the difficulties in penetrating the property management field, and the low turnover of property within the black community. Thus, Dearborn Real Estate Board members did most of their business in changing neighborhoods. The council knew that the most profitable place for black brokers to operate was in changing neighborhoods where turnover rates were high; still, with educational programs, it hoped to broaden their scope of operation. One of DREB's assets, it was felt, was its powerful president, Dempsey Travis, president of Sivart Mortgage Corporation in Chicago.

Several benefits were anticipated by the Leadership Council from this association. The overriding goal was to provide a channel through which black homeseekers could make effective choices from the total metropolitan housing market. The Dearborn Real Estate Board was to become a "fast, efficient clearinghouse" through which individuals who were interested in moving out of the black community could be referred to the council and was to encourage black brokers to apply for memberships in suburban real estate boards and multilisting services to assist black homeseekers in securing housing in white suburban areas. Much effort was spent on trying to reach those objectives, without much success.

NARRATIVE HISTORY: THE FIRST FIVE MONTHS (JANUARY THROUGH MAY 1970)

In January 1970, Mrs. Helen Fannings,[1] in charge of "special programs" for the Leadership Council, was assigned to work with DREB "[to] be instrumental in helping the new office to be a success . . . ."[2] The basic mechanics of setting up the new DREB office proved somewhat complicated, however. The board had been operating out of the office of Sivart Mortgage Company, and there was some resistance on Dempsey Travis' part to moving it to a separate location. However, the council felt that DREB should set up an office at a new address to allay any criticism of partisanship as the contract work developed. Paralleling this, a search for a "director" or "executive secretary" was begun. Here, too, there was some disagreement, since Travis felt that an "executive secretary" at $650 a month or so could handle the job at hand, whereas the council's position was that it was essential to get a thoroughly competent professional person and that it would be necessary to pay at least $850 a month. Both of these conflicts were resolved in the council's favor, and in the early months of the contract, an office was opened at 8609 South Cottage Grove Avenue, Chicago, and Ted Saunders hired as executive director at $850 a month in February 1970.

Saunders tried to work with the DuPage County Board of Realtors for the purpose of setting up a multilisting service within DREB to cooperate with the DuPage board, but his only contact was with the director of the DuPage board, and no relationship developed. DREB had no functioning program committee at that time and the board needed organizing badly. The few seminars that Saunders put together were not well attended, and Dempsey Travis became unhappy with his lack of ability to pull people in and organize programs. Saying he wanted a more "high-powered" director, Travis fired Saunders at the end of the three months, on May 30, 1970, and notified the Leadership Council after doing so. Thus, between finding and furnishing an

---

1. Mrs. Fannings resigned from the Leadership Council at the end of 1971.
2. Memorandum, March 16, 1970, from F. Willis Caruso of the Leadership Council to Michael Schneider of the Department of Housing and Urban Development.

office and hiring and firing a director, months passed without producing any program results.

MR. HICKS' FOURTEEN MONTHS AS DREB
DIRECTOR (JUNE 1970 THROUGH JULY 1971

In June 1970, Malcolm Hicks became the new executive director of DREB. Hicks' hiring is described by him as follows:

> On Friday, May 29, 1970, Mr. Dempsey J. Travis called me at home at 7:30 A.M. and advised me of the need for an Executive Director for the DREB. He also advised me of the existing relationship of the DREB with the Leadership Council and *expressed some fears about its continuance* (italics added), because of, (1) the rapidly deteriorating condition of the board vis a vis its inability to comply with the critical contract provision that at least four members of DREB volunteer to actively seek membership in all white real estate boards and their multiple listing service adjuncts. (2) The failure of the Board of Directors to generate a precipitate increase in memberships to which they had committed themselves. (3) Also, in his description and explanation he alluded to the following facts:
>
> 1. That the relationship of DREB and Leadership Council were a result of the funding of Leadership Council as a prime contractor for a demonstration project designed to expand the housing options of blacks within the Chicago metropolitan area.
> 2. To provide more ready and greater and more profitable access for black brokers to the housing inventory now monopolized by all white local boards and multiple listing services.
> 3. Through financial assistance to enable the DREB to pursue a vigorous policy of stabilizing and upgrading predominantly black neighborhoods through programs of tenant education, attacks on vandalism and crime. Finally, through legal and legislative assistance to stem the rising tide of restrictive housing practices.
> 4. That we were part of a triumvirate composed of the Leadership Council as prime contractor and the DREB and University of Chicago as subcontractors.
> 5. That he was empowered to offer me as president of the board an employment contract until the expiration of his term in March, 1971, under terms to be mutually agreed upon .... [3]

It is obvious, then, that at the end of May 1970, Dempsey Travis was apprehensive that DREB would not be able to meet its contract commitments. Its board of directors was lethargic and did not work

3. Memorandum, July 1, 1970, from Malcolm L. Hicks to Edward L. Holmgren, executive director, Leadership Council.

as a team. Travis had during his tenure run DREB; in fact, DREB had always operated like a private club under the direction of each succeeding president.[4] It served more as a protective agency for those "in the know" than as a service organization for its members; it was viewed by DREB members as the president's personal feifdom. Old guard membership was retained, but new members joined and then resigned when they became aware that DREB could not serve their needs.

Who was Malcolm Hicks? He was a long-time friend of Dempsey Travis and worked for him as a salesman for eleven years; he had no executive experience. One of DREB's members described him as a "messenger" for Travis. However, if Travis felt the contract was in jeopardy, he must at this time have decided either to continue to run DREB himself, to run it through Malcolm Hicks, or to abdicate in favor of Hicks.

Up until this time, June 1970, the evaluation team, at the request of the Leadership Council, had made no contact with the Dearborn Real Estate Board. The council felt that if the team entered the picture before DREB clearly understood its role, the ultimate success of the program might be jeopardized. The team therefore had its first meeting with Malcolm Hicks at the Dearborn board office on June 29, 1970.

[The meeting] served the dual purpose of an exchange of information regarding the role to be played by each subcontractor and set the stage for a successful, mutually beneficial working relationship between them.
It was possible to identify separate responsibilities as follows:

1. Mr. Hicks and Mrs. Fannings are to set up and plan activities for implementation of the Leadershp Council's contract with the Dearborn Real Estate Board;
2. Mr. Koenig and Mrs. Smith will assist Professor Berry in evaluating the effectiveness of both programs. In addition, they will provide Mr. Hicks and Mrs. Fannings with access to any information they might have which might be useful.

Additionally, the evaluators agreed to:

1. Formulate a questionnaire to sample attitudes of its members toward Dearborn Real Estate Board,
2. Provide interviewers to make sample survey, and

---

4. "The Dearborn Real Estate Board," Appendix A to *Brokers at Bay* (Chicago: Center for Urban Studies, University of Chicago, March 1971).

3. Prepare a map for Dearborn Real Estate Board showing predictions of black population movement in the Chicago metropolitan area.

Hicks, for the Dearborn board, agreed to assist the center in its data collection and monitoring.[5]

The evaluators completed their survey of members of DREB in August of 1970 and furnished copies of it to Mr. Hicks as well as to the Leadership Council and the Department of Housing and Urban Development. Some of the more important conclusions were as follows:

1. The great majority of black brokerages remain one man operations with few salesmen.
2. Black brokers operate mainly in racially changing neighborhoods where property turnover rates are high.
3. There was no clear consensus of DREB's purpose nor awareness of current activities of the board.
4. Few of the DREB members were financially able to set up offices within the geographic boundaries of suburban boards, and fewer still were convinced that it would be profitable to operate in those areas.
5. Revocation or reformation of Illinois' antisolicitation law was the primary concern of black brokers.
6. The Leadership Council lacked credibility to DREB members.
7. Communication and elaboration of the Leadership Council's program to DREB's membership were virtually nonexistent.

These were stumbling blocks to contractual performance on DREB's part.

DREB in the summer of 1970 was set up for internal struggles. Hicks felt that he had to try to become spokesman for DREB; Travis had to take a back seat. The old members had to make way for younger, more progressive members. Some of the members agreed with Hicks, some felt that the executive director was "merely an employee, an administrator to carry out the president's mandates." Travis also had his followers, who felt that what was needed was a "lobbyist, force, you know . . . he [Travis] has a loud voice." But this very forcefulness and drive that brought Travis to prominence in the community also worked against him in eliciting cooperation;

5. Memorandum, July 2, 1970, Katherine Smith, Center for Urban Studies, to Malcolm L. Hicks (copy to Helen Fannings).

many people respected and envied him but did not necessarily like him.

Hicks' concern about Travis controlling DREB proved groundless. In the fall of 1970 Travis discontinued playing an active role in DREB and announced that he would not again run for the presidency. The board of directors of DREB, who had been content to let Travis run the show, now let Hicks take over. By silent mandate, it now placed itself in Hicks' hands, and he took full advantage of the situation.

First of all, he wanted a new president whom he could control. At "Black Expo," held in November of 1970, he was favorably impressed with a relatively new member of DREB, Jefferson R. Perry, president of his own Chicago real estate firm, Park Grove Realty, and encouraged him to seek the presidency. From later events, it would seem that he saw Perry merely as a figurehead and undoubtedly painted a rosy picture for him in his role as DREB's president. Hicks said, "I imposed on Mr. Perry to be a candidate because I thought he was receptive to new ideas." The election went off smoothly, and Perry was elected in December of 1970, taking office in March of 1971.

At the end of 1970, the Leadership Council felt quite bullish about the DREB contract. In its end of year report, the council reported that "roots in the black real estate market suddenly became much stronger as a result of the subcontract with DREB." But then there were signs of trouble. Repeated attempts to obtain information from Hicks by Helen Fannings were largely unsuccessful. To each request, he responded by stressing the need for DREB to increase its membership. He decried brokers' commitment to the idea of segregation, espousing democracy in housing as imperative. Crusading against anti-solicitation laws remained high on his "list of priorities." However, when confronted with actual contract obligations and asked to comment on progress being made on each point, he could at no time give any clear statement as to what was being done. Seemingly, he could not or would not respond to contract requirements; in short, he was either not competent in the situation in which he found himself or his "list of priorities" actually included things that had no relevance to the contract.

As Mrs. Fannings tried to force Hicks to work on program implementation, Hicks expressed reservations about his relationship with the Leadership Council. He felt that he and Mrs. Fannings had a personality conflict and was annoyed that he did not have authority to dispense the funds provided for in the HUD subcontract. He could not understand the council's refusal to accept as real the concerns of DREB members about the antisolicitation law, its "equivocation" about making a public statement about the issue, or its refusal to explain its hesitancy. He said that he was upset about the intimidating effect the Leadership Council staff had on the executive committee of DREB. According to him, complaints aired to him privately were not expressed openly during meetings with the council, even though he tried hard to get the committee members to express their reservations with the program.

DREB's and Hicks' preoccupation with the Illinois antisolicitation law (Illinois Public Act 76-1389) is itself revealing. Interviews with DREB members brought forth a variety of quite pointed responses. "I exist," said one, "as do 99 percent of other brokers, i.e., members of DREB, on the transition of neighborhoods from white to black." Another said that "panic peddling was a result of the current system" and indicated that he saw operations in transitional neighborhoods on the periphery of the black and white communities being threatened by new, repressive laws aimed at preventing alleged panic peddling and block busting. One broker went further and predicted that such laws would become even more repressive, meaning that some broker, probably a black one, would be prosecuted under the law and given severe punishment as an example to other brokers working in the same communities.[6] DREB members, then, clearly saw their

6. *Chicago Daily Defender*, September 21, 1971. This issue did not go away. In August 1971, two DREB brokers were alleged by the South Lynne Community Council to be panic peddlers. The two men were Stacey Smith, Midwest Realty, and Marion Maner, Maner Real Estate. Mr. Smith was one of the Leadership Council's original applicants to a white suburban board; he dropped out when, among other things, he told the Leadership Council that it was possible he might be accused of blockbusting. Mr. Maner took office as DREB's president on March 1, 1972. The second vice president of DREB in 1971, Frank J. Williams, also was portrayed as a blockbuster by the *Southtown Economist*. According to Williams, he was visited early in September 1971, by fifty white residents of the North Beverly area of Chicago, who tried to "pressure" him into signing a document stating that he would not solicit business in their neighborhood. Mr. Williams said:

There is a very tenuous line between blockbusting, which involves repeated phone calls, threats, and intimidation, and legitimate soliciting, where prospects are sought in a ripe housing market . . . as a black man I couldn't get away with scare tactics in a white neighborhood even if I wanted to . . . besides I don't usually get any business in an area until the racial change is well along. I'm limited to the areas where I can buy and sell. Big southside agencies, like Russ Pocock, or S.A. Van Dyke can sell on Kedzie or in Oak Lawn and South Holland. They can do business anywhere, but I can't. Yet representatives from Beverly told me they plan to allow "good-guy" realtors, like Pocock, to continue to do business in their area.

However, in 1974 Williams was accepted into the Beverly-South Suburban Real Estate Board.

current fortunes as being linked to the pace of ghetto expansion, not to access to suburbia.

What, actually, did Hicks do during his term of office? He alleged that he increased membership by as much as 500 percent and gave a membership figure of 136 as of January 1, 1971. However, when interviewed about this Ripley Meade of DREB said, "I have been secretary of DREB six years. There has been a lot of talk about the way membership is generated. We thought it had increased 100-200 percent. We actually got about twelve to fifteen members."

The board of DREB did not have or want any control over Hicks. Expenditures were made under the guise that they were approved by the board, when in fact they were not. For $125 a month a xerox machine was installed in DREB's offices, as was a "touch type" Pitney Bowes mailing machine, which cost $37 a month. Excessive mileage charges were turned in by Hicks, according to Helen Fannings; his parking fees were taken out of petty cash.

DREB maintained two checking accounts: one, a general account, at Independence National Bank, which was not under Hicks' control; the other an account set up at Seaway National Bank that was to contain only moneys coming to DREB from the Leadership Council from its HUD grant. The latter account required two signatures on every check. However, some checks went through with only one signature—Hicks. As he explained it, "the bank calls to see if the check is okay, and when I tell them it is, they pay it with just my signature." To the evaluators' knowledge, DREB did not pursue the legalities of this situation with Seaway National Bank.

Membership fees allegedly collected by Hicks were not turned over for deposit in DREB's general account; some checks representing proceeds from a banquet held by DREB also failed to go into this account. As Meade related it, "All moneys from the banquet were to go into the general account. Everyone knew that. I made it my business to collect checks. On one occasion Mr. Hicks came by and I told him to present checks. They had not been recorded or stamped. After the banquet I asked for additional checks and he said there were none. There are no records kept in his office."

There also were countercharges made by Hicks in his letter of August 2 addressed to "Dear Dearborn Real Estate Board Members":

> I have complied with the request of the Leadership Council by delivering to them on this 31st day of July, 1971, required materials, reports, programs and plans for the period August, 1971 to February, 1972 inclusive.
>
> I respectfully request your presence on Wednesday, August 4, 1971, to discuss and evaluate the CPA report which indicates that the secretary, Mr.

Ripley B. Meade, Jr., with the apparent acquiescence of the treasurer, Mr. Albert H. Johnson, failed to give proper accounting of the DREB monies, commingled the DREB funds with his own and withheld for his own purposes hundreds of dollars from the National Organization.

This strong language and revelation is necessitated by the fact that in spite of the record of progress made in the past year which the membership has not been made aware of:

- A minimum of 100 additional members were obtained in one calendar year
- An increase in net worth from $51.00 to apparently several thousand dollars
- Renegotiation of the Leadership Council Contract in the amount of 50,000-20,000 dollars in excess of previous contract negotiated before the present director took over
- Revisions of the accounting procedures which your new billings indicate
- Establishment of an image in the industry commensurate with the size and quality of our membership.

In spite of these accomplishments, I have not been able to secure for the membership an accounting of their money. Therefore, if after examining the financial statements enclosed you would like to know why: 1) there are no proper records for the last four years other than those developed by the present director, 2) our tax liabilities to the Internal Revenue Service is unclear 3) that after many petitions, resolutions and demands the membership has not been able to obtain a reconciliation of the two bank accounts which would enable the director to unravel and isolate the DREB's actual money from the liabilities to the Leadership Council, the IRS and the membership; then please take this opportunity to be heard on these subjects at a special membership meeting on Wednesday, August 4, 1971 in the DREB offices, 8609 S. Cottage Grove, Chicago, Illinois 60619 at 7:30 P.M. promptly.

I have enclosed for your examination and response, copies of the CPA's Report and a copy of this letter is being sent to all DREB Directors who hold the stewardship of the organization for the membership. If this is an unsatisfactory and unrevealing record of accomplishment compared to the "old way" of a voiceless membership unaware of what goes on inside the organization, I shall willingly submit my resignation effective August 13, 1971.

It was intimated that Hicks was actively selling real estate during the time he was executive director of DREB; indeed, some people interviewed felt that it is possible that he was funneling off calls made to DREB for this purpose. In addition, the office secretary told of callers asking for "Mr. Hicks the appraiser."

After an April 1971 evaluation conference, F. Willis Caruso of the Leadership Council issued a memorandum to DREB, "Recommendations of Additions to Program Report":

1. Careful monthly reports including:
   a. Statements on each of the items of the Contract
      i. what has been come
      ii. what are plans to complete
   b. What deviations from contract
2. Report on financial situation
   a. All moneys
   b. Problems
   c. Changes in budget
   d. Actual, proposed remaining
3. Report on Board participation
   a. Who
   b. How many
4. Program
   a. Who participates
   b. Who does not
   c. Was it valuable
5. How have you contacted Leadership Council?
   Why have you asked it for?

(It should be noted that a new budget for DREB had been prepared by Mr. Hicks, calling for $50,000 a year rather than $30,000. It was approved on April 27 and increased Mr. Hicks' salary from $12,500 to $14,500 after six months as executive director of DREB.)

Problems persisted into the second quarter of 1971 and were delineated in a July 14, 1971, memorandum from Mrs. Fannings:

I. Program Implementation
   A. Educational programs for community consumption.
      During this interim the executive director and the president appeared on "Opinion". As far as we were able to determine from interviews and other reports from the executive director no specific plan for service or follow-up was spelled out on the program.
   B. There have been no educational leaflets, or brochures made available to the public or membership. There have been no seminars or forums for the public or general black community
   C. There have been no referrals of individuals seeking housing information outside of the black community.
II. Broker-Salesman Training Institutes
   A. One institute held during the first quarter, no program during the second quarter.

B. No sales courses or otherwise training sessions for brokers or salesmen.

C. No other service information or otherwise provided for the membership.

III. General Meetings Open to the Public
One general meeting during these six months open to the public. Very few non-real estate persons involved or in attendance.
No dissemination to the community of information relative to service.

IV. Operative and Functional Office

A. The office is plagued by various types of personnel problems. During the past six months there have been three persons who performed some office work, however, none are there at this time. The office is frequently closed during work hours and telephones are not answered.

B. Monthly reports have not been submitted by the executive director on the first of each month. When reports are received after repeated written and verbal requests, they tend to be vague and deal with philosophical viewpoints rather than program specifics.

C. Vouchers and request for reimbursements are never submitted prior to the first or earlier than the second week in the following month.

D. It has been impossible to ascertain even a general understanding of the executive director's activities or calendar of events he has participated in relative to the board.

E. We have not received from the executive director an accurate accounting of the total membership with a breakdown of brokers, salesmen and others.

F. There is no evidence that regular membership meetings are scheduled monthly and the membership is notified in ample time to attend meetings.

G. Although there are separate accounts for membership funds and others and one for HUD of Leadership Council, there is evidence that funds have been co-mingled without proper authorization. Further in this same area, checks have been dispersed with one signature while the account calls for two.

V. Mutual agreements and/or Board of Directors approval on program, large expenditures and additional personnel other than those designated by the contract budget

A. Personnel hired without authorization:
1. Mrs. Dorothy Carpenter
2. Mrs. Anne Blair of Hurley Green Associates

B. Equipment Expenditures
The total amount allowed for equipment for twelve months was spent in three months plus $127.00 deficit. A large piece of equipment rented with a "use charge" of $125.00 per month without the Board of Directors authorization.

C. Newsletters

Two newsletters were published during the past six months. The second newsletter cost $365.00 for 2500 copies. There is no indication that these letters were forwarded to any organization or individual other than the board membership.

According to Mrs. Fannings, until late spring of 1971, there was no sense of panic either in the Leadership Council or the board of directors of DREB, which was not willing to recognize that it had to get things in order: "the board was not alarmed about petty things like money."

However, when DREB's May vouchers and request for reimbursement were received on June 10, 1971, the Leadership Council began a review of all expenditures from January 1, 1971. Following this, a letter was written to Hicks detailing the problem areas later spelled out in Mrs. Fannings' July 14 memorandum. He gave neither a verbal nor a written response. On June 16, Mrs. Fannings met with Jefferson Perry, president of DREB; Mr. Crank, its attorney; Mr. Meade, secretary; and Mr. Johnson, treasurer. They were told that funds would be withheld until a satisfactory explanation was made to the council. Mr. Holmgren following this up with a letter to Mr. Perry dated June 23 requesting specific information within ten days. Mr. Perry, in turn, on June 25 requested Mr. Hicks to submit such information by July 8. Two reports were submitted by Mr. Hicks, neither of which spoke to the specifics at hand. This was the situation when a quarterly evaluation meeting was called for July 15, 1971.

At this meeting Hicks attempted to ride roughshod over Perry. Some of Perry's comments follow.

I will admit I am quite inexperienced in this type of activity, and I am somewhat bewildered in the last few days. I can and cannot understand the position we are in at this time, particularly the quarter I have been president, and that is why I haven't been on top of things. I admit I was in a jungle trying to find a way out. I found myself in situations I really knew nothing about. I am learning that things have not been done properly . . . . I am speaking over a period of long duration, prior to my coming . . . . Very frankly, we are at a juncture where I don't know what to do, but I must do something . . . I am concerned. For the three months I have been president, I have taken a lot of time away from my business . . . . I have left things undone . . . . I must make a determination. Where the problems lie, I don't know. I am not going to place the blame except on myself because I have not been completely unaware. I got the thrust for the past three months of how things should have been done for over a year, before I got into this position . . . even before I was a member of the board.

Things were lax and undone, and everything fell on me before I got my feet wet. *I came into a situation which was quite different from what I had been led to imagine* (italics added) . . . . I haven't been doing anything but holding meetings; I don't even get to my office. Meetings on meetinge on meetings, *and with only one or two people there* (italics added). Officers do not function according to the constitution and bylaws . . . the treasurer was not functioning. . . . I have not signed any checks because I have not had the support of the board. . . . I cannot continue unless I get coopera- tion from the board. . . . I am going to have to make a decision quickly . . . I can't go through this day in and out.[7]

However, despite DREB's contact with Mrs. Fannings, despite the contract and the April 30 memorandum from the council to DREB, its board members at this meeting kept raising the question of what DREB was supposed to do. As Mr. Crank, DREB's lawyer said, "There is not a clear understanding of what DREB is to implement with the aid of the Leadership Council."[8]

One board member put her finger on the problems when she said:

There is limited involvement. Malcolm Hicks appears as an individual. How is this benefiting board and members? Membership is as unaware as general public as to what we are supposed to do . . . . We have liaison with the Leadership Council [but] I am concerned that there was no close working relationship . . . . We must cooperate with the Council . . . . There is a wealth of information available [from the Council] as to how the board should function . . . but there is a lack of organization and participation. These are serious defects.[9]

Holmgren summed up the situation by saying:

It seems clear that there are many problems here, not the least of which is the performance of the contract. There are problems on questions of the board itself and relationships between officers, members of the board, and hired help. No outside agency can tell DREB . . . how to run its business. On the other hand we do have a responsibility to be concerned with performances and execution of contract and its terms. The fact that these other issues have emerged so forcefully shows the gravity of the situation . . . .

Thereupon Holmgren announced that the contract between the council and DREB would be cancelled as of July 31, 1971. The door

7. Katherine Smith from the Leadership Council Quarterly Evaluation Con- ference of DREB, July 15, 1971.
8. Ibid.
9. Ibid.

was left open, however, so that if DREB could demonstrate that it could work as a unit and actually fulfill contract obligations, a renewal could be initiated.

As far as the HUD-funded contract was concerned, Hicks' employment was terminated as of July 31st; he remained on DREB's payroll until the end of September. During his last two months in office, he kept busy; he wrote letters to "selected" board members eliciting their support, suggesting that a new real estate board be set up in competition with DREB—a board which he, of course, would head. He also removed all records from the office, including the mailing list, membership cards, reports, letters from and to Mrs. Fannings, correspondence with brokers, and the Rolodex containing pertinent telephone numbers—in short, everything of importance. In a visit to the Center for Urban Studies he indicated that he might contact George Romney, secretary of the Department of Housing and Urban Development and "blow the whistle on the Leadership Council." He then vanished from the scene, with not one contractual requirement fulfilled.

DREB RESTRUCTURES ITS PROGRAM (AUGUST AND SEPTEMBER 1971)

Apparently the cancellation of its contract was enough to produce something of a shakeup in DREB. During August and September, Jefferson Perry, together with Albert Johnson, treasurer, and Ripley Meade, secretary, was able to motivate the board enough to put together a positive program and a new budget to be presented to the Leadership Council. With some budget adjustments, these were both approved. DREB began assuming responsibility not only for program content but for a percentage of the funding; it received $37,375 through the Leadership Council, and itself supplied $8,525. In addition, the board's office was relocated in larger quarters, the rehabilitation of which was handled by services and money solicited from area businessmen.

Dearborn Real Estate Board presented the following 1971-1972 program to the Leadership Council:[10]

Services
1. Library of pertinent real estate materials—publications, books, films, slides.
2. Monthly Newsletter—To contain exclusive information on federal pro-

10. Letter to Edward L. Holmgren, November 26, 1971, from Jefferson R. Perry.

grams, funding, financing, FHA discounts, etc. Also inquiries and NAREB news. To be edited by a Board Editorial Committee.

3. Clearing House—re financing such as second mortgages, basic mortgage procedures, referrals from buyers and sellers.
4. Legislative information and reference materials.
5. Referral service to Leadership Council of all prospective cases of discrimination.
6. Group insurance for all members—real estate brokers and salesmen.

Schools and Training Institutes

1. Weekly school for salesmen in salesmanship—starting in January— Tuesday nights for 3 months—6:30 P.M.-8:00 P.M. (certificates will be given for full completion).
2. Weekly school on Basic Principles of Real Estate—starting in January— Tuesday nights from 8:00 P.M.-9:30 P.M. or beginners with a view towards securing a salesman's license.
3. Weekly school for property management—starting in January—Wednesday nights for 3 months—7:00 P.M.-9:00 P.M. Course #1 Basic Principles in Real Estate Management (elementary procedures). Registration fee to cover materials.
4. Course #2—Advanced course in management—to begin in April— Wednesday nights for 3 months—7:00 P.M.-9:00 P.M.
5. Course #3—Commercial and Industrial Management—to begin in September—Wednesday nights for 3 months—7:00 P.M.-9:00 P.M. Credit will be given for these courses towards a Designation as a Certified Real Estate Manager.
6. Appraisers Institute—starting January—Monday nights for 3 months— 7:00 P.M.-9:00 P.M.
   Educational Committee, setting up the schools, will select a Dean and Assistant Dean.

Communication and Public Relations

1. Board will set up Lobbying Committee to work with Legislative Committee.
   To attend hearings on ordinances and legislation affecting the profession—being held in City Council, state legislature, etc.
   Also to organize sessions with public officials and state legislators to present our viewpoint. Press conferences to be held with media personnel.
2. Full use of media for coverage of DREB programs, schools, and events. Radio-TV-Press.
3. Full use of press releases. Press release in support of member F.J. Williams, example of support that will be given to all members *unfairly* accused of panic-peddling and other unethical practices.
4. Observance of Realtist Week in February, being coordinated on a national level by the NAREB. Beginning with a Realtist Breakfast in

February, followed by a Realtist Week. Representatives of Media, public officials, and state legislators to be our guests at Breakfast.

Seminars and Panels (to be open to the public)

In light of very serious attacks on the real estate profession mainly concerned with legitimate real estate practices which are being condemned as panic-peddling, block busting, etc., the officers and Board members of the Dearborn Real Estate Board, have planned a number of seminars directed to this problem as well as to other vital phases of real estate.

Thursday, October 14   — HOW HUD AFFECTS YOU TODAY
Thursday, November 11 — LEGISLATION AFFECTING REAL ESTATE
Thursday, December 9   — Xmas Party to be held. Election of Officers for the coming year. (Nominations Committee Report will have been made to the General Membership Meeting, November 11, at 7:00 P.M.)
Thursday, January 13   — PANEL ON REAL ESTATE PRACTICES IN OUR CHANGING SOCIETY
Thursday, February 10 — PANEL ON SUBURBAN BOARDS AND MULTIPLE LISTING SERVICES
March   — 1972 INSTALLATION BANQUET
Thursday, April 13   — TENANT AND LANDLORD RESPONSIBILITIES
Thursday, May 11   — RENT SUBSIDIES
Thursday, June 8   — COOPS AND CONDOMINIUMS

SHORT-TERM THIRD DIRECTOR (OCTOBER 25, 1971 TO JANUARY 7, 1972)

On October 25, 1971, DREB hired its third director, Dudley A. Emmons. By December his effectiveness was seriously questioned in a letter sent him by Mrs. Fannings:[11]

We have carefully reviewed the report you submitted on November 30, 1971. The packet contained a report of activities of the Dearborn Board Real Estate, a membership list, a yellow ledger sheet itemizing expenses for August and September. You indicated in your letter that a report from the building committee was also included, however it was not found.

We found your report unsatisfactory and deficient in its account of activities of the Board since you became Executive Director. The figures listed for August and September expenses were not clearly outlined by each month—to indicate expenses for each month. Cancelled checks, vouchers, and unpaid bills should provide complete information on these expenditures.

11. Letter to Dudley A. Emmons from Mrs. Fannings, December 22, 1971.

The report submitted to the Leadership Council's evaluation and new contract discussion meeting should have been submitted to your Board prior to the meeting. A monthly report (as stated in the contract) should be forwarded to the Leadership Council relative to program implementation and future programming. It appears that you are still unclear as to the functions of your role with the committees and also your relationship to the Board of Directors of the Dearborn Board. There is little or no evidence of your interest in the programs of the Board or evidence of any initiative shown in the position of Executive Director. Further, we are concerned about your lack of rapport with the membership and the Executive Board members. Your approach to new members and your unwillingness to cooperate with members on projects, will serve to hamper a smooth-operating board.

Since all of the above mentioned negative factors will impede the progress of the Dearborn Real Estate Board and create difficulty in our mutual program, we are extremely concerned about the future of the Board.

We sincerely hope that you and the Dearborn Real Estate Board of Directors can come to some agreement as to future planning for the Board and made a final determination as to whether you and the Board members can continue in your present relationship.

CHRONOLOGY OF EVENTS DURING 1972

Emmons was discharged on January 7, 1972, to be followed on January 17 by Samuel Dixon, whose main responsibility, aside from setting up and maintaining a smooth-flowing office, was to aid the Dearborn board in finding a suitable permanent director. Mr. Dixon, a semiretired man, said he would assume the directorship for not more than one and one-half years but would gladly step down when DREB found a director. The personnel committee continued its search for such an executive.

Jefferson Perry was succeeded as DREB's president in March 1972 by Marion L. Maner, president of Maner Realty Company, Chicago. The board moved its headquarters in April to a new location that provided it with sufficient space for its educational programs and conferences. Mid-July saw the hiring of Ms. Jean V. Gay as DREB's new executive director. Mr. Dixon left on August 1, after briefing Ms. Gay on her new duties.

The most significant event during the year was probably a special meeting that was called for June 29 to discuss the sixty-day moratorium on loan applications for existing homes in Chicago imposed by John Waner, Chicago area director of the U.S. Department of Housing and Urban Development.

Marion Maner . . . said the 60-day moratorium unfairly discriminates against blacks who finance 90 percent of their home purchases in Chicago through the FHA.

. . .

Maner, pointing out that the moratorium does not affect new housing and housing in the suburbs, said that the impact has been primarily on black home buyers and black real estate brokers.

. . .

He [Waner] ought to life the moratorium or impose the moratorium throughout the Chicago area . . . . Maner said he believed that Waner imposed the moratorium because of pressures from white community groups who are opposed to black families buying homes in predominantly white areas.[12]

Realtists present at the meeting agreed that something must be done immediately because the situation was crucial to their livelihood:

An emotional, spontaneous plea was made to the group by John B. Knighten (age 63, broker 35 yrs.). Mr. Knighten related the history of DREB from his perspective. He indicted them for apathy as well as lack of masculinity . . . . Mr. Knighten ended his speech with the question, "What will you tell your children and grandchildren about why you were afraid to stand up and be men?" Mr. Knighten served as the catalyst that provided the spark needed for the group to decide that they would picket John Waner's office on the following morning.[13]

DREB's June 30 meeting with Mr. Waner convened as twenty-five persons picketed in the street below. At the end of the two hour meeting Mr. Waner made the following concessions:

1. The moratorium would be shortened to forty days.
2. He would hire more black appraisers.
3. He would be willing to provide the mechanism whereby black appraisers would be able to take academic courses for full credit applicable to qualification.
4. The establishment of an ad hoc committee consisting of DREB persons and members of his staff to work out problems.
5. He would consider DREB the spokesman for the black real estate community.

12. *Chicago Daily News,* June 29, 1972.
13. Memorandum, July 3, 1972, Magdalen Redmond to Kale Williams.

6. He will meet with the committee on July 5 in a further effort to quash the moratorium.[14]

When the July 5 meeting did not produce a lifting of the moratorium, DREB contacted Senator Charles Percy and asked him to intercede with Mr. Waner, sending copies of its letter to PUSH, SCLC, NAACP, and the Urban League. Mr. Maner called George Romney, secretary of HUD.

Mr. Waner announced the week of July 16 that the freeze, originally scheduled to continue through August 16, would cease instead on July 24. He said that the moratorium was shortened because of more efficient processing procedures by his staff. But "[p] ressure from the Dearborn Real Estate Board was principally responsible for the lifting of an announced 60-day ban on applications for Federal loans in Chicago, according to Marion Maner, president of the Board."[15]

Following this success, DREB's programs finally seemed to fill in during the final months of 1972. DREB published its first monthly newsletter in November and sponsored a seminar on "How Does the Northeastern Planning Commission Concern the Minority Broker?" Increasing numbers of brokers were contacting DREB for information, and on December 13, DREB finalized its agreement with Home Investment Fund whereby HIF would provide the board, exclusively, with listings of houses for sale in the city and suburbs that were available to HIF.

PROGRAM PERFORMANCE

The foregoing would seem to indicate that during 1972, DREB was to some extent able to strengthen itself as a professional organization, but the question remained as to whether this enabled it to mobilize toward the goal of its subcontract with the Leadership Council. There was very little indeed to show for two years of support; the reed had been too weak. The main goal of the subcontract with the Dearborn Real Estate Board was to provide a channel through which black homeseekers could make effective choices from the total Chicago metropolitan housing market. Yet the interests of DREB's members were otherwise. The great majority of black brokerages remained one man operations with few salesmen. They operated mainly in racially changing neighborhoods where the volume of property

14. Ibid.
15. *Chicago Daily Defender*, July 20, 1972.

turnover was high. Those black brokers who relied primarily on property sale commissions depended on the pace of ghetto expansion to survive. As small businessmen, they remained relatively power-less seriously to affect the forces that restricted them and hindered the development of large-scale business operations.

Reasons for the precarious existence and traditional reliance on the process of neighborhood change are not hard to find. Low volume of property turnover in black neighborhoods meant few commissions for the broker who restricts his scope of operation to the black com-munity. Racial prejudice and a reluctance of whites to patronize black-owned businesses effectively barred the black broker from working in all white neighborhoods. In addition, most black brokers lacked the business skills necessary to diversify into related areas such as property management, appraisal, insurance, financing and so forth. Those members of the board who had become successful businessmen generally seemed to have done so by concentrating on aspects of real estate other than sales.

DREB was formed to help serve and protect the interest of black brokers at a time when conditions were even more hostile to the black businessman than they were in 1970. Over the years it success-fully fought many battles for the benefit of its members and the black community, as it did with HUD in 1972. There was a small nucleus of members who had been with it through the years and who remained members because of DREB's past accomplishments. Even among younger members there existed a great deal of respect for the founders of the board. But there was a feeling among these younger members that the board no longer effectively served their interests.

GAINING ACCESS TO SUBURBAN REAL ESTATE BOARDS

The program to gain entrance for DREB members into white sub-urban real estate boards was, of course, designed to benefit members of DREB. But there were major objections among members to the program's goals. The bulk of black brokers' experience had been working in racially changing neighborhoods. There appeared to be much hesitancy on the part of DREB members toward leaving the kind of area in which they have been most successful in the past to embark on an ambitious project in all white suburban areas far from their current places of business. Few of the DREB members seemed financially able to actually set up additional offices within the geo-graphic boundaries of the thirteen suburban boards in metropolitan

Chicago (Figure 4-1), and fewer still were convinced that it would be economically profitable to try to operate actively in those areas.

Yet there were some signs of change. In 1971 two black brokers became members of suburban boards: Mrs. Ruby Blake of S. Ray and Blake Realty, Harvey, joined the South Suburban Board and also was accepted into the Homewood-Flossmoor board; Mrs. Lynnasacks Guice of Penny's Real Estate, Maywood, obtained membership in the West Suburban Board of Realtors. Each woman was already operating in a suburban community with a sizable concentration of blacks. In addition, there were four other attempts to gain membership. Jefferson Perry was accepted into the Homewood-Flossmoor board. He did not submit his fees, however, because he felt the pressures of the presidency of DREB would preclude expanding his personal business at the time. Therefore, his membership was not finalized, although it was assumed that he could reactivate his application at any time. Ripley Meade, secretary of DREB, applied to the Evanston–North Shore board, but despite the fact that this board already had three black members, was "reluctant to pursue the issue." A second applicant to the Evanston–North Shore board withdrew her application when she accepted a job with the Federal Housing Administration.

Stacey Smith, applicant to the South West Suburban board, made two trips to the board to be interviewed, "got the run around," and decided not to follow through when it appeared that he might be subject to blockbusting charges.[16] Clyde Parrish did make every effort to enter the Northwest Suburban board. His first application was returned by the board, which told him that he had filled out the wrong form. His second application and check were returned with the comment that he did not have an office in the area of the board's jurisdiction and could not be considered for membership until he established such an office.

What, then, of the suburban initiative? In conversations with Mrs. Ruby Blake, she revealed that she felt that she had to go slowly to build up a representative black buyers' market since she would be working in areas such as Dolton, South Holland, Hazelcrest, Chicago Heights, South Chicago Heights, Matteson, and Park Forest, where houses sold for higher prices than they did in Harvey's black neighborhoods (her home base). She felt the need to expend money for an advertising campaign to reach the interested market but said she was not able to do this at the present time. She hadn't yet been able to take advantage of the multiple listing service, although she felt that she got complete listings on computer printouts. Two changes in

16. *Supra* note 6.

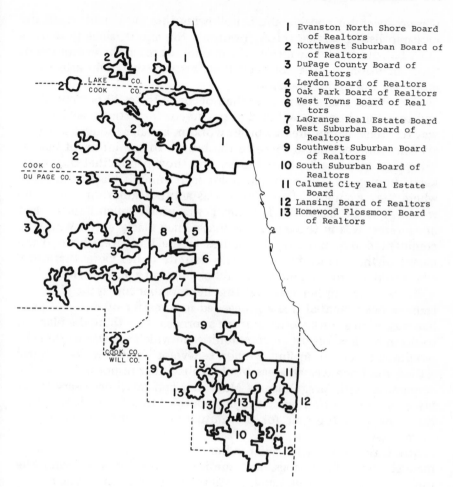

1 Evanston North Shore Board of Realtors
2 Northwest Suburban Board of Realtors
3 DuPage County Board of Realtors
4 Leydon Board of Realtors
5 Oak Park Board of Realtors
6 West Towns Board of Realtors
7 LaGrange Real Estate Board
8 West Suburban Board of Realtors
9 Southwest Suburban Board of Realtors
10 South Suburban Board of Realtors
11 Calumet City Real Estate Board
12 Lansing Board of Realtors
13 Homewood Flossmoor Board of Realtors

Figure 4-1. Areas Served by the Thirteen Suburban Real Estate Boards in Metropolitan Chicago.

her organization were foreseen by Mrs. Blake—a beefing up of management and a change to a "low key" sales approach. "You can't sell people a lovely home using the huckster approach," she said.

The South Suburban board's attitude toward her had been pleasant, and some board members had "leaned over backwards" to be nice to her; "What more can you want?" She did feel, though, that when she tried to sell a home in a "hand's off" area, they [the board] might "get tough." Asked for an example, she said that she might be told that an offer had already been made on a specific house. If she wanted to push it, she then would ask if she could give the name of her prospect for consideration. Following this she would watch her multiple listing service (MLS) printouts for results, since properties must be sold, withdrawn from the market, or reach the expiration of their inclusion in MLS. She felt that this way she could effectively monitor cases of discrimination.

Mrs. Blake said that Harvey had become 15 to 20 percent black and that the people were "mad at the mayor for letting blacks in." It was too sensitive an area to begin work in, and her thought was that all communities should "receive the brunt" of the influx of blacks. "It would take the heat off Harvey and show people that they can't keep running . . . what is the point in running if blacks can move where they want to?" Park Forest was another suburb in which she wouldn't work, since she felt that it was pretty much "open," and her interest was in those suburbs that denied blacks entry. While she commented that most of the houses in the MLS were beyond the means of the average black, she was definite in her views that those who could afford such moves should be helped to make them.

In the long run her view was that her membership in the MLS had tremendous potential if she proceeded in a matter of fact, business-like way, with a constructive positive approach. One thing she planned to do in her ads was list all communities in which she was working so resentment and ill feeling wouldn't develop in one white suburb; rather, the hope was all areas would realize their responsibilities. She cooperated with Mrs. Guice of Maywood and felt it necessary to get black brokers all over the city and suburbs into MLS services so that they can work together for the mutual benefit of their clients and themselves.

Mrs. Guice was much briefer in her comments. She had sold houses through her MLS listings, and she hoped to sell many more. She thought there would be much hostility and resentment as she moved into white communities but that she would deal with them as they come along. She felt that she had deep roots in her community polit-ically and socially and that these would stand her in good stead when the going got rough. Contrary to Mrs. Blake's feelings, she thought that the houses listed in her MLS were realistically priced for blacks.

The first steps in gaining access to suburban boards had, then, been achieved (but largely by Leadership Council rather than DREB initiative). The ability to progress beyond this point depended upon the attitudes and practices of those boards without black members and the willingness of black brokers to branch out from the city. As noted earlier, in the suburbs of Chicago there are thirteen real es-tate boards. Interviews with members of three of these boards sug-gested that each was beginning to approach the issue of admitting black members and selling on a nondiscriminatory basis with care. Responses to questions about integration were often strictly formal, relating to agreed upon national objectives and standards circulated by the NAREB (National Association of Real Estate Boards) and to their own constitutions.

Their function, they said, was to promote wise use of land and property and to protect the interests of the property-owner. Emphasis was placed upon the necessity for strictest ethics in the services needed in property transactions and in their own capacity for self-policing. Conspicuously absent in their comments were references to open housing or open housing groups, and the question of admitting a black member was interpreted strictly in terms of each Board's membership requirements and procedures. Further, if acts of discrimination occurred, respondents felt that these were acts of individual salesmen, not of the boards, which did not take stands on such issues and explicitly avoided setting guidelines for their individual members.

Contrasts between these responses and the perceptions of Dearborn Real Estate Board members were apparent. While the suburban boards agreed that they did not exert significant influence on other organizations in the community, nor did they indicate that they should, members of DREB felt that their organization should be the powerful political force it had been in the past. Suburban board spokesmen simply glossed over or ignored the problem of discrimination in housing, but this was the main issue with DREB members, who verbalized at length about what DREB should be doing, whereas suburban board members were content with the status quo.

Both groups were in agreement on the advantages of educational programs and the importance of raising professional standards. All felt that the small broker would be forced out of business in the future. However, the suburban boards thought that this would come about through increased complexity of management, increased professionalism and the like: DREB members felt that they would be swallowed up by white brokers as new laws restricted black brokers' present mode of operation and means of making profits.

While DREB members constantly talked about the duality of the real estate market, suburban boards were completely unconcerned with the issue. According to the suburban boards, ethnicity was not a requisite or deterrent to membership, yet half of the DREB members interviewed were in agreement with the broker who expressed the fear that he would get only "third class scraps if he joined a white MLS."

Black brokers seemed indifferent to moving into all white suburban areas; white brokers did not give the idea even a passing thought. These same white brokers said their boards would not sanction them for selling to a black buyer in a white neighborhood, but that neighbors, friends, and so forth might pressure them; black brokers stated that they might be the target of violence for such action—"they're still burning houses out there!" And why, then, take the risk, since business was getting much better in the inner city as ghetto expansion accelerated apace.

Figures 4–2 through 4–5 reveal the pace and extent of ghetto spread between 1968 and 1972. These maps again use school enrollment data supplied by the Chicago Board of Education. In the year 1970–1971 alone, the accelerated flight of the white community is revealed by the fact that, while the total school population decreased by 3,184 pupils, this was made up of an 11,357 decrease in white students and a 4,086 increase in blacks along with a 3,404 increase in Spanish-surnamed pupils (Table 4–1). It is to the other side of these shifts, white attitudes and white flight, that I now turn, because it is clear that the weakness in black demand for suburban homeownership stemmed from this flight and an accompanying growth of black homeownership via accelerating ghetto spread, rising black incomes, and declining prices at homes in the abandoned communities. The profits to black brokers were in doing business as usual in the many changing neighborhoods. For black homeseekers the traditional constraints were lifting; to be an integration pioneer was no longer the only route to better housing. This is the topic of the chapters that follow.

Table 4-1. Race of Students Enrolled in Chicago's Public Schools.

	1970		1971		Difference in Number
	Number	Percent	Number	Percent	of Students
Caucasian	199,669	34.6	188,312	32.8	−11,357
African or Negroid Origin	316,711	54.8	320,797	55.8	+ 4,086
American Indian	1,042	0.2	1,184	0.2	+ 142
Oriental Origin	3,883	0.7	4,424	0.8	+ 541
Spanish-surnamed Americans	(56,374)	(9.7)	(59,778)	(10.4)	(+ 3,404)
Mexican Origin	24,066	4.2	25,314	4.4	+ 1,248
Puerto Rican Origin	26,176	4.6	27,303	4.8	+ 1,127
Cuban Origin	2,673	0.4	3,510	0.6	+ 837
Other Spanish-surnamed Americans	3,459	0.6	3,651	0.6	+ 192
TOTAL	577,679	100.0	574,495	100.0	− 3,184

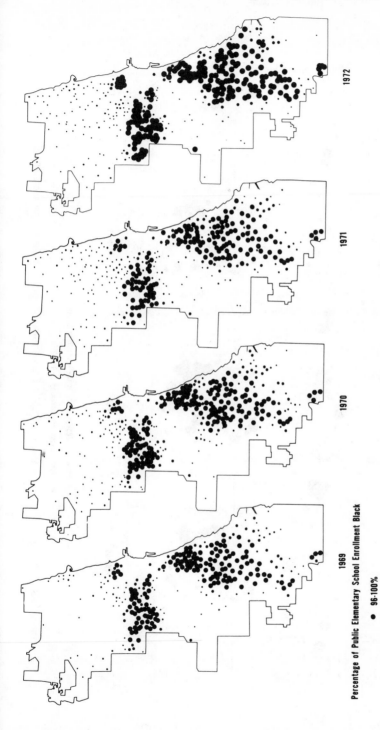

Percentage of Public Elementary School Enrollment Black

● 96-100%
· 50-96%
· 10-50%
· Less than 10%

1969   1970   1971   1972

Figure 4–2.   Racial Headcounts in the Public Elementary Schools, 1969–1972.

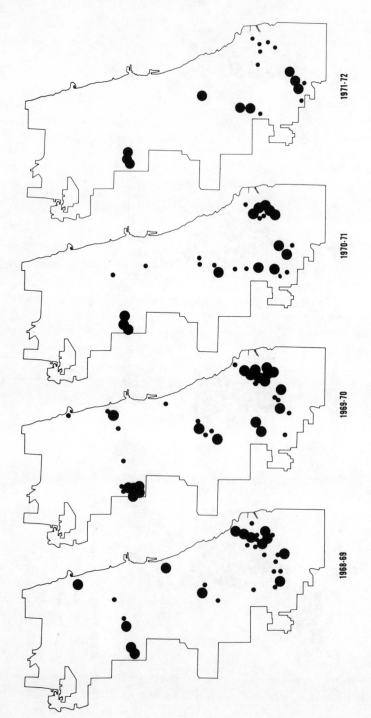

● More than 20% increase in the percentage figure
   School headcount increased by 10-20%

● More than 20% increase in the percentage figure
· School headcount increased by 10-20%

1971-72

1970-71

1969-70

1968-69

Figure 4–3.   Changes in the Percentage of Public Elementary School Students Who Were Black, 1963–1972.

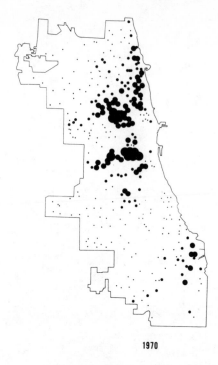

1970

Percentage of Public School Enrollment Spanish Surnamed

● **More than 80%**

• **25-80%**

· **5-24%**

· **Less than 5%**

Figure 4–4. Percentage of Pupils in Chicago's Public Elementary Schools Having Spanish Surnames in 1970.

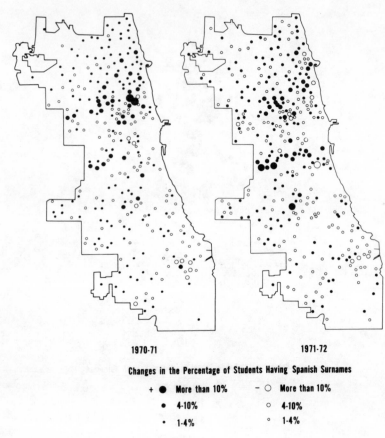

1970-71   1971-72

Changes in the Percentage of Students Having Spanish Surnames

+ ● More than 10%   – ○ More than 10%

   ● 4-10%   ○ 4-10%

   • 1-4%   ° 1-4%

Figure 4–5. Changes in the Spanish-surnamed Elementary School Population, 1970–1972.

✳ *Part II*

**Attitudes to Integration: White
Response to Racial Change**

✳ *Chapter 5*

The Black "Threat" to White Neighborhoods: A Continuing American Dilemma

In 1944, Gunnar Myrdal discussed the dilemma faced by Americans regarding race:

> The "American Dilemma" is the ever-raging conflict between, on the one hand, the variations observed on the general plane which we shall call the "American Creed," where the American thinks, talks, and acts under the influence of high national and Christian precepts and, on the other hand, the valuations on specific planes of individual and group living where personal local interests, economic, social and sexual jealousies, considerations of community prestige and conformity; group prejudice against particular persons or types of people; and all sorts of miscellaneous wants, impulses, and habits dominate his outlook.[1]

This American dilemma remained a continuing characteristic of the Chicago scene in the decade under study. While, on the one hand, the Leadership Council pursued open housing under the banner of Myrdal's "American Creed," racial confrontation continued as the normal way of life in Chicago's neighborhoods. Only in a few more cosmopolitan, national-regarding suburbs did some easing of racial fears occur and a modicum of integrated living emerge and then not without great difficulty.

It is to this confrontation that we turn, for the continuing dynamic of the American dilemma and the occasional assertion of the

---

1. Gunnar Myrdal, *An American Dilemma* (New York: Macmillan, 1944), p. iiii.

American creed form part of the backdrop against which the limited success of the Leadership Council's efforts is to be gauged.

A RESEARCH FRAMEWORK

In parallel with our monitoring of the Leadership Council's activities, a program of community studies was launched in metropolitan Chicago to develop a more intimate understanding of the dynamics of neighborhood change and particularly of whites' perceptions of the black threat to their neighborhoods. A set of research cues was developed in collaboration with S. Golant to help guide these studies of residential adjustments that are continually being made in response to critical events associated with passage through different stages of the life cycle or with occupational career trajectories. Leaving home, marriage, the development of a larger family, retirement, and upward social status resulting from job change and income increase are all accompanied by a search for new, more suitable residential accommodations and a more appropriate neighborhood setting. However, what is also clear is that many white American households continue to make residential adjustments in response to the prospective presence of black families in their neighborhoods, whether this entry comes in the form of a single black family planning to move into the all white residential neighborhood, the planned development of a low income (black) housing project in a middle class white neighborhood, or the creeping spread of the boundaries of a black ghetto into adjacent white residential areas. We therefore asked ourselves what guidance we might give our participant observers in a variety of Chicago central city communities and outlying suburbs.

Generally, racial change takes place in an area in three phases. The first occurs well in advance of the actual turnover. Residents become aware that change is impending and react in various ways. Young families with children, concerned about schooling, move to the suburbs. Other residents have concerns about declining property values, about confrontations in racially changing schools, about increasing crime, and about numerous other threats that are more often rumor than fact. Often these concerns are promoted by real estate agencies, many of which already have set up offices in the neighborhood.

The second phase is the turnover period when blacks move into a neighborhood. For sale signs spring up on front lawns, and quite often blockbusting, panic selling, and questionable real estate manipulation become commonplace. The instability of this phase has a long-term effect on property upkeep. The third phase occurs in the wake of transition when the area is all black. Some neighborhoods retain their original character, with little change other than that of occupancy. In most areas, however, the uncertainties and turmoil of the previous two stages have taken their toll. Postponement of long-term investment on the part of original owners, departure of many supporting services and institutions, and deterioration during the turnover process, coupled with the financial inability of some new-comers adequately to maintain property, have all had their effects on the neighborhood. The legacy of these complex events is that the third phase of racial change often is associated with blight.

Whatever the mode of entry, black entry continues to be viewed by many white residents as threat. The presence of threat implies that within the psychological environment of an individual are stress-ful stimuli associated with an imminent event or situation that is re-garded as being in some way harmful to well-being. Whether or not the source of the threat is in fact realistically capable of harm is of minor importance in understanding the resulting pattern of behavior. Threat finds its genesis through such cognitive processes as percep-tion, learning, memory, judgment, and thought. An individual's ap-praisal of a forthcoming event, accordingly, is related not only to the magnitude and direction of external stimuli but also, and more im-portantly, to the manner in which these stimuli have been assimilated through these mediating cognitive processes. An appreciation of what constitutes a threatening event for a particular individual therefore must be derived from his personal appraisal of a set of stimuli, how-ever irrational and contrary to objective reality such an evaluation may appear to an outside observer.

In the terminology of living systems theory the existence of a threatening event results in the steady state of the living organism being disturbed. An individual is most comfortable when the strains resulting from stressful situations are kept to a minimum. Possessing adaptation mechanisms, he will therefore be motivated to initiate coping strategies designed to reduce to a minimum outside threats. Thus, a decisionmaking schema can be postulated in which there is a major distinction between the appraisal process and the coping process, further subdivided into five principal divisions and ten steps or stages. This individual behavioral schema, it is suggested, helps clarify the issues involved and served as the framework for our com-munity studies, as well as being a means of identifying underlying causes, as is shown by the following outline:

A. The Appraisal Process
    I. Recognition
        (a) the perception of information about the threat

II. Definition
   (a) an estimate of the probability of the event occurring
   (b) an estimate of the nature of such an event
   (c) an estimate of the severity to the individual of such an event
B. The Coping Process
   III. Strategy and Evaluation
   (a) an estimate of the means of coping with the threat
   (b) an estimate of the probability of success of the means
   (c) an estimate of the cost to the individual of the means
   IV. Commitment
   (a) a resolution and decision about behavior
   (b) a testing of behavior
   V. Progressive Uses of a Lattice of Defense
   (a) a selection of behaviors that are nonadaptive to aspects of the organism but preservative and defensive for part of the organism's integrity.

Let us discuss the elements of this schema in turn, as we discussed them with our participant observers.

Recognition: Perception of Information About the Threat

Initially the individual is exposed to stimuli or cues signifying the imminence of a forthcoming event or situation. The degree to which the information received is perceived as threatening is a function of three sets of factors—the input of information; the psychological predisposition of the receiver; and the degree to which the psychological predisposition of the individual either supports (reinforces) or contradicts the information input.

The information input can be examined in terms of the following categories: types of communicators; frequency of communications; credibility of communicators; degree of ambiguity of communications; fear-arousing level of communications. Communicators are either "formal" or "informal," the former referring to such sources as newspapers and radio broadcasters, the latter to such sources as primary group discussions or neighborhood association meetings involving word of mouth communication. While the influence the information has on the individual will depend on how frequently messages are emitted, of greater importance is the receiver's respect for the communication source. One would expect that information received from a respected figure in the community would be likely to be assigned greater validity and to be given greater significance than that received from a less important figure. However, in any communication process, who is viewed as an important figure can vary considerably and will likely depend on the community setting. While some communications will include neutral or unbiased messages, still others, in presenting the same information, are likely to reveal a clear policy position with regard to black residential integration. It is also clear that information can be presented on the one hand objectively and calmly and on the other, heavily laden with emotion and fear.

Of comparable importance is the degree of ambiguity of such messages. The interpretation of an ambiguous message is less predictable as it will depend to a larger degree on the nature of the individual's belief system. It is of considerable importance to be able to evaluate and predict how different communication media transmit a similar item of information. Information transmitted by informal communication sources, such as by word of mouth, is often more fear arousing, less factual, and more likely to be laden with personal value judgments than information transmitted by formal sources. The rate of diffusion of such information is directly related to the social cohesiveness of the community. Word of mouth communications are initially more influential, but with time, more formal communications, such as those transmitted by local newspapers or newsletters, assume greater importance.

Before receiving any cues or stimuli via new information inputs, the individual will possess a system of beliefs or attitudes that will influence the manner in which new inputs are processed. The strength of the belief system can be evaluated in reference to the following categories:

1. Extremeness of belief system—the degree of tenacity with which beliefs are held;
2. Integration of belief system—the degree to which the beliefs are interconnected, are mutually supportive, and are in agreement with each other;
3. Relationship of individual's belief system to his needs and goals— the degree to which the acceptance of particular beliefs supports the various motives and goals of the individual;
4. Relationship of an individual's belief system to that held by his reference groups—the degree to which the reference group influences or sanctions the individual's belief system;
5. Value orientation of individual's beliefs—the degree to which the individual's beliefs are value or emotionally oriented.

Beliefs held by an individual are strongly influenced by evaluation of what is believed to be expected of the individual by relevant reference groups. The likelihood of this conformity will increase to the extent that the individual is dependent upon these groups for the satisfaction of motives and goal attainment. The greater the probability, therefore, that the entry of black families will jeopardize the attainment of an individual's goals, the greater the impact of the belief system on the perception of the information. If the beliefs held by the individual are based on a strongly integrated set of values, it is also more likely that his belief system will dominate the appraisal of any information. This is especially the case if the value system provides a device by which the individual's ego strength or superiority is enhanced.

The individual's belief system is related to socioeconomic characteristics. Individuals with higher intelligence, intellectual resources, and sophistication are thought to possess a more flexible belief system that is more susceptible to change and are less likely to view information about the entry of black families as threatening. The individual's belief system also is related to the degree of previous personal contact with black persons. The greater the amount of interracial contact, the more flexible are the beliefs of white persons and the less likely it is that the prospect of new black neighbors will be viewed as a threatening event. Ethnicity and cultural identity also are reflected in an individual's belief system. "Self-segregation" tends to be highly valued by some Jewish groups, for example.

The perception of information regarding the prospective event ultimately depends on the degree to which the psychological disposition of the individual supports or contradicts the information input:

1. The stronger a belief system, the greater its likelihood of arousal in a given situation.
2. The greater the strength of a belief system, the less the amount of appropriate information necessary to confirm it.
3. The greater the strength of a belief system, the more the amount of inappropriate or contradictory information necessary to inform it.

The relationship between a set of new information inputs and the hypotheses (belief system) held by an individual can be further elucidated by the following example: Given the statement, "The new Negro family is an unfavorable event," assume that the information inputs and the individual's hypotheses either:

1. Strongly support the statement,
   or

2. Are uncommitted to the statement,
>   or
3. Strongly contradict the statement.

Let: HI = very high degree of threat,
      MH = moderately high degree of threat,
      ML = moderately low threat,
      LO = very low threat,
      ZE = zero threat.

Then a "threat-degree" matrix can be hypothesized representing all possibilities of information perception, as shown in Table 5-1. In the cases where the hypothesis is strongly supportive and the information input is either neutral or strongly supportive (Al, A2, C2, and C3), the perception of information about the threat would appear to be fairly predictable. This is also the case when the hypothesis held is neutral and the information input is neutral or contradictory (B2 and B3). Less clear is the situation when the information input is strongly supportive and the hypothesis is uncommitted (B1). The least predictable situation would appear to occur when the hypothesis is in direct opposition to the information input (A3 and C1).

Definition: Estimating the Probability of the Impending Event

Following initial perception of information regarding the threatening event, the available inputs are organized within the existing context of the individual's belief system, and a determination is made of the probability of occurrence, form, and seriousness.

This estimate will be based largely on the individual's interpretation of the information just received. The intensity and direction of subsequent appraisal and copying behavior would appear to be directly related to the size of the probability assigned to the forthcoming event.

Table 5-1. A Threat-Degree Matrix.

			Information Input		
			1 *Strongly* *Supportive*	*2* *Uncom-* *mitted*	*3* *Strongly* *Contradictory*
	A	Strongly Supportive	HI	HI-MH	MH-LO
HYPOTHESIS	B	Uncommitted	MH-ML	ZE	ZE
	C	Strongly Contradictory	ZE-LO	ZE	ZE

An Estimate of the Probability of such an Event.   What is it about prospective black families in a white neighborhood that results in this situation being viewed as threatening? One general approach to this question is provided by content analysis of various situations viewed as threatening, from which the following qualities of kinds of response may be derived:

1. *Restriction*—Restriction or construction of the area of free movement in one's life space.
2. *Impotency*—Loss of potency in coping with the various situations with which one is confronted.
3. *Isolation*—Isolation from all stimuli, social isolation, and so forth.
4. *Irrationality*—Lack of understanding about what is going on, such as occurs in ambiguous situations, uncertainties, ignorance about cause and effect when such information seems necessary for behavior.
5. *Conflict*—Conflict in demands, needs, or authority.
6. *Nonacceptance*—Loss in acceptability of oneself by oneself or others.
7. *Discomfort*—Physical (and social) discomforts of minor or extreme nature.

Several authors have identified the threatening aspects of a black resident's entry into a white neighborhood. Each of these examples is associated with one or more of the threat categories just outlined.

1. Fear on the part of many white people that the presence of black persons in the neighborhood will cause serious depreciation of existing property values.
2. Reluctance of some whites to share public and community facilities with black persons.
3. Fear of losing social caste by living in a neighborhood with black persons.
4. Apprehension lest change in racial composition will upset existing political balance.
5. Fear that existing homogeneity of neighborhoods will be disturbed.
6. Resentment against alleged efforts of municipal or federal governments superimposing social changes upon a local community.
7. Entrenched racial prejudice.
8. Fear of having social contact with black persons.
9. Fear by some whites of their children having social contact with black children.

10. Fear by white individuals of becoming a member of a minority group in their own neighborhood.
11. Fear that associated with new black families will be a higher incidence of crime.
12. Fear on part of many white people that occupancy of housing by black families will result in earlier physical deterioration of these structures.

An Estimate of the Severity, to the Individual, of such a Development. The period of time within which the threatening event will occur appears to have considerable importance in the individual's judgment of its severity. In this regard, two hypotheses that appear relevant:

1. Signs of urgency and imminence are more likely to be present in precipitant than in nonprecipitant disasters. The precipitant disaster occurs rapidly as opposed to the nonprecipitant disaster, which builds up slowly.
2. Precipitant disaster may be regarded by most as more dangerous and more difficult to escape than nonprecipitant disaster, which builds up slowly.

The literature supports both hypotheses. When one or even two black families entered white neighborhoods, the event was treated much less like a calamitous event than when a dozen or more black families were pushed on the community, all at once. However, examples can be cited where only one new black individual planning to enter a white neighborhood is treated as if it were a major catastrophe.

Closely related to the timing of the threatening event as a measure of severity is the degree to which the white resident believes that the admittance of one or more black families represents the beginning of a mass influx of black families as opposed to representing only a single isolated incident. The former belief, it can be hypothesized, will lead to a more severe appraisal of the event.

There appears to be a close relationship between the severity of the event and the stake that the white resident has in the neighborhood. More permanent neighborhood dwellers, homeowners in contrast to apartment renters, appear to express greater interest in any developments that affect the future of the community. This is especially the case for white residents with public-school-aged children who often relate an influx of black residents to a subsequent decline in school quality. It can be hypothesized that the greater the stake that the white resident has in the neighborhood, the more likely that new black residents will be viewed as a severe threat.

The severity of the event appears to be closely related to the white resident's perception of social distance. The greatest concern of some white residents is where (relative to themselves) the black resident or residents will locate. While some white residents would prefer that a large social distance be synonymous with actual physical distance— that is, "at a good distance"—others are willing to have them next door providing "they keep in their place".

Finally, there appears to be a close relationship between the severity of the event and the perceived social status of the white resident. Certain individuals and segments of the population will be so located in the social structure as to be especially likely to attach the meaning of threat, injury, deprivation, or punishment to the presence of one or more ethnic groups. Thus, integration is a greater threat to the relatively uneducated urban proletariat in the process of uncertain transit to the suburban middle class. This group, especially, sees the "Negro move" as doing potential damage to the social status of its community members. Thus, the already existing insecurity of the white resident is increased by the arrival of a new black resident.

Process of Coping: Strategy and Evaluation

The essence of the coping process is that when the individual is threatened, motor actions and psychological activity will be aroused to ward off anticipated harm. Unless something is done to protect the psychological system, a damaging state of affairs will occur (by the definition of threat). The individual may attempt, for example, to avoid the danger, to overcome it by attack on the harmful agent, or to engage in a rich variety of self-deceptive, defensive activities, reappraising the danger even in defiance of reality. Following the initial or primary appraisal of the threatening event, the individual will have developed a certain level of urgency or fear. In order to understand and predict the coping strategies that follow, a further consideration is required of the cognitive processes more directly related to alternative courses of action. This secondary appraisal involves the separation out of a complex assortment of cues—those that are relevant to threat appraisal, those relevant to the action tendencies that are generated, and those relevant to both. The cues for the secondary appraisal process concern the consequences of any action tendency that might be activated in the face of the given conditions. Primary and secondary appraisal may overlap in time, since features of the stimulus configuration relevant to secondary appraisal may be noted even before threat is appraised.

Before attempting to cope with a threatening event, the individual must have a clearly defined "agent of harm." however unrealistic such an identification may appear. In the case of the entry of new black residents, the agent of harm is generally well defined. However, since a confession of racism or prejudice is considered unacceptable even among the most conservative members of the white population, one set of cognitive processes associated with secondary appraisal consists of a rationalization by which the white resident is able to justify his subsequent actions. One such example involves a reinterpretation of the Judaeo-Christian tradition with the contention that since Negroes have low IQs and education levels, it is just and merciful to segregate them and keep them with their kind. An alternative strategy is to transfer the "agent of harm" to another more reconcilable scapegoat. Thus, the white resident's focus may be redirected from the black threat to other "unconstitutional," "illegal," or "corrupt" objects. Typical are these three:

- Levittown, Pennsylvania: the black family is merely a "pawn" for purposes of "blockbusting" by Communists or the NAACP organization.
- Deerfield, Michigan: white residents direct their attack on the private developer (Progress Development), who, it was claimed, violated the constitutional rights of the residential community with its interracial housing project.
- Seattle, Washington: hostility and pressure toward the potential white seller to a Negro family.

It can be hypothesized that the white resident who is evaluating a set of coping strategies (secondary appraisal) will engage in a course of action believed to provide the greatest probability of success at lowest personal cost. Two principal areas of inquiry related to this appraisal suggest themselves, and they comprise variables describing the personality of the individual and the situation constraints and incentives within which the individual functions:

1. Personality Variables—certain forms of coping may not be in the "response repertoire" of individuals.
2. Situational Constraints or Incentives—variables describing conditions outside the individual creating either barriers or incentives to different coping strategies.

An understanding of the coping strategies selected by the individual requires an understanding of internalized values—that is, what is believed to be morally right and wrong. This value set in turn is related to a large number of psychological characteristics and previous experiences. The importance of these variables for understanding the coping strategies of the white resident has received relatively little attention.

The literature suggests that the most important source of influence exerted on the white resident originates from community groups or associations. It is necessary further to distinguish whether the individual is a member of a group whose coping strategies are consistent with the individual's values and goals or whether the individual's coping strategies reflect external pressures from a group that is not enthusiastically supported. The white resident contemplating selling a house to a black family may receive considerable pressure, if not hostility, from neighborhood groups or associations that "encourage" the avoidance of such a sale. The neighborhood organization may also provide a means by which the white resident can "transfer" responsibility for actions to that of the formal group. There would appear to be relatively little "cost" in signing a petition or in delegating authority for action to a group leader for the purposes of initiating coping strategies. In focusing on the coping strategies of the white resident, therefore, considerable attention should be directed to the role played by institutions and organizations in the white resident's secondary appraisal.

When alternative opportunities for coping action are available by which the white resident can avoid direct confrontation with the threat, such strategies may be adopted if the personal cost is not too high. One such coping action includes a change of residential location ("white flight"). Those who are wealthier and/or self-employed are likely to be among the first to move when they are faced with the prospect or existence of new black residents in their neighborhood. This type of coping action is particularly noticeable in periods when the supply of metropolitan housing is plentiful.

Commitment

On the basis of primary and secondary appraisals, various types and intensities of coping responses are possible. At least four major types of coping strategies involving "assertive" or "direct action" behavior can be defined.

Actions Aimed at Strengthening the Individual's Resources Against the Anticipated Harm.   These actions are characterized by considered and controlled selection of some form of strategy for strengthening the means available to master the threat. Such a behavior response is "vigilance"—namely, adopting a vigilance set involves cognitive as well as action changes—scanning the environment for signs of danger, attending to information pertinent to the danger, planning alternative courses of action for dealing with emergency contingencies, and the like. Simple examples of this form of coping action include more frequent and intensive reading of local newspapers, more frequent interaction with members of reference groups, the joining of a community organization or association, and attainment of a leadership role in a neighborhood association.

Actions Aimed at Attacking Agent or Agents of Harm. In this case, the modification (eliminating the object of hostility) is to be effected by destroying, injuring, removing, or restricting a person or class of persons considered responsible for the evil at hand. Examples of this type of coping behavior are abundant—for example, local political and other institutional pressure; financial inducement; economic boycott (on stores, etc. not to sell to Negroes); symbolic violence (burning of a cross); direct violence against property (rock through window); direct violence against person; climate of terror (hate literature); threatening phone calls; letters; loud noises; (automobiles carrying Confederate flags).

Actions Aimed at Avoiding Agent of Harm. In this coping response, confrontation with the agent of harm is accomplished by avoiding it completely. The most extreme response is exemplified by white flight—the residential relocation of the white resident.

Inaction. This implies the complete absence of any action tendency for coping with the threat. "Apathy" is the term used to connote the affect or attitude associated with inaction. Such a condition can come about only when the individual is totally resigned to the belief that there are no direct ways of preventing the harm or when he makes successful reappraisal that there is no danger. The degree to which this coping response is affected by white residents deserves attention for its obvious implications for understanding morale level.

Progressive Uses of a Lattice of Defense
Defenses are psychological maneuvers in which the individual deceives himself about the actual conditions of threat. In this way, harm is not anticipated either from an external or internal source. A variety of defenses are identified by such descriptive names as denial, isolation, rationalization, and the like. They represent various types

of strategies for this self-deception, most of which have the common quality of producing a benign appraisal of the situation rather than a threatening one. The degree to which this coping strategy has been adopted by white residents is not clearly documented in the litera-ture, but some light is cast on it in the series of community studies to which we now turn. These community studies were conducted by a variety of evaluation team members, frequently as participant ob-servers, working within the broad framework of research cues just described but open-endedly, so as not to preclude any consideration relevant to understanding the process of community change.

✳ *Chapter 6*

South Shore: Community Action to Control Racial Change

The first of the studies of community response to racial change was undertaken in South Shore, a community within the city of Chicago, and located some ten miles south of Chicago's Loop (Community Area 43, see Figure 1-1). We began with South Shore because Molotch had recently finished his analysis of the area, and we could simply update his work while training our own investigators.[1] Bounded on the north by 67th Street and Jackson Park, on the west by Stony Island and South Chicago Avenue, on the south by 83rd Street, and on the east by Lake Michigan, South Shore's population in 1970 numbered almost 90,000 persons. An area that had been undergoing racial change since the early 1960s, South Shore at the time of the 1970 census was nearly 57 percent black. Of the foreign born residing in the area, persons from Poland predominated, followed by persons from Germany, the USSR, Ireland, and Sweden. Fifty-one percent of the area's families earned in 1969 between $10,000 and $25,000 annually, and 57 percent of the population were at least high school graduates. Largely an apartment-dwelling community, 75 percent of South Shore's housing stock was renter-occupied.

Within South Shore several distinct neighborhoods can be identified. Located in the northwest corner of South Shore, Parkside was the first area in the community to "go black." By 1964, when the rest of South Shore was still predominantly white, Parkside was con-

1. See Harvey L. Molotch, *Community Action to Control Racial Change* (Ph.D. dissertation, University of Chicago, 1968).

165

sidered a black residential area. Largely an area of apartment dwellings, Parkside had been described by the South Shore Commission, the area's major community organization, as an area where widespread deterioration is occurring. Jackson Park Highlands, a solidly white upper middle income area, is located directly east of Parkside between Cregier and Jeffrey. Although it contains only 2 percent of the community's population, Jackson Park Highlands holds some of South Shore's most impressive single family residences. East of the Highlands and bounded by Jeffrey and South Shore Drive is an area of mixed housing in which apartment houses predominate. O'Keefe, as this area is known, is racially mixed. Directly south of O'Keefe is Bryn Mawr East, which in 1970 was a biracial area of mixed housing. Almost half the housing is owner-occupied, and Bryn Mawr residents have tended, perhaps because of this, to be disproportionately active in the South Shore Commission. An area of small apartment dwellings and single family homes, Bryn Mawr West is located south of the Highlands and Parkside and is bounded on the west by Stony Island. By 1967 blacks had become the predominant racial group in Bryn Mawr West. The South End is an amorphous area including South Shore's southern neighborhoods. Composed of small single family homes mixed with walk-up apartments, this area until recently has identified least with the rest of South Shore. Still predominately white in 1967 and represented by its own community organization, the Chelwin Association, the South End throughout the 1960s often opposed the integrationist goals of the South Shore Commission. Somewhat distinct from South Shore but nevertheless belonging to it is South Shore Drive. The luxury high rises that line South Shore Drive along Lake Michigan's shore are inhabited primarily by middle income whites.

At the time of Chicago's Columbian Exposition in 1893, South Shore was a sparsely settled area composed of several neighborhoods. In spite of the impact that the fair was expected to have on the area, it was not until 1900 that apartment buildings in large numbers began to be constructed. By 1920 South Shore was experiencing a building boom. Between 1920 and 1930 the population increased to almost 80,000. The completion of Lake Shore Drive and the development of beaches along Lake Michigan stimulated the construction of high rise apartments along the lake shore from 51st to 79th Streets. During this same period the ethnic composition of South Shore's population changed. Into the southeastern areas that had earlier been heavily Swedish and English moved large numbers of Irish Catholics and Jews, many of the latter from the Washington Park area to the west. Still a middle income apartment house community, by 1940 South Shore had grown little in size, although Russians now became the leading nationality among foreign born stock, a position they were to hold during the next two decades.

In 1960 South Shore was a solidly middle class residential community inhabited by a relatively well-educated population. According to the 1960 census, South Shore's median income was above that of the city as a whole ($7,888 versus $6,738). Only 2 percent of the area's housing was substandard, and there was no heavy industry in South Shore. There were indications, however, that South Shore was no longer a choice area for white middle class residence. It possessed, according to Harvey Molotch, many of the traits of an area likely to undergo racial change. For example, the South Shore community contained a high proportion of apartment housing at a time when middle class families by and large desired single family residences. Moreover, since much of South Shore's housing had been built in the 1920s, 1930s, and 1940s, many of South Shore's structures, although sound, were old fashioned and no longer in keeping with the tastes of contemporary middle class families. The apartment character of the community, furthermore, meant a certain amount of inherent mobility and community instability, thus making black inmigration more likely. Most important in labeling South Shore as an area likely to undergo racial change was the fact that South Shore was contiguous on the west (Greater Grand Crossing) and northwest (Woodlawn) with already existing black residential areas. The middle class area of South Shore was, thus, ripe for racial change. As Pierre de Vise has noted:

The Negro Belt does not typically expand in the areas of oldest and lowest quality housing. It expands along the paths of least resistance, typically into upper- and middle-income areas adjacent to the Negro Belt, even though the housing in these areas is better, larger, newer and less convertible to low income use than the housing of low income white areas. One reason for the succession of higher income areas is that the higher income people can more easily move to other parts of the city or to the suburbs, whereas the lower income whites are more limited in their choice of housing areas.[2]

2. Pierre de Vise, *"Chicago's Widening Color Gap,"* Chicago: The University of Chicago, Interuniversity Social Science Research Committee, Report No. 2, December 1967, p. 42.

PERCEPTIONS OF CHANGE

By the mid-1950s it was apparent to some South Shore residents that black inmigration was a distinct possibility in the near future. In 1954 a priest, a minister, and a rabbi decided to use the South Shore Ministerial Association as the basis for a more extensive community organization. The South Shore Commission emerged from this reorganization. The members of this new organization liked living in South Shore and wanted to remain in the community. Given this fact, one of the major problems faced by the commission was how to respond to South Shore's imminent racial change. Because the commission leaders wanted to avoid alienating South Shore's white residents, they were reluctant to take a specific stand on integration for their community. A division existed within the organization between the "exclusionists," who wanted South Shore to remain white, and the "integrationists," who wished to maintain a balance between white and black residents. Eventually the integrationist viewpoint prevailed, and in 1966 integration was explicitly mentioned as an organizational goal. Although this statement upset many South Shore residents, it was necessitated by the realization that a large proportion of South Shore's population was already black. Once integration became a goal, commission leaders focused their efforts on maintaining a racial balance between blacks and whites. The South Shore Commission believed that South Shore could avoid the pitfalls of racially changing communities such as violence, panic peddling of real estate, and the mass movement of whites out of the community and become an integrated middle class community modeled on its neighbor to the north, Hyde Park. The commission decided that it was both desirable and possible to intervene in the changing community in such a way as to produce racial stability.

Although the South Shore Commission described itself as a democratic grassroots organization, it was always characterized by a class bias. Low income and blue collar persons were not represented in the commission leadership even though 27 percent of the 1960 population of South Shore was engaged in blue collar work. Also, blacks were represented on the commission board and executive committee only after 1963 and remained underrepresented throughout 1967. In 1967, for example, six of seventy-five board members were black, despite the fact that one-third of the community's residents were black. The positions of executive director and president were throughout the 1960s occupied by white males. Organizational power, therefore, remained in the hands of whites. Up until 1969 blacks never played a major role in commission activities.

THE NATURE OF THE RESPONSE:
ORGANIZATIONAL GOALS
AND PROGRAMS

The major goal of the South Shore Commission throughout the 1960s was to make South Shore a community in which white middle class individuals and families would choose to live. The kind of environment thought attractive to middle class whites was characterized by "safety, quiet and the kind of people whose status and life style make them 'good neighbors' and whose children make good pupils and schoolmates."[3] In making South Shore *"the* place to live" two major strategies were used by the commission:

1. An attempt was made to create neighborhood and community conditions felt to be desirable to whites; and
2. The Commission tried to facilitate white moveins by recruiting white, middle class residents through actual intervention in the real estate market.

To create more desirable living conditions in South Shore, several specific programs were instituted dealing with the areas of crime prevention, education, community amenities, and housing. Between 1964 and 1966 there was a dramatic increase in the' number of "serious" crimes (homicide, rape, major burglaries, thefts, and assaults) in South Shore north of 76th Street. Emergency treatment for gunshot wounds, gang activity, and an increased number of police beats were all signs of increased antisocial activity in the area. The South Shore Commission responded to this rise in crime by creating a citizen-manned radio patrol that operated on weekends, the time when the largest number of crimes tended to occur. The mobile patrol would radio any information about irregular activities it observed to the district police. It was not to engage in actual enforcement of the law but rather to provide better surveillance of the South Shore area and to increase the efficiency of the police.

Another commission effort designed to deal with increased crime in South Shore was the following of cases through the courts once arrests had been made. In this capacity the commission acted as a watchdog agency to see that "justice was done" and reported results back to the community. It also served to make the court aware of the community's interest in the outcome of the case. Between June 1966 and June 1967 the commission appeared in court over sixty

3. Molotch, p. 95.

times in regard to criminal cases and attempted to insure that charges were pressed, witnesses were found to testify against the accused, and maximum sentences pronounced. It was especially anxious that something be done about the Blackstone Rangers, a youth gang operating in the area, and to this end exerted pressure on the police to ferret out the gang leaders. The commission also ran a "Youth Guidance Program" for juveniles who committed crimes not serious enough to result in jailing, while encouraging other area organizations (YMCA, Young Men's Jewish Center, churches) to expand programs for teenagers.

Only 32 percent of South Shore's population was directly affected, or likely to be so in the future, by the state of the area's public schools. In 1968, only 23 percent of the population had children under eighteen, as many of South Shore's whites were middle aged or older. Moreover, because of the large number of Catholic residents, only 15 percent of South Shore's inhabitants had children who attended public schools. Nevertheless, for those people whose children did attend public schools, the future state of the area's public schools was an issue of overriding importance. The schools also had a symbolic importance for the area as a whole, since the reputation of the schools in South Shore affected its image and its ability to attract white families with children.

Consequently, the commission made strenuous efforts to improve the quality of education offered by South Shore schools. Moreover, it worked to provide white residents in the area with neighborhood schools containing large numbers of white children. The "Bryn Mawr Petal Plan" was one such scheme of managed integration. Through a system of permissive transfers, the Petal Plan aimed at achieving racial balance. This plan was never put into operation, however, and was eventually dropped on the advice of the commission's legal committee.

Another and more successful effort focusing on the area's schools was the South Shore School-Community Plan. Worked out in cooperation with the Chicago School Board, the plan was designed to give South Shore priority over other school districts, hopefully making the area's educational facilities so attractive to whites that they would remain in the community. Construction was authorized for a second South Shore High School before relief was promised to four other southeast schools, all of which were significantly more overcrowded than South Shore. Other aspects of the South Shore School-Community Plan included district "educational saturation centers" with programs for high school computer science training, creation of an evening junior college, establishment of reading clinics, and remedial classes for below grade level students.

The commission enthusiastically supported efforts to bring South Shore those amenities like parks and shopping centers that were felt likely to attract and retain whites. Eventually it formulated a comprehensive plan modeled on the urban renewal program for Hyde Park. On the whole, the response to this plan was not particularly encouraging. First, because of the large amount of time involved in developing such a plan, this strategy was not felt immediate enough to deal with South Shore's problems. Second, the likelihood of attracting government funds for such an effort seemed poor since South Shore was already in danger of losing its status as one of the city's five "Demonstration Cities." And, finally, South Shore had the additional problem of being a community unlikely to attract prospective developers, being relatively distant from downtown Chicago and not adjacent to any major institution such as the University of Chicago in Hyde Park. South Shore was neither interesting nor convenient as was, for example, the Near North, nor safe and modern like Evanston. Other areas in the Chicago metropolitan area had, in short, more to offer white middle class residents than did South Shore.

Maintaining the existing property in South Shore was considered of prime importance to the commission's goal of keeping and attracting white middle class families to the community. City building code enforcement was, thus, always a part of the commission strategy. Between June 1966 and June 1967, the commission received over 1,000 citizen complaints involving local street, alley, and building conditions. Although South Shore's housing stock was basically sound, attention to landscaping, building exteriors, and trash removal had noticeably declined. But "in terms of the more subtle forms of building maintenance, the Commission seemed not able to function as efficiently as when dealing with illegal practices."[4]

The second major strategy used by the commission to attract whites to South Shore involved its actual intervention in the housing market. The commission first attempted to create alliances with real estate agencies in the area both to discourage panic peddling and to encourage a high level of property maintenance. During the 1966–1967 period the commission held two mass education meetings for real estate men, rental agents, janitors, and the like, which attempted to convert the local real estate industry to constructive attitudes toward neighborhood change. This meant more explicitly changing

4. Ibid., p. 125.

some of the beliefs held by the real estate industry. Most white building managers, for example, felt that after property "goes black," the most profitable course to follow was either to lower the level of maintenance expenditures or to modify maintenance practices in such a manner that "beautification" suffers. Since the black demand for housing is great, blacks would pay higher rents and be satisfied with fewer services.

The Commission also tried to control to a certain extent the actual selection of tenants. It wanted the blacks entering South Shore to be equal or superior in occupational and educational status to the whites whom they replaced. To influence the type of tenants rented to in South Shore, the commission created a central screening agency to which real estate agents were to submit the names of questionable apartment applicants. A member of the commission's staff was then sent unannounced to inspect the living conditions and housekeeping practices of the applicants. The information gathered by this staff member was then referred to the real estate agent. A list was thereby begun of "undesirable" tenants.

The major program of the commission to recruit white residents for South Shore was the Tenant Referral Service. Through this service the commission attempted to insure that housing was brought to the attention of as many white prospects as possible. The service operated in the following manner. Persons interested in South Shore apartments visited the commission's office where they specified the size of the apartment desired, the top rent they could pay, the family's composition, and the names of personal references. The commission presented the applicant with six available apartments appropriate to the means, needs, and race of the individual. The Tenant Referral Service did not refer tenants randomly to buildings and neighborhoods in South Shore. Instead referrals were made with the goal of moving whites into integrated buildings. This necessarily created certain problems in regard to the treatment of black applicants. The commission did not want to refer blacks to a mixed building if a white tenant could be found, since the continued integration of a building would eventually result in resegregation. However, the commission was also reluctant to refer blacks to buildings that were all white. An attempt was made to increase the number of whites in South Shore by contacting major institutions in Chicago and by placing ads in the *Hyde Park Herald* and the *Chicago Maroon*, the University of Chicago newspaper. But a similar attempt was never made to seek potential black tenants. In fact, the commission hoped to discourage additional black occupancy by supporting in 1967 a Fair Housing Center in South Shore. Operated by the Leadership

Council for Metropolitan Open Communities, the Fair Housing Center attempted to make blacks aware of housing opportunities in all white communities throughout the metropolitan Chicago area.

How effective was the Tenant Referral Service in achieving its goal? Seven hundred fifty families were served by TRS, and of these, 675 located in South Shore. Two hundred of these 675 families were black, and the remainder were white. Two hundred came from outside the city, while ninety came from Hyde Park, indicating the success of the commission's advertising campaign in connection with the University of Chicago. Processing the number of persons it did, TRS became a major force in the local real estate market. It gave the South Shore Commission bargaining power with local realtors, apartment managers, and so forth that could be used to enlist cooperation with various commission programs. Realtors were asked to hold units vacant until white renters could be found rather than rent to blacks. Landlords who did not cooperate with the commission could be excluded from the TRS or provided with lower quality prospects than they would otherwise receive. By bringing together all available apartments and prospective tenants in one location, TRS served primarily to make market mechanisms operate in a more efficient manner than they otherwise would have. It did not, however, significantly alter the overall speed or the pattern of racial transition. In fact, the most striking trend in TRS's history was the increasing proportion of those served who were black.

EVALUATION AND CONCLUSIONS

The South Shore Commission's goal of a stable integrated community for South Shore assumed some interaction among blacks and whites in the community. In fact, interaction between blacks and whites during the period of racial change was minimal. Racial shopping patterns tended to follow racial residential patterns. Thus, businesses in predominantly black residential areas were patronized by blacks, those in white areas by whites, and those in mixed areas by both races. This carried over into restaurants, beaches, and churches. Biracial contacts, when they did occur, were most likely to take place in public and impersonal locations like stores and schools. Differences between the two races were, however, likely to deter further contacts. Compared to South Shore's whites, its blacks were likely to be younger, to be of lower socioeconomic status, to have more children, to have two breadwinners rather than one, and to have lived in the area a shorter period of time. As a general rule, then, the more personal and intimate the setting, the less the likelihood of integregation occurring.

Three indicators of the success of the South Shore Commission's intervention to achieve racial stability were (1) the racial composition of the schools, (2) the speed of change compared to other changing areas, and (3) the nature of the South Shore Commission itself in 1970. The central goal of the South Shore Commission was to retain and attract white residents to South Shore, thus altering the usual pattern and the speed of racial change where previously all white areas become almost completely all black. In examining the racial composition of the schools, the data do not suggest that integration was achieved or that South Shore was experiencing anything other than the classic invasion and succession cycle. In 1970, 57 percent of South Shore's population was black. But racial change had occurred at a normal pace for such an area without excessive property turnover or a massive flight of white residents, the absence of which may indicate the partial success of the South Shore Commission programs.

Perhaps the greatest indication of the racial change that occurred in South Shore is the composition of the South Shore Commission itself. In 1970 about 50 percent of the commission's membership was black, as were the executive director and his staff. And in 1972 the first black president of the commission was elected. The change in leadership, which commission officials refer to as the "new regime," was paralleled by a change in the major goals and in many of the programs of the commission. No longer was the organization's prime objective the attraction of white residents to South Shore. Instead, it focused on attacking the problems that plague a racially changing community. The commission's programs changed, to deal with specific community problems such as the deterioration of housing in the South Shore area and the resource drain caused by the movement of businesses from South Shore. The commission also attempted to involve the community's renters in the work of the organization and to give them a stake in the community by organizing tenant unions on a widespread scale. The tenant unions, along with the enforcement of building codes, have constituted the commission's major response to deteriorating housing and lack of maintenance of apartment buildings. Other commission programs included the continuation of the citizen radio patrol, Project Whistlestop, a sickle cell anemia testing program, and the formation of a nonprofit housing corporation. One concern was the potential move of the

South Shore National Bank from the community; this was prevented, and an attempt was made to organize the citizens of South Shore around this crisis, reflecting the more Alinskylike mood of the South Shore Commission of the 1970s.

Several explanations can be offered as to why the South Shore Commission did not succeed in achieving integration in the South Shore community. First, South Shore in the 1960s was simply not one of the more desirable areas of the city for whites. Both the predominance of apartment dwellings as opposed to single family residences and the age of the housing stock combined to make South Shore less attractive to whites than others in the city and the suburbs. These factors, together with the absence of any large institution (e.g., research center, industry, or university) dependent upon white professionals in the area, combined to make South Shore less attractive to whites than to blacks. Moreover, the commission's attempts to make South Shore more desirable to whites—increasing security; improving education and the physical environment—made the area equally if not more desirable to blacks.

The fact that blacks did find South Shore attractive was directly related to the dynamics of the rental housing market. Having fewer rental choices within Chicago and willing to pay more for those choices, blacks were more likely to take over available rentals in South Shore than whites. In fact, blacks in South Shore did appear to be paying more for rentals than whites. This color tax, which averaged about 20 percent on rentals in the late 1960s was high enough to influence realtors to rent to blacks rather than to search for white applicants. Because a high rate of mobility was characteristic of South Shore due to its predominately apartment house character, it made the racial transition more likely to occur rapidly, since a large number of persons would have changed their residence regardless of the racial conditions existing in the area. As Molotch notes, "Normal mobility makes neighborhood change *possible;* when markets are structured in such a way that blacks continuously constitute the bulk of those who move into the vacancies which result, racial change is made inevitable."[5]

Molotch also mentions problems of timing as possible reasons for the failure of the commission to achieve its goals. Most of the South Shore Commission's programs were not established until racial transition was well underway. Had the Tenant Referral Service been de-

5. Ibid., p. 275.

veloped in 1960, for example, the ultimate outcome might have been different. Molotch suggests two programs that might have been particularly effective had they been initiated earlier:

1. The attraction of a major educational or research institution to the area would have resulted in increased white demand for housing; and
2. A scheme to transfer large contiguous blocks of apartment housing to a single management firm that could have been trusted to maintain property and to operate under a racial quota system might have helped to achieve racial balance in South Shore.[6]

But whether or not these programs might have been able to achieve racial stability in South Shore will never be known. In 1972 South Shore was becoming increasingly a black residential community, a testimony to the failure of the South Shore Commission to alter the ecological processes of city growth and the dynamics of the dual housing market.

6. Ibid., p. 320.

Chapter 7

West Englewood: Father Lawlor's Defensive Network

In South Shore, there was an attempt to create an integrated community. Nearby in West Englewood (Community Area 67, see Figure 1-1), there was a very different response. A Catholic priest, Father Francis X. Lawlor, organized instead a defensive network of block clubs to try to contain racial change.

Originally part of the town of Lake, West Englewood shared in the growth of the entire south side that followed the Chicago fire of 1871. The first settlers located in the area of 63rd and Ashland. West Englewood was annexed to Chicago in 1889 and grew rapidly as a result of the building boom that accompanied the 1893 Columbian Exposition. By 1896 the area was within convenient commuting distance of downtown Chicago by means of the streetcar lines that operated on its major streets. Two principal neighborhoods developed: South Lynne, extending south between Ashland and Western Avenues from 59th to 67th Streets, and Murray Park, from 67th to 74th Streets. East of Ashland Avenue was a more amorphous residential territory, however, without well-marked neighborhood definition, and it was here that black entry was most rapid in the late 1960s.

The original settlers were working men, largely of German and Swedish origin. Early in the 1900s Italians also began to move into the South Lynne neighborhood, settling first on Wood Street and spreading south to 71st and east to Ashland Avenue. North and west of this Italian settlement was an Irish district. By 1920, West Englewood's population was 53,000, and its leading foreign born groups were Germans, Irish, and Italians. In addition, a small black population had lived there since before the turn of the century. Concentrated near 63rd and Loomis, this black community was large enough by 1900 to support four area churches. When the Englewood branch of the elevated trains was extended westward to Loomis in 1907, even more blacks were attracted to the area.

After 1940 the population of West Englewood decreased with each census until, in the late 1960s, racial change occurred. In the white neighborhoods the decline in population continued, but this was offset east of Ashland Avenue by rapid population increases in areas newly occupied by black families. In 1970, the community was already 50 percent black. Murray Park remained predominantly white and Catholic, however. The community remained one of working men with somewhat lower income levels than the city as a whole and with a relatively high homeownership rate of its modestly priced homes, most of which had been built before 1930.

PERCEPTIONS OF CHANGE

When we began our studies of West Englewood, racial change was already proceeding apace. Ashland Avenue marked the dividing line between white neighborhoods to the west and black neighborhoods in the east, and even this dividing line had been breached north of 67th Street as blacks moved westward into South Lynne.

Few residents could fail to perceive the crooked spine running through the community separating white from black areas. To the west of West Englewood were the predominantly white communities of Gage Park and Chicago Lawn; to the east, the predominantly black communities of Englewood and Greater Grand Crossing. The neighborhoods to the east were poorer and more dilapidated; those to the west were better cared for.

In answer to the question—Do you expect much change in the community in the next five years?—asked during a 1971 survey, 70 percent expected major changes, most of which were evaluated negatively. The principal change foreseen in 1971 was racial. Despite this, however, 80 percent of the respondents said they did not plan to leave the area.[1]

The perceptions of those interviewed appear to be fairly accurate. In a study prepared by the Chicago Real Estate Board for the board of education, nearly complete racial turnover was predicted for West Englewood by 1975. The community was 13 percent nonwhite in

1. "Report on Community Survey—Holy Cross Hospital," (Chicago: Holy Cross Hospital) August/September, 1971, p. 4.

1960 and almost 50 percent nonwhite in 1970. According to the CREB study, it would be 85 percent nonwhite in 1975. The consequences of racial change are clearly visible to both white and black residents of West Englewood—particularly in the areas of education, real estate practices, housing, crime and safety, and community services.

The schools in West Englewood were a source of major community conflict. In 1968 schools east of Ashland Avenue were overcrowded, virtually all black, and equipped with mobile units, whereas the west side schools were operating at about capacity without mobile units.

The board of education responded to the overcrowding in black schools by changing the boundaries of attendance areas and assigning some black students to adjacent schools. In fringe areas this led to overcrowding of the schools in already tense white communities near the ghetto and a hastening of the racial transition process. Seeing black students enter white West Englewood neighborhoods to attend school aggravated white fears of eventual takeover by blacks as well as contributing to racial incidents between white and black students.

Proposals were made that overcrowding on the fringe of the ghetto be relieved by the busing of pupils to vacant classrooms in remote schools. Nevertheless, the school board continued to deal with each school on the fringe of the ghetto individually, and only after the overcrowding had grown acute was there juggling of the surplus students between schools in the newly black areas and schools in the neighboring white community and by providing mobile units.

As early as 1963, the South Lynne Community Council (SLCC) became concerned about panic peddling in its area and invited area brokers to meet with it to discuss real estate practices and their effect on the community. The tactics were simple: a Ms. Smith or Jones would call a South Lynne resident, introduce herself as a member of "Blank" Realty, and announce in a "Negro dialect" that her company had just bought so and so's house down the street and just happened to have some leftover buyers in case the owner was interested in selling.

In the fall of 1969, complaints concerning this kind of panic peddling increased greatly in South Lynne. The SLCC received numerous phone calls from residents in the northeastern section of South Lynne reporting harassment from real estate agents in the form of phone solicitations, letters, and business cards saying, "Sell now. The neighborhood is going."

In August of 1971, the SLCC surveyed homeowners and found that many residents had been solicited by real estate agents. In September of 1971, the owner of Miller Realty was involved in an argument with a local resident. Miller charged that he was being harassed for alleged panic peddling. The harassment began when a southside homeowner singled him out as responsible for "encouraging black moveins and ruining the neighborhood."[2] Miller adamantly denied the charge, accusing the resident of unfairly attacking him. Yet, almost a year later, Judge Richard Austin enjoined Lee Miller from panic peddling in West Pullman, an area several miles southeast of West Englewood.

When asked by a *Sun Times* reporter in 1971 whether he thought blockbusting was the cause of most the racial tensions in the area, the president of the Murray Park Civic Association, Henry Coppolillo, answered:

> Absolutely. One hundred percent. It's the agitation that goes with it. And not the colored families, the person who's working for a living, because, let's fact it, we're no better than they are in some respects. You know? We realize they've been handicapped through education and other means.[3]

When the reporter asked, "Do you ever get satisfaction from the city if you find a blockbuster?" Coppolillo said, "Absolutely not. We don't get any satisfaction from the city because it's a political issue and they want the black votes." As of 1970, in fact, not one Chicago real estate firm in the previous seven years had had its license revoked for panic peddling, and while there had been suspensions, the longest had been for only forty-five days.

The fact that the Chicago Department of Development and Planning designated the east side of Ashland Avenue as an urban renewal area indicates the physical deterioration that had already set in. A prominent concern of West Englewood's major civic organizations thus had been keeping up the appearance of homes by subtly applied pressure on nonconformers and by finding and investigating building code and zoning violations in an effort to prevent overcrowding and deterioration of housing. A home survey conducted by the South Lynne Community Council in 1969 revealed that many properties owned and managed by absentee landlords are neglected and in violation of housing and zoning codes.

Yet plans for public housing in the area were strongly opposed by West Englewood's white population. Public housing was feared because residents felt it would bring low income blacks into the area

2. *Daily Defender*, September 29, 1971.
3. Joseph Reilly, *Chicago Sun-Times*, March 15, 1971.

and precipitate even greater racial change. A 1971 *Sun Times* survey revealed that residents favored neighborhood control of Chicago Housing Authority (CHA) locations and that none thought housing should be built near them.[4]

Crime was also of continuing concern. Local police commanders in racially changing districts offered two possible explanations for crime rises in changing neighborhoods:

1. Many of those arrested for crimes were blacks who did not live in the area, but who apparently went to changing neighborhoods for criminal purposes, especially for burglary and robbery.
2. Crime may not increase as much as reported crimes do in these changing neighborhoods, since transition upsets many whites and leads them to call the police about things they would otherwise ignore.

The perceptions of residents concerning crime may then have been more important than the actual volume of crime. Police surveillance in and around West Englewood's two high schools did increase, but not enough to satisfy whites, who had recently established their own citizens' patrol. Even so, demands for more police protection continued.

Alongside crime, there was concern about declining community quality. Residents of neighborhoods like South Lynne and Murray Park leave their houses for reasons in addition to panic peddling and fear of crime. The slowness of commercial urban renewal, poor city services, and the growth of problem businesses such as taverns have all played a part in the racial transition of the West Englewood area.

In 1969, for example, the SLCC noted the sudden appearance of numerous taverns in the area between 61st and 66th Streets, Ashland and Paulina. It opposed this rash of taverns by holding a local option election in the fifty-second and thirty-eighth precincts with the result that nine taverns in the first precinct were closed while only three in the latter remained open.

In the same year there was also some concern over the new elevated train ("L") extension that was to be constructed at 63rd Street. While providing inexpensive transportation for the area's residents, the "L" extension seemed likely to attract more blacks to the community. Murray Park residents opposed the "L" extension precisely for this reason.

4. Ibid.

NATURE OF ORGANIZED
COMMUNITY RESPONSE

There were three different community responses to the changes taking place. In South Lynne, there was an attempt to achieve integration; but in Murray Park, a defensive network of block clubs was organized by a Catholic priest, and a more aggressive exclusionary policy was pursued by the neighborhood's civic association.

South Lynne Community Council

The SLCC was formed in 1957 as a liberal-oriented community improvement association before the imminence of racial change was recognized. It expanded its activities in the 1960s in response to the demand for a free rent referral service and also became a center for rumor clearance and general civic information. In 1963, the SLCC came out for open housing. Its aim had always been balanced integration as opposed to inundation of an area by blacks and the simultaneous flight of whites.

In 1969 the council developed a housing policy with two main objectives: (1) to encourage white residents to remain along racial borderlines and to aggressively recruit other white families to move in as vacancies occur; and (2) to encourage and assist economically capable black families who desired to move into South Lynne to locate to the west of the racial border in predominantly white areas. To achieve the former goal, the SLCC operated a free referral service because, as one of the SLCC's members, Reverend Bohm, noted in 1968, the only way to halt block-by-block racial change was to have blacks jump over fringe areas and settle farther west.

The SLCC's decision to accept integration made it vulnerable to blockbusting efforts. South Lynne had been plagued by panic peddling, and much of the council's efforts had been directed toward halting this practice. In 1963 the council tried to discuss blockbusting practices with area real estate brokers. Four years later, several black families moved into an apartment building at 62nd and Marshfield. This was a significant event, since it was the first such movein west of Ashland Avenue. In 1968, as blacks began to move further west, the SLCC noted the simultaneous increase in the number of complaints about panic peddling.

Throughout the following year, the incidence of complaints about panic peddling increased even more. Property turnover was especially great in one area, in the southwest section of South Lynne. Area residents complained of solicitations by mail and in person by real estate agents. The SLCC investigated the complaints of the residents and eventually charged Gem Realty Company with panic peddling. Ms. Lois Ann Rosen, then SLCC executive director, said that the organization had received dozens of complaints of panic peddling directed against a Gem salesman within a five day period.[5] The SLCC responded with "Operation Fight Back." Four residents filed complaints against Gem Realty with the Chicago Commission on Human Relations, which urged Mayor Daley to suspend Gem's license for three months. Although the mayor acted upon the commission's recommendation, the suspension was appealed by the company and eventually revoked.

The SLCC also had a number of committees dealing with housing zoning, mental health, schools and education, and youth. Periodic property surveys were carried out and pressure brought to bear on negligent owners and absentee landlords. Reports of zoning and building code violations were received and investigated. Concern was expressed over the form that urban renewal would take in the area of 63rd and Ashland. In 1969 a letter was sent to the Chicago City Bank informing it that brokers working through it were showing homes on Paulina and Marshfield only to black buyers and asking it to support the SLCC's efforts to maintain racial balance in the area. The SLCC also supported quality schools for the area. The education committee made periodic reports on the state of the area's schools and attempted to pressure the school board and the state into providing more financial support for education.

In keeping with its objective of integration, the SLCC also tried to welcome black families into the community and generally to prevent any racial violence. In 1969, for example, the *SLCC News*, the organization's publication, reported that the SLCC Housing Committee and Executive Board had met with twelve new black families to acquaint them with the work of the SLCC. And later that year, when a smoldering mattress was found in the garage of a home recently purchased by a black family, the *SLCC News* decried such actions. As it turned out, the SLCC was so successful at welcoming black families that by the early 1970s, there were few whites left to welcome new blacks. Today, the SLCC is largely black in both membership and leadership and is concerned with the problems of posttransition areas —namely, crime and gangs, property maintenance, and the condition of the schools.

5. *Chicago Tribune*, October 9, 1969.

Father Lawlor and the South West
Associated Block Clubs

Francis Xavier Lawlor, a priest for twenty-five years and dean of St. Rita's High School in West Englewood, became increasingly concerned about fears of black expansion expressed by parishioners of his part-time parish base at St. Mary of Mount Carmel Church in West Englewood. Initially, in 1967, in sermons and private talks, he was sympathetic, helpful, and knowledgeable.

> If he had learned anything from his earlier campaigns, in which he had forced department stores to display modest dresses, forced (the book) "Sex Goddess" off Loop book shelves, coaxed disk jockeys into a "decent disk" drive, forged teen-age seminars on communism, he had learned *organization*.[6]

In December of 1967, the first block clubs were formed. In February of 1968, Cardinal Cody informed Fr. Lawlor that "he was requesting the provincial to transfer me because I opposed the archdiocese's integration policies. The request, of course, was an order."[7] Fr. Lawlor was transferred to an Augustinian school in Tulsa, Oklahoma, where he stayed only a short time before returning of his own volition and against orders to his block club activities in Chicago. He was subsequently forbidden to perform his priestly functions in the Archdiocese of Chicago. However, Fr. Lawlor's personality was crucial in organizing many white residents of West Englewood. Signs in southwest side windows announced "Jesus Loves Father Lawlor."

Fr. Lawlor's South West Associated Block Clubs (SWABC) were overtly home improvement associations, but their implicit objective was to "hold the line at Ashland Avenue." While Fr. Lawlor maintained that he was not a racist, SWABC aimed at a policy of excluding blacks totally from West Englewood until certain preconditions that formed the basis of his exclusion policy had been met. These preconditions were primarily to rectify what Fr. Lawlor believed to be inherent "socioeconomic, cultural"[8] differences between whites and blacks. Fr. Lawlor described his constituents as "hard-working, lower middle class," many of whom had invested their lives into owning their own homes.

> We are fully aware that the black people need housing, jobs, and an education for their children. We sincerely want them to have these advantages in

6. *Chicago Sun-Times*, March 9, 1969.
7. Ibid.
8. Interview with Father Lawlor, November 14, 1972.

this urban environment. We do not believe that it is just to take these same needs from our people in order to give it to the black population. We must live, too. We must have a home to shelter our families. We must see that their educational needs are provided for. This is not hatred or prejudice.[9]

He identified himself very closely with his constituents and with what he believed to be their culture. The white community, likewise, seemed to accept him as its leader. He characterized the black community as essentially riddled with crime, lacking respect for either persons or property, and completely "unprepared" for such responsibility as homeowning. He described many of the blacks moving into the area as "opportunistic," desiring only to make the relatively small down payment required by the Federal Housing Authority but having no actual intention of maintaining the property.

In regard to the "problems" that he believed to be facing the black community, he felt it was up to them to get together their own moral courage and solve their own problems. As for himself, he said, "I am only one man and can't be everywhere at the same time. I'm only trying to improve this neighborhood. There are 3,000 other priests who can work in black areas."[10] Until such time as the black community did solve "their own problems," he suggested buffer zones and black-imposed quotas for each block.

Fr. Lawlor's essential point was that the races are simply unsuited for mixing. Once "differences" had been overcome, reconciliation and integration could proceed smoothly and, in his words, "present no difficulties." This much was made clear in an article written by Fr. Lawlor entitled "Do Block Club Members Object to Blacks Living in the Community among Whites?" The answer to this question was: "If they obey the law and want to get along with the neighbors on a friendly and mutually respectful basis, there would be no objection."[11]

Fr. Lawlor worked to foster a sense of community among the whites living in West Englewood. He stressed the common culture that they had come to share, despite the diversity in their European ethnic backgrounds. He considered this culture to be distinct from both middle class white culture and black "ghetto" culture. His values centered mostly around traditional, church-oriented morality. This included the importance of being a good neighbor who would not sell to either panic peddlers or blacks and betray his neighbors. For example, an article in the *ABC News* asked readers to "join with

9. Ibid.
10. *Chicago's American*, August 18, 1968.
11. *ABC News*, (SWABC bimonthly newsletter) October 27, 1972.

us in prayer for the community. . . . We all need His help and providential care in this time of community crisis. He can do all things. May we merit His blessings at this time."[12]

Father Lawlor was elected as an independent alderman of the fifteenth ward in Chicago in 1971. In running, Fr. Lawlor failed to carry his own precinct because of the changing character of the neighborhood, however. And as it turned out, as the area continued to change, he was a one term alderman. During his period of service, a shaky alliance between him and black alderwoman Anna R. Langford (of the sixteenth, all black ward, immediately east of Fr. Lawlor's fifteenth ward) developed. Ms. Langford, a civil rights lawyer, was elected to her first term at the same time as Fr. Lawlor. Newspapers reported meetings between Ms. Langford and Fr. Lawlor in efforts to solve their mutual problems. Ms. Langford was quoted as saying:

> We have these meetings where we bring 10 or even 100 people from each of our wards to talk. . . . He'll tell me about his strategies. I tell him, "You're going to fail, so let's go on to step two and see what we can do about it."
> He's hung up on the idea of the clash of cultures, that black people will try to force their ways upon whites. I tell him, "Do not worry, if you don't bother us, we won't throw our barbecue bones on your front lawn."[13]

The period of harmony was, however, short lived. Incidents of arson in West Englewood and differences concerning education policies divided the two. In April 1972, Fr. Lawlor and Ms. Langford clashed in a meeting of the city council regarding board of education policies, which Fr. Lawlor blamed for racial change in white neighborhoods. Fr. Lawlor also charged that Mr. Langford had helped black people move across Ashland Avenue into houses in his ward. "And you burn them down!" she responded. After the council session Ms. Langford said:

> That bigot. There have never been any conciliatory moves. We just sat down to move toward togetherness. But I am sick and tired of his whole bigoted, ignorant attitude. . . . He is doing what he was elected to do—polarize people and keep blacks out of the community.[14]

12. Ibid.
13. *Chicago Tribune*, August 29, 1971.
14. *Chicago Sun-Times*, April 6, 1972.

Alderman Thomas E. Keane, Mayor Daley's floor leader, then arose to remark, "The honeymoon is over, the marriage is hereby dissolved."[15]

Fr. Lawlor wanted to have a screening process to ascertain a new resident's qualifications before he or she was allowed to move into an established community. Ms. Langford, on the other hand, believed that the only "screening" process necessary was whether or not the buyer could afford to pay for the house. If he could afford it, he was just as qualified to buy it as a white man and was as likely to care for his investment. As to the cultural differences Fr. Lawlor spoke of, Ms. Langford felt that these were created by segregation. To agree to separate into two camps would only perpetuate the cause of the problem.

To stabilize white fringe neighborhoods, Fr. Lawlor focused on three issues—crime, school enrollments, and real estate practices. To offer protection against crime, the block clubs instituted nightly mobile patrols that reported suspicious events to the police, and they regularly demanded increased police protection.

SWABC's education committee frequently monitored school enrollments and aggressively worked for "high quality neighborhood schools." Fr. Lawlor and SWABC considered the board of education's integration policies their major enemies and resorted to picketing to present their realization. Fr. Lawlor publicly charged the school board with changing school boundaries, approving "permissive transfers," and contemplating school additions that would racially change Chicago neighborhoods. "James Redmond is a ruthless individual. . . . the Board of Education is the biggest block-buster in Chicago," he was quoted as saying.[16]

O'Toole School in West Englewood became in 1970 the center of a dispute between Fr. Lawlor and the school board. Between 1967 and 1970 the school had changed from all white to 36 percent black. To relieve overcrowding at O'Toole, the board of education ordered the building of sixteen prefabricated classrooms on the school playground. Fr. Lawlor and his followers felt that the new buildings would accommodate so many black pupils that white families in the O'Toole area would be forced to move. Instead of mobile units, they urged the school board to consider sending many of O'Toole's black students to other schools. The failure of the board of education to act upon Fr. Lawlor's suggestion led him and his supporters to picket

15. Ibid.
16. Anthony Monahan, *Chicago Sun-Times*, March 9, 1969.

the school to prevent construction of the units. Although the outcome of this strategy was unsuccessful, Fr. Lawlor did manage to delay the construction.

Two years later Fr. Lawlor again tried to prevent construction of new classrooms—at this time at Barton Elementary School—for similar reasons. The black parents protested the delay in construction of a twenty-room modular addition to Barton and charged Fr. Lawlor with attempting to prevent construction. Again Fr. Lawlor proposed busing black students to other area schools instead of increasing the capacity and percentage of blacks at Barton.

All of the area's high schools had histories of racial violence as the black enrollment increased. Perhaps the most intense of the disputes involved Gage Park High School in 1972-1973 (see Chapter 8). In addition to the Chicago Board of Education, SWABC identified as enemies of stable housing panic-peddling brokers, the federal government, Chicago politicians, and large developers.

The main factor in black expansion was panic peddling, according to Fr. Lawlor. But, he said, panic peddling could not succeed were it not for the lack of courage and pride in the neighborhood on part of the residents. One objective of the block clubs was thus to promote solidarity in the face of solicitations by real estate agents. As vacancies occurred, SWABC tried to fill them with, as Father Lawlor liked to repeat, "persons of the same cultural, social, and economic background as our own community." This meant trying to prevent the sale or rental of properties to blacks. Thus SWABC's block clubs could be seen as restrictive covenants on a smaller scale.

The emphasis of the SWABC on self-help and grassroots organization derived in large part from the feeling that there was a lack of responsibility on the part of the federal and city governments when it came to dealing with interracial problems. Federal programs were seen as directed solely toward blacks. Thousands of signs bearing the message "We are going to STAY—down with FHA" could be seen in the windows of homes on the southwest side of Ashland Avenue in 1971. Fr. Lawlor's followers were protesting the subsidizing of home mortgages by FHA that made it "too easy" for low income blacks to move into white neighborhoods. According to Fr. Lawlor:

> We must stop the FHA. If only restrictions could be enforced so that the blacks who move in were those who want to integrate, who can afford to pay for the homes, who will live by the same standards. But most of them don't want to integrate.[17]

17. *Chicago Tribune*, August 29, 1971.

The city government was viewed by SWABC with even greater distrust than the federal government. The Chicago Housing Authority slated 311 public housing units from 47th to 74th Streets between Ashland and Cicero Avenues. SWABC hoped to prevent the construction of any of these units in its area. In April 1972, *ABC News* informed its readers, "Don't worry about CHA sites. None of them can be built in the block club area. . . . "[18] City politics were, moreover, suspected of being influenced by private interests. Fr. Lawlor's explanation of what occurred was as follows:

> The powers-that-be have decided that the part of the city that counts is the lakefront, and they are determined to save it. The big realtors, the downtown politicians, the business community . . . are united in this situation. To them the part of Chicago that matters is the high rises of Lake Shore Drive, the high income districts in and around the Loop, and the string of institutions on the south side running from Michael Reese Hospital to the University of Chicago. The rest of city? Let that go to the swiftest and strongest, be he black or blue-collar white. Provided, of course, that their squabbles do not spill over into the enclave of civilization and high property values that the smart money boys have decided to save.[19]

Murray Park Civic Association

A third community organization operating in West Englewood was the Murray Park Civic Association (MPCA). Subsumed by the SWABC, the MPCA included some of Fr. Lawlor's strongest supporters. Containing some 1,800 members, or 53 percent of the community according to its own estimates, the MPCA encompassed an area whose inhabitants were chiefly of Italian descent.

As to why communities undergo racial change, Henry Coppolillo, president of MPCA, had a theory very similar to that of Fr. Lawlor. He felt that areas are "mapped out" as "risk areas" in the following way: "Key people like bankers, real estate dealers, elected representatives, our civic government sit down and figure out that they're going to map out a certain community as a risk area."[20] Coppolillo remained vague as to the motives of this power elite for selecting risk areas, however. "Here's an area where people pay high taxes, like everywhere else, the crime rate is practically nil, and yet somebody suggests that this is a risk area. What authority do they have to do this?"[21]

18. *ABC News*, April 1972.
19. Ronald Grossman, *Chicago Journalism Review*, February 1973, p. 14.
20. *Southtown Economist*, July 25, 1971.
21. Ibid.

In defense, Murray Park took a wild west approach to black encroachments into its community. In 1971, four homes in the fifteenth ward into which black families were moving were destroyed by fire. Arson was clear in three of the cases. Ms. Bernice Hight's home, for example, was burned down in an all white neighborhood in April of 1971. A two gallon gas can was found forty feet from her home.

The year before, shots were fired and bricks thrown through the windows of a home occupied by blacks in a white block organized by SWABC. And several years earlier a storefront church was bombed. About the same time, there were three days of rioting around a new townhouse when it was rumored that blacks were planning to move into the building. Murray Park had a history of racial violence.[22]

The attitudes of the leadership of MPCA apparently mirrored those of the area. Coppolillo, commenting at an MPCA meeting on the fire that destroyed Ms. Hight's home, called it:

> an incident whereby a militant family tried to move into a brand new home, bringing with them a truckload of kids with baseball bats in their hands and cursing. . . . We here in Murray Park are a different type of people. We are not going to allow that type in our community, whether they are white or black.[23]

He then asked for donations to defray the legal expenses of a fourteen-year old area youth arrested in connection with the fire.

Coppolillo also mentioned at the same meeting the fire that destroyed the Banwich home. He charged that Ms. Banwich was selling her home to black people in order "to get revenge on neighbors she couldn't get along with." Summed up Coppolillo: "When you hear of an incident in this community of a garage being burned or a house being bombed, it's not because the people in this community are doing it for kicks. We're letting everyone know we mean business."[24]

EVALUATION

It was in South Lynne that blacks first broke the Ashland Avenue boundary into West Englewood. Once the barrier was broken, black inmovement accelerated. Why did the SLCC fail to achieve its goal of stable integration? The members themselves were puzzled by their

22. *Commentary Publications*, July 7, 1971.
23. *Southtown Economist*, September 5, 1971.
24. Ibid.

lack of success. The apparent immunity to black inmovement of similarly composed neighborhoods such as Murray Park was noted at an SLCC meeting. The general feeling seemed to be that blacks avoided moving into such areas because they knew that they would be opposed violently. In fact, SLCC's integration policy paved the way for black takeover. Whereas blacks perceived South Lynne as more desirable that their other alternatives and a step away from the ghetto, whites viewed South Lynne as a changing area and therefore undesirable. Whites with children were not attracted to vacancies in an area with a deteriorating school system and proximity to the ghetto. The inevitable result was that more blacks than whites applied for vacancies in the area when they occurred, and vacancies increased as whites perceived their area changing.

SWABC and MPCA were more successful than SLCC in preserving the status quo, although the Ashland dividing line was ultimately breached at a variety of points. SWABC's success must be credited to the powerful organizing ability of Father Lawlor and the vigilance of the block clubs. The SWABC was a mass-based organization focused on a few issues, and black moveins were resisted violently. Blacks were therefore more willing to move into South Lynne, where less resistance was to be encountered.

Murray Park remained a tightly knit ethnic neighborhood. Many of its families had been residents of the same area, according to Coppolillo, for "four even five generations." There were very low turnover rates, a high degree of homeownership, but relatively low incomes. Because of this there were fewer options for Murray Park residents, a fact that made their fight for their area even move desperate. As one resident noted in 1971: "Most of us have lived here all our lives. We own property and we can't afford to buy another house someplace else."[25]

How long SWABC and MPCA could continue to hold the line was problematic. In 1975, however, the condition of the neighborhood schools was of crucial importance. As black enrollment continued to rise, whites with children continued to move away or to enroll their children in parochial or other schools. Fr. Lawlor and SWABC were unable to change the school board's integration policy. The best they could do is delay. Said one parent in May of 1971:

You bet we're worried about racial tension . . . but what can we do about it? Our kids are supposed to go to Harper High School. We can't afford $1000 for parochial school. We can't transfer our kids to another school.

25. Sandra Pesman, *Chicago Daily News*, May 27, 1971.

Are we supposed to send little girls and boys into Harper, where we know they'll be molested and beaten up?[26]

The perceived safety of the area remained an additional factor in precipitating white flight as the percentage of blacks to the immediate north and east of Murray Park increased. Several Raster PTA mothers told a *Chicago Daily News* reporter in 1971 that they didn't allow their children to go out alone in the evenings. They also told them to "ride west only" when they went out on their bicycles. Said one mother:

We can't walk outside our houses either day or night because we never know what's going to happen. One neighborhood boy was hit by a brick thrown from a passing car. Another man was shot in the back by two holdup men. But we can't stay inside all the time.[27]

The real question then was when the situation would be seen as too serious to fight any longer. When that perception became generally widespread, Murray Park seemed destined not only to undergo racial transition but to undergo it very rapidly.

26. Ibid.
27. Ibid.

Chapter 8

Gage Park: A Battleground in the Schools

Gage Park lies north and west of West Englewood (see Figure 1-1, Community Area 63), bounded on the north by 49th Street, on the south by 59th Street, on the east by the Pennsylvania railroad tracks (2200 W.), and on the west by the Grand Trunk Western railroad tracks (3600 W.). At first glance, the community is not much different from a host of other Chicago area communities. Situated on narrow, deep lots lining tree-lined streets are neat one and two story brick homes and small apartment buildings with well-manicured lawns.

To the north, west, and southwest, Gage Park is bordered by communities very much like it—white, ethnic, and working class. To the east, however, the situation was different in the late 1960s. On Gage Park's southeast corner is West Englewood where Ashland Avenue (1600 W.), once Chicago's Mason-Dixon line, had been blurred by black movement west. Gage Park was only eight blocks west of Ashland.

The ghetto's westward expansion had become increasingly apparent to Gage Park's residents in 1965, when Gage Park High School was integrated by extending its attendance boundaries as far east as Racine (1200 W.) and as far south as 63rd Street. The school district set up thus encompassed several black feeder schools. The implications of this boundary change and the response of Gage Parkers are the subject of this chapter.

Settled originally by German farmers, Gage Park did not experience its main growth until 1905-1919. By 1920 its population exceeded 13,000, almost one-third foreign born Czechoslovakians, Poles, and Germans.

Much of Gage Park's growth during this period reflected the industrial development occurring both within Gage Park itself and in nearby communities. The building of the railroad tracks, three of Gage Park's most prominent borders, spurred the growth of industry.

During the 1920s, as now, Gage Park was a working class community, its residents employed in the car shops of the Grand Trunk Western railroad, the Crane Company plant in Brighton Park, the Stockyards, and various factories and plants in the area.

Throughout the 1920s Gage Park experienced a great deal of growth. By 1930 its population had more than doubled, reaching 31,500. Few vacant lots remained in 1929, and the outlines of today's community had been established.

After 1930 Gage Park experienced a slow but steady decline in population. Between 1950 and 1960, it decreased from 30,149 to 28,244. By 1970 Gage Park had a solidly white population of 26,698. Of these, approximately half were of foreign stock, with Poles constituting 25 percent, Czechoslovakians 16 percent, Irish 10 percent, and Germans 8 percent.

Between 1950 and 1970 the community also aged, as children left home and families with young children moved away. The consequences of this aging process did not go unnoticed, especially by the area's churches. One clergyman noted that while his congregation numbered some 300 persons, only two births had occurred among his members in a year. He felt that families with school age children had begun to leave the area. "Sometimes it's so bad," he confessed, "that it seems like I'm ministering to a parade."[1]

Solidly blue collar, in 1970 Gage Park was not an area of high educational achievement. Gage Park High School had one of the city's highest dropout rates even prior to its integration. Always heavily dependent on nearby industries, most of Gage Park's breadwinners were employed as craftsmen and foremen, operatives, and clerks in southwest side manufacturing and retail enterprises.

Yet despite the impressions of the churchman who felt that he was ministering to a parade, about 65 percent of Gage Park's residents lived in the same house in 1970 as in 1965, giving Gage Park a lower rate of turnover than that for Chicago as a whole. Twenty seven percent of those who were not in the same house in 1965 as in 1970 came from other parts of Chicago. Ronald Grossman

1. Ronald Grossman, "Report from Gage Park," *Chicago Journalism Review*, February 1973, p. 13

suggests that many of Gage Park's residents have followed a pattern of moving farther and farther west to escape the expanding black ghetto:

> A priest at a local church says that some of his parishioners have been unwilling participants in this process so many times that by now they have come to accept it as an unpleasant fact of life. . . . when the advance of the black community overtakes their neighborhood, they often tend to take an apartment just a little further on, and hope to squeeze out two or three years there before they have to move on again.[2]

About 60 percent of Gage Parkers owned their own homes in 1970, compared to 33 percent of the white Chicago population. The median value of a home in Gage Park was a moderate $18,200 in 1970, lower than the median $21,200 for Chicago as a whole. For those 38 percent who rented units, the median contract rent was $105.

Most of Gage Park's housing stock, much built during the 1920s, was already old, although well maintained. And the community had a definite reality for its inhabitants, geographically identifiable, encompassing an easily defined area marked on the three sides by natural barriers—railroad tracks. Residents not only defined their territory; they also identified strongly with it. Besides the area's churches (most of them Roman Catholic), Gage Park's most important institutions were the park after which the community is named; Talman Federal Savings and Loan Association, which occupied several blocks on both the east and west sides of Kedzie Avenue and was a prominent actor in the area's real estate transactions; and Gage Park High School, a factorylike red brick building. These institutions served as important sources of community identity and as rallying points for community action. Grossman noted:

> The people of Gage Park may well lose the present dispute over the school district's boundaries. They might lose control of the school entirely. In the end they might lose much more. But they are never going to be dissuaded from the idea that the school, like everything else in the area bounded by Western and Kedzie, 49th and 63rd, is theirs.[3]

Perhaps the best indication of the depth of the Gage Parkers' loyalty to their community was their response to what were per-

2. Ibid., p. 7
3. Ibid., p. 4

ceived as outside threats to their continued way of life. Attempting to explain the Gage Parker's psychology, Rick Soll said:

> when foreigners . . . invade and threaten to take the neighborhood and school you've called "mine" for two decades more than half a century, you don't wait until tomorrow to move on it. You move now and you move quick and you stop it. Before it gets too big and bad to handle. The way you've seen it happen to other neighborhoods, as old as yours.[4]

The image of Gage Park presented in the mass media was far from favorable, however. The community has consistently been viewed as an area inhabited by racists and violent extremists. The media has persisted, for example, in identifying Gage Park as the community where Dr. Martin Luther King was stoned during his 1966 open housing march through Chicago's west side. Because the attack actually occurred in Chicago Lawn, an area south of Gage Park, Gage Parkers have tried to defend themselves—often unsuccessfully— against this slur. One young respondent interviewed by Grossman said: "Well, if that's what people want to think about us, let them. We didn't do it. But what the hell, maybe we should have! They're going to think it of us anyway!"[5]

Gage Parkers were well aware of their community's negative image and felt that to some extent they had been unfairly portrayed. As one southwest side resident wrote:

> I am bored with the indignation of newspaper editors and others affluent enough to live in lily-white suburbs or in Lake Shore Drive high-rise apartments telling those who have not made it so well financially that they must send their children to schools where chaos reigns or be prosecuted.
>
> Do you believe for one minute that if Gage Park opens its doors to hundreds of black students who do not reside in Gage Park that those of the white populace who are financially able will not move out and that others, steeped in frustration, will make for a climate where reason will prevail? It has happened in Englewood, Woodlawn, and elsewhere; why should Gage Park be any different?[6]

PERCEPTIONS OF CHANGE

Gage Park was in the early 1970s a solidly white residential community. Erroneously labeled a "changing neighborhood" by the

4. Rick Soll, "At Night, Gage Park Belongs to Neighbors," *Chicago Tribune* (November 26, 1972).

5. Grossman, p. 15

6. Cited in Grossman, p. 14

news media during the 1972 school boycott, Gage Park in 1973 had virtually no black residents. For a number of years, moreover, it had considered itself far enough west to be secure from the expanding black ghetto. According to a long-time Gage Park resident, "when the colored people were at Halsted, I didn't think about them."[7]

By the early 1970s it was not as easy to dismiss thoughts of the impending approach of the black ghetto along with its attendant problems of crime, drugs, and gangs, and deteriorating housing, services, and schools. Notes Grossman:

> when the people of Gage Park look down 55th Street, . . . they perceive a landscape strewn with violence, decay, and social disorganization. When they chance to drive through the neighborhoods where they formerly lived they find the streets now run by gangs, and schools more like armed camps than educational institutions. They see wall after wall and building after building covered with all of the scrawled obscenities and bitter hatreds which poverty and despair cultivate.[8]

It is this perception of the black movement west that Father Francis X. Lawlor so effectively exploited by speaking of the "cultural differences" between blacks and whites.

By the late 1960s the ghetto was beginning to approach Gage Park's southeast corner. At several places in West Englewood, blacks had crossed to the west of that historic Chicago black-white division line, Ashland Avenue. Gage Parkers could thus observe firsthand the well-publicized battles of Fr. Lawlor in West Englewood to set up block clubs to keep areas from "tipping" and to prevent the inundation of white neighborhood schools in the area with black students. Nor were many unfamiliar with West Englewood's South Lynne Community Council, its attacks on panic peddlers, and its transition from a white liberal-oriented community betterment association in the 1950s to a largely black community organization in the 1960s.

Yet up until 1965 most Gage Parkers could feel relatively immune from the threat of racial change. In that year, however, there was an event that was to have enormous consequences for the area. In 1965 the attendance boundaries for Gage Park High School, until then all white, were changed to include black students from the West Englewood area.

The reason for the boundary change was the conversion of West Englewood's Lindblom High School from a general to a technical

7. Grossman, p. 8.
8. Ibid., p. 7.

school. As a consequence, some of the schools that formerly fed their graduates into Lindblom were included in Gage Park High School's district.

John Hahn, who became principal of Gage Park High School the year it was integrated, felt that his supervisors were unaware of the implications of the boundary change—namely, that some of the West Englewood feeder schools included in Gage Park High's district were largely black. Whatever the case, Gage Park High School opened its doors in the fall of 1965 to its first eighty-eight black students. Each year thereafter, the percentage of black students increased and the imminence of the threat of black movement into the community itself became increasingly apparent. Especially for the residents living near the high school, the sight of hundreds of black students must have seemed the precursor of even more significant neighborhood changes.

Significantly, the percentage of black students at the Gage Park High School branch located one block away from the main building and housing the school's freshmen increased more rapidly than that in the main high school. For example, in 1972, blacks constituted 50.3 percent of the student body in the main building, whereas 60.9 percent of the branch's student body was black. The black feeder schools contributed rising numbers of students. On the other hand, the number of whites attending Gage Park High School declined from 2,249 in 1965 to 761 in 1972.

Where did the white students who no longer attended Gage Park High go? The shrinking white student enrollment reflected (1) increased parochial school enrollment, (2) enrollment in public and private schools outside the area, and (3) movement of families with high school age children away from Gage Park. In 1970 public high school enrollment in some Gage Park census tracts was as low as 42.2 percent.

VIOLENCE IN THE SCHOOL

During the first two years following Gage Park High School's integration, no major racial incidents occurred. In December 1966, John Hahn, the high school principal, reported that altercations between students at the school had been about the same in number and type as in preintegration years. However, as the number of black students enrolled at Gage Park High School increased, so did the number and gravity of racially motivated disturbances. Several violent incidents that occurred on buses transporting black students to and from school early in 1967 culminated late in October in a school walkout and boycott by blacks.

In May and June trouble again broke out. A three-day period of unrest was sparked when a black student was seriously injured in a fight. At the close of May, the black students presented the administration with a list of demands, two of which were to become themes in subsequent disorders:

1. an end to racist language by teachers and
2. the need for more police protection.

The administration's response to the violence was to increase disciplinary measures. Additional police were also assigned to the school through June.

In the spring of 1969, severe disruptions occurred on the streets and in the schools. These disorders followed a similar pattern. Whites would attack black students as they entered Gage Park going to or coming from the high school, and the blacks would retaliate within the school walls. Incidents between blacks and whites that would result in trouble the following week in school also occurred on weekends in parks and other public places.

Black students and their parents again complained that Gage Park High School teachers were racist and that police protection was inadequate. Gage Parkers, on the other hand, urged the principal to "expel the troublemakers" and supported the police.

In May, two policemen and twelve students were injured during several days of fighting at the school. Twenty black students were arrested. In retaliation for the alleged unfair treatment of the blacks involved, two-thirds of the black student body walked out of the school. Hahn ordered suspensions for those involved in the fight. The pattern of dealing with the school's racial problems continued to be one of harsh discipline by the administration and the police.

The school year 1969–1970 was the year of the worst disruptions, as the black student body increased to 400. A fight in a school washroom between blacks and whites—apparently in retaliation for the stoning of a bus—led to an outbreak of racial violence that continued into November and December.

Gage Park High School officials and the police responded to the outbreak by canceling off campus lunch privileges, since much of the trouble tended to occur outside the school in nearby streets and at a bookstore where students gathered, and by increasing police security. During 1969 a great many complaints could be heard concerning the police and their tactics. The police were criticized for not providing surveillance adequate to prevent student ambushes and for descending en masse when violence did occur. Perhaps the greatest amount of criticism was aroused, however, when the police maced a bus carrying black students at 59th and Ashland.

Racial incidents continued despite the efforts of the administration and police. In early November a black effigy and sign saying "die nigger" were hung in a tree near 57th and Rockwell for all Gage Park students to see. During three successive days of violence in the same period, eighty-nine students were arrested and charged with disorderly conduct.

In December incidents and arrests continued to occur. When seventy black students staged a walkout protesting their treatment at Gage Park High School, thirty-eight of them were barred from re-entering the school. A delegation of black students sought reinstatement of those barred and a memorial service for Black Panther leader, Fred Hampton, who was slain during a police raid on Panther headquarters. When their demands were refused by administration officials, the black student body staged a sit-in. In response, 750 white students sponsored their own sit-in.

In the spring of 1970 the situation at the school worsened. Fights continued and the buses carrying blacks to Gage Park High School remained a focus of conflict. In March, for example, two Chicago Transit Authority buses carrying ninety-seven students were driven to the Chicago Lawn police station. The students were charged with disorderly conduct after missiles were thrown and obscenities shouted from the buses at 59th and Rockwell.

Besides the growing number of black students attending Gage Park High School, there were additional factors that contributed to the frequency of racial incidents. One factor was the new mood of militancy in the black community. "Black Power" was a recurrent theme in the late 1960s, and urban disorders in cities across the nation dominated the news media in the summer of 1967. The militant mood of the black revolution filtered down to high school students. Whites as well were highly conscious of this development. For example, a spokesman for the Gage Park Civic Association, attending an advisory council meeting in 1968, asserted that white children were attending Gage Park High School in an atmosphere of fear and pointed to statements by black militants that "takeover" was imminent.

Undoubtedly there were also problems present in the school prior to its integration—as indicated by its high dropout rate—that were aggravated by the influx of black students. For example, Gage

Park High School operated on a track system that in essence guaranteed education for the few. The needs of working class youth and "greasers" were ignored in the process. Dropouts felt that to a large extent they were "pushouts." Interestingly, much of the trouble at Gage Park High School was instigated by dropouts and adults loitering around the school. In the opinion of the eighth district police and school officials, "outsiders" who were not a part of the school were responsible for much of the trouble. In November, Hahn and the Chicago Law Police Commander publicly blamed the fighting on "small minorities of whites and blacks spurred by various extremist groups," and later that month Commander O'Connell attributed many of the incidents at the school to juvenile and adult "outsiders" who encouraged students to violence. This frequently repeated theme was true to a certain extent.

However, the outsider theme was also a way of avoiding school responsibility for the incidents. According to the University of Michigan's Mark A. Chesler:

It is comfortable for school officials to blame racial tensions for school outbursts rather than examine the shortcomings of the school program or offering to grant students some of the power and dignity they require. . . .

School people have a self-interest in seeing things racial. . . . That way they don't appear to be at fault. That way they can blame the outside community.[9]

That there were problems inherent in the organization and administration of the school that were not directly related to the integration of the student body is indicated by a report on Gage Park High School released by the state's public education office early in 1973. In that report it was stated that lack of communication between the school system's central office and the Gage Park High School administration hampered operations at the school.

One characteristic of Gage Park High School, and perhaps of the Gage Park community, in dealing with students should be noted— its authoritarianism. In February of 1972, for example, the Gage Park High School Advisory Council opposed a "Student Bill of Rights and Responsibilities" that had been proposed by a Chicago school board member. Irene Shrader, then President of the Gage Park High School PTA, noted that fifteen pages were devoted to student rights, whereas only half a page was concerned with student responsibilities. The council was unanimous that the implementation

9. Henry DeZutter, *Daily News*, November 5, 1969.

of the ideas in this booklet would cause chaos in the schools. Principal Hahn later said that his comments had prompted the council's decision.

This authoritarian attitude toward students was displayed by both the high school administration and the police when dealing with student racial problems. The school frequently responded to disorders with strict disciplinary measures and, in this, was supported by the larger community.

Police tactics, too, were often harsh and demeaning to students. In 1966, when violence occurred at Gage Park High School, the administration and police decided that surprise searches of school lockers should be made and that checks should be run to determine if students were carrying concealed weapons. One of the six policemen assigned to watch Gage Park High School's lunchroom that same year said violence occurred because:

> There's no respect. I got whipped when I was a kid. I've never been sorry for it. It was a doubleheader, I got it at home and in school. Now they'd get a lawsuit if they hit a kid. There's no discipline.[10]

In 1969 when many street fights occurred, complaints were frequent that the police treated black students roughly. Many "police brutality" complaints came during this period from the black community.

In 1972, however, when whites boycotted the school, Ms. Shrader complained of differential police behavior, charging that blacks received more favorable treatment. In part these conflicting perceptions could be a reflection of the fact that whoever is marching or boycotting is more likely to have conflict with the police. In 1969 blacks boycotted, in 1972 the whites.

The police also came under attack for frequent mass arrests and physical and verbal abuse of both blacks and whites. The local newspapers were often filled with pictures of Gage Park High School students being loaded en masse into police paddywagons. Certain incidents, such as the macing in 1969 of a busload of black students, aroused the ire of both the black and the white communities.

Underlying the advent of integration, of course, was the persistent fear of Gage Parkers that a growing black student body would eventually change the racial composition of the community. In 1969, after a fall of racial disruptions, thirty-eight businessmen and businesswomen in the area of West 59th Street met with the executive

10. *Daily News*, February 4, 1966.

members of the Chicago Southwest Property and Homeowners Protective Association to solve the problems of student violence in the area. Disturbances in and around Gage Park High School had forced the stores in the area to close, resulting in a loss of business. Two demands were made by the association: (1) that CTA buses load students on Gage Park High School grounds, and (2) that the high school attendance boundary be shifted east to Ashland Avenue.

For Gage Park's businessmen, particularly, the approach of the black ghetto had grave consequences. As Grossman has noted:

> If the ghetto overtakes him he will be faced with an agonizing choice. Either he can just let go of something he has built up by sheer hard effort, and twelve hour days, or he can learn how to operate it under ghetto conditions. He could call in a contractor to cover his shop windows with protective grating, and hire a guard to stand at its door during business hours.[11]

It is not surprising then that the fight for Gage Park High School came to symbolize the fight for the entire community. As Ms. Proust, president of the Gage Park Civic Association, remarked when interviewed: "as the school goes, so goes the neighborhood."

THE COMMUNITY RESPONSE

Because the initial threat focused on the area's schools, it is not surprising that school organizations were among the first to perceive and respond to the responsibility of racial change. One organization, the Gage Park High School PTA, was extremely important in rallying community support to preserve the status quo. One other school-related organization should be mentioned as well, however, since its very lack of influence is revealing.

The Biracial Parents Committee was formed in 1969 when racial trouble began to escalate. The purpose of the committee was to discuss racial problems with both white and black parents and to advise the principal on appropriate actions. About twelve blacks were invited from a group who had met with Hahn and were from the beginning suspicious of him because he had surreptitiously taped their initial interview. Hahn recruited the twelve white members from a Gage Park Civic Association meeting. Thus, from the beginning, the policy was set of ignoring the large number of white families in the Gage Park school district who lived in the neighboring

11. Grossman, p. 7

communities of Back-of-the-Yards, South Lynne, and Marquette Park.

The Biracial Parents Committee provided advice to the principal and served to channel information from the school administration back to the community. Its members even served in biracial parent patrols in the halls and lunchroom during the months in 1969 when the violence peaked. But although the committee met through 1970, it became inactive in 1971, largely because the black members stopped attending. Blacks felt that information was not always accurately presented to the group by the administration, and they also eventually lost faith in the ability of the group to accomplish anything significant.

An important outgrowth of the Biracial Parents Committee was the Concerned Black Parents of Gage Park, a black parents' group from West Englewood formed by some of the black members of the Biracial Parents Committee. There was a good deal of misunderstanding between white and black parents on the Biracial Parents Committee as to why the new group used the words "of Gage Park" rather than "of Gage Park High School." A leader of the Concerned Black Parents said they chose the name because they were concerned not only with the high school, but also with the community from which most of the problems derived.

In November of 1969, the Concerned Black Parents presented a nine-point statement to the board of education demanding, among other things, fair treatment for both black and white students, special police, the removal of Principal Hahn, a full day of school (black students had been bused home early many times when violence occurred), and investigation of white hate groups' activities in the Gage Park area. Christine Leak became the spokesman for the Concerned Black Parents and presented their viewpoint throughout the 1972 school boycott.

The Gage Park High School PTA was the local Gage Park organization that played the most critical role in responding to the high school's problems. Although the PTA had been dominated by moderates, its relation to black parents has always been one of little or no communication. While a few black parents occasionally attended PTA meetings, no black had ever served on the PTA executive board. In fact, like the Biracial Parents Committee, very few whites who served on the board lived outside the Gage Park neighborhood, thus denying representation to the large number of students from areas other than Gage Park who attended Gage Park High School.

In 1970, following a year of increasing black enrollment and numerous racial incidents, the PTA for the first time called for a boundary change. By 1971, with the election of Irene Shrader as president, a change in the Gage Park High School attendance boundaries had become a priority concern of the PTA. The strategy used by the PTA was to emphasize physical overcrowding in the high school as the major reason for changing the school boundaries. Ms. Shrader tried to avoid the "racist" label by arguing: "some parents feel that students within walking distance of Gage Park are attending other high schools, while other students who attend Gage Park could be better served by uncrowded schools closer to home."

The PTA was not very successful, despite its strategy, in its aim. "Racist" was an adjective that frequently appeared in the press in connection with Gage Park, and it was a charge openly made against the PTA and the community it represented by the South Lynne Community Council, the Concerned Black Parents, Anna Langford (black alderwoman, sixteenth ward), Operation PUSH, and the Chicago Urban League.

The ultimate goal of the PTA was to move Gage Park High School's eastern boundary further west, thereby disinheriting much of the area containing Gage Park High School's black students. Several plans for boundary changes were offered between 1970 and the school boycott of 1972. The eastern boundary shifted between Racine and Hoyne, depending upon the group that proposed it.

A second part of the PTA's plan was the use of underutilized high schools to receive overcrowded Gage Park High School's excess students. The PTA suggested that students removed from the Gage Park High School attendance district by its proposed boundary change be assigned to schools nearby that were operating below capacity. Englewood High School, then operating at 73 percent of its capacity, was often suggested as the school whose empty seats could be filled by Gage Park's disinherited students.

The board of education was, however, reluctant to assent to the Gage Park High School PTA's proposed boundaries. Two considerations governed its decision. The first was the fear, expressed by Julien B. Drayton, the Area B Superintendent, that changing the boundaries in order to remove 660 students (519 of whom were black, 113 white, and 28 Chicano) from Gage Park High School would violate the Armstrong Act, which prohibits moving school boundaries so as to encourage racial segregation. The second consideration that influenced the board of education was the disfavor with which the plan was greeted outside the Gage Park community.

Opposition to the Gage Park High School PTA plan came from Anna Langford, the Concerned Black Parents, the South Lynne

Community Council, the North Englewood Improvement Association, the PTA of Earle Elementary School, and even Father Lawlor (alderman, fifteenth ward). Said Alderwoman Langford, although blacks had requested relief from overcrowding many times, "when we asked, we got 'Willis Wagons.'[12] Isn't it odd that it [boundary change] seems to follow the black people who are moving into the area?" She also contended that racism, not overcrowding, was the reason for the PTA proposal and that Englewood High School (built in 1897) should not be operating at 73 percent capacity but at zero capacity. The Earle PTA President, Darnell Carter, said that the boundary change was proposed because blacks were moving in through the east. Richard Parker, chairman of the South Lynne Community Council, saw the action as "another attempt to exclude black citizenry from a quality education" and, moreover, threatened a lawsuit on the basis of violation of the Armstrong Act if the boundary were moved. Fr. Lawlor, on the other hand, objected to the Gage Park High School plan because he felt the boundary was not far enough west.

According to the board of education, this united protest from Englewood illustrated a lack of community support ("community" defined as Gage Park and West Englewood) for the plan, and the Gage Park High School PTA plan was tabled as a potentially explosive political issue. The board decided that nothing more could be done until the "community" agreed upon a plan.

From the viewpoint of the Gage Park community, a battle that they had been waging since 1970 had been lost. Darrell T. Littrell, a Republican candidate for state senator for the twenty-fifth district, must have articulated what many felt when he said to our interviewer:

> The Chicago Board of Education is once again attempting to fool the people of the Gage Park High School area. . . .
> The justice of the request is apparent when it is realized that Gage Park High School is jammed to overcapacity while at the same time Englewood High School to the east has 600 empty seats. . . .
> The school board's form of blockbusting must end if we are to stabilize our communities.

The Southwest Community Congress, an umbrella group operating in the area, echoed Littrell in the following public statement:

> There seems to be a policy of ignoring only recommendations made by people from our area. It is a copout for the board of education to write

12. Mobile units named after former Chicago Board of Education Superintendent Benjamin F. Willis.

off our solutions as racist and do nothing themselves to resolve our school problems.

After rejecting the Gage Park High School PTA's boundary change proposal, the board of education suggested mobile units to relieve overcrowding at Gage Park High School. The threat of mobile units and double shifts at the school in the 1972–1973 school year united all factions of the white Gage Park community. The Gage Park High School PTA, the Gage Park Civic Association, the Nightingale School PTA, and the Gage Park Little League agreed that the only acceptable relief for overcrowding at Gage Park High School would be through boundary changes. Given West Englewood's unwillingness to agree to the changes, neither side could reach an accord.

In July of 1972, the United Community Organizations of Gage Park planned a mass rally for August to demand a boundary change. Further pressure by Gage Parkers was seen as essential, since no action had been taken by the school board in response to the request for a boundary change. Ms. Shrader urged the community to support the rally because the "future of your home, school, and community is at stake."

In August a general boycott of Gage Park High School was urged at a United Community Organizations-sponsored mass rally attended by 600 persons. Ms. Shrader told the group that the PTA executive board, after exhausting all other approved channels, had decided that sit-ins and mass walkouts were the only answer to overcrowding and boundary problems. She urged all parents to boycott the school when it opened in September.

On September 3, a mass meeting voted to boycott and picket Gage Park High School. The first two days of school, more than 1,000 persons boycotted the Gage Park High School in an action that was to continue for eleven weeks. In its boycott, the Gage Park High School PTA was joined by thirteen other community organizations, the most important of which was the Gage Park Civic Association (GPCA). A militant organization that does not hesitate to take to the street with picket signs, the GPCA considers the board of education its archenemy and believes strict discipline, expulsions, and suspensions will best end fighting in the school.

While the original leadership of the GPCA came from moderates (including PTA leaders), it began almost from the beginning to move toward the right. A local news article in October of 1968 reported a split within the leadership of the GPCA. One group felt that GPCA's purpose was to change the Gage Park High School boundaries to block the entry of blacks, while another group felt that the organization's primary function was to "serve the community."

Robert Erickson, a spokesman for the first faction, said, "You're not going to have a lot to save if you don't do something now."

Each year the GPCA has moved further to the right, and the leadership has led the way. In March of 1972, for example, at a GPCA meeting, a John Birch Society-produced film, "Anarchy—U.S.A.," was presented. Two years earlier, GPCA members had viewed a film called "In the Name of Peace," a documentary that examined the motivations of various groups connected with the peace movement. In 1970 Joe Lodato, then president of GPCA, announced that a mobile parent radio patrol had been active in Gage Park for some time but added, "we don't want to be advertised in the newspapers." In fact, said Lodato, he doubted if even the association's executive board was aware of the patrol until his announcement. In 1972, thirty-five area residents walked past the school to protest the ban on assembling in streets near the school. The "fresh air walks" were organized by S. Thomas Sutton, a Kane County lawyer and head of Operation Crescent, a white segregationist group. Sutton was quoted at one meeting as comparing the Gage Park whites' dispute with the blacks as "a bunch of Scots fighting a tribe of Zulu warriors in Africa—you're different from those people over there!"

In January, GPCA withdrew from the Gage Park coalition because it objected to the coalition's refusal to support the "fresh air walks" and private meetings being held between some coalition members and a group of black parents. However, several days later, the GPCA membership overruled the earlier action by the association's leaders and voted to stay in the United Community Organizations of Gage Park.

The GPCA had early recognized the importance of changing Gage Park High School's attendance boundaries. In March of 1966, GPCA approved a resolution to review the high school boundaries, with a view to placing the western boundary farther west and the eastern line "further west to any unnamed point." The goal of the boundary change was stated as relief of overcrowding.

In 1969, the education chairman of GPCA requested that the board of education restore the eastern boundaries of Gage Park High School to South Ashland Avenue to relieve overcrowding and suggested that some of the vacant seats at Englewood High School be utilized for students removed from the old district.

Several months after this request, GPCA urged concerned residents and parents in the area to stage a white boycott of Gage Park High School and to march en masse on the board of education, protesting racial conflict at school. It again suggested that the older (pre-1965) Gage Park High School boundaries set on the east at Ashland Avenue should be reinstated. The boycott was quite successful—between

300 and 400 persons picketed the board of education, and 44 percent of the students were absent from school.

In 1971 GPCA joined with the PTA to demand a boundary change and in 1972 enthusiastically supported the school boycott.

As the school boycott continued and received increasing publicity, other community groups and individual spokesmen became involved in the conflict. In the Gage Park community itself, the Concerned Clergy of Gage Park was formed with the objective of ending the boycott and protecting the academic standing of the boycotters. Most of the area's politicians, who tended to support the PTA boycott and the demand for a boundary change, at one time or another participated in the dispute, siding with the Gage Park community against the board of education. As early as 1969, Representative "Babe" McAvoy had said, "I am thoroughly convinced that if the blacks at Gage Park High School were removed, there would be no violence and education would again be number one."

During the Gage Park school boycott, several organizations from outside the southwest area became involved in the controversy. Tom Sutton and his Operation Crescent tried to exploit the Gage Park situation by encouraging the right wing factions present in the community. The United Patriots, a militant white youth group whose members wear white berets, participated in and encouraged the physical and verbal abuse of Gage Park High School's black students. Even the Nazi Party held a rally in Gage Park during the height of the turmoil.

Two city organizations entered the Gage Park school dispute. Operation PUSH picketed for a time during the high school boycott and provided aid and support to various West Englewood organizations. Gage Parkers very much resented this interference by a non-local "professional" organization. The Chicago Urban League also entered the dispute when it investigated the events leading up to the boycott and reported in a public study that "racism," not overcrowding, was the actual reason for Gage Park's requested boundary change.

The leadership and organization of the boycott was surprisingly good. Every morning for eleven weeks in the autumn of 1972, women, children, and teenagers, numbering from under a hundred to several thousand, could be seen marching in front of Gage Park High School carrying placards demanding a boundary change. However, when the boycott ended in November, the eastern boundary still remained at Racine. Moreover, the boycott resulted in a lower enrollment that the PTA had projected and weakened its overcrowding argument.

The end of the boycott was followed by a new series of racial incidents marked by attacks on blacks by whites at Gage Park High School. During the third week in November, twenty-five students were arrested because of racially motivated fights around the school. The black students were eventually escorted home on buses as "white berets" pelted them with rocks and bottles. After two days of sporadic violence and more than forty-five arrests, the school was closed.

When Gage Park High School reopened, more than one hundred police had been assigned to patrol both inside and outside the school, and lunch privileges had been canceled. No major incidents occurred until March of 1973, when white students and residents congregated to taunt black students boarding buses for home. Violence erupted, and twenty-six persons were arrested.

CONCLUSION

Put simply, Gage Park's major effort to preserve the status quo, its eleven-week school boycott, was unsuccessful. The boycott actually precipitated a decline of white enrollment.

The failure to achieve the boycott goal and the community's inability to formulate a viable strategy for maintaining its existence in the changing southwest side can be attributed to several factors. First, the boycott strategy was a divisive one that precluded joining forces with West Englewood to achieve some form of compromise. The antagonism between Gage Park and West Englewood engendered by the Gage Park High School PTA boundary plan and boycott made any sort of mutually acceptable plan difficult to achieve. The failure of the two areas to agree also gave the board of education a convenient excuse for tabling the proposed Gage Park High School boundary change plan and withdrawing from the controversy.

Second, the boycott strategy was a single issue battle, a battle that was lost. The inability of the more moderate forces in the community to bring about desired changes opened the way for increased support of individuals and groups who offered more radical solutions.

Finally, Gage Park's location must be considered. It lay directly in the path of Chicago's expanding ghetto. The traits of the community—its aging white, ethnic, working class population consisting largely of owners of moderately priced homes—made it vulnerable to change. The age structure was especially important, making it difficult to attract and retain young families with children. And since holding families with children depends upon the quality of the area's schools, the prognosis for a white Gage Park appeared poor. In too many ways, Gage Park appeared ripe for racial change and likely, therefore, to follow the standard invasion-succession pattern.

Chapter 9

Garfield Ridge and the CHA: Erection of Defensive Barriers

Three miles west of Gage Park, on the western city limits, is Garfield Ridge (Community Area 56; see Figure 1-1). The community[1] is generally bounded by the Stevenson Expressway and Chicago Sanitary and Ship Canal to the north, the tracks of the Belt Railway to the east, Midway Airport and 59th Street to the south, and Harlem Avenue to the west. Small detached frame and brick homes are fronted by carefully tended patches of lawn arranged along clean, tree-lined streets; the quiet and greenery offset the harshness of the gridiron street pattern and imbue the community with a stereotypically suburban atmosphere. Total population in 1970 was 42,984; of this total, 39,298 (91.4 percent were white and 3,386 (8.6 percent were black.[2]

Racial transition in Garfield Ridge has differed from the pattern of expansion into contiguous areas described in the preceding chapters. Located at the outskirts of the city, Garfield Ridge differs from many communities experiencing racial change in that it is a relatively new community, it is far from the central ghetto, and it has housed

1. The designation of Garfield Ridge as a "community" is based largely on its identification as such in the *Community Fact Book, 1960,* Evelyn Kitagawa and Karl E. Taeuber, eds. (Chicago: Chicago Community Inventory, University of Chicago, 1963). Although the *Fact Book* delineation of "communities" has come under considerable criticism, the extent to which the residents of Garfield Ridge exhibit a marked homogeneity of socioeconomic characteristics, share a similar system of values, and profess to perceive their area as a "community" offers significant support to the validity of this designation.

2. These and all subsequent statistics for 1970 are from the U.S. Bureau of the Census, 1970.

both black and white families for a considerable number of years. Black families first moved to Garfield Ridge in the early 1950s as residents of the Chicago Housing Authority's Leclaire Courts public housing project. Typical of what Robert Park referred to as "a mosaic of little worlds which touch but do not interpenetrate,"[3] whites co-existed peacefully with their black neighbors as long as the blacks were confined to the two story row house apartments of Leclaire Courts. White panic and subsequent racial transition began in the decade of the 1970s when black families emerged from the public housing ghetto to purchase homes in the surrounding area.

Despite the apparently atypical manner in which this community was drawn into the confrontation between whites and blacks over housing, it seems to exhibit the full range of problems associated with racial change. The fabric of daily life in the community is influenced by the presence of racial conflict. It would not be an exaggeration to maintain that the future of Garfield Ridge will be determined by the outcome of the racially dominated processes that were being played out in the housing market in the early 1970s.

As late as 1930, much of the area now known as Garfield Ridge was undeveloped prairie and vacant subdivided land. Garfield Ridge began developing as a residential community largely after 1940 and particularly in the post–World War II period. Total population in 1950 was still only 12,858. Between 1950 and 1960 the population more than tripled—to 40,446. In 1960, fully 50.1 percent of residents over five years old were reported to have lived in a different house in the central city of Chicago in 1955.[4] This population growth through inmigration was a response to the general outward expansion of the city and the continuing development of industrial facilities in the area that provided employment for residents. In 1960, almost 70 percent of working males were employed in blue collar occupations. The surrounding industrial areas still provide employment for the bulk of the community's labor force. In addition, it is estimated that some 2,500 to 3,000 city of Chicago policemen and firemen are residents of Garfield Ridge.[5]

Today it is a quiet community of working families who own the homes they live in. Most residents work nearby, and shopping facilities on main streets and a small neighborhood shopping center within the community are adequate for day-to-day needs. Residents describe

3. Robert E. Park, "The City: Suggestions for the Investigation of Human Behavior in the Urban Environment," in Park, *Human Communities: The City and Human Ecology* (New York: Free Press, 1952), p. 47.
4. U.S. Bureau of the Census.
5. Information from neighborhood respondents.

the elementary schools and the high school as among the best in the city. Churches play an important role in this 90-95 percent Catholic community, providing an element of neighborhood cohesion and a meeting place for social affairs and community activities. The ethnic composition of the community is predominantly Polish, Italian, and other Eastern European; residents claim, however, that compared to many other Chicago communities, ethnic loyalties are minimal, that differences among ethnic groups have disappeared, and that the various nationalities have "blended."

There was a rapid overall increase in population in the 1950-1960 period as new families moved to the community. The decade of the 1960s was marked by a general aging of the population and a concomitant loss of the very young and those in the family-forming years, however.

Median family income in 1960 was $7,896. The figure for 1970 had risen to $12,603, which is slightly higher than the $10,242 median for the city of Chicago. Interestingly, residents estimate family income for the community in 1970 to range from $8,000 to $20,000, with a median income around $13,500. This suggests that residents have a positive image of the community, perceiving it to be slightly better off than the objective facts would warrant.

In 1970, 83 percent of all housing units were single family units, 81 percent of occupied units were owner occupied, and the mean value of all owner-occupied units was $22,800. This is slightly higher than the $21,200 median value of owner-occupied units for the city of Chicago as a whole. In 1960, only sixteen owner-occupied units (0.002 percent of all such units) were occupied by nonwhites. By 1970, this figure had increased to 126 owner-occupied units (0.13 percent of all such units). Although the 1960-1970 decade saw the greatest increase in homeownership by black families, blacks had been resident in Garfield Ridge for a considerably longer period of time and in some cases antedated the development of much of the area for white occupancy.

INITIAL PERCEPTION OF
COMMUNITY CHANGE

The first black families came to Garfield Ridge in 1950 when the Chicago Housing Authority completed construction of Leclaire Courts, a low income public housing project financed by city and state funds. The 315 one to four bedroom units were arranged in two story row houses located on vacant land in the northeastern corner of Garfield Ridge. At the time of construction, the area surrounding the project was still vacant, since most of the private residential development was taking place in the western section of the community. In 1951, 276 (88 percent of the families in Leclaire Courts were white and 39 (12 percent were black.[6] In 1954, federal funds financed the construction of 300 additional units directly adjacent to the original project and similar in design. With tne opening of Leclaire extension, of the 600 units rented in 1954, 467 (78 percent were occupied by white families and 133 (22 percent) by black families.[7]

The site chosen for the Leclaire project was far from an ideal residential location and was a product of the racially dominated site selection controversy that clouded the public housing issue throughout the history of the program.[8] A report on potential sites by the Chicago Plan Commission to the Chicago City Council describes the site proposed for Leclaire extension is less than glowing terms:

> To the north across the railroad are extensive refuse dumps, chemical industries, oil terminals, tank farms, and the Sanitary and Ship Canal. To the northeast is Leclaire Courts, a relocation housing project (316 dwelling units) now in construction by the CHA (residential density: 9½ units per gross acre). The balance of the area to the east and directly south is vacant land, being built up with single-family homes. The Chicago Midway Airport is 1½ miles south of the subject site. To the west across the city limits are vacant lands (in Stickney Township), and further southwest, extensive railroad yards.[9]

Despite the seeming inutility of the site for most purposes, there appears to have been substantial opposition in the community to construction of the public housing project. As is still the case today, racial antipathy dominated the site selection controversy; in the public mind, public housing was synonymous with blacks, and whites did not want blacks in the community, no matter how marginal the location. According to Meyerson and Banfield, the alderman at the time (Tourek) claimed to object to the project on the grounds that a number of veterans living in trailer camps in the ward would be ineligible for housing in the project. The *Chicago Sun-Times*, editorializing in favor of public housing, took issue with this objection, asking: "What's your real reason for objecting to construction of a

6. Chicago Housing Authority, *Annual Report,* 1951.
7. Ibid., 1954.
8. For a detailed discussion, see Martin Meyerson and Edward Banfield, *Politics, Planning and the Public Interest* (Glencoe, Ill.: Free Press, (1955); and Harold M. Baron, *Building Babylon* (Evanston, Ill.: Northwestern University, Center for Urban Affairs, 1971).
9. Chicago Plan Commission, *City Planning Report on 15 Suggested Public Housing Sites* (Chicago, 1950).

housing project in a sparsely populated area that private enterprise isn't the least bit interested in developing?"[10] Tourek subsequently voted against the project in the city council, "because the people in the ward do not want it." However, he later noted that "I was able to get it cut down in size, but not to stop it."[11]

Black residents of Leclaire Courts were in the minority for the first five years after the project opened for occupancy in 1950. By 1956, half of the families resident in the project were black.

Significantly, the privately developed white residential area adjacent to the project was built up subsequent to the opening of Leclaire Courts and at a time when the racial composition of the project had dramatically shifted to a black majority. As reported in a newspaper account: "By 1957, when much of the neighborhood housing was going in, Leclaire Courts was 62 percent black."[12] Data arranged by census tract indicate the high proportion of housing units built since 1950 in the tracts closest to Leclaire Courts. In the tract within which the project is located (5602), 98.5 percent of all housing units in 1960 were built since 1950; the mean for the three adjacent tracts is 92.6 percent and the mean for the remainder of tracts in the community area is 54.1 percent.[13] In other words, at the same time that the population in Leclaire Courts was rapidly turning all black, the surrounding residential area was being developed with single family homes that contained a population that was all white. The evidence seems to suggest that the presence of an increasingly black public housing population was not a deterrent to the rapid development of the area as housing for whites.

The explanation for the complete racial turnover in Leclaire Courts is not immediately evident. Original city council approval of construction of public housing on the site rested on the imposition of a quota system restricting the black population of projects in white areas to 10 percent.[14] This quota system allegedly developed as a

10. *Chicago Sun-Times*, August 4, 1950, quoted by Meyerson and Banfield, p. 337.
11. *Chicago Tribune*, November 1, 1970.
12. Ibid.
13. *Community Fact Book*, p. 127
14. Baron reports (p. 50):

Mayor Kennelly and the key leaders of the Chicago City Council . . . did not find these [vacant land] sites acceptable. From an economic angle they wanted to preserve for private development vacant sites on which a profit could be made. From a racial angle they sought to maintain the lily-whiteness of their wards. A period of over half a year was taken up in negotiating a compromise package . . . . The aldermen for these wards assented to project locations only on the basis of an understanding with the Chairman of CHA that there would be a 10 per cent quota on blacks in the white areas. P. 50.

compromise measure to achieve approval of the vacant land sites in outlying areas and was consonant with official CHA philosophy designed to maintain a biracial population in the projects. In 1954, however, after construction of Leclaire Courts was completed, the leadership of CHA changed hands, and the new executive director reportedly abolished the quota system in an attempt to eliminate vacancies.[15] CHA documents, however, indicate that of Chicago's five other projects in all white areas, one, in Mayor Daley's home community of Bridgeport, has maintained a 100 percent white population since initial occupancy in 1943, one has been 100 percent black, and three others have maintained a black population of 15 percent throughout their thirty of more years of occupancy. Clearly, CHA has maintained a racial quota in all its projects in white neighborhoods except for Leclaire Courts. The reason for this exception, however, is not easily forthcoming. A plausible explanation, although admittedly highly conjectural, can be suggested. Altgeld Gardens, located on Chicago's far southern boundary, was designed and built as relocation housing for blacks displaced by slum clearance in the inner city; it was intended for entirely black occupancy from its inception and was located in an undeveloped area still within city limits but as far removed from the center of the city as possible. The political rationale for Bridgeport Home's white occupancy is self-explanatory. Of the other projects, all but Leclaire experienced extensive racial turmoil when the first black families moved in. The white reaction to integration at Trumbull Park was particularly violent. It is conceivable that CHA imposed and maintained a 15 percent quota in these projects to forestall or minimize the likelihood of continued or renewed racial violence in these neighborhoods. Only the unusual circumstances under which Leclaire Courts was constructed and the surrounding area subsequently settled explain the absence of conflict between the black public housing tenants and the surrounding community.

The period in the late 1950s during which the eastern portion of Garfield Ridge was developed comprised years characterized by both high demand for and rapid construction of housing. The single family detached bungalows built in the area were sold rapidly with VA financing, and the presence of nearby Leclaire Courts was not a deterrent to buying.[16] The extreme physical isolation of Leclaire Courts must provide at least partial explanation for this latter fact, and iso-

15. Harry Schaffner, Public Information Department, Chicago Housing Authority, personal interview, May 4, 1972.
16. Information from neighborhood informants.

lation of the public housing site is intensified by the combined impact on the city limits, major thoroughfares, and surrounding land uses.

To the north and west, access and contact are terminated by the impassable barriers of railroad tracks, a six lane expressway, the Sanitary and Ship Canal, and a vast industrial area devoted to truck terminals, warehousing, and manufacturing. To the east, Leclaire is bounded by the six lanes of Cicero Avenue, which carries extremely heavy automobile and truck traffic to and from the expressway interchange immediately to the north; the area east of Cicero Avenue is marked by vacant lots, abandoned structures, substandard housing, and industrial uses. Current plans for construction of the Crosstown Expressway along Cicero Avenue would serve to isolate the area still further. It can easily be seen, then, that Leclaire Courts is physically extremely isolated from the remainder of Garfield Ridge. Physical isolation permitted and fostered social isolation. A local newspaper reports that "it is doubtful that black residents of Leclaire Courts and neighboring streets consider themselves as living in an integrated community."[17] The present ward committeeman (and former alderman) has flatly stated:

> They [the CHA] set up a naturally segregated area by their action. Even the whites who lived there did not share the social mores of their middle class neighbors. They were isolated, and the blacks are even more so isolated. They find it hard to become a part of the community.[18]

A SECOND PHASE: 1968 AND AFTER

The physical isolation of Leclaire Courts is such that it is only to the south that residents in the project have contact with the rest of Garfield Ridge. In 1968, black families began moving out of Leclaire Courts and buying homes in the blocks directly adjacent to the project to the south. The events associated with the movement of black families out of the isolation of Leclaire Courts and into the community have forced the residents of Garfield Ridge, both black and white, to confront the problems of racial change and racial competition for housing that are the product of the dual housing market and the American social system.

As black families began moving out of Leclaire and buying homes in Garfield Ridge and others took their places in the project, the total

17. *Southwest News-Herald*, October 28, 1971, p. 1.
18. *Chicago Tribune*, November 1, 1970.

black population of the community increased dramatically. Between 1960 and 1970, while the white population of the community increased by 4.3 percent, the black population increased by 32.9 percent. With the exception of a few families moving into the poor housing east of Cicero Avenue, the black population is concentrated in the census tract (5602) that includes Leclaire Courts and several square blocks of adjacent housing.[19] Within tract 5602 the black population increased from 52.3 percent of the total population in 1960 to 65.1 percent in 1970.[20] The proportion continued to increase thereafter as most of the homes adjacent to Leclaire north of the 47th Street boundary of the census tract were bought by black families. The magnitude of population change is such that between 1960 and 1970 the white population decreased by 580, a loss of 23.4 percent, while the black population increased by 827, a gain of 30.4 percent.[21] This racial turnover was entirely restricted to tract 5602 containing Leclaire Courts. The discrepancy of 247 individuals reflects the larger size of the black families who replaced the departing whites.

It should be recalled that the white population leaving tract 5602 between 1960 and 1970 had just arrived during the previous decade. When Leclaire Courts was initially occupied in 1950 and 1954, the surrounding area was vacant land; the white families who left in the 1960s were themselves relatively recent arrivals. The possibility exists that the area experienced a very high rate of turnover throughout the period; this would only serve to accentuate the brevity of white occupancy of the transition area. The recency of development of the entire area is reflected in the very high increase in white population throughout the area from 1950 to 1960. The only exceptions are the tracts immediately adjacent to Midway Airport (5605 and 5606) that were presumably developed in conjunction with airport-related activity.

The first black families to move out of the project and to buy homes in the community were generally upwardly mobile, older, and politically moderate and tended to have been long-term stable residents of Leclaire Courts. These black families were prompted to move out of Leclaire Courts by what they perceived to be drastic changes in the characteristics of more recent arrivals in Leclaire. Residents maintain that following the assassination of the Reverend Dr. Martin Luther King, Jr., and the subsequent passage of the Housing Act of 1968, the Chicago Housing Authority changed its selection

19. Information from neighborhood informants.
20. U.S. Bureau of the Census.
21. U.S. Bureau of the Census.

process for screening prospective tenants for public housing. Black respondents report that the change in CHA's screening of applicants eliminated questions relating to attitudes and behavior and admitted tenants on the basis of income criteria only.

Historically, Leclaire Courts has been a preferred location for public housing tenants, due to its distance from the inner city ghetto, proximity to blue collar employment, and low rise, garden apartment type design. With the reported change in CHA's screening procedures, however, incoming tenants began to differ substantially from longer term residents. The black families who moved out of Leclaire Courts into the community say that they were prompted to move because of this alleged change in the "type" of tenants living in the project. More recent tenants were considered to be transient types, uninterested in Leclaire as a permanent place to live. Thefts were said to increase within the project, maintenance and garbage removal became problematic, and life in the project began to take on the atmosphere of the slum ghetto that Leclaire's earlier residents had tried to escape. Ironically, the complaints, usually voiced by whites unwilling to live in proximity to blacks—complaints relating to safety, property maintenance, atmosphere, life style—were being voiced by the upwardly mobile black population of Leclaire Courts who were unwilling to live with the new type of "Westside ghetto"—namely, poorer—tenants coming into the project.

New black homeowners in Garfield Ridge maintain that homes became available when whites began moving out because they objected to the growing black pedestrian traffic through the area. As the black population of Leclaire Courts neared 100 percent, they say, black children going to school and others using shops and transportation facilities on 47th Street became increasingly visible to the white homeowners south of Leclaire. Significantly, they tend to deny any awareness of undue conflict accompanying the process of racial transition.

THE NATURE OF THE RESPONSE

Reflecting conflicting group perceptions of the situation, the description of the course of racial change offered by white residents of the community differs in important respects from that reported by black residents. James T. Heffernan, white president of the Midway Organization, a moderate, integrationist citizen's action group, stated in an interview that the initial white reaction to the first few black families to move from the project and buy homes in the community was positive. These first black families were perceived as older, politically moderate, and upwardly mobile as compared to the newer, more militant, and more aggressive residents then coming to Leclaire. The stated intention of the white Garfield Ridge Civic League was to "make it [integration] work." These initial attempts to cope with the problem peacefully, however, were thwarted by white panic and flight instigated by real estate agents from outside the community. Although respondents among the black homeowners deny knowledge of blockbusting or panic peddling in the area, the present white residents of Garfield Ridge blame these outside real estate agents for the panic of the white residents who fled. Agents reportedly distributed leaflets, solicited door to door, and warned white residents of a coming black "takeover" and of falling property values. Local realtors refused to deal with properties in the area; if asked to list a house for sale, they reportedly claimed that they did not handle properties in the area (north of 47th Street) or gave the listing to a black broker.[22]

The unwillingness of local white real estate agents to deal in the area north of 47th Street reflects a more general policy of isolation of the black population in Garfield Ridge. Whites have established the barrier between white and black residential areas at 47th Street; the area to the north of this dividing line has been abandoned by the white community. Whites no longer patronize stores north of the line. Bus drivers on Cicero Avenue are reported to occasionally fail to stop for passengers waiting between 43rd and 47th Streets.

In 1970, the ward boundary was redrawn at 47th Street; this had the effect of removing the area north of 47th Street from the twenty-third ward, to which it is contiguous, and annexing it to the twelfth ward, from which it is separated by a vast expanse of railroad yards and industrial facilities. This change was made despite the fact that Leclaire was considered a traditionally heavily Democratic area and redistricting meant the loss of some ten "sure" precincts for the twenty-third ward Democratic organization.

In line with the above attempts to isolate the black population, school district lines also were redrawn to add further to de facto segregation. As in most communities experiencing racial change, the schools became a major arena of confrontation between blacks and whites in Garfield Ridge. Hearst elementary school, which draws students from Leclaire Courts and the surrounding blocks, became increasingly more segregated over the past decade. This in part reflects the growth of the black population within Leclaire Courts itself and also reflects the continuing racial turnover in private homes

22. Information from neighborhood respondents.

in the Hearst school area. In the summer of 1971, the boundaries for Hearst school were redrawn to conform with the racial distribution of the population, thus assuring the complete segregation of Hearst school. The decision to make 47th Street the dividing line between whites and blacks is evident from the fact that the school district line was moved only one block, from 48th to 47th Street. In arguing for the redistricting before the board of education, white parents claimed that their request was prompted by heavy truck traffic on 47th Street, which posed a danger to school children having to cross the street on their way to school. It is significant, however, that this danger only became manifest when the area north of 47th Street was experiencing racial change and the proportion of black students in Hearst school had reached a very high level.

Interestingly, conditions in Hearst school have been used as an organizing issue by black community leaders as well as by segregationist white organizations. Earl Alberts, black president of the Hearst Education Council, reported in an interview that in 1972 Hearst school was 800 students over capacity and that while 95 percent of the students were black, 95 percent of the teachers were white. The quality of education at the school is said to have declined considerably in recent years: while good teachers were said to be on waiting lists for assignment to Hearst school a few years ago, the turnover rate among teachers now is very high, and many substitutes are used. Alberts has expended considerable energy attempting to organize the black population in Garfield Ridge around these issues. Ironically, he has been able to use white fear of black expansion as a tool for improving facilities at Hearst. When Hearst requested portable classrooms from the board of education to ease overcrowding, Alberts wrote to the other (all white) schools in the district asking their support for the request. With the realization that continued overcrowding at Hearst might cause the reassignment and dispersion of black students throughout the district, all the schools in the district supported Hearst's request for additional classrooms.

Other ironies pervaded the educational facilities of Garfield Ridge. While parochial schools have frequently provided white parents in other communities with an alternative to integrated public schools, the reverse seems to be the case in Garfield Ridge. Black families both inside and outside Leclaire Courts joined Our Lady of Snows parish on 49th Street in order to provide quality education for their children and to avoid the poor conditions at Hearst school. Our Lady of Snows parochial elementary school became approximately evenly divided among white and black students; then, white families began removing their children from integrated Our Lady of Snows school and enrolling them in Mark Twain school, a public, but still segregated, elementary school on 51st Street. The white community was adamant in its policy of "containing" the black population north of 47th Street. James Heffernan reported in an interview that whites would react with panic if black students were to begin utilizing any of the other elementary schools in the area.

The problems stemming from white policy in regard to elementary education served to magnify the problem at the high school level. The overcrowding and poor quality of education received by black students at Hearst school forces them into remedial classes in Kennedy High School, with the resulting stigmatization and lack of competitiveness with white students. While the number of black students at Kennedy increased slowly, they still constituted a very small minority of the student body by the mid-1970s.

White students at Kennedy remained a decidedly hostile majority. A black respondent reported that his children have to "run for the bus" at the end of the school day and are afraid to stay after school to participate in extracurricular activities. On April 6, 1972, 250 black students left the school when white students massed to attack blacks in retaliation for a fight between a black and a white student. Continuing clashes between whites and blacks led to the suspension of twenty students on April 12. A local newspaper reported that "many of the black students are afraid to stay around after school."[23]

White reaction to the racial clashes at Kennedy was mixed. A small number of both blacks and whites seized upon the issue as a possible organizing tool for bringing whites and blacks together; Kennedy High School was one of the few community institutions where blacks and whites could interact on the basis of common interest. The interracial Kennedy Parent's Council was formed following the disturbances in April, and for a brief period blacks and whites cooperated in patrolling the halls at Kennedy in an attempt to ward off further clashes. Formed as it was in response to a specific incident, however, the parent's council was unable to develop a long-range program and soon became ineffectual. In general, the white students' expression of hostility reflected the attitudes of their parents. Many white parents in Garfield Ridge felt that school integration was synonymous with poorer education and were therefore extremely hostile to the black students at Kennedy, whom they viewed as detrimental to their children's education.

23. *Southwest News-Herald*, April 13, 1972.

ATTITUDES TOWARD INTEGRATION

The population of Garfield Ridge divided into several clearly identifiable groups delineated solely in terms of their placement in the
racial confrontation over territory. These include:

1. The all black population in Leclaire Courts;
2. The all black population of homeowners in the area north of 47th
   Street;
3. The all white population of Vittum Park, the neighborhood just
   south of 47th Street; and
4. The all white population in the rest of Garfield Ridge.

These groups are identified as such by neighborhood residents, both
black and white, and discussion of racial problems in Garfield Ridge
is invariably phrased in terms of these four groups.

Whites in Garfield Ridge distinguish between the blacks in Leclaire
Courts and black homeowners in terms of the immediacy of the
threat posed by each of these groups to the white community rather
than in terms of differences in characteristics within the black population. In spite of significant differences in income, occupational
characteristics, and attitudes within the black community, whites in
general in Garfield Ridge tend to view all blacks as poor and as a
threat to their community. In May 1972, a coalition of white civic
organizations, aiming to keep blacks out of the southwest side area
that includes Garfield Ridge, filed a class action suite in federal district court in opposition to construction of proposed scatter site public housing in the area. Included among the plaintiffs in the suit were
the Garfield Ridge Beautification Commission and the Garfield Ridge
Council of Organizations. A local newspaper account summarized the
argument presented to the court:

> The suit ". . . alleges that differences in life-style between the middle-class
> residents of the neighborhoods where the housing is proposed and the low-
> income families which would occupy the housing would cause significant
> deterioration in property maintenance and in increased crime rates in those
> neighborhoods."
>
> Compared to the class of people filing the suit, low-income family mem-
> bers as a whole " . . . possess a higher propensity toward criminal behavior
> and acts of violence than do the social classes of the plaintiffs," the suit
> states.
>
> "As compared to the social class characteristics of the plaintiffs, such

low-income family members possess a disregard for physical and aesthetic maintenance of real and personal property which is in direct contrast to the high level of care with which the plaintiffs' social classes treat their property," the suit adds.

Further, the suit states, "Low-income family members possess a lower commitment to hard work for future-oriented goals with little or no immediate reward than do the social classes of the plaintiffs."

Largely as a result of these "social class characteristics," the suit states, the neighborhoods where low-income families reside "as a statistical whole possess higher levels of physical violence, as well as physically and aesthetically dilapidated housing structures, while "the neighborhoods where the plaintiffs reside possess physically and aesthetically well-maintained housing structures, as well as much lower crime rates and levels of physical violence."[24]

In spite of this stereotyped view of all blacks as poor, violent, and a threat to their community, the black population of Garfield Ridge was in fact far from monolithic. The black population in "the Courts" continued to bear the same marginal relationship to the remainder of Garfield Ridge that it has throughout the existence of the project. As suggested above, planned construction of the Crosstown Expressway along Cicero Avenue was likely to isolate project residents even more than is now the case. Leclaire Courts, despite its location in a white middle class neighborhood rather than in the ghetto, despite its two story rather than high rise construction, and despite its reputed attractions for public housing tenants, still engender the same reaction from its tenants as had been voiced by residents of public housing throughout the country. Isolation, alienation, regimentation, stigmatization, and the absence of motivation—these terms aptly summarize residents' descriptions of life in public housing. All changes in family income must be reported to the project management; this includes income from children's part-time jobs. Residents expect that if they fail to report changes in income themselves, their neighbors will. One resident's attempt at gardening was thwarted by neighbors' thefts and opposition from project management; some plants were destroyed by project maintenance men. Interior design and construction of project apartments is such that annoyances are commonplace: storage space is nonexistent; instead of sliding vertically, windows open outward letting in rain and snow; the only electric outlet in the kitchen is behind the refrigerator; and so forth. Life in public housing is excessively regimented; the project management tells residents "how to live" and what they "better not

24. *Southwest News-Herald*, May 18, 1972.

do." Regulations instill the notion that "nothing is mine"; pride of ownership is absent. In the words of a former resident, "Anything is better than the project."

The blacks in Leclaire refer to the area to the south of the project as "the homes." To the former Leclaire residents who have bought houses in the area, the homes are considered to be a great improvement over the courts. Many of the families who moved from the courts to the homes had tried previously but without success to find adequate housing elsewhere in the private housing market. Racial restrictions prevented access to other than substandard housing or housing at exhorbitant rental levels. It is likely that public housing in many cities contains a sizable population that would prefer to live in decent private housing if it were available to them at a reasonable rent.

The response of black families in the homes to the question, What are the three or four most important reasons why people like living in this neighborhood? was enlightening. Low population density— that is, lack of crowding—the presence of trees, grass, and flower gardens; and garage space for cars (cars parked on the street in the courts were said to be "sitting ducks" for vandals and thieves) were mentioned as important attributes of the neighborhood. The point most stressed, however, was that living in the neighborhood provided the opportunity of owning one's own home. Homeownership, especially in the near suburban atmosphere of Garfield Ridge, is clearly the antithesis of life in public housing. The emphasis placed on home improvements and maintenance is readily apparent. The condition of lawns and gardens and the general outward appearance of property is clearly a significant concern of residents of the homes. Considerable amounts of money have been spent on landscaping and maintenance. Lawn competitions are held among neighbors and within block clubs; some block clubs have specified days on which their members are to mow their lawns. One resident described this concern on the part of his neighbors as an overreaction to the white stereotype of neighborhood deterioration following black occupancy. Excessive concern for the outward appearance of homes may, indeed, reflect a concerted effort to demonstrate the inaccuracy of white stereotypes. An additional factor may be the newness of the homeowning experience for these long-time residents of public housing.

When asked to discuss what they considered to be the major problems in the neighborhood, black homeowners expressed concern about the behavior and appearance of the new tenants in Leclaire Courts. They feared that what they considered to be improper behavior on the part of some blacks—namely, loitering near neighborhood liquor stores, gambling in public view, and so forth—would reflect poorly on them and detract from what status gains they had achieved as a result of the move out of public housing into the homes. Significantly, black respondents in the homes consistently failed to mention any of the factors such as transportation and taxes that white residents of Garfield Ridge listed as problems with the neighborhood. Compared both to Leclaire Courts and to any alternatives available elsewhere, the homes provided an almost unhoped for measure of status and security. The black respondents expressed a certain amount of bitterness, however, in their inability to escape the stereotype of inferiority that is imputed to them because of race. In addition, they felt that they might never be able to escape from racial tensions and confrontations. Their move from Leclaire and the ghetto was designed to remove them from racial problems and from the problems of the low income black population; this had clearly been denied them as racial tensions in Garfield Ridge became intense.

Further, the white antipathy demonstrated the fact that homeownership had not brought them status equalization with their white neighbors. Rather than being granted the status recognition that they felt should be associated with ownership of a home, the black families in the homes experienced the results of white society's efforts to isolate the black community—homeowners and public housing tenants alike—in a physical, social, political, and institutional ghetto.

In spite of these considerable differences in the problems, perceptions, and aspirations present within the black population of Garfield Ridge, white residents reacted as though faced with a monolithic threat to the character and stability of their community. To black residents, the neighborhood south of 47th Street, known as Vittum Park, was a hostile area. A black respondent reported that the community is like a tinder box. A white resident similarly described the area as "a bomb about to explode." The white residents of Vittum Park organized themselves into the Vittum Park Civic League with the primary objective of preventing racial turnover in the area. Located immediately adjacent to the black residential area north of the 47th Street barrier, residents of Vittum Park felt themselves to be the most threatened by the expansion of the black population. They organized street patrols to guard against outside blockbusters soliciting in the neighborhood and to safeguard themselves from what they perceived as a threat of crime and violence from the black community. Meetings of the Vittum Park Civic League were closed to nonresidents and the press. Emotions at meetings ran high, and several meetings ended in disorder when residents disagreed over policy or methods. All homes that came up for sale in the Vittum

Park area were listed with the civic league and not advertised through normal real estate channels. White respondents outside of Vittum Park estimated that up to a hundred homes in the area were up for sale due to normal causes—for example, job transfers, growing families, and so forth—but suggested that the civic league was unable to find buyers. These respondents expected "the bomb to explode" imminently.

The white residents in the rest of the community took a wait and see attitude. Located at somewhat of a distance from the black concentration in Leclaire Courts and the homes, they felt less threatened by immediate racial transition. Racial tensions, however, remained high. The continuing controversy over scatter site public housing kept the issue of race and housing alive throughout the community. An unofficial public hearing organized by local political candidates held in June 1972 attracted 800 residents opposed to construction of scattered single unit public housing in the community. A sample of the statements made is instructive:

> These liberals come on with these beautiful programs that are going to integrate us. . . . How are you going to integrate when they just inundate us . . . . Their kids got better bikes than we got. Why? They come across 47th Street and steal them.[25]
>
> I'm against CHA housing because I simply have no where else to run. I came from an integrated community.[26]
>
> If this CHA housing comes in, the people in this room within five years will be gone, but people like me who just bought a home will have to stay.[27]
>
> I was pushed out one before; I'll be damned if I'll be pushed out again.[28]
>
> I want the privilege of living in an all white neighborhood.[29]

Opposition to scatter site public housing is only one of the areas in which white antipathy to racial integration has become manifest. Maintaining the racial homogeneity of the community is clearly an overriding consideration for the white residents of Garfield Ridge. In October 1971, the Common Counsel of Participating Organizations, an umbrella group of southwest side civic associations including representatives from Garfield Ridge, passed a resolution opposing the pro-

25. Mrs. Phyllis Rogers, reported in the *Chicago Sun-Times*, June 6, 1973.

26. Unidentified resident, reported in the *Southtown Economist*, June 7, 1972.

27. Mrs. Beverly Atton, reported in the *Southtown Economist*, June 7, 1972.

28. Vincent Teresi, reported in the *Southwest News-Herald*, June 8, 1972.

29. Mrs. Dorothy Lupinski, reported in the *Southwest News-Herald*, June 8, 1972.

posed city ordinance banning "For Sale" and "Sold" signs on houses. According to a newspaper account:

> The resolution . . . charged that the ordinance would "give people a mandate to sneak out into the night, leaving their neighbors high and dry."
> The signs were defended as a means for community organizations to keep watch on mobility in the neighborhoods and investigate why people are moving, as an indication of what real estate dealers are operating in a neighborhood, and as a "possible check on sales to blacks."[30]

Community paranoia over racial change is such that residents feel the need to institutionalize mechanisms for keeping watch over one another lest someone burst the dam by "selling out" to a black family.

CONCLUSION

In describing the attributes of the neighborhood—what they liked best about living there—white residents mentioned its peacefulness, quiet, and neat appearance and stressed the common backgrounds and shared values of their neighbors. The threat of racial change was viewed by whites as a threat to these community attributes and presented the potential of complete disruption of community life. The white residents of Garfield Ridge shared close ties to the community and were vehemently concerned with protecting neighborhood status. They felt that they had "made it," that Garfield Ridge was a community that satisfied their status aspirations, at least for the present. Many of them had moved away from changing neighborhoods at least once before and echoed the sentiments of the resident who publicly declared that he would "be damned if I'll be pushed out again." Integration, to most white residents of Garfield Ridge, was a term completely devoid of the positive connotation given it by liberal intellectuals.

The competition between the races in Garfield Ridge was clearly defined in terms of territory. As suggested earlier, the future of the community is described in terms of the racial characteristics of its population; the determinant of its character will be the pattern of distribution of whites and blacks and the manner in which it is achieved. Because of the absolute refusal of whites to share residential space with blacks, white residents continued to leave Garfield Ridge in step with the continuing arrival of black families. Because

30. *Southwest News-Herald*, June 8, 1972.

of the backlog of fear and antipathy, even a small infusion of black families on an all white block resulted in the rapid evacuation of the area by whites. Thus, while the eventual transition of the community depends on the rate of growth of the black population, only a small increase in the number of blacks appears sufficient to place the entire area within the boundaries of the black housing market. The vehemence of white opposition ironically has served to speed transition in the area.

Chapter 10

Beverly Hills–Morgan Parks: BAPA's Language of Political Power

Other communities along the western city limits also experienced rising racial tensions as the 1960s drew to a close, among them Beverly Hills and Morgan Park on the city's southwest side (Community Areas 72 and 75; see Figure 1-1). Early growth in the area, which includes within their boundaries some of the most elevated land in the city—a zone about six miles long and two miles wide rising forty feet above the marshy Chicago plain to the east—was due to the location of several educational institutions there and the fact that the Rock Island Railroad provided convenient transportation to the Loop for professional and business men who wanted to live in the "Suburb in the City." Elegant homes were built along "the ridge," while to "the valley" areas of eastern Morgan Park came house servants and railroad workers. There too, a black enclave of stucco and frame houses developed. This enclave, extending from 107th to 119th streets east of Vincennes Avenue, grew to make up 35 percent of Morgan Park's population in 1930.

In 1970 Beverly Hills was a solidly upper middle class community, with the second highest median income level and percentage of professional workers in Chicago and the third highest educational level; its 27,000 people were virtually all white, two-thirds were white collar employees, over 70 percent were of heavily Catholic Irish or Swedish extraction (the two largest Catholic parishes were probably the most powerful in the city), and reflecting the high degree of homeownership, the residential mobility rate was among the lowest in Chicago and the median age of the population among the highest. With curving tree-lined streets and carefully tended lawns, such diversity as existed was between the large solid pre-1930s homes of Dutch, English, or Colonial style—each different from its neighbor— and the postwar Georgian or contemporary style developments of nearly uniform size and value along the western side of the ridge, culminating in the newest, smaller, more boxlike houses in the south-western corner of the area.

Morgan Park was more diverse. In the west, it shared "ridge" characteristics with Beverly Hills, but further east were the less ex-pensive frame and stucco homes of the valley, generally well pre-served but occasionally run down. In 1970 Morgan Park ranked twenty-second among Chicago's seventy-five community areas in socioeconomic status, and only 40 percent of its workers were em-ployed in white collar occupations. Mobility rates were higher, in-comes and educational levels lower. Fifty-six percent of its 30,000 people were black.

Beverly Hills–Morgan Park residents were politically conservative, but not necessarily Republican. The nineteenth ward had consis-tently sent a Democratic alderman to city hall, always an inhabitant of Beverly, although the ward covers much more territory than that. However, in national elections BH-MP had always voted Republican, except in 1960 when it gave John F. Kennedy a majority.

The distinctiveness of the ridge has brought about an equally dis-tinctive sense of community. BH-MP families, some second and third generation residents, appreciate the community's amenities—thirty minutes commuting time to the Loop; the individuality of the houses, priced lower than comparable suburban homes; the magnificent trees; and extensive shopping facilities along 95th Street and in Ever-green Plaza Shopping Center. Recreational facilities include three major parks, the private Beverly Tennis Club, and three country clubs. Cultural activities are provided by the community-built million dollar Beverly Art Center, which houses the major portion of the John H. Vanderpoel Memorial Collection of twentieth century art. One artist in the area summed up the feeling:

Our sense of history doesn't pull the community down to a sleepy village more interested in the past. It makes us alive in the contemporary sense. This is an age when people are looking back to find their roots, and a new community has no roots. BH-MP is like a small town in a big city, where people are of sufficient means and educational level to take an avid interest in their community. The average resident thinks his community is something very special in its better-than-usual communication between residents who all know that their community has a good thing going. Its citizens think of themselves first as from BH-MP and then from Chicago, with many wishing they could forget about the existence of the rest of the city.[1]

PERCEPTIONS OF COMMUNITY CHANGE

It was this distinctive sense of community that was threatened in the late 1960s. In 1968, the Chicago Board of Education had prepared a series of projections for city schools for 1970 and 1975 that had not gone unnoticed in Beverly Hills. Point four of the board's report stated that:

> it appears extremely likely that the vast majority of the non-white population growth in the city will continue to occur through transition outward from the fringes of the existing ghetto. . . . The southwest sector will experience 39.8% of the non-white increase during 1960-70, and 47.8% during 1970-75 . . .
>
> With no regard for the velocity of transition, it is possible to determine the direction of non-white transition, identifying the barriers to it, and the impact of these barriers on the direction of the movement . . . influenced greatly by the characteristics of the housing stock in areas at and beyond the ghetto fringe, i.e. ethnic composition, age of owner occupied units, and income level. . . .
>
> Factors of ethnic solidarity and owner occupancy are much more likely to cause a diversion in the path of racial transition if a non-residential barrier exists. These barriers include commercial and regional parks, R.R. tracks, industrial districts, and major commercial streets. The obvious projection problem presented by a barrier is that it is extremely difficult to forecast the time which will elapse before racial transition will occur beyond the barrier. . . . Existing and future barriers include:
> 1) Austin Blvd.–Oak Park city limits
> 2) East and North boundaries of Cicero
> 3) C.B. and O. Railroad of near southwest side
> 4) Ashland Ave.: Non-white transition reached Ashland at 59th St. in the late 1950's. At that time, the transition turned and has been moving southward all along the east side of Ashland with great velocity. As succeeding blocks east of it have become black, the pressure on the Ashland Ave. barrier has increased steadily. *Moreover, as the southwest expansion of black families encounters large numbers of higher price housing in the Beverly area, the demand for units will be further strengthened. By the early 1970's Ashland Ave. should no longer be a significant barrier to transition.* This southwest area shows a significant increase in its share of black growth between 1970 and 1975, an indirect result of Oak Park's migration squeeze,

1. Personal interview, 1972.

which makes the southwest side growth proportionately higher. *Also, it reflects the opening up of new residential areas west of Ashland and those south of 87th St.*[2] (Emphasis added)

The study suggested that areas west of Ashland Avenue, including BH-MP, were prime targets for residential succession and made predictions for each community area's racial composition as shown in Table 10-1. Between 1967 and 1972, the valley schools of Barnard, Vanderpoel, and Esmond did indeed change drastically in racial character, while the ridge schools of Clissold, Sutherland, and Kellogg remained white.

Esmond school, in southeast Morgan Park, grew in black enrollment from 312 to 1,132 from 1967 to 1972 with black expansion from east of Vincennes Avenue west to the Rock Island Railroad. White enrollment dropped from 282 to 52. Barnard School went from no blacks in 1967 to 46 percent in 1971, but dropped to 39 percent in 1972 when a new, all black school was opened at 96th and Racine in Brainerd. North of Barnard, Vanderpoel school was virtually all white in 1967, over half black in 1971, and 44 percent black in 1972, because of the new school at 96th and Racine. Morgan Park High School, 56 percent black in 1972, experienced a threefold increase in the rate of black enrollment growth after 1970 as white residents sent their children to the Catholic schools or to private Morgan Park Academy.

The pattern in the elementary schools was the same. Each of the schools became overcrowded, as the percentage of black children increased and the use of mobile classrooms became necessary. It was at this time that white residents chose to enroll their children in private schools, having little faith that the public schools would remain quality institutions. The quality of the local private schools did encourage existing white residents, especially the Catholics, to remain in the valley, but whites who might otherwise have moved in did not do so because they saw racial change in the schools as a precursor of residential succession, and frictions developed between the Catholic and the non-Catholic residents of the area. One concerned resident of BH-MP stated:

the Catholics . . . sure aren't helping things by sending all their kids to Catholic schools. They'd probably have closer ties and much more contact with the total community and care more about acting on the total com-

2. Chicago Board of Education, *Projections of School Enrollments, 1970 and 1975*. Chicago: by the Board, 1968, p. 14.

Table 10-1. Projections of Racial Mix in the Schools, 1970 and 1975.

Community Area	Percent Nonwhite in 1970	Percent Nonwhite in 1975
Beverly Hills	0.1	3.4
Morgan Park	50.7	62.1

Source: Chicago Board of Education.

munity's problems if they went to public schools. The same goes for Morgan Park Academy.[3]

Yet many of the community leaders and residents felt that the cheaper homes of the surrounding communities of Evergreen Park and Mt. Greenwood made them much more ripe for racial change than the more exclusive residential areas of the ridge, and they therefore sought to transform their community organization to ensure that the ridge would remain a cultural as well as a geographic island. The Beverly Hills–Morgan Park Protective Association (BAPA) was to become an organization devoted to the containment and deflection of racial transition.

AN ORGANIZED RESPONSE: BAPA RESTRUCTURED

BAPA had been established in 1946 as a voluntary organization devoted to the preservation of the quaint small-town character of BH-MP. But as the valley schools changed in complexion, the then unsalaried leaders of BAPA realized that BAPA's original purpose of maintaining and improving the area's unique character would have to be redirected if an effective response were to be made to the impending crises of racial confrontation.

BAPA was restructured in 1971. A new constitution and a larger budget allowed the hiring of a professional, full-time director, Philip Dolan, and five paid staff members. A strong campaign was launched, and in a short time BAPA recruited over 200 volunteers from some fifteen suborganizations. Among the most active of these suborganizations were:

Beverly Improvement Association
Beverly Manor Homeowners Association

3. Personal interview.

Longwood Manor Improvement Association
Morgan Park Improvement Association
Ridge Homeowners Association
Southwest Beverly Improvement Association
West Morgan Park Improvement Association
Business in Beverly
95th Street Merchants Association
Evergreen Plaza Merchants Group
Western Avenue Merchants Group
Rich Civic Council
Citizens Action for Morgan Park
Esmond Block Clubs

These small groups, except for the business organizations, have since slowly dissolved, as their goals were assumed by larger BAPA.

Funding was the first concern. Every financial institution in the area made major pledges to BAPA. Churches, mainly Catholic, contributed large amounts. Homeowners' organizations that had delegates on the BAPA council approved giving major portions of their own dues to BAPA. The largest BAPA benefactor, Arthur Rubloff and Co., a large Chicago real estate firm (see Chapter 3), donated over $20,000 and outlined a plan to revitalize the 95th Street business strip and remodel the interior of Evergreen Plaza, which was managed by the Rubloff company. Mr. Rubloff reported that statistics showed that BH-MP is "in the enviable position of being the second most important economic center in Chicago, second only to downtown," and he said that the purpose of his donation was "to prove my confidence in the area and to bring about a complete rejuvenation of this strategic location."[4] Individual contributions made up the rest of a budget of over $125,000.

New services were introduced, including a rumor control desk. In the beginning, about sixty calls a day were received. BAPA's monthly newsletter kept residents informed of progress made toward stabilization and promoted its programs. The publication was the heart of BAPA's effort to eliminate the fears of white residents of BH-MP and to bolster faith, confidence, and a sense of responsibility in the community. To this end the BAPA hired a professional in psychology to assist in preparing the newsletter.

A real estate practices committee had as its prime concern the solicitation of homeowners. It established an ethics code for real estate agents operating in BH-MP and explored ideas for dealing with

4. Quoted in BAPA press release, n.d.

agents who refused to show white clients homes in racially mixed neighborhoods. The code enforcement committee had members from each civic association and surveyed businesses, homes, and new construction, noting any substandard situations. Recruited from the dozens of lawyers living in the area, the law, legislation, and taxation committee gave legal aid to citizens who were willing to testify against real estate agents violating antisolicitation laws. In addition, local lawyers have made it possible for BAPA to become amicus curiae in antisolicitation cases, going all the way to the Illinois Supreme Court.

Underpinning all of this activity was a belief that BAPA's new purpose was to ensure that the ridge would remain a predominantly white community. Most BH-MP residents conceived of BAPA as a protector devoted to preserving the area as a predominantly white, minimally integrated community with the same amenities it had always had. A distinct minority in BH-MP, mostly from the west side of Western Avenue, were exclusionist. They favored standing firm and resisting all forms of black immigration. One small constituent group, the Rich Civic Council, the oldest civic group in BH-MP, composed of businessmen, advocated a policy of complete containment. Five percent of BAPA's membership were middle class blacks from the ridge, and they too appeared to have the same goals as the white members, wishing to keep the village atmosphere and to avoid the physical and social deterioration of the ghetto. They felt that they had escaped from exactly what BAPA was trying to avoid. BAPA welcomed such middle class blacks, but in its drive to find good leaders it wooed the wealthy, people with contacts, and experts in the field of public relations. In terms of power and prestige, the local blacks were in a poor position to compete for major roles in the BAPA.

Director Philip Dolan was quite explicit about the goals of the organization he led. "This community must remain predominantly white, or everyone will run away, the schools will go downhill, crime rates will skyrocket, and the city of Chicago will be nothing more than the haven for the old, poor, and the black."[5] He denied that BAPA was pursuing isolationist policies.

This is a massive national experiment to demonstrate that we do not need an institution like the University of Chicago to stabilize an area. People themselves can do it, if they're organized. We knew that if we sat on our behinds, with nothing done at all, the neighborhood could very well go.

5. Personal interview.

But people have great pride and stake in the community so we couldn't just sit and see it occur. We see no signs of giving up either.[6]

In trying to attract whites of the same social class as the present residents, BAPA spent many thousands of dollars. Executive transferees and residents of other parts of the city and suburbs in particular, were sought by BAPA, and the organization actively lobbied for a requirement that all city of Chicago employees live in the city. To attract the right kind of families, a brochure listed the advantages of the area; a twenty-five-minute slide presentation was made available for showing at civic affairs; and a direct mail package of promotional material was sent to artists, university professors, newlyweds, lawyers, and professional and trade groups. The most costly part of the promotion included newspaper, radio, and magazine advertising, including ads in the *New York Times*, the *Wall Street Journal*, and the *National Observer*, reading: "Moving to Chicago? Investigate Beverly Hills, the village in the city. Easy commuting. The city's best public schools. A house for every taste and budget."[7]

Dolan took a strong position against any kind of change in the area's basic character. In an interview he listed the factors that he felt made BH-MP different from other communities faced with racial change, factors giving the area a far better chance to survive—high level of education and cosmopolitanism, few apartments, high income level, large numbers of city officials as residents, easy communication within the community, strong sense of community, and the existence of a hired professional to guide the BAPA. Dolan said:

> Our greatest asset is the strong family orientation and community identification in BH-MP. These people love this area and will fight to maintain its stability. In the end, the success of the association's efforts will rest with the dedication of our residents. . . . We aren't like South Shore. It's obvious why it couldn't have possibly stabilized. Seventy-seven percent of the dwellings were apartments. Our community is 90 percent single family homes, and we have a chance unlike any other community in Chicago to maintain a quality community.[8]

Dolan described himself as a combination city manager and chamber of commerce. In the city manager role, he was in constant contact with city leaders who had the power to act in ways favorable to BH-MP, both publicly and behind the scene. Dolan said, "I talk

6. Ibid.
7. Ad copy was supplied by BAPA.
8. Personal interview.

the language of political power. . . . We can either push and praise certain actions, organizations, and people, or do the opposite. The first thing worked, since we've got so much power, political power and people power."[9]

BH-MP, because of BAPA's pressure, became an overserviced community. Dolan argued that "This is the key to doing away with deterioration."[10] He stressed most emphatically that BAPA was not a "Saul Alinsky organization," as he termed it. "We are not throwing rocks at city officials, we are *using* their power to keep our city services at the present high level. . . . We're walking softly and carrying a big stick, with powerful people behind that stick." Coming very close to being exclusionist, he never gave the impression that BAPA's work was racially motivated. At all times he stressed the wish to have only "desirable" people replace those whites who move; the impression was that no blacks in the area would be the happiest situation, with managed integration second best. But he was quite clear about his role. As he said: "I control this community."[11]

Clearly, the reshaped community organization was having its effect. The exact location of a community's boundaries, the degree to which they are agreed upon, and the significance of the territory they enclose are of great importance to an area anticipating racial change. For a community organization attempting to keep whites living in an area, the question of whether it should engender a common perception of community boundaries arises. Community action may be facilitated when residents perceive themselves as belonging to the same geographical unit, since perception of common boundaries may help create community feeling and bolster morale in the face of racial change. However, fuzzy boundaries also may have certain advantages for a group trying to stabilize a neighborhood. If rigid community boundaries are not perceived, the threat of racial change moving across these boundaries may be minimized.

The Chicago Real Estate Board's *Chicago Neighborhood Maps* set the boundaries of Beverly Hills and Morgan Park as 87th Street on the north, Western Avenue from 87th to 99th Street, California Avenue from 99th to 119th Street, 119th on the south, Ashland Avenue from 119th to 115th, Halsted Avenue from there to 107th Street, 107th to Vincennes, Vincennes to Beverly Avenue back to 87th Street again.

BAPA disagreed with this definition and chose instead to define

9. Ibid.
10. Ibid.
11. Ibid.

"its" community as one that excluded the entire eastern (black) half of Morgan Park. One result was that as new black residents moved into the valley homes in western Morgan Park, the average white BAPA member's perception of BH-MP's eastern boundary moved west to continue to exclude the black residential areas. BAPA explicitly avoided talking about racial percentages within the community, and by defining certain ghettoizing areas as beyond the path, they were able to reinforce their exclusionary orientation. As one middle class black ridge resident said: "What we don't need are those welfare families in the 235 shacks who have a million kids and nobody to keep the place up. My neighbors and I think we must keep the whites that are here right now and bring in more suitable blacks."[12]

The pressure to increase city services clearly paid off. BAPA publications point out that area crime decreased an overall 23.6 percent in only three years, with auto theft down 22.4 percent, robbery down 22.9 percent, and burglary down 26.8 percent. Compared to the national average of ten crimes per 10,000 people, BH-MP has 10 crimes per 12,000 people. There was little racial violence in the area, although there were two publicized fire bombings of black families who moved onto the ridge and two murders involving blacks and whites in 1972.

BAPA, and virtually all residents of BH-MP, believed that their efforts to bolster the quality of what they believed to be a unique community were preserving its substantially white character. However, they felt that its very desirability and proximity to a black area would turn out to be its greatest liabilities. Middle class black families, who could well afford such housing, were gravitating to BH-MP, thus posing a threat to its white residents, who had greater freedom of movement in the metropolitan housing market.

Thus, BAPA concentrated much of its power on influencing the actions of real estate firms inside and outside the area. It was most concerned about "outside" real estate men, particularly those from black areas who solicited listings in BH-MP. It was less concerned with local firms, since they were unlikely to sell to large numbers of blacks as long as white demand remained high.

BAPA pressured brokers outside the area who sell homes to blacks in BH-MP to avoid BH-MP as a market, not to solicit in the area, and to sign a document that they would not "advertise" their services. When Illinois' antisolicitation law was pronounced unconstitutional, BAPA appealed to the Illinois Supreme Court and continued its antisolicitation campaign in BH-MP. A number of black real estate firms located east of BH-MP were visited by officials from the state Depart-

12. Personal interview.

ment of Registration and Education and warned not to solicit in the area as a result of BAPA's activities. One real estate weekly commented that the officials were acting under community pressure and without official sanction. When one of these firms, according to BAPA, refused to cooperate, BAPA initiated a telephone campaign tying up the company's phones day after day. The same weekly said that the Austin community may be pushed to second place as the city's worst hotbed of community groups' anti-realty activities. Dolan, in a reply, argued:

> Suggestion of mob rule, inflammatory rhetoric, and intimidation of BH-MP residents very clearly demonstrate the paranoia of the real estate industry, which now ranks second to used car dealers in arousing public distrust. Most people in our community would find it difficult to sympathize with your stalwart defense of "honest business firms" doggedly abused by violence and mob action. In fact, our observation would be quite the opposite: avaricious, panic peddling real estate salesmen from disreputable firms preying on the anxieties of BH-MP homeowners. . . . Rather than berating the community for its strong and proud stand, we would suggest that you review your position in regard to state licensing and enforcement of anti-solicitation legislation. . . . [13]

One of the real estate firms visited by representatives of the state Department of Registration and Education, Maner Realty Co. (see Chapter 4), said they were soliciting in Beverly and would continue to do so. They denied, however, that they were panic peddling or blockbusting, since the salesmen avoided homeowners who had registered with the city as not wanting to sell. Maner said that "Black families who have achieved some economic stability have a right to move to better neighborhoods, and Beverly represents an attractive neighborhood."[14] A second firm, Owens Bros., denied soliciting in BH-MP and said that the homes they have sold have been through referrals. One of these homes was at 11756 Longwood Drive and was sold to a black family for $40,000; the owner's car was firebombed, and a Molotov cocktail was thrown onto the porch but failed to ignite. A third black broker complained that she was:

> having a running battle with the Beverly Improvement Association [sic] and the Illinois Commission on Human Relations in a letter that I sent out offering my services to owners should they desire to sell their homes or buildings. This letter is not offensive and is merely offering my services. . . . How are owners going to know about brokers and real estate firms if we can't advertise?[15]

13. Personal interview.
14. Personal interview.
15. Personal interview.

One BH-MP broker commented, "There are a number of excellent realtors in our community, and property owners have dealt with these reputable firms. The concern of BAPA is those 'Johnny come latelys' from Chatham and Roseland. It is this type of broker using scare tactics in an attempt to do business in changing areas where the action is."[16]

Local real estate men felt that a sure sign of the efficacy of BAPA's campaign was that housing values were up in all areas of BH-MP. One broker said,

> When blacks moved into Brainerd, housing values dropped since everyone was fleeing. But the people in BH-MP aren't afraid like they were in Brainerd, and they know that with the help of the BAPA they can keep BH-MP just like it's always been. Even though blacks have moved in from the east, property values haven't dropped at all since there's plenty of white demand and no one is fleeing. Blacks aren't moving in block by block, which has decreased most white fear . . . and it doesn't give whites the feeling that they've been invaded.[17]

In BAPA's struggle to stabilize BH-MP, the issue of the federal government's role as a source of community change also arose. Director Dolan said, "If we cannot be relieved from the conceptually proper but practically destructive federal pressures that hold a dagger to the heart of our community, our area will not survive."[18] He therefore took a strong stand against FHA policies as well as the Section 235 scattered site housing program. In a speech to the Senate Housing Subcommittee Hearing on March 30, 1973, he stated, among other things:

> That FHA, marvelous in its conception of helping Americans into home ownership and the middle class, becomes not the program that allows escape from the ghetto, but, rather the only funding available to foster white flight from the city.[19]

According to Dolan:

> FHA impacted sales have come to mean the economic deterioration of neighborhood after neighborhood in Chicago. On the fringes of our community, as the economic level of the inhabitants has decreased, the businesses that have depended on middle class sales have been forced to flee to

16. Personal interview.
17. Personal interview.
18. Personal interview.
19. Copy of speech provided in personal interview.

more productive markets. The disintegration that they have left behind is disastrous.[20]

Figures given by Dolan for FHA sales during "one sixteen month period" were broken down roughly into three BH-MP areas. In the first easternmost area, Beverly Avenue to Racine Avenue, which had been largely black since the 1920s, he listed 158 FHA sales out of a total of 187 sales. In the "threatened" area, Beverly Avenue–Vincennes Avenue to the Rock Island Railroad, Dolan said that out of 77 sales, 36 had been FHA financed. The third area, the Rock Island Railroad to Western Avenue, encompassing the ridge, had only 2 FHA sales out of 104 total sales.

As regards Section 235 housing, Director Dolan said:

> An example of the impact of 235 housing is clearly evident in one section of our community, the . . . Esmond area.
>
> This area was characterized by modest homes, open space and excellent schools, integrated since the early 1900's. Within a short time, 211 235 housing units were impacted in the area, bringing 800 new children on to the rolls of Esmond Elementary School. An addition was finally built on the playground, reducing play space to zero. The impact on the high school has yet to be felt. Since Section 235 guidelines call for families to have three or more children, it is no wonder that our city's school boards are increasingly in financial trouble.
>
> Without being anti-poor, marginal buyers often cannot afford, nor can they realize the importance of, proper home maintenance. . . . [21]

Both black and white residents of BH-MP and Brainerd united in opposition to the Section 235 homes along Beverly and Vincennes Avenues, most of which were in Morgan Park. More were planned, but residents and BAPA waged a successful campaign against them. Residents felt that they should influence the quality of construction and the type of people who moved in. A leader of the anti-235 group stated:

> In many cases a mother is the head of the house. A woman with six children can't possibly take care of work around the home and doesn't know how to fix things that frequently go wrong in these homes. What happens is after a couple of months, the new homeowner finds he can't afford to keep his new home and abandons it. We are stuck in the neighbothood amidst abandoned homes and overcrowded schools.[22]

20. Ibid.
21. Ibid.
22. Personal interview.

OTHER VOICES, OTHER VIEWS

BAPA's aggressive and apparently successful tactics were not without their critics in the early 1970s. One distinguished ex-member of the BH-MP community had much to say about BH-MP as it started to resist the pressures of the ghetto. He was the Reverend Andrew Greeley, who at the time was director of the Center for the Study of American Pluralism at the National Opinion Research Center of the University of Chicago and former associate pastor of Christ the King parish in Beverly Hills. In October 1972, Greeley wrote a series of articles on BH-MP for *Chicago Today* that raised a storm of controversy in the community because of their pessimistic flavor. He reiterated his arguments in a personal interview:

> Some residents vigorously insist that their neighborhood, of all neighborhoods, will not be swept by panic following black immigration. But others assert that they are going to move as quickly as possible to someplace where they will be safe from seeing another neighborhood go down the drain. . . . The explanation that the citizens of Beverly . . . don't want to live with people of black skin has a certain amount of plausibility to it, because even if there was not another black face within a hundred miles and not the slightest possibility of community change, there are unquestionably some people in Beverly who would not want a black face in the house next door or down the street. . . . But I suspect that the overwhelming majority of them are not bigots in the sense that bigotry is the all-controlling force in their lives. If there were some way in which BH could be permanently integrated, some way in which the appearance of the first black face did not set into motion a chain of causal events turning the area completely black, most of those who presently live in Beverly would not move.

Greeley went on to say:

> But while I am under no illusions about the enlightenment of Beverly, I think that I can understand their fears, and I think I also understand that the sophisticated university intellectual world in which I have lived since I left Beverly is afraid. It is afraid of change, change of any sort—political, social, religious, economic. . . . But there are special dimensions to the fear of change in BH. The older citizens are the new rich, [who] feel they have "earned" the comfort, the affluence, and respectability in their community by long years of hard work. . . . The younger generation has been touched by [the Depression], for all through its childhood it was filled with fear of failure and the need to strive. The children of Beverly have very fragile egos and vast amounts of self-hatred. . . .

In the same personal interview he later stated: "Both the younger and older generations of Beverly may be innovative, but their homes and neighborhood are bastions of security that are threatened by the prospect of change."

> The journalists and the lawyers who support the ACLU may dismiss them as absurd. Social turf is not a reality and therefore concern about it is stupid [they say]. . . . Desire to protect one's community is reactionary, an obstacle to social change and to the improvement of the conditions of the poor and oppressed, and is therefore culpable. On almost any ground imaginable the liberal elites will dismiss the fear of change in Beverly as neurotic, thus not to be taken seriously. . . . Even if men better and wiser than they tell the citizens of Beverly that their fears are unreal, they have considerable historical precedent for insisting that those who gainsay fear simply do not know what they are talking about. We cannot ignore the classic dictum of W.I. Thomas that when people define something as real, the definition itself is a reality with which we must deal. Fear of financial loss is a response which cannot be denied. While there exists considerable literature showing that in the long run housing values go up after black immigration, *there is no doubt that in the short run they go down.* Furthermore, it is in the short run that most people must live, since even in Beverly few families are likely to be able to afford two homes.

Greeley said that blockbusters would not be successful in Beverly because the residents were too sophisticated, but he upset BH-MP residents by saying that "The housing market is *already soft* in Beverly. . . . Property values are no longer what they used to be, and Beverly is *no longer a desirable neighborhood*" (emphasis added). For he may have been expressing their secret fears as faits accomplis. He also talked of the fear of crime and violence.

> An increase in the amount of murder, rape, and burglary in the neighborhood may not be something that is accepted as just punishment for the sins of the white race. To tell the Beverlyites that most blacks are not criminals would be to state something they would not deny, but it only takes one or two stabbing murders such as occurred in Beverly's sister neighborhood South Shore to create an atmosphere of intense fear that no community can long survive. The terror in white neighborhoods at the time of black immigration may very well be excessive, but again, terror has never been known to decrease in the human population simply because pious liberals arrive on the scene to announce that terror is excessive. . . . And there is also fear of what happens to schools. . . . In other words, most of the arguments against moving out of Beverly say you should be willing to expose yourself to dangers, financial loss, and poor education for your children because injustices have been done and are being done to

black people in other neighborhoods. This may be a form of argumentation that has appeal for some sophisticated liberals (though I notice that the U. of C. lab school is very crowded), but it is not, I think, successful among most human beings at the present state of the evolution of the race.

And he believed that the only solution is the diffusion of minority groups throughout the metropolis via a system of subsidized quota integration. His main point was that "few neighborhoods, not even one as affluent and sophisticated as Beverly, can solve its own problems."

As a Catholic priest, he also felt that the Catholic church could be a positive force rather than a refuge for fearful whites but, he added, "Cardinal Cody thinks the whole south side is gone, and that they shouldn't spend any more time or money on those parishes." Although Catholic blacks now lived within the boundaries of his former parish of Christ the King, whites had not panicked because and only because the Catholic fortress had not been pierced yet. "There isn't a ghost of a chance that Beverly will solve the problems of the oncoming black ghetto unless the two groups [Catholic and non-Catholic] are willing to cooperate intensively," he said.

Greeley also felt that community organizations such as BAPA were ineffective in a rapidly changing but still dualistic housing market:

Similar efforts have been disastrously unsuccessful in the threatened neighborhoods over the last 15 years. This is of course the tragedy of it all. At this point in time nothing can be done in Beverly. . . . As it stands now, it may survive, but only by chance. There may not be enough blacks to buy homes in Beverly, even in the present soft real estate market. The peculiar dynamics of ghetto expansion may carry the ghetto in other directions. The younger generation may, more out of stubbornness than organized virtue, simply refuse to move. . . . Oh, there are likely now to be all kinds of frantic efforts at community organization, but I have the sinking feeling that they will do more harm than good. . . . I would estimate the chances of Beverly's survival as a more or less permanently integrated neighborhood to be moderate at best. . . . If Beverlyites are smart, they will lean on Mr. Nixon and his HUD to do everything in their power to integrate the upper middle-income suburbs beyond the city limits.

During the interview he maintained that "Fear, bigotry, and uncertainty have been ingrained into the new rich mind of Beverly. The fact that Kellogg is a fifth black means that blacks must walk to school through the all white sections, meaning more biracial contact, more fear instilled in whites when they perceive that their neighbor-

hood has been invaded." He disagreed with Dolan's statement that
BH-MP is in its final stage of changing:

> Beverly will undoubtedly change much more. The homes on the hill will
> be much more affordable to blacks in a depressed market. Beverly resi-
> dents have less reason to move, but that's not going to stop the chain of
> events, only slow it down. The BAPA is catering to the need for hope in
> the community but can't affect the dual market. The BAPA is certainly
> integrationist; however, a more exclusionist policy would probably be the
> most desirable to them, if it were workable.[23]

BH-MP residents took strong exception to Greeley's view that they
could opt to abandon their area if the black population increased. A
series of quotations from our interviews with them follow:

> I certainly don't agree with Greeley that nothing can be done in Beverly.
> Integration laws exist today and I don't think any community is going to
> be immune from the law. Our goal is to make BH-MP the best place to live
> for those who stay and those who move here.
>
> . . .
>
> I don't think Father Greeley knows what he is talking about. Today we
> have good neighbors and I don't expect it to change. If we have black
> neighbors, we'll take them in and enjoy their company as we would any-
> one else. Greeley talks about panic peddling. I think he is panic peddling in
> the press.
>
> . . .
>
> We're not running. We moved to Beverly nine years ago because our
> Negro neighbors in our old neighborhood weren't even allowed to buy gas
> except at two service stations. But the stuff Greeley is writing about might
> bring a situation we don't want in BH-MP.
>
> . . .
>
> Naturally, there can be no immigration into this neighborhood without
> an exodus. That is logic. But all of the people I have talked to say they
> want to stay, even if the black population becomes ten families to a block.
>
> . . .
>
> I don't worry. I've been here for forty years. Changes? I haven't noticed
> any changes. Maybe in Brainerd, but not here. It's stabilized. The married
> children are coming back.
>
> . . .
>
> Some customers have moved out of the area through the years. I don't

23. Cited in personal interview with Greeley.

know why. Maybe some of them got tired of the neighborhood. I'm not a bit worried. There's always that talk.

. . .

The older people who can't take care of their large homes and grounds are the only ones to move out now. And they have to go elsewhere for elevator apartments. When they move out, young couples move in. They're buying these homes hand over fist. [Young white couples is assumed.]

. . .

We are concerned about the image of Beverly. We want people to move in here, particularly white, so it will stay like it is now, with a good balance. The community is tremendously desirable for both black and white. We live in an integrated world, and BH-MP gives us the opportunity to enjoy it.

. . .

I think that the black movein will be stopped at the edge of the ridge, since this is where the home values skyrocket. The good thing about it is that these moveins, at least past the Rock Island, have been good middle class blacks who have a sense of responsibility to their homes and community. Blacks are moving south toward the integrated south suburbs, anyway, so that relieves the pressure on us a little bit. Therefore I think that blacks won't move past the older and more modestly priced sections up to the natural ridge, and whites will stay on the ridge.

. . .

What offends me is the implication that people are running away. It just isn't true. These people here are ready to deal with the real problems of changing neighborhoods. This isn't to say that some people haven't moved out, when faced with an influx of people of lower economic status. We have had a lower number of professional people moving in, while many affluent professionals are moving out. We have to campaign to get the professionals back.

. . .

I think we're neither pro- nor anti-integration. But we want to work to stop any blockbusting before it gets moving. We want to maintain a stable viable community with the right mix, I guess.

. . .

I'm not sure I disagree with Greeley. He is talking about humans and how they act. I really can't say for sure how people will react here to change. But I can make this guess: I came here because I have the sense that this community has a generosity of spirit and a tradition that should permit it to absorb a substantial amount of change without modifying its essential attractive character.

. . .

There's a strong devotion to this community. It has characteristics that make the people very openminded. Perhaps it is the income level, or educational level, or the fact that many people grew up here.

. . .

All I know is that most of us are tough to budge. And there is something else about Beverly. It is suburban but also has the vitality of the city. That makes it so ideal. Change? I think we'll handle it as we have in the past.

. . .

In past years we tried to convince people that the time for integration was before the black community is next door. We succeeded in convincing a number of people, but not the community as a whole. But I'm optimistic about the stabilization of the community. If the overcrowding at the elementary schools could be solved, it would be a tremendous step in the right direction.

. . .

The question is whether a community that is so handsomely endowed, that is so devoted to its own history and to a particular kind of lifestyle, can steer through the turbulence created by some of those fellows on Western Ave. I'm sure it can.

But other residents were less optimistic:

The first black families began moving into this block about two years ago, and the panic peddlers began to harass me and everybody else. We told them all to get lost, and eventually they quit calling. But others began selling. Then some money hungry builders built those cheap crackerboxes on every vacant lot and sideyard they could find.

. . .

and then there was this incident. One morning we found all the tires on cars for blocks slashed in the night. With a couple of exceptions, the cars were those of the whites. Not a word got into the papers. I wondered if such systematic vandalism had been arranged by the blockbusters to panic the whites into selling faster and cheaper. The boys who did it were eventually caught and they were all black. . . .

. . .

Of course, the people who live in those [Section] 235 homes ought to have homes, and the program they're under is a tool for implementing integration. That's fine. The hint is that somebody must be making a lot of money from this. Those homes sell for $24,500!

. . .

If you controlled the type of shops that were in the community, it might help. It seems there is a big turnover in the type of shops around Morgan

Park. Liquor stores are coming in, bars are coming in, little things like this which are directed toward a certain ethnic group instead of for the whole community.

. . .

The most serious problem is trying to take people of a different cultural level, regardless of who they are, and cram them into a culture that they're not capable of adapting to. And by not being able to adapt to it they become frustrated and they project guilt and want people to pull them up by the bootstraps and they don't get the gratification of doing it themselves. . . . I think that people better quit kow-towing and being gutless and apathetic and stand on their haunches, and say, "Look, this is how it is: we give you schools, you bust them all up; we give you good books, you tear them up; if you don't want to learn, don't blame us and don't blame color, creed, or anything else for the predicament you put yourself in."

. . .

The most serious problem is forced integration. I've lived in this neighborhood all my life, and none of us like [forced integration]. Father Lawlor has the right idea to stick [with it], but people just don't do it. I mean, after all, one or two in a neighborhood is fine, but when you get overrun, it's not safe. I've had personal experiences where my boys have been jumped.

. . .

I know that there was a plan that proposed checkerboard integration of the area in which only homes in scattered areas would be shown to black families. The plan might work north of 95th Street, where homes are priced as high as $100,000, but it would run into trouble south of 95th where some sell in the low 20s. Doctors and lawyers will move north of 95th, but less desirable blacks would move into my area. . . . When teens are on the rampage in Gresham, and once people are robbed and women are raped, the whole plan will go out the window. Why hasn't stricter police enforcement been stressed in the plan?

. . .

We've got to convince people not to run, especially in the fringes of the racial change along the east boundary. If people want to move, it's one thing, but they should not feel they are being forced to leave. Nothing is wrong if blacks move in, except if they move in en masse while the whites move out. We've got to convince the local residents that if blacks move in it's not the end of the world.

. . .

I heard that real estate values have been dropping off at an almost alarming rate in the high-priced home category. A house that once sold for $50,000 now may be sold for $40,000 whereas in another area it might go for $60,000. [Dolan said there is no documented evidence backing this up, but any "softness" in the market in the high-priced areas might be due to the closing of the Union Stockyards when many executives moved out of town.]

. . .

It isn't that I object to the neighborhood's being mixed, but that's just not what happens. I think that the whites are being forced out of Chicago. I think it's just a matter of time before Chicago is gone. I don't know as the city can do a thing about it.

. . .

The neighborhood, whether anyone will admit it or not, is terrified, and trying to keep all the black moveins quiet. The large houses along Longwood are such a big barrier to the blacks, though. [The people in those homes] are all large Catholic families who would be the last to move. They'd never be able to find other houses as big in other places for the same money. It's just too expensive to move.

. . .

I remember a racial incident between Morgan Park Academy, which is almost all white, and the University of Chicago Lab School, which is pretty well integrated. The Lab School demanded that the academy, as part of the Prep School Association, recruit more blacks, and of course the academy and all the students' parents said no. I think it would hurt the community if more blacks went to the academy. It would just promote more fear and result in a faster changeover.

. . .

The area is changing much faster than outsiders and the press know about and report, since it is kept so quiet within the neighborhood. . . . The Baptists in the area have been doing the most, in my opinion, because of their primary vulnerability of being integrated. You know that most blacks are Baptist and not Catholic. [Every church except for one in BH-MP is all white, but most all of them have taken a public stand that they will gladly accept blacks as members.]

CONCLUSION

By the mid-1970s the valley was essentially abandoned by BAPA as ghetto spread continued, but the organization still hoped for stabilization of the real estate market on the ridge. White brokers were willing to cooperate with BAPA as long as white demand for housing remained high, but wherever white demand showed signs of dropping, white brokers' self-interest necessitated placing business before loyalty to the community, as had already taken place in the valley.

And "outside" black real estate men had every reason to try to penetrate the BH-MP market. As one black broker put it:

> Unless the citizens of Beverly are willing to work with us and not against us, the neighborhood will go all black just like so many others have gone. . . . the solution to rapid racial turnover is not harassment and intimidation of black brokers, but cooperation and a long-range view . . . such tactics [of intimidation] are futile and only lead to more aggressive approaches by the black brokers.[24]

24. Personal interview.

Chapter 11

Austin: Reactions too Late

Also located on the western city limits, Austin (Community Area 25, see Figure 1-1) tried to react in the manner of BAPA, but too little was accomplished and too late. One of the largest of Chicago's seventy-five community areas (1970 population 128,000), Austin's development had been intimately related to the extension of the railroads. The construction in the 1840s of the Galena and Chicago Railroad (later the Chicago and Northwestern) promoted the subdivision of much of what is now central and southern Austin. By 1874, Austin had a population of about 1,000, mostly English and native Americans. Many substantial Chicago businessmen built homes in the area of Central and Lake where the handsome old town hall still stands.

Improved suburban service on the Chicago and Northwestern line and the proximity of several manufacturing companies and the railroad yards and ships stimulated the growth of the area during the 1880s. The Lake Street branch of the elevated line was begun in 1893, while the Garfield Park branch was completed to Cicero Avenue two years later. When Austin became part of the city of Chicago in 1899, it was a relatively well to do community of approximately 4,000 people. Austin, through annexation, gained the distinction of being the choice neighborhood on Chicago's west side.

Austin's greatest growth occurred between 1900 and 1930, when its population rose to 131,114. The development of the "L" brought many Chicago Loop workers into this attractive residential community. Austin grew particularly rapidly during the 1920s. Columbus

Park opened in the early 1920s, and the neighborhood around its grassy malls was built up mainly with apartment buildings.

The northern part of Austin developed as a result of the building of the Division streetcar line, which was extended to Austin Boulevard in 1915, and growth in this area reached boom proportions after 1920.

Early Austinites were a cosmopolitan group that included native Americans, Scots, English, Germans, European Jews, Swedes, and Irish. These Irish settlers were to play a predominant role in Austin's social and political life. The Roman Catholic churches became the hubs around which community life revolved. Parishes, rather than addresses, often were used by Austinites to indicate where they lived.

During the 1930s, large numbers of Italians began moving into Austin from the more crowded and deteriorated neighborhoods to the east and, by 1960, were the leading nationality group. However, the Irish remained the predominant group in the central part of Austin around the town hall and, likewise, continued to dominate Austin's social and political organization.

In 1970, 30 percent of Austin's population was of foreign stock, with Italians comprising the largest single group (25 percent), followed by the Irish. Ethnic areas were readily identifiable, but racial change had disrupted the former settlement pattern. Many of the Irish had moved north of Division Street, where Italians also were congregated. Spanish-speaking people, comprising 3.6 percent of Austin's total population, were found mostly along Austin's eastern border, from Lake Street to Chicago Avenue, with growing concentrations on the fringe of black ghetto expansion. The Greek residential community, which centered around the Greek Orthodox Church of the Assumption, had been almost completely displaced although the church still operated. The Jews had also left their homes in south Austin, and the former synagogue on south Central Avenue housed a black Baptist congregation. In 1972, 34 percent of Austin's population was black. The greatest concentrations of black population were found in the southeastern census tracts, but blacks lived as far west as Austin Boulevard and north of Chicago Avenue.

Austin's rate of natural increase in 1960 was 8.3 percent (as compared with 12.4 percent for the city of Chicago). Only ten of Chicago's seventy-five community areas had a natural increase rate as low as Austin's. This low rate was primarily a function of Austin's age structure, which in turn was influenced by outmigration of younger families and individuals.

During the mid-1960s, the pattern changed dramatically, however. The most marked shift occurred in the eighteen and under age bracket, which increased sharply between 1960 and 1970. The percentage of persons forty-five and older declined in the same decade. This shift toward younger age groups also was reflected in the rising total population of Austin, up almost 3,000 since 1960. Both the shifting age structure and the population increase reflected the large-scale black inmigration as the ghetto spread west, and indeed, the changes were largely confined to the tracts that had undergone racial transition, while in Austin's white tracts population aging and decline continued.

The largest group of residents in 1970 were white collar workers, 31 percent being engaged in clerical and sales jobs and 14.3 percent occupying professional and managerial positions. Austin's median income in 1970 was $10,630 (versus Chicago's $10,242). The highest median incomes were found in the northernmost tracts of Austin, and the largest percentage of families with incomes below the poverty level was localized in tracts with the greatest black concentrations.

About 77 percent of Austin's dwelling units were built prior to 1939. Residential construction was negligible after 1930 except in northernmost Austin. Most of Austin's dwelling units—some 60 percent—were renter occupied. The median value of Austin's homes in 1970 was $20,900 (versus $21,200 for Chicago as a whole), while the median rent was $130.

Austin's best housing is located in its Galewood section. East of Harlem Avenue there are single family brick homes on large lots, and the area exudes a feeling of suburban affluence. Past Natchez, traveling east on Wabansia, there is a decided shift in housing and neighborhood characteristics. More apartment buildings are in evidence, and the single family homes are smaller. The northeastern part of Austin above Chicago Avenue generally seems to be composed of well-maintained single family homes and two- and three-flats.

Leamington, north of Chicago Avenue, is an area of single family frame homes in need of maintenance. The streets are in poor condition. However, the struggle to maintain the area goes on, and between Chicago and Iowa signs announce, "Welcome from the North Leamington Block Club." Lamon, in a mixed area just west of Cicero, is lined with deteriorating housing. Some blacks are living just north of Chicago Avenue in single family homes and small apartment buildings.

PERCEPTIONS OF COMMUNITY CHANGE

Austin in the early 1970s was an area of marked diversity. It still showed signs of former, better times—graceful homes, splendid churches, and plentiful large trees—but its past glory was marred by deterioration. The public face that Austin had tried to maintain was one of a self-contained, sedate residential area with a "small-town" atmosphere. However, this image had been severely threatened by the racial change Austin had been undergoing since the middle 1960s.

In 1960, the major problems facing Austin were its aging housing stock and its declining population. By 1966 Austin was confronted with new problems as blacks had begun to move into the area's southeastern corner. Directly in the path of the expanding black ghetto, Austin was much more vulnerable to black inmigration than its hostile neighbor, Cicero. Blacks entered Austin along Jackson Boulevard from the black communities of West Garfield Park and North Lawndale. By 1967 Austin was about 12 percent black, and this black population was concentrated in the southeastern part of Austin.

The steady movement of black residents into southern Austin was reflected first in the area's schools. Austin High School had only one black student in 1963. In 1964, when its boundary was moved east to relieve overcrowding in all black Marshall High School, Austin High School received 84 black students, and that number jumped to 405 (14 percent of the entire enrollment) in 1965. The greatest change occurred between 1968 and 1969, when Austin High School went from 49.3 percent white and 48.6 percent black to 25.3 percent white and 73.5 percent black. In 1972, Austin High was, for all intents and purposes, completely black.

> While defiantly fighting the influx of more blacks into the north half of Austin, the whites who live there are just as defiantly refusing to send their children to almost all-black Austin High School. In a kind of chicken-or-egg confusion, Austin High School is all-black because practically none of the 1,200 to 1,400 [white] children who live in its district go there.
>
> Instead, many of them falsify addresses to go to out-of-district schools or, if they're lucky, they go with the Board of Education's blessing to "receiver" schools under the permissive transfer program, or if they're Catholic (as many are), and if their parents can afford the tuition, they go to a parochial high school.[1]

Along with the increase in black students, overcrowding also occurred. In 1963, 2,895 students were enrolled in Austin High School; by 1972 the school contained over 4,000 students.

1. *Chicago Today*, September 24, 1972.

Racial change in Austin was mirrored in the elementary schools as well. May and Spencer schools were the first to receive blacks, followed by Emmet. Emmet school, 97.6 percent white in 1967 was 20 percent black in 1968 and 67 percent black the following year. By 1972, Emmet's student population was 100 percent black. Moreover, by 1969, crowding at Emmet was so serious that three branches were set up to accommodate its overflow students.

In 1969, when Key school had an 8 percent black enrollment, parents first became aware of friction at that school:

> A few black kids had started attending the school and some of the whites would harass them on the way home. Soon the blacks started bringing chains for protection . . . there was an awful lot of tension in the school grounds. . . . Some of them [blacks] would tease my daughter about her blond hair, or cut it. As the black kids got older, they were getting completely out of hand, and the teachers weren't coping with it. . . . Some of the black kids were coming in late with their radios blaring. . . . By the summer of 1971, we could see the writing on the wall. The school wasn't going to make it. People started moving.[2]

The movement of black families north could be seen in the changing school enrollments in the area's more centrally located schools. Howe school's enrollment, for example, had changed from 100 percent white in 1967 to 89.5 percent black in 1972.

By 1967, the southern half of Austin was in the throes of racial change, experiencing all the problems associated with the invasion-succession syndrome—overcrowded schools plagued by racial tensions, deteriorating housing and declining municipal services, the loss of commercial facilities and community institutions, and increasing crime and gang activity.

In 1969, Austin became the target of widespread panic peddling. White homeowners on Chicago's west side, including Austin, were beseiged by real estate firms with phone calls, door to door solicitations, and offers in the mail to sell their homes. Residents became increasingly concerned about the dozens of real estate operations that had sprung up in the area to profit from racial change.

A major campaign was launched by a number of west and northwest side community organizations, including Austin's Organization for a Better Austin (OBA), against the blockbusting tactics of some real estate men. In May of 1970, after much citywide publicity and constant local pressure, salesmen from two area realty firms—Sky

2. *Chicago Tribune*, October 14, 1973.

Realty and Belltone Realty Company—had their licenses revoked by the city, an almost unprecedented action. However, the two salesmen were, by August of 1970, operating their own business "as usual" in Austin. The license of Sky's president, John Luitgaarden, was supended for two years. On January 4, 1971, Circuit Court Judge Edward Egan upheld license revocations for Belltone and its former president, John W. Dice. However, the city collector's office issued an individual broker's license to Mr. Dice, at the same North Avenue address, the next day, January 5. Acting City Collector Lawrence J. Goss said:

> a broker must only sign an affidavit saying he has a state broker's license to obtain a city license. Dice still has his state license.
>
> Goss said that if he had known Dice had a previous revocation, his office would not have issued the present license . . . the corporation counsel's office failed to notify him of the revocation. . .[3]

Belltone apparently folded in November of 1970 and was replaced by a "front" company, Realty USA, which closed down in May of 1971, only to pop up in Austin again under the name RKO Realty.

In 1971, at the insistence of such groups as OBA, the city council passed an ordinance banning "For Sale" and "Sold" signs from being displayed throughout the city. In that same year Austin had been covered with such signs when

> more than 200 outside real estate companies, who have come here to prey on the racial fears of people living in a chinging community, and have descended on Austin for the sole purpose of making big, quick, panic money off of each and everyone of our Austin home buyers and sellers[4]

deluged the community with "For Sale" placards. The removal of signs, however, did not sidetrack panic peddlers and block busters. Said one Austinite, "You can get a neighborhood worked up into a frenzy without posting 'For Sale' or 'Sold' signs all over the place."[5]

> A West Side real estate operator [said] . . . "We don't care if the whites run all the way to Hong Kong as long as they run. . . . I go where the money is. I'm a money-oriented guy. It's good business for us when they're frightened. It helps out business."

3. *Chicago Today*, February 28, 1971.
4. Fifth Annual Austin Convention, Organization for a Better Austin, May 1, 1971.
5. *Chicago Tribune*, December 4, 1972.

Another West side broker . . . assessed the change in Austin: "Chicago Avenue is the demarcation line right now. . . . No, I don't know how they form. . . . But one of these days some black will move in north of Chicago Avenue. When one of them jumps, that's the green light. Then it's open season."

Sky Realty Co., Inc. uses this message in its mailings: "If you want to be a former neighbor fast, call Sky Realty Co., Inc."[6]

As Austin underwent racial change, residents reported that they found conventional loans more difficult to secure and FHA-insured loans more available. The area's financial institutions were accused of "redlining," refusing to make loans in the Austin area, although this was generally denied by lenders. The president of Austin Federal Savings and Loan placed the following ad in the June issue of *The Austinite*, a local community newspaper:

I would like to dispel another rumor that there is no conventional mortgage money available in Austin for mortgages. This is definitely a rumor and not true. In the year 1972, Austin Federal made 151 conventional mortgages and rejected only 14, and during the first 5 months of 1973 we made 80 conventional mortgages and rejected 9.

However, based on a sample furnished by a reliable real estate industry source, there is little doubt that there was a withdrawal of conventional mortgages from Austin's fringe and black areas in 1971.

Many of the homes and apartments insured under the federal Section 235 and 203 programs contained numerous building code violations and required extensive and costly repairs. In 1971, for example, the Able Construction Company built seven brick bungalows in Austin that were financed by the FHA Section 235 program for low income homebuyers. The houses, which were said by area residents to look like oversized outhouses, sold for $24,200, but were worth, according to OBA, only $12,000 to $16,000 because of their poor construction. Each house stood on a thirty-foot lot. None had a basement, a garage, or proper insulation in the attic.

In 1973, FHA abuses continued. The black buyer of a house at 5051 West Superior Street said she bought a "dream house that turned into a nightmare."[7] The timbers of her FHA-approved home were rotting, there was sewage in the bathtub and sinks, and there were only two electrical outlets in the $16,000 house. Evidences of corruption in the administration of the FHA programs came to light.

6. Excerpts from a series of articles, *Chicago Tribune,* August 8–12, 1971.
7. *Chicago Sun-Times,* March 31, 1973.

In January 1972, the *Chicago Sun-Times* reported, for example, that two Austin real estate men had been accused of making false statements in securing a $21,850 FHA-insured loan the previous October. The loan had been sought to enable a couple to purchase a property that the agents had acquired for $13,500.

As Austin went through this process of racial transition, insurance, like conventional loan money, also became more difficult to secure, and rates were higher. Insurance companies in the city were accused of redlining certain geographic areas and charging their inhabitants double or triple the amount normally paid for insurance. The highest insurance rates were allegedly charged in black and Spanish-speaking areas, and the amounts charged in these so-called "high risk" or "disaster" zones were, it was argued, not necessarily related to actual crime rates. Until 1960, all Chicago area residents were considered to be in the same type of residential area and therefore paid the same rates. Thereafter, however, the city was divided into zones, and residents paid accordingly. For example, a single male, under age twenty-five, living in the northern portion of Austin had to pay $280 every six months to insure his car, while a single male, under twenty-five, living in south Austin, paid $363.[8] A local insurance agent was quoted as saying that it was "more than a coincidence" that an increase in insurance rates occurred in areas considered to be changing racially.[9]

Concomitant with racial change in Austin was the loss of local businesses and community institutions. In April of 1973, three local savings and loan companies announced plans to open suburban "branches"—Laramie Federal Savings and Loan in Schaumberg; St. Paul Federal Savings and Loan in Franklin Park; and Austin Federal Savings and Loan in Bloomingdale. While these proposed moves were interpreted as a loss of faith in Austin's future, all three companies denied any intention of permanently withdrawing from the community. Despite these reassurances, in August of 1973, *The Austinite* reported that Laramie Federal Savings and Loan in Schaumberg would operate as First Federal Savings and Loan while Laramie Federal Savings and Loan in Austin would operate as the Laramie branch of the First Federal.

In addition to businesses and local financial institutions, other organizations felt the impact of racial transition in Austin. Many of the area's churches were sold as their old congregations moved away; others tried to adapt to a changing constituency.

8. *The Journal*, January 16, 1972.
9. Ibid.

An example of the latter is St. Thomas Aquinas Church, a 1923 Italian Gothic à la Chicago. At its peak in the 1940s and 1950s it served between 2,000 and 3,000 families. In 1972, however, St. Thomas Aquinas had between 300 and 400 families on its register. Nearly all its parishioners were then black, although a few elderly whites and a few Spanish-speaking people lived in the area. St. Thomas Aquinas holds a Spanish mass every Sunday to meet the needs of the latter group. Two of the church's priests were active in OBA, and all were committed to serving the changing needs of the neighborhood. Housed in the church basement, for example, is the "Soul Patrol," a two-way radio network that enables neighborhood residents to contact the police quickly.

St. John's Reformed Episcopal Church is an example of a church that did not adapt to the social changes in its area. St. John's had only a dozen worshipers in August 1973, when it closed, and they were spread out in suburbs like Villa Park and Morton Grove, with only one family living in Austin. After operating forty-six years, the church shut down when its minister of thirty-four years retired: no one else from the seminary wanted to take over St. John's.

Symbolic of what was happening to the entire community were the changes taking place in the area around Austin's Town Hall, the traditional "heart of Austin." The Austin Methodist Church across the street from the town hall was sold to a black congregation. Several of the parochial schools in Austin, which once served the large Irish Catholic population, were forced to close or to curtail their programs due to declining enrollments. St. Lucy's Roman Catholic Church, serving the town hall area, lost three quarters of its parishioners from 1960 to 1973 and closed its school in 1973, sending its pupils to St. Catherine's, which had a 1972-1973 black enrollment of 45 percent. Many commercial establishments fled the town hall area, to be replaced by shops catering to black patrons. The town hall area stood, in the early 1970s, as an example on a microlevel of what was occurring throughout the entire area, and its problems were further exacerbated by an urban renewal project scheduled for 30.2 acres adjacent to the town hall. The city's DUR acquired and razed part of this area before a freeze on federal urban renewal funds was announced. Thereafter, except for a new middle school that has been built on one block, no redevelopment took place, and homeowners in the project area found it difficult either to sell their homes or obtain home improvement loans.

Since the mid-1960s, Austin has experienced a steadily rising rate of crime. In June of 1973, *Chicago Today* reported that Austin, with thirty-five murders, led all other districts of the city for the same period (January 4 through May 23, 1973) and had the fifth highest total crime rate in the city. The south part of Austin was classified as one of twelve "most dangerous" areas, while central and north Austin fell into the "high crime area" category.

Part of Austin's rising homicide rate may be traced to the increase in gang activity that had occurred in the area. The police estimate the presence of ten major gangs in the fifteenth Police District, which includes Austin and the surrounding neighborhoods. Among the known gangs in Austin were the Four Corner Hustlers, the Insane Vice Lords, the Undertakers, and the Gangsters.

The strip of small bars and restaurants along Cicero Avenue from Lake Street to the Expressway became the locus of street crime and vice activities. By the time blacks began moving into the southeastern part of Austin, these establishments were already frequented by blacks. Newspaper editorials decried crime along Cicero, which they linked to "outsiders," as distinguished from Austin's own black residents.

Black and white Austinites were continually taking the police to task for failing to reduce crime in the area. At a meeting in Resurrection Church in December of 1971, Commander Thomas Frost of the patrol division was

> criticized for emphasizing traffic problems and statistics when violent crime is plaguing the area. He was asked to bring back foot patrols, which he said would be investigated.
>
> "Some say the crime rate in Chicago is going up, but we are getting fewer calls. I would say something is really wrong," Frost said.
>
> A black man rose and sarcastically exclaimed, "There sure is."[10]

In 1972 a parents' committee sent out a questionnaire through a local Catholic church, asking what people felt should be improved in the community.

> Everyone complained about security. There was a whole rash of purse snatching at the elevated, a couple of people were beaten up, and all of a sudden, everyone's bikes started disappearing. We had two stolen from in front of our house. A black family would get a house in the neighborhood, put three or four locks on the doors, and lock up their bikes, but we weren't used to that. All of a sudden, everything that wasn't nailed down was gone.
>
> . . .

10. *Chicago Today*, December 1, 1971.

The kids on the block beat up my daughter. . . . I used to send her to the Y with a dime for a towel. They wanted the dime. After that, she was terrified to go out by herself. The older boy was selling candy for the Y and was robbed. They went thru his pockets and knocked him down.[11]

Another resident complained that "In the past 5 years much of Austin has lost established businesses due to unexplained fires, window-breaking, and vandalism."[12]

NATURE OF THE COMMUNITY RESPONSE

Two major community organizations, Organization for a Better Austin (OBA) and Town Hall Assembly (THA), were formed in the late 1960s to deal with the problems resulting from racial transition. The organizations were very different in membership, leadership, and, most important, style.

Organization for a Better Austin

OBA was founded in 1967, when a group of Austin clergymen and religious leaders decided that the community needed a strong, representative organization if it were to withstand the threat of the approaching ghetto. In order to create such a community organization, they hired Thomas Gaudette, a Saul Alinsky–trained organizer, who remained OBA's director until 1972. Some 1,200 to 2,000 delegates, representing block clubs, church organizations, voluntary organizations, and civic groups, attended the community congress in 1967. At that congress it was decided that a permanent organization should be formed to represent the community. OBA was the result; it is an umbrella group for over 180 black, white, and biracial associations ranging from churches to block clubs.

Each year at an annual community congress, a new board is elected, and a new program worked out. OBA had three full-time, salaried staff members and several organizers who were assigned to OBA for internships in 1972. The formal leadership of OBA was composed of five senior officers plus seventeen vice-presidents and seventeen committees. Clergy and religious leaders were notable among the officers and community organizer trainees of OBA. In 1973, OBA's board and vice-presidents reflected the increasing involvement of local black citizens. The president, as well as his predecessor, was black.

11. *Chicago Tribune*, October 14, 1973.
12. Letter to *Northwest Passage*, August 2, 1972.

The organization's funding came from four major sources: (1) business and industry, (2) churches, (3) foundations, and (4) benefits and fund-raising events. Church contributions were in the past the largest single source of OBA revenue.

In its first six years of existence, OBA was involved in controversies that had implications at one time or another for most of Austin's residents. This facet of OBA gave it a more or less "floating membership," as people participated in or ignored specific issues.

Like its membership, OBA's methods tended to change depending on the issue at hand. As OBA's mentor, the late Saul Alinsky, once noted:

> The real question has never been, "Does the end justify the means?" The real question is, and always has been, "Does this particular end justify these particular means?" The ethics of means involves a lot of things, such as who is the judge, the times, and whether you're winning or losing.

Following Alinsky, OBA's policies were based on the principles of confrontation and conflict. Critics of OBA said its tactics were to rub the wounds of society raw:

> "Alinsky tactics are to keep chopping, to continue accusations," said a former public relations director of the Chicago Commission on Human Relations. . . ." OBA tactics are to keep their feet up the government's ass," said another CCHR official. "We will never be able to satisfy them no matter what we do."[13]

Most of the time OBA tried to meet directly with landlords, real estate agents, and city officials to solve problems and arrive at some mutual agreement while acting within the law. But OBA members also became involved in several unsavory incidents, and they were known to take matters into their own hands if resolutions did not meet their expectations.

In 1970, for example, an OBA vice-president was charged with arson when the Sky Realty office, which had been accused of panic peddling in Austin, was firebombed. When asked about this incident, Thomas Gaudette

> "grins, looks at me, and shakes a finger in mock sternness, 'If I ever catch the bastard who did that to those poor real estate people. . . .' The grin on the good face widens."[14]

13. *Chicago Tribune*, December 5, 1971.
14. Ibid.

A housewife who had been active in OBA said:

> The fire-bombing of the Sky office—you bet we did it. A woman did it,
> as a matter of fact, threw it right thru the window and burned the bastards
> out. Not the woman the cops got and charged with arson, then found not
> guilty. . . .
> We just burned out those creeps' real estate office. Real estate people
> here in Austin'll do anything to make a god-damned dime, but we got
> them that time and burned them out. They deserve everything they get.[15]

The following year another OBA vice-president, Thomas Gradel, was
found guilty of panic peddling by the Chicago Commission on
Human Relations when he sent a letter to area homeowners linking
various community problems with black inmigration. The letter
said in part:

> You probably bought a home in Austin for the same reason many of us
> did—excellent transportation and a stable residential community away
> from the loop but not miles out in the suburbs.
> Some things are starting to change, however, Many people are com-
> plaining about crowded schools, deteriorating property values, unsafe
> streets, declining city services, etc. Some of these problems can be traced
> to the rapid turnover from white to black in Austin.[16]

Mr. Gradel said he didn't feel he did wrong in writing the letter,
since he felt it could not be construed as panic peddling. However,
when asked "whether the same letter, if written by a real estate man,
would be considered panic peddling . . . [he said] 'yes, I would consider it panic peddling.'"[17]

The complaint against Gradel was filed by a vice-president of
Town Hall Assembly. She also contended that OBA acts as a real
estate agent through its housing referral service, a charge that has
been echoed by some real estate brokers. Said one:

> It's OBA is the only panic peddler there is in Austin. But instead of
> driving every legitimate real estate man out of Austin and keeping the
> business all for themselves, these community organizations should be in
> the real estate business in a clean manner. . . .
> Listen, I sold pots and pans once, and I called regularly on this whore-
> house. . . . There was this Eunice who lived above the whorehouse . . .
> when her husband was off at work, she would drop down occasionally

15. Ibid.
16. *The Austin News*, June 16, 1971.
17. *The Austinite*, June 16, 1971.

and turn a trick for spending money. I came in one day, and Eunice and this other whore were having at each other, one with a bottle and one with a knife. One of the girls grabbed one, and the pimp got between them, and I tried to make light of it. "What's this world comin' to if we can't trust two whores to be nice to each other?" Eunice got real indignant. "Don't call me no whore! She's the whore. I do it just for spending money, and she's full-time!" . . . The people of Austin have been duped, conned, and swindled by OBA. OBA is like Eunice.[18]

Following the Alinsky premise that the way to mobilize people is to appeal to their self-interest and emotions, OBA never shied away from using racism and scare tactics to involve Austinites in its programs. OBA members also were accused of extorting "contributions" for the organization from local businesses. Several west side businessmen complained that solicitors for OBA used pressure tactics. A spokesman for OBA said, "As for threats, or anything like that, there is nothing to it. We've never been involved in violence. It's not a part of our program."[19] However, an Austin businessman said a delegation from OBA had "demanded $1,500," and left with shouts of "pay up or get out."[20] He added that he wouldn't give 15 cents for the whole OBA group. Another businessman complained that he was told to contribute $500 or his place of business would be picketed. "I really don't know what to call them; dues, I guess. We paid them $250 because we're vulnerable."[21] "They came to see me and they had a price on my head," said the operator of a small restaurant.[22] Thomas Gaudette, speaking for OBA, said, "the establishment only reacts to pressure. . . . I get great joy in seeing people stand up for their rights and only people can solve people's problems."[23] And, while Saul Alinsky has said, "Most conflict will take place in orderly and conventionally approved legal procedures," he added, "But there come times when 'the law spoke too softly to be heard in such a noise of war.'"

Such tactics hardly endeared OBA to many local businesses and residents. However, OBA firmly believed that in some situations only direct confrontation would produce results. It picketed the homes and churches of real estate men accused of panic peddling and harassed landlords and real estate agents into making repairs and

18. *Chicago Tribune*, December 5, 1971.
19. *Chicago Today*, July 15, 1970.
20. Ibid.
21. Ibid.
22. *Chicago Today*, July 17, 1970.
23. *Chicago Tribune*, December 5, 1971.

giving refunds. A March 1973 OBA flyer, for example, headlined "Liutgaarden Lied" goes on to say:

> John Liutgaarden, of Sky Real Estate, promised us he would fix up Mrs. Edwards' house completely. All he has done is unstop the sewer. Mrs. Edwards is left with thousands of dollars in repair work. We want Sky Real Estate to finish the repairs. Bad wiring, rotten window frames, rotten bathroom floor. Call John Liutgaarden at 275-3400 and tell him to fix Mrs. Edwards' house.

Over the years OBA has changed its particular aims. Before 1970 there was more emphasis given to stabilization and to the effort of attracting middle class white families into Austin. As this goal slipped away, more attention was devoted to housing problems, crime, and preventing financial institutions from leaving the area.

At the first all Austin congress in 1967, the following resolutions designed to stabilize community life in Austin were adopted: (1) support for low density housing zoning, (2) support for better police control of Cicero Avenue, and (3) a campaign to attract white families to Austin. In its first year OBA carried on a campaign against panic peddling and operated a housing referral service. OBA's strategy was to discourage white persons from moving out of changing or fringe areas and to encourage referral of black home and apartment seekers to predominantly or all white areas well beyond the racially changing area. OBA claimed to have placed more than 2,000 white applicants in homes and apartments south of Lake Street, but it had little success in placing blacks in outlying white neighborhoods and suburbs. Furthermore, the referral service of OBA had to compete with several hundred real estate agents in the area, all of whom were willing to place black families in fringe areas. Rather than wait for openings in the suburbs, black buyers and renters were more likely to take advantage of the accommodations immediately available in Austin. When questioned as to why OBA's referral service was no longer in operation, on OBA spokesman said that, while it had been the "most successful such service in the city," it was difficult to operate because of "manpower shortages." However, a past OBA president said that severe overcrowding in the schools precluded finding white families to replace those who moved out.

A major accomplishment during OBA's first year of operation was its prodding of the board of education to bus school children from two overcrowded (and largely black) southeastern Austin schools instead of using mobile classrooms that eliminated needed playground space. In 1968, in the first such busing program in Chicago, 317 children from May school and 256 from Spencer school were bused to eight schools in hostile white working class and lower middle class areas on the northwest side of the city. The plan was protested by angry parents of children in the receiving schools and as late as 1971 their attitudes toward the program remained negative.[24]

OBA remains concerned about overcrowding in the area's schools. Busing, demountables, mobile units, and additions are all used to deal with the problem. OBA takes credit for having brought in more new demountables than any other area organization. It was, moreover, largely responsible for the purchase of Sienna Catholic Girls' School by the board of education to be used as a branch for 1,000 students from overcrowded Austin High School. OBA also supported the middle school concept for Austin.

Despite its continuing interest in the area's educational problems, OBA focused most of its efforts on housing. Abandoned buildings became an increasing problem in Austin as whites left, and OBA tried to "encourage" the city to tear down buildings in bad condition and to renovate dilapidated buildings, but felt that the city departments had been dragging their feet.

> By order of a kangaroo building court held on the bed of a rented truck, Austin area residents yesterday launched an assault on an abandoned building in their neighborhood.
> The self-appointed judge, Timothy Harding, 58, a 46-year Austin resident (dressed in a dark robe resembling a judge) signaled the beginning of the effort with a raised fist, the drop of a sledge hammer, and a loud cheer.
> Accompanied by shouts of "right on," the "jury" . . . marched toward a vacant house at 4652 W. Ohio St., which OBA officials said they had unsuccessfully asked the city building department to tear down.[25]

OBA continued to oppose FHA financing of buildings in need of major repairs and tried to force FHA to reimburse buyers for repairs made on housing that had between $2,000 and $10,000 worth of code violations.

After an initial furor, there was a diminishing focus on panic peddling, perhaps due to the perception that the most formidable enemy was not the small-time real estate operator but the lending industry, including the federal government, whose policy of redlining threatened any possibility of stabilization.

OBA fought against the tendency of banks and savings and loan

24. *Northwest Passage*, March 22, 1972.
25. *Chicago Tribune*, January 28, 1973.

associations to refuse conventional loans to businesses and home-owners in changing areas. Excerpts from an OBA Resolutions Meeting on March 3, 1972, comment directly on policies of savings and loan associations:

> Whereas, Savings and Loans have different criteria for giving mortgages in our communities compared to the standards for the suburbs, and
>
> Whereas, Savings and Loans don't even look at buildings in our communities before saying "no mortgage,"
>
> Therefore, Be It Resolved that Savings and Loans be required to investigate each application without red-lining certain communities or neighborhoods.

In the April, 1972, issue of the *OBA Advocate*, Dorothy Malone, who was trying to sell two apartment buildings, complained that she could not get a conventional mortgage for her qualified buyer and that FHA did not apply to large buildings that did not need rehabilitation.

> She and the buyer have been to 8 mortgage companies that have said "OBA is controlling real estate in that area and we're not going to fight them . . . no mortgage money in that area. It's changing neighborhood. If it were all white or all black we would be glad to do business with you . . . that area is a bad area, the FBI is investigating and there is too much publicity."

The organization worked actively to prevent financial institutions from leaving the area. In July of 1973, due to OBA's efforts in fact, one Austin savings and loan association was denied its request to establish a branch in the suburbs.

The Town Hall Assembly

Austin's second major community organization and OBA's archrival was the Town Hall Assembly (THA). Composed of approximately sixty-five member organizations in the area around the town hall (bounded by Long, Austin, Lake, and Chicago), THA was founded soon after OBA in 1967 and is perhaps best understood as a reaction to OBA. Strictly a volunteer agency, manned by Austin residents, THA did not consider OBA to be the local, grassroots organization it claimed to be because of the "outsiders" and professional organizers associated with it. A THA officer said that THA was founded to provide a "catalyst" for the block clubs that were forming in the central part of Austin and not as an opposition group to OBA, but the obvious implication was that OBA was not seen as fulfilling this need. In addition to these block clubs and other organizations located within THA's boundaries, Austin groups that had a recognized interest in the town hall area also were eligible to join. Unlike OBA, THA was supported by and worked in close alliance with Austin's major community institutions such as the Austin Business Council, the Kiwanis and Lions clubs, and *The Austinite* newspaper. In fact, THA enjoyed from the outset a near monopoly in the center of Austin, both geographically and institutionally. It was of the establishment and worked through the establishment. While this led to some allegations that THA was prone to manipulation by politicians, it did not participate in electoral politics as does OBA, which was actively involved in the Walker and McGovern campaigns in 1972.

THA's original major goal, like that of OBA, was to stabilize the community. THA did not operate a housing referral service— "there is already one in every Catholic church in the area," said a THA spokeswoman. It did not inaugurate any specific programs designed to monitor code violations or to encourage building maintenance; in fact, it looked askance at OBA's tactics and refused to be part of "snooping around" looking for violations in slum buildings.

THA emphasized education rather than real estate practices as a key factor in stabilizing Austin. It worked for more schools and classrooms and for the maintenance of a fifty-fifty racial balance in Austin High School. THA demanded, to no avail, that the Austin High School district boundaries be returned to their pre-1964 location. In the absence of a boundary change, THA tried to create other alternatives for Austin's white high school students. For example, Lane Tech was opened to Austin students due in part to THA pressure, and THA supported a program of permissive transfers for Austin high school students. More recently, THA demanded a high school for North Austin residents. In the spring of 1973, THA provided information for parents of eighth graders interested in enrolling their children in Prosser Vocational High School, a former boys' school that THA had succeeded in opening to girls as well. To accomplish these goals, THA worked quietly with the board of education; it never, according to a spokeswoman, resorted to "yelling kangaroo-court tactics."

THA's program for stabilizing Austin also included working with local employers to encourage their employees to seek housing in Austin and support for the Crosstown Expressway, which OBA opposed. THA's endorsement of the Crosstown was based on the hope that it would bring new vitality to Austin, in the form of motels, large stores, and perhaps even a city college or sports complex. It would also entail demolition of some of Austin's most deteriorated structures and, in turn, displace some of Austin's black population.

THA did numerous other "constructive" things for the Austin community. It was responsible for lowering Austin's property taxes by bringing about a property reassessment of the area. For a number of years THA ran a tutoring program in reading and math manned by volunteers. In the area of crime, THA sponsored a drug program and generally tried to encourage better communication between the police and the area's youth. According to THA, the organization had good relations with the local police, with whom a THA committee meets once a month.

Apart from programs designed to deal with specific local problems, THA engaged in a public relations effort to build up Austin. It attempted to counterattack the negative image it felt Austin had in the press due to the actions of "other groups in the area."

"I'm so tired of old people being frightened out of their wits by the OBA, of people being used," says Eileen McCaffrey [a vice-president of THA]. "OBA claims they want stability in Austin, but they only get bad publicity for it. I get flyers from OBA. If I didn't know better, I'd say, My God, this must be a terrible place. I'd move out. It is demoralizing to have picketing in your community, and these flyers they are always sending out—this is not conducive to residential living. There is a lot to be proud of in Austin, beautiful homes and beautiful architecture. . . . We have rich and we have poor, but THA wants to attract middle-class people to this area. Our methodology is very different from OBA's. We have positive programs while OBA takes a germ of truth and exploits it.

"OBA brings in organizers to train in Austin. They create problems so organizer trainees can get their experience. . . ."

. . .

"It think we ought to try to bring out the best of what everybody is, not the worst. No one at OBA accepts responsibility for what is being done, no one at OBA owns up."[26]

In response to these charges, a spokeswomen for OBA said:

THA says we only cause dissension in Austin, but if it weren't for our activism, THA wouldn't exist. They exist only to attack everything we do. They favored bussing until OBA backed it, and then the opposed it. But THA is not even public. They have their token blacks while we work with

26. *Chicago Tribune*, December 5, 1971.

blacks and they work with us. THA has a buzzer on their door. You have to buzz to get in like a funky private club, and that screams fear to me.[27]

After 1970 THA, together with the Austin Business Council and *The Austinite*, sponsored a communitywide festival called "Old Austin Days which sought to promote "the good things about Austin." The same spokeswoman for OBA did admit that "THA does things this community needs. They have a parade, they have dinner dances, the nice and healthy things. Things OBA doesn't have time to do."[28]

THA and Austin's established organizations and institutions made strong efforts to preserve the status quo. One important offshoot of this was the division of Austin into two communities, North and South Austin, separated by the Lake Street elevated tracks. This cleavage emerged while South Austin was still predominantly white and represented the unspoken assumption that South Austin was "gone," while North Austin might still be "saved." While racial change in itself would probably have produced such a division, it was institutionalized by the actions of community leaders and institutions at a very early stage in the transition process, probably precluding any small hope South Austin may have had of stabilizing. Redlining by banks and insurance companies and the demand for a North Austin High School have already been mentioned. THA, for example, never attempted to represent that part of Austin south of Lake Street. *The Austinite* began referring increasingly to North and South Austin, until those terms were used to the virtual exclusion of just "Austin." There was considerable editorial speculation over whether the trend of racial turnover would be directed north or whether it would cross the city limits and continue in its westward course along the Eisenhower Expressway, eventually linking up with suburban Maywood's ghetto. A projection by the Real Estate Research Corporation that the latter was most likely was well publicized, and *The Austinite* wrote of the possibility of a "biracial" Austin, with blacks and whites living in separate neighborhoods but sharing certain institutions and facilities. While *The Austinite* still purported to serve the entire community, blacks seem quite underrepresented in its coverage of social and organizational news.

The secession of North Austin was roughly paralleled by changes in ward boundaries. In 1970, the thirtieth ward was redistricted so that white Alderman McMahon could continue to control it. The

27. Ibid.
28. "Austin: Civil Rights and Integration in a Chicago Community," Report Number 3, Community and Family Study Center, University of Chicago, August 1, 1968.

twenty-eighth ward, directly to the south, was "given" to a black alderman, as was the southernmost twenty-ninth ward. This left Alderman Thomas Casey and Committeeman T.A. McGloon in control of the thirty-seventh ward, covering the predominantly white and safely Democratic center of Austin. Redistricting also left Austin's state senators and representatives with much smaller black constituencies than they previously had.

While Lake Street, because of its central location, had always been the site of the offices of Austin's major organizations, such as the Democratic headquarters, *The Austinite*, the later THA, all of these moved north, at least as far as Chicago Avenue.

Yet new institutions also emerged in both sections of Austin. *The Northwest Passage*, *The Austinite's* sister paper, dealt specifically with the North Austin community, giving extensive coverage of THA activities, area crime, and community events. In South Austin, new black organizations were created to serve the specific needs of this area.

CONCLUSIONS

Austin's two major community organizations were entirely different in character and strategy, and these differences led to a marked hostility between them. OBA supporters considered THA ineffective and cemented to the status quo, while THA partisans considered OBA leadership "outside agitators" who were devious and divisive in their tactics.

It would seem that OBA, since its inception, had misread the character of the Austin community. Its aggressive flamboyance and attempt to involve Austinites on the basis of fear ignored the fact that overt race prejudice was contrary to the prevailing self-image of its residents, who resented being characterized as bigots. However, in reality, the typical white Austinite's attitude toward integration was less than favorable, according to a 1968 study:

> At best [his] attitude may be described as ambivalent. . . . In part, then, it appears that ambivalence toward integration is based on the expectation that the Negroes moving in would be of lower socio-economic status or—more to the point—characterized by markedly different styles of life. [It is] also based on the expectation that integration would soon become Negro invasion.
>
> . . .
>
> Yet the *anticipation* of rapid racial turnover is clearly associated with the fact that 44 percent of the white residents of Austin expect to be

moving away from a community which they now regard as a satisfactory place to live.[29]

Many Austinites viewed OBA's involvement with pro- and anti-integrationist constituencies as hypocrisy and as self-serving agitation by people who had no deep or lasting interest in the community. They also rejected the militancy of OBA. Moreover, the indigenous social network and leadership in Austin was either bypassed by OBA or could not be enlisted by it. The bringing in of outside organizers became a source of deep community resentment toward OBA.

OBA's underlying premise was that Austin was a community in the process of racial change, a change that would result in a new social character and new needs. However, this premise was not generally adopted by residents of North Austin. The North Austin establishment operated on the theory that, since the advent of black inmigration, Austin is two social and territorial communities. Rather than change its conception of the general social and cultural character of the community and redefine its values and norms, it decided to redraw and, if necessary, to keep on redrawing the shrinking boundaries where the status quo applied.

OBA adapted to the changed social and economic needs of its constituents and vociferously tried to attack the problems at hand—deteriorating housing, FHA violations, redlining and rate zoning, the loss of community institutions, and school and crime problems.

However, OBA was an organization ahead of its time. It did not fit the community in which it operated. Only when Austin had its back to the wall could *The Austinite* editorialize that, "Austin was forced to accept OBA tactics only because of its extreme frustration with regular channels but it did not like or approve them." But by the time Austinites began to feel that OBA's strategies were their hope of survival, OBA had lost the advantage of time. Thus it would seem that OBA's Alinskylike character could only have been embraced by Austinites at the specific time when they perceived that they were in a fight for territorial survival. Unfortunately, by this time, much of Austin had gone from white to black. However, it is extremely doubtful, given Austin's proximity to the black ghetto, its aging and declining population, and its obsolescent housing stock, that OBA could have stabilized Austin—even if it has been wholeheartedly backed by the community from 1967.

THA fitted Austin's self-concept to a much greater degree than did OBA. THA moved in ways that Austinites considered "proper."

29. Ibid.

It did not engage in shouting matches with officials; it never aired its dirty linen in public. THA never embarrassed the community; it never took a bold step or a chance. It was an organization of local people who behaved in a "rational" manner. THA stressed the good, positive reasons for staying in or moving to Austin—the beautiful homes and other amenities that could be found there. By so doing, it maintained an aloof, dignified profile in Austin, far removed from the turbulence that was reality. The very things about THA that appealed to Austinites doomed it to a position of weakness. Since THA received part of its funds from area banks and businesses, it could not attack them even when their policies threatened Austin's ability to stabilize. In fact, THA's relationship to these institutions seemed to blind it regarding the consequences of such policies. By trying to preserve the status quo, THA failed to come to grips with the rapidity of racial change that overtook Austin.

Thus the two community organizations that were set up to stabilize Austin failed: one because it could not generate community acceptance until it was too late to test its tactics; the other because saving Austin's public face took priority over developing an action-oriented program.

Austin, as a result, continued to see racial change above Chicago Avenue as far north as Division Street and thence on to North Avenue. The area's aging housing, combined with its gradual loss of services and commercial, financial, and community facilities, its high crime rate, and its overcrowded, racially changing schools, could not attract the young white families necessary for it to achieve racial stability.

Chapter 12

Oak Park: Reverse Steering and Racial Quotas

Just over the city limits from Austin is Oak Park, one of the first of Chicago's suburbs to face the prospect of ghetto expansion as South Austin underwent racial succession. Oak Park is a middle income, white collar dormitory suburb, with most of its labor force employed in Chicago in professional and technical occupations. Its 1970 population of 62,506 resided within a rectangular-shaped area of 4.7 square miles located at the western border of the city of Chicago, nine miles due west of the Loop. Situated on the Eisenhower Expressway, the Lake and Congress rapid transit lines, and the Chicago and Northwestern Railway, Oak Park has excellent access to the Loop, the Illinois Medical Center complex, and the University of Illinois Chicago Circle campus. In 1970, the median income of Oak Parkers was $13,319, and the median home value was $26,200. While Protestants outnumbered Roman Catholics by about two to one in earlier times, the majority of immigrants to Oak Park in the last decade had been young Roman Catholics fleeing ghetto expansion on Chicago's west side, and the two groups were in 1970 about evenly split, with a little over 40 percent each. Jews and Orthodox Catholics together made up about 5 percent of the religiously affiliated population. In 1970, 30.2 percent of the population was foreign born or of foreign or mixed parentage, and only 132 Oak Park residents were black. Other nonwhites accounted for about 1 percent of the population.

While single family homes occupied 45 percent of Oak Park's total land area and 79 percent of its residential land area, they constituted only 42 percent of the total dwelling units. The largest single category of dwelling units were those located in large apartment buildings—namely, structures of six or more units. These constituted 44 percent of the total dwelling units, while they occupied only 5 percent of the total land area, giving the village the misleading visual appearance of a typical suburb of single family homes. Only 46 percent of the total dwelling units were owner occupied, a very low figure for a suburb.

Oak Park was almost completely developed by 1930 and has changed little in land use or physical characteristics since that time. Thus, aging and obsolescence of structures and land uses is one of its major problems today. The village is completely enclosed by other municipalities, and there is very little internal open space for new construction. Like many older suburbs, the problem of obsolescence of its commercial areas has been compounded by successful competition from new shopping centers located elsewhere. While it is generally conceded by community leaders and public officials that change and modernization are urgent necessities, those elements of change that evoke the image of the "big city"—high rise buildings, for example—are perceived by many residents as threats to Oak Park's way of life that are perhaps as great as the threat of continued aging and obsolescence.

The population has also aged. The community had reached the end stage of its life cycle by 1960. However, after 1960 there was a large influx of young white families, bringing the median age down from 40 in 1960 to 36.7 in 1970 and producing a massive increase in numbers of children in the schools. The percentage of residents in the sixty-five years and older age group is still extremely high (16.3 percent). However, the proportion of the population in the younger age groups has also increased, while the middle age groups have been decreasing.

Oak Park's symbolic image can hardly be inferred from quantitative data of the sort that has been presented so far. Oak Park's relative prestige among Chicago's western suburbs had declined considerably by 1970, a combined effect of the obsolescence of its housing stock and the rapid growth of new developments farther west. Nonetheless, its image as a well-established, affluent, white Anglo-Saxon Protestant community had remained surprisingly durable, despite what the "objective" facts and figures showed to the contrary. First of all, it must be recognized that the northern and southern halves of Oak Park were two very different communities from the standpoint of social and housing characteristics. The northern half was generally more affluent, composed primarily of single family homes and few apartments. Several blocks were lined with very large expensive homes, a few of them valued at more than

$100,000. Frank Lloyd Wright lived in Oak Park and did much of his early work there, and much of north Oak Park was designated a historic preservation district because of its architectural landmarks, including the Wright homes and over forty other buildings of major significance. On the other hand, the southern half of Oak Park consists primarily of modest bungalows and two story frame homes and also contains most of the village's large apartment buildings.

Other factors also enhanced the community image. The central business district was small, but it had stores such as Marshall Field, Peck and Peck, and Bramson's, offering high-priced merchandise, as well as moderately priced chains such as Montgomery Ward and Wieboldt and small shops in all price ranges. The historical and cultural heritage contributed to the image. One could not remain in Oak Park long without being made aware that it was the one-time home not only of Frank Lloyd Wright, but also of Ernest Hemingway and Edgar Rice Burroughs, or that it had won a National Beautification Award for four consecutive years. One of Oak Park's grand old estates and part of the grounds of another had been preserved as public parks. The image of the community held by its residents and promoted through the local media rested far more on its "better" stores, expensive homes, architectural landmarks, affluent citizens, and famous sons than on any kind of average measure of population and housing characteristics. Even for residents of south Oak Park, for whom this imagery should be least salient, Oak Park was at the very least a community of homes, schools, and churches—and a familial, suburban lifestyle—sharply distinguished from the central city, despite the fact that homeowners were in the minority and that in many other social characteristics Oak Park more resembled the city of Chicago than the rest of the suburban ring.

Since 1953, Oak Park had a village manager form of government. The board of trustees, consisting of six trustees and a village president, was elected every four years in a nonpartisan, at large election. The Village Manager Association dominated local politics, with its endorsed slate having won every election for the past twenty years. Sometimes opposition parties emerged at election time, but they dissolved after the election.

The village government enjoyed considerable prestige and respect. "Good government" and official integrity were assumed without question by the local citizenry. The most serious charge that had been brought against the trustees was that they allowed their decisions to be influenced too much by local commercial and financial interests. Those elected to the village board were invariably business and professional men and were thought of as such and not as politicians.

A 1971 survey of Oak Park homeowners gave evidence of overall satisfaction with the level of local public services. A majority of respondents rated all services except street lighting as at least "adequate." A majority of respondents rated as "excellent" the high school, elementary schools, fire department, parks and playgrounds, police department, and garbage pickup (listed in order of the percentage responding "excellent" from highest to lowest).[1]

In county, state, and national elections, Oak Park cast a Republican majority, but the margin steadily decreased after 1965. The Republican and regular Democratic parties had precinct organizations that were weak by city standards. The independent Democratic Organization was strong enough to be taken very seriously by candidates. The League of Women Voters also was very active and apparently influential in local decisionmaking.

Oak Park had ten public elementary schools and one public high school, all reputed to be very good. The high school, shared with River Forest, an affluent suburb to the immediate west, was college preparatory in its orientation. There were black students enrolled in all of the elementary schools, but the black enrollment was concentrated in Hawthorne and Longfellow schools in the east central sector of the suburb. In the 1971-1972 school year, three black teachers were employed by the elementary school district. In the same year, the high school had about twenty-five black students out of a total enrollment of over 4,000 and no black teachers. Both the elementary and the high schools made the hiring of black teachers a high priority goal for 1972 and succeeded in hiring a few new black teachers.

There were also four Roman Catholic elementary schools, a Catholic boys' high school, a Lutheran elementary school, and a Montessori school located in the village. (Actually, since parish boundaries cut across municipal boundaries, Oak Park Catholics are served by a total of eight elementary schools, while some of the Catholic schools located within Oak Park are shared with neighboring municipalities.) It is indicative of the social-geographic cleavage of Oak Park that only one of the four Roman Catholic parishes is located in the northern half of Oak Park. This parish is located within a high income neighborhood, and its school is noted for its excellent facilities, equipment, and educational program. St. Catherine's elementary school, located on the eastern border of Oak Park at Washington Boulevard, serves both Chicago and Oak Park children and

---

1. Roberta Raymond, "The Challenge to Oak Park: A Suburban Community Faces Racial Change" (M.A. Thesis, Roosevelt University, January 1972).

had a 1972-1973 black enrollment of 45 percent, giving it by far the highest black enrollment of any school in the suburb.

PERCEPTIONS OF COMMUNITY CHANGE

The First Phase of Local Race Relations:
1900-1969

Around the turn of the century, as many as one hundred black families lived in two small residential areas in Oak Park. One enclave was located adjacent to the central business district, and the other was located in the northwest corner of the village. As the use of domestic servants declined and the growing CBD invaded the neighboring black area, Oak Park's black population dwindled, reaching its low point of fifty-seven in 1960. Most of the remaining blacks were domestic servants, many living in the homes of their employers, and they were such an inconspicuous part of the population even by 1950 that a noted black scientist who moved with his family into the community in that year has often been called Oak Park's "first black resident." He was able to move into the community only with much difficulty, finally obtaining a home on one of the suburb's most affluent blocks by repurchase from a white friend who acted as "straw buyer." A firebomb did minor damage to his home, and he was also subjected to various types of less serious harrassment, but the hostility subsided, and he remained in Oak Park.

Race did not become an important issue again until the early 1960s, when Oak Park, like communities across the nation, had its share of whites involved in the civil rights movement. The issue became an inescapably local one when the community symphony orchestra hired a black musician but fired her before her first public appearance, allegedly for reasons of race. This incident gave the impetus of clear local relevance to the civil rights activities that were already taking place. The heightened concern pursuant to the incident culminated in the formation of the Oak Park-River Forest Citizens' Committee for Human Rights, a voluntary group that led the drive for local open housing and civil rights for the rest of the decade. The Village Community Relations Commission, consisting of fifteen citizens appointed by the village board, was also established soon after the incident. Although the trustees had been considering the establishment of such a commission before this, the incident of the musician precipitated its formation.

Between 1963 and 1968, the citizens' committee and other involved organizations used a variety of tactics to educate the community in the area of race relations and to establish fair housing in Oak Park. These included newspaper advertisements, public meetings, marches and demonstrations, and "open house" tours for black Chicagoans seeking suburban dwellings. Real estate brokers agreed to provide for an "M" listing service whereby a seller or landlord could offer his property without regard for race. However, at any given time, only about 10 percent of the total listings were available on this basis, and these in fact were not always shown by agents to minority prospects.

By the end of 1967, there were only eleven black or interracial families living in Oak Park, and the housing market was clearly all but tightly closed to blacks. Pressure was initiated for a local fair housing ordinance, and such a law was passed in May 1968, despite strong organized opposition and apparent negative public opinion. The Referendum Group, an ad hoc organization demanding a public vote on the issue, secured over 10,000 signatures on a petition supporting their demand, and they unsuccessfully brought the issue to court after the village board passed the ordinance. The local real estate industry, at first strongly opposed to "forced housing"—the catchword of fair housing opponents—subsided in its opposition when the Federal Civil Rights Act was passed in April 1968, possibly feeling that compliance with a local ordinance might decrease their susceptibility to prosecution under the stricter federal law. Community leaders and activists at the time considered passage of the law a brave and unpopular decision on the part of the trustees, and even now it is sometimes cited as evidence of the courage and integrity of the village board. Nevertheless, the incumbent local party, the Village Manager Association, swept the elections the following spring, despite the fact that they ran against candidates promising a referendum on the fair housing law, a major issue in the campaign.

The Oak Park Fair Housing Ordinance, as originally enacted, prohibited discrimination "against any person in the terms, conditions, or privileges of sale or rental of a dwelling, or in the provision of services or facilities in connection therewith, because of race, color, religion, or national origin."

In addition, this ordinance prohibited:

any form of advertising which indicates discrimination on the basis of race, color, religion, or national origin.

refusal to deal with or misrepresentation of facts to a prospective buyer or renter because of his race, color, religion, or national origin.

any form of "Panic Peddling" on the grounds of present or prospective entry into the neighborhood of persons of any particular race, religion, or national origin . . . .

extending differential treatment in financing because of an applicant's race, color, religion, or national origin.

solicitation by real estate brokers when an owner indicates in writing that he does not desire to sell or be solicited.[2]

The ordinance did not apply to the rental of rooms or apartments in owner-occupied buildings of up to four units and to the nonpublic offering of property by a private owner. Furthermore, "certain locations, buildings, and transactions could be declared exempt if a plan of development designed to prevent or eliminate de facto segregation is submitted to the Community Relations Commission and found to be reasonable and pursued in good faith." This "exempt location" clause in effect legitimized an informal quota system at the discretion of the Community Relations Commission, and it became particularly controversial. Community Relations Commission members suspected that it was unconstitutional and discussed deleting it from the ordinance. When this issue was again brought up at a commission meeting in the summer of 1972, the consensus was that it should be left in the ordinance, if only because deleting it might lead to the impression that the commission was abandoning its commitment to prevent resegregation of some parts of the community.

The fair housing ordinance also provided the Community Relations Commission with a staff of one and one-half full-time employees (since doubled) to administer the law. The following paragraphs from a Community Relations Commission pamphlet describe enforcement procedures:

Persons who are aggrieved by what they consider an unfair real estate practice may file a complaint with the Oak Park Community Relations Commission. The Administrator will attempt to eliminate it by conference, conciliation, and persuasion within thirty days. If this fails, the Commission will hold a hearing at which both parties in the incident may appear and present testimony.

If it is the opinion of the Commission that there has been a violation of the ordinance, they may recommend to the Village Board of Trustees that the license of the real estate broker who has committed the unfair real estate practice be suspended or revoked, and that proceedings shall be filed against any person who has committed an unfair real estate practice.

2. Village of Oak Park Community Relations Commission, "Fair Housing Oak Park," undated pamphlet.

The court will determine the outcome of the case and in the event of a violation, will levy a fine of not more than $500.[3]

(The section relating to local licensing of brokers and power to suspend or revoke licenses was later superseded by state law negating the power of municipalities to regulate professions.)

By the end of 1971, the Community Relations Commission had handled thirty-eight discrimination complaints, resulting in four litigations, of which there were three convictions and fines and one dismissal. In addition, one broker was prosecuted for operating his business without a local license and in a residentially zoned area, raising the total number of litigations under the ordinance to five. Eighteen complaints were not forwarded by the administrator to the full body of the commission for various reasons, including lack of substantiation and disinterest of the complainant in pursuing the complaint further. Eleven complaints were satisfactorily conciliated.

As a matter of policy, the Community Relations Commission did not engage in testing for discrimination through the use of bogus prospects, and without this it was difficult to substantiate discrimination complaints. Therefore, the Citizens' Committee for Human Rights did much of the investigation and preparation of evidence for the litigated complaints. In addition, the citizens' committee helped prepare several cases that were subsequently brought before the federal court by attorneys of the Leadership Council for Metropolitan Open Communities (see Chapter 2).

Passage of the local fair housing law induced the citizens' committee to step up its program to attract blacks to the community. To this end, the citizens' committee cooperated with the Leadership Council for Metropolitan Open Communities and with the Home Investments Fund. Repeated advertisements were also run in the *Daily Defender*. By 1970, the net gain in black or interracial families in Oak Park since the passage of the Fair Housing Law two and one-half years earlier was twenty-eight, a figure that has been variously touted as success or disparaged as failure, depending upon the speaker and the occasion.

The Second Phase: 1970 and After

1970 marked the end of the first phase of Oak Park's attempt to come to grips with the issue of race and housing. By 1970, the classic pattern of block by block invasion and succession had swept through much of the southern part of the neighboring Chicago com-

3. Ibid.

munity area of Austin. The westward expansion of the ghetto was taking place at a rate of about two blocks per year between 1965 and 1970, fanning out to the north as well, as the industrial areas that had confined it lapsed into residential land uses in Austin. Clearly, if the transition were to continue westward at the same pace, Oak Park could soon expect a sizable ghetto of its own. Much "official" notice was also taken of the fact that the ghetto had reached the Chicago city limits and appeared headed through the suburbs. "Expert" projections of the future racial composition of Oak Park were made and well publicized in the local and metropolitan press. Real Estate Research Corporation, for example, predicted that Oak Park would have 2000 blacks by 1975 and would be 25 percent black by 1980. Such predictions were generally known to the residents of Oak Park and Austin.

Oak Parkers were ambivalent in their assessment of the prospects for racial change. On the one hand, expressions of the long-standing rivalry and invidious comparisons of Oak Park and Austin (comparisons favorable to Oak Park) were heard less frequently than were comments emphasizing the essential similarity of the two communities and remarks to the effect of "what a nice neighborhood Austin used to be." Oak Parkers were dismayed at the speed of transition in Austin. One local official commented in a personal interview that, "Fifteen years ago Austin and Oak Park were practically indistinguishible in physical characteristics. No one would have thought that Austin was going to go down the drain—if you want to call racial change 'going down the drain.'"

On the other hand, it became common for Oak Parkers to react to the prospect of substantial black residency in the village with remarks such as: "But how can they afford it?" and "What I want to know is where do they get the money?" Such beliefs were based on a combination of racial stereotyping and the assumption that housing costs in Oak Park were somewhat inflated, that one paid a premium to live in the community over and above the cost of comparable housing in Austin, for instance. One Oak Park woman said when interviewed, with reference to high rents in the suburb, "They[?] want it that way. They want to keep the colored out." However, rents and home prices seemed more in line with similar quality housing in other areas by 1970 than they had been in the past, as housing costs remained more nearly stable in Oak Park than in much of the metropolitan area.

Some of the perception of the prospects of racial change must be seen in the context of Oak Park's earlier experience with fair housing. While integration was strictly minimal, the pattern of black residence was well dispersed, and the village's fair housing efforts had received considerable good publicity outside of Oak Park. This bolstered local pride and the sense of the community's "uniqueness" and led to the falsely secure belief on the part of some residents that Oak Park would have little difficulty in maintaining integration while absorbing more blacks into its population.

The typical black family who moved to Oak Park before mid-1971 also left white Oak Parkers ill prepared for black immigration from Austin. Blacks who moved to the suburb before this time came largely from outside the Chicago metropolitan area or from nonghetto areas within Chicago. They were superior in socioeconomic status to most white Oak Park residents. Two-thirds purchased homes, according to a Community Relations Commission survey. There was a clear preference on the part of these black "pioneers" for blocks with higher than average housing values. Ten out of the seventeen black homeowners chose blocks where the average home value was at least $30,000, while the average home value on most of Oak Park's blocks was less than $30,000.

After 1970, however, new and different black residents began moving into southeastern Oak Park's rental properties as the ghetto reached the city limits in south Austin. In October 1972 the Community Relations Commission estimated Oak Park's black population at 180 families. Based on a ratio of four individuals to one family, this would set the black population of Oak Park at approximately 760.

Officials were hesitant to single out the southeast quadrant for any special attention for fear that this would call attention to the existence of a "problem" and lead to panic on the part of present white residents or frighten prospective white residents away from the area. Officials were faced with the dilemma of finding solutions for a problem while publicly denying its existence. Local leaders commonly used the term "minority person" when they meant "black," and they emphasized that these "minority persons" constituted only a very small percentage of the population. By the end of 1971, community relations officials had decided that this was a counterproductive strategy. It was considered offensive to black residents, and furthermore, it seemed to imply that there was no reason for alarm only because and as long as blacks were a tiny minority of the population. Yet in the spring of 1972, the Community Relations Commission distributed a newsletter in which it was asserted that Oak Park's minority population was under ½ of 1%, well-dispersed in all parts of the Village. The substitution here of "minority" for "black" results in a statement that is untrue, if taken literally, for the figure cited is correct for Oak Park's black population but understates the total nonwhite population. Further evidence of reluctance to give official notice to the issue of racial change is seen in the fact that the plan commission and its voluntary citizen advisory body, the Citizens' Action Committee, despite stated intentions to deal with the goal of racial integration and means of achieving it, released a comprehensive plan in 1972 that failed to give more than passing mention to the subject. After public criticism of the omission, the trustees called for the development of an integration plan for the village.

Voluntary groups and local activists involved in the race and housing issue were consistently more willing to admit publicly the existence of a problem, and they insisted that the village government openly commit itself to dealing with it. Residents of southeast Oak Park demanded and received from the village government special attention to their "special problems," including more police protection, physical redevelopment, better housing inspection, and the like.

Indeed, the most disturbing issue for most Oak Parkers became crime. They were well aware of the dramatic increases in the crime rate that had occurred in Austin, In 1971, Oak Park's index crime rate was up only 6 percent over the preceding year. In 1972, it rose another 8 percent. In mid-1972, however, it was also reported that robberies, the type of crime that was of major concern to residents, had tripled in three years. Press coverage of crime may have been more important in inciting anxiety than the actual crime rate. One community newspaper in particular gave prominent coverage to crime news, in one instance devoting most of the front page to five separate headlined items about street robberies and assaults. This also was the only local paper to print the race of the offender. The chief of police consistently maintained that racial change in Austin or Oak Park had not been a significant factor in increased crime in Oak Park, but there is no doubt that the two phenomena were directly linked in the minds of many residents.

THE NATURE OF THE RESPONSE: ORGANIZATIONS, GOALS, AND PROGRAMS

The responses to prospective racial change were a function of the types of organizations in the community. Beginning at the grassroots level of the community power pyramid, the first organizations to be considered are the block clubs, or One Hundred Clubs, as they are called in Oak Park. These were actually instituted by the village government under the auspices of the Village Beautification Commission. They were intended to serve as home improvement organizations and channels of informal control and communication among neighbors. While the majority of Oak Park's blocks were organized— that is, they had officially designated volunteer block chairmen— many were dormant. The most intense block club activity occurred in the southeast quadrant, particularly in the area in which black penetration had occurred or seemed imminent. These block clubs met regularly, often sending delegations to public meetings or private conferences with village officials, and there was considerable communication among the more active residents of the different blocks of this area. A regular newsletter also was published by and for residents of this area.

These southeast block clubs did not overtly attempt to keep blacks out of the area, but they did attempt to prevent panic and flight of white residents through informal communication and persuasion. In addition, they functioned as pressure groups on the village government, working primarily to gain attention for what they saw as their particular needs—physical rehabilitation and maintenance, strict housing code enforcement, redevelopment of the deteriorating Madison Street commercial strip, additional police protection, and, in general, a commitment from village officials that their area was not to be "written off." Village government acceded to these demands.

Another group of major importance in Oak Park was the local chapter of Citizens' Action Program (CAP). CAP, a dues-supported, issue-oriented pressure group, was extremely active and enjoyed considerable grassroots support. Structurally, it consisted of a salaried community organizer assigned by the parent organization and an executive board composed of local volunteers. While its actual paid membership was not large, on particular issues it was able to mobilize as many as 200 residents at a time, including highly respected members of the community—for example, local professionals, pastors of large churches, and members of village commissions.

CAP strove to be a broad-based organization, neither integrationist nor segregationist, able to unite people representing the entire range of the social and political spectra. Its success in this regard was only partial. While it was supported by some whose avowed desire was to keep blacks out of Oak Park, the membership in general was of a liberal complexion. CAP's major support came from residents of the southern half of Oak Park, and it was especially strong in the southeast quadrant. On the other hand, it had virtually no active support from the northwest sector of Oak Park.

CAP's major activities in its first two years of existence were support for a ban on "for sale" signs; organized opposition against zoning amendments to allow development of a high rise apartment building; pressure on local lenders suspected of redlining and on the village government to outlaw redlining; and pressure on the village government to provide funds for the hiring of additional policemen. CAP was successful in each of these endeavors but one: it was not able to prevent approval of the high rise construction, although CAP has assumed major credit for trimming down the proposed size from fifty-four to thirty-seven stories. CAP's major operating tactics included publicity through local newspapers and mimeographed leaflets, persuasion of local officials in private meetings, testimony at open meetings and hearings, and mobilization of large numbers of supporters to attend relevant public meetings to give a show of grassroots support for CAP's positions. CAP deliberately avoided tactics of direct confrontation. Other than mass attendance at public meetings, the most direct action CAP took was the leafletting of a savings and loan bank alleged to be redlining, and though CAP's supporters packed the lobby of the firm while CAP leaders met with savings and loan officials, the purpose was apparently only mild intimidation, and there was no intention stated of remaining after the meeting if the outcome was not satisfctory (which it was).

Passing mention should be made of the Oak Park-River Forest Citizens' Committee for Human Rights, the group that was so active in the earlier phase of open housing activity. While the group was still in existence and occasionally attempted to exert its influence on local governmental decisions, it had lost the vigor that it had in the period of agitation for a fair housing law. It apparently suffered from the complacency of success and the inability to reorient itself to suit the altered circumstances—that is, the need to attract whites rather than blacks to the community if integration was to be achieved.

The organizations discussed so far served the function of crystalizing issues, mobilizing and serving as vehicles for public opinion, and applying pressure on those with the power to act effectively. These organizations also functioned to raise public morale by instilling the belief that "something can be done," although this morale could be expected to dissipate quickly if "something" in fact was not done. Because the function of these groups was ultimately contingent upon what other actors could be persuaded to do, primary attention must now be focussed on the activities of those agencies that did have some capacity for direct action with regard to racial change. Principally, this means the village government and, to a lesser extent, the Oak Park Housing Center and the schools.

The Elementary Schools

Prompted by school incidents involving assaults by white children upon black children and by reported harrassment of black families in the neighborhood, parents from the Lincoln School area (located in south Oak Park, but not in the area of major black influx) urged school officials to take some action on the issue of race relations, including implementation of a formal race relations program and the hiring of black teachers and staff. School officials responded with a human dignity policy, adopted by the elementary school board in March 1972. The document covered four major areas.

1. Hiring Practices: Consideration in hiring and evaluation of teachers and teacher aids shall be given to knowledge of human relations and sensitivity to cultural differences. The administration is also to expand its efforts to hire minority group individuals in professional and paraprofessional positions.
2. In-Service Training: Teachers and administrators shall receive in-service training in minority group studies and human relations skills.
3. Safeguarding Human Dignity in the Schools: Grievance procedures and faculty-student grievance committees are to be instituted.
4. Implementing and Reporting: This section urges full communication among the schools of the district regarding their experiences with human relations programs and plans for the future.

The elementary schools moved quickly to implement the policy, initiating some in-service training and other cultural awareness programs even before the 1971–1972 school year ended. However, other planned programs received a serious setback when the board was refused a request for a federal grant to be used for teacher training and coordination of school and community integration efforts.

Oak Park–River Forest High School

With ten schools within its jurisdiction, the elementary school board was impelled to act by the clear potential for de facto segregation, which would place the district in violation of state school Superintendent Michael Bakalis' directive on school integration. However, the single high school, serving all of Oak Park and River Forest, was faced with no such immediate threat and lagged far behind in race relations policy.

On October 29, 1971, an argument between a black student and two white students in the school erupted into a fight. The police were called, and four arrests resulted. Reports and rumors of the incident spread rapidly throughout the community, but the panic was short lived, as school, youth, and community relations officials were successful in reducing the incident to what they considered its proper perspective. Nonetheless, there was enough concern to result in several meetings among parents, school officials, and community agencies. Immediately after the fight, a group of black and white parents met with school officials and formed a committee to assist in the case of further disturbances. A teacher human relations committee was also formed as a result of the incident.

Oak Park Housing Center

The Oak Park Housing Center, which went into operation on May 1, 1972, operated as a housing referral service with the primary objective of encouraging dispersed integration and discouraging residential clustering of blacks in any single area. The idea for the center began as a proposal in August 1971 by the Oak Park–River Forest Citizens' Committee for Human Rights that the Community Relations Commission open up a storefront type neighborhood center in the east central part of Oak Park where anxiety over racial change was high. The commission discussed the proposal, but took no action, because it was felt that the important thing was diffusion out into all parts of the community rather than concentration in a localized area in which the commission would draw criticism. When the commission refused to act on the proposal, the prime mover behind the housing center, Roberta Raymond (its director) and other supporters decided to go ahead independently with the idea.

The Housing Center was staffed by local volunteers in office space provided by a downtown Oak Park church, and was supported by private contributions, including a three year, $24,000 grant from the Wieboldt Foundation.

The housing center sought listings from private landlords and cooperating real estate firms and solicited clients through magazine and newspaper advertising and through direct contact with major employers, professional associations, and educational institutions. The housing center's newspaper and magazine promotion program included advertising in *Ms.*, *Chicago Guide*, *Saturday Review*, and the Lerner chain of newspapers, which serve Chicago's north side and north suburbs and include *Skyliner*, which is distributed to north side high rise dwellers. The target of the publicity, as the choice of advertising media and direct contacts would suggest, was the young, college-educated person or family desiring, or at least willing, to live in a racially integrated community. While the housing center's sixteen page brochure made no explicit reference to the biracial character of the suburb, several of its photographs showed blacks and whites engaged in common activities. The center operated on the assumption that there is a large enough demand for racially integrated community living to maintain stable integration in Oak Park if only this market could be successfully tapped. This was a belief which Ms. Raymond had earlier tried unsuccessfully to impress upon local real estate men, who generally tried to sell the community as essentially all white.

By February 1973, the housing center had cooperated with eleven local real estate firms and numerous private landlords in placing new residents in 141 apartments and twenty-four single family homes. Of these 165 family units, 80 percent were white and 20 percent were black, interracial, or other nonwhite. The occupational distribution of family heads was:

Medical professionals	42
Business and clerical workers	37
University staff members	18
Social workers	13
Other (including teachers, entertainers, reporters, and retired)	55
TOTAL	165

While whites continued to move into the area threatened by transition, the housing center had a very difficult time persuading whites to buy homes in the small area that was most affected by racial change, particularly the 600 block of South Humphrey Avenue and immediately surrounding blocks. Several homes on this block had already changed from white to black ownership and occupancy, and in February 1973 there were ten additional homes for sale on this one block according to the housing center. A housing center spokesman reported "absolutely no success" in interesting white buyers in homes on this block. However, later in February, a white family did purchase one of the homes, and another white family purchased a home two blocks west.

Community relations and housing center staff said that it seemed less difficult to attract white renters than buyers to the area in the immediate path of transition. On the other hand, reports and comments by local observers and residents of the area suggested that white emigrants, some of them long-time Oak Parkers leaving specifically because of racial change, were often being replaced by a white population that is likely to be more transient (younger, unmarried, student, etc.) and unlikely to be strongly committed to staying.

Village Government

The village government was probably the local organization with the greatest potential for affecting the future of the village, if only because it had the resources—money, legitimate authority, and prestige—to act. Three major goal areas characterized the activities of the village government relative to racial change: (1) Directly relevant to the issue of racial change were activities aimed at controlling the real estate industry, including lending institutions. (2) A second goal area, physical and economic redevelopment, was extremely significant even though its relation to racial change was less direct. (3) Finally, managing the image of the suburb—affecting perceptions of the community held by residents and potential residents—was a purpose that can be seen as underlying much of local government's activity. Naturally the effectiveness with which the village government accomplished the other two goals directly affected perceptions of the community. However, certain programs, such as the public relations efforts of the Community Relations Commission and some particular aspects of physical planning, could be seen as having little or no other purpose than image influence.

The remainder of this discussion will be organized in terms of these three goal areas. While attention is focused on the village government, the discussion must also include attention to the participation and involvement of other local organizations in these goal areas.

Controlling the Real Estate and Lending Industries. A discussion of attempts to control the local real estate and lending industry logically begins with the passage of the local fair housing ordinance, which has already been dealt with in some detail. By 1973, however, the issue was no longer the exclusion of blacks from housing in the suburb, as it was when the law was passed, as much as it was certain other real estate and lending practices that typically surface when a number of blacks have already entered a community—"steering," "blockbusting," "panic peddling," "redlining," and so forth. Amendments to the ordinance adopted in 1972 were aimed at dealing more explicitly and effectively with these new problems.

Local real estate men and the local real estate board had enjoyed a relatively good reputation among local fair housing and race relations people. There had been no known cases of discrimination in the sale of single family detached homes since the passage of the fair housing ordinance, although the developer of a townhouse complex was charged in federal court with discrimination in that he refused a unit to an Indian couple, both of whom were medical doctors.

The Community Relations Commission had always tried to maintain a good working relationship with the local real estate industry and to emphasize persuasion rather than coercion or threat of coercion in its dealings with real estate men. Some critics felt that the commission had leaned too far in the direction of persuasion and voluntary cooperation and had been too timid in displaying and using its legal power. Furthermore, the commission's first administrator, who left that post in August 1972, was himself in the real estate business, a fact capable of raising some eyebrows. However questionable the appointment of a real estate man to administer a fair housing law may be, it must be admitted that in this particular case the administrator's connections, influence, and popularity in the real estate industry were probably major factors in securing the cooperation and compliance of local brokers.

Community relations staff occasionally spoken of noncooperation by "problem" brokers, but they were generally careful to emphasize that the problems were with "outside" brokers and not with the local members of the Oak Park River Forest Board of Realtors. The board had about forty-five members, who must have offices either in Oak Park or in River Forest, and the majority of these brokers also resided in one of the two suburbs. However, there were over 200 brokers and agents doing business in Oak Park, and it was primarily because of concern over the potential practices of these outside brokers that the Community Relations Commission recommended new legislation. In particular, the experience of Austin, where there had been much publicity over alleged panic peddling and blockbusting, made Oak Park officials extremely wary lest the movement of blacks into Oak Park attract such fringe operators and speculators.

The major new legislation passed in 1972 included a ban on residential "For Sale" and "Sold" signs, prohibition of redlining or of extending differential mortgage terms based on the racial composition of the neighborhood in which the property is located, and strengthening of the antisolicitation provision by requiring that the real estate operator assume the burden of obtaining a list of homeowners who had indicated in writing that they did not wish to sell or to be solicited for the sale of their homes. Previously the Community Relations Commission had to send the list by registered mail to every broker and salesman, a procedure so costly as to render it nearly inoperable.

The ban on "For Sale" and "Sold" signs was passed by the trustees in February 1971, only after several months of conference between the Community Relations Commission and the Board of Realtors, attempting to work out a voluntary plan. The commision finally decided that the situation had become urgent, due to the appearance of an inordinate number of signs along Austin Boulevard and in other "sensitive" blocks. Some commission members felt that the potential for panic in the southeast part of Oak Park warranted total prohibition of signs from this area, while real estate men would agree at most to limitation of the number of signs to one or two per block. And while commission members did not consider the elimination of signs throughout the village a necessary measure, they felt that singling out particular areas for special treatment might do more psychological damage than the proliferation of signs. Further factors that influenced the commission to recommend the sign ban were the history of noncooperation by a few particular brokers, delay by the Real Estate Board in adopting a voluntary sign limitation program, doubts that the board could use its informal influence to control practices of nonboard members, and refusal of the chairman of the Real Estate Board to acknowledge the priority of community interests over the dictates of "good business practice."

Suspicions of redlining had beset the Community Relations Commission and other local activists throughout 1971 and 1972, but despite rumors, no substantiated complaints had been received. In 1971, the Community Relations Commission undertook a three stage project to evaluate lending practices. The first stage involved meetings with local lending officials. Next, a survey of approximately fifty new homeowners was conducted. Finally, local real estate man were questioned about their knowledge and experience of local lending practices. By completion of the project, at the end of 1971, no evidence of discriminatory lending practices or of redlining had been disclosed, and the commission issued a highly optimistic statement regarding lending practices in the village.

Not as convinced as the Community Relations Commission appeared to be, the Citizens' Action Program also began in the spring of 1972 to monitor lending practices. They turned up no evidence of unethical practice from telephone calls to new homeowners. However, when members of CAP contacted savings and loan firms, posing as prospective sellers, an official of one firm, after some pressure, finally admitted that the probable decision of his firm would be to finance with FHA guarantee in Oak Park and finance conventionally in the adjacent, all white suburb of Forest Park. The firm later denied restricting conventional mortgages in Oak Park in any way. CAP prepared a formal pledge, promising nonrestriction of mortgages and allowing CAP access to certain records, which was circulated to all the local savings and loan institutions with a request for them to sign the pledge. The firm that CAP had alleged was engaged in redlining signed the pledge only when around eighty CAP supporters packed the building, while CAP leaders met with the firm's officials. Other institutions refused to sign, while unanimously denying redlining practices.

The issue generated a great deal of local interest and controversy. The Trib charged that the word "redlining" had disappeared from the pages of the other local newspapers due to pressure from local financial interests. The lending firms formed a new organization, Financial Institutions Special Committee on Area Leadership (FISCAL), which became the representative of member institutions in dealings with CAP. The Community Relations Commission was also involved in mediation between the two groups, and it passed a resolution of support for CAP's request that loan data, excluding personal credit information, be made available to ensure that no redlining was taking place. Eventually FISCAL agreed to provide data concerning types of mortgages granted and their locations for a period of six months. The village board also amended the fair housing law to prohibit redlining. CAP continued to survey new residents, particularly those moving into the area of immediate concern over racial change. Neither the lending data nor the telephone surveys turned up any clear evidence of redlining, although a CAP leader claimed that while conventional mortgages were being granted throughout the village, the few FHA mortgages that were granted were confined to the southeast section.

Despite the lack of substantiation of illegal real estate and lending practices, few if any knowledgeable people in Oak Park were convinced that the practices were nonexistent. Members of the Oak Park Real Estate Board, including one of its officers, admitted that racial "steering" was going on, and there were some reports of panic peddling, although no legal action was being taken. The real estate rental industry has never been assumed to be nondiscriminatory, of course, and several cases of discrimination in rentals were successfully prosecuted in court. The Oak Park Housing Center was instrumental in discovering even more cases of discrimination in rentals than were previously suspected, and its director stated candidly when interviewed, "If a black person goes looking for an apartment in Oak Park, he's going to run into discrimination." On the other hand, a black could rent a unit in any part of Oak Park with much greater ease than in any of the all white areas surrounding Oak Park.

The Community Relations Commission has also tried to exert some mild informal pressure on housing choices through what it termed its "counseling program." The program was intended to encourage dispersed integration and to discourage concentration of blacks in particular neighborhoods by persuading black homeseekers not to buy homes on blocks that were considered especially susceptible to panic. Blacks expressing interest in homes on these blocks were to be given a form letter from the commission explaining the sensitive character of the immediate neighborhood and asking them to contact the Community Relations Commission, where a staff member would encourage the prospective buyer to consider housing in other Oak Park neighborhoods. It was nevertheless stressed that buyers were entitled to purchase any property they wished. The commission was worried from the beginning that the program in itself would be seen as discriminatory, and the counseling program was therefore expanded so that all prospects and not just blacks were invited to contact the Community Relations Commission.

Physical and Economic Redevelopment. In March 1973, the Oak Park Board of Trustees adopted a comprehensive plan for the village. In addition, several major public and private construction projects were planned for the immediate future, notably a thirty-seven-story, twin tower, privately developed residential building, a public senior citizens' residence, a shopping mall for the central business district to be financed by a special taxing district, and a new municipal center.

The overall aim of the physical planning program was to increase commercial vitality and the economic base of the village. As a means to this end, the comprehensive plan called for more intensive residential land use, eventually bringing the population to 75,000. The shopping mall, together with expanded and more flexible commercial zoning, were intended to retain old businesses and to attract new ones.

The extent to which economic revitalization is achieved will be a major factor in determining the future of the village. The quality of the housing stock is also a major issue because of its age and the lack of open space for new construction. Building inspection has reputedly been graft-free and fairly adequate, and the village relies on an intensive inspection program to maintain the quality of older housing. The housing stock will be renewed primarily through multiple dwelling construction, and land bordering the central business district and the major thoroughfares is being rezoned for high density residential use. Some critics have charged that the high density rezoning proposed along Austin Boulevard is intended to erect a barrier between Oak Park and Austin. While this purpose may be served, heavy traffic on Austin makes the land hardly suitable for single family homes.

The criticism that Oak Park was trying to seal itself off from

Austin is probably better taken if applied to another feature of the proposed physical plan—that is, extensive construction of cul-de-sacs. Cul-de-sacs were proposed for all four boundaries of the village, confining automobile traffic entering the village to the major thoroughfares. More cul-de-sacs to be constructed along these major thoroughfares were proposed to curtail traffic through residential neighborhoods. Initial cul-de-sac construction was proposed for the area adjacent to Austin, a plan that drew heavy criticism, including some from members of the Community Relations Commission, that Oak Park was "turning its back on Austin." The chairman of the Community Relations Commission, without expressing an opinion on the wisdom or ethics of such a tactic, agreed with critics that the planners probably had just that object in mind. On the other hand, the cul-de-sacs may be seen simply as part of an overall attempt to create a visual identity for Oak Park as a distinct community and not just another mass of streets and homes making up some ill-defined part of the metropolitan area. To this end, rustic-looking markers were also to be placed at the major entrances to the suburb, announcing the "Village of Oak Park." Presuming that the aim of the village was simply to create its own visually defined identity and to distinguish itself from neighboring communities, there seemed little doubt that one neighboring community from which Oak Park wanted very much to distinguish itself was South Austin, as evidenced by the fact that the first village markers were erected at this border, and the first cul-de-sac construction also was begun there.

The relocation of the village hall served two purposes. The present village hall, near the central business district, was to be demolished to allow commercial development of this valuable site, and the new municipal plaza was to be constructed in southeast Oak Park, right in the area of present racial change. Abandoning the old site was expected to increase the tax base. The selection of the new site was explicitly motivated by village officials' desire to raise resident morale in the area and to demonstrate that this sector of the village was not to be "written off" as some had charged, particularly after the historic preservation district was established in north Oak Park. A cynical slogan is still frequently heard: Conservation for the north, and urban renewal for the south.

Image Management and Morale Building.   The physical and economic redevelopment aims were designed to reinforce the belief that "Oak Park is a good place in which to live," the ultimate aim of the planning program diagrammed in Figure 12–1, taken from Oak Park's comprehensive plan.

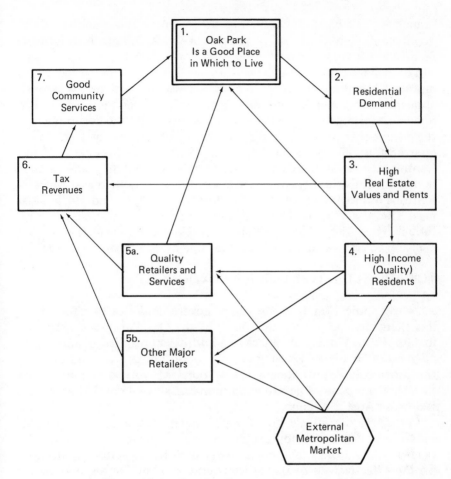

Figure 12-1. The Oak Park Residential Demand Model.

But there was ample evidence of anxiety among residents in spite of the efforts at image building. Occasional racial incidents and inter-racial fights or assaults were inflated through rumor. The Community Relations Commission continually received reports, mostly unsub-stantiated, that only blacks were being shown a house for sale on a particular block. It was "common knowledge" that Oakbrook Shop-ping Center had drawn much trade away from Oak Park's higher quality stores. Community morale was in no way enhanced when Peck and Peck announced the closing of their Oak Park store, and the rumor that Marshall Field was leaving was in constant circulation. Oak Park's major savings and loan institution applied for permission to relocate the main office in a suburb farther west and to maintain a branch in Oak Park. Facts such as these, which in less anxious times might be perceived as part of normal business, did much to feed the fear that Oak Park was becoming a less good place in which to live.

The village government tried to deal with these problems of morale by making its officials more accessible, particularly through appearances at block club meetings and other community affairs. Special informational meetings were sponsored by the government at the neighborhood level. Publication of an official newsletter, mailed quarterly to all residents, began in 1972. In southeast Oak Park, Community Relations Commission members and staff made visits to homes of individual residents, primarily those who had expressed intentions of moving or those who did not regularly attend block meetings. The effect of such visits is hard to gauge, but commission staff thought that the visits may have made the difference between the decision to stay or to move in at least one or two cases.

TOWARD SELECTIVE DISCRIMINATION

An early indication that the village government's early efforts were less than successful came in studies of the Oak Park housing market in late 1972. While both blacks and whites continued to move into all parts of Oak Park, housing sales in the southeastern quadrant were the most volatile, producing a new round of worries in spite of the fact that the pace of ghetto expansion had slowed considerably once it crossed Austin Avenue.

Certainly, the village board was concerned, for in April 1973 it passed a policy resolution calling for the maintenance of stable "dispersed integration." The board had come to see serious limitations on the effectiveness of its earlier voluntary plans for dispersed black residency. While the village authorities had condoned discrimination by the housing center, they did not officially sanction it until November 1973, when the "exempt location" clause of the fair housing ordinance was applied for the first time. This provision, written into the 1968 fair housing ordinance, allowed the village government to exempt areas from prosecution if it was determined that serious attempts at integration were being made and that their success might be jeopardized by strict enforcement of the fair housing ordinance. The board granted exemption to one block and one apartment building, both over 50 percent black, when petitions signed by over half of the white and black residents were presented. This action by the board did not prevent black moveins; it merely permitted racial discrimination in the two exempt locations. Soon after the board's action, however, another move that would legally prevent black moveins to certain areas was receiving serious consideration.

In December 1973, an amendment to the fair housing ordinance putting into operation a quota system was proposed by a trustee and referred to the Community Relations Commission. If it had been enacted into law, this quota provision would have held the black population of the village to 30 percent. Public hearings turned up much opposition to the new quota plan, though it is probable that a majority of residents, most of whom do not attend such hearings, supported it. The quota system was finally tabled, and apparently killed, primarily as a result of the extreme adverse publicity that the plan received from the metropolitan news media. Then, in May 1974, the village board began discussion of a multifaceted, but quotaless, integration maintenance program. However, selective discrimination has already replaced nondiscrimination as official policy.

While it may be too early to draw final conclusions, it is nonetheless possible to indicate the variables that may be expected to retard or accelerate racial change and therefore to affect this new and different policy direction. It is not likely that the most affluent neighborhoods in the heart of north Oak Park will undergo transition in the very near future. It is conceivable that this area could become open to black occupancy on the typical block by block basis. If, as Molotch suggests in the case of South Shore, the presence of large apartment buildings is conducive to racial transition,[4] Washington Boulevard presents an ideal path of change in Oak Park.

Stable integration might be maintained if particular market conditions prevail—if the black demand for housing of the type available is low relative to supply; if the white demand for housing of the type available is high relative to supply; or if the community possesses some feature making it unusually attractive to whites.[5] The first two conditions do not prevail in Oak Park. As to the third, most of the attractive features of Oak Park are the normal amenities that make the community attractive to both blacks and whites, but that whites can readily find in other communities—that is, good services, good schools, convenient transportation, and so forth. Whether the image of a liberal, heterogeneous community with strong cultural traditions can be considered a feature that will sufficiently increase white demand for housing in Oak Park remains to be seen, but this is the image that the local government, and particularly the housing center, are trying to promulgate.

Demographic factors also suggest the probability of racial change. A study of racial change on the southwest side of Chicago found that

4. Harvey Molotch, "Community Action to Control Racial Change" (Ph.D. Thesis, University of Chicago 1968).
5. See Eleanor Wolf, "The Invasion-Succession Sequence as a Self-Fulfilling Prophecy," *Journal of Social Issues* 13, 4 (1957): 7-20.

neighborhoods where the population was older than average and those where there were a concentration of families with young children were more likely to undergo transition. The young and the senior citizens are the two groups overrepresented in Oak Park's age distribution. The same study also found that native white neighborhoods were more likely to undergo transition than neighborhoods with a concentration of foreign stock.[6] Oak Park has no neighborhoods that could be described as white ethnic. Finally, if Pierre DeVise's conclusions are correct, the influx of a younger population into Oak Park in the middle and late 1960s was a result of white flight from transitional neighborhoods on the west side of Chicago.[7] The behavior of these residents when faced with racial change a second time is indeterminable. A comparative attitudinal survey of these new residents and of old Oak Park residents found that, if anything, the newcomers were more liberal in their racial attitudes than the old residents.[8] Actually, the relatively "liberal" reputation of Oak Park is projected by its elite and does not necessarily characterize the general population. There is little reason based on attitude alone—an admittedly questionable basis—to expect white Oak Parkers to remain when substantial numbers of blacks move in.

On the other hand, Oak Park has some features that suggest that stable integration is a possibility. First of all, local government and all other organizations presently involved are committed to the goal of stable and dispersed integration. This concentration and coincidence of efforts in a local area distinguishes the suburb from city neighborhoods where transition has taken place. Secondly, Oak Park's political arena is characterized by consensus. There is none of the intergroup conflict and concommitant publicity that accompanied racial change in Austin. No organized effort to exclude blacks from the community—a factor which Wolf,[9] for one, suggests may encourage racial change—has emerged. The local real estate industry is reasonably cooperative with the integration effort. Many local real estate men seem to have concluded that containment is futile and that scattered integration serves their own best business interests. As

6. Peter Negronida, "Rolling Residential Resegregation: A Study of What Makes Neighborhoods Change," (University of Chicago, unpublished, June 1971).

7. Brian J.L. Berry and Frank Horton, *Geographic Perspectives on Urban Systems* (Englewood Cliffs: Prentice Hall, 1970), De Vise research cited, p. 413-19.

8. James Rohrich, "Attitudinal Differences between Selected Residents of an Established Upper Middle Class Suburb" (M.A. Thesis, DePaul University, Chicago, February 1969).

9. Wolf.

long as north Oak Park and River Forest remain white, the high school should also remain substantially white. To be sure of this, it would be necessary to know how many north Oak Park and River Forest families actually send their children to the public high school and, further, how likely they would be to withdraw their children as black enrollment increases. Finally, the existence of the housing center may have a positive effect, though similar referral services have failed in Austin and in South Shore. It goes almost without saying that none of the factors above will be meaningful if Oak Park does not achieve the economic and physical redevelopment goals set by the comprehensive plan.

A conservative prediction is that at least part of south Oak Park will resegregate. No part of Oak Park will remain all white. Stable, though possibly minimal, integration may be attained in the northern neighborhoods of higher than average social standing. It must be conceded that much of south Oak Park also has at least a chance, slim perhaps, of stabilization. The rate of change so far has been slow, compared with Austin, and while stabilization efforts have not prevented some black concentration, neither have the results been wholly discouraging.

✳ *Chapter 13*

Evanston: A Suburban Ghetto Expands

At the time that west side ghetto expansion spilled over the city limits into Oak Park, Chicago's northern suburban neighbor, Evanston, was also experiencing racial change of its own. No new suburb, Evanston was named after an early settler, John Evans, a professor of obstetrics at Rush Medical College in Chicago, and became a town in 1857, a village in 1863, and a city in 1892. Northwestern University, developed and administered by the Methodist Episcopal Church, was founded in Evanston in 1851 and became a major factor in the city's growth as well as in its character as a community. During the 1860s Northwestern University sold land at low prices to attract residents to the area. Purchasers were warned that the land would revert back to the university if the owner permitted intoxicating drink to be manufactured, sold or given away on the premises, or allowed any gambling to be carried on.

Many churches early settled in the community; at present over seventy of all denominations, including four synagogues, serve Evanston and are dominant in its landscape. Evanston is home to the national headquarters of the Women's Christian Temperance Union, and until 1972, no liquor was sold within city limits. An aura of intense respectability has always been projected by the city.

Starting in 1856, the Chicago and Milwaukee Railroad's train service helped develop Chicago's north shore, which encouraged the growth of Evanston. As Chicago grew as an industrial and transportation center, Evanston became increasingly popular with businessmen seeking a small town lifestyle for their families.

Evanston's first known black resident, a shoemaker, settled there in the 1850s. Other early black settlers also were engaged in trades and crafts as well as in service occupations. The city is alleged to have been a northern depot of the Underground Railroad, a fact that would account for its growing black settlement around the time of the Civil War. While the size of the early black population is not known, by 1900 a black residential area had developed in what is now census tract 8092, although some blacks lived in homes scattered throughout the city or in service quarters of their white employers' estates. This first black residential concentration has remained the nucleus of Evanston's black community. Inside this black enclave there arose separate black businesses, organizations, and institutions, setting a pattern of racial separation and minimal contact between Evanston's whites and blacks that still endures.

The period of greatest population growth, white and black, followed World War I. The opportunity for blacks in service occupations, particularly domestic service, increased as the population grew and as the foreign immigrants who had filled many of these posts moved up to better jobs. By 1930, about 5,000 blacks lived in Evanston, and as their numbers increased, the pattern of segregation became even more rigid. Except as a source of needed labor, the black community was virtually ignored by white Evanstonians. The 1970 census showed Evanston's population to be 79,808, of whom 12,861 (16 percent) were black.

Tree-lined streets characterize this "City of Gracious Living," and homes in the city reflect their era. Some Evanston homes are more than one hundred years old, but styles of all decades are represented. However, the city had 56.6 percent of its housing stock in rental units,[1] with an average rent of $174 in 1970. Home prices ranged in that year from slightly under $20,000 to over $100,000, the average value being $36,500.

Sixteen public elementary schools, four junior highs, and the Evanston Township High School serve the city. There are four Catholic elementary schools, one Catholic high school, one Lutheran elementary, and one private coeducational school located in Evanston. Busing of public elementary school children, used along with redrawn attendance boundaries to achieve desegregation, was started in 1967.

The city of Evanston has had a council-manager system of municipal government since 1952. The mayor and aldermen are elected

1. "with growth came change. Apartment houses began to 'rear their ugly heads among the noble trees and victorian spires,' wrote David Streeter in 1928." Harold M. Mayer and Richard C. Wade, *Chicago: Growth of a Metropolis* (Chicago: University of Chicago Press, 1969).

officials, as are the city clerk and city treasurer. The aldermen constitute the city council, which appoints the city manager and passes on appointments made by the mayor.

1970 census figures gave the median family income in Evanston as $13,932, with 44.4 percent of the families having incomes of $15,000 or more. Only 3.6 percent of the families had incomes less than the poverty level, while 73.2 percent were employed in white collar occupations. Seventy-five and one tenth of Evanstonians had completed 4 years of high school or more. Seventeen percent of the city's population was sixty-two years of age or older, while 26 percent was under eighteen years of age. Evanston's median age was 34.8 years.

PERCEPTIONS OF COMMUNITY CHANGE

Evanston NAACP president Carl Davis was quoted in the June 7, 1973, *Evanston Review* as saying, "But for all [the problems], we've got a stable black community. . . ." And that is exactly the reason that white Evanston has, since its inception, been able to ignore its black citizens. Two stable, but divided communities have coexisted in Evanston for many years. White Evanston has reacted to black Evanston only in periods of real or fancied crisis.

For example, in 1945, the Evanston Council of Social Agencies responded to nationwide postwar interracial tensions by commissioning a study on "The Economic and Cultural Problems in Evanston, Illinois, as They Relate to the Colored Population."[2] The report indicated that most of the jobs available to blacks in Evanston were in the domestic and service fields and that problems of overcrowding and housing deterioration were apparent in the "west-side ghetto." After this study appeared, Evanston's City Council announced the formation of a Commission on Human Relations, but, since Evanston experienced no racial trouble, this remained a "paper" commission.

In May of 1953, the Evanston Interracial Council conducted an "Inventory of Human Relations."[3] This survey was undertaken because the World Council of Churches, which planned to hold meetings in Evanston in August 1954, had specified in preliminary negotiations that there be no discrimination against delegates or observers in any facilities. This 1953 inventory showed that the employment

2. Warren M. Banner, "The Economic and Cultural Problems in Evanston, Illinois, as They Relate to the Colored Population" (Washington, D.C.: National Urban League, January-February, 1945).

3. Evanston Interracial Council, *Human Relations in Evanston* (Evanston, 1953.)

situation for blacks had changed little since the 1945 study, that black residents not only lived in more crowded quarters in worse repair than similar units occupied by whites, but also that they paid more for such units. According to this report, the pattern was further aggravated during the post-World War II years by the shortage of available housing, a shortage especially acute for blacks since they were prevented, primarily by the practices of the North Shore Board of Realtors and of lending institutions, from obtaining housing in white areas. Residential segregation naturally led to segregation in areas of education, health services, recreation, and religion.

While these conditions were documented, then, in 1953, there seems to be no evidence that any corrective action was taken. The emergence of a strong national civil rights movement in the early 1960s probably precipitated the formation of the Evanston Community Relations Commission in April 1961. An excerpt from the ordinance establishing the commission stated its purpose to be "an effort to equalize opportunities and lessen prejudice and discrimination because of age, religion, or ethnic differences among Evanston residents."[4] Using the 1953 "Inventory of Human Relations" as a stepping stone, the Commission produced, in 1964, its one hundred-page *Inventory '64*.

While *Inventory '64* covered essentially the same topics as the 1953 inventory (employment, housing, recreation, health, and education, plus a section of the administration of justice), its tone was dramatically different from the 1953 report. Much more militancy was expressed by both whites and blacks. The social changes of the ten years intervening between the reports are reflected by the participants: in 1964 they confronted one another openly and identified discriminatory companies and institutions. The issue of racism in Evanston was pushed to the forefront, as the following quotations reveal.[5] For example, Dr. Warren Spencer, representing the National Association for the Advancement of Colored People, said:

My presentation has a title: "Two Down—Ninety Eight to Go." This Commission has been in existance approximately two years. And if we wonder how the Negro has been able to achieve nothing in a hundred years, we can tell from this Commission that they have done nothing to date, and if they keep going for the next 98 years, they still will not have accomplished anything.

---

4. *Inventory '64: A Study of Human Relations in Evanston*, ed. Richard J. Thain, Jr. (Evanston: Evanston Community Relations Commission).
5. Ibid, for the quotations that follow.

It is the feeling of this organization [NAACP] that the whole Inventory is a trick to delay the proposed Open Occupancy Resolution . . . .

Mrs. Mildred W. Robinson, of the Evanston North Suburban Urban League commented:

"Evanston's 7,000 Negroes live in a segregated community." This is the opening statement of the section on housing in the 1953 Inventory of Human Relations in Evanston. The Commission's Report of its findings on housing in this 1963–64 Inventory could accurately make the same statement, changing only the words "7,000 Negroes" to "9,300 Negroes."

. . .

still true is the statement of the 1953 Inventory that "the greatest deterrent to the occupancy by Negroes of houses in so-called 'white parts' of Evanston is the real estate profession."

Another participant commented that:

One need only to glance at the pages of the classified section of the *Evanston Review* where such genteel phrases as "non-racial" and "inter-racial" vie with "for colored," and "for ambitious colored families" [for] irrefutable evidence that the pattern of racial exclusion is deeply ingrained into the mechanism by which homes are sold and apartments rented . . . . Nor is deliberate, systematic exclusion restricted only to race. The term "exclusive neighborhood" . . . which means "Jews need not apply" appears with less, but stubborn frequency.

The Reverend S.A. Gathings of the NAACP concluded:

The NAACP feels that Evanston's housing situation is a little Birmingham, Alabama. We think that because in Birmingham they have the biting dogs and high-powered water hose . . . . In Evanston we have the real estate brokers to deal with . . . . some of these people [are] "little Wallaces."

Oscar Lindstrand, whose organizational affiliation was not noted, replied: "I am proud of the real estate people of the City of Evanston." Whereupon a black woman retaliated, "I don't mean to call you 'bigot,' I don't know what else I can call you." Mr. Lindstrand then exclaimed, "I don't care what you call me. I am defending human rights."

While members of the North Shore Board of Realtors apparently did not attend these meetings either to make clear or to defend their position, it was mentioned that they had recently published a "very scathing document called 'Fair Housing, Forced Housing' which was distributed to its renters and anyone who came into their offices."

Perhaps the issues were summed up best by Dr. Grace M. Jaffee, representing the Urban League of Evanston, when she said:

> The title, "Athens of the Middle West" has, on occasions, been conferred upon our City by some of its leading citizens . . . . however, another title has come to the minds of some members of the Urban League, namely, "Sybil or the two Nations" . . . . the title of Disraeli's great book . . . . [that pointed out] that the England of his day was divided, economically, socially, and educationally into two separate nations . . . .

The Community Relations Commission's conclusions stated, in part:

> Although no attempt will be made here to detail a blueprint of action, it is clear to the Commission that the problem of highest urgency and priority is housing. We believe it to be imperative if Evanston as a maturing community is to continue to provide an inspirational cultural and moral environment that all of our citizens regardless of their race, color, or creed have access to housing of their choice and capability to purchase . . . .

In November 1962, The Reverend Dr. Martin Luther King spoke to an audience of 1,500 in Evanston's Unitarian Church. The essence of his talk was that:

> The old idea of segregation has exhausted itself, and the American society is trying to orient itself around the new idea of integration . . . . The problem is not limited to the south, it is a national problem . . . . No section of the land can boast of clean hands in brotherhood . . . . [in the north] discrimination [takes on] a hidden and subtle form in the twin evils of housing and employment segregation.[6]

Apparently Dr. King's message created only a brief flurry in complacent Evanston: "The Evanston Human Relations Council, the descendent of the Interracial Council established almost 40 years before . . . went to work on the integration problem of which he had spoken."[7] The council's response, in 1963, was an attempt to appease the black community by integrating the Grove Street YMCA, a gesture that seems ludicrous in retrospect. However, 1963 was a racially quiet

6. Rubin, Jack and Sandy Eichengreen, "The History of the Negroes in Evanston, Ill." (Northwestern University, May 1968; Unpublished).
7. Ibid.

year for Evanston; if the blacks were unhappy, they were quietly so, and Evanstonians again settled back in the belief that the status quo could prevail. For example, only fifty people turned out in October 1963 for a discussion of the integrated neighborhoods at the Unitarian Church. One panelist representing the Dewey Community Conference, an organization that then characterized its neighborhood as biracial, said, "Discussion of integration is a self-conscious thing . . . . It is easy to tear a neighborhood apart over integration."[8]

Evanston experienced its first racial sit-ins in the summer of 1964, and more were to follow in 1965. The targets of the sit-ins were Evanston real estate firms, who were asked by the civil rights picketers to stop using "the term 'forced housing' to refer to open occupancy in north shore newspapers . . . to 'cease appealing to prejudice . . . .'"[9] Some of the 400 pickets recruited by the North Shore Coordinating Council, an umbrella group made up of fifteen organizations, were pelted by eggs thrown by a group of juveniles. Thirty-six persons were arrested in May 1964, during a simultaneous sit-in at three Evanston real estate offices.

In December of 1964, the Northwest Evanston Homeowners Association, whose membership numbered 700, urged the Evanston City Council not to pass proposed ordinances "designed to control the activities of realtors. It called suggested city laws a 'sacrifice [of] the freedom enjoyed by all of its citizens in a questionable attempt to benefit a few.'"[10] The group went on record against any proposals to regulate real estate brokers, either by requiring local licensing or by passing an antiblockbusting ordinance then under consideration. The association stated in a letter to the City Council that "This type of action tends to impugn the ethics and integrity of these realtors both individually and as a group and is unwarranted in view of the realtors' conduct in this regard in the past."[11] The group also opposed the enforcement of such ordinances by the Community Relations Commission, stating "that thereby an administrative agency would become 'investigator, prosecutor and judge in determining the guilt or innocence of the accused realtor.'"[12] Also in December, the officers of the Evanston Human Relations Council submitted a proposal for a fair housing bill to the Evanston City Council: "The seven-page ordinance submitted . . . would prohibit discrimination in the showing, sale, or lease of property."[13]

8. *Evanston Review,* October 24, 1963.
9. *Chicago Tribune,* July 10, 1963.
10. *Evanston Review,* December 17, 1964.
11. Ibid.
12. Ibid.
13. Ibid.

The Evanston City Council, in spring of 1965, adopted a resolution by a fifteen to two vote, which said in part:

This City Council favors a measure which would forbid real estate brokers, their agents, and employees from taking any independent action to discriminate against any person on the basis of race, creed, color, or national origin in the sale or rental of residential real estate.

This City Council favors a measure to forbid lenders of money for the purchase or mortgaging of residential real estate from discriminating against any person solely on the basis of race, creed, color, or national origin and apart from any financial considerations, in the lending of funds.[14]

Roy Wilkins, executive secretary of the NAACP, spoke to a crowd of over 600 Evanstonians in May 1965:

the Civil Rights Movement was finally on its way to victory in Evanston, but it would have to step fast to keep up . . . . [he] used the word "peculiar" to describe the way it had taken Evanston so long to get in step with the national movement . . . . [he] especially criticized real estate agents for segragated listings and banks for refusing to loan money to Negroes.[15]

When the city council's resolution on open housing did not bring about effective legislation, about 500 persons, including ministers, priests, and nuns, marched from Kenilworth to Evanston on August 30, 1965, to assemble at a rally in Bent Park. From there the procession moved to the offices of the Evanston–North Shore Board of Realtors for an all night vigil to protest its real estate practices.

The Reverend Emory G. Davis, pastor of Bethel A.M.E. Church, headed up a campaign in October of 1965 to open Evanston apartment buildings to persons of all races. Said the Reverend Davis at one meeting, "Evanston is losing many good Negro citizens by its closed-door policy."[16] A new music teacher at Evanston Township High School added that his experiences in seeking an apartment in Evanston were "dehumanizing."[17]

Paralleling the thrust for open housing, 1965 also saw the beginnings of school desegregation plans, which became an actuality in 1967 (see section on school desegregation, below).

Black demands for open housing continued throughout 1966 and into 1967. In October 1967, Evanston passed a fair housing ordinance prohibiting discrimination by brokers and owners using bro-

14. Rubin, Eichengreen.
15. Ibid.
16. *Chicago Tribune*, August 30, 1965.
17. Ibid.

kers' services. Despite this, by 1968, the black community felt that little actual progress had been made, and early in March of that year:

> a panel of high officials was already forecasting a "gloomy summer" in Evanston. They cited the summer riots of 1967, Black Power, and especially the poor housing situation as reasons for the coming trouble. The only area where integration was becoming a reality was in the public schools.[18]

In April, after Dr. King's assassination, more open housing marches were organized by whites and blacks in Evanston and pressures were brought to bear on the Evanston City Council to adopt an all-encompassing open occupancy ordinance. An editorial in the April 25, 1968, *Evanston Review* stated, in part:

> The pressure is being applied by a new group called NOW. The group, which was formed after the murder of Dr. Martin Luther King, Jr., is leading daily marches that it says will continue until the Council adopts a stronger ordinance . . . . The vast majority of NOW's marchers are white. It is significant that the movement has not won the active support of those it would affect most—Evanston's Negro resident . . . . Threats of violence have been made clear. Literature distributed before Monday's Council meeting said: "Violence is necessary; it is as American as cherry pie."

Giving in to pressures, The Evanston City Council did adopt a stronger fair housing ordinance in late April of 1968 amid cheers from its backers.

Nevertheless, in May 1969:

> Black leaders interviewed in recent weeks unanimously charged that many of their race in Evanston are restricted to housing which is abysmally inadequate. . . . The charges are not new. But they are accented by a tone or urgency, a sense that time for redressing these grievances may be running out. . . . These conditions are producing a situation where many blacks may die. And maybe some whites will die, too.[19]

But as late as 1970, the *Community Opinion Journal* reported that of Evanstonians surveyed "35% . . . talk about maintaining the status quo or reverting to the past . . ." when asked what they would like to see happen.

Real estate practices, which have always been exclusionary in Evanston, in 1972 continued to be in forefront of the city's racial

18. Rubin, Eichengreen.
19. *Evanston Review*, May 12, 1969.

problems. Real estate firms' tactics changed, but their goals remained the same—to keep north Evanston, lakeshore Evanston, and
other northern suburbs white (see section on real estate practices,
below).

Black Residential Expansion

Between 1950 and 1960, and again between 1960–1970, the black
population of Evanston increased about one-third (from 9.5 percent in 1950 to 11.5 percent in 1960 and 16.1 percent in 1970).
From 1950 to 1960, the numerical growth of the white population
(+3,232) exceeded that of the black (+2,132), as the total population increased from 73,641 to 79,283. During the next decade, this
overall growth came to a near halt, with the population reaching
79,808 in 1970. This slow total growth rate actually represented a
white population decline of 4,253, while the black population grew
by 3,723.

Since its beginning, Evanston has had natural boundaries that have
helped form its schizophrenic character. This chapter will concern
itself primarily with a triangle of the city bounded on the west by
the North Shore Channel, on the east by the Chicago and Northwestern Railroad tracks, and on the south by the Chicago Transit
Authority tracks and Howard Street. One resident characterized
these bounds as the "Great Wall of China," while another old-time
Evanston resident commented that "I live in South Evanston and
that was 'the other side of the tracks,' compared with the lakeshore
area—that was Evanston."

By 1900 the northern tip of this triangle formed the nucleus of
Evanston's black ghetto. As early as 1930, 83.7 percent of the
city's black population lived in this area, while to its immediate
south lived the city's main concentration of foreign born, Germans
predominated, followed by Swedish, rather large groups of Polish
and English, and small groups of Norwegians, French, and Southern
Europeans.

This triangle was ideally suited to contain within its limits blacks,
"foreigners," and Jews—that is, to shunt them away from north
Evanston and lakeshore Evanston. A strip of land at the base of the
triangle, between the CTA tracks and Howard Street, remained a
heavily Jewish enclave in 1973.

In 1970, tract 8092, the heart of the historic black community,
was over 97 percent black, up almost 3 percent from 1969, although
this tract has been nearly all black for many years. Between 1969
and 1970, the ghetto expanded southeastward in a wedge-shaped
path, into areas containing mostly single family and small multi-

family structures, with very few large apartment buildings. Blacks in these transitional areas were more likely to rent than own their own homes, so that homeownership presents no obstacle for blacks moving into these neighborhoods.

The core of a second ghetto developed immediately to the south along the C & NW railroad tracks, also in an area composed of both moderately priced single family homes and apartment buildings of all sizes. Blacks in this area also were more likely to rent than to own. Some of the blacks living in this newly ghettoizing area came from a six block minighetto on Chicago's northern border—an overbuilt slum on Juneway and Jonquil Terraces, where six and eight room flats were cut up into two, three, and four room flats.

The major exception to the rule that blacks had been contained by the "Great Wall" was in the northern part of the triangle, adjacent to the oldest portion of the ghetto, where the four city blocks west of the C & NW tracks were 50 percent or more black in 1970. However, blacks had lived in this area since before 1930, and it was not an area of expansion. The black population in these blocks remained stable between 1960 and 1970.

Thus, in 1970, there were two vectors of black expansion in Evanston, south and southeast from the old black community and northwest from the newer ghetto area centered around Main Street and the Chicago and Northwestern tracks. Both of these areas exhibited signs of the classic transition pattern, with blocks of high black occupancy rates flanked by blocks of rather abruptly decreasing percentages of blacks. This drop in black population in "fringe" blocks was not as sharp as is typical in transitional neighborhoods in Chicago and ran a rather jagged course. And while it may have appeared to residents or on site observers as integration rather than transition, it was clear that southwest Evanston's "mixed" neighborhoods were merely the vanguard of ghetto expansion.

More up to date information gathered from interviews, on site observation, and a partial census of the southwest side conducted by St. Nicholas parish in the summer of 1972 confirms this projection of likely transition. (The parish boundaries cover roughly the southern half of Evanston's triangle area.) The fringes of predominantly black areas in 1970 had by 1972 become predominantly black. Indeed, the entire neighborhood between Dempster and Oakton Street, Ridge Avenue, and the Chicago Transit Authority tracks had become heavily black. Transition seeemed to be led by black moveins to certain apartment buildings, for the St. Nicholas census reported that most of the single family homes were occupied by whites and that while some apartment buildings were all white, some were all black, but most were mixed. The area was reported as extremely unstable. Rapid transition also was occurring farther west, indicating movements likely to cause Evanston's two ghettos to link up with one another along Main Street.

The southern part of the southwest Evanston triangle remained nearly all white, but this white area had contracted as block by block ghetto expansion occurred with but little alteration in the Dewey School area, where the expansion appeared to have been retarded. The Dewey Community Conference had been active in stabilization efforts, including a housing referral service, and had been successful in retaining both elderly residents and many Northwestern University students.

Similar stabilizing influences were not present elsewhere in southwest Evanston. The two predominantly white areas in the immediate path of transition were occupied by young married couples with children who had replaced older families.[20] These residents' perception of change fed the process of neighborhood transition. For example, in November of 1972, two families in the square block defined by Oakton, Florence, Seward, and Wesley put up "For Sale" signs. Within two weeks, seventeen out of thirty-five houses were up for sale. In another instance where a black family moved into an all white block, seven nearby homes immediately went up for sale. A resident characterized the mood of southwest Evanston as "periodic episodes of panic which immediately calm down when a white family moves in."

Expectedly, the sense of threat on the part of the residents seemed to vary directly with the nearness of the front of transition. The impressionistic comments of St. Nicholas' census takers indicate little anxiety, a "live and let live" attitude, on the part of Brummel Street residents on Evanston's far south side, blocks away from black and changing neighborhoods. In the area south of Main Street and well to the west of Ridge Avenue, which by 1972 had experienced some scattered black moveins, the attitude seemed more cautious. "All agreed that the black families were good neighbors and were liked. However, some people did express anxieties about 'others' coming in who would ruin the neighborhood."[21] This anxious but still calm mood did not prevail among whites living farther to the east, in the area between Ridge Avenue and the CTA tracks. Transition there had been rapid, and the situation was nip and tuck. The blacks moving

20. *Evanston, Illinois. Selected Studies of Its People, Its Economy and Its Human Services* (Center for Urban Affairs, Northwestern University, 1972), pp. 24-26.
21. St. Nicholas parish census, July-August, 1972.

into the area's older apartment buildings were of a lower socioeconomic status than those moving in west of Ridge Avenue. Building maintenance had deteriorated in some of the larger apartment buildings, and inspection codes were not being enforced. Comments were made that "It just costs too much to inspect apartments, so they work on single-family homes."[22] The neighborhood was described by St. Nicholas' census takers in such terms as "sounds unstable" and "residents are worried . . . more will probably leave in the spring."

Ridge Avenue, lined with large, expensive homes, seemed an important perceptual barrier. While Ridge was only a block west of predominantly black neighborhoods at some points, the blocks immediately adjacent to Ridge were all white in the summer of 1972. On the east side of Ridge, residents "seem to think that the area east will start moving west and be a part of their condition in a very short time."[23] But residents only a block away on the other side of Ridge had a "sense of stability and content with [their] neighborhood . . . no fear of blacks moving in."[24]

The people living comfortably beyond the North Shore Channel or in the high-priced dwellings along the lakefront remained largely removed from the problems of the triangle. As one southwest Evanstonian put it, "The perception up there is 'what problem?'" The same person said, "I fully expect to go up there some day and find they've erected a drawbridge across the Channel." Residents of the northern section of Evanston were reported to relate more to Wilmette than to the remainder of their own city.

The sense of inevitability of change was certainly not felt by all residents of Evanston's threatened neighborhoods. Some believed that stable integration was a possibility, and a few even believed that it was an actuality. It was likely that many were willing to live in an integrated community, if it was truly integrated and not racially changing. A priest of a southwest Evanston parish contrasted the community with a changing Chicago neighborhood (South Austin)

22. In so doing, it has been alleged by some white homeowners that:

city inspectors themselves contribute to the indignation of the black community by enforcing the zoning laws unequally. . . . When a city inspector goes to the imposing house next door to me, he's postively deferential. But when he inspects a black home . . . the first thing he does is to count the toothbrushes to check on the number of people living there. . . . [However] the city's planning and development director is dubious of the validity of these charges. . . .
Evanston Review, June 5, 1969.

23. St. Nicholas parish census, July-August 1972.
24. Ibid.

in which he had previously lived: "There you didn't find a positive value placed on living in a multi-ethnic, diverse neighborhood. That feeling is definitely here on the part of some people." While he conceded that these people might constitute a minority, he said they were "a fairly significant minority—not just 10%."

The June 7, 1973, issue of the *Evanston Review* quoted a white newcomer as saying, "Our main concern is to raise our children in a place with real diversity—old and young, black and white, blue collar and white collar. We feel this will give them a more meaningful education." But the liberal attitudes of some residents could not offset fears of total racial transition. There were repeated assertions that integration was great, but that "I don't want to be the last white man on the block." If Evanston could not communicate a sense of stability to its present, and most importantly, prospective white residents, even "liberals" were likely to avoid the community.

Real Estate Practices

Real estate practices in Evanston seem to have remained constant. As early as 1930, firms were steering Jews, "foreigners," and blacks into the triangle. *Inventory '64* comments directly on this problem, naming several real estate firms as being blatant discriminators.

In late 1971, the Evanston Human Relations Commission became concerned over the widespread practice among local Evanston real estate brokers to undersell Evanston to prospective white buyers and to oversell Evanston to prospective black buyers. There also seemed to be evidence of panic peddling, as well as attempts to list property below its recognized market value.

On July 10, 1972, after nine months of extensive investigation of real estate practices in Evanston and in other north shore suburbs, the Human Relations Commission released its report of findings: "Activities of Real Estate Firms in Evanston and Surrounding Communities."

Of sixteen real estate firms visited by thirty couples, black and white, four companies had been mentioned in *Inventory '64* for racial discrimination. And more than half of the tests revealed some divergence from proper practice—a violation of the letter or the spirit of the Evanston Fair Housing Ordinance.

Discrimination took much the same form as it had thirty or forty years before. Real estate men were no more subtle in their references to religion than in those to race. One checked a buyer's choice of listings to make sure that they were not located in a "Jewish, colored, or student area." Most made the assumption that the critical factor in the buyer's choice would be the racial or religious composition of the neighborhood.

Because of Evanston's desegregated schools, one salesperson suggested a house in northwest Evanston rather than one in central Evanston, because there were fewer blacks in the schools: "I don't know what your views are, but it's my job to tell you these things." This particular person made subsequent suggestions for showing houses in Wilmette, Kenilworth, and Glencoe. Another saleswoman, discussing a particular area in Wilmette said: "These houses are in a largely Jewish area. They're nice people, but you want to live with people like yourself, don't you?"

The Evanston school situation was mentioned by several real estate agents as an undesirable one. One said that people were no longer interested in Evanston because of the schools, while another cautioned a buyer: "I don't know if you'd want your children to go to the high school. I know I wouldn't." Still another commented: "Evanston is killing itself . . . . There are some good neighborhoods . . . . it's mainly the schools." The assumption seemed to be that the number of black pupils could be correlated with the quality of the schools and, therefore, of the neighborhood.

Testers were told that "real estate in Evanston isn't going anywhere—it'll go down." Houses located in the triangle were generally characterized as being in a "colored" or questionable area.

People who expressed an interest in houses in integrated areas were discouraged, "for investment purposes." One broker, when confronted with such a request, said in a puzzled tone, "What is this, integration?" In general, whites were steered to houses in north and lakeshore Evanston or out of Evanston entirely, while blacks and, presumably, Jews were shown houses in the triangle.

Real estate agents in general seemed to have little actual perception of the racial composition of various Evanston areas. One agent described a house as being in a black area, another said the same house was in an integrated area, and a third said it was in a white area.

The Evanston Human Relations Commission found that "although some Realtors are aware of and willingly comply with the Fair Housing Ordinance, a substantial number are either ignorant or deliberately defiant of its provisions."

Crime

As the ghetto expanded, there was a growing fear of street crime in Evanston neighborhoods where crime was once rare. Priests and ministers reported an unwillingness on the part of their congregations to venture out to attend evening meetings. The presence of groups of young black males on the streets or in public facilities, such as laundromats, was viewed with alarm by whites. There seemed to be an increasing belief that violence in the schools had become commonplace, although school officials claimed that these rumors were magnifications of relatively minor events. In general, one could describe the situation as sensitive.

In the rate of increase of "index crimes" (murder, rape, robbery, aggravated assault, burglary, grand larceny, and auto theft), Evanston scored relatively high during 1965-1969. The national rate of increase was 73 percent; Evanston, 62 percent; Illinois, 38 percent; and Chicago, 19 percent.[25]

On the other side, black Evanstonians had long felt the interplay of racial prejudice within the Evanston administration of justice. In 1973, it was alleged that there were numerous cases of police brutality toward black youths ("breaking nigger heads") and that police did not want to answer calls in black neighborhoods. When they did answer such calls, it was charged that they went in with riot helmets, shotguns, and so forth and proceeded to escalate the difficulties. Underrepresentation of blacks in the police department was charged. Out of a total of 200 policemen, Evanston had only 1 black captain and 17 black patrolmen.

School Desegregation

The segregated housing pattern in Evanston created a pattern of segregated schools, with perhaps a little help from school district officials, since it has been reported that "the Foster school district was originally gerrymandered to confine the Negro children to one elementary school."[26] The Evanston Interracial Council's 1953 inventory called attention to the segregated condition of Foster school and advocated that "each school district be restudied and, if necessary, redrawn so that children be required to attend the school nearest their homes without regard to race or creed," implying that these had been criteria for the assignment of pupils to schools. But racial and religious segregation persisted in Evanston's grammar schools in 1964.

In December 1964, the District 65 Board of Education, serving all grammar and junior high schools of Evanston and part of Skokie, resolved to eliminate de facto segregation in its schools. 1965 was a year of planning and discussion. Community groups and individuals

25. *Evanston Review*, April 15, 1971.
26. *Inventory '64*, p. 36.

suggested plans for desegregation. Superintendent Oscar M. Chute formulated two alternative plans designed to conform to three major objectives: (1) desegregation of Foster school, (2) integration of the school district, and (3) adherence to the neighborhood school concept.[27] These plans provided for a combination of strategies, including redrawing of attendance boundaries, construction of new facilities located on the fringe of black neighborhoods where they could easily receive an integrated student body, transfer of black students out of all black Foster, and a voluntary plan for the exchange of white and black students.

In September 1965, an eighteen member citizens' advisory commission was charged with formulating a specific and detailed plan for desegregating the elementary schools. The commission set to work redrawing school attendance boundaries with the aid of a computer, to achieve "maximum integration with minimum disruption of neighborhood school patterns."[28]

While integration was controversial in itself, the seeds of one of the greatest controversies in Evanston's history were sown later that same school year. Superintendent Chute had announced his decision to retire, after twenty years in the Evanston schools. The school board sought a replacement who would be a strong and capable administrator of the new desegregation program, and they found Dr. Gregory Coffin, graduate of Harvard University, Boston University, and the University of Connecticut, and superintendent of schools in Darien, Connecticut, where he had implemented a teacher and student exchange program between Darien and Harlem, New York schools. Coffin, one of more than eighty applicants for the job, was hired in March 1966.[29] The board was soon to become disenchanted with its new superintendent, but he was welcomed at the outset, according to one resident, as a "snob's dream' by school-proud, heritage-conscious Evanston. . . . He was a Harvard man and a member of a prominent New England family going back to earliest colonial days." Coffin himself agreed; "I had the right pedigree . . . . I had studied Latin."[30]

While an overall desegregation plan had not yet been completed, Coffin proposed opening an experimental kindergarten at Foster school to spur the voluntary desegregation of this school that had been proposed during the Chute administration. This kindergarten,

27. *Evanston Review*, May 20, 1965.
28. *Chicago Sun-Times*, July 2, 1967.
29. *Evanston Review*, July 14, 1969.
30. *Chicago Daily News*, April 3, 1970.

offering small classes, salaried teacher aides, and subject matter specialists, among other attractions, opened in September 1966 and proved so successful that 139 white children attended on a voluntary basis,[31] while still others were on waiting lists.[32]

In the meantime, the advisory commission's integration plan had been unveiled. After a series of public meetings in each of the elementary school neighborhoods, the plan came up for deliberation by the school board. The final desegregation program was to include:

1. The new computer-developed school attendance map, with some minor modifications resulting from objections and suggestions raised at the public hearings;
2. Busing of about 450 children, most of them blacks attending Foster and Dewey, where black concentrations were too high to be adequately reduced by redistricting alone; and
3. The conversion of Foster school into an ungraded, team-taught laboratory school, utilizing experimental programs and techniques. This aspect of the plan can be credited to Dr. Coffin, who proposed it and backed it strongly, although such an idea had been considered and laid aside during the Chute administration. The lab school project was accepted by the board after some debate and was realized with the aid of a federal grant and the cooperation of Northwestern University.

The desegregation plan would give each school a black enrollment ranging from 12 percent to 25 percent, designed to approximate the 22 percent total black enrollment of District 65. A total of about 650 students would change schools. Consideration of the plan was on the agenda of the October 1966 school board meeting. A record crowd of 450 attended, many to voice their disapproval,[33] but the controversy had hardly begun, and this attendance record was to be broken several times in the three years to come.

Despite opposition from some parents, the integration plan had substantial support from community groups and institutions. The School board reported that it had received as of November 5, 1966, 181 letters from individuals, 136 of them in support of the desegregation plan. In addition, the board had received statements from twenty-six community groups, PTAs, and school faculties favoring the plan, and only three petitions against it, and these from newly

31. *Chicago Tribune*, September 20, 1966.
32. District 65 Board of Education, *School Outlook*, November 14, 1966, p. 3.
33. *Evanston Review*, July 14, 1969.

formed, ad hoc groups.[34] Save Our Schools, operating in the all white Orrington school area, had distributed a newsletter stating that Evanston children "get plenty of integrated education in the 6th through 12th grades." 467 residents of the ninth ward, located in South Evanston and mostly white, signed a petition against the plan, as did twenty-four College Hill school parents. A survey of parents whose children were to be bused found that 92 percent approved the plan.[35]

A final decision on the plan was put off until the November board meeting, which was again attended by a standing room only crowd. This time most of the audience seemed to favor the plan, although a small group hissed and booed as the board gave school desegregation its unanimous approval.[36]

Evanston's elementary schools, fully desegregated for the first time, opened uneventfully in September 1967. The lab school, which was to represent, as far as possible, a social, cultural, religious, and racial cross-section of the community, proved sufficiently attractive to whites, despite its location in an all black neighborhood, that the black enrollment was kept near the desired 25 percent level during its first year.[37] Evanston became nationally renowned for the peaceful desegregation of its schools.

While relative tranquility reigned in the community, an internal conflict had begun to develop in the schools, at the center of which was Dr. Coffin. The conflict was to culminate in his dismissal in 1969 and to divide the community into bitter factions.

The rift between Coffin and the board can be traced back at least as far as the fall of 1967. No sooner had the elementary schools been integrated than the issue of discipline surfaced. The charges of a "deterioration of pupil conduct" and a "double standard" in dealing with black and white misbehavior were to continue off and on throughout Dr. Coffin's tenure.

In May 1968, friction between Dr. Coffin and Dr. Vance Frasier, principal of the lab school, ended in Dr. Frasier's resignation and the sympathy resignation of four lab school teachers. This became one of the important charges leveled against Coffin when he was fired, for the board claimed that it had been kept ignorant of the dispute until it was too late to do anything about it. The board was especially chagrined, since it considered the lab school the keystone of the

---

34. District 65 Board of Education, *School Outlook*, November 14, 1966, p. 3.
35. *Evanston Review*, November 17, 1966.
36. *Chicago Sun-Times*, November 22, 1966.
37. *Chicago Sun-Times*, July 2, 1967.

whole integration program. On many other issues, the board claimed that it had been kept in the dark, suggesting that Dr. Coffin deliberately concealed or misrepresented matters of concern to the board.

Dr. Coffin's contract was due to expire in June 1969. At the end of the 1967–1968 school year, he asked the board to negotiate a new contract, a year in advance of expiration, as called for by the guidelines of the American Association of School Administrators. The board refused this request, stating in a letter to Coffin dated June 25, 1968, that being forced to decide on renewal of his contract at that time would precipitate a "crisis" in the school district. The letter also outlined particular grievances that the board had against Coffin, centering around

1. The superintendent's concept of superintendent-administration-board relationship;
2. Absence of trust between the superintendent and the board; and
3. The superintendent's too grequently insensitive manner.

In addition, the letter expressed a "growing feeling that we are not dealt with truthfully, openly or reliably," while at the same time expressing full support for the way in which Coffin was implementing integration.[38]

The board did not make its dissatisfaction public, and the community at large did not become involved in the dispute until the fall of 1968, when it was leaked to the public that Coffin had been offered a one year contract renewal offer with no salary increase. Such terms are commonly interpreted in academic circles as an invitation to resign, though the board denied this intention. The Committee for Better Education, which had been formed during the formulation period of the integration plan, distributed pamphlets in Coffin's behalf and submitted to the board a petitition with 721 signatures, calling for a three year contract and a pay raise for Dr. Coffin. The South West Evanston Community Club sent the board a telegram supporting Dr. Coffin, stating "Integration is here to stay; let's live it together and support your policy against de facto segregation."[39]

Bennett Johnson, co-chairman of the Citizens' Coordinating Committee on Zoning and Housing, an umbrella group of twenty-five black organizations, set the tone of the real battle to come when he

38. Letter reprinted in the *Chicago Tribune*, June 25, 1969.
39. *Evanston Review*, October 31, 1968.

said that the black community (of which the group claimed to represent 75 percent)

> believes with some justification that Dr. Coffin is being punished for carrying out the integration plan which he did not originate . . . . Although [racism] may not be the main issue in this controversy, it is part of the mixture . . . . [Dr. Coffin is] the hero of the black community. He should be the hero of the white community because he has saved our city from benumbing racial disruption and he has provided all of our children with a better education.[40]

Within less than a week after the rumor of the no raise contract began to circulate, it was reported that the board had changed its offer to a one year "continuing tenure" contract (meaning that the board was required to give Coffin a one year notice if it did not intend to renew his contract) with a $2,000 salary increase.[41] Six hundred people filled the meeting room at the October 28 board meeting, at which the board was to vote on Dr. Coffin's contract.[42] The revised offer was approved by a vote of five to two. J. Thomas Buck and Franklin C. Gagen, the two dissenting board members, referred to a letter from Dr. Coffin in which he had stated his intentions to accept the earlier contract offer. They maintained that the letter was a bona fide acceptance to which Coffin should be held.

The matter was far from closed. At the next school board meeting, Buck accused Coffin and the school board secretary, Kenneth Orton, who was also on Coffin's staff, of distorting the minutes of the October meeting. Instead of quoting accurately from the statement issued by Buck and Gagen that Coffin had "accepted" the no raise renewal offer, Orton had substituted directly from Coffin's letter to the school board, "it is my intention to accept those terms at the board meeting scheduled October 28." Coffin and Orton maintained that this eliminated the confusion over the proper interpretation of the Coffin letter and that quoting the Buck-Gagen statement directly would attribute a statement to Coffin that he did not in fact make. Buck replied, "If a board member says down is up or vice versa, he has a right to have it recorded."[43]

In February 1969, Dr. Coffin fomented another crisis when he told a seminar at the annual convention of the American Association

40. Ibid.
41. Ibid.
42. *Evanston Review*, July 14, 1969.
43. *Evanston Review*, December 19, 1968.

of School Administrators that the accreditation of his school system was in jeopardy because some of his administrators were not certified by the state. A *Chicago Tribune* reporter was on the scene, and his subsequent article was the first that school board members knew of the uncertified staff members. The incident added new fuel to two of the by then familiar complaints against Coffin: that he was not open with his school board and that he was willing to engage in distortions of truth to suit his purposes. According to an interview with an Evanston resident present at the seminar:

> The session Coffin participated in was on pupil integration. With his experience, he had a good record. The question of staff integration came up—the bringing in of black teachers and administrators—and Coffin stated the necessity of getting black professionals into the school system. He went on to say that in Evanston he was in trouble with the state over accreditation because he had five black principals who had not gone through all certification necessary to be principals. As it turned out, the five he referred to were white. He could not have forgotten this. The conclusion that must be drawn, based on this and other things I have seen and heard, is that Coffin deliberately and gratuitously misrepresented things for his own purposes. Initially I liked him professionally, but I began to find him overbearing, arrogant, and playing for ego aggrandizement.

The school board was more concerned with the accreditation threat than the race of the principals involved. Digging into the files of the mandatory reports to the state, it found that where asked if all administrators and faculty were certified, Coffin had checked the box for "yes," adding the note "some in process," and where asked if the report had been approved by the school board, Coffin had also answered "yes," when in fact the board had never seen any such reports.

Dr. Coffin maintained that the first response was entirely accurate and that, while the second was false, the reports were of a completely routine nature and sending them out without board approval was standard and traditional practice. It also turned out that the accreditation of the school system was not in danger at all. The real source of the anger of board members seemed not to be that Coffin had "falsified" reports, although this charge was one of those brought against him when he was fired, but that he had again kept the board in the dark, causing them the embarrassment of finding out about the supposed accreditation threat no sooner than the rest of Evanston's *Chicago Tribune* readers.

Since Dr. Coffin's contract required a one year notice of termination, a decision had to be made by the summer of 1969, and the matter was set on the agenda of the June 23 meeting. A movement to oust Coffin had already developed, with the Northwest Evanston Homeowners Association at its core. The northwest section of Evanston is virtually all white and has been described as "ultraconservative." There were also rumors, denied by the board and never substantiated, that the local John Birch Society had applied pressure for Coffin's removal.

Forewarned by these rumblings, 500 people attended the school board meeting. More than fifty spoke in favor of retaining Dr. Coffin, and less than a dozen spoke against his retention.[44] What is more, no organizations were represented by the anti-Coffin speakers, while groups represented as being for Coffin included:

District 65 teachers
District 65 administrators
Evanston Human Relations Commission
Evanston-North Suburban Committee for an Urban League
Citizens Advisory Committee for District 65 Integration
Evanston Ministerial Association
Ecumenical Action Team
Evanston Black Caucus
Evanston Democratic Club and Democratic Party
Dewey Community Conference
East Evanston Community Conference
Smith Park Neighborhood Association
Ridgeville Neighborhood Association
Main Street Neighborhood Association
Neighbors at Work (a mostly black OEO-funded community center)
Evanston NAACP
Evanston Human Relations Council

Individual speakers included Dean B.J. Chandler of Northwestern's School of Education, who was to remain one of Coffin's most prominent supporters.[45] Another prominent supporter in the struggle ahead was the Reverend Jacob Blake of the Ebenezer A.M.E. Church, one of Evanston's oldest and strongest black institutions. Other groups, both established and ad hoc, would also add their backing, among them the League of Women Voters, several PTAs, the Rabbis of District 65, the District Educators Council (the school system's

44. *Chicago Daily News,* June 24, 1969.
45. *Evanston Review,* June 26, 1969.

professional organization), the South West Action Group, and North Evanston West, which was formed, according to its chairman, "to give another voice to northwest Evanston."[46]

Despite the pro-Coffin sentiment of the crowd attending the meeting, the District 65 board voted four to three to dismiss Coffin at the end of the 1969–1970 school year and placed the immediate search for a successor at the top of its list of priorities.

At the meeting, after the decision to fire him, Dr. Coffin stated:

> I have been hung in a kangaroo court. I understand when someone stands accused, he has a chance to defend himself. I ask that charges be placed in writing and that I have ample time for my defense. When all the facts are out, the democratic process will prevail. My record is an open book.[47]

Dr. Donald Lawson, an Evanston Urban League official, put it mildly when he said, "This town is up in arms." Dr. Allwyn H. Gatlin, the school board's only black member, and the second in its history, said: "Every time we find a champion, he is blown away. Don't make this man another martyr. Here is a man with soul."[48] But another black man said more cynically after the meeting, "I'm glad they voted that way. It's a good education for the black people. It will make things happen just that much faster."[49]

On June 27, a pro-Coffin rally was attended by 1,000 people. A telegram from Roy Wilkins pledging the full support of the NAACP in the campaign to retain Dr. Coffin was read, and the crowd heard numerous fervent speeches in support of the superintendent.[50]

Two thousand people turned out for the July school board meeting, much of the overflow crowd listening to loudspeakers outside the auditorium. When the board retired to another room to reconsider in private the decision to fire Coffin, the waiting audience passed the time singing "We Shall Overcome." A total of twenty-six speakers was heard, twenty-three in favor of retaining Dr. Coffin. Joel Summer of the *Evanston Review* wrote: "The pros and cons were heard. Speakers were cheered and jeered, and there were ovations and catcalls. It reminded one of the left field bleachers in Wrigley Field during a crucial series with the Mets."[51] A Coffin supporter said, "We want no compromise. We want a three-year contract and

46. *Evanston Review*, June 30, 1969.
47. *Chicago Daily News*, June 24, 1969.
48. Ibid.
49. Ibid.
50. *Chicago Daily News*, June 28, 1969.
51. "Songs Fill Gap in Lengthy Meeting," *Evanston Review*, June 17, 1969.

we want it now. That board will never hold another meeting without finding us here."[52] The session was so stormy and so bitter that the board members were given a police escort home, and police guards were stationed at the homes of the school board president, who voted to terminate Coffin's contract, and of J. Thomas Buck, who, in addition to being one of the most vehement Coffin critics on the board, was also a *Chicago Tribune* reporter and was accused by Coffin backers of planting unfavorable stories in that paper and with influencing its editorial position, which was unfavorable to Coffin.

The school board did grant one concession to the Coffin supporters. They agreed not to seek a successor for Coffin until after the school board election, to be held in April 1970. The pro-Coffin faction hoped that the three seats becoming vacant then would be filled by candidates favoring retention of Dr. Coffin and that the decision of the board would be reversed.

While the board's concession may have eased tensions, which were reaching a perilous level, it also ensured that the furor would continue at least until the April election. Numerous marches, rallies, meetings, and auto caravans were held. There were pro- and anti-Coffin bumper stickers, buttons, and posters, and images of turtles—a reference to a plaque hanging in Coffin's office that read, "Behold the turtle . . . he makes progress only when his neck is out"—began to appear all over. There were hints of possible violence, which never materialized beyond noisy disruptions of meetings and the shouting down of unpopular speakers. One of the more militant groups was the Evanston Black Caucus, which, according to a spokesman, was led by a cadre of about fifty members dedicated to direct action. Said the spokesman, the Black Caucus would not accept "anything less than total victory . . . . We are prepared to escalate our efforts by any means necessary."[53] In the end, however, the Black Caucus had to accept less than total victory, and the hopes of the pro-Coffin camp, which had been kept alive by the school board's concession, were thwarted in an election that resulted in defeat of the pro-Coffin slate.

The controversy became more than a local issue, involving national organizations, including, in addition to the NAACP, the U.S. Civil Rights Commission, which wrote a letter to the school board praising Coffin's "leadership" and "creativity" and stating that District 65 under Dr. Coffin "has become one of the few systems showing the way"; the head of the Chicago Roman Catholic Archdiocesan School System, who wrote, "Dr. Coffin's loss to the educational

52. Ibid.
53. *Evanston Review*, July 28, 1969.

community of our metropolitan area would be a tragedy";[54] and the National Education Association, which adopted a resolution at its national convention condemning the firing.[55] The NEA was later to conduct an investigation of the whole affair. There were reports that the Department of Health, Education, and Welfare was watching the situation closely, and Dr. Coffin requested and received a HEW audit of the District 65 financial records to counter charges of mismanagement.[56] There was widespread media coverage, and Coffin himself accepted invitations to speak all over the country.

While individual aldermen were active in both camps, the city council refused to involve itself officially in the debate. The Human Relations Commission voted eight to three to ask the school board to reconsider the firing,[57] and the commission offered to meet with the board. The major result of this meeting, which was held in closed session on August 19, while 300 people watched on closed circuit TV outside the meeting room, was that the board agreed to release to the public a report detailing its objections to Dr. Coffin. A minority report would also be included.

The reports, which came out in late August 1969, were elaborations on the themes already expressed publicly by the school board's pro-and anti-Coffin factions. Summarizing a few of the complaints itemized within, the majority report alleged:

> Test scores have dropped. Excellent teachers have felt forced to leave the district. Educational programs have been ignored. Needed classroom materials have been lacking. Suggestions of a PTA and principal have been ordered burned. Uncertified and perhaps unqualified personnel have been allowed to teach and to supervise teachers.
>
> Money has been diverted from the district to pay for above-budget deficits in federal programs. Federal money has been misapplied through the use of false vouchers. The board has been bypassed and misinformed. Items requested by board members have never been made available. Suggestions of board members have been ignored.
>
> Questions asked of the administration remain unanswered. Board access to staff members has been thwarted and discouraged.

While stating full support for integration, the majority report went on to say:

> In our view, Dr. Coffin has failed to be effective as an educator and because of this, he has failed as an integrator. For integration—once again—

54. *Chicago Daily News,* April 2, 1970.
55. *Chicago Today,* July 2, 1969.
56. *Evanston Review,* September 22, 1969.
57. *Chicago Tribune,* July 3, 1969.

means quality integrated education. Quality integrated education can only be achieved where the superintendent has the confidence of the board and where the board is satisfied with the educational progress of the district. We are not satisfied.

And the report repeated indirectly the charge that Dr. Coffin had polarized the community, when it described the qualities sought in a new administrator:

We would seek a man who would heal the wounds of this community, not through appearances but through accomplishments. Would seek a man who would gain the trust of the black community, not through press releases but rather through programs.

The minority report was an "appraisal of the kinds of things we were led to believe bothered the majority prior to June 21, 1969":

The claim that a sudden general deterioration of pupil conduct followed Dr. Coffin's arrival is, to us, simply not credible . . . .
As for the buzzing about class scores on standard achievement tests and student performance generally, it is almost scandalously partial and ill-informed . . . .
About the "good teachers are leaving" talk . . . there may be room for discussion about how good, in terms of present needs, some of the teachers were who recently have lapsed out of the system.

These and similar issues were taken by the minority report to be smoke screens, while the real issue, the report suggested, was that Dr. Coffin had pursued integration too vigorously and that he had pursued it outside of the school and into the community at large:

There remains the question of the superintendent's political activity: His conspicuous support for open housing, his well advertised endorsement of a particular candidate for the high school board, and we include occasional sharp sentences in his public statements dealing with the sociology of Evanston.

Reaction to the reports was as predictable as the reports themselves. A *Chicago Tribune* editorial said, "the majority report makes numerous substantial points," while the "minority report is brief and couched in general terms." On the other hand, Dean Chandler called the majority report a "nitpicking, illogical, partly after the fact, propagandistic, self-righteous, self-serving diatribe."[58]

58. *Evanston Review*, September 8, 1969.

The school board majority and minority reports in some ways summarized the divided sentiments of the community, but they did not reveal the depth and complexity of the controversy. After the initial flurry of pro and con activities and statements by the numerous existing and newly formed community groups, two major alliances crystalized. The main pro-Coffin group, the Citizens Committee for Coffin and District 65 (later simply Citizens for 65), was an umbrella organization claiming about 12,000 members. On the other side of the dispute was the Northwest Evanston Homeowners Association and the ad hoc Community Education Committee, chaired by the wife of the First Ward (northwest) alderman, C. Lyman Emrich, Jr., and claiming 1,000 members.[59]

In the school board reports, as in the larger community dispute, it is clear that the two forces never quite met in a head-on confrontation on the issues, for they never agreed on the terms of the debate. On the surface, it seemed to be a standoff between one side, which claimed that Coffin was ineffective as an administrator, and the other side, which responded with charges of racism. But underlying this quarrel were questions of the representativeness of the school board candidate selection procedure and hence the legitimacy of the board itself. Even deeper than this, the controversy opened wide the issue of representation and participation in the total community political structure, and the intensity of the conflict may be partly accounted for by the fact that the Coffin issue became the battleground for a much more far-reaching power struggle. Finally, Dr. Coffin's personality was no small factor in the dispute.

Thus, the multiplicity and complexity of the issues involved meant that one might support either Coffin or the school board for any one of a number of reasons, and the cleavages resulting were molded into alignments that were far less than perfect. In 1973, three years after the conflict subsided, a resident said that the dispute

split the community in such a way that it still has not recovered. It is still polarized. There are damn few moderates—either liberals or conservatives. And the community is split black/white, liberal/conservative. When I am with liberals they consider me a conservative and vice versa.

Another resident, himself an administrator in Chicago's schools, seemed similarly uncomfortable with having to choose up sides. While he described Coffin as "totally incompetent" and complained, "My kids are not getting an education," he thought that he still might

59. *Chicago Sun-Times*, August 27, 1969.

vote for the pro-Coffin school board ticket because of the racism he perceived in the opposition to Dr. Coffin: "A lot of the people who are against Coffin are against him for the wrong reason: They don't like black people."[60]

Superintendent Coffin did not initiate integration in the Evanston schools, but there is no doubt that he became its foremost symbol, especially to the black community. Ross Adams, of Concerned Blacks for Quality Education, summed up this feeling when he said: "It's not the man but what the man stands for that is at issue here. Let's call a spade a spade. Evanston is attempting to reverse the process of integration."[61] And while J. Thomas Buck accurately represented the position of the majority members of the board when he said, "Integration has nothing to do with it. Integration has the full support of the board," Reverend Blake told the board and the audience on the night Coffin was fired, "Part of the issue is integration because you have been so influenced by some conservative elements in this town." He made it clear that he referred mainly to the Northwest Evanston Homeowners Association.[62] Even before the firing, Dr. Donald Lawson, an Urban League officer, claimed, "This move to oust Coffin is primarily coming from a small segment of the school district—the northwest property owners."[63] Thus, the issue was identified from the beginning as a fight between the liberals and the conservatives, as Coffin himself described it, and "northwest" and conservative seemed synonymous to many people. The liberal-conservative theme is echoed in a letter to the *Evanston Review:* "[The] firing of Coffin [was] the arbitrary action of an arrogant public body determined to turn the clock back several generations. Or even to throw the clock away."

Dr. Coffin also believed that his stand on integration was responsible for his firing, that his differences with the board were the result of his going "too far, too fast" with integration.[64] In an interview with Casey Banas of the *Chicago Tribune,* Coffin agreed that all of the board members were for integration, but

My quarrel with the majority of members of the board is in the definition of integration. You have heard me talk about the difference between desegregation and integration, and indicate that desegregation—which is redrawing the map of school attendance boundaries—is step number one

60. *Chicago Daily News,* April 3, 1970.
61. *Chicago Today,* June 24, 1969.
62. *Evanston Review,* June 26, 1969.
63. *Chicago Sun-Times,* June 23, 1969.
64. *Chicago Sun-Times,* September 16, 1969.

toward integration. Integration is step number 10. Nine intermediate steps must take place . . . . Integration is a psychological condition which exists in the minds of children and adults . . . . I don't think some members of the board—and I won't say one, two, three, or four—really understand everything that must be done and how it must be done in the eyes of a professional, and I do claim to be a professional educator and my staff members are all professional educators. I don't know whether they agree with the kind of integration I am talking about, but I don't think they understand. The fact that they don't understand is my failure . . . . I have failed to educate four members of my board, and that's a bad batting average.[65]

It is important to remember that Dr. Coffin was not just a progressive, integrationist educator with a great deal of popularity among blacks and liberals. He was most of all a symbol, and for many of his supporters, his administration was a promise of change and of increased participation by blacks and liberals in community life. When this promise seemed to be revoked by the firing of Coffin, his supporters attacked the issue on a more basic level—namely, the "caucus system" by which school board candidates were chosen.

The District 65 caucus is composed of two delegates from each of thirty-two organizations and twenty-four elementary and junior high school PTAs. Since the number of participating organizations is fixed, nonmembers wishing to join must wait for a member group to withdraw and create a new opening. This meant that the composition of the caucus reflected a social and political order established in the past, an order that many people felt was essentially WASP, conservative, and totally out of step with reality. Blacks and liberals were not completely unrepresented in the caucus, but both sides tended to agree that they were underrepresented. The NAACP was a member, but so were the Daughters of the American Revolution, King's Daughters, the Evanston Historical Society, Kiwanis, Lions, and Rotary clubs, and the North Shore Board of Realtors, while the League of Women Voters was still waiting for an opening at the time of Coffin's firing.[66] The caucus-selected slate of candidates could, in theory, be challenged in the open school board election, but in practice, endorsement by the caucus almost assured one's election.

When Dr. Coffin was fired, a number of delegates and groups voiced their dissatisfaction by withdrawing from the caucus. Seven

65. *Chicago Tribune*, June 29, 1969.
66. *Chicago Daily News*, March 30, 1970.

black delegates who withdrew on July 11, 1969, issued a joint statement, alleging, in part:

> [The caucus system] has for 40 years acted as a screening committee for those candidates who expressed a desire to serve on the board. For white candidates, it has served as a legitimizer, saying in effect, that this is the main qualification of the man we want: he is white. In 40 years it has allowed only two blacks to penetrate its racist fabric.[67]

Albert Burroughs, a member of the District 65 Citizens' Committee on Rights and Responsibilities resigned, saying that he felt, "as a black man, that my services are not wanted or needed."[68] Another delegate resigned, saying, "The system was created in order to perpetuate government by the few. The obvious entrenched white racism of this community will not prevail. I can't do anything about it; I hope to God my five children will."[69]

The fight for power extended beyond the realm of school affairs. Caucus Chairman Raymond E. Willemain described the "Citizens for 65," which had slated three pro-Coffin candidates to challenge the caucus' anti-Coffin slate, as "an entirely different breed—the white liberals, the militant blacks . . . . They are interested in political control of this community." Dr. Dow Kirkpatrick, pastor of Evanston's First United Methodist Church and a Coffin supporter, agreed that more than either the issues of integration or school board composition was at stake:

> What is under challenge is the way we [whites] organize this community as if we are better than other people.
> What is regrettable is that we still haven't admitted there are racist attitudes in this community so that they can be rooted out . . . .
> The old order is finished.[70]

Dr. Coffin had publicly challenged the Evanston establishment. He had participated in fair housing marches and allowed petitions to be circulated in the schools. He aroused the ire of some segments of the community when at the National Conference on Equal Educational Opportunity in America's Cities he called the North Shore Channel "our Mason-Dixon Line," continuing, "This housing pattern appears

67. *Evanston Review*, July 14, 1969.
68. Ibid.
69. *Chicago Sun-Times*, June 25, 1969.
70. *Chicago Daily News*, April 3, 1970.

to be protected by the realtors as though it were sacred."[71] He told the same conference:

> Don't think for a minute that we had a lot of extreme liberals on our board of education. We didn't and don't . . . .
> The white power structure of the city never became involved [in school integration], it remained aloof. The mayor, the city council, the downtown service clubs, and the big businessmen remained completely aloof, at least in terms of the public record.[72]

He reacted to the termination of his contract in an even more outspoken manner, vowing that he would "help break the stranglehold the white power structure has on this city."[73] Later he expressed regret over the hasty words, but elaborated on the underlying theme and the appropriateness of political activism for a school superintendent:

> One of the faults I have seen in Evanston is that a relatively small minority controls the town. They control the real estate and the commerce. How many stores in the downtown Evanston area are owned and operated by blacks? The black people of this town have not had, until recently, any control over their own destiny. Grant Shockley, who was on this board when I was hired and no longer lives in Evanston, was the first black man to sit on this board of education, I believe . . . .
> What does this have to do with education? Everything. If what a child sees outside negates what we teach, then the effectiveness of our education of that child is negated . . . . If a small element, a minority in the city, controls all the institutions—which indeed it does and I don't think anyone can dispute this—and maintains the status quo of white management and white leadership, then our efforts in the long run will probably go for nought.[74]

One of District 65's eleven black principals (there was only one when Coffin took office) said:

> The overriding issue is that integration is on trial in Evanston and do we as residents believe that blacks should have the same opportunity in our society as whites. What we're talking about is power distribution—will blacks really be allowed to exercise power. There are a lot of people in this community who don't want blacks to have any control over what happens in this town.[75]

71. *Chicago Sun-Times*, November 17, 1969.
72. *Evanston Review*, July 14, 1969.
73. *Chicago Sun-Times*, June 25, 1969.
74. *Chicago Tribune*, June 29, 1969.
75. *Chicago Daily News*, March 31, 1970.

Roosevelt "Bru" Alexander, one of the more militant voices in the effort to retain Dr. Coffin and later a successful candidate for fifth ward alderman, theorized that the anti-Coffin forces thought that once they had gotten rid of Coffin, "everything will go back to being quiet and being the way it was. They are greatly mistaken. They don't want any change, but they're damn betcha going to get change."[76] He went on to say that what was going on in Evanston was a "progression of institutional changes toward a piece of the action for black people."[77]

While it is an oversimplification to characterize the dispute simply as a liberal-conservative or a black-white split, that those distinctions were clearly operating is suggested by two polls conducted by Evanston's *Community Opinion Journal.* The results show that blacks overwhelmingly favored retaining Coffin and that long-term and older residents were less likely to support Coffin than were newer and younger residents. Coffin had the solid backing of virtually all of the black community's institutions and organizations. And while one of the anti-Coffin school board candidates was a black woman, she received few black votes.[78]

Still, many people chose sides for reasons that had little to do with ideology or racial identification. Such easy categories as old Evanston–new Evanston, black-white, liberal-conservative, did not always apply, and one of the factors that tended to blur these distinctions was Coffin's personality. The 1968 edition of *Who's Who in America* called Coffin "very much a man of the hour," but critics more frequently described him in such terms as "insensitive," "dictatorial," "arrogant," "abrasive," "high-handed," "stubborn," and "self-serving." It was such qualities, according to the school board, that had done much to destroy its working relationship with the superintendent. Some of these charges are probably true, as Coffin himself confessed to being "abrasive" and "stubborn,"[79] and one of his supporters conceded that personality probably had something to do with the firing, explaining, "You either love him or you hate him." The *Chicago Tribune* editorially compared Coffin to Benjamin Willis, the former Chicago school superintendent who had also been the center of a long and heated controversy: "Like Willis, Coffin also has excellent credentials as an educator. His weakness is that he tries sometimes to dictate programs rather than sell them."[80] This opinion

76. Ibid.
77. Ibid.
78. *Evanston Review,* April 16, 1970.
79. *Chicago Tribune,* June 29, 1969.
80. *Chicago Tribune,* June 25, 1969.

was shared by a teacher who had left the district after Coffin's arrival and who said he had felt that the prevailing attitude in the schools had been "Get with Dr. Coffin's thinking or get out." A parent commented, "When someone asks a question, Coffin behaves as if no one had the right to ask a question."[81]

A final battle in the campaign to keep Coffin was fought in April 1970, when the caucus-endorsed, anti-Coffin school board candidates defeated the Coffin supporters slated by Citizens for 65, but it was already a lost cause. The election was held on April 11. April 16 was the first day of a two day school boycott protesting the outcome of the election. Four thousand fourteen students out of a total enrollment of 10,800 were absent, including more than 90 percent of the district's 2,300 blacks. All seventy black teachers stayed away from school. "Freedom schools" were set up around the city for boycotting students, and they were staffed by boycotting teachers. Emotions ran especially high among parents of black children being bused to Willard school in Evanston's far northwest corner, where the Citizens for 65 slate was overwhelmingly defeated. The black parents of Willard stated:

> We can no longer trust that those not accountable to us are capable of setting educational goals for our children . . . . [The vote] indicates to us that the white majority is only willing to accept a program of integration which is totally planned and controlled by whites. Black parents are sick and tired of this. This is not acceptable and we will no longer tolerate an education plan in which we have no say.[82]

One Willard black parent requested that his daughter be transferred to the lab school:

> If they can get that many bigots and racists out to vote, God only knows what they may do to my daughter . . . . Let Norma Eason [successful black anti-Coffin school board candidate] send her kids up there . . . .
> If Gov. [Claude] Kirk can take over a Florida school system maybe we should too.[83]

Peace was reached by compromise at the school board meeting later that month, when the board adopted in revised form a resolution proposed by Alderman "Bru" Alexander. The resolution pro-

81. *Chicago Daily News*, April 1, 1970.
82. *Evanston Review*, April 16, 1970.
83. Ibid.

vided that the Ad Hoc Committee of Concerned Black Parents and the Citizens for 65, a "body representative of the black community, will participate equally at all levels of determination with all members and with all committees appointed by the board."[84] But according to the *Evanston Review*'s reporter, it was clear that the board did not intend to relinquish any of its formal authority and that the resolution left control firmly in the hands of the board.

By 1973 it was possible to look back upon six years of fully desegregated education in Evanston's grammar schools. The picture of mixed success and disappointment, though the disappointment some residents expressed may have resulted from having pinned unrealistic hopes on desegregation in the beginning. Dr. Coffin told the school board soon after integration began, "If you thought you solved our problems by voting for integration, forget it. It was only a beginning."[85]

At least two serious problems remained in the aftermath of desegregation. One was the old and unresolved issue of black representation and participation. The other was the reciprocal relationship of school racial composition and neighborhood transition.

The findings of a three year study of integrated education in Evanston, conducted by Educational Testing Service with Rockefeller Foundation support, were released in 1971. In May 1972 the U.S. Civil Rights Commission also conducted an evaluation. The conclusions of both reports were similar and generally positive, but there were two findings that tended to disturb black parents. First, both reports talked of a decline in black "self-concept" after having been placed in schools with whites with a higher achievement rate. Second, both reports found some gains in achievement of both blacks and whites, but the Rockefeller report found them to be insignificant, and the Civil Rights Commission report concluded that Evanston's blacks still achieved below national norms.

The Rockefeller report represented the first feedback on the academic effect of integration in Evanston, and black parents reacted with alarm, as indicated by comments:[86]

Integration is not doing anything for anyone . . . . Evanston kids are being selectively de-educated.

. . .

84. *Evanston Review*, April 27, 1970.
85. *Evanston Review*, July 14, 1969.
86. *Evanston Review*, November 18, 1971.

I fought for desegregation. But our kids aren't being educated. They're being trained to the white man's way of thinking. I used to be against all-black schools, but I'm not any more. I say let's go back to the old way.

. . .

[Regarding Martin Luther King Laboratory School, formerly Foster] We want it back. You improved it, thank you, now give it back.

This discontent was echoed in 1973 by some black parents who now oppose the quota system that limits black enrollment in any elementary school to 25 percent. One black community leader further complained: "There's no identity for the black child who attends school all over town, and black parents are never strong enough to have a voice in the PTA."[87] It seems, then, that at least those blacks most strongly identified with the black community came to find that their power was diluted by integration. For these blacks, the statement made by the director of Neighbors at Work about the city council applied just as well to the Evanston schools, if not all of Evanston's institutions: "The City Council calls it controlled diversity. What they mean is 'We didn't mind those other folks as long as we have control over them.'"[88]

However, these selected comments could not be taken as representative of all or even most of Evanston's blacks. The Civil Rights Commission investigators interviewed black parents and found that: "The majority strongly favored the educational experience in desegregated schools. Only a handful felt their children had been inconvenienced by busing."[89]

In 1973, the school system was still substantially integrated, but the district was faced with the state-imposed necessity of further redistricting as the black enrollment of one school approached the 50 percent mark. Continuing neighborhood transition in Evanston meant that redistricting would be an ongoing process, and there was the risk that continued redistricting would speed white flight from the district. An evaluation of school integration conducted by the U.S. Civil Rights Commission in May 1972 concluded that integration had been successful but said of the decline of white enrollment in the district: "some . . . may be attributable to such factors as birth rates, but several school officials view the decline as white flight from newly desegrated districts."[90]

87. *Chicago Tribune*, June 17, 1973.
88. Ibid.
89. *Evanston Review*, February 1, 1973.
90. Ibid.

Comments by outmigrating whites left no doubt that there was white flight attributable to school integration, however, although the amount was impossible to determine on the basis of the evidence available. Certainly, there was no mass exodus of whites from the suburb, and in 1970, the great majority of Evanston's children, black and white, attended the public schools. District 65's nonwhite enrollment for the 1970-1971 school year was 25.3 percent, only slightly higher than the 22 percent black figure existing at the start of the integration program. The crucial questions were whether Evanston's schools would remain attractive to potential white residents and whether they would remain attractive to both old and new residents if increasing black population and continuing neighborhood change raised the black enrollment and caused boundary changes to be regular, periodic necessities.

Race Relations in the High School

Evanston Township High School (ETHS), founded in 1883, was in 1970 four separate schools located on one campus. Each school had its own principal and teachers but shared with the others facilities such as laboratories, sports equipment, and parking lots. ETHS was in the center of the black ghetto, and as one black resident put it, "I'm sure if they'd known that would happen, they never would have built it there."[91] During the 1970-1971 school year, nonwhite students comprised 22 percent of ETHS' total enrollment.

A *Chicago Daily News* article of May 5, 1965, pointed out that negro and white students interacted very little socially with one another. Several black and white students expressed positive opinions about the integrated school situation (ETHS was about 10 percent black at the time), but others reacted negatively: "It's a tense situation. It makes me feel uneasy to go to school with Negroes—you have to be so careful about what you say, or it might make them mad." Lloyd S. Michael, then the school's superintendent, commented that "It is hard to force mixing. We give our students a choice and they tend to sit with their friends. We finally had to tell them where to sit during assemblies, just to mix them up a bit."[92] Black students, in 1965, rarely participated in student activities, for fear of ostracism by their peers. One black student dropped out of a school play after receiving a number of calls from civil rights groups protesting his participation.

Negro honor student Oliver Henry, student council vice president, who

91. *Chicago Tribune,* June 17, 1973.
92. *Chicago Daily News,* May 5, 1965.

works for the NAACP on weekends, said, "Believe me, intermarriage is not a thing with us. It is not the Negroes aim. What we want are equal opportunities—in jobs, and education, and housing."[93]

Since there were few interracial neighborhoods at the time in Evanston, it was natural that both black and white students would continue patterns of segregation established since grammar school.

Students coming from all black Evanston grammar schools did not do as well scholastically as white students, in fact: "The go-go-go emphasis on scholastic achievement in Evanston leaves most Negroes . . . struggling to catch up. The critics say this attitude has resulted in 'de facto segregation.'"[94] ETHS' track system was widely criticized for a number of years, since black students were predominant in low tracks. It was not until September of 1967 that ETHS began its modular scheduling program, a program that also was severely criticized by blacks. In 1973, Carl Davis, president of the Evanston NAACP, stated that the high school dropout rate for black students at ETHS was 33 percent as a result of modular scheduling. "The high school is operating like a college . . . . The students change classes, have more control over their own time. That means a lot of students—many of them black—are going to be graduates of the hallway."[95]

The black enrollment of ETHS in 1967 was 700 (15 percent) out of a total enrollment of 4,800. Black students then were complaining about ability grouping, the fact that white students' views tended to predominate in situations of stress, and the fact that greater attention should be given in the curriculum to accomplishments of the American Negroes.[96]

In 1968, ETHS found it necessary to establish a rumor control center to counteract "rampant rumors about racial tensions at Evanston High School."[97] The then superintendent, Dr. Scott D. Thomson, wrote parents in November of that year:

The situation . . . was one of physical assault, of petty extortion surrounded by an atmosphere of racial tension. The assaults were primarily, but not entirely, by black students against white. The assaults occurred at the rate of one to three a day for two weeks except on Blue Monday, Oct.

93. Ibid.
94. Ibid.
95. *Evanston Review*, July 7, 1973.
96. *Chicago Daily News,* October 31, 1967.
97. *Evanston Review*, November 21, 1968.

28, when seven were reported. The assaults were not severe beatings. . . . The Negro students as a group are not to be blamed . . . . Of approximately 750 black students . . . fewer than 40 caused the difficulties.[98]

Dr. Thomson labeled totally false the rumors that gangs of Negro students were freely roaming the halls, that a student was stabbed, and that faculty cars were overturned.

In December of 1968, Black Organization for Youth (BOY), whose membership consisted of one hundred black students at ETHS, submitted a list of ten demands to Dr. Thomson. These demands ranged from curriculum reform to the hiring of more black teachers, counselors, and staff members to the request that 20 percent of black products be incorporated into use in the cafeteria, the janitorial service, and the library and resource centers. One board member said: "the board is sympathetic to the demands. They are practically all good demands. We would like to, and will, respond to them positively."[99] However, board president Donald W. Ferguson said that the board was "absolutely not planning to abdicate its powers to the students. Decision making is the board's."[100]

In January of 1969, 300 black students held a sit-in at Superintendent Thomson's office protesting the school's policy of requiring a note from parents to explain their absences to attend memorial services for Dr. Martin Luther King. While this policy was consistent with general school policy regarding absences, the administration made an exception in this case.

The best that can be said for the solution is that it prevented a more violent form of protest. The worst that can be said is that it could have far-reaching, damaging effects by establishing a precedent of capitulating to unreasonable demands if the protest is forceful enough . . . . We only hope that the response to the protest on absences has not hindered the chance for meeting other expectations that cannot be solved so simply [BOY demands].[101]

Twenty-five black students were suspended in March of 1969, and seven white students were asked to bring their parents to school in the aftermath of a racial incident in the senior lounge. In addition, about seventy-five black students walked out of the school for sev-

98. Ibid.
99. *Evanston Review*, December 16, 1968.
100. Ibid.
101. *Evanston Review*, January 27, 1969.

eral hours in support of a new list of demands presented to Dr. Thomson by four adults. Dr. Thomson said:

The whole incident is a symptom of a generally high level of apprehension and suspicion in the community. When such a high level exists, the chances for any minor incident to become a major issue are vastly increased. [He added that] black students now are turning "all discipline cases into racial incidents." . . . This community can't expect the high school to absorb all of the dissatisfaction and discontent that exist.[102]

ETHS, in 1970, was characterized as being "Like the city around it . . . organization-oriented—sort of a training camp for North Shore living . . . there are enough groups for everybody to belong somewhere. But learning the proper niche can take some searching."[103]

Blacks, in 1973, remained critical of Evanston Township High School. One called the high dropout rate for blacks "an instant indictment of the schools . . . . White people seem to think it's their school and they're allowing us to go there."[104] A black administrator said, "We have successful desegregation but no integration; cultural pluralism rather than integration."

Fiscal Instability

"Like numerous other cities and older suburbs across the country, Evanston is faced with an impending fiscal crisis . . . . A blunt recognition of the problem's intensity is a first, difficult but very necessary, step."[105] What was the nature of the crisis Evanston faced and how was it likely to speed or hinder racial transition?

The Center for Urban Affairs at Northwestern University in its *Evanston, Illinois. Its Economy and Its Human Services*[106] compared Evanston's economic performance with that of six other nearby suburbs whose size and demographic composition were similar to Evanston. Two of the suburbs studied, in addition to Evanston, were Skokie and Wilmette, both all white and bound by Evanston on the west and north, respectively.

In 1955, Evanston's total annual retail sales were $123.6 million, Skokie's sales were $40.9 million, and Wilmette reported $22.3 mil-

102. *Evanston Review*, March 3, 1969.
103. *Evanston Review*, September 28, 1970.
104. *Chicago Tribune*, July 17, 1973.
105. *Evanston, Illinois. Selected Studies of Its People, Its Economy and Its Human Services* (Evanston: Center for Urban Affairs, Northwestern University, 1972).
106. Ibid.

lion in sales. In January of 1971 Evanston's total had risen to $179.2 million, Wilmette's annual sales went up to $70.8 million, while Skokie's total volume soared to $312.1 million. The report said, "These trends appear even more dramatic when one considers that Evanston had the largest population of all six suburbs throughout the period under consideration."

Further, as the study pointed out, "Two ways to increase retail sales are to . . . increase the number of consumers, and to increase the number of viable retail and service-providing outlets . . . . Evanston does not fare well in either of these respects." Evanston grew in population from 79,283 in 1960 to 80,010 (Center for Urban Affairs' figure) in 1970, a 1 percent change; Skokie had a population of 59,634 in 1960, 68,404 in 1970, a 15.2 percent change; while Wilmette grew from 28,268 in 1960 to 31,987 in 1970, a 13.2 percent change. During the same period Evanston lost 17.7 percent in "Average number of taxpayers for retailer's occupation tax, use tax and service occupation tax," while Wilmette gained 5.7 percent, and Skokie, 31.9 percent.

These declines occurred during a period when sales in general merchandise and apparel increased greatly in other suburbs, such as Skokie. One possible reason for the poor performance could be the lack of a mall-type shopping center in Evanston, which seems to attract suburban buyers in large numbers. Evanston's "downtown" shopping area, which used to draw consumers from the entire North Shore area plus Chicago's north side, now has a shrinking market area (fifty per cent of which is in Lake Michigan) despite the population growth of that area. The obvious success of Skokie's Old Orchard Shopping Center makes the point.[107]

The report further stated that the probable trend was for even further deterioration in sales and employment. And, in fact, if remedial steps were not taken, Evanston soon would rank last among the suburbs in the sample, and the gap between Evanston and the per capita sales leaders could be expected to widen over time.

During the time period 1955–1970, the report added, Evanston had the smallest percentage growth in general revenue of the six suburbs studied, and Evanston relied most heavily on property tax of all six. The Center for Urban Affairs continued, "the relatively slow growth of the retail trade sector would necessitate a greater reliance on property taxes."

Evanston, then, was faced with several alternate courses of action

107. Ibid.

in solving its problems of economic viability, according to the Center for Urban Affairs:

It could maintain the present property tax rates and reduce the level of city services . . . [which would] ultimately lead to a deterioration in Evanston's quality of life. People would emigrate . . . [which would] tend to cause land values to fall and confront the city with a greater fiscal crisis.[108]

If whites emigrated and liberal white replacements were in short supply, blacks would be likely to enter at a relatively rapid rate. First, Evanston was known to be one northern suburb that was open to blacks, and second, some deterioration in city services might not be perceived by blacks as a deterrent, given Evanston's good housing and schools, location, and presumably somewhat better city services than they might encounter elsewhere.

Evanston, by increasing its property tax rates, could maintain its current level of city services. However, as the Center for Urban Affairs' study pointed out, this strategy could work only if surrounding suburbs also raised property taxes, an unlikely event since such suburbs' retail trade taxes bring them relatively higher revenues. This tactic could also cause outmigration, perhaps leading to an even higher property tax to compensate for population loss and a greater fiscal bind for the city.

However, since middle class black families had restricted access to quality suburban housing, Evanston might still be very attractive to them. As one black professional put it, "Evanston is one of the few places that upper or middle-class blacks can move and fine a decent community."

A third alternative for Evanston would encompass diverse methods of gaining additional revenue. But liquor sales, legalized in Evanston in 1972, could be expected to generate more than $60,000 in additional revenue per year. If the state adopted a tax policy in which the per capita level of revenue from the municipal sales tax was equalized throughout the state, Evanston would receive only an additional $144,000, based on fiscal 1970 sales. There were two other measures that conceivably could enable Evanston to alter its financial position—a statewide municipal income tax collected and administered by the state and the encouragement of discount stores and shopping centers to locate in Evanston. The first tactic required the support of other communities to ensure passage by the state legislature, which

108. Ibid.

seemed unlikely. The second strategy, given Evanston's limited room for expansion and real estate taxes that were "roughly twice as high as that of the newer suburbs . . . [puts] the city at a competitive disadvantage in wooing developers."[109] Evanston's fiscal position, not unique among Chicago suburbs, did seem to jeopardize further its chances of stabilizing.

NATURE OF THE RESPONSE

In a special review of the decade 1963–1973, the June 7, 1973 *Evanston Review* commented on the "staggering increase in the amount of organizations and individuals lobbying in local government. At least eight sizable neighborhood organizations were formed since 1963." This upsurge of organizations was indicative of the new mood of anxiety and concern in Evanston. The issues and events that brought the various organizations into being differed; some were founded explicitly to deal with the threat of neighborhood transition, and others incorporated this purpose into their agenda. As early as 1964, the Dewey Community Conference had established nondiscriminatory listing of housing available for sale or rental in its area, and it had contacted all of Evanston's real estate brokers in an effort to persuade them to promote the Dewey area as a highly desirable integrated neighborhood.[110]

The West End Neighbors Organization, serving the area between the North Shore Channel, the C & NW Railroad, Dempster and Main Streets, was formed in 1963 "as a result of occupancy changes" in the area.[111] The group held discussions among residents, pressured real estate brokers and the *Evanston Review* to refrain from listing or advertising housing in the area on a racial basis, and proposed an ordinance for nondiscriminatory advertising of housing. However, it is clear that by 1970 the group's efforts had failed, for the neighborhood was then largely black.

Other neighborhood organizations followed similar tactics. Some engaged in testing of real estate practices. Others concentrated on zoning and housing code violations. A list of neighborhood organizations active in Evanston includes the South West Action Group, the Smith Park Neighborhood Association, the Main Street Neighborhood Association, the Ridgeville Neighborhood Association, the South West Evanston Community Club, the East Evanston Com-

109. *Chicago Tribune,* July 19, 1973.
110. *Inventory '64.*
111. Ibid.

munity Conference, the North West Home Owners Association, North Evanston West, and North Evanston East, as well as the Dewey Community Conference and the West End Neighbors Organization. While there was a proliferation of groups involved with issues on a local neighborhood basis, their efforts were fragmented and appear in most cases to have amounted to too little, too late. Nothing even resembling a concerted, communitywide attack on the problem of neighborhood transition existed until 1973, when some residents active in neighborhood groups united in an informal coalition to put pressure on the real estate industry to end racial steering. They conducted interviews with local real estate operators, from which they planned to publish a "white list" of brokers who appeared not to engage in objectionable practices. The group deliberately refrained from establishing itself as a formal organization in order to have maximum flexibility in its actions and to escape accountability to a membership. However, at best these efforts can be seen as tentative steps toward an organized response to the threat of racial change.

CONCLUSIONS

Thus by 1973 Evanston found itself faced with an expanding black area in the triangle, a problem that hindsight tells us it could have recognized as early as 1945. Yet Evanston remained overall a very passive community. Evanstonians did react in great numbers during the controversy surrounding the firing of Dr. Coffin, and that issue fragmented Evanston into angry camps of blacks, whites, liberals, and conservatives and created a battleground for a local power struggle. But thereafter, except for a small minority of activists, Evanstonians retreated from headon confrontations in favor of a laissez faire policy. Most of those living out of the triangle either perceived no problem or did not wish to deal with it. No program for stabilization came from the city government, from Evanston's central institutions, or from the grassroots level. The very lack of response to the possibility of racial change left Evanston extremely vulnerable to it.

The compelling question, given the forewarning Evanston should have had, is why there had been this nearly total absence of any kind of active response. Although the question cannot be answered conclusively, some factors that seem important may be pointed out.

It has been noted frequently in the media as well as by residents that Evanston had been undergoing significant social change after 1960. The conservative influence in Evanston had been gradually eroded as more liberal newcomers replaced the old Evanstonians.

Elections were no longer "safe" for Republican candidates, and both political organizations had been weakened by the growing trend away from party affiliations. The shaky black-white coalition that formed around the Coffin controversy dissolved, and columnist Ann Pollak wrote in the January 20, 1971, issue of the *North Shore Examiner*, "Black people don't seem too interested anymore in getting together with Whites in what Whites believe are common interests."

In the wake of the Coffin controversy, Evanston remained divided, and the divisions permeated the community from the city council and both school boards down to the local neighborhood organizations. It would be wrong, however, to say that the Coffin dispute created these divisions; it merely brought them to the surface. While much of Evanston no doubt settled back into its accustomed complacency, willing to let community leaders carry on business as usual, divisions in that leadership seem to have rendered the community all but immobile. In short, the Coffin issue catalyzed something of a moral disintegration in the community. While the conservative element emerged the immediate victor, its legitimacy had been challenged. The struggle for power appears to continue, with no side holding a balance of really effective power.

Real estate practices in Evanston are not conducive to maintaining the triangle as an integrated area; in fact, they threaten its limited integration pattern. Furthermore, Evanston seems to have no ability to control the practices of real estate brokers operating in the city. This fact alone would justify the prediction that blacks seeking north suburban homes will locate predominantly in the triangle.

After six years, integration in the elementary schools may have displayed enough stability to make the community attractive to families actively seeking an integrated setting for the education of their children, but this potential demand had to be weighed against Evanston's diminished attractiveness for whites, who were inclined to avoid integrated schools.

Aggravating all its other troubles was the economic decline clearly evident in Evanston in the early 1970s. Evanston had many years to mobilize itself to deal with the issue of integration. What seems most remarkable is the apparent lack of direction and unity in Evanston's response to the continuing threat of neighborhood transition. While it could have been a forerunner in promoting racial integration, it found itself, in 1973, actually behind other communities that had only recently begun to attempt strategies of intervention. Its "do nothing" approach could not help but accelerate the process of change.

Chapter 14

Park Forest: A Program of Integration Maintenance

While Evanston was retreating to a situation of divisive laissez faire, another suburb far to the south in Cook County, Park Forest, was struggling to develop the metropolitan area's only successful program of open housing maintenance. Developed after World War II by American Community Builders (Philip Klutznick, Nathan Manilow, and Samuel Beber), Park Forest gained nationwide fame as one of the first planned communities in the Chicago area. Containing moderately priced two and three bedroom rental units within commuting distance of Chicago, Park Forest was attractive to young families competing for housing in the limited market after World War II. In addition to building more homes, long range plans for the village included schools, parks, stores, churches, and an industrial park. However, industrial development did not take place, and Park Forest remained a suburban community, a satellite of Chicago.

When Park Forest originally opened, 3,000 of its rental units were row houses grouped around large, open courts, each unit having a picture window facing the court. Such was the environment of William Whyte's *The Organization Man*, which was written there. Park Forest during the 1950s was home for a number of persons employed by large business firms. Throughout this period Park Forest remained at about the same age level primarily because it had a turnover rate of 50 percent. While there were several explanations for this high turnover, one of the most important was that many Park Forest residents employed by large corporations were frequently transferred to other locations, creating vacancies for other young families.

While Park Forest in the early days was a young, upwardly mobile community composed of people beginning their careers and their families, the Park Forest of the 1960s and 1970s has tended to be closer to the average in age, education, and income. The turnover rate today is about half that of the 1950s, and both the village and its residents have aged.

In 1967 the typical Park Forest resident was between thirty and thirty-five years old. Nineteen percent of the population was under five and 48 percent under eighteen. The median family size was 3.6. Park Forest's residents ranked well above average educationally and higher than would be expected on the basis of their incomes. Fifty percent of the male residents and 25 percent of the female residents were college graduates. The median Park Forest income in 1970 was $13,951. Homeowners (6,553) greatly outnumbered renters (1,887); the average home value was $23,000. Homes in the $35,000 to $40,000 plus category had been built in the northern (Lincolnwood) section of Park Forest, but the original rental units, some of which are now cooperatives and condominiums, were very reasonably priced. Of the 1970 population of 30,638, 613 were black. By 1973 the black percentage had risen to 7 percent.

EARLY HISTORY OF SUCCESSFULLY MANAGED INTEGRATION

One of the few integrated southern suburbs, Park Forest strongly supported open housing from the early 1960s. However, according to Harry Teshima, one of the early proponents of integration in the village, it was difficult initially to prevent areas within Park Forest from becoming ghettoized. In order to prevent whites from perceiving the introduction of blacks into the area as an "invasion," some manipulation was needed in the early stages of integration. The actual process of integration was begun by several Park Forest residents acting independently of any organization. White residents would buy houses in Park Forest neighborhoods and then transfer them to blacks. Black persons interested in living in Park Forest were recruited by contacting fair housing groups in Chicago and by attending black churches on the south side. Encouraging blacks to buy or rent in areas other than those where blacks already lived was the most difficult aspect of integrating Park Forest. In locating blacks for homes in the village, no effort was made to evaluate their backgrounds, personal tastes, or lifestyles. The sole criterion was economic. If an individual could afford an available house or apartment in Park Forest, he could live in it.

As early as July of 1959, the village government of Park Forest issued instructions to village employees, "For answering questions with respect to local residence of members of the Negro race," stating, in part:

> The Village Government must extend equal services and protection of the law to all its citizens without any discrimination between them. The Village Government neither encourages nor discourages the residence in the Village of members of the Negro race. However, the Village Government carefully investigates all information which reaches it, so that preparations can be made to avoid any undesirable incidents. In the event that a Negro family should make its home in Park Forest, the Village Government will assure that family the same protection of the law that is afforded to any other resident or property owner in the Village.

In October of 1959, the Park Forest Commission on Human Relations forwarded to the Board of Trustees "A Policy on Minority Group Residence in Park Forest," reporting that, "If patterns evident in other parts of the country are repeated, integration of Negroes into Park Forest is likely to occur . . . [and] it cannot be said with certainty that integration would or would not be accomplished . . . without incident." The commission presented a "flexible outline to cover some of the contingencies." Briefly, this included recommendations that:

1. The village government and the commission should keep informed of any contemplated or actual real estate transactions that might immediately or ultimately involve Negro families.
2. Prompt, efficient, and intelligent police action was vital in the event of a Negro family moving into Park Forest, but no action, other than emergency, should be taken except under the direction of the director of public safety. Special instruction in handling interracial incidents should be given all regular and auxiliary police personnel.
3. Negro families moving into the village should be assured of the good will of the village government and asked to keep in touch with the Commission on Human Relations or the police in the event of questions or problems.
4. In the event of a Negro movein, the village government should be prepared to hold neighborhood meetings to give information concerning data on the incoming family to quell fears and rumors and to discuss property values.
5. In an effort to keep a neighborhood from becoming all black, it

was recommended that realtors encourage succeeding sales in scattered areas of the village.

The first black movein occurred in December of 1959, when Charles Z. Wilson, a DePaul University business school professor, bought a single family home. However, "managed" integration proceeded at a slow pace, for in 1965 the village reported only eighteen black families living in single family homes, nineteen in multifamily (rental) areas. It should be pointed out that a great deal of cooperative effort was required to peacefully absorb even this limited number of blacks. As each movein occurred, memoranda were circulated by the village government and the Commission on Human Relations to all Park Forest clergy and rabbinnate, as well as to real estate brokers, giving general information about the family and the location of the property. It was hoped that brokers would take note of the addresses and concentrate on selling surrounding houses to whites to avoid clustering. (This practice was continued until 1968 when Federal Civil Rights Laws were passed.)

When a particularly difficult situation was anticipated, members of the Human Relations Commission made personal visits to the neighbors involved. In these interviews they stressed the legal right of the black family to move in and furnished the interviewees with copies of the state of Illinois civil rights booklet. They pointed out that the village neither encouraged nor discouraged residents of any race, color, or creed, but that violence would be the worst thing that could take place, since it would not only discourage future home purchases but would also accelerate selling in the area. On occasion, members of the Human Relations Commission arrived at the home when the moving van pulled in to keep the situation under control. Despite all the efforts made, there were black-white confrontations: Epithets such as "niggers are moving into that house," "black nigger," and "white trash" were hurled; "unobtrusive" [police] surveillance on a black-owned home provoked comments such as "if tax monies can be used to provide police protection for a nigger, then a policemen can escort my son to kindergarten"; the burning of a cross near a home owned by a black was found to be the work of juveniles whose motivation was "a scene enacted on TV when the Ku Klux Klan burned a cross"; and a fence facing a black's home was painted black. One successful black movein was described as "moved in today; no cakes and no problems."

In 1963 and 1964, because of large numbers of VA and FHA foreclosures, the village was faced with the possibility of clustering, but, probably because of the small number of black families at that time in Park Forest, the community was stable and attractive enough to draw white families into the threatened areas.

In the village president's *Annual Report for 1966*, dated April 22, 1967, it was reported that, "Since (1959) 80 others (Negro families) have purchased homes, joined the coops, or rented townhouses. Eleven have moved out since 1962."

The Park Forest Star of November 9, 1969, noted with evident pride that "the village is now home to an estimated 160 Negro families, making it the most integrated of Chicago's predominantly white suburbs. These are mostly middle-class families who dwell in the townhouses or in a house acquired through an FHA foreclosure. In January, 1968, the village adopted an open housing ordinance deemed to be among the strongest in the state."

BEACON HILL-FOREST HEIGHTS: A THREAT TO THE OPEN COMMUNITY

However, as Park Forest tried to maintain an open door policy over the years, outside factors came into play that were possibly to jeopardize its future as an integrated community.

Adjacent to the Eastgate area of Park Forest and included within its School District 163 lies a section of Chicago Heights whose proximity has had profound implications for Park Forest's effort to remain stably integrated. Beacon Hill-Forest Heights is an area of over 500 homes, 87 percent black-occupied, isolated both from Chicago Heights, the city of which it is legally a part, and from its nearest neighbor, Park Forest. A city of some 42,000, Chicago Heights is about 20 percent black, but its black population is located predominantly in the east, whereas Beacon Hill-Forest heights is located in western Chicago Heights. Bounded on the east by a forest preserve, on the north and south by railroad tracks, and on the west by Western Avenue, Beacon Hill-Forest Heights is connected with surrounding areas by only three streets.

The land upon which Beacon Hill-Forest Heights is built was once owned by the developers of Park Forest, American Community Builders, and was intended for eventual development as an industrial park. When in 1952 Park Forest consolidated its four school districts into one district, that land was included in the annexation in the hope that future industry there would augment the school district's tax base. In 1959, when it became apparent that no industrial development was likely to occur in Park Forest, the land was transferred to the Andover Development Corporation, a subsidiary of American Community Builders, and was rezoned and platted for about 550 houses.

In 1960, Andover Development Corporation began to build the Beacon Hill development, but two years later it sold out to United States Steel Homes Division. By 1963, 270 homes had been completed, ranging in price from $17,000 to $18,000. All of the original purchasers were white, and many worked in the steel mills in the south suburban area. Shortly after Beacon Hill was completed, some of the houses in the project were abandoned and eventually were placed on FHA foreclosure lists. Black buyers purchased several of the foreclosed homes in 1963. Although there was some concern that the area would become a black ghetto, by 1969 the housing situation had stabilized, and the population at that time was 25 percent black, 75 percent white, while the vacancy rate was low.

In 1970, Kaufman and Broad, a national construction company, began to develop the land to the east of Beacon Hill. Between 1970 and 1971 about 270 low cost ($23,000 for a three-bedroom house) frame houses were built. The FHA allotted Forest Heights' developers 255 Section 235 mortgages—about 95 percent of the total development. Thus, homes could be bought for as little as $200 down and $135 a month by persons eligible under HUD criteria. All available land in Forest Heights was used for homes. No provision was made for parks, community centers, playlots, or churches.

Although advertised as an integrated development, the majority of the homes were sold to blacks—many from Chicago's south and west side ghettos. Given the fact that Kaufman and Broad placed the bulk of their advertising in the black media, the volume of black buyers in Forest Heights is not surprising. The Section 235 financing was particularly attractive to low income families as it offered them an escape from the inner city and entrance into the promised land of suburbia. By 1972, the population in Forest Heights was 99 percent black and among the new residents were

> families from the city, women and children without fathers in the family. . . . The majority of these people had never before owned a house. . . . for most of them the transition was from a high-rise slum to a one-family house (that) began deteriorating because they had no experience in keeping a place up. . . . [1]

Racial turnover in Beacon Hill resumed as a result of the situation in Forest Heights, and by 1972 Beacon Hill–Forest Heights was 87 per-

1. *Chicago Sun-Times* July 9, 1971.

cent black, 7 percent Spanish surnamed, and 6 percent white. In short, with a giant assist from HUD, Beacon Hill–Forest Heights had all the ingredients necessary for a suburban ghetto.

Soon after Forest Heights was completed, a number of complaints were made by residents concerning faulty construction. A reporter for the *Chicago Daily News*, visiting a Forest Heights' family in its $23,250 bi-level home, leaned against a steel column that provided the main support for the living room as well as for the load-bearing wall in the upstairs hallway and found that it swung loosely from the beam overhead. This was only one of many such examples of shoddy construction in the subdivision. Faulty plumbing; bowing floor braces; sinking foundations; improper lot grading; erosion of gravel driveways; no doorbells, screendoors, or streetlights; and no recreational space were among the most common complaints of residents in Forest Heights. As of March 1972, thirty-two Forest Heights homes—or more than 11 percent of the year old development—were vacant and boarded up. When added to vacant houses in the Beacon Hill area, a total of fifty-four homes had been abandoned. Targets for vandals, the vacant houses were not only eyesores but dangerous as well.

In the spring of 1972 the *Chicago Daily News* ran a series of articles exposing the poor quality construction of Forest Heights' homes and the failure of the builders to repair problems despite frequent requests by residents. The area director for HUD, John Waner, toured Beacon Hill–Forest Heights in March and, distressed by what he had seen, warned Kaufman and Broad to correct structural deficiencies in the subdivision. However, a spokesman for the company blamed "many of those complaints on home buyers who are not familiar with the maintenance and housekeeping habits necessary for home ownership." And the president of the firm, Royal Faubion, had earlier denied that Kaufman and Broad had failed to repair structural defects. Blaming residents for not contacting the firm about complaints, Faubion said:

> It's hard to say this, frankly, but many of the people who bought homes in Forest Heights don't know how to read or write. . . . Although all of our developments are open to any buyers, we have learned that we made a terrible mistake in Forest Heights. If we had it to do over, we would try not to sell to ADC people. . . . [They] just don't have the pride and ability to take care of a home.[2]

By May of 1972, however, due to continuing pressure from the

2. *Chicago Sun-Times* July 19, 1971.

Beacon Hill–Forest Heights Community Organization as well as from Park Forest and Chicago Heights, some concessions were wrung from Kaufman and Broad and HUD. An executive with Kaufman and Broad declared, "if it is justifiable, we will fix it," but that items of normal maintenance would be pointed out to the people involved. Asked how a determination could be made as to what is the result of faulty construction and what is normal maintenance, he said, "a trained eye can tell." Kaufman and Broad also agreed to create, with federal assistance, a day care center in two of the vacant houses in Forest Heights, to make arrangements to install streetlights, and to pave driveways. By November 1972, driveways had been paved and streetlights installed by the city of Chicago Heights, but as of December 1972, the two houses promised to the community by the developers for a day care center had not been renovated.

Problems similar to those in Forest Heights have been experienced throughout the country in connection with the Section 235 program. HUD has been criticized because low-priced homes financed with Section 235 money are often among the worst examples of poor quality construction. Problem areas within the Section 235 program include lack of proper administrative procedures, improper use of site criteria with indiscriminate placing of Section 235 housing adversely affecting local school districts and employment patterns, and gross mismanagement in the administration of inspection procedures involving this housing. Moreover, in more than one instance HUD has been accused of perpetuating through this same program racial concentration—for example, *Shannon v. HUD*. To quote from a report of the U.S. Civil Rights Commission:

The pattern developed by Kaufman and Broad in the South Suburban area is typical of the operation of the 235 program all over the country. Kaufman and Broad, one of the nation's largest corporate builders, built the all-white development of "Appletree" in Country Club Hills and eight miles away in Chicago Heights built the amonst all black "Forest Heights." This was not an accident. The marketing procedures must have been carefully designed to produce this result. HUD not only did not question these procedures but aided the builder by allotting 255 section 235 mortgages to the builder to be used in Forest Heights. This is over 90% of the new homes in lower income subsidized mortgages. In Appletree they allotted some 113 and black buyers going to Appletree were told that 235 mortgages were not available in Appletree. These two projects were built at the same time with almost identical houses at the same price level. HUD and FHA made no attempt to help or inform low-income buyers, but left this entirely in the hands of the builder.

During the summer of 1972, concurrent with the Beacon Hill-Forest Heights publicity, several Chicago papers began to probe an FHA land scheme in which substandard housing was being fraudulently approved for FHA-insured loans. On December 12, 1972, the *Chicago Sun-Times* carried a story that provides a telling footnote to the Beacon Hill-Forest Heights controversy. The headline reads "Two Plead Guilty in Bribes of Housing Inspectors." The article disclosed that the former controller of Kaufman and Broad's Illinois division had pleaded guilty to charges of bribing housing inspectors, while the supervisor of FHA inspectors in the single family division had pleaded guilty to accepting bribes. It also mentioned that Royal Faubion, "former president of Kaufman and Broad," had pleaded guilty two weeks earlier to bribery charges.

The failure of HUD-FHA to properly administer the Section 235 program resulted in the creation of an almost all black ghetto of low income families in what had previously been an integrated moderate income area and of a racially identifiable school in Park Forest's formerly integrated school district. By 1971 it was apparent that because Beacon Hill-Forest Heights was part of Park Forest's school district, its problems would inevitably affect the village. At a Park Forest Human Relations Committee meeting one of the members noted:

> the commission faces more difficult problems in Forest Heights than in any previous integration efforts. In the past . . . blacks moving into the community were of the same social class as their white neighbors; but now those coming have different life styles and backgrounds than the whites, making adjustment a major problem for both groups.[3]

The first major interaction between Beacon Hill-Forest Heights and Park Forest residents did in fact occur in the area's schools. Grammar school children from Forest Heights attended Beacon Hill School, which, built originally for 350 students, was by September 1971 serving almost 700 children. During the fall of 1970 the school received an average of fifteen new students a week due to the large number of families moving to Forest Heights. Three mobile units were installed, and additional children were housed in the teachers' lounge. Eventually about 200 children from the Beacon Hill School had to be bused to neighboring grammar schools in Park Forest.

The school found itself faced with problems other than overcrowding as a result of the influx of children from Forest Heights.

3. *Park Forest Star*, June 13, 1971.

According to then Principal Pauley, "Most have come from the South and West sides of Chicago—some from Chicago Heights and a few from Harvey but most from Chicago." The previous educational beckgrounds of many of their new students required numerous adjustments on the part of the administration and teaching staff at Beacon Hill School. As one teacher noted: "Many of the families have moved here to get away from crowded, bad schools and unnecessary fighting. So our first problem in working with these children is one of socialization."[4]

Beacon Hill School students reflected these problems in their performance on standardized tests. For example, the school ranked below district and national averages on reading comprehension tests given in 1970. While sixth graders across the country averaged 6.9 on tests, pupils in Park Forest's Wildwood School scored 8.3. Beacon Hill School sixth graders, however, scored only 5.6.

During 1970-1971 the Beacon Hill School changed from 25 to 90 percent black. This massive racial change in the neighborhood school undoubtedly was a contributing factor in the flight of whites from Beacon Hill, which went from 75 percent white to over 80 percent black during the same period. Thus, Beacon Hill School became a racially identifiable school—the only one in Park Forest's School District 163.

As a result of Beacon Hill–Forest Heights children attending junior high school in Park Forest, black enrollment in Blackhawk and Westwood Junior High Schools increased from almost zero in 1969 to 15 percent in 1971. Thus, interaction between the two areas took place first in Park Forest's two junior high schools, and not surprisingly, the first conflicts occurred there as well.

In May of 1971 a fight between a black student and a white student at Blackhawk Junior High School resulted in a well-attended school board meeting where problems at the school were discussed. Many of the remarks made by Park Forest and Beacon Hill–Forest Heights residents at that meeting indicate an awareness of racial tensions between the two areas. The father of the white boy involved in the fight told the audience that he had gone to Beacon Hill–Forest Heights to talk about racial relations at Blackhawk. He added: "I have yet to meet a parent or a child in Beacon Hill who thinks he's getting a fair break. Unless we start to deal with these problems we'll have more and more."[5] Another person, referring to discipline at Blackhawk, said, "two years ago [1969] all hell broke loose." And

4. *Park Forest Reporter*, October 28, 1970.
5. *Park Forest Reporter*, May 27, 1971.

John Zager, co-chairman of the Beacon Hill-Forest Heights Concerned Citizens Committee, said that problems were occurring not only at Blackhawk, but in all schools, including Beacon Hill School. The outcome of the meeting was the formation of a Citizens Task Force on Educational Problems, which was charged with the task of looking into problems in the area's junior high schools.

A month later the president of the board of education for District 163 announced: "The problems are caused by overcrowded junior high schools, and the changing racial structure of junior high schools, together with what was [sic] normal, but now is [sic] magnified student behavioral problems."[6] In July the task force issued its statement. In the area of race relations it suggested among other things:

1. Open enrollment for Park Forest Children in Beacon Hill School.
2. Additional black teachers for junior high school staffs—especially at Westwood, where there were no black staff members but where black students numbered 20% of the student population.
3. Black history.
4. A social worker to be assigned to Forest Heights-Eastgate during the summer to gain an understanding of the tensions existing between those two areas.

Conflicts even more serious than those at Blackhawk occurred at Rich Central High School in Olympia Fields, where Beacon Hill-Forest Heights students were sent after completing junior high school in Park Forest. As a result of this assignment, Beacon Hill-Forest Heights students, 250 in number and some from families receiving welfare, came into contact with classmates from an area that has a median income of almost $30,000 a year.

In June of 1971 fist fights broke out on the Rich Central campus. A more serious disruption occurred the following September, when eleven students were injured and twenty-five suspended. While the overt cause of the disturbance was the alleged unfairness of suspensions for fighting involving a black student and a white student, the actual explanations appeared to be rooted in long-standing tensions both within the student body and between the students and the administration of Rich Central.

The September disturbance provoked responses from both white and black parents. A group of some thirty Olympia Fields residents presented a list of grievances and demands concerning the safety of their children who attended Rich Central. Members of the group

6. *Park Forest Reporter*, June 16, 1979.

cited reports of weapons allegedly brought to school, violence in wash rooms, and a child being chased home from school by a black as cause for their concern. Responding to the same incident, an organization of black parents pointed to the principal of the school as the cause of racial tension that erupted into the conflict in September. A representative of the organization said fuel for the flareup had existed a long time in the form of the physical and psychological abuse of black and Chicano students.

The black students themselves presented at a School Board District 227 meeting a list of grievances that included unfair student suspensions, the failure of the principal to implement formal grievances presented by black students the previous spring, and the small number of black staff and faculty members (6 out of 135). The students also said:

> Black students are separated from the majority of the student body by virtue of the tracking system . . . the majority of the black students are placed on a low level track without adequate programs to help them advance. . . . tracking is a major factor contributing to black and white conflicts because there is no opportunity to interact.[7]

The Rich Central administration replied to the criticisms leveled against it by parents and students by saying:

> A year ago, no one realized there would be an influx of children from the inner city into the Forest Heights subdivision and into Rich Central. The increase in the number of students from this area was gradual. It took six months to realize that many of its newcomers were badly in need of remedial help.[8]

Rich Central attempted to alleviate some of the problems by adding an Afro-American history course, hiring more black teachers, and adding a black social worker to its staff. Cook County sheriff's police were also hired to patrol the Rich Central campus as a result of the September disruption.

Incidents, however, continued to occur at Rich Central throughout the school year 1971-1972 despite these precautions. In February there was a fight in the cafeteria involving white and black students, and in May 250 white students participated in a walkout triggered by objections to recalling a student council election after black students

7. *Park Forest Reporter*, October 6, 1971.
8. Ibid.

complained that there had been a vote fraud. Finally, on May 8 vandals caused an estimated $8,000 worth of damage at Rich Central.

The high school was thereafter put on half sessions, with freshmen-sophomores attending one session and juniors-seniors attending the other. The administration also called on parents to aid in campus supervision, planned a staff training session for the opening week of school in September, and instituted a number of curriculum changes. Despite these efforts, however, tension between Forest Heights students and pupils from Olympia Fields persisted.

The situation in the area's junior high schools and high schools provoked a strong response from Park Forest residents but not as strong as that called forth by the decision to desegregate the Park Forest elementary schools. In 1970 none of Park Forest's eleven elementary schools fulfilled the racial guidelines of 80 percent white–20 percent black laid down by State Superintendent of Education Michael Bakalis. The pupil population of Beacon Hill School was 83 percent black while the other schools averaged 7 percent black. This racial imbalance occurred between 1969 and 1971 when black families began moving into Beacon Hill–Forest Heights. By 1970 the board of education of District 163 realized that it had a problem and began to undertake plans to voluntarily desegregate the district.

Throughout the spring of 1972 various integration plans for District 163 were examined by a community task force. In April the board of education adopted a voluntary magnet school plan wherein Beacon Hill School would have become the laboratory school for the district, which students would have voluntarily requested to attend. Mandatory grade reorganization was accepted as the backup plan. By April the magnet school had failed to attract sufficient volunteers from either Park Forest or Beacon Hill–Forest Heights, and the grade reorganization plan had to be implemented.

In September 1972, the grade reorganization appeared to be operating successfully. About 1,500 of 4,600 students in Park Forest were bused from their neighborhoods. Of the Park Forest children who attended the Beacon Hill School, eighty-five were drawn from Sauk Trail, twenty-eight from Wildwood, one hundred from Lakewood, and ninety-two from Algonquin (the neighborhood school for the Eastgate section). Some 500 children from Beacon Hill–Forest Heights are bused to Park Forest schools, while 90 Beacon Hill–Forest Heights children attend Beacon Hill School.

Park Forest's school desegregation plan was implemented in an orderly manner without violence but the attitude of many Park Foresters toward busing was, to say the least, ambivalent. The following incidents give some indication of the negative responses to busing in the village:

1. In the spring of 1972 four candidates for the board of education in District 163 campaigned as two teams—one team supported de- segregation and busing if necessary to achieve it, while the other supported the neighborhood school concept and opposed "forced busing." The antibusing ticket won, though by a small margin, and only 25 percent of eligible voters participated in the election.

2. Also in the spring of 1972 about 400 Park Forest parents filed a suit against District 163's Board of Education Superintendent Ivan Baker and State Superintendent Michael Bakalis challenging the right of Bakalis to set up rules for eliminating segregation in schools and the right of local officials to implement those rules. The court refused to hear the case.

3. In June of 1972 Representative Don Moore (R–Midlothian) pre- sented a bill that would have ended busing as a tool of desegrega- tion in the state legislature. "Despite a packed house of busing foes from Park Forest, the Senate welfare committee, without hearing an opposing witness . . . tabled the bill."[9] Despite this setback, Senator Moore introduced a bill designed to prevent Bakalis from authorizing "forced busing" of students in racially identifiable public school districts in the 1973 legislative session. Busing was, moreover, a key issue in Moore's successful campaign against former State Representative Anthony Scariano of Park Forest.

4. A study of Park Forest desegregation found that 95 percent of teachers expressed approval of the grade reorganization plan. But "Brown expressed some small uneasiness that some questionnaires which were mailed in August have just now been returned [and] the responses have been 'negative' and they have come from Beacon Hill–Forest Heights as well as Park Forest."[10]

Perhaps the greatest amount of criticism concerning busing came from a section of Park Forest known as Eastgate. In August the *Park Forest Star* reported that some Eastgate residents had asked the board of education "to make the distribution [of Park Forest stu- dents bused] equitable." Members of the Eastgate Residents Asso- ciation and residents of Park Forest Cooperative II (Area A), both groups from the two areas closest to Beacon Hill–Forest Heights,

9. *Park Forest Star*, June 1, 1972.
10. *Park Forest Reporter*, November 29, 1972.

came to object to the fact that the majority of primary students assigned to Beacon Hill School were from their section of the village. They claimed that the section of the village fighting hardest to maintain stable housing conditions, the Eastgate area, where the least expensive housing is located, was disproportionately involved in desegregating Beacon Hill School. The objections voiced to the assignment method were based on the fear that housing patterns would change. Realtors had spoken to neighborhood groups in Eastgate and had told residents that the value of their property would decline because of the Beacon Hill School assignments. One resident, pointing in the direction of Eastgate, exclaimed: "That whole area could go black!"

In January of 1973, after supporting an unsuccessful bid to halt the busing through litigation, many Eastgate residents are still upset by what they feel are inequitable methods of busing children. A *Park Forest Star* article reported that several persons in the Eastgate neighborhood had expressed dissatisfaction with busing arrangements for children who are attending Beacon Hill primary school.[11] One woman said that grade reorganization was causing problems in the Eastgate, Norwood, and Co-op A areas. A particular concern she expressed was that people who were trying to sell their homes in the area felt handicapped because of the busing of children in the area.

Eastgate, separated from Beacon Hill–Forest Heights only by the Elgin, Joliet, and Eastern Railroad tracks, was an area of low cost single family residences planned originally for people who held service jobs in Park Forest such as policemen, firemen, and store clerks. Because of the reasonable cost of the housing, Eastgate was accessible and desirable to black families wishing to leave Beacon Hill–Forest Heights in search of better quality housing. It was equally desirable to other blacks seeking housing in Park Forest.

In 1971–1972 one street, Apache, at the eastern extreme of Eastgate had several black families move in. A Midlothian real estate agent, not licensed to sell in Park Forest, sold one of the Apache homes to a black family with nine children. Soon after, the house next door was sold to another black family with eleven children. Both houses began to deteriorate, and the police were called in on several occasions to settle disputes between the two families. Rumors began to circulate that the Eastgate area was going black. Many whites wanted to sell their houses, and brokers began to steer whites away from the area—a sure sign that it had been labeled undesirable.

At this point, the Eastgate Residents Association, an organization

11. *Park Forest Star*, January 14, 1973.

of some 350 homeowners, originated in 1968 to protest a proposed highway and since restructured to encourage home maintenance and beautification of the Eastgate area, met with the village and Park Forest real estate agents. At that meeting the ERA noted their concern over certain real estate practices—especially the grouping of two or three black families in the same area. A representative for the organization stated:

> In recent months there has been a turnover of houses, and many new families have moved here . . . . in this instance we do not feel that "clustering" is in our best interest.
>
> With the housing market so short of low-income housing, and our homes being the lowest priced in Park Forest, we are particularly vulnerable at this time to become another racially dominated area such as Beacon Hill–Forest Heights. The fact that our village practices "open housing" and surrounding villages apparently do not do their share makes us more vulnerable than ever.
>
> Representatives of ERA will be personally calling on all licensed realty firms, asking them to cooperate with us in this matter . . . . ERA will be monitoring very closely the transactions in our area.[12]

The situation did stabilize, however. The houses that turned over were largely white occupied, and at the beginning of 1972, 23 homes out of a total of 350 were for sale. Several events may have contributed to this stabilization.

In June of 1972 a Responsible Housing Practices Day sponsored by the Park Forest village government was attended by 175 persons. Topics discussed in small groups included the need for (1) better standards of selection of housing for federally financed low and middle income families throughout the south suburbs, (2) legislation that would permit two or more communities with a combined population of 25,000 or more to form their own local housing authorities, (3) counseling low income families in home maintenance procedures, and (4) financing public schools on some basis other than real estate taxes. The Housing Day gave Eastgate residents an opportunity to air some of their fears and to discuss them with real estate firms as well as offering Park Foresters in general the chance to discuss the implications of the Beacon Hill–Forest Heights situation for the village as a whole.

One indirect result of the Housing Day was the village board's decision in November 1972 to investigate the possibility of establishing a not for profit housing corporation that would have as its

12. *Park Forest Star*, May 11, 1972.

priority concern the rehabilitation of substandard housing. The ERA vigorously supported the housing corporation because:

> One of the most important results of such a corporation would be the stabilizing factor. Once people know of the housing corporation and its function, they will feel much more secure in their present community, knowing that if a specific problem arises there will be a place to turn for help.[13]

Nevertheless, many residents of Eastgate still feared inmigration from Beacon Hill–Forest Heights. A survey conducted in 1972 by the ERA revealed that residents of Eastgate were disappointed with the school situation and the busing program. According to the survey, if things did not change for the better, many residents would move away from Park Forest.

Crime had also been a concern of the Eastgate residents. Many houses on Apache had been burglarized, although the situation had been brought under control by the extra police patrols that had been assigned to the area as a result of the action of the ERA.

Tensions between Eastgate and Beacon Hill–Forest Heights had been recognized since 1971. One of the recommendations of the educational task force commissioned to investigate problems in the junior high schools was the assignment of a social worker to the two areas to gain a better understanding of the hostility between juveniles from the two communities. The following examples illustrate the problems:

1. June 6, 1971—Two white youths, one from Park Forest Co-op C, were arrested in connection with a shooting incident in Forest Heights.
2. June 10, 1971—A black youth was attacked by eight or nine white youths while riding his bike on Beacon Boulevard near Western Avenue.
3. June 10, 1971—A fight in the forest preserve between Park Forest and Chicago Heights youngsters ended in bloodshed.
4. October 28, 1971—Two Park Forest youths were reportedly attacked and beaten by four other youths at Boston and Cambridge Streets in Chicago Heights.
5. November 14, 1971—A ten-year old girl, a fourteen-year old boy, and a fifteen-year old girl—all residents of Eastgate—complained of beatings in three separate incidents.

13. *Park Forest Star*, November 30, 1972.

During the summer of 1971, Chicago Heights police found a sharp increase in juvenile problems, and residents of both races complained of vandalism and extortion of money from children. Merchants in nearby Richton Park began to lock their doors to prevent shoplifting by black children attending nearby Park Forest schools.

Crime for the Park Forest areas as a whole began to increase. 1970 ended the decrease in serious crimes that had occurred in 1968 (154) and 1969 (142). In that year "serious crimes" (aggregate of murder, rape, robbery, aggravated assault, burglary, larceny over $50, and auto theft) increased from forty-one to fifty-six and thefts of property valued at $50 or more increased from sixty-eight to seventy-three.

Although the crime rate increased for Park Forest, it remained comparatively low. The official crime rate computed by the FBI for Park Forest was 6.3 per thousand as compared to 38 per thousand for the city of Chicago or 21 per thousand for Matteson. Somewhat disturbing, however, was the fact that Park Forest's neighbor, Chicago Heights, had a crime rate of 45 per thousand (1,835 serious crimes)—higher than that for Chicago—and all black East Chicago Heights had an even more alarming 50 per thousand.

In 1971 Park Forest's crime rate continued its upward trend, but dropped somewhat in 1972. Serious crimes increased 48 percent, from 189 in 1970 to 289 in 1971, but decreased to 252 in 1972. Major increases in 1971 involved crimes against property—burglary, theft over $50, and auto thefts. Burglaries jumped from fifty-six in 1970 to ninety-eight in 1971, decreasing to ninety-one in 1972. Thefts over $50 rose from seventy-three in 1970 to eighty-seven in 1971 and one hundred in 1972. Eighty-three auto thefts were reported in 1971 compared to forty-nine in 1970; police figures showed 1972 vehicle thefts down to forty-eight. Juveniles—whom both Park Forest and Beacon Hill–Forest Heights had in abundance—were disproportionately involved in cleared crimes. However, while in 1971 62 percent of the crimes cleared by arrest involved persons under age, in 1972 only 53 percent of juveniles were so involved. The Park Forest police report for 1972 indicated that clearance of serious crimes was 32.9 percent in that year, up 13.3 percent over 1971. In 1971 Chicago Heights' crime rate decreased slightly but still remained high.

In respect to crime, Chicago Heights and Park Forest conformed, of course to a nationwide trend. FBI statistics showed that suburban crime rates were increasing much more rapidly than were rates in the cities. Nationally the 1971 suburban crime rate was 11 percent higher

than 1970's, and locally the suburbs' crime rates rose 6 percent faster
than that of Chicago.

RESPONSE TO THE EXPANDING THREAT:
INTEGRATION MAINTENANCE

While Eastgate residents were vocal about their concerns for the stability of their immediate area, other Park Foresters also began to feel
threatened by the influx of blacks. Since Beacon Hill–Forest Heights
had no stores, its residents shopped primarily in Park Forest. Blacks
thus became highly visible in the community, and some whites began
to shun Norwood Plaza Shopping Center, a small complex situated
nearest to Beacon Hill–Forest Heights, because they felt it had begun
to take on a "ghettolike" look.

In cooperation with the Human Relations Commission it was felt
necessary in 1971 to establish a "rumor control" telephone service
that would:

> give citizens a system to check out rumors relevant to problems within the
> community . . . on a 24-hour a day basis. It is hoped that the system will
> help offset the effect of rumors which may escalate or aggravate already
> tense or potentially tense conditions.
>
> Working hand in hand with Rumor Control will be a new Human Relations blotter program in the village Police Department. The blotter consists of a notebook for recording a summary of any incident relative to the
> safety and security of residents . . . . This summary book will be maintained by the Police Department and the information will be given to the
> Human Relations Commission.[14]

Renters in some of the cooperative units just south of the Eastgate
area became apprehensive as moveouts occurred; they felt, also, very
vulnerable to black unnundation. 1970 census figures show that ten
courts in this area were, at that time, 4, 5, 6, 6, 7, 9, 9, 12, 18, and
19 percent black, respectively.

The Beacon Hill–Forest Heights situation and the busing of grammar school children created dilemmas for Park Forest, but another,
perhaps graver, threat to the overall community began to surface.

Because of the fact that Park Forest had been well publicized as an
integrated community and many of the communities around it were
known to be highly resistant to black inmigration, more and more
blacks from Chicago and out of state attempted to locate in Park

14. *The Park Forest Bulletin*, 5, no. 4 (Fall 1971).

Forest. At an April 11, 1973, meeting at the village hall, one broker remarked that, "We are getting more and more blacks; almost more than whites in the offices."[15]

This particular meeting had been initiated by some residents of the Lincolnwood area, where many of Park Forest's highest priced homes are located, because of what they felt was a problem of clustering on Gettysburg and Illinois Avenues. At the meeting it was stated that:

> We are talking about three separate transactions and the possibility of a fourth. On the north east corner of Gettysburg and Illinois, house sold to a black family; two months later at 508 Illinois another house sold to a black family. There is another house on Gettysburg available for sale. [Note: This house has since been sold to a black family.] There is a difference between integrated housing and clustering. No one has objections to colored.

A broker replied that:

> Representatives of the Human Relations Committee used to send us lists of black move-ins so we could scatter blacks . . . this was 7 or 8 years ago; it was steering in reverse. With the multiple listing service we can't keep track of where people live by race. We could be accused of violation if blacks asked to buy a specific house and we did not show it. Anyway, colored prefer not to live next door to one another . . . and I find if I know there are other black families right there and I mention this to them and suggest they would be happier in another location in the village they will agree with me.

Another broker said:

> I am not going to lose my license over this. Maybe if we made it public record or something it would be okay, I don't know, but I couldn't even call up any broker legally and ask him where he is selling to colored.

One resident remarked that:

> I once approved the rate of integration here, but it is getting reckless now . . . . Park Forest is a soft touch for colored . . . . The community has made a big mistake in publicizing integration so we have been attracting more than our share of what we are trying to get away from.

15. However, another broker commented that he "guessed" that a minimum of 80 percent of Park Forest houses were sold to other than minority groups. The contradiction posed by these statements is open to a variety of interpretations.

A woman commented that her husband worked for a major oil company that was transferring large numbers of families to the Chicago area, but that "no one is interested in moving into Park Forest, mainly because the problem of integration has come up." A realtor added, "Most transferees generally object to the southern suburbs. They not only try to steer clear of Park Forest but the south suburban area. The word is out; people come in knowing the integration situation."

Although brokers pointed out that properties in Park Forest had appreciated in value by approximately 50 percent in the past ten years, residents persisted in asking for relief of the perceived problem. One suggested that the village should provide by ordinance a definition for resegregation and make it illegal for real estate brokers to sell property to minority group representatives within a geographic distance as spelled out by the village code. Another resident said that the village should supply the realtors, as it had in the past, with information as to where minority residents are located. In a letter dated April 13, 1973, the village attorney replied to both points:

> Such a Village ordinance would be considered to be discriminatory and in violation of the Bill of Rights and the amendments under the United States Constitution, in view of the rulings of the United States Supreme Court. It would also be in violation of the new Illinois Constitution.
>
> . . .
>
> This information [addresses of minority residents], under the public nature of the Village's operation and its fiduciary relationship with its residents, should not be made available.
>
> . . .
>
> In effect . . . the laws respecting clustering and allowing realtors to regulate the racial nature of the community would in most instances be illegal . . . .

In a letter to the village president, also dated April 13, one Lincolnwood resident pointed out:

> I feel that it may have been a waste of time to have the meeting. Many of the residents attending . . . have lived [here] for 10 years so they were living here when the integration movement began . . . . However, as clustering develops the burden of complaint rests with these stable and solid citizens who have now been accused of being bigots . . . . I felt little was accomplished at the meeting due to the passive attitude and little concern projected by the brokers and the village administration. I firmly feel a positive approach is possible without violating the law. A concerted effort by the brokers and the village can control this problem . . . . There are

other communities near us with desirable homes . . . yet only Park Forest has the clustering problem. These areas should be brought to the attention of prospective buyers. Also there are other ways, I'm sure, of keeping clustering to a minimum. This problem can be corrected only if the brokers and the village administration stop "sweeping the problem under the rug." The problem is *real* and some immediate positive action should be taken toward solving it . . . .

It was clear that some Park Forest residents felt it possible to "manage" integration—that is, to manipulate and control locations and numbers of black families moving into the village, as was done in the early 1960s. They felt that local authorities or real estate brokers could circumvent open housing laws to stop black moveins. they found it hard to believe that they had no control over it themselves—other than their right to move when they felt sufficient pressure. The fact that the blacks who moved into the Lincolnwood area were middle class and could afford $30,000 plus houses did not alter the reactions of some of the white Lincolnwood residents. They reacted as strongly as did the Eastgate residents to possible black encroachment from Beacon Hills–Forest Heights.

However, while brokers enunciated strongly their feelings that they could not legally steer black clients out of certain areas, there were some reports that whites who visited Park Forest real estate firms were being steered. Two Park Forest real estate firms advised one woman in 1971 not to consider property in the Eastgate area. Another prospective buyer was told in 1973 that since he couldn't afford the Lincolnwood area, a nice neighborhood would be "west of the Park Forest Plaza Shopping Center, maybe something on Rocket Circle." Still another individual was told to avoid buying property abutting the cooperative and rental units or near Norwood Plaza, since these areas might be in a transitional stage.

Meetings held in late May and early June of 1973 reflected Park Forest's increasing concern with the integration issue. Then, on June 4, the village board's Community Relations Committee presented a series of recommendations to the entire board for maintaining Park Forest as a viable, open community. These included adopting an ordinance "prohibiting the steering of majority and minority home buyers or tenants to, from or within Park Forest"; establishing a fair housing review board; maintaining up to date listings of all housing as it becomes available on the market; establishing a current list of all existing housing by race and color; keeping a record of all real estate brokers and sales personnel doing business in the village; setting up a testing program to determine housing practices in general and steering in particular; providing counseling and information to prospective buyers, sellers, landlords, and tenants; producing a brochure outlining the advantages of living in Park Forest; and exchanging information periodically with area real estate firms.

Some of these suggestions proved unworkable, even undesirable, but in connection with its testing program, the village enlisted the aid of the Leadership Council for Metropolitan Open Communities. The Leadership Council had previously assisted the Evanston Human Relations Commission in such an endeavor, which resulted in publication, in June 1972, of "Activities of Real Estate Firms in Evanston and Surrounding Communities" (see Chapter 13). And on June 12 the Park Forest Human Relations Commission unanimously approved a resolution urging surrounding communities to implement open housing policies in the hope of relieving the perceived racial pressures on Park Forest.

Then, on November 26, 1973, after lengthy discussion of the June proposals, Park Forest confirmed its position as an equal opportunity community by passing into law a package of "integration maintenance" ordinances calling for:

1. Prohibition of "steering" prospective homebuyers into or out of neighborhoods on the basis of religious or racial composition.
2. The establishment of a Fair Housing Review Board, a quasi-judicial body with the powers of subpoena to revoke brokers' licenses and to refer complaints to court.
3. Reorganization of the Human Relations Commission, establishing for it an advocacy role and granting it subpoena powers.
4. Authority of the village manager to take administrative action on housing discrimination complaints before referring them to any other bodies.
5. Prohibition of "redlining" by lending firms.

These ordinances backed up the other efforts of the village government to eliminate discrimination. It has been characteristic of the village's official response, since the first fair housing ordinance was passed in 1968, that the emphasis had been on enforcing the constitutional right of minorities to housing of their choice, while stopping short of attempts to "manage" integration by direct intervention in the locational choices of individuals, despite considerable external and internal pressures to do so. Suggestions that there be legal restrictions on "clustering" or pressure on real estate brokers to actively discourage it had consistently been rejected. A proposed "exempt location" provision in the new set of ordinances, which would have permitted "steering" for the purposes of maintaining racial balance in certain areas, created a furor among black residents and a controversy among whites, and it was dropped from consideration. Nor were village officials persuaded by popular sentiment and the exhortations of real estate people to maintain a lower profile with regard to open housing. Commented one broker on the ordinances: "I wish they would be more quiet and wouldn't make so much noise." On the contrary, the Human Relations Commission chairman felt that "the revision of the current ordinances moves our village into the ranks of municipalities that have the most forward-looking and workable structure for dealing with today's very real problems." For Park Forest officials (as implied by their use of the term "integration maintenance" for their new laws), the assumption seemed to be that integration can occur naturally in a housing market that is free from racial bias. If fair housing brings with it some perils, the solution is more fair housing.

Chapter 15

The Role of Status in Community Response to Racial Change

The foregoing cases reveal a broad range of white responses to black entry into their communities, from accelerating flight in Austin and violence in West Englewood to the erection of defensive barriers in Garfield Ridge, minimal organizational response in Evanston, reverse steering and managed integration in South Shore and Oak Park, and an avowed commitment to unrestricted open housing in Park Forest. *Yet across this range of white responses the general conclusion must be that, at each income level and regardless of socioeconomic characteristics, a concentration of black families is perceived negatively by whites.*

Why did it matter to communities like these that their new residents were black rather than white? How did the symbolism of race determine the definition of a black residential concentration as undesirable for whites? And what are the implications for the housing market and for the efficacy of fair housing programs? In order to seek explanation of processes manifest at the macroscale of community and region, it is necessary (as was noted in chapter 5) to focus on individual response at the microlevel of face to face confrontation of blacks and whites as homeowners and neighbors. The status consciousness of white residents is viewed as a basic factor underlying their perception and evaluation of racial change and their individual and organized attempts to cope with it.

Status is defined in the Weberian sense of the "social estimation of honor" and as such is clearly distinguished from the concept of "class."[1] Status consciousness is "the degree to which status considerations are important to the individual, the extent to which he is concerned about his own relative status or to which status factors tend to color his interaction with others."[2] The concept thus represents an attitude that one's status should be maintained and protected; this attitude is made manifest through explicit expedients designed to maintain social distance between individuals of unlike status.

It is with these definitions in mind that we argue that the desire for status protection lay beneath the white behavior in racially changing neighborhoods that we have documented and that this desire was usually manifested as avoidance behavior based on status consciousness—that is that the mechanism precipitating white flight was white status consciousness. Our focus here will be on the social and cultural mechanisms that prompt an individual's latent status consciousness to become manifest. This takes place within the context of the residential structure of the city, which we view as a spatially arrayed stratification system. City residents (individuals) and city neighborhoods (areas) are seen as being ranked in congruent hierarchical systems, with the mechanisms of social status serving to relate the "vertical" structure of social stratification to the "horizontal" structure of urban residential areas ranked by "exclusiveness" and "desirability." A reciprocal relationship thus is seen between an individual's residential location and his position (status) in the social stratification system, and residential mobility is viewed as a sifting process whereby like-statused individuals tend to cluster in distinguishable subareas of the city.

This notion of a direct relationship between the city's residential structure and its status hierarchy is a venerable ecological principle that stems from the observation, first noted by Robert Park,[3] that social mobility is often reflected in residential mobility: the upwardly mobile improve their "residential status" to keep pace with improvements in their social status. Individuals tend to choose a residential location that, within the constraints imposed by available resources, satisfies their desire for symbolic expression of their self-conceived status.

1. S.N. Eisenstadt, ed., *Max Weber on Charisma and Institution Building* (Chicago: University of Chicago Press, 1968), p. 177.

2. H.M. Blalock, "Status Consciousness: A Dimensional Analysis," *Social Forces* 37, no. 3 (March 1959): 243.

3. R.E. Park, "The Urban Community as a Spatial Pattern and a Moral Order" (1926), in R.M. Turner, ed., *Robert Park on Social Control and Collective Behavior* (Chicago: University of Chicago Press, 1967), p. 61.

In contrast to the emphasis placed on locational shifts associated with improved status, less attention has been paid to the corollary process by which individuals, having selected a residential location, strive to protect their status, however. Two processes ultimately account for the sociospatial structure of the city: (1) the tendency toward mobility and change, and (2) the tendency toward stability and resistance to change. Racial transition encompasses both, with the friction between arriving blacks and resisting whites attributable to differential perspectives of the environment. Upwardly mobile blacks view the contested area as compatible with both their housing needs and their self-conception of status and seek to enter. The resident white population, having in some earlier period identified the area as congruent to their status needs, opposes changes perceived as leading to status deterioration, either resists black encroachment or seeks to manage compatible integration, and if these strategies fail, flees to "safer" territory.

These interactions must be understood from the perspective of an American cultural context in which "black"carries the imputation of status inferiority and a black or integrated neighborhood is considered low status.[4] In an insightful discussion of the social and psychological factors involved, Fishman notes that: "After all is said and done, an interracial . . . neighborhood is a step-up for most Negroes. Any white who is appreciably concerned for his status in the larger white world . . . may conclude that for him such a community is a step down."[5] And a similar point has been made by Mayer: "Our culture has developed in a direction where persons who view themselves as related to the dominant cultural norms cannot afford to live in a bi-racial neighborhood. This means most people, including those who are not prejudiced individuals, as we now measure prejudice."[6]

Despite their general veracity, these statements must be examined in detail. Careful questioning would suggest that numerous factors intervene in the relationship between the individual's social and cultural environment and his attitudes toward and perceptions of the residential environment during the course of racial change. Which "dominant cultural norms" come into play? How are individuals

4. E.C. Hughes, "Dilemmas and Contradictions of Status," *American Journal of Sociology* 50, no. 5 (March 1945): 353-59; C. Abrams, *Forbidden Neighbors* (New York: Harper and Bros., 1955).

5. J.A. Fishman, "Some Social and Psychological Determinants of Intergroup Relations in Changing Neighborhoods," *Social Forces* 40, no. 1 (October 1961): 46.

6. A.J. Mayer, "Race and Private Housing: A Social Problem and a Challenge to Understanding Human Behavior," *Journal of Social Issues* 13, no. 4 (September 1957): 264.

"related" to these norms, and where and how large—from a few blocks to the scale of an international fraternity—is the "larger white world?" How do individuals and groups vary in their perceptions of a neighborhood as being "biracial?" In the attempt to deal with these questions, the discussion that follows is organized into two major sections.

First, attention is focused on the social and cultural milieu that imbues meaning to the sociospatial setting. It is argued that the status implications of residential proximity depend on the cultural definitions of the social and spatial symbols manifested in the sharing of residential space.

Second, emphasis is placed on the specific cultural environment in which the individual lives and the particular social group(s) of which he is—or aspires to become—a member. The overall cultural setting outlined above defines the "dominant cultural norms" and the "larger white world" to which Mayer and Fishman make reference. Within this general framework, the immediate social group provides both positive and negative reinforcement for the individual's attitudes toward status. These attitudes influence his attitudes toward the residential environment, which in turn influence perception of and response to racial change.

STATUS AS AN ORGANIZING PRINCIPLE

In 1926, Harvey Zorbaugh noted the central role played by the quest for status in American urban life:

> Now, in the intimate economic relationships in which all people are in the
> city everyone is, in a sense, in competition with everyone else. It is an im-
> personal competition—the individual does not know his competitors. It is
> a competition for other values in addition to those represented by money.
> One of the forms it takes is competition for position in the community.[7]

And Charles Abrams remarked some thirty years later: "The suburb and the quest for status are shaping the American personality of the future as the frontier once shaped the American personality of the past."[8] Zorbaugh's concept of "position in the community" reflects the significance of status as an element of the individual's definition of self in society. In turn, individuals sharing a designated status con-

7. H.W. Zorbaugh, "The Natural Areas of the City" (1926), in G.A. Theodorson, ed. *Studies in Human Ecology.* New York: Harper & Bros., 1961, pp. 46-7.

8. Abrams, p. 140.

stitute status groups, which are characterized by "communal action" arising from the "feeling of the actors that they belong together". Aspired or achieved membership in a particular status group has the behavioral implication that " status honor is normally expressed by the fact that above all else a specific *style of life* can be expected from all those who wish to belong to the circle."[9]

Hence, status groups are characterized by (1) an externally derived and perceived measure of "honor" within a ranked hierarchy of status groups; (2) an internally shared sense of belonging to the group; and (3) symbolic expression of status group membership through a characteristic lifestyle. The significance of status as an organizing principle in American life thus derives from the importance of status as an element of self-identity. Status expresses the individual's sense of his position in the city's ranked social hierarchy, recognition of this position by others in the social system, and sharing of the position with other members of the same status group. Finally, it includes an important element of what Park termed "self-consciousness": "the fear . . . that we shall not be able to live up to the conception of ourselves, and particularly, that we shall not be able to live up to the conception which we should like other persons to have of us. This is the impelling force underlying the very literal 'struggle for status' in which every individual finds himself."[10]

"MEASURES OF HONOR": SPATIAL PROXIMITY AND SOCIAL DISTANCE

Status rankings are operationalized in society through the imposition of social distance.[11] In turn, there are complex interrelationships between social distance and physical proximity that depend upon the cultural definition of the situation. Normally, propinquity engenders social interaction, but the social distance between individuals can control the quantity and quality of their social interaction. Thus, Tillman writes that in race relations, "physical proximity is the issue only insofar as the 'presumption of equality' is superimposed upon it."[12] Examples abound: The close physical proximity allowed a Negro servant[13] or the residential proximity allowed an on-premises

9. Eisenstadt, p. 178.
10. Park, p. 68.
11. Ibid.; J.A. Beshers, *Urban Social Structure* (Glencoe, Ill.: The Free Press, 1962), p. 50.
12. J.A. Tillman, "The Quest for Identity and Status: Facets of the Desegregation Process in the Upper Midwest," *Phylon* 22, no. 4 (Winter 1961): 734.
13. E. Franklin Frazier, "The Status of the Negro in the American Social Order," *Journal of Negro Education* 4, no. 3 (July 1935): 293-307.

black janitor,[14] to cite only two instances in which proximity was not a threat because social distance maintained status differences. Indeed, the Jim Crow restrictions imposed upon blacks in the South regarding the use of public accomodations were designed largely to prohibit the symbolic assumption of equal status rather than to prohibit the use of the specific facility per se:

It is not the sitting next to a Negro at a table or washing at the next basin that is repulsive to a white, but the fact that this implies equal status. Historically, the most intimate relationships have been approved between black and white so long as status of white superiority versus Negro inferiority has been clear.[15]

Social distance, symbolically imposed through uniforms, separate facilities, and the like, can maintain status differences despite physical proximity. On the other hand, as van den Berghe has shown, complete spatial segregation will be imposed in those instances where "etiquette"—the recognition of social distance symbols—breaks down as a means of maintaining status differences.[16] Examples of situations in which physical separation is used to enforce social distance include migrant port of entry areas in the city that segregate individuals who might not be cognizant of local social distance symbols and areas undergoing marked social change, such as Southern cities in which residential segregation increased in direct ratio to blacks' economic progress.

The extent to which physical separation is required to maintain social distance between individuals or groups of unlike status depends on the ability of the dominant higher status group or individual to manipulate symbols that determine the cultural definition of the situation. Tensions become severe when the relevant symbols contradict the dominant group's claim of higher status. The equal status connotations of residential proximity then assume special importance for the maintenance of social status. An insightful explanation of the social-psychological mechanisms involved is offered by Tillman:

In the United States, the majority group has sought to compartmentalize by gradually and grudgingly giving and imputing equality to minority

14. Abrams.

15. Kenneth Clark, Dark Ghetto: Dilemmas of Social Power (New York: Harper & Row, 1965), p. 11.

16. P.L. van den Berghe, "Distance Mechanisms of Stratification," Sociology and Social Research 44 (January 1960): 155–64.

peoples in the fields of education and employment. The granting of equality of opportunity in these fields, indeed, did not require the majority
group to impute equality to the total or whole personalities of minority
group members. Fair housing will make it impossible for this condition of
compartmentalized equality and inequality to continue. Fair housing will
require the majority group to view minority people as whole and complete
personalities.[17]

That residential segregation tends to persist long after the barriers
have come down in schools and workplaces has often been noted.[18]
Westie, for example, measured social distance between blacks and
whites by occupation, using four different dimensions of social distance: residential distance; "position" distance (related to white
respondents' willingness to have blacks in positions of power or prestige in the community); interpersonal physical distance; and interpersonal social distance.[19] He concluded that as black occupational
status improves, whites are more willing to decrease position distance
and interpersonal social distance, while maintaining interpersonal
physical distance and residential distance regardless of the occupational status of blacks.

The most important implication of the above is the notion of a
special significance of the home and neighborhood environment and
the individual's personal space in maintaining social distance between
individuals of unlike status and of a lesser significance of spatial separation in other contexts of daily contact. Physical proximity and
residential proximity communicate an imputation of status equality
to third party observers, regardless of the feelings or intentions of the
participants that the presumption of inequality is always maintained
and communicated to others. In social contexts, boundaries between
status groups can be maintained and even allowed to fluctuate within
limits through social conventions of posture, facial expression, con-
descension, language, and so forth. In impersonal physical contexts,
however—those of interpersonal physical distance and residential distance—individuals tend to lose the ability to manipulate symbols and
thus to determine the definition of the social situation. Instead, in-
animate symbols of equality—the home and neighborhood or the adjacent seat on the bus—become manifest and dominate the definition

17. J.A. Tillman, "Rationalization, Residential Mobility, and Social Change,"
Journal of Intergroup Relations 3, no. 1 (Winter 1961-2): 32.
18. C. Bauer, "Social Questions in Housing and Community Planning," *Journal of Social Issues* 7, no. 1 (1951): 250; H. and D. Rosen, *But Not Next Door*
(New York: Obolensky, 1962), p. 67.
19. F. Westie, "Negro-White Status Differentials and Social Distance," *American Sociological Review* 17, no. 5 (October 1952): 550-58.

of the situation. In these cases, then, status conscious whites must resort to spatial separation of all blacks regardless of occupation, in order to prevent what would be interpreted as equal status contact by third party observers.

STATUS AND NEIGHBORHOOD IDENTIFICATION

The individual's sense of membership in the residentially based status group derives from his perception of and identification with the neighborhood. Perception of the local residential environment comprises two complementary scales: macroscale perception provides the individual with an image of how his residential area fits into the city-wide hierarchy of neighborhoods ranked in terms of status; micro-scale perception focuses on the residential area itself as home, turf, or territory and relates to the individual's personal identification with and use of the local neighborhood. The confluence of these two perceptual streams produces the individual's cognitive image of the internal structure of his residential area and its place within the city.

Microscale perception provides the individual with a cognitive and evaluative image of his local residential environment, including the extent to which the area constitutes an element of his personal identity. Oak Park's residents' attempts to maintain a viable community in the face of racial change were thus at least in part impelled by a sense of possessiveness for its tree-lined ambience and unique architectural heritage, just as residents of Beverly Hills fought to maintain a particular type of community on the ridge. The importance of the individual's personal identification with his house and neighborhood has been alluded to by numerous writers. As Rainwater points out, "The house acquires a sacred character from its complex intertwining with the self and from the symbolic character it has as a representation of the family," and he adds that this conception of the house is "readily generalized to the area around it, to the neighborhood."[20] Weber writes: "The physical place becomes an extension of one's ego."[21] The individual's personal identification with his local neighborhood environment, engendered through the mechanisms of his microscale perceptions, thus contributes to his sense of belonging to the neighborhood.

The macroscale level of neighborhood perception derives from

20. L. Rainwater, "Fear and the House-as-Haven in the Lower Class," *Journal of the American Institute of Planners* 32, no. 1 (January 1966): 24.

21. M. Weber, "Culture, Territoriality and the Elastic Mile," *Papers and Proceedings of the Regional Science Association* 13 (1964): 63.

what Suttles has referred to as the "foreign relations" of neighborhoods:

> Residential groups gain their identity by their most apparent differences from one another . . . Residential identities, then, are imbedded in a contrastive structure in which each neighborhood is known primarily as a counterpart to some of the others, and relative differences are probably more important than any single and widely shared social characteristic.[22]

Relative differences between residential areas give each area an identity and a "place" in the city's residential hierarchy. Thus, the working class white residents of Chicago's northwest and southwest side communities violently opposed integration of the local high schools, not because of their concern for the quality of education per se, but because they feared that integration and a possible drop in the quality of education would reflect poorly on their community's image in the rest of the metropolitan area. Because of the linkages between a city's residential structure and its social structure, an address carries firm connotations of the individual's position in the city's status hierarchy. The sense of social position is shared with one's neighbors by simple virtue of residential propinquity; on the scale of the metropolitan area, residents of a neighborhood are "all in it together."

While the two perceptual dimensions contribute independently to the individual's sense of membership in the residential status group, they also interact in complex ways. Gans' description of the mechanisms by which microscale perceptions contributed to a macroscale sense of place in suburban Levittown deserves to be quoted at length:

> The feelings about the black neighbors, friends, and favorite organizations were sometimes translated into a more general identification with Levittown as the best possible place to live, and some people took pride in a winning football team or an organizational achievement that lent distinction to Levittown. These feelings were neither intense nor of long duration; they were generated less by intrinsic qualities of the community than by the desire to put Levittown "on the map" in the unending competition with other communities. "The map" was usually Burlington County, but when L.Y.S.A. [Levittown Youth Sports Association] asked the Township Committee to finance a local team to play in the county baseball league, it pointed out that this league was regularly scouted by the majors, so that a $1,000 municipal subsidy might one day enable a Levittowner to represent the community in the American or National League. Even the name change that transformed Levittown to Willingboro was justified largely by

22. G.D. Suttles, *The Social Construction of Communities* (Chicago: University of Chicago Press, 1972), p. 51.

the negative headlines about the town in the Philadelphia area press, and reflected less a concern about the community than the belief that the name created a community image (and a *persona* for its residents) which they wanted the outside world to respect.[23]

The individual's experience of the residential area on the micro-scale contributes to a concern for the neighborhood's status on the macroscale level of the metropolitan community. On the one hand, satisfaction at the microlevel leads to a desire to protect (or even boost) the neighborhood's macrolevel image; on the other hand, concern for the macrolevel image of the community leads to a desire to protect against harmful change at the microlevel. The culmination of the individual's perception of his residential area along both dimensions is a sense of membership or belonging in the neighborhood.

Identification with the neighborhood as a status group has direct and obvious consequences for white response to the arrival of blacks. Since blacks are viewed as detrimental to neighborhood status, their arrival upsets the harmony between the white resident's cognitive image of the neighborhood and his status claims based upon self-image. The more congruent these images, the greater the likelihood that white residents will oppose black entry. With the continued presence of blacks in the neighborhood and consequent confirmation of the discrepancy in neighborhood status, satisfaction with the residential environment decreases and the likelihood that whites will begin to move out increases.

The earlier discussion of equal status connotations of residential proximity stressed the inability of residents to manipulate environmental symbols in order to indicate status differences to third party observers. Residents can manipulate the symbols of home and neighborhood to augment their own status or that of the neighborhood; they can do little, however, to prevent others, whom they might consider of lower status, from manipulating residential status symbols in the same way and thereby claiming status equality. Further, status conscious individuals can do little to directly manipulate the home and neighborhood symbols of others perceived as lower status to advertise the status differences to third party observers. Aside from the obvious terror tactics involved, it is possible that at least part of the motivations for the defacing of homes of unwanted "low status" neighbors derives from the conscious or subconscious desire to prevent a family perceived as low status from claiming equal status through the symbol of the home and to graphically indicate to others

23. H.J. Gans, *The Levittowners. Ways of Life and Politics in a New Suburban Community* (New York: Random House, 1967), pp. 144-45.

that the "intruders" are not of equal status. Thus, white residents of
Chicago's Garfield Ridge community tolerated the presence of a large
black population while it was confined to the nearby LeClaire Courts
public housing project; the stigma of residence in public housing is
so pervasive that it would be clear to all that any black person in the
area was a public housing tenant and therefore not of equal status
with white residents of the neighborhood. White opposition became
intense, however, as soon as blacks purchased homes in the neighborhood and thus claimed equal status with whites on the basis of the
immutable symbolism of equal property ownership. The difficulty in
manipulating the status symbolism involved in residential proximity
suggests that the greater the visibility of the black families in a neighborhood the greater the likelihood that status conscious whites will
move out in an attempt to avoid inclusion in the status group that is
in conflict with their self-perception of status. Thus, as Wolf cogently
argues, white opposition to the initial arrival of one or a few black
families is based on the fear of a future inundation of blacks that
would give the area the image of a "black neighborhood."[24]

There is a presumption in the foregoing of a preference for neighborhood homogeneity. This similarity of lifestyle within residentially proximate groups derives from the spatial distribution of
housing types and the widespread preference held by most residents
for similar neighbors. But neighborhood homogeneity is clearly a
relative concept: there is no doubt that "homogeneous" neighborhoods contain a population with an often broad range of occupations, educational backgrounds, and even class affiliations. When
viewed in terms of the citywide or metropolitan population pool
from which residents of a given neighborhood are drawn, however,
it is clearly demonstrable that residents of the neighborhood are more
similar to each other than to other people in other neighborhoods.
Such population homogeneity in residential areas connotes a compatibility of values concerning the use of the residential environment.[25]

Concern for having the "right kind of neighbors" is of major importance in the decisionmaking relative to residential mobility. First,
the social composition of a neighborhood is a prime consideration in
choosing a home. Wolf and Lebeaux conclude that:

the physical standards of an area seem to play a minor role in the residential decision of white households, at least in comparison with the importance of the social characteristics of the area's population. There are, of

24. E. Wolf, "The Tipping Point in Racially Changing Neighborhoods," *Journal of the American Institute of Planners* 29, no. 3 (1963): 217-22.
25. Gans, pp. 165-174.

course, a number of largely Negro-occupied areas in many cities which present an excellent appearance. However, this was not sufficient to maintain the racial mixtures which such areas did possess at one time in the past.[26]

And Abrams has noted: "It is no longer the type of house but the type of neighborhood which reflects social standing. . . . Fine looking homes in Chicago may be still as fine looking but are considered blighted when Negroes or other minorities live in the neighborhood."[27] Because of limitations in both the individual's resources and the supply of appropriate housing, the decisionmaker must, of course, "trade-off desirable properties on a less important criterion for desirable properties of a more important element."[28] A national survey by Butler et al. indicated the prominence of the social characteristics of the neighborhood as such over criteria such as the desirability of the house itself and the accessibility of the neighborhood.[29] From similar data, Stegman found that when offered a choice between a dwelling in an accessible but less desirable neighborhood and an equal-priced dwelling in a more desirable but less accessible neighborhood, 83 percent of a suburban sample and 61 percent of a city sample of recent movers chose the latter neighborhood.[30]

Neighborhood "attractiveness" is clearly associated with the type of social relationships desired in the neighborhood. Status aspirations seem to supersede all or most other considerations in residential mobility in as much as alternatives for housing are only considered within those neighborhoods that are consistent with the individual's or family's conception of its own status. While this conception often reflects a commitment to upward mobility, in general residents tend to choose neighbors at a roughly similar level of status. The Levittowners studied by Gans were not seeking higher status through home and neighborhood but were nonetheless highly status conscious—fearful, Gans explains, of their "self-image".[31] What Gans refers to as "fears about self-image" derived from the desire for status protection or maintenance. While residents were not necessarily seeking higher status (else they would presumably move to a higher

---

26. E. Wolf and C.N. Lebeaux, "Class and Race in the Changing City: Searching for New Approaches to Old Problems," in L. Schnore and H. Fagin, eds., *Urban Research and Policy Planning* (Beverly Hills: Sage, 1967), pp. 101–102.
27. Abrams, p. 139.
28. E.G. Moore, *Residential Mobility in the City* (Washington, D.C.: Association of American Geographers, 1972), p. 14.
29. Ibid., for discussion.
30. M.A. Stegman, "Accessibility Models and Residential Location," *Journal of the American Institute of Planners* 35, no. 1 (January 1969): 22–29.
31. Gans, pp. 414–15.

status area), their concern was most often with maintenance of their present status and the integrity of the residentially based status group.

Maintenance of residential homogeneity over time may be problematical in light of the extremely high rate of intraurban mobility characteristic or urban areas. Twenty percent of the population changes residence from one year to the next, and two-thirds of all moves are within the same metropolitan area.[32] Concern for homogeneity requires residents to continually monitor the characteristics of new arrivals in the neighborhood. White residents of Chicago's southwest side, for example, opposed a municipal ordinance banning "For Sale" signs on homes because, despite the usual fear that a blossoming of such signs engenders a rash of panic sales, residents felt that they could better monitor the characteristics of new homeowners with the aid of signs identifying those homes available for sale.[33]

The persistence of residential homogeneity is, however, simplified by the general stability of the pattern of population distribution in the city. Thus, Simmons notes that "perhaps the most remarkable aspect of intra-urban mobility is the stability of the spatial structure of social characteristics despite high rates of mobility throughout the city."[34] Continuity over time in the characteristics and the price of housing in an area tends to attract an incoming population similar to the outgoing population in respect to income and other socioeconomic characteristics, and this is true whatever the color of the newcomers.[35]

Despite this general similarity of characteristics between incoming blacks and resident whites, however, racial differences clearly suffice to dispel a perception of neighborhood homogeneity in changing areas. Immigration of blacks differs from the more general process of residential mobility in that the incoming population is perceived as substantially different by the resident white population. The perception of a critical difference in the incoming black population stems from the imputation of low status as a result of the "master status-determining trait" of skin color. While the arrival of an equal status white family is viewed with equanimity and possibly even ignored,

32. J.W. Simmons, "Changing Residence in the City: A Review of Intra-urban Mobility," in B.J.L. Berry and F.E. Horton, eds., *Geographic Perspectives on Urban Systems* (Englewood Cliffs, N.J.: Prentice-Hall, 1970), p. 395.

33. *South West News Herald,* October 19, 1971.

34. Simmons, p. 409.

35. O.D. and B. Duncan, *The Negro Population of Chicago* (Chicago: University of Chicago Press, 1957); K.E. and A.F. Taeuber, *Negroes in Cities* (Chicago: Aldine, 1965).

the arrival of a black family is noted as a substantial change in the residential environment. In four study areas in Philadelphia, Rossi reports that incoming families were only perceived as "different" when they were also perceived as of lower status than the families they were replacing.[36] Thus, the imputation of status inferiority to blacks results in a perception of black inmigrants as different and a threat to neighborhood homogeneity; the perception of a lack of residential homogeneity in turn influences white attitudes toward the neighborhood, engenders opposition to the arrival of blacks, decreases satisfaction with the area, increases the desire to move out, and produces an attitude on the part of other residents of the city that the neighborhood is inadequate for felt status needs and therefore no longer to be considered a desirable place to move to. Thus, the sentiment voiced by an outspoken Garfield Ridge resident that he didn't "want no neighbor throwing no garbage and barbecuing no beef out in the back" stemmed from the frequently expressed fear of the neighborhood going "downhill" and reflecting badly on remaining residents. The often-noted tendency for white residents to redefine the boundaries of their neighborhoods to exclude areas that have "gone black" reflects the perhaps subconscious realization of shared group membership among residentially proximate individuals.[37] The same process is very likely at work in the attempts by residents of West Englewood and Beverly Hills to impose defensive barriers along particular thoroughfares and to block, by force if necessary, minorities from crossing that barrier.

In fact, shared opposition to the intrusion of low status groups may be the strongest communal bond in an otherwise unorganized locality. Thus, Tillman, reporting on a study of integration in nine suburban communities in Minneapolis, concluded that "many inhabitants viewed homogeneity based on color as one of the important mechanisms of community cohesion."[38] And similarly, Isaacs noted in his criticism of the traditional "neighborhood concept" in urban planning that "in many residential areas, the only real basis for solidarity is the fear of Negro infiltration";[39] "the fear of minority

36. P.H. Rossi, *Why Families Move* (Glencoe, Ill. The Free Press, 1955), p. 53. "Indeed," Gans concluded in his own work p. 174, "The major barrier is effective integration is fear of status deprivation."

37. See for instance A. Hunter, "Symbolic Communities" (Paper presented at Metropolitan Forum, University of Chicago, 1971); and H. Molotch, *Managed Integration: Dilemmas of Doing Good in the City* (Berkeley: University of California Press, 1972).

38. Tillman, "The Quest for Identity and Status," p. 333.

39. R. Isaacs, "The Neighborhood Theory, an Analysis of its Adequacy, *Journal of American Institute of Planners* 14, no. 2 (Spring 1948): 21.

group infiltration is substituted for a common denominator of neighborhood consciousness."[40]

THE ROLE OF REFERENCE GROUPS IN RESPONSE TO RACIAL CHANGE

Residentially proximate groups fulfill Weber's characterization of communities as capable of "communal action" derived from the feeling that members "belong together." Within any given residential area, however, significant variation is likely to exist in the extent to which the common bond of shared status group membership is acknowledged. While on the one hand perception of status threat influences attitudes toward the neighborhood, on the other hand, a unique constellation of past experiences and future expectations provides each individual with a unique set of attitudes that may lead one individual to perceive a status threat where another perceives none or to strive to attain membership in a residential status group that another individual is striving to repudiate. It is again necessary, however, to specify that explanation of such variations need not be sought in the internal psychological states of the individuals involved. Individuals tend not to make outlandish status claims; their expectations are related to the perceived experiences and situations of individuals of similar status. A particular set of past experiences, sense of present status, and aspirations for the future determines the individual's selection of reference groups. Thus, Merton notes the systematic nature of reference group selection:

> Presumably, there will be distinct shifts in reference [groups and] individuals and role models as people move through sequences of statuses during their life cycles. This would again imply that much of such selection is not idiosyncratic but is patterned by structurally determined and statistically frequent career sequences, actual, anticipated or desired.[41]

The individual derives his status claims from within this patterned framework; on the basis of these claims, he relates to a set of membership and nonmembership groups that he evaluates either positively or negatively, and these reference groups in turn provide positive or negative reinforcement for the individual's status claims. A status claim is clearly a claim for membership in a particular status group.

40. R. Issacs, "The Neighborhood Unit as an Instrument for Segregation," *Journal of Housing* 7-8 (July-August 1948): 219.

41. R.K. Merton, *Social Theory and Social Structure*, 3rd ed. (New York: The Free Press 1968), p. 357.

If a member of this status group, the individual strives to maintain membership; if claimed status is represented by a nonmembership group, the individual strives to repudiate membership in his present group and to attain membership in the sought for status group. Membership groups seen as detrimental to status claims are repudiated; nonmembership groups seen as detrimental to status claims are avoided; membership groups seen as supportive of status claims are maintained; and nonmembership groups seen as supportive of status claims function as status goals that the individual strives to attain.

It follows from the above that the neighborhood is a status group with which the individual is identified by virtue of his residential address and with which the individual identifies in defining his place in society. In both senses, the neighborhood operates as a reference group, and the individual evaluates membership in his neighborhood-based status group in the same terms as he does other reference groups. Membership in the neighborhood cum reference group is weighed against membership in all other neighborhood-based reference groups known to the individual in the present, remembered from the past, or aspired toward in the future.

In evaluating his environment, the individual, rather than operating *in vacuo*, refers to a set of reference groups to establish both a normative set of values and guidelines and a comparative framework against which evaluation can be made. The individual's attitude toward membership in the neighborhood group is derived from how well it contributes to his status claims—to what extent there exists a "harmony of consensus" between the individual's status claims and the status image of the neighborhood environment.

Evaluation of the neighborhood cum reference group is accomplished by means of a subjectively determined utility threshhold, defined by Wolpert as "a weighted composite of a set of yardsticks for achievement. . . . The threshhold functions as an evaluative mechanism for distinguishing, in a binary sense, between success and failure, or between positive or negative net utilities."[42] The utility threshold is thus seen as an attitudinal boundary: evaluated as above the threshold, the neighborhood environment supports the individual's status claims and is viewed as a positive reference group, membership in which the individual strives to maintain; evaluated as below the threshold, the neighborhood environment detracts from the individual's status claim and is viewed as a negative reference group, membership in which the individual seeks to repudiate.

In examining the mechanisms by which the individual relates to

42. J. Wolpert, "Behavioral Aspects of the Decision to Migrate," *Papers and Proceedings of the Regional Science Association* 15 (1965): 161–62.

the neighborhood as a reference group, it is possible to identify several key factors related to status that seem to influence both the determination of the threshold of utility and the individual's evaluation of the neighborhood's utility. By influencing the relationship between the individual and the neighborhood environment, each of these attitudinal dimensions also influences the individual's perception of racial change as a process that alters the residential environment. The three factors, which will be considered in turn, include reliance on the residential environment for status, orientation to the residential neighborhood, and attachment to the neighborhood.

For example, individuals and groups vary in the extent to which they rely on the symbolism of the neighborhood environment to substantiate their status claims. Evidence indicates that the upwardly and downwardly mobile, sensing the insecurity of uncertain status group membership, rely more heavily on the neighborhood environment as a source of status than do the nonmobile. Similarly, individuals facing incongruence in their status-determining traits tend to rely on the neighborhood as a visual symbol of status group membership.

An example of the significance of neighborhood status in substantiating status claims and the consequent influence of this relationship on the perceived meaning of residential integration is provided in a study of white response to integration in suburban Levittown, Pennsylvania. Bressler reports that the arrival of the first black family was met with mass demonstration, highly vocal and prolonged opposition, and considerable community polarization. The most vocal opponents were those who, upwardly mobile and with a strong sense of status incongruence, relied heavily on the physical symbolism of the residential environment to substantiate claims to middle class status. As Bressler notes:

> A skilled or semi-skilled laborer employed by the United States Steel Company, Kaiser Metal Products, or other local enterprises might well sense the disparity between his relative economic affluence and his modest occupational prestige. One method of resolving this ambiguity consists of *borrowing prestige from his community* which if it is to serve this purpose satisfactorily must then represent a pure distillate of middle-class lifestyles.
>
> The working class addiction to the coy middle-class symbolism so prevalent in Levittown, its "Sweetbriar Lanes" and "cook-outs", its "patios" and enthusiastic agronomy, is to an appreciable extent a simultaneous exercise in self-persuasion and ritualistic affirmation whose purpose it is to demonstrate that *life patterns in the community, and not the job, constitute the only valid basis for class assignment.*[43]

43. M. Bressler, "The Myers Case: An Instance of Successful Racial Invasion," *Social Problems* 8 (March 1960): 133 (emphasis added).

To the opponents of integration, the neighborhood was well above the utility threshold as long as it continued to support claims of membership in the middle class reference group. Arrival of blacks was interpreted as lowering the utility of the neighborhood by changing the image. For individuals who rely on the status symbolism of their environment as a source of status—at whatever level in the status hierarchy—the arrival of blacks is clearly perceived as a status threat.

Related to the dependence on the residential environment as a source of status is the broader question of the individual's orientation to the local neighborhood as a normative reference group to which the individual turns in establishing a set of values and standards. This orientation has often been described in terms of a scale continuum from localism to cosmopolitanism. Localities are generally said to be lower status and less mobile and to seek their social contacts from among relatives, friends, and associates located within the local community. As a result of this orientation, localites tend to express the greatest concern for "desirable neighbors,"[44] and they are most likely to vocally oppose black entry into the neighborhood; an example is Chicago's "no-CHA" coalition, discussed below. Cosmopolites, in contrast, have a less restricted range in which they establish social contacts, carry out daily activities, and derive a set of values; cosmopolites thus tend to relate to reference groups outside the local community, as in the liaison between suburban fair housing groups in Chicago's Regional Housing Coalition, also discussed below. Bressler reports that supporters of integration in Levittown, Pennsylvania, were "cosmopolitans, persons who refused to define the situation primarily and exclusively in terms of its impact on the tight little island of suburbia."[45] Much the same can be said of integrationists in Park Forest and Oak Park and, indeed, of the entire open housing movement.

In a case study that provides an interesting contrast to the situation described by Bressler, Gans reported that integration in Levittown, New Jersey, occurred relatively uneventfully. While residents of the New Jersey community were not necessarily supportive of integration, their concern was to avoid visible demonstrations against new black families, fearing that such demonstrations would reflect poorly on the community. Gans reported that "as it turned out, Levittowners favored peace and order even more than segregation. . . . Many knew that racial conflict might well begin to reduce

44. Gans.
45. Bressler, p. 137.

Levittown's prestige, and even those who opposed integration often said it was preferrable to a riot." The racial conflict in the Pennsylvania community, which occurred prior to integration in the New Jersey Levittown, was described by the New Jersey residents as a "stone-throwing riot, giving the older Levittown a worldwide reputation as a riot-torn community and placing a blot on its escutcheon which the residents of the newest one wanted desperately to avoid."[46]

While the local orientation of opponents in Pennsylvania and the cosmopolitan orientation of supporters in New Jersey had different outcomes in terms of influencing white response to the arrival of blacks, both responses are to be explained in terms of residents' concern for status. Opponents in Levittown, Pennsylvania, were responding to localized reference groups that stressed the importance of the physical image of the neighborhood and visible characteristics of their neighbors. The cosmopolitan orientation of supporters of integration led them to respond to reinforcements provided by reference groups located outside the community; what reached these groups was not the physical image of the neighborhood, which requires visible contact to be evaluated, but rather the press and media-related public image that is transmitted to friends and associates outside the community. Oriented to reference groups outside the local area, attitudes toward integration on the part of the cosmopolitan in Levittown were prompted by a concern that the community not get a "bad press."

"No-CHA" versus the Regional Housing Coalition

A similar contrast in orientation is to be seen as the primary factor differentiating nineteen local community organizations that grouped together to form "No-CHA" in Chicago from the regional entities represented in the area's Regional Housing Coalition. Indeed, the variations in attitudes to be found in the case studies detailed in Chapters 6-14 are encapsulated in these contrasting responses.

In the early years of the nation's public housing program, the Chicago Housing Authority (CHA) sought to build public housing scattered throughout Chicago. The city council, in the belief that most prospective public housing tenants were black, proposed, however, to restrict such housing to ghetto areas. Since each alderman had a veto over site selection in his ward, CHA had to go along with the city council if any public housing was to be constructed; Chicago's

46. Gans, pp. 375, 382.

public housing was constructed and rented on a racially segregated basis.

As a result, CHA administered regular (family), elderly, and Section 23 (leasing) public housing in a manner that kept blacks out of white areas. Regular public housing was located in ghetto neighborhoods to minimize the number of blacks displaced by slum clearance, and the other programs were located in all white neighborhoods. In the four housing projects in white neighborhoods, quotas kept the number of black tenants at zero or a minimal level. In projects for the elderly, tenant assignment policies ensured that white elderly occupied most of the housing in white neighborhoods. Only in racially changing areas were "integrated" projects—namely, those with a second racial group of more than 10 percent—to be found, and these projects and areas ultimately became all black. Leased housing was treated in the same fashion. Tenant selection was delegated to landlords by CHA, giving them the right to refuse tenants because of "undesirability." Landlords were allowed to select tenants who were not on CHA's almost all black waiting list. In sum, the white elderly were placed in public housing in white areas, while blacks were located in ghetto projects.[47]

Throughout the 1960s federal civil rights laws and regulations were valueless in producing any changes. While HUD was aware that CHA was violating HUD regulations covering racial discrimination, it opted to serve rather than regulate the local constituency. Finally, in August 1966, fair housing interests filed suit in U.S. District Court accusing CHA of discrimination against blacks (*Gautreaux v. CHA*). Judge Richard B. Austin in February 1969 found CHA guilty as charged and issued an order designed to promote integration by construction of public housing in all white areas. As a result of CHA's refusal to abide by the court's directive and HUD's refusal to enforce compliance, all public housing construction in Chicago ceased during the 1969–1974 period.

It was only under continuing pressure from Judge Austin that CHA finally announced plans in 1973 for a program of scattered site public housing in the white northwest and southwest sides of the city. Residents of the white neighborhoods were aghast, for another element in their web of territorial defense was threatened. The attitudes that lay behind the ward politicians' earlier vetoes of public housing surfaced in an attempt by a consortium of nineteen northwest and southwest side white community organizations to use the National

47. F.A. Lazin, "The Failure of Federal Enforcement of Civil Rights Regulations in Public Housing, 1963-1971," *Policy Sciences* 42, no. 2 (1973): 263-73.

Environmental Policy Act of 1969 to prevent the Chicago Housing Authority from acting in accordance with Judge Austin's ruling. The argument of the Nucleus of Chicago Homeowners Association (No-CHA) was that:

> As a statistical whole, low-income families of the kind that reside in housing provided by the Chicago Housing Authority possess certain social class characteristics which will and have been inimical and harmful to the legitimate interests of the plaintiffs.
>
> Regardless of the cause, be it family conditioning, genetics, or environmental conditions beyond their control, members of low-income families of the kind that reside in housing provided by the Chicago Housing Authority possess, as a statistical whole, the following characteristics:
>
> (a) As compared to the social class characteristics of the plaintiffs, such low-income family members possess a higher propensity toward criminal behavior and acts of physical violence than do the social classes of the plaintiffs.
>
> (b) As compared to the social class characteristics of the plaintiffs, such low-income family members possess a disregard for physical and aesthetic maintenance of real and personal property which is in direct contrast to the high level of care with which the plaintiffs social classes treat their property.
>
> (c) As compared to the social class characteristics of the plaintiffs, such low-income family members possess a lower commitment to hard work for future-oriented goals with little or no immediate reward than do the social classes of the plaintiffs'.
>
> . . . .
>
> By placing low-rent housing populated by persons with the social characteristics of low-income families described above in residential areas populated by persons with social class characteristics of the plaintiffs, defendant CHA will increase the hazards of criminal acts, physical violence and aesthetic and economic decline in the neighborhoods in the immediate vicinity of the sites. The increase in these hazards resulting from CHA's siting actions will have a direct adverse impact upon the physical safety of those plaintiffs residing in close proximity to the sites, as well as a direct adverse effect upon the aesthetic and economic quality of their lives.

U.S. District Court Judge Julius J. Hoffman ruled on November 26, 1973, in dismissing the suit that "It must be noted that although human beings may be polluters, they are not themselves pollution." Assistant U.S. Attorney Michael H. Berman added, "Public housing residents are not untouchables and the judge rightly accepts this view." However, the suit indicated clearly enough that Chicago's northwest and southwest side communities did not; to them, the threat to their status was real.

While this was going on, in certain suburbs and in metropolitan-wide civil rights organizations two sets of interests came together in a contrasting Regional Housing Coalition designed to promote "fair shares" of "low income" (=minority) housing throughout the six county area. On the one hand, this reflected the liberals' desire to ensure civil rights, equity of treatment, and access to housing under conditions of accelerated decentralization of employment from the central city. On the other hand, there was a growing awareness in certain suburbs that unless a regional solution to low income minority housing was found, the more liberal communities like Park Forest would be beggared by their recalcitrant neighbors. Instead of confrontation and defensive territoriality, Chicago's cosmopolites sought to minimize status incongruities by promoting managed integration. Yet whatever the motivations of its backers, the RHC strategy of dispersal and "fair share," developed in response to continued racial and economic segregation, stood in sharp contrast to the containment strategy pursued by No-CHA.

The Regional Housing Coalition (RHC) was a partnership consisting of the Leadership Council for Metropolitan Open Communities and the Northeastern Illinois Planning Commission, with a steering committee of suburban mayors and village presidents and business, religious, and civic organizations. It announced its "Interim Plan for Balanced Distribution of Housing Opportunities for Northeastern Illinois" on October 1, 1973. The plan pointed out the immediate need for 167,600 housing units for people of low and moderate income throughout the six county metropolitan area.

While housing for minorities was nowhere mentioned in the RHC proposal, its intention was to provide housing for blacks and other minorities in suburbs other than those few to which most suburban-bound blacks were migrating. It represented the convergence of interests of the Leadership Council and such suburbs as Oak Park and Park Forest, which also had committed themselves to active integration efforts that seemed destined to falter if the surrounding areas would not accept their "fair share" of the responsibility of providing housing for minority groups. Thus the RHC plan was motivated simultaneously by ideology and self-interest. It appealed to those whose ultimate goal was increasing the number and proportion of blacks living in the suburbs—namely, the Leadership Council and local fair housing groups; at the same time it appealed to those whose concern was limiting the numbers of blacks moving into their own area—for example, Oak Park, Park Forest.

Clearly, if the RHC plan had been expressly formulated as a plan for integrating the suburban area, the opposition would have been far greater than the support. Therefore, it was also designed to appeal to yet a third set of interests—that is, the need to provide a labor supply for the growing industrial and commercial base of the suburban area. Yet even phrased as a plan to encourage economic as opposed to racial integration, the RHC plan faced formidable resistance from suburban whites, and indeed, it ultimately foundered on their failure to support low income housing, for any such development continued to be viewed as a status threat by suburbanites, many of whom had fled the city not too long before.

CONCLUSIONS

What might be said from all of this? Locally oriented individuals most fearful for their own status were the first to oppose black entry to their neighborhoods. Those with the greatest neighborhood attachment were the most active in organizing to prevent black entry. Cosmopolitans, on the other hand, were more likely to organize to encourage peaceful integration while maintaining neighborhood stability if they had strong neighborhood ties or simply to move away if their ties were weaker.

It has been often taken for granted that as ghetto encroachment threatens, the whites in adjacent neighborhoods either resist vigorously or rapidly abandon the area or both, with flight following temporary resistance. But such exclusionary tactics seem to have dominated only in the blue collar ethnic communities bounding ghetto areas. These neighborhoods were among the first to feel the pressure of black expansion, and their characteristic response was too rapidly assumed to be the dominant form. With the continuing enlargement of Chicago's ghettos and the parallel expansion of suburban minighettos, the threat also came to be felt in the formerly safe refuges of higher status inhabitants. The experience of these communities indicates that the traditional "fight and run" pattern is not necessarily typical. Only when such communities as South Shore, or the suburbs of Evanston, Oak Park, and Park Forest, became threatened did the range and variety of responses begin to emerge.

How effective have the higher status communities' alternatives been? Across the range of white responses, the general conclusion remains the same: at each income level and regardless of socioeconomic characteristics, a concentration of black families is perceived negatively by whites. This is true regardless of the fact that to afford the housing, incoming blacks must be equal in achieved socioeconomic status to their white neighbors.[48] Put crudely, while the localites' defensive response was directed to protecting those characteristics of their neighborhoods that they deemed to be important, the cosmopolites' alternative of managed integration was more often than not directed to maintaining their own neighborhoods' status in the eyes of others. And in both cases the ultimate resolution was the same—a breached defensive line or too much integration to manage both precipitated white flight. With only limited exceptions in Park Forest and Oak Park, dwellings once occupied by black families have rarely reverted to white occupancy. When an "integrated neighborhood" was defined as one attracting both blacks and whites, a national survey found a median black population of only 3 percent in such neighborhoods.[49] This finding not only calls into question much of that survey's subsequent analysis of "integrated neighborhoods" but also, and more importantly, graphically portrays the result of myriad white decisions to shun residential integration on other than a token basis. It also goes a long way toward explaining why, on the white side, the Leadership Council's programs received such minimal support. As the National Academy of Sciences reported: "There is no ratio of blacks to whites that is known to ensure success in racial mixing."[50] But the Leadership council's programs also foundered because there was very little black interest in integrated living. It is to the reasons for this that we turn in Part III of this book.

48. Taeuber and Taeuber, p. 112.
49. N.M. Bradburn, S. Sudman, and G.L. Gockel, *Racial Integration in American Neighborhoods*, NORC Report No. 111-B (Chicago: National Opinion Research Center, 1970), p. 30.
50. National Academy of Sciences, *Freedom of Choice in Housing: Opportunities and Constraints* (Washington, D.C.: by the Academy, 1972).

 *Part III*

Consequences of White Flight

Ghetto Expansion and Single Family Housing Prices: Contributing Forces and Contrasting Theories

Two other forces combined with the unwillingness of Chicago's white residents to share their neighborhoods with blacks, facilitating white withdrawal and ghetto expansion and, in turn, materially affecting the housing opportunities of Chicago's black population. First among these was the pace of new housing starts, far in excess of the growth of demand for additional housing units. Second was the general orientation in the population to seek better homes in better neighborhoods and especially to look to the single family home in the suburbs as an ideal.[1] The excess supply made it possible for many families to trade up. The resulting game of musical chairs produced accelerated filtering of both homes and neighborhoods as departing residents adjusted their housing consumption upwards, and new incoming residents satisfied their mobility aspirations by moving into the vacated homes. In the departing whites' status system, "invasion" and "succession" by black homeseekers was but another case of filtering, as whole neighborhoods were transferred from the white housing market to the black housing market. To the incoming blacks, the transferred neighborhoods were places in which they could begin to realize their housing aspirations (see Chapter 2). Obviously, such realization was

---

1. This orientation remains strong. As the final draft of this book was being edited in March 1979, Market Opinion Research Inc. of Detroit reported on the results of its late February national panel survey: 34 percent of the national sample said one of their top priorities was to move to a new location; of that 34 percent, three-quarters wished to live in a single family home, either to buy a first home, to buy a better home, or to buy a bigger home.

constrained by the pace of white exodus (i.e., the quantity of housing units being transferred from white to black occupancy), by the nature of the neighborhoods being vacated (i.e., the quality and variety of the housing types becoming available), and by the selling prices of the properties. And because of whites' continuing unwillingness to share neighborhoods with blacks, the movements preserved the racial segmentation of Chicago into dual housing markets.

HOUSING STOCK AND OCCUPANCY CHANGES, 1960-1970

The statistics are these: between 1960 and 1970, 481,553 housing units were built in metropolitan Chicago, 129,496 in the city of Chicago and 352,057 in the suburbs (Tables 16-1 and 16-2).[2] Some 257,590 of the new units were occupied by white homeowners in 1970 and 146,029 by white renters, another 13,849 by black homeowners and 27,153 by black renters, and 27,934 of the new units were vacant, presumably awaiting the arrival of their new tenants. Yet as these 481,553 housing units were being built, the net household growth in metropolitan Chicago was only 285,729 (the net increases were white homeowners, 143,174; white renters, 25,797; black homeowners, 45,065; and black renters 49,573), implying that for each new household entering Chicago's housing market, 1.7 new units were added to the housing stock! The new construction alone provided the opportunity for most households in metropolitan Chicago to change their homes at least once in the decade.[3] Lansing has estimated that for each 1,000 new dwellings constructed in American metropolitan areas, a sequence of moves is set in motion that ultimately enables 3,545 households to shift their residence.[4] Applying this finding to Chicago, new housing construction may have generated 481.553 × 3,545 = 1,707,105 moves. There were 1,897,916 households in metropolitan Chicago in 1960 and 2,183,645 in 1970.

Housing vacancy chains—the sequences of moves by which a vacancy is transferred from one unit to another as a household leaves its existing residence to move into the vacant one—have a symmetric

2. This compares with the 427,375 new units built between 1950 and 1960 (123,764 in the city and 303,611 in the suburbs) and a pace of housing starts after 1970 that, if maintained, would have added more than 600,000 new units in the decade 1970-1980.

3. There are, of course, many other reasons why housing units become available on initiate sequences of moves—emigration from the metropolitan area; the termination of a household through death, divorce, and so forth; and default.

4. John B. Lansing, Charles Wade Clifton, and James N. Morgan, *New Homes and Poor People* (Ann Arbor: Institute for Social Research, University of Michigan, 1969).

Table 16-1. Changes in the Suburban Housing Stock, 1960-1970.

	1960 Stock	New Construction 1960-1970	Withdrawn from Stock 1960-1970	Net Change in Stock 1960-1970	1970 Stock
Total Housing Units	812,652	352,057	83,980	+268,077	1,080,729
Occupied Housing Units	740,508	335,135	29,841	+305,294	1,045,802
Owner Occupied	561,170	223,845	26,275	+197,570	758,740
White Owners	555,480	219,657	34,998	+184,669	740,179
Black Owners	8,690	4,188	(3,208)[a]	+ 7,396	16,086
Renter Occupied	176,338	111,290	576	+110,714	287,052
White Renters	167,964	107,578	4,859	+102,719	270,683
Black Renters	8,374	3,712	(2,153)[a]	+ 5,865	14,239

[a]Net increase over new construction due to transfer of units from white to black occupancy.

Table 16-2. Changes in the Central City Housing Stock, 1960-1970.

	1960 Stock	New Construction 1960-1970	Withdrawn from Stock 1960-1970	Net Change in Stock 1960-1970	1970 Stock
Total Housing Units	1,214,598	129,496	145,988[b]	- 5,492	1,209,106
Occupied Housing Units	1,157,409	118,484	138,039[b]	-19,555	1,137,854
Owner Occupied	396,727	33,745	34,115[b]	- 370	396,357
White Owners	360,117	24,084	65,609	-41,525	318,592
Black Owners	36,610	9,661	(28,008)[a]	+37,669	74,279
Renter Occupied	760,682	84,739	103,930[b]	-19,191	741,491
White Renters	564,029	61,298	138,220	-76,922	487,107
Black Renters	196,653	23,441	(20,267)[a]	+43,708	240,361

[a]Net increase over new construction due to transfer of units from white to black occupancy.
[b]These 138,039 units were demolished in the decade. Of the demolitions, 63,000 were in areas occupied by black residents in 1960 and 75,000 in white areas.

quality: as households "trade up" to more desirable homes, the vacancies "filter down" the housing stock, from newer and/or better quality to older and/or less desirable units. If an excess of new housing units is being built, the surplus must come to rest somewhere, presumably where the least desirable housing units are concentrated—namely, in the oldest neighborhoods around the city's core. Such was the case in metropolitan Chicago between 1960 and 1970.

In suburban Chicago in the decade, 352,057 new housing units were constructed, largely for whites. In the entire six county suburban area, only 4,188 out of 223,845 new homes were sold to blacks, and only 3,712 out of 111,290 new apartments were rented to blacks. In addition, some 3,208 blacks purchased homes previously owned by whites. In contrast to the net increase of 287,000 white families in suburban Chicago, only 13,261 new black families were able to obtain residences in suburbia, and many of these residences were in or contiguous to suburban "minighettos."[5] On the other hand, there was a net decline of 41,500 white homeowners and 76,900 white renters in the central city in the decade as whites fled to the "safety" of segregated suburbia or left the Chicago region altogether. Net increases in the central city black population consisted of 37,669 new homeowners (more than doubling of black home ownership in the decade)[6] and 43,708 new renters.

The complex dynamics of white-to-black filtering accompanying ghetto expansion were as follows: some 128,829 units were transferred from white to black occupancy in the decade, allowing net increases over new construction of 28,008 in black homeownership

5. Some 12,168 of the new black families moved into or adjacent to the traditional ghettos of the crescent of industrial satellite communities ringing the metropolis (Waukegan, Elgin, Aurora, Joliet, Harvey, and Chicago Heights) or into those suburbs with long-standing black enclaves, such as Evanston and Wheaton. The increase in black families elsewhere in suburbia was only 1,093, bringing the total from 1,217 to 2,310. Of this increase, 20 percent was in two communities, Park Forest and Oak Park (which together absorbed an additional 976 black families in the next four years 1970–1974). Only 569 of the remaining 2,084 black families lived in suburbs with over 2,500 residents in 1970; the remaining 1,515 families lived in smaller places or in isolated rural backwaters that have had black populations for many years. In 1970, sixty-eight of one hundred forty-eight suburbs with more than 2,500 population had no black families in residence, fifty-four had a token four or less, fifteen had between five and nine, nine had ten to twenty-four, and only two had more than fifty. There were so few blacks in suburban DuPage County that they formed their own organization, the Black Suburbanites Club, to provide a social outlet and a basis for mutual aid amidst white indifference or enmity.

6. There had been 15,928 nonwhite homeowners in the city of Chicago in 1950. The number rose to 36,610 black homeowners in 1960 and to 74,279 in 1970.

and 20,267 in black rental of good quality flats and apartments. In addition, 63,000 black families moved into better quality housing from dilapidated and other units that were demolished in the decade within the area of the 1960 ghetto, and finally, there was a net increase by 1960 of 17,554 units vacant in the black residential area of 1970 (see Table 16–3).

Put quite simply, there was a vast increase in housing available in the metropolitan area, and a combination of accelerated filtering and rapid residential relocation (whites to the suburbs, ghetto expansion into former white neighborhoods) produced a substantial sag in demand in areas of traditional minority residence. As white families withdrew to the suburbs, black families gained access to large numbers of good quality housing units in previously white areas. There, population increased, and school enrollments escalated as black child-rearing families replaced whites at later stages in the life cycle. In turn, the traditional black belt was depopulated. The population living within the boundaries of the 1960 ghetto declined 19 percent in 1960–1970, and it was in the communities in which population declines in the decade were greatest that the greatest amounts of abandoned housing began to appear. Increasing the pressures on substandard private market housing that would otherwise have to be occupied by the welfare poor, 13,250 of 19,000 units of public housing built in the decade were located within the 1960 ghetto. Manifesting the changed market conditions, Chicago's overall vacancy rate increased from 3.7 to 4.6 percent, with the rate exceeding 6 percent within the 1960 ghetto limits.

Table 16–3. Dynamics of Chicago's Dual Housing Market.

	White Market	*Black Market*
Occupied Housing Units in 1960	924,146	233.263
New Construction 1960–1970	85,382	33,102
Demolitions 1960–1970	75,000	63,000
Housing Stock in 1970 of 1960 Market Areas	934,528	203,365
Housing Stock in 1970 of 1970 Market Areas	805,699	314,640
Transfers from White to Black Market 1960–1970	(-128,829)[a]	+111,275[a]

[a]Difference between these figures represents a net increase in vacancies in black residential areas of 17,554 units by 1970, a growing surplus of property associated with abandonment.

THEORIES OF PRICE MOVEMENTS DURING GHETTO EXPANSION

It was the assertion of those who created the Leadership Council for Metropolitan Open Communities that racial segmentation of Chicago's housing into dual markets, one for whites and one for blacks, linked by the unidirectional supply shifts accompanying ghetto expansion had resulted in lower housing quality, less services, and higher housing prices for the city's black population than if the metropolitan housing market had been nondiscriminatory. Yet the failure of the council to achieve its goals was not simply a matter of white recalcitrance. Blacks, too, as we saw in Part I, had little inclination to make use of the council's services, preferring instead to occupy neighborhoods newly vacated by whites, where they said that "good buys" were available, without all the hassles that were encountered by pioneer integrationists (see above, footnote 5).

The literature on relative price levels for comparable homes in the white and black communities and on property price movements during ghetto expansion is ambiguous on this point, however, and is worth reviewing before the evidence for Chicago is analyzed in Chapter 17, because the civil rights advocates argue that segregation imposes a price surcharge—a "race tax"—of some 10-15 percent on the black homebuyer, cutting homeownership rates and reducing consumption of housing services, and that this fact alone is justification for such programs as those pursued by the Leadership Council. Yet Chicago's black homeseekers appear to have been telling us something else about the period in question.

Let us begin our review of the Chicago literature in 1922, with the publication of *The Negro in Chicago*, a report undertaken by the Chicago Commission on Race Relations following the bloody race riots of 1919. As we noted in Chapter 1, the south side black belt had emerged in the previous decade as the city's white residents showed increasing reluctance to share their neighborhoods with a growing black population. Neighborhood "improvement" or "protective" clubs were formed by the white population. Black residents were forced out of white neighborhoods, and real estate dealers were pressured by white organizations to confine blacks to designated "districts." A residential segregation ordinance was proposed to the city council in 1911, and when that failed, restrictive housing covenants came into use—and along with them both dual housing listings and racial steering as normal features of the "legitimate" real estate industry and a much despised character, the "panic-peddling" and "blockbusting" real estate agent who was willing to convert a marginal building from white to black occupancy, demanding rents that were higher than had previously been received.

The development of a physical ghetto in Chicago, then, was not the result chiefly of poverty; nor did Negroes cluster out of choice. The ghetto was primarily the product of white hostility. Attempts on the part of Negroes to seek housing in predominantly white sections of the city met with resistance from the residents and from real estate dealers. Some Negroes, in fact, who had formerly lived in white neighborhoods were pushed back into the black districts. As the Chicago Negro population grew, Negroes had no alternative but to settle in well-delineated Negro areas. And with increasing pressure for Negro housing, property owners in the black belt found it profitable to force out white tenants.[7]

The first major explosion of racial hostility came in the riots of 1919, and in 1922 the Chicago Commission on Race Relations reported that racial attitudes and housing prices were closely intertwined as causes of the violence:

One of the strongest influences in creating and fostering race antagonism in Chicago is the general belief among whites that the presence of Negroes in a neighborhood inevitably and alone depreciates the market value of real estate. . . . The principal influence of Negroes upon property values in a neighborhood is psychological, due to the deep-seated and general prejudice of whites against Negroes which begets and sustains the belief that Negroes destroy property values[and] is directly reflected in the unwillingness of whites to buy property close to that occupied by Negroes and in their desire to sell, even at a sacrifice, when Negroes move into the immediate neighborhood. . . . the understandable bitterness of feeling on this question . . . has been intensified in some cases through exploitation, by both white and Negro real estate operators, of anti-Negro prejudice and fear of loss on account of Negro occupancy. In brief, Negro occupancy depreciates the value of residence property in Chicago because of the social prejudice of white people against Negroes, and because white people will not, and Negroes are financially unable to buy at fair market prices property thrown upon the market when a neighborhood begins to change from white to Negro occupancy.[8]

The commission also noted that

When values fall extremely due to a selling panic among white owners, it is often followed by a decided recovery as the Negro demand grows. Such

7. Spear, *Black Chicago*, p. 26.
8. *The Negro in Chicago*, pp. 608–11.

a new market among Negroes, however, seems never to have been strong enough to send prices for residence purposes back to original levels.[9]

Homer Hoyt seems to have been ambivalent in his studies of property values and residential change in Chicago as to whether the basic mechanism was one of push from the center or pull to the suburbs, but he was instrumental both in putting questions of ghetto expansion and housing prices into a broader race-ethnic framework and in suggesting that change at a racial frontier was simply a special manifestation of broader growth and filtering processes operating in metropolitan housing markets as a whole.

To repeat our discussion in Chapter 1, on ethnicity and housing he wrote:

> While the ranking given below may be scientifically wrong from the standpoint of inherent racial characteristics, it registers an opinion or prejudice that is reflected in land values; it is the ranking of races and nationalities with respect to their beneficial effect upon land values. Those having the most favorable effect come first in the list and those exerting the most detrimental effect appear last: 1. English, Germans, Scotch, Irish, Scandinavians. 2. North Italians. 3. Bohemians or Czechslovakians. 4. Poles. 5. Lithuanians. 6. Greeks. 7. Russian Jews of the lower class. 8. South Italians. 9. Negroes. 10. Mexicans.[10]

These ideas found speedy expression in the underwriting manuals of the Federal Housing Administration both before and after World War II, significantly affecting attitudes to mortgage risk that were supportive of racial segregation:

> Areas surrounding a location are investigated to determine whether incompatible racial and social groups are present, for the purpose of making a prediction regarding the probability of the location being invaded by such groups. If a neighborhood is to retain stability, it is necessary that properties shall continue to be occupied by the same social and racial classes. A change in social or racial occupancy generally contributes to instability and a decline in values.[11]

. . .

> If the occupancy of the neighborhood is changing from one user group to another, or if the areas adjacent to the immediate neighborhood are occupied by a user group dissimilar to the typical occupants of the subject

9. Ibid., p. 211.

10. Homer Hoyt, *One Hundred Years of Land Values in Chicago* (Chicago: University of Chicago Press, 1933).

11. United States Federal Housing Administration, *Underwriting Manual* (Washington, D.C.: United States Government Printing Office, 1938), Par. 937.

neighborhood or a change in occupancy is imminent or probable any degree of risk is reflected in the rating.[12]

To be fair to Hoyt, he was responsible not simply for the federal attitudes to mortgage risk, but also for key elements of the filtering concept—housing filtering down the income scale and families filtering up the scale of housing quality:

The erection of new dwellings on the periphery of a city . . . sets in motion forces tending to draw population from the older houses and to cause all groups to move up a step leaving the oldest and cheapest houses to be occupied by the poorest families or to be vacated. The constant competition of new areas is itself a cause of neighborhood shifts. Every building boom, with its new crop of structures equipped with the latest modern devices, pushes all existing structures a notch down in the scale of desirability. . . . The high grade areas . . . tend to preempt the most desirable residential land by supporting the highest values. Intermediate rental groups tend to occupy the sectors in each city that are adjacent to the high rent area. . . . Occupants of houses in the low rent categories tend to move out in bands from the center of the city mainly by filtering up into houses left behind by the high income groups. . . . Within the low rent area itself there are movements of racial and national groups . . . thus . . . there is a constant dynamic shifting of residential areas. There is a constant outward movement of neighborhoods because as neighborhoods become older they tend to be less desirable. . . . A neighborhood composed of new houses in the latest modern style, all owned by group married couples with children, is at its apex. . . . The owners will strenuously resist the encroachment of inharmonious forces because of their pride in their homes and their desire to maintain a favorable environment for their children. The houses . . . are marketable at approximately their reproduction cost. . . . Physical depreciation of structures and the aging of families are constantly lessening the vital powers of the neighborhood. Children grow up and move away. Houses with increasing age are faced with higher repair bills. The steady process of deterioration is hastened by obsolescence; a new and more modern type of structure relegates these structures to the second rank. The older residents do not fight so strenuously to keep out inharmonious forces. A lower income class succeeds the original residents. . . . There is often a sharp decline in value due to a sharp transition in the character of the neighborhood. These internal shifts . . . cause shifts in the location of neighborhoods. When, in addition, there is poured into the center of the urban organism a stream of immigrants or members of other racial groups, these forces also cause dislocations in the existing neighborhood pattern.[13]

12. United States Federal Housing Administration, *Underwriting Manual* (Washington, D.C.: United States Government Printing Office, 1947). Par. 1320 (2).
13. *The Structure and Growth of Residential Neighborhoods in American Cities* (Washington, D.C.: Federal Housing Administration, 1939), pp. 120-22.

Such filtering works well and has positive welfare consequences if, as Kristof has noted, (1) new construction exceeds the rate necessary to house normal growth, producing an excess housing supply at the point where the filtering originates; (2) such new construction exerts a downward pressure on the rents and prices of existing housing, permitting lower income families to obtain better housing bargains relative to their existing housing quarters; (3) any such upward mobility is apart from any changes caused by rising incomes and/or declining rent-income ratios: (4) a decline in quality is not necessarily forced by reductions in maintenance and repair to the extent that rents and prices are forced down; and (5) a mechanism exists to remove the worst housing from the market without adversely affecting rents and prices of housing at the lowest level.[14]

If such conditions are met, filtering and its associated price changes may clearly be viewed as a mechanism for social progress, a point about which Little has demonstrated that there is both confusion and disagreement.[15] Indeed, arguing against just such a unitary view of the housing market consisting of homes, households, and neighborhoods changing over time due to filtering, postwar Chicago sociologists favored instead the compartmentalized notion of a dual housing market in which minorities pay more, not less, per unit of housing. Concluding their study of the period 1940-1950, the Duncans wrote that:

In summary, non-white housing conditions are less satisfactory than white; the difference appears to have increased . . . over the 1940-50 decade . . . ; and the difference is by no means accounted for solely by the relative economic advantage of the white population. . . . non-white housing conditions reflect both the economic disadvantage of the Negro and the noneconomic restrictions of his access to the housing market. Partly in order to pool incomes and partly because of the limited housing supply, Negroes resort to doubling-up . . . expending a larger proportion of aggregate in-

14. Frank S. Kristof, "Federal Housing Policies: Subsidized Production, Filtration and Objectives: Part I," *Land Economics* XLVIII (1972): 309-20; Part II, *Land Economics* XLIX (1972): 163-74.

15. James T. Little, "Housing Market Behavior and Household Mobility Patterns in Transition Neighborhoods," *Working Paper* HMS 1 (Institute for Urban and Regional Studies, Washington University, 1973); "Household Preferences, Relocation and Welfare: An Evaluation of the Filtering Concept," *Working Paper* HMS 2 (Institute for Urban and Regional Studies, Washington University, (1974); "Residential Preferences, Neighborhood Filtering, and Neighborhood Change, *Working Paper* HMS 3 (Institute for Urban and Regional Studies, Washington University, (1974).

come for rent. . . . But the quality of housing received for this expenditure is inferior.[16]

Soon after came the explanation:

[t]hat given the high degree of residential segregation which obtains in the City of Chicago, white and non-white households are not competing in the same housing market. Instead, white households are competing in a white housing market and non-white households are competing in a non-white housing market. If this were the case, supply and demand factors in the white housing market would be more or less independent of supply and demand factors in the non-white housing market; and relationships among quality, size, and rent might be different in the two markets.[17]

Taking up the theme, the Taeubers concluded their studies of the 1950s with the feeling that:

The concept of a dual housing market is helpful in explaining certain facets of the relationship between race, residence and income. . . . the supply of housing for non-whites is restricted in both terms of number of units and quality of units. For non-whites, then, demand is high relative to supply and this situation is aggravated by the rapidly-increasing urban Negro populations. Housing within Negro areas can command higher prices than comparable housing in white residential areas.[18]

Such is the Chicago contribution to the Kain-Quigley conclusion that "evaluation of the diverse empirical studies leads us to conclude that blacks may pay between five and ten percent more than whites in most urban areas for comparable housing."[19] Yet even to support such a conclusion, two different theories have been advanced. One is the Becker (1957) conjecture that in fact the housing market is homogeneous, but the black-white differentials arise from a discrimination coefficient in the supply function that reflects a desire for both social and physical distance from blacks on the part of whites and leads to whites restricting minority access to the overall housing supply.[20] The alternative concept is one of a segmented housing

16. O.D. and B. Duncan, *The Negro Population of Chicago* (Chicago: The University of Chicago, 1957), pp. 83-84.
17. B. Duncan and P.M. Hauser, *Housing a Metropolis-Chicago* (Glencoe, Ill.: The Free Press, 1960), pp. 203-204.
18. Karl and Alma Taeuber, *Negroes in Cities* (Chicago: Aldine Publishing Company, 1965), p. 25.
19. J.F. Kain and John Quigley, "Housing Market Discrimination, Home-ownership and Savings Behavior," *American Economic Review* (1973): 263.
20. Gary S. Becker, *The Economics of Discrimination* (Chicago: University of Chicago Press, 1957).

market, in which excess demand or supply in each market segment determines the price of housing.[21] The justice or equity in the latter situation depends upon the nature of the barriers between markets that affect an individual's mobility.[22] This second concept requires that the city be viewed as a spatially arrayed stratification system in which relatively homogeneous neighborhoods are differentiated not simply by race and ethnicity, but simultaneously by socioeconomic status, stage of households in the life cycle, and similar sources of differences in tastes and housing preferences (see Part II).[23] If black-white segregation is accompanied by discrimination, then at the interface:

> the seller soon realizes that he has a great advantage, and prices reflect this knowledge. In instances where sales are made in panic "because the Negroes are coming" the process works indirectly: the seller receives a low price but speculators size the situation up, acquire the property and unload at high prices. The result is that *colored people usually pay higher prices than were current prior to their occupancy.*[24]

But this may be transitory, for the argument continues that it is

> inevitable that after the transition in racial occupancy has been completed *selling prices in the area will ultimately decline in accordance with property values in the particular section. The speed with which this will take place depends largely upon the basic factors which determine prices everywhere: the relationship between effective demand (as determined by the size of the Negro population seeking and able to pay for shelter) and the supply of housing available to them (determined largely by the availability of housing for whites elsewhere in the city).*[25]

This conclusion, although consistent with the Chicago Commission on Race Relations and Hoyt, runs counter to the findings of both the Duncans and the Taeubers as well as the Kain-Quigley assertions, yet it is at odds neither with work by other Chicago sociologists in the 1950s and 1960s nor with the consumer preference hypothesis

21. R.A. Haugen and A.J. Heins, "A Market Separation Theory of Rent Differentials in Metropolitan Areas," *Quarterly Journal of Economics* 83 (1969): 660-73.

22. N. Walzer and D. Singer, "Housing Expenditures in Urban Low-Income Areas," *Land Economics* L (1974): 224-31.

23. Such is the conclusion of urban social geographers studying the city.

24. Robert Weaver, *The Negro Ghetto* (New York: Harcourt, Brace and Company, 1948).

25. Ibid.

developed by Chicago economists and later elevated by Little to the status of the "arbitrage model of neighborhood succession."[26]

The central proposition, posed and verified in Schietinger's 1953 analysis of property values and racial change in Chicago, was the familiar one of threat-decline, invasion-recovery.[27] Schietinger showed that price movements with respect to race can be investigated with considerable success by using public records and relying on documentary tax stamp estimates for property value. He further showed that problems of comparability may be partially met by standardizing against assessed valuations, and he stated that a price recovery after initial decrease following the entry of blacks is well documented.

Luigi Laurenti made the earliest use of the methods developed by Schietinger and arrived at two conclusions:

First, price changes which can be connected with the fact of non-white entry are not uniform, as often alleged, but diverse. Depending on circumstances, racial change in a neighborhood may be or it may not be stimulating to real estate prices and in varying degrees. Second, considering all of the evidence, the odds are about four to one that house prices in a neighborhood entered by non-whites will keep up with or exceed prices in a comparable all-white area. These conclusions are chiefly based on observations of real estate markets in a period of generally rising prices. This period, moreover, was characterized by unusually strong demand for housing, particularly by non-whites who had been making relatively large gains in personal income. These conditions seem likely to continue into the foreseeable future, and therefore the main findings of the present study may be valid for many neighborhoods certain to experience the entry of non-whites.[28]

Reacting to this work, Rapkin and Grigsby offer a dissenting view:

It appears that the studies of price movements in racially mixed areas have fallen short of their basic objectives because they have focused on the price shifts themselves rather than on the full array of underlying causes of these shifts. In essence they have failed to provide any real foundation for

26. Frederick E. Schietinger, "Racial Succession and Residential Property Values in Chicago" (Ph.D. dissertation in Sociology, University of Chicago, 1953).

27. Frederick E. Schietinger, "Racial Succession and Changing Property Values in Residential Chicago," in *Contributions to Urban Sociology*, E. Burgess and D. Bogue, eds. (Chicago: University of Chicago Press, 1964), p. 99.

28. Luigi Laurenti, *Property Values and Race* (Berkeley: University of California Press, 1960), pp. 52-53.

a change in attitudes or practices toward Negroes by brokers, appraisers, mortgage lenders, and home-owners.

However, they go on to say:

In all fairness . . . it must be stated that the principal and permanent value of these studies may be in erasing the primitive folk notion that Negroes have an inherent taint which inevitably cause[s] house prices to decline in any area that they may enter. If this belief has fewer adherents as a result of these studies, then an important contribution has been made to the improvement of race relations and to the ultimate goal of equality for Negroes.[29]

Complementing this were Helper's conclusions in her 1958 and 1964-1965 studies of the racial policies and conceptions of Chicago's real estate brokers: "According to the majority of the respondents, the pattern of effect on values of residential property when Negroes enter an area is: downward before entry, when Negroes are approaching the area; upward upon entry and/or for a period after entry; downward after entry to a lower level of value than existed in the area before Negro entry."[30]

It was at the same time that Bailey developed what Muth has termed the customer preference hypothesis—that whites have a continuing aversion to living among blacks because of the advantages they perceive white neighborhoods to possess.[31] Even if whites and blacks originally paid the same amount for housing, this would have the effect that whites would be willing to pay more to live in segre-

29. Chester Rapkin and William Grigsby, *The Demand for Housing in Racially Mixed Areas* (Berkeley: University of California Press, 1960), pp. 104 ff.

30. Rose Helper, *Racial Policies and Practices of Real Estate Brokers* (Minneapolis: University of Minnesota Press, 1969), p. 95.

31. Martin J. Bailey, "Notes on the Economics of Residential Zoning and Urban Renewal," *Land Economics* XLII (1966): 215-20; Richard F. Muth, *Cities and Housing* (Chicago: University of Chicago Press, 1969). Actually, Bailey posits that blacks desire to live near whites more than they desire to live near other blacks (although, clearly, this may simply reflect demand for the better housing available in white areas), so that price differences reflect the nuisance of people themselves when they live adjacent to other people whose tastes, habits, and incomes are markedly different from their own. The argument is that people do not want to live near others with social status lower than their self-perceived status. This results in two possible situations. One is where neighboring people are a mutual nuisance. The solution is the eventual gravitation of members of each group to homogeneous areas with minimum borders with the other, mutually repulsive, group's area. The other situation is one of unilateral repulsion. In this case, only members of the repulsed group eventually gravitate to homogeneous residential areas, and they are continually chased by members of the other group, in a follow the leader fashion.

gated white neighborhoods and less to live adjacent to or integrated with blacks, whereas some blacks would be willing to pay more for residence adjacent to whites. Owners on the white side of the boundary line would have an incentive to sell to blacks, and the boundary would shift into the white area. In the absence of external forces preventing the movement, and assuming that white and black demands for housing are changing at the same rate, as the boundary shifts and the supply of housing to blacks grows relative to the white supply, housing prices paid by blacks will fall relative to those paid by whites. The only possible equilibrium is with identical prices on the white and black sides of the boundary and with housing prices in the interior of the black area lower than those in the interior of the white area. On the other hand, if black demand were growing at a sufficiently faster pace than white demand for housing and the rate of expansion of the ghetto into formerly white areas, it could maintain and even increase initial price differentials in the two zones of racial occupancy.[32] Bailey produced evidence for both the 1940s and 1950s apparently supporting the latter hypothesis in southside Chicago, as did Muth, who concluded that blacks generally paid about a third more for housing, at a given income level, than whites and that average values in neighborhoods changing from white to black occupancy increased 18 percent more than the value in tracts remaining white, an observation reiterated in one Chicago community by Molotch.[33]

A related explanation is offered by Smolensky, Becker, and Molotch, who use a version of the Prisoner's Dilemma model to construct a payoff matrix that they conclude will explain neighborhood transition.[34] Imagine the following situation: There is a neighborhood of single family dwellings. The owners of these dwellings are normal economic men in that if they rent their houses they will do so at rates that will yield maximum profits. Two adjacent houses in this neighborhood are vacant. A black presents himself as a prospective tenant to the owner of one of the houses. The owner of the adjacent house does not know this, since it is assumed that there is no communication between the owners.[35]

32. Ibid., pp. 109-10; and Susan Rose-Ackerman, "Racism and Urban Structure," *Journal of Urban Economics* 2 (1975): 83-105.

33. Harvey Molotch, "Community Action to Control Racial Change: An Evaluation of Chicago's South Shore Effort," (Ph.D. dissertation, Department of Sociology, University of Chicago, 1968).

34. Eugene Smolensky, Selwyn Becker, and Harvey Molotch, "The Prisoner's Dilemma and Ghetto Expansion," *Land Economics* XLIV, no. 4 (November 1968): 419.

35. Smolensky, p. 420.

The question is, then, Will the owner rent to the prospective black tenant and, if so, at what price? In other words, is there a circumstance in which the owner should not rent, even if the prospective tenant is willing to pay prevailing or premium rent?

The answer depends entirely upon the owner's expectations of future profits.[36] He must ask himself what he thinks will happen to future profits if he does rent to the black as well as what will happen if he does not rent to the black.

To answer these questions we must understand the events that might occur and their consequences:

1. Rents will increase with respect to costs if the owner rents to the black.
2. The black is willing to pay premium rent for the house as long as he is the only black in the neighborhood. But if another black moves into the neighborhood both will insist upon rents below those paid by the whites.
3. Should the owner rent his house to a black, whites will rent the adjacent unit only at a reduced price.

The owner is now faced with the dilemma illustrated by the payoff matrix shown in Table 16-4.[37] If Owner 1 rents to the black and Owner 2 does not rent to another black (southwest corner of the matrix), Owner 1 will receive $110 in rent every month, and Owner 2 will receive $80 in rent every month. Opposite actions taken by the owners (northeast corner) result in the reversed outcome.

Competitive behavior by one owner implies renting to the black, yielding the owner higher rent and higher short-run profits. The same action taken by the second owner has him renting also to a black. The result is that both owners will have lower long-run profits (southeast corner). If they cooperated with each other and excluded blacks, both of their long-term profits would be maximized (northwest corner). The conclusion is that competitive behavior is the cause of unstable housing situations. Generalizing, the model would seem to explain the reason why neighborhoods open to blacks in succession. When a black neighborhood is adjacent to a white neighborhood, the probability increases that blacks will reside ultimately in the all white area.[38]

It is realized that the Prisoner's Dilemma model might not have great explanatory power. But even if the payoff matrix does not

36. Rents are interchangeable with profits in this model.
37. Smolensky, p. 421.
38. Ibid., p. 422.

Table 16-4. Payoff Matrix: Prisoner's Dilemma

		Owner 2	
		Not Rent	Rent
Owner 1	Not rent	$100, $100	$80, $110
	Rent	$110, $80	$90, $90

characterize the housing market, there are still advantages in using it to help answer questions such as:

1. What are the profits in racial transition?
2. Are black rents greater than white rents in transitional neighborhoods?
3. What is the relationship between rents (and profits) when the neighborhood is all white as opposed to when it becomes all black?[39]

The overriding implication is that if the model is perceived and overt or tacit communication between owners is possible, the result will be black exclusion from white neighborhoods.[40]

Both Bailey's welfare formulation and the Prisoner's Dilemma model assume that blacks are willing to pay more to live near whites than whites are to live near blacks. This makes blockbusting not only possible, but profitable.[41] The key economic factor in a transitional neighborhood appears to be that housing that comes on the market is worth more to blacks than to whites.[42] White demand continues to decrease as the neighborhood is perceived to "deteriorate" and as black demand increases; the racial price differential grows and induces more and more whites to rent apartments or sell homes to blacks. This economic explanation takes place independent of "panic" situations involving blockbusting or other similar techniques.

David Karlen explains this very clearly in terms of supply and demand. In South Shore, which was undergoing racial transition when he studied it, Karlen found that white demand decreased drastically before blacks moved in (Figure 16-1). White Demand 1 slipped to white Demand 2, with an associated price decrease. During the transition period, he found new black housing demand unable to

39. Ibid.
40. Ibid., p. 429.
41. Ibid., p. 422.
42. Molotch, p. 167.

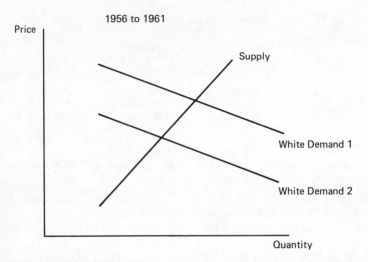

Figure 16-1. Supply and Demand for Housing in a Transitional Neighborhood: First Phase—White Demand Declines.

offset the decrease in white demand. There were only a few blacks moving into the neighborhood at this time. Then, as blacks began moving into the neighborhood in increasingly large numbers, their increased demand eventually more than compensated not only for the decreasing white demand, but also for the increase in white supply of houses for sale (Figure 16-2). White Demand 1 slipped to white Demand 2, but black Demand 2, added to the decreased white Demand 2 and compared to the increased Supply 2, accounts for an increase in price from P_1 to P_2.[43]

And so we return full circle to the patterns reported by the Chicago Commission on Race Relations, but elevated to the status of the arbitrage model of neighborhood succession, which itself is viewed as a special case of the concept of neighborhood filtering in a segregated (segmented) housing market. As formulated by Little, the arbitrage model assumes that the housing market is segregated by race and income. Such market segmentation depends upon the pref-

43. David H. Karlen, "Racial Integration and Property Values in Chicago" (Department of Sociology, University of Chicago, April 1968), pp. 12-13, 26. Mimeo.

Another explanation for the disparity between the equilibrium points in adjacent black and white areas is that blacks (and whites, for that matter) perceive trends in the expansion of black areas. This can lead to a "self-fulfilling" prophecy. The perception of the trend will encourage attempted black ingress and white egress. See Helper.

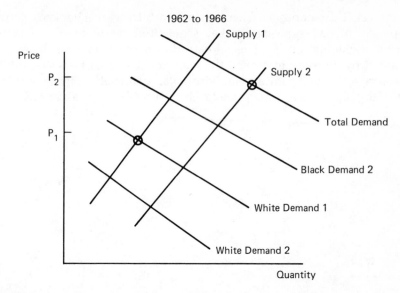

Figure 16-2. Supply and Demand for Housing in a Transitional Neighborhood: Second Phase—Black Demand Enters and Housing Supply Shifts.

erences of households for the kinds of neighborhoods in which they want to live and the distribution of income. For a variety of reasons, families prefer to live in homogeneous neighborhoods. Higher status families discount housing adjacent to low status neighborhoods because of the likely loss in status imparted by contiguity. Lower status families are willing to pay a premium to live close to high status neighborhoods because of the greater amenities there and because of the neighborhood effect of proximity. Equilibrium occurs when the boundary price is the same for the two groups, but for this to be so, the price within high status neighborhoods must be higher, and within lower status neighborhoods it must be lower. The arbitrage mechanism[44] involves the transfer of housing from one group to another, either because growing demands in low status areas raise prices along the boundary to a level greater than higher status families are willing to pay, in which case they leave and the low status area expands, or because a rapidly growing supply of new housing causes rapid filtering and a lowering of the price that high status families are willing to pay for the now less desirable older housing along the boundary, in which case arbitrage will be the instrument whereby filtering takes place, transferring housing from one

44. Little, p. 13.

submarket to another. Clearly, such arbitrage mechanisms should operate in any housing market segmented by income and tastes; racial segmentation is a special case that may or may not be accompanied by discrimination and the maintenance of barriers that inhibit arbitrage, protect white neighborhoods, artificially restrict minority housing supply, and raise price levels in the minority submarkets.

Chapter 17

Price Levels and Price Movements of Single Family Homes in Chicago, 1968-1972

What actually happened to property prices in Chicago during the period that the Leadership Council was attempting to create a colorblind housing market? Did they move in ways that created such good buys in neighborhoods newly shifted from white to black occupancy that they satisfied the mobility needs of black homeseekers without the need to become pioneers in integrating white communities? A variety of analyses were completed in the attempt to answer these questions: (1) a pilot study in which a large number of determinants of selling prices were examined for a small sample of 275 single family homes sold in the city of Chicago in 1971; (2) a broad-gauged analysis of every single family sale taking place in city in the period 1968-1972, in which relative price levels of comparable units were analyzed across a series of submarkets; and (3) an examination of the same data set, involving over 30,000 real estate tranactions, in which relative price changes of comparable units in different racial submarkets within Chicago were determined. Choice of equations was determined, first, by the form of the classical Muth-Alonso residential location model and, second, by the Lancastrian concept of a hedonic price index that can be used to operationalize the classical model.

THE CLASSICAL RESIDENTIAL LOCATION MODEL

Traditional residential location theory, as formulated by Muth and Alonso, focuses on the role of relative location in determining hous-

421

ing prices. The derivation begins by separating the market price of a house into two components—the price per unit of housing and the quantity of units purchased. The product of those two components is the total expenditure on housing by a family, and it can be derived using what are now traditional utility maximization procedures. Assume that a consumer's level of welfare depends upon the quantity of housing that he consumes, H, and the quantity of all other goods, X.

$$U = U(H,X) \text{ where } U_{h'} U_x > 0. \tag{17-1}$$

He also faces a budget constraint such that his total expenditure on housing $[P(k) \cdot H]$, where $P(k)$ is the price of a unit of housing, which is a function of the distance, k, from the central business district, plus his total expenditure on all other goods $[PxX]$, plus his expenditure on travel (assumed for simplicity to depend only upon distance) $[T(k)]$, must equal his income (Y).

$$PxX + P(k) \cdot H + T(k) - Y = 0 \text{ where } T_k > 0. \tag{17-2}$$

This can be maximized by setting up the Lagrangian multipliers and taking the first derivatives.

$$\frac{\partial L}{\partial X} = U_x - \lambda Px = 0, \tag{17-3a}$$

$$\frac{\partial L}{\partial H} = U_h - \lambda P(k) = 0, \tag{17-3b}$$

$$\frac{\partial L}{\partial k} = -\lambda(H \cdot P_k + T_k) = 0, \tag{17-3c}$$

$$\frac{\partial L}{\partial \lambda} = Y - [X + P(k) \cdot H + T(k)] = 0. \tag{17-3d}$$

From the third utility maximization condition (17-3c), it is apparent that the marginal change in the cost of a given quantity of housing is given by

$$H \cdot P_k = -T_k. \tag{17-4}$$

In order to determine the price at any given distance K_o from the

CBD of one unit of housing it is necessary to integrate equation (17-4) with respect to k,

$$\int_{o}^{K_o} H \cdot P_k \, dk = [A_o - T_{K_o}] H, \qquad (17\text{-}5)$$

where T_{K_o} is the travel costs from distance K_o and A_o is the cost of the housing in the CBD ($k = 0$). Defining the price of one unit of housing at the center of the city as equal to unity, then

$$H \cdot P_{K_o} = H(1 - T_{K_o}). \qquad (17\text{-}6)$$

The way in which the price per unit of housing declines in response to distance depends upon the way in which travel costs increase. They might increase linearly, in which case the price of a unit of housing would decline linearly from the CBD and equation (17-6) could be rewritten as

$$H \cdot P(k) = H (1 - \beta k) \text{ where } \beta > 0. \qquad (17\text{-}6a)$$

There is considerable evidence that the price per unit of housing does not decline linearly but in some negative exponential fashion (implying that transportation costs increase less than proportionately). In this case equation (17-6) would be rewritten (redefining A_o) as

$$H \cdot P(k) = H \cdot e^{-\beta' k} \text{ where } \beta' < 0. \qquad (17\text{-}6b)$$

Measuring H, a "unit of housing," poses a problem. There is no clear way of constructing a priori a weighting scheme that would determine exactly how many bathrooms were equivalent to one garage or to a bedroom, since separate prices of the components of a parcel of housing units (i.e., a complete residence) are not available. The number of housing units that any one house contains is a function of the number of separate components that it contains.

$$H = \Pi_i A_i^{\alpha i}, \qquad (17\text{-}7)$$

where A_i is the quantity of the ith component (bathroom, degree of modernization, age, etc.). This functional form has the intuitive appeal that it explains why the continual addition of a given component (e.g., the number of bedrooms) does not add a constant dollar value to the residence. The complete form of the model is then

$$\text{PRICE} = e^{-\beta'k} \left[\Pi_i A_i^{\alpha_i} \right], \tag{17-8}$$

where PRICE is the market price of the residence, or, in Log form,

$$\text{Log(PRICE)} = -\beta'k + \Sigma_i \alpha_i \text{Log} A_i + U, \tag{17-8a}$$

where U is a random disturbance term.

DEFINITION OF HOUSING ATTRIBUTES

Having established the functional form in equation (17-8a) the next step is to determine the relevant attributes that enter into the definition of H. The potential list is enormous since it includes not only the physical properties of the building itself but also all possible "neighborhood amenities" and disamenities as well.

That the value of a housing unit depends on its characteristics and those of the neighborhood surrounding it is easily grasped by thinking of the dwelling as an asset that satisfies certain needs of its occupants, such as shelter, privacy, and recreational space. It is the specific bundle of characteristics of the housing unit that determine what needs the dwelling can satisfy. It is obvious that some characteristics (benefits) will satisfy needs and that others (disbenefits) will hinder satisfaction. Furthermore, thinking of a housing unit in this way gives one a method of evaluating the relative importance of various characteristics initially. The task of choosing specific variables to explain the value of a dwelling is still formidable, however, and the choice varies greatly with the researcher with respect to both the types and the numbers of variables chosen, as Table 17-1 reveals.

For example Evans, interested in the influence of distance from CBD on property value, limited his independent variables to log of distance to CBD, log of floor space, and years of lease expired. By confining his sample to houses of one type located in neighborhoods with similar environmental and socioeconomic characteristics, thereby holding those variables constant, he was able to account for 84 percent of the variance of the dependent variable. In another example, Kain and Quigley took a different approach. They began by collapsing thirty-nine neighborhood and housing characteristics to five factors using factor analysis. Two regression models were then constructed, one for owner-occupied units and one for rental units. In the rental model, the five factors, along with twenty-three other independent variables, were regressed against monthly rent. In the

Table 17-1. Summary Table of Recent Work on Housing Value.

Author	Date	Dependent Variable	Locational Variable(s)	Racial/ Ethnic	Neighborhood Variables		Housing Variables	
					Neighborhood Characteristics	Environmental Pollution	Housing Characteristics	Housing Improvements
RIDKER and HENNING	1968	House Price	Travel time To CBD Access to Main Highway	Percent non-white	Housing Density School Quality Socioeconomic Group Index Persons per Dwelling unit Mean Family Income	Air Pollution Index	Number Rooms Average House Age	
KAIN and QUIGLEY	1970	House Price	Distance To CBD	Percent White	Median Schooling Crime Index		5 Factors Produced from 39 Measurements: Age Number Rooms Lot Area	Number Baths
		Monthly Rent	Distance To CBD	(Same Variables as Above Plus The Following)			Type of Structure	Heat, Water, Appliances, Furniture Included in Rent Hot Water Central Heat Owner Occupied

Table 17-1 continued

Study	Year	Dependent Variable	Accessibility	Race	Neighborhood / Socioeconomic	Environmental	Structure	Amenities
LANE	1970	House Price	Accessibility Index				Floor Area House Type Number Floors	Garage
MUTH	1970	Housing Expenditures per Month		Percent Black	Number Manufacturing Establishments Percent Housing Built Before 1940 Percent Owner-occupied Housing Units Percent Population over 20 Years Income Migration Median Years schooling Percent Workforce in white collar jobs Population Growth			
ANDERSON and CROCKER	1971	House Price	Distance To CBD	Percent Nonwhite	Mean Family Income Percent Dilapidated Buildings Number Buildings Older Than 20 Years	SO_2 Levels Particulate Level	Number Rooms	
APPS	1971	House Price	Accessibility to Employment Accessibility to Schools				Floor Area Story Height Age Condition Lot Area Structure Type	Garage
MASSELL and STEWART	1971	House Price			Neighborhood Quality Index		Structure-Size Index	
WABE	1971	Average House Price	Rail Travel Time and Cost To CBD		Social Class Population Density Distance to Greenbelt		Floor Area Date of Construction	Garage Central Heating

WILKINSON	1971	Factor Analysis	Distance to CBD	Socioeconomic Index Residential Density Number schools per population	House Type Age Number Rooms Area	Attics Bedrooms Garage Garage Space Bath Inside toilet
EVANS	1973	Asking Price	Distance to CBD		Floor Area Number of Years Lease Expired	

Sources:

R.J. Anderson, Jr., and T.D. Crocker, "Air Pollution and Residential Property Values, *Urban Studies* 8 (1968).

P. Apps, "An Approach to Modelling Residential Demand," (Unpublished paper, 1970),

J.S. Cubbin, "A Hedonic Approach to Some Aspects of the Coventry Housing Market," Warwick Economic Research Paper 14, 1970.

A.W. Evans, *The Economics of Residential Location* (London: Macmillan, 1973).

J.F. Kain and J.M. Quigley, "Evaluating the Quality of the Residential Environment," *Environment and Planning* (1970).

_____. "Measuring the Value of Housing Quality," *Journal of the American Statistical Association* 65 (1970): 330.

R. Lane, "Some Findings on Residential Location, House Prices, and Accessibility" (Unpublished paper, 1970).

B.F. Massell and J.M. Stewart, "The Determinants of Residential Property Values" (Standford University, Program in Urban Studies Dicussion Paper #6, 1971).

R.F. Muth, "Permanent Income, Instrumental Variables, and the Income Elasticity of Housing Demand" St. Louis: Washington University, Institute for Urban and Regional Studies Working Paper EDA 12, 1970).

J.S. Wabe, "A Study of House Prices as a Means of Establishing the Value of Journey Time, The Rate of Time Preference and the Valuation of Some Aspects of Environment in the London Metropolitan Region," *Applied Economics*. (1971).

R.K. Wilkinson, "The Determinants of Relative House Prices" (Unpublished paper, 1971).

owner-occupied model, nine more independent variables were added to the five factors. Many of the variables proved insignificant, and R^2 were lower than those of Evans' model.

If a broader overview of past empirical work is attempted, it will be seen that most of the models seem to include at least a few variables from each of three general categories—locational measurements, housing characteristics, and neighborhood characteristics. Within the last two categories, such features as neighborhood quality, environmental pollution, the type of improvements made to the property, and the like are frequently considered. Whether or not each subset is included seems quite random, however. Many studies neglect at least one of the three categories. For example, Apps, Cubbin, and Lane included no neighborhood characteristic variables in their regressions, while Massell and Stewart omitted locational variables. Muth, attempting to determine the income elasticity of housing demand, formulated several models with housing value as the dependent variable but included no independent variables that measured housing characteristics.

Even when similar independent variables are included in several studies, they often behave very differently. For example, Evans and Wilkinson both included the locational variable "distance to CBD" in their models while attempting to explain house price. In both cases the variable was significant, but in Evans' study its coefficient was negative while in Wilkinson's it was positive. To compound the situation further, Kain and Quigley found distance to CBD insignificant at the 5 percent level.

MODELING STRATEGY: INITIAL SAMPLE STUDY

It seems apparent that there has been both arbitrariness and expediency in the variable selection process in most previous studies. Often, it appears as though the most important factor determining a variable list is simply the availability of data or a high level of significance of a variable's coefficient where larger models were run initially and only smaller "significant" models were published. Neither of these decisionmaking processes seems adequate.

The approach taken here is to include the "conventional" locational variable, distance to CBD $[k]$, and to divide the bundle of housing characteristics (H) into two groups, one including properties of the house itself and another reflecting neighborhood factors. These two classes of variables are then further subdivided, with a distinction being drawn in the first case between standard housing characteristics and the nature of housing improvements that have been made while the second is divided into neighborhood socio-economic status and mobility characteristics, racial and ethnic characteristics of the residents, and environmental pollution.

The next step was to collect the variables for each of the subcategories that are listed in Table 17-2. Three sources served to supply these data. The housing characteristics and housing improvement variables were provided by the Society of Real Estate Appraisers' Market Data Center publication *Chicagoland Residential Sales Data* for a sample of 275 single family homes in the city of Chicago in 1971. This publication consists of very detailed information concerning the type and condition of a sample of residential properties that sold in the Chicago area during the period 1970 to 1972. Besides the terms of the sale (price, mortgage, data, and type of financing), twenty-seven characteristics of the building and land are recorded for each property.

The neighborhood characteristics and the racial and ethnic variables are census data. These figures pertain to the census tract in which the property is located.

Both the pollution variables and the distance measure are the result of Argonne National Laboratory's air quality display model. This pollution simulation program is capable of generating a daily sulfur dioxide and suspended particulates reading for every cell of a one kilometer square grid covering the city of Chicago. This grid also makes calculation of straight line distance from downtown Chicago relatively simple.

Finally, building and land assessments for the properties were obtained from the figures published by the Cook County Assessor's Office. Every property in a township is reassessed every four years (one fourth of Cook County being assessed each year), and the results are published in a paper serving the appropriate township.

These variables were tested for their association with other variables and their contribution to the model itself. Once a tentative group of variables was chosen, a choice concerning the order in which the groups of variables were to enter the model had to be made. The final decision was influenced by several considerations. First, in attempting to determine the relative importance of the various subgroups, it was helpful to consider the decision process of potential homeseekers (see Chapter 2). It was felt that the basic characteristics of the structure (i.e., housing characteristics) were the first factors to be taken into account by people trying to make a choice among houses. Next, more specific details of the house (housing improvements) become important. Finally, the prospective buyer examines the neighborhood (neighborhood characteristics) and the type of people living in the area (racial and ethnic variables). The

Table 17-2. List of Variables.

Category	Variable	Code	Description
HOUSING CHARACTERISTICS	Floor Area	SQUARE FEET	Floor area of the dwelling in square feet
	Age of Dwelling	AGE	Age of the building in years
	Lot Area	LOTAREA	Area of the property's lot in square feet
HOUSING IMPROVEMENTS	Air Conditioning	AC	Dummy variable for presence of central air conditioning
	Garage	GARAGE	Dummy indicating presence of a garage
	Improved Attic	ATTIC	Dummy indicating an improved attic (containing rooms or a bath)
	Improved Basement	BASEMENT	Dummy indicating basement with rooms or bath
	Number of Baths	NUMBER BATHS	Number of bathrooms
NEIGHBORHOOD CHARACTERISTICS	Median Family Income	MFI	Median family income of census tract in which property is located
	Multiple Family Dwellings	APARTMENTS	Percentage multiple family dwellings in the census tract
	Migration	MIGRATION	Percent of families in property's tract living in a different tract five years before
RACIAL AND ETHNIC VARIABLES	Percent Blacks	BLACK	Percent black in census tract
	Percent Cubans-Mexicans	CUBAN-MEXICAN	Percent Cuban and Mexican in census tract
	Percent Irish	IRISH	Percent Irish in census tract
ENVIRONMENTAL POLLUTION	Sulfur Dioxide	SO_2	average yearly sulfur dioxide intensity (micrograms per cubic meter)
	Particulates	PARTIC	average yearly suspended particulates measurement (micrograms per cubic meter)
ACCESSIBILITY	Distance to CBD	DISTANCE	distance in kilometers from downtown Chicago

order in which the groups of variables were entered into the model was consistent with this interpretation as well as with statistical interpretation of the groups' relative importance.

Thus, housing characteristics and improvements were entered first, because it was felt that the most important characteristics that determine the value of a housing unit are the properties of the house itself. The order in which the neighborhood variable groups were added to the model also reflected their relative importance: socioeconomic levels preceded racial characteristics and environmental pollution.

In the case of distance from CBD, interrelationships among the variables dictated that it be entered into the equation last. As can be seen from the simple correlation coefficients in Table 17-3, many of the characteristics of single family dwellings are related to the unit's distance from the CBD. Entering distance last in the model allowed its effect on other variables to be determined after some idea of the importance and sign of the nondistance variables had already been acquired. The two pollution measurements were treated in substantially the same way since, in effect, they almost serve as proxies for the distance variable (simple correlation coefficients between the two and distance are -0.40 and -0.74). Because of the high correlation between the two pollution variables themselves (0.51), they were not entered together in any of the model runs. Similarly, the last run of the model was made with distance but with neither of the pollution measurements.

DETERMINANTS OF SELLING PRICES IN THE 1971 SAMPLE CASE

Tables 17-4 and 17-5 present the results of the analyses, with the groups of independent variables regressed first on the selling price of the housing unit and second on the price per square foot of the unit. A series of nine regression models is presented in each case:

1. $P = f\,((1)$ housing characteristics)
2. $P = f\,((1) + (2)$ housing improvements)
3. $P = f\,((1) + (2) + (3)$ neighborhood characteristics)
4. $P = f\,((1) + (2) + (3) + (4)$ racial and ethnic variables)
5. $P = f\,((1) + (2) + (3) + (4) + (5a)\ SO_2\,)$
6. $P = f\,((1) + (2) + (3) + (4) + (5b)$ Particulates)
7. $P = f\,((1) + (2) + (3) + (4) + (5a) + (6)$ distance)
8. $P = f\,((1) + (2) + (3) + (4) + (5b) + (6)$ distance)
9. $P = f\,((1) + (2) + (3) + (4) + (6)$

Table 17-3. Simple Correlation Coefficients Among Model Variables.

		Price	Price Per Square Foot	Sulfur Dioxide	Particulates	Distance From CBD
HOUSING CHARACTERISTICS	Floor Area	0.43	-0.40	0.11	0.17	0.05
	Age of Dwelling	-0.43	-0.52	0.14	0.29	-0.34
	Lot Area	0.37	0.06	-0.07	-0.22	0.31
HOUSING IMPROVEMENTS	Air Conditioning	0.38	0.32	-0.13	-0.15	0.22
	Garage	0.11	0.02	-0.01	-0.07	0.01
	Improved Attic	0.08	0.13	-0.01	-0.10	0.07
	Improved Basement	0.31	0.20	-0.15	-0.09	0.16
	Number of Baths	0.34	-0.18	0.03	0.13	0.05
NEIGHBORHOOD CHARACTERISTICS	Median Family Income	0.73	0.61	-0.21	-0.37	0.58
	Multiple Family Dwellings	-0.18	-0.37	0.14	0.35	-0.28
	Migration	0.02	-0.27	0.03	0.15	0.03
RACIAL AND ETHNIC VARIABLES	Blacks	-0.40	-0.57	0.25	0.50	-0.40
	Cubans-Mexicans	-0.19	-0.22	0.13	0.24	-0.34
	Irish	0.29	0.25	-0.19	-0.29	0.29
ENVIRONMENTAL POLLUTION	Sulfur Dioxide	-0.18	-0.28	1.00	0.51	-0.40
	Particulates	-0.36	-0.50	0.51	1.00	-0.74
ACCESSIBILITY	Distance from CBD	0.61	0.58	-0.40	-0.74	1.00

Table 17-4. Factors Influencing the Price of Single Family Homes.

	Model	1	2	3	4	5	6	7	8	9
	R^2	0.474	0.568	0.741	0.772	0.772	0.773	0.788	0.790	0.787
	Constant	5.113	5.762	-2.641	-1.455	-1.455	-0.381	-0.410	-2.061	-0.347
HOUSING CHARACTERISTICS	Square Feet	0.457 (0.058)	0.318 (0.069)	0.247 (0.057)	0.323 (0.055)	0.323 (0.055)	0.330 (0.056)	0.338 (0.054)	0.336 (0.054)	0.344 (0.054)
	Age	-0.252 (0.023)	-0.209 (0.022)	-0.135 (0.020)	-0.127 (0.019)	-0.127 (0.019)	-0.126 (0.019)	-0.122 (0.018)	-0.123 (0.018)	-0.123 (0.018)
	Lot Area	0.308 (0.053)	0.309 (0.050)	0.201 (0.040)	0.163 (0.038)	0.163 (0.038)	0.155 (0.039)	0.123 (0.038)	0.128 (0.038)	0.123 (0.038)
	AC		0.211 (0.047)	0.082 (0.039)	0.070 (0.037)	0.070 (0.037)	0.070 (0.037)	0.079 (0.036)	0.080 (0.036)	0.078 (0.036)
	Attic		0.178 (0.051)	0.155 (0.040)	0.149 (0.038)	0.149 (0.038)	0.144 (0.039)	0.122 (0.037)	0.126 (0.037)	0.124 (0.037)
HOUSING IMPROVEMENTS	Basement		0.116 (0.037)	0.087 (0.029)	0.085 (0.027)	0.085 (0.027)	0.084 (0.027)	0.078 (0.027)	0.074 (0.026)	0.074 (0.027)
	Number Baths		0.148 (0.073)	0.152 (0.057)	0.137 (0.053)	0.137 (0.053)	0.140 (0.054)	0.133 (0.052)	0.124 (0.052)	0.130 (0.052)
	Garage		0.068 (0.038)	0.065 (0.030)	0.062 (0.029)	0.062 (0.029)	0.062 (0.029)	0.70 (0.028)	0.073 (0.028)	0.071 (0.028)
NEIGHBORHOOD CHARACTERISTICS	Median Family Income			1.019 (0.077)	0.814 (0.086)	0.814 (0.086)	0.820 (0.086)	0.713 (0.086)	0.683 (0.089)	0.720 (0.086)
	Apartments			0.044 (0.022)	0.027 (0.022)	0.027 (0.022)	0.036 (0.023)	0.060 (0.022)	0.055 (0.023)	0.061 (0.022)
	Migration			-0.030 (0.035)	0.044 (0.037)	0.044 (0.037)	0.031 (0.039)	-0.033 (0.040)	-0.030 (0.040)	-0.034 (0.040)
RACIAL AND ETHNIC VARIABLES	Black				-0.031 (0.006)	-0.031 (0.006)	-0.028 (0.006)	-0.022 (0.006)	-0.025 (0.006)	-0.022 (0.006)
	Cuban-Mexican				-0.026 (0.007)	-0.026 (0.007)	-0.023 (0.007)	-0.013 (0.007)	-0.014 (0.007)	-0.013 (0.007)
	Irish				-0.016 (0.010)	-0.016 (0.010)	-0.016 (0.010)	-0.015 (0.010)	-0.015 (0.010)	-0.016 (0.010)
ENVIRONMENTAL POLLUTION	SO_2					-0.002 (0.074)	-0.002 (0.205)	0.033 (0.032)		
	Particulate								0.415 (0.242)	
ACCESSIBILITY	Distance							0.024 (0.006)	0.030 (0.007)	0.023 (0.005)

Table 17-5. Determinants of the Price Per Square Foot of Single Family Homes.

	Model	1	2	3	4	5	6	7	8	9
	R^2	0.281	0.391	0.552	0.629	0.631	0.635	0.654	0.654	0.654
	Constant	2.750	2.371	-4.915	-2.524	-2.280	0.107	-1.049	-1.686	-1.078
HOUSING CHARACTERISTICS	Age	-0.267 (0.026)	-0.238 (0.027)	-0.164 (0.026)	-0.145 (0.024)	-0.145 (0.024)	-0.142 (0.024)	-0.139 (0.023)	-0.139 (0.023)	-0.138 (0.023)
	Lot Area	0.125 (0.056)	0.151 (0.055)	0.044 (0.049)	0.012 (0.046)	0.010 (0.046)	-0.004 (0.046)	-0.032 (0.045)	-0.032 (0.045)	-0.032 (0.045)
HOUSING IMPROVEMENTS	AC		0.210 (0.055)	0.077 (0.050)	0.060 (0.046)	-0.058 (0.046)	0.061 (0.046)	0.070 (0.045)	0.071 (0.045)	0.070 (0.045)
	Attic		0.157 (0.060)	0.122 (0.052)	0.116 (0.048)	0.116 (0.048)	0.105 (0.048)	0.087 (0.047)	0.087 (0.047)	0.086 (0.047)
	Basement		0.047 (0.042)	0.024 (0.037)	0.035 (0.034)	0.028 (0.034)	0.032 (0.034)	0.021 (0.033)	0.022 (0.033)	0.022 (0.033)
	Number Baths		-0.296 (0.066)	-0.300 (0.059)	-0.249 (0.054)	-0.246 (0.054)	-0.232 (0.054)	-0.241 (0.053)	-0.246 (0.053)	-0.242 (0.052)
	Garage		0.075 (0.045)	0.067 (0.039)	0.054 (0.036)	0.056 (0.036)	0.054 (0.036)	0.065 (0.035)	0.066 (0.035)	0.065 (0.035)
NEIGHBORHOOD CHARACTERISTICS	Median Family Income			0.913 (0.099)	0.589 (0.105)	0.596 (0.105)	0.608 (0.105)	0.483 (0.106)	0.465 (0.109)	0.480 (0.105)
	Apartments			0.035 (0.029)	0.005 (0.027)	0.010 (0.027)	0.026 (0.029)	0.049 (0.028)	0.046 (0.029)	0.049 (0.028)
	Migration			-0.107 (0.045)	0.017 (0.046)	0.009 (0.046)	-0.015 (0.048)	-0.081 (0.050)	-0.080 (0.050)	-0.081 (0.050)
RACIAL AND ETHNIC VARIABLES	Black				-0.048 (0.007)	-0.046 (0.007)	-0.041 (0.008)	-0.036 (0.008)	-0.037 (0.008)	-0.036 (0.008)
	Cuban-Mexican				-0.032 (0.009)	-0.030 (0.009)	-0.026 (0.009)	-0.016 (0.009)	-0.016 (0.009)	-0.016 (0.009)
	Irish				-0.017 (0.013)	-0.019 (0.013)	-0.019 (0.013)	-0.018 (0.012)	-0.017 (0.012)	-0.018 (0.012)
ENVIRONMENTAL POLLUTION	SO_2					-0.056 (0.040)	-0.532 (0.253)	-0.014 (0.040)		
	Particulate								0.146 (0.304)	
ACCESSIBILITY	Distance							0.028 (0.007)	0.031 (0.008)	0.029 (0.007)

Table 17-6 shows the accumulative and incremental explanatory power of these successive regression models in the two cases. All of the groups of variables with the exception of environmental pollution always make a significant contribution to the explanatory power of the model. The results are in accordance with expectations.

Turning to the specific coefficients, the first model run, using selling price as the dependent variable, yielded results that in general are not difficult to explain. The signs of the coefficients, for example, are those one would expect, at least for the first three groups of variables. However, the coefficients of each of the racial variables are negative. Some researchers in the past have estimated that if housing quality and income levels are held constant (as is done in our model), blacks pay more for housing in the ghetto than nonblacks outside the ghetto. The results from this study show the opposite relationship between a neighborhood's blackness and housing prices and reiterate the parameter for Spanish Americans and Irish Catholics in the city. Each of our racial variables measures the percent of the housing unit's census tract population that is found in each subgroup. The negative relationship between price and the first two minorities in particular are emphasized by the small standard error and the relative stability of the coefficient.

The second sign that is different from that found by most other studies is the positive sign attached to distance from CBD. Although this result is unusual, it is not inexplicable. In fact, a modified form of the Muth-Alonso model is able to handle a positive price-distance relationship without difficulty. In this modified form, the price-distance gradient is shown to depend on two quantities. One of these is negative, the transport cost; one is positive, an amenity influence

Table 17-6. Increases in Explanatory Power with the Addition of Variable Groups.

Variable Group Added	Price Model R^2	Price Model F^a	Price Per Square Foot Model R^2	Price Per Square Foot Model F^a
Housing Characteristics	0.474	81.30	0.281	53.17
Housing Improvements	0.568	11.54	0.391	9.66
Neighborhood Characteristics	0.741	58.60	0.552	31.60
Racial and Ethnic Variables	0.772	11.89	0.629	17.89

[a]F test of hypothesis that all coefficients in group equal zero.

that increases with distance from the CBD. If the amenity increase outweighs the transport cost increase, a positive distance coefficient results.

Before we turn to these differences, however, several other features of the results presented in Tables 17-4 and 17-5 should be remarked. Of particular interest are changes in the size or significance of coefficients as other variables are added to the model. For instance, the coefficient of APTS that is significant at the 5 percent level when it enters suddenly becomes insignificant when the racial and ethnic variables enter the equation and then regains significance as distance enters. This large degree of interaction with other variables indicated by this sort of instability in a coefficient makes it difficult to determine the true relationship between the dependent and independent variables. It seems likely that in this case APTS initially was serving as a partial measure of the racial and ethnic variables, and thus, when the latter entered the model, the effect of APTS became small. Several other examples of this sort of behavior of coefficients can be found. The coefficients of AC, AGE, LOT AREA, and BASEMENT are all reduced when MFI and the other neighborhood characteristics enter the equation. Possible explanations for these changes of magnitude come to mind immediately. It is not hard to believe that air conditioning is highly associated with median family income and that the variable received undue importance in explaining price before the income variable entered. The slower depreciation rate indicated by the reduction in the size of the coefficient of AGE when MFI is added is not surprising either, since the more affluent should be able to maintain their homes more effectively. That LOT AREA is associated with affluence is what one would expect from the usual interpretation of the theory of land value, which states that the wealthy should be expected to consume more land at a greater distance from the city center while the poor consume less at a shorter distance. Finally, in the case of BASEMENT it seems entirely possible that this measurement is a reflection of basement family rooms or dens, which once again are probably correlated with income.

All of these variables, then, react in the same way when MFI enters the model: that part of their effect due to the underlying income component is reassigned to the actual income variable, MFI. In every case the size of the specific housing characteristic coefficient falls appreciably.

The same type of changes occur in the coefficients of LOT AREA and CUB-MEX when distance enters. The possible explanations for this behavior are also similar. It should be expected that the lot size depends on distance and that excluding distance from a model will inflate the coefficient of a lot size variable embodying a distance component. The population distribution of Cubans and Mexicans appears also to be related to distance (simple correlation coefficient of -0.34). Once again, when the distance component of the variable is subtracted (by entering distance among the independent variables), the size of the coefficient of CUB-MEX decreases.

The results of the model with price per square foot as the dependent variable are quite similar to those described above. This should not be surprising, since floor area was included as an independent variable in the first formulation. The coefficients of AGE and LOT AREA are reduced in size when MFI enters the equation, just as in the first model. Likewise, the CUB-MEX coefficient decreases when distance is added. A few differences are worth noting, however. One of these is a highly significant negative coefficient attached to # BATHS. This negative relation is probably caused by the high degree of correlation between the floor area and # BATHS (0.64). If dividing price by square feet of floor space is tantamount to dividing by # BATHS, then the negative relationship is not hard to understand. Every time the value of the independent variable is increased, the size of the dependent variable decreases since, in fact, it is being divided by the former. The negative relationship is almost automatic as a result. Another difference is that the variable MIGRTN is significant (5 percent) when it enters but becomes insignificant when the racial and ethnic group are added. One hypothesis to explain this is that MIGRTN is serving as an indicator of neighborhoods undergoing racial turnover. Thus, in areas undergoing racial change, the values of MIGRTN will be high, since many of the residents are newly arrived. These new arrivals will be minority group members. When the racial and ethnic variables enter and are in a sense held constant, the importance of MIGRTN lessens, and much of its influence is assumed by BLACK and CUB-MEX.

In both models, all of the groups of variables added significantly to the explanatory power of the formulation except environmental pollution. The high correlation between distance and particulates (-0.74) leads to great instability in the pollution measurement's coefficient. For example, in the price per square foot model, the coefficient of PARTIC changes from a significant negative to an insignificant positive parameter. Unfortunately, PARTIC is also highly associated with many independent variables. Perhaps the common underlying component of all of these variables is distance, and if the dual nature of this component could somehow be extracted—the negative effect of transport costs and the positive relationship of neighborhood and environmental amenities to distance—the true nature of the relationship of several of the independent variables to the dependent would become apparent. It is to this question that we now turn.

THE CLASSICAL MODEL RECONSIDERED

To reach our objective—a reasoned explanation for positive distance exponents for single family housing prices in the central city—we should first reconsider the basics of property value theory and then try to reformulate the Muth-Alonso model.

It was Sir Henry Maine who pointed out, over a century ago, that one of the essential ingredients in the emergence of modern urban-industrial society was a change in the concept of property ownership. Originally held in common by traditional social groups, property—particularly land and the capital invested on it—has been transformed into another exchangeable commodity with a price determined by competition among prospective users.

The value of property is not simply the value of the physical object, however; it is the value of a bundle of rights that property ownership conveys. Exchange of a piece of property involves the transfer of this set of rights from one individual to another. The rights derive their significance from the fact that they help a man form expectations that he can reasonably hold in his dealings with others—expectations that find expression in the laws, customs, and mores of society. An owner expects the community to protect his rights—which include rights to benefit or harm himself or others—and to permit him to act in those ways not prohibited in the specification of the rights.

The right to benefit or harm others, and its complement, to be benefited or harmed by others, is important because it involves externalities—the effects of each land user's activities on others—and their internalization—how the costs and gains are accounted for in property prices and land use. An individual property owner will try to maximize present value by assessing the future time streams of costs and benefits associated with alternative land uses, selecting that use that he believes will maximize the present value. In doing so, he will take into account the benefits conveyed to him by others and the costs imposed on him by others. Society does not, however, require the converse—that he receive rewards for the benefits he conveys to others and pay for the costs he imposes on them.

Hence, in any well-functioning competitive property market in which there are few constraints on the mobility of purchasers of property, the price of each piece of property should reflect the present value of the future stream of net benefits expected to flow over the useful life of the "highest and best" improvements—namely, those land uses that maximize returns, consistent with the societal definition of property rights. This generalization is, however, subject to the workings of time. Many capital investments cannot be changed overnight. A commitment to a particular land use may therefore be a commitment for several decades, and one that is fixed rather than mobile. Where major capital investments are involved it will only be in the new property market that one sees uses being established that at any given time are risk takers' estimates of the "highest and best." Elsewhere the toll that depreciation takes of fixed capital investments before their economically useful life has run out will be apparent.

As noted, the value of any site will be enhanced by benefits conveyed by others (both "windfalls" of particular actions and, in the longer term, positive externalities such as a "good neighborhood" and a "fine school district" or "excellent accessibility"). Likewise, they will be reduced by costs imposed by others (immediate "wipeouts" and longer term negative externalities such as air pollution or the swath of noise associated with airport landing patterns). The private property market produces an "internalization" of many of these externalities in that the consumer bears the costs. Thus, a new highway will provide windfall profits to some landowners, while property owners along a bypassed route will suffer losses and even what we have termed wipeouts. Subsequently, a new owner will be willing to pay more to occupy and use a site well endowed with positive externalities, while the price paid for properties that bear a heavy burden of negative externalities will be much lower.

One result is land uses that are patterned geographically because the purchase or rental of the physical commodity, land, conveys the exclusive right to occupy a particular location and to use a particular set of site amenities. One can thus distinguish between the locational value and the amenity value of the property. Both are relative values, in that they involve interdependencies and reflect externalities.

Locational value is determined by relative accessibility to the activity centers that serve as points of focus within any spatial organization; the lines and channels of movement to and from these centers; and the identifiable neighborhoods, communities, districts, and regions that are the essence of human territoriality. At any given time, these are a matter of inherited spatial organization, although over a span of time they will be affected by both public and private decisions. But since different uses have different needs for access to different things, the result is a mix of competing uses that varies from one location to another. As a result, both land use and land value vary systematically with relative location, a product of the desire to be as close as possible to certain things to benefit from their positive spillovers and as far away as possible from others to avoid the negative externalities.

Amenity value is in part a matter of the relative worth to prospective users of the physical attributes of the site, such as a waterfront location, and in part also a matter of the acquired social attributes of the site, such as neighborhood quality. Again, both land use and land value vary systematically with the relative worth of the amenities. Those best able to pay will preempt the better endowed sites and will relegate to those least able to compete the least desirable sites in the least desirable locations.

It is the interaction of amenity value and locational value that is of particular interest. Setting aside the fact that the classical formulations assume only a single center—the CBD—in an increasingly multicentered pattern of urbanization in which access to peripheral locations seems as meaningful as access to the city center, there are still other interdependencies that are important. If, as Alonso maintains, the rich will preempt the periphery, putting expensive homes on large lots and relegating the poor to the city center, there are definite amenity value consequences: status-derived amenities will increase with distance, while poverty- and crowding-related disamenities will decrease with distance. Thus, it was seen in Table 17-3 that income levels showed a strong positive relationship to distance from Chicago's CBD while particulate pollution showed a strong inverse relationship. We thus see the dilemma of intertwined positive and negative distance effects on amenity value that cross-cut the conventional negative exponential CBD-related patterns of locational value. Clearly, a more general framework is required.

THE ROLE OF AMENITY VALUE IN POSITIVE DISTANCE EFFECTS

It is possible to reconstruct the classical Muth-Alonso type of model to achieve the desired result of simultaneously including distance-related locational and amenity values as housing value determinants. First, assume that the consumer's welfare depends on the quantities of housing, H, other goods, X, and amenities, A, he consumes:

$$U = U(H,X,A). \tag{17-9}$$

Adding the budget constraint as before we can write

$$P_x X + P_h(k)H + T(k) - Y = 0, \qquad (17\text{-}10)$$

where P_x is the price of other goods; $P_h(k)$ is the price of housing, which is dependent on K, the distance from the CBD; $T(k)$ is the expenditure on travel; and Y is income.

Lagrangian maximization yields:

$$\frac{\partial U}{\partial X} = -\lambda P_x = 0, \qquad (17\text{-}11a)$$

$$\frac{\partial U}{\partial H} = -\lambda P_h = 0, \qquad (17\text{-}11b)$$

$$\frac{\partial U}{\partial K} = \frac{\partial U}{\partial A}\frac{\partial A}{\partial K} - \lambda\left(H\frac{\partial P(K)}{\partial K} + \frac{\partial T(K)}{\partial K}\right) = 0. \quad (17\text{-}11c)$$

Let P_h be the price of a unit of housing. Then, in order to obtain an observable housing price, $P_h H$, we may multiply in equation (17-11c) by P_h/P_h and rewrite the equation as:

$$-\frac{1}{\lambda}\frac{\partial U}{\partial K}\frac{\partial A}{\partial K} + \left(\frac{P_h}{P_h}\right)H\frac{\partial P(k)}{\partial k} = -\frac{\partial T(k)}{\partial k}. \qquad (17\text{-}12)$$

Thus

$$\frac{P_h H}{P_h}\frac{\partial P(k)}{\partial k} = -\frac{\partial T(k)}{\partial k} + \frac{1}{\lambda}\frac{\partial U}{\partial A}\frac{\partial A}{\partial k}. \qquad (17\text{-}13)$$

In other words, the housing price–distance gradient now depends on two factors, one negative and one positive. The negative term is the familiar transport cost. The positive term involves the rate of change of amenities with respect to distance (along with the marginal utility of amenities and λ).

If constant prices are assumed, λ may be interpreted as the marginal utility of income since, in the general case, we can write:

$$U(X_1, X_2, \ldots, X_n) \text{ and} \qquad (17\text{-}14)$$

$$\Sigma_i P_i X_i = Y, \qquad (17\text{-}15)$$

where the X_i are goods and P_i their prices. Then using the Lagrangian technique,

$$\frac{\partial U}{\partial Y} = \lambda \Sigma P_i \frac{\partial X_i}{\partial Y}. \tag{17-16}$$

From equation (17-15) we know that

$$dY = \Sigma_i P_i dX_i, \tag{17-17}$$

and therefore,

$$\Sigma P_i \cdot \frac{dX_i}{dY} = 1. \tag{17-18}$$

Finally, substituting into equation (17-16), we have

$$\frac{dU}{dY} = \lambda. \tag{17-19}$$

From equations (17-11a) and (17-11b) we know

$$\frac{\partial U}{\partial X} \frac{1}{\lambda} = -P_x \text{ and} \tag{17-20}$$

$$\frac{\partial U}{\partial H} \frac{1}{\lambda} = -P_h. \tag{17-21}$$

Following the analogy for amenities, write

$$\frac{\partial U}{\partial A} \frac{1}{\lambda} = -P_a, \tag{17-22}$$

where P_a is the amenity shadow price. Now equation (17-11c) can be rewritten as

$$-P_h H \frac{\partial P(k)}{P_h \partial k} = \frac{\partial T(k)}{\partial k} + P_a \frac{\partial A}{\partial K}. \tag{17-23}$$

In other words, change in housing prices is subject to two influences—the toll taken by transport costs and the positive effect of amenity values (argued earlier to increase with distance).

Now assume that the amount spent on housing, the transport cost gradient, and the change in amenities with respect to distance are invariant. Furthermore, let us say that $P(k)$ depends only on k. Then equation (17-23) may be rewritten as

$$-\frac{D\dfrac{dP(k)}{dk}}{P_h} = b + g, \qquad (17\text{-}24)$$

where D is the amount spent on housing, b is the transport cost gradient ($b < 0.0$), and g is rate of change of amenity with respect to distance (generally $g > 0.0$). Multiplying both sides of equation (17-24) by dK and integrating yields:

$$-D \ln P_h + C = (b + g)K. \qquad (17\text{-}25)$$

In exponential form, we can write

$$P_h^{-D}\, e^C = e^{(b+g)k}. \qquad (17\text{-}26)$$

Thus,

$$P_h = e^{(b+g)(k/-D)} \cdot e^{-C/-D} \qquad (17\text{-}27)$$

or

$$P_h = \alpha e^{bk/-D} e^{gk/-D}. \qquad (17\text{-}28)$$

This last equation is a form that can be estimated using standard statistical methods. It is not necessary to limit the amenity measurement to a single term. Addition exponential terms may be included with no difficulty.

The Chicago Data Reconsidered

If the foregoing is correct, then we can postulate the following: in the absence of amenity values, housing prices should decrease because of the toll taken by transport costs; however, with significant amenity values that increase with distance, housing prices will vary in a manner determined by the relative influence of the negative and positive components. If the distance exponent is positive, it should be greater in any model that does not hold constant amenity factors than in one that does, and the more comprehensive the accounting of the amenity component, the more likely will be the emergence of a negative distance factor.

This was tested in the Chicago case. For the stepwise models, the beta coefficients and F levels for inclusion of the distance variable in the model were examined after regressing the dependent variables only on subset (1) housing characteristics, then (1) + (2) housing improvements, and so forth (see Table 17-7). As more and more amenity factors were controlled, there was a progressive decrease in the beta coefficient for distance and in the F-level for including distance, indicating that distance was indeed serving as a surrogate for amenity variables positively related to distance from the city center. Or, to put it another way, as one proceeds into the central city there is a progressive increase in neighborhood and environmental disamenities whose toll on property values is far greater than the positive contribution to value of inner city location.

RELATIVE PRICE LEVELS AND MOVEMENTS, 1968-1972

Another way of looking at the amenity–positive distance question is with reference to the Bailey-Muth consumer preference formulation discussed in Chapter 16. In the 1968–1972 period during which the

Table 17-7. Variations in the Standardized Coefficient of Distance with the Addition of Variable Groups.

Variable Group(s) in Equation	Price Model Beta	F^a
(1) Housing Characteristics	0.440	106.09
(1) + (2) Housing Improvements	0.391	92.58
(1) + (2) + (3) Neighborhood Characteristics	0.264	41.26
(1) + (2) + (3) + (4) Racial and Ethnic Variables	0.197	18.49
Price Per Square Foot Model		
(1)	0.471	84.16
(1) + (2)	0.433	78.25
(1) + (2) + (3)	0.366	48.99
(1) + (2) + (3) + (4)	0.253	19.04

[a]F level to enter model as next independent variable.

Leadership Council was struggling to implement its programs, over 10 percent of Chicago's stock of single family homes, more than 30,000 units, changed hands. The greatest concentrations of these real estate transfers were to be found in the zones of black or Latino expansion shown in Figure 17-1, as whites relinquished one neighborhood after another to members of minority groups expanding outward from the traditional ghetto communities within which they had previously been confined. Departing whites moved either to the suburbs or to suburblike inner city neighborhoods, so that a rough concentricity emerged, coinciding with status conscious whites' perceptions of the associations between suburblike residential environments and amenity. Analysis of the full 30,000+ transaction data set enables us to say much more definitively what happened to housing prices as ghetto expansion took place, both within the "cores" of the white, black, and Latino submarkets and in the "threatened" and transitional submarkets, the salient characteristics of which are described in Table 17-8.

As in the case of the pilot study, a series of hedonic price index models was fitted to the data. These models were formulated on the assumption that the market price of a single family home (P) is composed of two elements, the market value of the structure (R) and the value of the lot on which the structure is built (V). The market value of the structure was assumed to be determined, in turn, by the bundle of services provided by the physical characteristics of the housing unit (H) and the improvements made thereto (I). On the other hand, lot value—the product of lot size (S) and land value (L)—reflects services to the household that vary with accessibility (A), with neighborhood characteristics (N), and with environmental amenities and disamenities (E).

In the linear form in which housing price is viewed as an additive composite of the prices of individual services, these relationships may be written:

$$P = R + V, \qquad (17\text{-}29)$$

$$R = \sum_i a_i H_i + \sum_j b_j I_j, \qquad (17\text{-}30)$$

$$V = SL, \qquad (17\text{-}31)$$

$$L = \sum_k c_k N_k + \sum_l d_l E_l + \sum_m f_m A_m, \qquad (17\text{-}32)$$

$$V = \sum_k (Sc_k)N_k + \sum_l (Sd_l)E_l + \sum_m (Sf_m)A_m; \qquad (17\text{-}33)$$

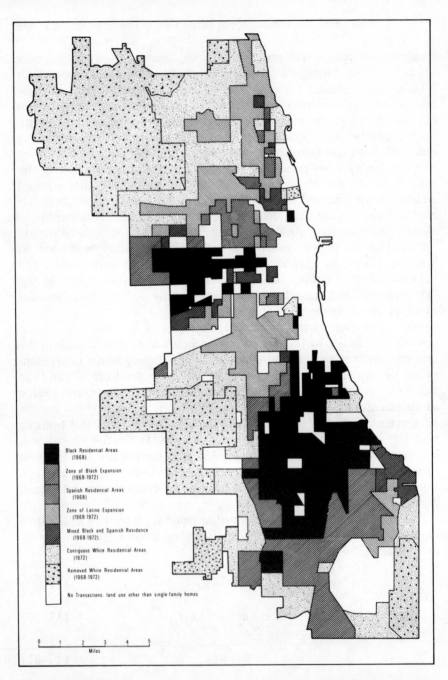

Figure 17-1. Type of Residential Area in the City of Chicago, 1968–1972. Six housing submarkets are identified, based upon continuous monitoring of the racial occupancy of housing conducted by the Center for Urban Studies, University of Chicago.

Table 17-8. Characteristics of Chicago's Six Racial Submarkets.

	City of Chicago	White Neighborhoods		Black Neighborhoods		Spanish Neighborhoods	
				Type of Area			
		Peripheral	Adjacent to Minorities	1968–1972 Expansion Zone	1967 Ghetto	1968–1972 Expansion Zone	1967 Ghetto
Percent Black							
1968		0	0	22	94	5	8
1972		0	0	63	99	8	10
Percent Spanish							
1968		0	1	4	1	6	43
1972		1	3	7	0	24	51
Mean Family Income	10,161	12,693	10,580	9,358	8,366	8,129	7,005
Percent Families Beneath Poverty line	12	<1	17	14	23	11	25
Percent Families in Different House 1965–1970	21	16	17	26	27	21	22
Percent Residences Multifamily	10	6	10	10	11	15	14
Pollution Levels in 1968							
TSP	124	115	122	126	125	134	138
SO_2	83	70	82	83	87	98	105
Average Sales Price Single Family Homes	22,463	27,369	24,324	19,395	18,658	19,794	16,341
Average Annual Price Increase, 1968–1972	3.8	3.7	3.1	4.3	2.8	4.3	5.2
Average Value of Structure	16,330	18,327	17,109	15,298	15,479	14,258	13,391
Land	6,133	9,041	7,215	4,097	3,178	5,535	2,950
Front Foot Land		255	226	133	106	185	113
Average Lot Width		35	31	30	29	28	26

so that

$$P = \sum_i a_i H_i + \sum_j b_j I_j + \sum_k (Sc_k)N_k + \sum_l (Sd_l)E_l$$

$$+ \sum_m (Sf_m)A_m. \tag{17-34}$$

If, on the other hand, P is viewed as a joint product of the bundle of services provided by the housing unit, rather than as a summation in which individual components such as bedrooms add constant dollar value to the residence, elasticities should be obtained by calculating hedonic indexes in the form

$$P = \Pi H_i^{a_i} I_j^{b_j} N_k^{Sc_k} E_l^{Sd_l} A_m^{Sf_m}. \tag{17-35}$$

When accessibility is indexed by linear distance to the central business district (CBD), the negative exponential form $e^{-Sf_m A_m}$ may be preferred, so that:

$$P = \Pi H_i^{a_i} I_j^{b_j} N_k^{Sc_k} E_l^{Sd_l} e^{-Sf_m A_m} \tag{17-36}$$

Equations (17-34) and (17-36) are the fundamental forms of model fitted to the data in what follows. There are further complications and elaborations though. Specific housing characteristics and improvements H_i and I_j were available only for the small sample of the total transactions discussed above. These sample data were used to test whether an available surrogate for the characteristics and improvements—the Cook County Assessor's estimate of the value of the structure (R^*)—could be used in place of these missing measurements. Since the tests confirmed that

$$R^* = \sum_i a_i^* H_i + \sum_j b_j^* I_j, \tag{17-37}$$

aR^* was substituted in what follows for all of the H_i and I_j terms in equation (17-34) and $(R^*)^a$ for all such terms in equation (17-36). Separate models also were run using structure value and lot value as dependent variables to further verify the argument that the former reflects replacement cost while the latter reflects the capitalized value of location, environment, and amenities.

The first goal of the modeling was to isolate the consequences for the selling prices of single family homes of the capitalization into land value of the location of an otherwise standard housing unit in the sequence of the six distinct housing submarkets mapped in Figure 17-1—in peripheral white neighborhoods, in white neighborhoods contiguous to expanding minority communities, in zones of black and of Latino expansion, and in the traditional black and Latino ghettos. To achieve this, in each of the models the last five neighborhood types were inserted into the equations as dummy variables. Thus, the intercept of the models refers to price levels in the peripheral white neighborhoods, and the dummy coefficients provide an estimate of the five other submarket price levels relative to these white areas. The estimates control for structure and other housing characteristics because a stepwise estimation process was utilized— housing variables first, other neighborhood characteristics next, followed by the racial-ethnic variables, and proceeding finally to the residual variance attributable to location and to environmental pollution.

It was but a simple extension of the technique to substitute the rate of housing price increase in the city's neighborhoods between 1968 and 1972 as the dependent variable in the models. In this way, spatial variations in appreciation rates could be related to differences in location, social environment, and the nature of social change to provide properly controlled estimates of price changes in the interior of the white, black, and Latino submarkets, in "threatened" white areas, and in the black and Latino expansion areas to complement the estimates of variations in price levels in these areas obtained previously. Figure 17-2 maps this second dependent variable. Note that the rates of price increase run far behind the Chicago construction cost index for the same period and that most (but not all) run behind Chicago's aggregate consumer price index.

A variety of experimental analyses were performed successively with the 1971 sample data set to enable overlapping variables to be pruned and surrogates to be inserted for missing information in the layer scale analyses of the 30,000+ transactions for 1968-1972. To repeat, the sales price of the transaction came from the tax stamp noted with each title transfer in the Cook County Recorder's Office. This service also provided the data of sale and the street address of the property, as well as the name and address of both buyer and seller. Olcott's *Blue Book of Land Values* provided a front foot land value figure that, when multiplied by front footage taken from Sanborn maps, gave an admittedly imperfect best available estimate of lot value. Subtraction of this lot value from the selling price yielded an estimate of the value of the structure. The Society of Real Estate Appraisers' (SREA) Market Data Center publication, *Chicago-*

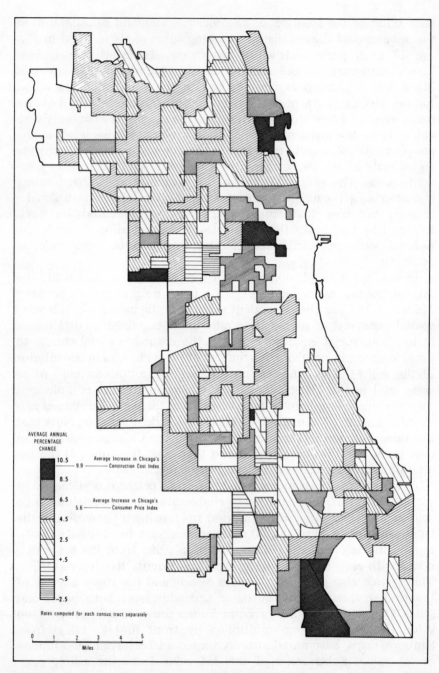

Figure 17-2. Average Annual Percentage Rate of Price Increase for Single Family Homes in Chicago, 1968-1972.

land Residential Sales Data, provided, for the 275 sample properties, twenty-seven different variables relating to type and condition of each of the residences. Quadrennial assessments published by the Cook County Assessor in local newspapers, as required by law, yielded assessed values of the structure and of the land—the former, following traditional assessment practice, supposedly being a constant percentage of replacement cost and the latter supposedly the true value of the land. Many characteristics of the social and physical environment were taken from the census tract statistics of the 1970 *Census of Population and Housing* to enable each property to be related to the census tract "neighborhood" in which it was located. Next, special studies conducted in the Center for Urban Studies of the University of Chicago provided a detailed record of racial changes in the city on a block-by-block basis for the years 1968-1972. Finally, the Argonne National Laboratory's Air Quality Display Model, which uses an "integrated puff" algorithm to distribute pollution from its sources, yielded sulfur dioxide and total suspended particulate pollution readings for each location, as well as a straight line accessibility measure of distance to the central business district.

These variables were tested for their association with each other and for their contribution to the model itself. Once a tentative group of variables was chosen to represent a particular bundle of housing services, a choice concerning the order in which the groups of variables also was made, as outlined earlier. With the sample data, final reduced form models were pleasing both from the standpoint of their power and because of the significance and consistent signs of the individual coefficients, as is revealed in Table 17-9. But more importantly, it was confirmed that tax assessments on improvements did in fact reflect structure characteristics and not characteristics of location or environment, as they should if the latter are capitalized in the value of the land. This finding permitted assessments to be substituted for the mass of Society of Real Estate Appraisers' data in the study of the full data set.

Submarket Differences in Price Levels

The experimentation completed, full data set analysis was undertaken. Sales price and assessment data were assembled for each of the over 30,000 transactions involving single family homes taking place in the years 1968-1972, as were all of the other variables noted in the previous section, excepting only the SREA data set, for which information on assessed valuations was substituted. Transactions were grouped into subsets—first census tracts and then racially and socially homogeneous groupings of census tracts—until 231 tracts or

Table 17-9.   Relationships Between Selling Prices and Housing Characteristics —Detailed Sample Data.

Independent Variables		Price of Property	Assessment on Improvements
		Dependent Variable	
Housing Characteristics	Square Feet	0.336*	0.551*
		0.054	0.098
	Age	-0.123*	-0.267*
		0.018	0.037
	Lot Area	0.128*	0.187*
		0.038	0.070
Housing Improvements	Air Conditioning	0.080*	0.036
		0.036	0.065
	Attic	0.126*	0.031
		0.037	0.068
	Basement	0.074*	0.020
		0.026	0.048
	Number of Baths	0.124*	0.026
		0.052	0.094
	Garage	0.073*	0.083
		0.028	0.051
Neighborhood Characteristics	Median Family Income	0.683*	0.546*
		0.089	0.161
	Percent Homes Multi Family	0.055*	0.021
		0.023	0.041
	Mobility	-0.030	0.040
		0.040	0.072
Racial and Ethnic Characteristics	Percent Black	-0.025*	0.010
		0.006	0.011
	Percent Latino	-0.014*	0.007
		0.007	0.014
	Percent Irish	-0.015	0.14
		0.010	0.018
Accessibility	Distance from CBD	0.030*	0.066*
		0.007	0.012
Pollution	Particulate Concentration	0.415	2.012*
		0.242	0.441
Intercept		-2.061	-12.488
R^2		0.79	0.65

Note: Asterisk (*) indicates that the coefficient is statistically significant at the 0.05 level.

tract groups were obtained, each of which had at least one hundred transactions within it. The rates of price increase mapped in Figure 17-2 were computed for the single family homes within each subset by regressing sales price on the assessment for improvements (to control for the within area differences in housing characteristics) and on the date of sale. The coefficients obtained for the date of sale variable were then converted into annual rates of price increase for average-valued homes within each subset. Average selling prices, structure and lot values, and neighborhood and environmental characteristics were also computed for each of the areas.

These 231 areas were then used as the units of observation in the full data set analysis that followed. Four different dependent variables (sales price, structure value, lot value, and annual rate of price increase) were regressed in turn on an identical set of independent variables in the stepwise fashion described in the successive models in Table 17-10. Both linear and logarithmic models were fitted, except that racial-ethnic types were entered as dummy variables in both forms, and distance to the CBD was entered in negative exponential form in the logarithmic model. The succession of models in each table is designed to reveal the incremental effects of different groups of explanatory variables on the dependent variable in question as well as the effect of substituting one variable for another—poverty levels for income levels, for example.

In Table 17-10, the average market price of single family homes in each of the 231 subareas of the city in the period 1968-1972 is the dependent variable. Approximately half of the variance is attributable to structure characteristics alone (model 1A—the surrogate assessment variable—is the only independent variable in the question). Only a modest increase in power is achieved by adding in three measures of the social environment—socioeconomic status as indexed by income levels, neighborhood stability as indexed by mobility rates, and pressure from more intensive land uses as indexed by the percentage of residences in the area in multifamily buildings, although each is statistically significant (model 1B). However, the power of the model receives a major boost in model 1C, adding in the dummy variables representing the various racial submarkets. Controlling for structural differences, for income differences, and for other variations in the social environment, a residence located in a neighborhood contiguous to a zone of minority expansion apparently sells for $1,633 less than the same residence located in a peripheral white area (model 1C). In the zone of black expansion, the value if $1,314 less, and in the interior of the black submarket, the price difference is -$4,974. Price drops by $3,072 in a zone of Latino expansion and

Table 17-10. Market Price Related to Property, Environmental, and Locational Characteristics.

Independent Variables			Dependent Variable Market Price			
	1A	1B	1C	1D	1E	1F
TOTAL ASSESSED VALUE	3.27[a]	3.30	2.87	2.78	2.80	2.43
	0.22[b]	0.22	0.21	0.22	0.22	0.21
	0.64[c]	0.56	0.52	0.51	0.51	0.41
	0.05[d]	0.05	0.04	0.04	0.04	0.04
ASSESSMENT ON IMPROVEMENTS (Replacement Cost)						
ASSESSMENT ON LAND						
MEDIAN FAMILY INCOME		0.13	0.07	0.07		0.06
		0.04	0.03	0.03		0.03
		0.30	0.20	0.18		0.13
		0.06	0.05	0.05		0.04
PERCENTAGE OF FAMILIES BENEATH POVERTY LINE					-592	
					301	
					-0.08	
					0.05	
MOBILITY: PERCENTAGE LIVING IN DIFFERENT HOUSE 1965 and 1970		-91	-73	-79	-50	-73
		24	24	25	26	22
		-0.08	-0.05	-0.05	0.02	-0.05
		0.02	0.02	0.02	0.01	0.02
PERCENTAGE OF DWELLING UNITS MULTIFAMILY		79	113	135	131	132
		42	42	47	44	43
		0.04	0.04	0.04	0.04	0.04
		0.02	0.01	0.01	0.01	0.01
LOCATION IN: CONTIGUOUS WHITE AREA			-1633	-1579	-1739	-1244
			688	691	688	618
			-0.05	-0.05	-0.05	-0.03
			0.03	0.03	0.03	0.02

ZONE OF BLACK EXPANSION			-1314	-1381	-1239	-1102
			322	239	329	296
			-0.05	-0.05	-0.05	-0.04
			0.01	0.01	0.01	0.01
BLACK NEIGHBORHOOD			-4974	-4953	-4559	-4305
			706	706	772	637
			-0.18	-0.18	-0.18	-0.16
			0.03	0.03	0.03	0.03
ZONE OF LATINO EXPANSION			-3072	-2914	-3301	-1826
			779	795	774	724
			-0.09	-0.08	-0.11	-0.04
			0.03	0.03	0.03	0.03
SPANISH NEIGHBORHOOD			-4767	-4416	-4484	-2985
			1150	1203	1178	1091
			-0.16	-0.13	-0.17	-0.09
			0.05	0.05	0.05	0.03
DISTANCE FROM CITY CENTER				114		81
				114		102
				0.05		-.03
				0.04		0.03
PARTICULATE POLLUTION LEVELS IN 1969						-149
						19
						-0.79
						0.12
CONSTANT	7,618	7,247	11,004	10,322	12,136	28,908
R^2	0.48	0.53	0.64	0.64	0.64	0.72
	(0.51)[e]	(0,61)	(0.67)	(0.68)	(0.67)	(0.75)

[a]Regression coefficient in the linear model.
[b]Standard error of the linear regression coefficient.
[c]Regression coefficient (elasticity) in the multiplicative model.
[d]Standard error of the elasticity.
[e]Coefficient of determination for the multiplicative model.

is $4,767 lower in the interior of the Latino submarket than in the peripheral white neighborhoods. Taking into account differential pollution levels, these price differences become, respectively, -$1,244, -$1,102, -$4,305, -$1,826, and -$2,985 (model 1F). The burdens of environmental pollution apparently bear down more heavily on the Latino neighborhoods, located as they are in the city, close to both the west and southside industrial complexes; a 10 percent increase in particulate pollution produces a 7.9 percent drop in property values in these areas.

Capitalization of the Submarket Price Differences into Land Values

To what extent are these sales price variations a product of variations in structure values on the one hand and lot values on the other? Are the benefits and disbenefits of location and environment capitalized into the value of the land, as existing theory argues that they should be? Tables 17-11 and 17-12 provide the relevant evidence, repeating the models of Table 17-10, but substituting structure and lot values as dependent variables, respectively.

A gratifying feature of Table 17-11 is that the power of the model is destroyed if the assessment on improvements, the assessor's surrogate for replacement cost, is deleted (as in models 2D and 2E). Over half of the variance in structure value (the quality of which is conditional upon the validity of the Olcott *Blue Book* valuations of front foot land values) is attributable to structure characteristics alone, and the only other statistically significant variables are income levels—more affluent residents occupy more expensive structures—and the dummy variables representing the Latino submarket and particulate pollution levels, both of which most likely indicate the miserably deteriorated quality of inner city homes, selling for an average price of $16,300, in areas that were the core of the Latino ghetto. In other words, the values of location and environment are not reflected in structure value, which is exactly what should be expected if structure value reflects replacement costs.

In fact, as Table 17-12 reveals, it is the value of the lot that expresses differences in the social environment, location in various racial submarkets, amenities (as indexed by distance from the CBD), and pollution. The assessor's estimate of land value reflects only part of the true value, however, for he overassesses land in minority submarkets and underassesses it in the peripheral neighborhoods (compare models 3A and 3B); an explanation of variations in price-assessment ratios in Chicago is provided in Chapter 18. Turning to model 3D, and controlling for income differences, variations in stability, and pressure from more intensive land uses, a lot located in a black neighborhood will be valued at $4,363 less than if located in a peripheral white area. $1,535 of this loss in value will be in the zone of black expansion. Similar figures for Latino areas are, respectively, -$2,495 and -$2,394. However, most of the difference in Spanish neighborhoods is due to pollution levels (model 3E).

To summarize the findings to this point, a "standard" single family home in an otherwise "standard" neighborhood will command the greatest selling price if located in the peripheral white submarket. The price will be lower in a "threatened" white neighborhood and significantly less in traditional black and Latino ghetto communities, although much of the price differential in the latter case is apparently due to excessive pollution burdens and structural dilapidation in Latino areas, because the coefficient for Spanish neighborhoods in model 3E is insignificant. Whether or not there is any price increase in a zone of minority expansion to a level above that in threatened white areas is ambiguous, however. Looking at what is capitalized into lot values, it appears that this is not so. Although the sign is in the right direction, the coefficient attached to the contiguous white area dummy is not statistically significant in model 3E, suggesting that lot prices overlap substantially with those in peripheral white areas. On the other hand, the coefficients for both the black and Latino expansion submarkets are large and significant, with negative signs.

Price Movements During Ghetto Expansion

These are cross-sectional comparisons, however, and we have yet to examine the varying rates of property price increase in the 231 areas during the four year period 1968-1972. The evidence is presented in Table 17-13. The power of each of the models is modest at best, but such is the nature of most analyses of change, and it also reflects the fact that all areas experienced similar strong inflationary pressures during this period.

The significant sources of variance were apparently twofold: first, appreciation rates were apparently greater for the lower-priced rather than the higher-priced structures in the city; and second, price changes were consistent with the arbitrage model in the case of black expansion, but were of a substantially different kind for the Latino community.

The first source of variance is to be explained in several ways. First, this was a period in which the Latino population was increasing very rapidly in the most modest neighborhoods in the city. Second, during the period 1968-1971, a variety of federal aids were available to

Table 17-11.   Comparative Structure Value Models.

Independent Variables	Dependent Variable Value of Structure					
	2A	2B	2C	2D	2E	2F
TOTAL ASSESSED VALUE						
ASSESSMENT ON IMPROVEMENTS (Replacement Cost)	2.17a 0.14b 0.42c 0.04d	2.06 0.17 0.36 0.04	2.06 0.17 0.36 0.04			1.98 0.17 0.36 0.04
ASSESSMENT ON LAND						
MEDIAN FAMILY INCOME		0.03 0.02 0.12 0.04		0.05 0.03 0.21 0.06		0.03 0.02 0.11 0.04
PERCENTAGE OF FAMILIES BENEATH POVERTY LINE			-126 194 -0.02 0.02		-336 245 -0.06 0.05	-15 16 -0.01 0.03
MOBILITY: PERCENTAGE LIVING IN DIFFERENT HOUSE 1965 and 1970		-17 16 -0.02 0.02	-11 18 0.00 0.02	4 20 0.02 0.04	18 22 0.07 0.12	
PERCENTAGE OF DWELLING UNITS MULTIFAMILY		1 30 0.00 0.01	4 30 -0.00 0.01	-14 38 -0.02 0.02	-7 38 -0.02 0.02	-1 2 -0.00 0.01
LOCATION IN: CONTIGUOUS WHITE AREA		-503 439 -0.02 0.02	-549 440 -0.02 0.02	-56 557 -0.00 0.06	-140 558 -0.00 0.05	-432 435 -0.02 0.04

	(1)	(2)	(3)	(4)	(5)	(6)
ZONE OF BLACK EXPANSION		-200	-194	-907	-853	-132
		210	218	256	268	210
		-0.01	-0.01	-0.04	-0.04	-0.00
		0.01	0.01	0.01	0.01	0.02
BLACK NEIGHBORHOOD		-917	-880	-1719	-1504	-768
		450	495	566	626	449
		-0.03	-0.05	-0.05	-0.07	-0.03
		0.03	0.03	0.02	0.02	0.02
ZONE OF LATINO EXPANSION		-765	-859	-1742	-1905	-518
		507	507	637	635	512
		-0.17	-0.18	-0.08	-0.10	-0.04
		0.03	0.03	0.02	0.02	0.04
SPANISH NEIGHBORHOOD		-2431	-2439	-3048	-2958	-2102
		765	777	971	986	768
		-0.17	-0.18	-0.20	-0.20	-0.17
		0.05	0.05	0.05	0.05	0.05
DISTANCE FROM CITY CENTER		-77	-80	263	243	-87
		73	76	86	90	72
		-0.01	-0.00	-0.00	0.01	-0.06
		0.04	0.04	0.00	0.00	0.05
PARTICULATE POLLUTION LEVELS IN 1969						-33
						13
						-0.23
						0.12
CONSTANT	8,695	10,219	10,617	14,423	15,177	14,354
R^2	0.51	0.56	0.54	0.26	0.26	0.56
	(0.45)[e]	(0.51)	(0.50)	(0.32)	(0.30)	(0.53)

[a] Regression coefficient in the linear model.
[b] Standard error of the linear regression coefficient.
[c] Regression coefficient (elasticity) in the multiplicative model.
[d] Standard error of the elasticity.
[e] Coefficient of determination for the multiplicative model.

Table 17-12. Factors Capitalized into Lot Values.

Independent Variables	3A	3B	3C	3D	3E
TOTAL ASSESSED VALUE					
ASSESSMENT ON IMPROVEMENTS (Replacement Cost)					
ASSESSMENT ON LAND	4.25[a]	4.25	4.12		
	0.51[b]	0.46	0.48		
	0.76[c]	0.80	0.71		
	0.12[d]	0.12	0.12		
MEDIAN FAMILY INCOME		0.04		0.06	0.04
		0.04		0.06	0.02
		0.46		0.60	0.34
		0.13		0.14	0.13
PERCENTAGE OF FAMILIES BENEATH POVERTY LINE			−272		
			239		
			−0.19		
			0.12		
MOBILITY: PERCENTAGE LIVING IN DIFFERENT HOUSE 1965 AND 1970		−54	−44	−56	−53
		18	21	22	19
		−0.15	0.02	0.01	−0.00
		0.05	0.05	0.06	0.06
PERCENTAGE OF DWELLING UNITS MULTIFAMILY		87	96	204	195
		37	38	42	36
		0.08	0.10	0.11	0.12
		0.03	0.03	0.04	0.04
LOCATION IN: CONTIGUOUS WHITE AREA		−987	−1048	−786	−560
		516	516	605	527
		−0.11	−0.11	−0.07	−0.03
		0.09	0.09	0.08	0.08
ZONE OF BLACK EXPANSION		−1364	−1324	−1555	−1166
		238	247	279	247
		−0.19	−0.19	−0.23	−0.18
		0.04	0.04	0.04	0.04
BLACK NEIGHBORHOOD		−4296	−4118	−4363	−3623
		524	583	615	543
		−0.68	−0.68	−0.68	−0.61
		0.09	0.09	0.09	0.08
ZONE OF LATINO EXPANSION		−2493	−2622	−2495	−1320
		590	587	692	619
		−0.30	−0.31	−0.27	−0.09
		0.11	0.11	0.10	0.09

Dependent Variable: Lot Value

Table 17-12 continued

| Independent Variables | Dependent Variable Lot Value | | | | |
	3A	3B	3C	3D	3E
SPANISH NEIGHBORHOOD		-2102	-2033	-2394	-933
		899	912	1055	935
		-0.33	-0.33	-0.43	-0.18
		0.15	0.15	0.16	0.14
DISTANCE FROM CITY CENTER		277	263	378	285
		80	83	93	82
		0.03	0.03	0.02	0.18
		0.12	0.12	0.12	0.11
PARTICULATE POLLUTION LEVELS IN 1969					-139
					16
					-2.54
					0.30
CONSTANT	1,798	827	1,491	3,026	1,956
R^2	0.23	0.53	0.53	0.35	0.52
	(0.22)[e]	(0.62)	(0.62)	(0.42)	(0.57)

[a]Regression coefficient in the linear model.
[b]Standard error of the linear regression coefficient.
[c]Regression coefficient (elasticity) in the multiplicative model.
[d]Standard error of the elasticity.
[e]Coefficient of determination for the multiplicative model.

enable low income households to move out of public housing and/or rental status into homeownership. Third, there was considerable upward mobility of minorities in the job market, as well. For all of these reasons, one would expect greater pressures on the lower price single family homes in the city, while availability of ample suburban alternatives kept filtering pressures, bearing down hard on the peripheral white neighborhoods.

Looking at the coefficients of the dummy variables, prices increased less rapidly in contiguous white neighborhoods than in the peripheral white submarket, rose again in zones of black expansion, and were substantially less rapid in black neighborhoods, the several intercepts in the linear model being:

- 5.49 percent (the intercept) in peripheral white areas;
- 5.49 percent − 0.58 percent = 4.91 percent contiguous white areas;
- 5.49 percent + 0.33 percent = 5.82 percent black expansion areas;
- 5.49 percent − 1.06 percent = 4.43 percent black areas.

Table 17-13. Factors Related to Variations in Rates of Increase in the Prices of Single Family Homes in Chicago, 1968-1971.

Independent Variables	Dependent Variable Average Annual Inflation Rate, 1968-1972 (X10)			
	4A	4B	4C	4D
TOTAL ASSESSED VALUE				
ASSESSMENT ON IMPROVEMENTS (Replacement Cost)	-.0004[a]	-.0003	-.0004	-.0003
	.0001[b]	.0001	.0001	.0001
	-0.32[c]	-0.27	-0.34	-0.24
	0.12[d]	0.15	0.15	0.15
ASSESSMENT ON LAND				
MEDIAN FAMILY INCOME		-.00001	-.00002	-.00001
		.00002	.00002	.00002
		-0.05	-0.13	-0.05
		0.17	0.17	0.17
PERCENTAGE OF FAMILIES BENEATH POVERTY LINE MOBILITY: PERCENTAGE LIVING IN DIFFERENT HOUSE 1965 and 1970		-.01	-.01	-.01
		.01	.01	.01
		-0.09	-0.01	-0.01
		0.08	0.08	0.08
PERCENTAGE OF DWELLING UNITS MULTIFAMILY		-.01	-.01	-.01
		.02	.02	.02
		-0.02	-0.01	-0.01
		0.05	0.05	0.04
LOCATION IN: CONTIGUOUS WHITE AREA		-0.58	-0.53	-0.58
		0.32	0.32	0.32
		-0.22	-0.20	-0.22
		0.10	0.10	0.10
ZONE OF BLACK EXPANSION		0.34	0.29	0.33
		0.15	0.15	0.15
		0.07	0.05	0.06
		0.05	0.05	0.05
BLACK NEIGHBORHOOD		-1.08	-1.07	-1.06
		0.33	0.33	0.33
		-0.50	-0.51	-0.50
		0.11	0.11	0.11
ZONE OF LATINO EXPANSION		-0.08	0.01	-0.01
		0.40	0.37	0.38
		-0.06	-0.02	-0.06
		0.12	0.12	0.12
SPANISH NEIGHBORHOOD		1.13	1.38	1.16
		0.53	0.56	0.54
		0.24	0.37	0.25
		0.20	0.20	0.18

Table 17-13 continued

Independent Variables	Dependent Variable Average Annual Inflation Rate, 1968-1972 (X10)			
	4A	4B	4C	4D
DISTANCE FROM CITY CENTER			0.08	
			0.05	
			0.23	
			0.16	
CHANGE IN PARTICULATE POLLU-TION LEVELS 1968-1972				0.017
				0.02
				0.15
				0.13
CONSTANT	5.14	5.41	4.91	4.59
R^2	0.09	0.20	0.20	0.20
	$(0.05)^e$	(0.18)	(0.19)	(0.18)

[a]Regression coefficient in the linear model.
[b]Standard error of the linear regression coefficient.
[c]Regression coefficient (elasticity) in the multiplicative model.
[d]Standard error of the elasticity.
[e]Coefficient of determination for the multiplicative model.

This is exactly the price behavior that one would expect if the arbitrage model holds true. In a housing market segmented by race and income, according to the preferences of households for the kinds of neighborhoods in which they want to live and the distribution of income, higher status families apparently prefer to live in higher status neighborhoods and discount housing adjacent to low status neighborhoods because of the likely loss in status imparted by contiguity. Lower status families apparently are willing to pay a premium to live close to high status neighborhoods because of the greater amenities there and because of the neighborhood effect of proximity. Equilibrium occurs when the boundary price is the same for the two groups, but for this to be so, the price within high status neighborhoods must be higher, and within lower status neighborhoods, it must be lower.

However, in the case of Latino expansion, the intercepts revealed in Table 17-13 are:

• 5.49 percent - 0.01 percent = no significant difference in expansion areas;
• 5.49 percent + 1.16 percent = 6.65 percent in Spanish neighborhoods.

In the case of Latino expansion, the arbitrage model fails in several respects. First, there is a high degree of integration of the higher status Spanish-speaking and/or Spanish-surnamed population in communities throughout the city and particularly on the northwest and north sides. Entry of well-educated Latino professionals apparently does not present itself as a threat to white residents. Second, the greater inflation rate in the more exclusively Latino neighborhoods is to be understood not simply in terms of the doubling in numbers of that minority group in Chicago in the past decade, but also in terms of pressures leading to displacement of poorer Spanish families on the north side, as part of the private market redevelopment of the Lincoln Park and New Town areas, and on the west and south sides by the expanding black community. A lower degree of perceived threat, rapid growth, and external pressures thus have all combined to produce different patterns of change in the Latino expansion submarket and in the more exclusively Spanish neighborhoods.

OVERVIEW

To summarize, controlling for housing characteristics, income differences, and so forth, price levels of single family homes in Chicago in the period 1968–1972 were highest in the peripheral white areas, dropped in "threatened" white neighborhoods, showed a modest increase in the zones of black expansion, and collapsed to their lowest levels within the traditional ghetto; the price changes maintaining these differences in levels were less in threatened white areas than in the periphery of "safe" neighborhoods, rose to produce the highest rates of price increase during the brief period of black succession, and then collapsed in the ghetto.

The differential changes in black and Latino areas confirm that a filtering model provides the most general explanation of differential housing prices movements, but that arbitrage mechanisms need to be invoked if the perceived status of a neighborhood group is threatened by the physical proximity and likely entry of another social group, as in the case of whites' racially related aversions to sharing their neighborhoods and schools with blacks. Compared with peripheral white areas, housing price levels were lower in zones of Latino expansion and still lower in the traditional Spanish neighborhoods; price changes, on the other hand, did not differ between the peripheral white and the Latino expansion areas and were higher in the traditional Spanish neighborhoods. The substantial degree of residential integration and the absence of any significant price change in the expansion areas doubtless reveals that Chicago's whites do not view the city's upper status Latinos as threats to their status, while the rapid appreciation within the older Latino areas reflects, as noted earlier, the doubling of the city's Latin population, as well as pressures for conversion of some Latin neighborhoods to other uses. On the other hand, the accelerated exodus of whites from the city did mean "good buys" for minority homeseekers and goes a long way toward explaining why the Leadership Council had so few minority homeseekers willing to integrate distant white neighborhoods and suburbs.

APPENDIX: DATA SET RERUN BY
RACIAL SUBMARKET

An objection has been registered by Robert Schafer[1] to the hedonic price indexes fitted in the preceding sections, on the grounds that single models run for the entire data set assume a unified housing market in which imputed prices of housing attributes cannot vary with location, thus obscuring important racial differences. Schafer argues that if the same models are computed separately for transactions occurring in each racial submarket, important differences in model parameters arise that reveal that, rather than paying less, blacks must pay more than whites for equivalent housing. The underlying theory that he favors in support of the latter view is one of a dual housing market with significant barriers between them such that the structure of relative prices of the attributes of the housing bundle may differ. The cost of comparable bundles of housing attributes may be compared across submarkets, according to this view, by solving the hedonic equations for each submarket and then applying the coefficients to the average characteristics of the properties in each submarket.[2]

Following Schafer's recommendations, we recomputed our hedonic price indexes for each racial submarket. Table 17-14 lists the average characteristics of houses in each submarket, and Tables 17-15 through 17-17 detail the hedonic equations for each, using sales price, land value, and house value as successive dependent variables. If those data are used to calculate what the average bundle of white housing characteristics would cost blacks, the results are the reverse of what Schafer found—that is, they are consistent with our previous

1. See for example, Robert Schafer, "Racial Discrimination in the Boston Housing Market," Discussion Paper D76-6, Department of City and Regional Planning, Harvard University, 1976.

2. Recomputing an earlier study of rental housing in Boston in this way, Schafer argued that, to cite one example, the average central city white area housing bundle cost 28.5 percent more in the ghetto than in white areas.

Table 17-14. Means and Standard Deviations of Variables in the Six Submarkets.

	White n = 71	Adjacent White 35	Spanish 10	Expanding Spanish 35	Black 33	Expanding Black 47
PRICE	27369.52[a] (4785.65)[b] 10.20[c]	24324.06 (4970.06) 10.08	16341.50 (2501.12) 9.69	19901.20 (3795.23) 9.88	18658.63 (2638.61) 9.82	19551.15 (3290.09) 9.87
LAND VALUE	9041.55 (3140.66) 9.04	7215.00 (3627.22) 8.77	2950.00 (457.20) 7.98	5615.71 (3611.15) 8.48	3178.79 (891.76) 8.03	4070.21 (1959.76) 8.23
HOUSE VALUE	18327.97 (3010.21) 9.80	17109.06 (3110.51) 9.73	13391.50 (2131.33) 9.49	14285.49 (2682.76) 9.55	15479.85 (2353.95) 9.64	15480.94 (2256.19) 9.64
TOTAL ASSESS- MENT	5030.93 (879.32) 8.51	4949.54 (1353.06) 8.47	3335.30 (767.68) 8.09	3866.31 (1016.75) 8.23	4449.06 (1168.51) 8.37	4296.96 (1167.12) 8.33
ASSESSMENT ON LAND	968.13 (347.28) 6.83	1087.29 (500.37) 6.91	801.10 (95.46) 6.68	1142.03 (520.89) 6.95	1033.45 (319.80) 6.90	987.79 (410.78) 6.82
ASSESSMENT ON STRUCTURE	4062.80 (740.46) 8.29	3862.26 (1123.18) 8.22	2534.20 (754.01) 7.80	2724.29 (648.63) 7.88	3415.61 (983.48) 8.09	3309.17 (1058.68) 8.05
PCT. BENEATH POVERTY LINE	1.09 (0.44) 0.02	1.49 (0.66) 0.30	5.57 (1.85) 1.66	2.85 (0.98) 0.99	4.31 (2.80) 1.19	2.68 (1.64) 0.82
PCT. OF STRUC- TURES MULTI- FAMILY	34.89 (22.38) 3.23	58.31 (26.93) 3.85	92.90 (1.78) 4.53	86.81 (6.97) 4.46	63.23 (28.99) 3.98	52.04 (28.78) 3.68
DISTANCE FROM CBD	9.98 (1.94) 2.28	8.52 (2.68) 2.10	3.70 (1.07) 1.27	6.04 (1.94) 1.75	8.85 (2.42) 2.14	9.66 (3.01) 2.21
PARTICULATE POLLUTION	107.26 (11.62) 4.67	112.63 (10.45) 4.72	126.54 (1.65) 4.84	120.88 (6.85) 4.79	116.82 (7.06) 4.76	117.80 (11.60) 4.76
RESIDENTIAL MOBILITY	30.61 (6.21) 3.40	35.24 (6.44) 3.54	47.81 (6.00) 3.86	44.84 (7.91) 3.79	49.14 (14.37) 3.85	48.97 (13.63) 3.85
MEDIAN FAMILY INCOME	11448.51 (1784.97) 9.33	10580.23 (1856.82) 9.25	7005.80 (1070.83) 8.84	8163.40 (947.78) 9.00	8366.85 (1965.10) 9.00	9442.98 (1697.92) 9.14

[a]MEAN.
[b](STD. DEV.).
[c]MEAN OF LOG.

Table 17-15. Dependent Variable is Selling Price (and log price).

	White		White Adjacent		Spanish		Expanding Spanish		Black		Expanding Black	
TOTAL ASSESSMENT	1.76* 0.59 0.21	0.07 .70 0.03	2.84* 0.41 0.62	2.63* 0.67 0.56	2.56* 0.94 0.51	3.52* 0.70 0.69	3.21* 0.38 0.55	3.13* 0.43 0.57	1.37* 0.22 0.30	1.37* 0.23 0.30	2.27* 0.35 0.41	2.60* 0.32 0.48
MEDIAN FAMILY INCOME		1.73* 0.43 0.51		0.65 0.65 0.38		-1.57* 0.53 -0.64		1.37* 0.42 0.45		0.17 0.29 -0.06		-0.62 0.36 -0.23
PERCENT BELOW POVERTY LINE	990.96 1194.13 -0.60		-1588.51 799.77 0.08		-479.54 406.47 -0.18		-1273.96* 301.82 -0.17		-254.66 145.36 -0.02		-166.93 263.18 -0.03	
MOBILITY	-15.70 81.00 0.04	161.70 84.57 0.18	57.49 99.61 0.14	37.08 106.89 0.12	197.62 182.61 0.71	154.59 101.95 0.49	65.38 50.85 0.19	113.00* 56.65 0.27	-4.57 15.01 -0.00	1.12 16.03 0.02	-10.35 25.55 -0.03	-16.02 24.23 -0.05
PERCENT MULTI-FAMILY	40.39 32.73 0.03	53.37 28.10 0.02	70.09 36.84 0.09	77.17 47.85 0.10	-520.97 874.73 -3.14	-1986.33* 727.50 -11.11	-62.50 55.04 -0.35	-47.15 56.63 -0.29	21.63 14.61 0.03	26.93 18.46 0.03	33.07 18.15 -0.02	3.20 24.03 -0.01
DISTANCE	304.76 315.14 0.03	88.60 283.95 -0.07	141.92 271.58 0.06	59.68 280.62 0.02	610.15 1377.07 0.15	709.12 781.28 0.23	-520.98* 168.85 -0.12	-536.67* 218.20 -0.13	481.48 290.79 0.25	702.31* 278.68 0.35	90.09 168.47 -0.02	83.32 162.99 0.03
PARTICULATES	-215.70* 41.08 -1.16	-198.87* 37.06 -1.10	-62.81 49.33 0.24	-67.91 51.72 -0.18	320.20 503.84 3.61	1017.21* 365.82 8.75	8.35 109.01 -0.23	-46.03 52.87 -0.59	10.11 50.10 0.06	25.67 53.10 0.24	20.10 28.67 0.05	23.79 27.52 0.10
CONSTANT	38750	21598	12380	5771	6615	61365	16769	4482	7060	196	5776	11245
R² (LIN)	0.46	0.56	0.83	0.81	0.92	0.96	0.88	0.88	0.85	0.84	0.63	0.65
(LOG)	0.49	0.55	0.83	0.82	0.94	0.97	0.84	0.84	0.81	0.81	0.67	0.70

*Significant at 0.05 level.

Table 17-16. Dependent Variance is Land Value.

	White (1)	White (2)	White Adjacent (1)	White Adjacent (2)	Spanish (1)	Spanish (2)	Expanding Spanish (1)	Expanding Spanish (2)	Black (1)	Black (2)	Expanding Black (1)	Expanding Black (2)
LAND ASSESSMENT	3.14*	2.09	1.23	2.56*	1.95	1.64	5.08*	5.29*	1.04*	1.15*	2.90*	3.57*
	0.95	1.42	1.25	0.98	1.09	1.42	1.18	1.19	0.41	0.44	0.75	0.65
	0.48	0.42	0.46	0.57	0.51	0.43	0.87	0.98	0.53	0.52	0.69	0.80
MEDIAN FAMILY INCOME FAMILY		0.34		0.17*		0.06		0.21		0.35*		-0.38
		0.35		0.43		0.18		0.39		0.14		0.27
		0.17		1.57		0.12		0.42		0.65		-0.32
PERCENT BELOW POVERTY LINE	17.50		-2008.81		4.00		-203.97		-242.29*		-150.40	
	783.79		667.43		77.40		37703		69.11		204.01	
	0.36		-0.30		-0.01		-0.29		-0.16		-0.10	
MOBILITY	-48.19	-5.79	98.21	106.38	-28.24	-21.28	-42.25	-42.28	22.55*	22.93*	-12.74	-17.79
	54.01	69.57	100.87	103.46	26.73	31.74	61.48	61.43	7.39	8.19	19.00	18.07
	-0.15	-0.06	0.28	0.31	-0.57	-0.48	-0.06	-0.15	0.24	0.26	-0.21	-0.27
PERCENT MULTI-FAMILY	25.24	39.88	99.79*	125.81*	111.77	132.27	26.37	25.17	-0.15	10.64	5.42	-19.86
	2094	23.88	31.87	37.12	120.05	125.26	54.60	54.13	7.74	9.88	14.45	19.63
	0.06	0.69	0.35	0.38	4.26	4.75	0.09	-0.07	-0.07	-0.00	-0.01	-0.06
DISTANCE	358.51	349.97	684.80*	567.67*	409.75	359.93	228.61	198.98	-150.15	-40.66	-23.08	-28.76
	205.39	201.76	229.72	230.84	246.30	268.54	194.81	218.69	125.79	125.07	123.53	121.40
	0.21	0.16	0.67	0.36	0.51	0.46	0.00	0.00	-0.17	-0.12	-0.07	0.05
PARTICULATES	-142.60*	-143.11*	-125.11*	-119.77*	-112.73	-138.52	-151.00*	-152.75*	4.44	5.25	6.61	11.60
	27.50	27.31	41.15	42.43	104.56	122.54	56.96	55.09	22.31	24.63	21.29	20.50
	-2.33	-2.31	-1.90	-1.39	-5.39	-6.29	-2.18	-2.89	-0.31	0.28	-0.15	0.06
CONSTANT	18293	13805	6389	-8971	5081	6150	16875	14799	2860	-2976	1395	4920
R^2	0.47	0.47	0.76	0.75	0.91	0.91	0.88	0.88	0.71	0.66	0.44	0.46
	0.61	0.61	0.75	0.76	0.94	0.94	0.85	0.84	0.72	0.68	0.49	0.49

*Significant at 0.05 level.

Table 17-17. Dependent Variable is House Value.

	White		White Adjacent			Spanish	Expanding Spanish		Black		Expanding Black	
IMPROVEMENT ASSESSMENT	1.81* 0.54 0.38	1.17* 0.58 0.30	2.39* 0.46 0.53	2.48* 0.59 0.53	2.43* 0.97 0.45	3.05* 0.82 0.56	3.28* 0.76 0.51	2.98* 0.73 0.50	1.29* 0.29 0.22	1.29* 0.27 0.23	1.78* 0.25 0.33	1.84* 0.25 0.35
MEDIAN FAMILY INCOME		0.71 0.27 0.35		-0.13 0.48 0.04		-1.29* 0.59 -0.67		1.29* 0.59 0.73		-0.18 0.29 -0.23		-0.18 0.23 -0.12
PERCENT BELOW POVERTY LINE	-720.21 839.75 -0.05		108.46 751.67 -0.00			-465.73 396.99 -0.23	-1006.89 597.73 -0.11		-16.75 157.95 0.01		-26.16 156.24 -0.00	
MOBILITY	11.43 57.07 0.06	72.76 58.91 0.13	-28.67 93.93 -0.04	-19.76 101.58 -0.05	209.95 188.57 0.94	150.93 127.93 0.56	48.32 76.03 0.06	93.13 78.92 0.24	-24.87 16.18 0.06	-20.13 16.33 0.04	3.48 15.99 0.01	2.99 15.71 -0.00
PERCENT MULTI-FAMILY	9.68 24.84 0.01	12.01 22.75 0.01	-26.47 35.40 -.04	-30.89 40.91 -0.04	-540.43 881.81 -3.99	-1662.54 843.15 -11.71	-120.01 80.83 -0.82	-100.38 79.79 -0.62	26.90 15.21 0.04	20.32 18.37 0.02	15.01 12.17 0.01	6.85 15.76 -0.12
DISTANCE	-74.73 225.34 -0.06	-176.45 215.71 -0.12	-454.46 258.84 -0.24	-449.86 251.66 0.09	275.29 1434.53 0.23	486.88 988.43 0.23	-963.25* 298.71 -0.32	-985.14* 279.18 -0.41	713.39* 318.46 0.38	815.64* 286.37 0.49	109.26 108.21 0.02	107.93 106.82 0.04
PARTICULATES	-60.54* 28.77 -0.05	-46.88* 28.03 0.44	42.29 46.19 0.33	41.29 46.38 0.34	378.23 476.17 5.00	903.67* 402.12 9.83	196.74* 88.16 1.19	165.15* 69.67 1.27	19.13 54.47 0.27	32.03 54.43 0.35	16.83 18.39 0.12	17.40 18.11 0.12
CONSTANT	18299	9624	9362	10551	1117	45790	-1508	-13874	2127	1341	5682	7459
R^2	0.31 0.31	0.37 0.35	0.59 0.61	0.59 0.61	0.90 0.92	0.95 0.96	0.48 0.29	0.51 0.35	0.78 0.74	0.79 0.76	0.67 0.62	0.68 0.63

*Significant at 0.05 level.

conclusions in the unified market model. The average price of the white house is $27,370 ($27,358 from coefficients of model with percent poverty [model 1] and $28,121 from coefficients of model with median family income [model 2]), while those same characteristics would cost $20,179 (model 1 and $19,771 (model 2) in the black housing market. The house value models yield the same sort of results. Average white house value is $18,328, while the black prices are $16,699 (model 1) and $16,190 (model 2). Schafer's assertion, which he apparently documented with rental properties in Boston, is unsupportable in the case of sales of single family homes in the city of Chicago between 1968 and 1972.

To be sure, there are differences in the coefficients of the hedonic price models between the various racial submarkets (in fact, seldom are more than three coefficients statistically significant in each case), but perhaps an alternative explanation should be sought.

The existence of a hierarchy of housing services would go a long way toward helping explain the differences between the black and white models. If residents satisfy their housing needs in some order, it would be reasonable to suppose that the high order services would be of little importance to those who had difficulty buying the more important (low order) housing qualities. If air quality is to be considered a housing characteristic, for example, it does not seem unreasonable to expect it to be a high order quality. It would not be surprising, then, if low income households were unable to reveal a preference for air quality, since their housing budget was consumed satisfying housing necessities. If the model of the black data is in fact a model of poorer homeowners, the regression results behave in the way one would expect. Blacks find the physical characteristics of the home the most important factor, as the size and significance of the regression coefficients indicate. None of the neighborhood, environmental, or access measures is statistically significant, with the exception of distance from the CBD (=proximity to the white community), which supports the consumer preference hypothesis. These higher order housing characteristics are ones for which this poorer group cannot show a preference because of their limited housing budget. The whites, on the other hand, have, as a group, satisfied these basic housing necessities and, still not having exhausted their housing budget, find the other characteristics important and so demonstrate their preferences. The white regression reflects this behavior; environmental quality has a relatively large significant coefficient.

The argument has been advanced that the differences between the black and white models is due fundamentally to a difference in the incomes and housing budgets of the two groups. If this assertion is true, subsamples of the two racial groups chosen to have similar economic positions should behave similarly when analyzed. To test this hypothesis, a subsample of the white data was constructed in an effort to isolate a group of whites whose housing budgets were roughly similar to those of the blacks. Since 99 percent of the homes in the black sample sold for less than $24,538, all white areas with a mean price less than this figure were selected to form a poorer white sample. This new data subset was then analyzed using the same regression equations applied to the black and white data and described above. In this case, the poorer whites behaved much more like the blacks than did the entire white sample.

Chapter 18

The Assessment–Price Ratio: Emergent Inequalities

One of the consequences of the price shifts described in the preceding chapter was the emergence of property tax differentials that bore down most heavily upon minority residents in the city. As selling prices declined, the quadrennial reassessment system was unable to respond quickly enough, and when reassessments were made, the traditional practice of assessing structures at a higher rate than land and of basing structure values on replacement cost rather than market value had the effect of maintaining higher price-assessment ratios in zones of minority expansion, especially since changing neighborhood externalities are capitalized into land rather than structure values. The continuing inequities were a source of discontent from which emerged a move to base assessments upon market values. What we therefore will examine in this chapter is the nature of the variations in the assessment-price ratio in Chicago in 1971 and the likely gains and losses that would flow from introduction of a system of assessments readjusted each year to reflect market prices.

There is a widespread belief that in most American cities that

a clear neighborhood pattern emerges in which poor-quality housing, occupied by low-income tenants, pays property taxes at a substantially higher rate than property in wealthy neighborhoods. Since legislation applicable to each of the[se] cities calls for uniform rates of taxation for all residential real estate, neighborhood rate differentials like these place a tax burden on low-quality housing which, by the standard of existing legislation, is inequitable.[1]

Certainly, significant variations in the ratio of property tax assessments to market values for single family homes (hereinafter termed the assessment-price ratio) do exist between neighborhoods within major cities. Figure 18-1, for example, shows that in 1971 the assessment-price ratio ranged from less than 15 percent to close to 30 percent in the city of Chicago. The lowest values were in a group of near southwest side neighborhoods centering on Mayor Richard Daley's home in Bridgeport, whereas the highest values were in several communities further to the south.

Responding to a growing public outcry about these apparent inequities, led by an aggressive citizen's action program (CAP) and following recommendations made by a Real Estate Research Corporation study group headed by Anthony Downs, the Cook County Assessor announced in 1973 that the assessment system would be changed. Henceforth, "to ensure equity," single family homes would be assessed at 22 percent of market value and other properties at similar uniform rates (apartment buildings at 33 percent of market value, commercial and industrial property at 40 percent, and vacant land at 22 percent).

This chapter therefore explores the question of who is likely to benefit from this change and who is likely to find that his taxes are increased. Factors determining the selling price of single family homes in Chicago are compared with factors related to variations in property tax assessments, to discover the ways in which the market and the assessor differ. The results of these comparisons are then combined to reveal those factors causing variations in the assessment-price ratio whose effects would be eliminated by uniform percentage taxation based on market values.

The technique is to use the hedonic price index for house values developed in Chapter 17 and then to repeat the method of index construction for land, improvement, and total property assessments and for the assessment-price ratio. This procedure enables direct comparison of the factors contributing to the variance of prices with those related to assessments and from this to note significant differences that produce variance in the assessment-price ratio.

The underlying rationale is, to repeat, that any commodity (such as a house) can be effectively disaggregated into a bundle of separately measurable characteristics, for which the relative contribution

1. George E. Peterson et al., *Property Taxes, Housing and the Cities* (Lexington, Mass.: D.C. Heath and Co., 1973).

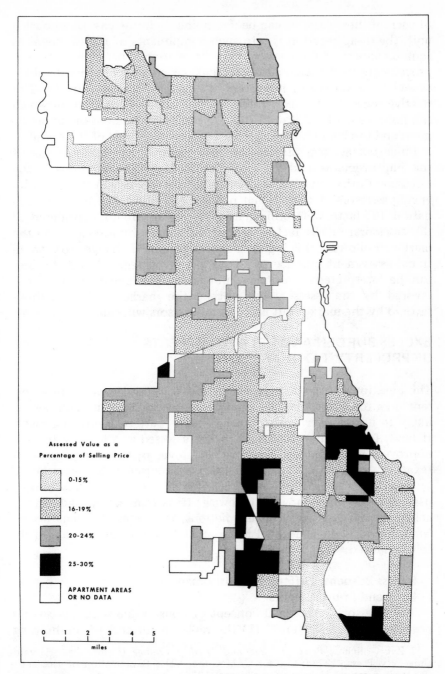

Figure 18-1. Assessment-Price Ratios for Single Family Homes Sold in the City of Chicago in 1971.

of each of these to price can be determined.[2] In the case of a housing unit, the disaggregation is into such components of improvement as square footage of floor space, number of rooms, baths, lot size, improvements to the attic and basement, air conditioning and the like, as well as a variety of indicators of neighborhood amenities and of relative location that contribute to the value of the land on which the improvement is located. It is the combined value of the improvement and the land that is reflected in the selling price of the house.

Since tax assessments are similarly based upon characteristics of the improvements and value of the land, spatial variations in the assessment-price ratio, then, can be attributed to: (1) factors influencing assessors' decisions that play no role in market price determination; (2) factors affecting market prices that are not considered by the assessors; or (3) factors valued differently by assessors and the market. Following this logic, Chicago's proposed change from traditional assessment practice to a constant percentage of market values can be interpreted as a change in tax burdens and benefits—those favored by the assessors but not by the market will lose; those favored by the market but not by the assessors will gain.

EXCESS BURDEN AND RELATED EFFECTS
OF PROPERTY TAX DIFFERENTIALS

The question of who will gain and who will lose is not an unimportant one, for it involves not simply a set of welfare issues, but also is likely to have longer run expression in the pattern of urban growth. If land, for example, traditionally was assessed at a lower rate than improvements, but this differential is removed by uniform percentage taxation, then the "excess burdens" (*sensu stricto*) that were borne by capital and which had the effect of changing the intensity of land use also will be removed. Likewise, if assessments varied among neighborhoods or political jurisdictions, the excess burdens (*sensu lato*) that arose and affected the spatial pattern of growth are likely to be changed.[3]

Excess Burdens: Differential Assessment of
Land and Improvements

The assessor's traditional concept of house value is that it is composed of several elements: (1) the replacement cost of the housing

2. Zvi Griliches, *Price Indexes and Quality Change* (Cambridge: Harvard University Press, 1971); Chester C. McGuire, "The Depreciation of Housing" (Ph.D. dissertation, University of Chicago, 1976).

3. Richard E. Slitor, "Taxation and Land Use," in C. Lowell Harriss ed., *The Good Earth of America* (Englewood Cliffs, N.J.: Prentice-Hall, 1974).

unit, less (2) an allowance for condition of the unit, and (3) an allowance for depreciation, plus (4) the site value. Replacement cost usually is estimated by professional real estate appraisers using a cost approach; detailed building characteristics are accounted at current costs. Site value, on the other hand, is assumed to reflect market value of the site exclusive of the improvements on it, and therefore is a product of the location of the property and neighborhood amenities.

The property tax thus has two components, part of it borne by the capital investments in buildings and land improvements and part of it resting upon the "pure" land value component of real estate values. One effect of the property tax, therefore, is to reduce the return to capital investments required in land utilization by increasing their cost; another effect is to reduce the return to land without any related effects on the land supply. If land is assessed at a lower figure in relation to fair market value than the building and other improvements, as is commonly the case, there will be resulting excess burden effects that produce a decrease in the amount of building and land improvement in the land-capital mix. This, in turn, should produce a centrifugal movement in land use to cheaper land at the periphery. The net effect will therefore be to reduce the intensiveness of land utilization and to slow investment in buildings and land improvements. There will be inducement to build smaller structures, sacrificing the potential benefits of larger construction economies that would permit lower per cubic foot costs, barriers to more intensive vertical land use, and a spur to horizontal expansion and sprawl.

Regressive Nature of the Tax on Housing:
The Issue of Differential Burdens

The property tax on housing also has serious regressive consequences. Exceeding 3 percent of fair market value, it is the equivalent of an excise or sales tax in the vicinity of 35 percent of the gross rental value of the housing unit, which clearly burdens low income budgets and at the same time acts as a disincentive to maintenance and rehabilitation in older neighborhoods, thereby accelerating deterioration and lowering the quality of life for the poor.

Consequences of Spatial Variations in
Assessments and Taxes

When spatial variations in tax assessments exist between neighborhoods within the same taxing jurisdiction, or in the tax rate between jurisdictions, consequences that are a combination of the excess burden effects and the regressive nature of the tax are likely. For example, as noted in a study by Arthur D. Little, Inc., of 228 owners of 420 properties in ten cities, "inequality of tax levels, as among neighborhoods of the same city, may contribute significantly to blight . . . [because] the chance to generate a substantial positive cash flow from property has substantially been destroyed."[4] Likewise, where separate jurisdictions have different tax rates, there is an apparent centrifugal move from the higher to the lower tax area, together with a reduction in intensity of use within the higher taxed area. One source of such interjurisdictional tax differences is, of course, differences in service need. Another is the differential location of property exempted from paying property taxes—shrinkage of the effective tax base by one-third requires a 50 percent increase in the property tax rate on the remaining property to produce the same revenue. Among recipients of exemptions are the following: (1) governmental bodies, federal, state and local; (2) nonprofit organizations; (3) individuals, usually veterans, widows, disabled persons, and senior citizens; and (4) politically favored groups. In each case, the exemption clouds the cost that would otherwise accrue to the tax exempt user from the use of the property, resulting, for example, in greater investments in educational structures or in churches than would otherwise occur. At the same time, both a lower intensity of use and a centrifugal move are indicated for those not exempted. More intensive site development is discouraged; capital is shifted into nontaxed areas including personal property, and there will be less saving because of the reduction in after tax rates of return on all capital investments on a shift from property to financial holdings.

VARIATIONS IN THE ASSESSMENT-PRICE RATIO

Hard analyses of variations in assessment-price ratios are difficult to come by, particularly on a neighborhood-by-neighborhood basis within cities. This is due both to traditional secrecy about assessments and to the difficulty of pairing sales price information for individual properties with assessments and with detailed property characteristics.

One recent analysis of detailed data for the Boston region by Oldman and Aaron concluded that the assessment-price ratio declines with property value in ways correlated with the distribution of political power.[5] However, two other possible reasons for the ratio dif-

4. Arthur D. Little, Inc., *A Study of Property Taxes and Urban Blight* (Washington, D.C.: U.S. Government Printing Office, 1973).
5. Oliver Oldman and Henry Aaron, "Assessment-Sales Ratios under the Boston Property Tax," *National Tax Journal* 18 (1968): 36–49; Atlanta Urban League, Inc., *Report on the Fulton County Property Tax* (1971).

ferences were suggested: (1) that, because of lags in the adjustment of assessed values to changing market values, regions in which values are rising will enjoy relative underassessment, while those in which property values are declining relatively will suffer overassessment; and (2) that assessors, consciously or unconsciously, are influenced by a "benefit principle" in which regions with relatively high population density per dollar of property value, needing and receiving more tax benefits, are taxed at a stiffer rate. In evaluating these alternatives, Oldman and Aaron concluded that to the extent that assessors employ a replacement cost concept in making assessments, properties that the market frowns upon, for special reasons ignored in the assessing process (changing character of a neighborhood, high vacancy rates, presence of negative externalities), tend to be assessed at higher rates. They also concluded that the harsher treatment of low price dwellings was consistent with the benefit principle, under the argument that the residents of low price dwellings do not receive proportionately fewer benefits (education, fire and police protection, etc.) than do residents of higher price properties. The conclusion was strong: "the observed pattern clearly indicates a bias in administration that probably makes the property tax in Boston highly regressive . . . small home owners suffer relative to large home owners." There were "systematic inconsistencies in property tax assessment in Boston, although inconsistency is explicitly rejected by the law."[6]

What of the situation in the city of Chicago? Before 1972, the Cook County Assessor, in keeping with commonly accepted practice, assessed land and improvements separately. No attempt was made to have the assessment figure represent some fraction of the selling price of the property. In the official assessor's publications, the assessor explained that the assessment on improvements was arrived at through the "application of unit building costs based on sound data, which includes determination of reproduction cost (new) of different types of buildings with allowance for age, condition and obsolescence. . . . " If the assessor's method is carried out correctly, neighborhood characteristics, racial or ethnic variables, and environmental externalities should have no effect on the assessment figures for the improvements. Identical physical properties in significantly different neighborhoods should still have identical assessments on improvements. The price of a property, however, may very well be affected by factors of this sort; indeed, it would be surprising if it were not. And to some extent, these factors should, of course, be reflected in the assessment applied to land and therefore in the total assessment of land and improvements, because land is supposed to be assessed

6. Oldman and Aaron, p.48.

on the basis of market value, and it is land value that expresses the benefits and disbenefits of environment and location to urban property.

Several models thus were formulated (1) to explore the determinants of variations in the selling prices, assessed values and the assessment-price ratio of single family homes in the city of Chicago in 1971; (2) to test the assessor's assertions; and (3) to find out what difference the change in the basis of taxation will make. In one of these models selling price was the dependent variable; in three it was assessed values—of the improvements, the land, and the sum of these two, respectively; and in one the assessment-price ratio was the quantity to be explained.

The independent variables included one locational variable (distance to the CBD) and a large group of measurements reflecting the bundle of housing characteristics embodied in a residential property. These housing characteristics were divided into two groups, one including properties of the house itself and another reflecting neighborhood factors. These two groups of variables were then further subdivided, with a distinction being drawn in the first case between "standard" housing characteristics and the nature of housing improvements made, while the second group was divided into neighborhood socioeconomic status and mobility characteristics, racial and ethnic characteristics of the residents, and two indicators of environmental pollution levels.[7]

Parameters in all equations were estimated by single stage least squares, using log-log models, so that the coefficients can be interpreted as elasticities, in a prescribed stepwise format.

Nine identically structured models are presented for each of five dependent variables in Tables 18-2 through 18-6. Table 18-1 summarizes the entire tableau of models that was run. The first four models include, first, basic housing characteristics and, additionally, housing improvements, neighborhood characterisitics, and racial-ethnic variables. The following five supplementary models combine these four subsets with different environmental variables and with distance.

Variations in Selling Prices

The results of the price regressions are discussed in detail in Chapter 17 and are in general not surprising. All of the groups of variables are statistically significant, with the exception of environmental pollution, which is significant only some of the time. (Table

7. The data and their sources were discussed in Chapter 17.

Table 18-1. Cumulative R^2 in Successive Regression Models.

Model[a]	Price	Improvement Assessment	Land Assessment	Total Assessment	Assessment: Price Ratio
		Dependent Variable			
1	0.474	0.440	0.444	0.506	0.115
2	0.568	0.466	0.457	0.518	0.144
3	0.741	0.514	0.647	0.592	0.188
4	0.772	0.521	0.655	0.599	0.236
5	0.772	0.522	0.655	0.600	0.237
6	0.773	0.523	0.662	0.603	0.251
7	0.788	0.536	0.667	0.617	0.240
8	0.790	0.554	0.696	0.645	0.279
9	0.787	0.536	0.666	0.617	0.240

[a]The four basic models are as follows:

1. $D = f[(1)$—housing characteristics]
2. $D = f[(1) + (2)$—housing improvements]
3. $D = f[(1) + (2) + (3)$—neighborhood characteristics]
4. $D = f[(1) + (2) + (3) + (4)$—racial-ethnic variables]

The five supplementary models are:

5. $D = f[(1) + (2) + (3) + (4) + (5a)$—$SO_2$]
6. $D = f[(1) + (2) + (3) + (4) + (5b)$—particulates]
7. $D = f[(1) + (2) + (3) + (4) + (5a) + (6)$—distance]
8. $D = f[(1) + (2) + (3) + (4) + (5b) + (6)$—distance]
9. $D = f[(1) + (2) + (3) + (4) + (6)]$

D is selling price of single family homes in 1971 in Table 18-2, the assessment on improvements in Table 18-3, the land assessment in Table 18-4, the combined total assessment in Table 18-5, and the assessment-price ratio in Table 18-6.

18-2). Furthermore, the signs attached to the coefficients are as expected, with two exceptions that were discussed in detail in Chapter 17.

Among the expected relationships, selling price increases with size both of house and of lot and decreases with age. Housing improvements add to value, but because larger homes are more likely to be improved and improved houses are likely to have depreciated less in value, the elasticities of the basic housing characteristic variables are reduced by adding housing improvements to the model. Housing prices are greater the higher the income level of the neighborhood (a clear status effect) and the greater the proportion of apartments (presumably reflecting land use competition). Again, addition of the neighborhood characteristics variables reduces coefficients associated with size of the housing unit, improvements, and depreciation; higher income neighborhoods have larger homes with more improvements in which the depreciation rate is less than elsewhere.

Table 18-2. Factors Influencing the Price of Single Family Homes.

		Model 1	Model 2	Model 3	Model 4	Model 5	Model 6	Model 7	Model 8	Model 9
	R^2	0.474	0.568	0.741	0.772	0.772	0.773	0.788	0.790	0.787
	Constant	5.113	5.762	-2.641	-1.455	-1.455	-.331	-.410	-2.061	-.347
HOUSING CHARACTERISTICS	Square Feet	.457 (0.058)	.318 (0.069)	.247 (0.057)	.323 (0.055)	.323 (0.055)	.330 (0.056)	.338 (0.054)	.336 (0.054)	.344 (0.054)
	Age	-0.252 (0.023)	-0.209 (0.023)	-0.135 (0.020)	-0.127 (0.019)	-0.127 (0.019)	-0.126 (0.019)	-0.122 (0.018)	-0.123 (0.018)	-0.123 (0.018)
	Log Area	0.308 (0.053)	0.039 (0.050)	0.201 (0.040)	0.163 (0.038)	0.163 (0.038)	0.155 (0.039)	0.123 (0.038)	0.128 (0.038)	0.123 (0.038)
HOUSING IMPROVEMENTS	Air Conditioning		0.211 (0.047)	0.082 (0.039)	0.070 (0.037)	0.070 (0.037)	0.070 (0.037)	0.079 (0.036)	0.080 (0.036)	0.078 (0.036)
	Attic		0.178 (0.051)	0.155 (0.040)	0.149 (0.038)	0.149 (0.038)	0.144 (0.039)	0.122 (0.037)	0.126 (0.037)	0.124 (0.037)
	Basement		0.116 (0.037)	0.078 (0.029)	0.085 (0.027)	0.085 (0.027)	0.084 (0.027)	0.078 (0.027)	0.074 (0.026)	0.074 (0.027)
	Number Baths		0.148 (0.073)	0.152 (0.057)	0.137 (0.053)	0.137 (0.053)	0.140 (0.054)	0.133 (0.052)	0.124 (0.052)	0.130 (0.052)
	Garage		0.068 (0.038)	0.065 (0.030)	0.062 (0.029)	0.062 (0.029)	0.062 (0.029)	0.070 (0.028)	0.073 (0.028)	0.071 (0.028)

		(1)	(2)	(3)	(4)	(5)	(6)	(7)
NEIGHBORHOOD CHARACTERISTICS	Median Family Income	1.019 (0.077)	0.814 (0.086)	0.814 (0.086)	0.820 (0.086)	0.713 (0.086)	0.683 (0.089)	0.720 (0.086)
	Apartments	0.044 (0.022)	0.027 (0.022)	0.027 (0.022)	0.036 (0.023)	0.060 (0.022)	0.055 (0.023)	0.061 (0.022)
	Migration	-0.30 (0.035)	0.044 (0.037)	0.044 (0.037)	0.031 (0.039)	-0.033 (0.040)	-0.030 (0.040)	-0.034 (0.040)
RACIAL AND ETHNIC VARIABLES	Black		-0.031 (0.006)	-0.031 (0.006)	-0.028 (0.006)	-0.022 (0.006)	-0.025 (0.006)	-0.022 (0.006)
	Cuban-Mexican		-0.026 (0.007)	-0.026 (0.007)	-0.023 (0.007)	-0.013 (0.007)	-0.014 (0.007)	-0.013 (0.007)
	Irish		-0.016 (0.010)	-0.016 (0.010)	-0.016 (0.010)	-0.015 (0.010)	-0.015 (0.010)	-0.016 (0.010)
ENVIRONMENTAL POLLUTION	SO_2			-0.002 (0.074)	-0.220 (0.205)	0.033 (0.032)		
	Particulate						0.415 (0.042)	
ACCESSIBILITY	Distance					0.024 (0.006)	0.030 (0.007)	0.023 (0.005)

483

Table 18-3. Factors Associated with Variations in Assessed Values of Improvements.

	Model	1	2	3	4	5	6	7	8	9
	R^2	0.440	0.466	0.514	0.521	0.522	0.523	0.536	0.554	0.536
	Constant	3.227	4.252	-1.734	-1.773	-1.572	-4.068	0.136	-7.694	0.136
HOUSING CHARACTERISTICS	Square Feet	0.727 (0.101)	0.577 (0.130)	0.526 (0.130)	0.508 (0.135)	0.520 (0.136)	0.493 (0.136)	0.541 (0.133)	0.504 (0.132)	0.541 (0.133)
	Age	-0.503 (0.039)	-0.481 (0.043)	-0.383 (0.130)	-0.383 (0.046)	-0.384 (0.046)	-0.385 (0.046)	-0.386 (0.046)	-0.378 (0.045)	-0.376 (0.046)
	Lot Area	0.135 (0.091)	0.107 (0.093)	-0.009 (0.092)	-0.019 (0.094)	-0.023 (0.094)	-0.002 (0.096)	-0.084 (0.095)	-0.064 (0.094)	-0.084 (0.095)
HOUSING IMPROVEMENTS	Air Conditioning		0.130 (0.087)	-0.010 (0.089)	0.003 (0.090)	0.002 (0.090)	0.003 (0.090)	0.018 (0.089)	0.026 (0.087)	0.018 (0.089)
	Attic		0.047 (0.096)	0.060 (0.093)	0.055 (0.093)	0.055 (0.093)	0.065 (0.094)	0.014 (0.093)	0.024 (0.091)	0.014 (0.093)
	Basement		0.087 (0.069)	0.079 (0.066)	0.072 (0.067)	0.066 (0.067)	0.076 (0.067)	0.054 (0.066)	0.054 (0.065)	0.054 (0.066)
	Number Baths		0.183 (0.136)	0.187 (0.130)	0.187 (0.130)	0.183 (0.131)	0.182 (0.130)	0.175 (0.128)	0.146 (0.127)	0.175 (0.129)
	Garage		0.161 (0.072)	0.148 (0.069)	0.159 (0.071)	0.161 (0.071)	0.159 (0.071)	0.174 (0.070)	0.184 (0.069)	0.174 (0.070)

		C1	C2	C3	C4	C5	C6	C7
NEIGHBORHOOD CHARACTERISTICS	Median Family Income	0.699 (0.177)	0.739 (0.209)	0.741 (0.209)	0.726 (0.210)	0.581 (0.213)	0.410 (0.217)	0.581 (0.213)
	Apartments	-0.124 (0.051)	-0.097 (0.053)	-0.094 (0.054)	-0.115 (0.056)	-0.043 (0.056)	-0.072 (0.056)	-0.043 (0.056)
	Migration	0.175 (0.081)	0.116 (0.090)	0.109 (0.091)	0.139 (0.094)	0.006 (0.097)	0.019 (0.095)	0.005 (0.097)
RACIAL AND ETHNIC VARIABLES	Black		0.014 (0.014)	0.016 (0.014)	0.009 (0.016)	0.028 (0.015)	0.015 (0.015)	0.028 (0.015)
	Cuban-Mexican		-0.028 (0.017)	-0.026 (0.017)	-0.033 (0.018)	-0.006 (0.018)	-0.012 (0.018)	-0.006 (0.018)
	Irish		0.017 (0.025)	0.015 (0.025)	0.018 (0.025)	0.016 (0.025)	0.021 (0.024)	0.016 (0.025)
ENVIRONMENTAL POLLUTION	SO_2			-0.049 (0.078)		0.001 (0.001)		
	Particulate				0.469 (0.506)		1.891 (0.596)	
ACCESSIBILITY	Distance					0.038 (0.013)	0.067 (0.016)	0.038 (0.013)

Table 18-4. Factors Associated with Land Assessments.

	Model	1	2	3	4	5	6	7	8	9
	R^2	0.444	0.457	0.647	0.655	0.655	0.662	0.667	0.696	0.666
	Constant	-4.334	-5.009	-14.881	-16.343	-16.397	-20.892	-14.891	-24.533	-14.772
HOUSING CHARACTERISTICS	Square Feet	0.869 (0.095)	0.905 (0.124)	0.583 (0.105)	0.528 (0.108)	0.525 (0.109)	0.498 (0.108)	0.542 (0.108)	0.509 (0.103)	0.554 (0.107)
	Age	0.027 (0.037)	0.055 (0.041)	0.044 (0.037)	0.033 (0.037)	0.034 (0.037)	0.029 (0.037)	0.041 (0.037)	0.036 (0.035)	0.039 (0.037)
	Lot Area	0.607 (0.086)	0.653 (0.089)	0.624 (0.074)	0.646 (0.075)	0.647 (0.076)	0.679 (0.076)	0.593 (0.076)	0.617 (0.073)	0.593 (0.076)
HOUSING IMPROVEMENTS	Air Conditioning		0.104 (0.083)	0.097 (0.072)	0.094 (0.072)	0.094 (0.072)	0.092 (0.071)	0.108 (0.071)	0.116 (0.068)	0.105 (0.071)
	Attic		0.043 (0.092)	0.052 (0.075)	0.062 (0.075)	0.062 (0.075)	0.082 (0.075)	0.026 (0.075)	0.041 (0.071)	0.028 (0.075)
	Basement		-0.010 (0.066)	-0.043 (0.054)	-0.052 (0.053)	-0.050 (0.054)	-0.045 (0.053)	-0.060 (0.053)	-0.067 (0.051)	-0.067 (0.053)
	Number Baths		-0.090 (0.130)	-0.069 (0.105)	-0.065 (0.105)	-0.064 (0.105)	-0.075 (0.104)	-0.070 (0.103)	-0.111 (0.099)	-0.074 (0.103)
	Garage		-0.134 (0.068)	-0.101 (0.055)	-0.072 (0.057)	-0.073 (0.057)	-0.072 (0.056)	-0.061 (0.056)	-0.047 (0.054)	-0.060 (0.056)

NEIGHBORHOOD CHARACTERISTICS	Median Family Income	1.079 (0.143)	1.282 (0.168)	1.281 (0.168)	1.256 (0.167)	1.139 (0.172)	0.938 (0.169)	1.151 (0.171)
	Apartments	0.226 (0.041)	0.247 (0.043)	0.246 (0.043)	0.213 (0.045)	0.291 (0.045)	0.256 (0.043)	0.292 (0.044)
	Migration	0.114 (0.065)	0.093 (0.072)	0.095 (0.073)	0.140 (0.075)	0.004 (0.078)	0.020 (0.074)	0.003 (0.078)
RACIAL AND ETHNIC VARIABLES	Black		0.015 (0.012)	0.015 (0.012)	0.004 (0.012)	0.026 (0.012)	0.010 (0.012)	0.027 (0.012)
	Cuban-Mexican		0.002 (0.013)	0.002 (0.014)	-0.009 (0.014)	0.020 (0.015)	0.012 (0.014)	0.020 (0.015)
	Irish		-0.021 (0.020)	-0.021 (0.020)	-0.018 (0.020)	-0.020 (0.020)	-0.015 (0.019)	
ENVIRONMENTAL POLLUTION	SO_2			0.013 (0.063)		0.060 (0.064)		
	Particulate				0.929 (0.403)		2.357 (0.465)	
ACCESSIBILITY	Distance					0.034 (0.011)	0.068 (0.012)	0.032 (0.011)

Table 18-5. Factors Correlated with Property Tax Assessments on Single Family Homes.

	Model	1	2	3	4	5	6	7	8	9
	R²	0.506	0.518	0.592	0.599	0.600	0.603	0.617	0.645	0.617
	Constant	1.219	1.525	-5.747	-5.824	-5.716	-8.736	-4.215	-12.488	-4.169
HOUSING CHARACTERISTICS	Square Feet	0.782 (0.079)	0.716 (0.103)	0.579 (0.099)	0.559 (0.103)	0.565 (0.104)	0.538 (0.103)	0.586 (0.102)	0.551 (0.098)	0.591 (0.101)
	Age	-0.358 (0.031)	-0.335 (0.034)	-0.269 (0.035)	-0.270 (0.035)	-0.271 (0.035)	-0.273 (0.035)	-0.263 (0.035)	-0.267 (0.033)	-0.263 (0.035)
	Lot Area	0.322 (0.071)	0.321 (0.074)	0.230 (0.070)	0.225 (0.071)	0.223 (0.072)	0.248 (0.073)	0.166 (0.072)	0.187 (0.070)	0.166 (0.072)
HOUSING IMPROVEMENTS	Air Conditioning		0.106 (0.069)	0.005 (0.068)	0.015 (0.068)	0.014 (0.068)	0.014 (0.068)	0.028 (0.067)	0.036 (0.065)	0.027 (0.067)
	Attic		0.047 (0.076)	0.060 (0.071)	0.057 (0.071)	0.057 (0.071)	0.071 (0.071)	0.019 (0.071)	0.031 (0.068)	0.020 (0.070)
	Basement		0.065 (0.055)	0.042 (0.051)	0.037 (0.051)	0.033 (0.051)	0.041 (0.051)	0.022 (0.051)	0.020 (0.048)	0.020 (0.050)
	Number Baths		0.058 (0.108)	0.068 (0.100)	0.068 (0.099)	0.065 (0.100)	0.061 (0.099)	0.059 (0.098)	0.026 (0.094)	0.057 (0.097)
	Garage		0.046 (0.057)	0.047 (0.052)	0.059 (0.054)	0.060 (0.054)	0.059 (0.054)	0.072 (0.053)	0.083 (0.051)	0.072 (0.053)

		(1)	(2)	(3)	(4)	(5)	(6)	(7)
NEIGHBORHOOD CHARACTERISTICS	Median Family Income	0.824 (0.135)	0.867 (0.160)	0.868 (0.160)	0.852 (0.160)	0.722 (0.163)	0.546 (0.161)	0.727 (0.162)
	Apartments	-0.019 (0.039)	-0.001 (0.040)	-0.003 (0.041)	-0.022 (0.043)	0.051 (0.042)	0.021 (0.041)	0.051 (0.042)
	Migration	0.164 (0.062)	0.139 (0.068)	0.135 (0.069)	0.176 (0.072)	0.023 (0.075)	0.040 (0.072)	0.023 (0.075)
RACIAL AND ETHNIC VARIABLES	Black		0.010 (0.011)	0.011 (0.011)	0.003 (0.012)	0.023 (0.012)	0.010 (0.011)	0.024 (0.011)
	Cuban-Mexican		-0.022 (0.013)	-0.021 (0.013)	-0.029 (0.014)	-0.003 (0.014)	-0.007 (0.014)	-0.003 (0.014)
	Irish		0.009 (0.019)	0.009 (0.019)	0.011 (0.019)	0.010 (0.019)	0.014 (0.018)	0.009 (0.109)
ENVIRONMENTAL POLLUTION	SO_2			-0.027 (0.059)		0.024 (0.060)		
	Particulate				0.596 (0.379)		2.012 (0.441)	
ACCESSIBILITY	Distance					0.035 (0.010)	0.066 (0.012)	0.034 (0.010)

Table 18-6. Factors Associated with Variations in the Assessment-Price Ratio of Single Family Homes from Legally Established Norms.

	Model	1	2	3	4	5	6	7	8	9
	R^2	0.115	0.144	0.188	0.236	0.237	0.251	0.240	0.279	0.240
	Constant	-3.895	-4.237	-3.106	-4.369	-4.270	-8.355	-3.805	-10.427	-3.822
HOUSING CHARACTERISTICS	Square Feet	0.325 (0.072)	0.399 (0.093)	0.332 (0.096)	0.236 (0.097)	0.242 (0.098)	0.208 (0.097)	0.248 (0.098)	0.215 (0.095)	0.247 (0.097)
	Age	-0.106 (0.028)	-0.127 (0.031)	-0.134 (0.034)	-0.143 (0.033)	-0.144 (0.033)	-0.147 (0.033)	-0.141 (0.033)	-0.143 (0.032)	-0.141 (0.033)
	Lot Area	0.015 (0.065)	0.012 (0.067)	0.029 (0.068)	0.062 (0.067)	0.060 (0.068)	0.093 (0.068)	0.042 (0.069)	0.059 (0.068)	0.042 (0.069)
HOUSING IMPROVEMENTS	Air Conditioning		-0.106 (0.063)	-0.077 (0.065)	-0.055 (0.064)	-0.055 (0.064)	-0.056 (0.064)	-0.051 (0.065)	-0.044 (0.063)	-0.051 (0.064)
	Attic		-0.131 (0.069)	-0.096 (0.068)	-0.091 (0.067)	-0.091 (0.067)	-0.073 (0.067)	-0.103 (0.068)	-0.095 (0.066)	-0.103 (0.068)
	Basement		-0.050 (0.050)	-0.045 (0.049)	-0.049 (0.048)	-0.052 (0.048)	-0.043 (0.047)	-0.055 (0.049)	-0.054 (0.047)	-0.054 (0.048)
	Number Baths		-0.090 (0.098)	-0.084 (0.096)	-0.070 (0.094)	-0.072 (0.094)	-0.078 (0.093)	-0.074 (0.094)	-0.098 (0.092)	-0.073 (0.094)
	Garage		-0.022 (0.051)	-0.018 (0.051)	-0.003 (0.051)	-0.003 (0.051)	-0.004 (0.050)	0.001 (0.051)	0.010 (0.050)	0.001 (0.051)

		(1)	(2)	(3)	(4)	(5)	(6)	(7)
NEIGHBORHOOD CHARACTERISTICS	Median Family Income	-0.194 (0.130)	0.053 (0.150)	0.054 (0.151)	0.032 (0.150)	0.008 (0.156)	-0.137 (0.157)	0.006 (0.155)
	Apartments	-0.063 (0.038)	-0.026 (0.038)	-0.024 (0.038)	-0.057 (0.040)	-0.010 (0.041)	-0.034 (0.040)	-0.010 (0.041)
	Migration	0.194 (0.060)	0.095 (0.064)	0.091 (0.065)	0.145 (0.067)	0.056 (0.072)	0.070 (0.070)	0.056 (0.072)
RACIAL AND ETHNIC VARIABLES	Black		0.041 (0.010)	0.042 (0.010)	0.031 (0.011)	0.046 (0.011)	0.035 (0.011)	0.046 (0.011)
	Cuban-Mexican		0.004 (0.012)	0.004 (0.012)	-0.005 (0.013)	0.010 (0.013)	0.007 (0.013)	0.010 (0.013)
	Irish		0.025 (0.018)	0.024 (0.018)	0.027 (0.018)	0.025 (0.018)	0.029 (0.017)	0.025 (0.018)
ENVIRONMENTAL POLLUTION	SO_2			-0.025 (0.056)		-0.009 (0.058)		
	Particulate				0.815 (0.355)		1.598 (0.429)	
ACCESSIBILITY	Distance					0.011 (0.010)	0.036 (0.012)	0.011 (0.010)

The fourth model indicates that part of the neighborhood effect also is expressed in racial-ethnic terms. While parameters of few of the housing variables shift when the fourth subset is added to the model, the income and apartment coefficients are reduced, and the sign of the migration variable is shifted, indicating that the racial-ethnic groups selected are disproportionately concentrated in the lower income categories and in neighborhoods with a higher apartment mix and in which mobility rates are high.

Each of the models that includes distance as a variable reveals that there is a statistically significant incremental effect of location with respect to the CBD on housing prices. This distance effect is, however, strongly correlated with other neighborhood patterns, as noted earlier. Inclusion of the distance variable (1) reduces the income coefficient (higher income neighborhoods ring the periphery of the city); (2) increases the apartments coefficient (higher density neighborhoods are more central); and (3) reverses the migration coefficient (lower mobility neighborhoods are farther out).

The first set of variables with unexpected signs are the racial-ethnic variables, particularly the percentage of black neighborhood residents, and the second sign which is different than expected is the positive sign attached to distance from CBD. Both of these cases were discussed in Chapter 17.

Variations in Assessments on Improvements

If the assessor's claims about the basis for calculating the building assessment are correct, one would expect many of the housing characteristics to be significant in similar regressions, but few if any of the other variables (except to the extent that they are correlated with housing size and improvements). To some extent this is true (see Table 18-3)—very little is added to the explanation by the third or subsequent models. Size of house, age, and the addition of garages are all significant with the expected sign. Furthermore, all three neighborhood characteristics enter the model with significant coefficients, but in every case become insignificsnt in one or more of the later models. In the case of the apartment and migration variables, it appears that they serve as a surrogate for the racial and ethnic variables, since both of their coefficients decrease markedly and become statistically insignificant when the racial and ethnic measurements enter the formulation (note that the coefficient for blacks is now positive). In the case of income levels, only the model including both distance and particulates results in a coefficient for income that is smaller than in the other models and statistically insignificant. But since income measures many of the household improvements and the amenities one usually associates with wealthier neighborhoods, and the wealthier neighborhoods are located farther out from the CBD, this is not altogether unexpected. Improvements are assessed on the basis of their quantity, nature, and quality, and reflecting the geography of the city, distance also is significant with a positive coefficient, because prices vary positively with distance, as do many amenities.

Variations in Assessments on the Land

Land assessments should reflect the quantity of land consumed, relative location, and neighborhood amenities. This is the case here. Lot area and square footage of the house, highly correlated with each other, are statistically significant with positive coefficients (see Table 18-4). No housing improvement variable is significant and neither are the racial-ethnic variables except when controlling for distance. On the other hand, highlighting the historical-locational structure of the city, the coefficient of age is positive; land developed at an earlier date has a higher value.

Holding quantity constant, both neighborhood characteristics and distance are highly significant. If income can be thought of as a surrogate for amenity values usually associated with higher income neighborhoods, then its positive significant coefficient is not difficult to explain. Lots in wealthier neighborhoods should be more desirable and thus merit a higher land assessment since, according to the assessor, the land assessment reflects the market value of the parcel. The same argument holds true for the locational value, distance. Recall that this variable's coefficient also was positive in the price model and that it was suggested that this relationship was due to the manner in which amenities vary with distance from the CBD. The positive sign on the coefficient for apartments also seems reasonable, since the presence of many apartment buildings in an area indicates a more intensive use of the land and therefore higher land values. Perhaps the garage coefficient serves as another measurement of the intensity of land use. If it is economically sensible to use land for garages, the value of the land cannot be too great. Therefore the negative sign attached to the variable seems reasonable. This explanation is supported by the fact that the coefficient drops from −0.134 to −0.099 and loses statistical significance when the apartments variable enters the model with a positive sign.

The coefficients for the black and particulates variables are a little more difficult to explain. Theoretically, race should have no effect on the land assessment, and thus, one would expect the variable to be insignificant in the model. In several of the formulations it is, but when distance enters the model in the absence of particulates, the coefficient is positive and significant. Since the black variable's simple correlation with particulates is 0.50, it may be that it serves as a surrogate for the pollution measure and gains some of its significance from the relationship between the land assessment and particulates. In the case of the pollution variable itself, its high degree of correlation with distance from CBD (simple correlation coefficient of −0.74) makes its true relationship with the dependent variable difficult to ascertain. The coefficient remains positive and significant (at more than the 0.05 level) with or without distance in the equation. It may be that this variable is serving as a proxy for access or proximity to industrial and/or commercial areas. The lots in these areas could be expected to be more valuable, and thus the positive coefficient might not be so surprising.

Variations in Total Assessments

When the same independent variables are used to explain the sum of the two assessments, the results are quite interesting. First, all of the housing characteristic variables are significant in all of the models as one should expect from the assessor's statement. After all, these basic physical properties should be very important in the calculation of any assessment figure, especially one depending heavily on replacement value.

Equally, many of the neighborhood variables also are significant. Median family income is statistically significant at better than the 0.01 level in all of the models. This is the same result found in the two previous assessment models, and the reasons for it are probably the same. The migration variable enters the equation significantly but loses its explanatory power when distance enters, because, as noted before, migration rates vary with distance from the CBD.

Two other variables are sometimes significant. Both, however, are strongly correlated with distance, which causes their coefficients to vary in importance depending upon whether the distance measure is in the equation. The black variable (simple correlation with distance of −0.40 and with particulates of 0.50) is significant when only distance is in the equation but not when both distance and particulates are included. Apparently the combination of distance and particulates explains much of black's variation, so that the racial variable adds little to the model over and above the other two. The pollution measure—particulates—behaves in a similar manner. Its simple correlation coefficient with respect to distance is −0.74, and as expected, distance greatly affects its coefficient. Without the distance variable, the particulates coefficient is 0.596 and insignificant. When distance enters, however, the coefficient jumps to 2.012 and becomes significant at better than the 0.01 level. It would seem that particulates is serving as a surrogate for some other factor excluded from the model, since, if the coefficient's positive sign is interpreted naively, the model indicates that housing units subjected to heavier pollution are assessed at a higher rate than those in cleaner neighborhoods. Perhaps this pollution variable is really measuring proximity to industry or commercial tracts that the assessor feels are likely to be converted to "higher and better" uses. Unfortunately, determining the true relationship between particulates and the dependent variable is very difficult since the pollution measure has a correlation coefficient of more than 0.25 (absolute value) with seven of the other independent variables.

Variations in the Assessment-Price Ratio

If assessment practice had responded to market values in Chicago in 1971, one would expect roughly similar statistical relationships in the models that were formulated to explain variations in the selling price and the total assessments on single family homes. Further, to the extent that this is true, one would also expect an identical set of dependent variables to have very little explanatory power in a model using the assessment-price ratio as a dependent variable, since the same factors would influence both numerator and denominator of the ratio and should presumably, cancel each other out.[8]

In many respects, this expectation is borne out by the results presented in Table 18-6. Many of the most powerful variables in the earlier equations, such as income levels, are statistically insignificant in the assessment-price ratio model, and the explanatory power of all nine models is low. Either other sources of much of the variance in the ratio must be sought, or one must admit to considerable random variation in assessment-price ratios. In most cases, the market and the assessor agree.

8. In log-log models, if $P = b + b_1 X_1 + b_2 X_2$, and $A = c + c_1 X_1 + c_2 X_2$, then $A/P = d_0 + d_1 X_1 + d_2 X_2$ with $d_0 = c_0 - b_0$, $d_1 = c_1 - b_1$, and $d_2 = c_2 - b_2$. Thus, the values of the coefficients in Table 18-6 are the differences between the values presented in Table 18-5 (the assessment models) and those in Table 18-2 (the price models), even though they were calculated by regression methods rather than by taking the differences. To cite one example, the coefficient for square foot in model 9 is 0.344 in Table 18-2, 0.591 in Table 18-5, and 0.247 (i.e., 0.591 - 0.344) in Table 18-6. The interpretation is that the market values a 10 percent increase in square footage with a 3.4 percent increase in price, whereas the assessor raises the assessment by 5.9 percent, and the assessment-price ratio therefore increases by 2.47 percent.

There are, however, some exceptions. For example, both size and age of housing unit are statistically significant: the positive sign indicates that assessments tend to run ahead of market prices for larger units (a pattern not related to improvements or income), and the negative sign reveals that the assessor depreciates property more rapidly than does the market.

A clear racial pattern also exists. The black variable is significantly positive in all nine formulations of the model. This suggests that not only are blacks assessed at higher rates, holding property characteristics constant, but that they are either overassessed in terms of the market value of their property or that assessment practice has not caught up with declining housing prices in black residential areas. The small standard error of black's coefficient and its stability suggest that the relationship between black and the dependent variable indicated by the coefficient is real and relatively precise.

The only cases where the black coefficient varies are those in which it appears in combination with the variables for migration, particulate pollution, and distance. The combinations of these variables indicate that the assessment-price ratio is greatest in black residential areas with relatively high mobility rates, in zones of substantial particulate pollution at some distance from the CBD. These are exactly those southside areas shaded full black in Figure 18-1; at the time of the 1970 census, these were the areas completing racial transition from white to black, and they were also reassessed in 1970 and 1971. One must conclude either that the reassessment represented use of some unknown combination of racial prejudice and the benefit principle on the part of the assessors (black immigration tends to replace aging white communities with child-rearing black families having escalating educational needs, for example) or that selling prices of single family homes have declined relative to those in other areas of the city (i.e., increased less rapidly), so that assessment practice lags behind actual price movements in the market.

Some element of racial prejudice cannot be denied, just as one is led to suspect favoritism on the part of the political machine. The low assessment-price ratio in Mayor Daley's Bridgeport neighborhood already has been noted; other low spots in Figure 18-1 correspond with the home neighborhoods of several other "machine" aldermen (although the "core" machine neighborhoods also tend to be neighborhoods of owners of small, relatively old homes—a combination reflected in the square foot and age variables). But, as noted earlier, the evidence of changing market conditions for black families in Chicago also is clear; removal of supply constraints and rapid departure of Chicago's white community to the suburbs has meant that black homeowners pay less than whites in the city for comparable units, but, for whatever reason, pay more property taxes in relation to market value. Black homeowners, then, had the most to gain from the change in assessment practices, whereas nonblack owners of the smallest oldest homes (the embattled blue collar white ethnics) had the most to lose.

Afterword

In the south they don't care how
close you are just so long as you
don't get too big; in the north they
don't care how big you are so long
as you don't come close.

                              Dick Gregory

Responding to the agenda of an earlier decade, the well-intentioned programs of the Leadership Council were unable to achieve their primary goal, the transformation of a dual housing market into a color-blind one in which the entire stock of housing in the metropolitan area was available to all of its citizens, regardless of race, on a nondiscriminatory basis. White central city residents refused to share their neighborhoods with blacks, withdrawing to the expanding suburban periphery. Most middle class black residents, finding an increasing array of housing opportunities at attractive prices in city neighborhoods abandoned by whites, were not inclined to become pioneer integrationists as they moved out of the traditional ghetto areas within which they had been confined.

There were exceptions, to be sure, and where whites overtly discriminated against black homeseekers, the council's legal action program became increasingly successful in getting satisfaction on a case-by-case basis. A body of open housing law was codified as a result. And other offshoots of the summit agreement were taking hold. For example, the Home Investments Fund, the Chicago Conference on Religion and Race's Housing Program, was indeed financing a growing number of black homeowners in suburbia. In 1975, 186 minority families were aided in moving into suburban homes (for a total of 671 families assisted in moving into ninety different suburban towns in the period 1969–1975) as a result of the provision of some combination of first mortgages, counseling, or downpayment loans.[1]

By middecade, too, there were signs of a modest relaxation of suburbanites' attitudes; many of Chicago's suburbs proudly displayed their one or two black tokens. The greatest growth of black moveins was in the newest residential areas, especially Park Forest South and Bolingbroke. Park Forest South, as a condition of its new town bond guarantee from HUD, was required to have a black percentage of at least that of the Chicago metropolitan area as a whole. In 1970 the black percentage was 3 percent, growing to 8.6 percent in 1972 and 16 percent in 1974. At that point white demand collapsed, and in the weaker housing market of the mid 1970s, the community went into federal receivership and showed signs of resegregating. Bolingbroke had only one black resident in 1970, but 161 in 1974.

Within Chicago, a special study by the Chicago Urban League completed in 1977[2] revealed that the ghetto had swept all the way to the southern city limits. Father Lawlor's defensive wall along Ashland Avenue had been breached all the way from 55th to 87th streets, and the new western edge of the ghetto was Western Avenue. Only the ridge in Beverly Hills and Morgan Park, where black brokers still found it very difficult to obtain listings, remained white. To the southeast, black expansion had circled Lake Calumet and reached the Calumet River. Across the city boundary, Calumet Park was gearing up to respond to prospective racial change with a program of managed integration while fear increased in neighboring Blue Island and Riverdale. These three are the only remaining white communities between the expanding Southside ghetto and the black suburbs of Dixmoor and Phoenix, biracial Harvey (already in the throes of polarization) and, beyond Homewood and Flossmoor, the old ghetto of Chicago Heights and, astride the southern Cook County boundary,

1. *Annual Report* of the Home Investments Fund for fiscal year 1975 (July 1, 1974 to June 6, 1975). FY 75 was the second year of HIF's affiliation with the Leadership Council, assuming the previously defunct role of the Leadership Council's Fair Housing Center. Potential client inquiries had grown, with demonstrated achievement, from 400 in FY 69 to 1,360 in FY 75. Much of HIF's efforts took place through a network of local fair housing centers, however, rather than through an open housing market.

2. *Where Blacks Live: Race and Residence in Chicago in the 1970's* (Chicago: Chicago Urban League, Spring 1978).

Park Forest and Park Forest South. The southside ghetto had expanded more than three miles, wavelike, across a succession of formerly white communities in scarcely more than a decade. At the same pace, it seemed destined to link up with Dixmoor and Phoenix before 1990 as the intervening suburbs resegregated.

On the west side, there was similar expansion of close to three miles, to reach the western city limits abutting Cicero and Oak Park and then moving north and west to North Avenue. Cicero adamantly resisted black entry, while Oak Park tried to preserve mixing by an implicit quota system; both approaches apparently led some blacks to skip these communities and to move into Bellwood and Maywood instead.

Ghetto expansion continued even though black population growth leveled off after 1970. The black population had been 812,000 in 1960 and 1,102,000 in 1970. By 1977, it was estimated to be only 1,184,000, as black immigration to Chicago came to a halt and then reversed. Meanwhile, the continuing white exodus from the central city resulted in a very soft inner city housing market and the depopulation and virtual abandonment of many areas within the pre-1960 ghetto limits.

Only on the north side was there evidence of increased mixing, both of blacks and Latinos within the expanding Spanish communities and in the apartment complexes edging the Lake that catered to young professional Chicagoans. It was in these areas, in particular, that the Leadership Council's Legal Action Program enabled many aggressive young black professionals to contest discriminatory behavior and to secure apartments that would formerly have been unavailable to them.

One dramatic consequence was that the new housing opportunities in new neighborhoods produced progressively more pronounced residential segregation *within* the ghetto: "within the Negro Community, there appears to be a deepening schism between the able and the less able, between the well-prepared and those with few skills."[3] For the black middle class, increasingly able to satisfy its mobility aspirations, the Leadership Council's programs became unnecessary; for the poverty-stricken black lower class that was being left behind they were irrelevant—satisfaction of basic needs had higher priority.

The remarkable coalition of black interests melded by the Rev. Dr. Martin Luther King, Jr. began to distintegrate, and such organizations as the Chicago Urban League, abandoned by the middle class, lashed

3. Andrew Brimmer, "Economic Progress of Negroes in the United States: The Deepening Schism" (Speech, Tuskegee Institute, March 22, 1970), p. 3.

out in frustration and anger. Trying to reactivate the old coalition, they reported in 1977 that:

> During the mid 1970s the economic conditions being experienced by black Chicagoans are so abysmal, so pervasive, and so starkly inferior to those facing whites in the region that they are having an insideously debilitating effect on the social, cultural, psychological, as well as material well-being of virtually the entire local black community. The causes and consequences of these economic conditions are sufficiently understood and so unequivocally devastating that fundamental changes in economic structure and policy at every level of institutional power and decision-making appear to be the only hope for escaping the present state of degradation and despair which permeates black Chicago.[4]

But the league's policy recommendations hardly seemed destined to induce the black middle class to rejoin the coalition:

> 1. The government at all levels should abandon its basic assumption that the stimulation of suburban construction is a viable means of enlarging and improving the housing stock available to the urban poor. Suburban building benefits the construction industry and middle class whites. *It also benefits an increasing number of middle class blacks* who were discovering, especially in the years since 1970, that very few Chicago suburbs are closed to them any longer.[5] (Emphasis added)

Apparently, to try to recapture the black solidarity of the late 1960s the league was willing to sacrifice the very programs that had laid the foundations for black middle class progress. The old battle cries were resounded: "The forces which fuel resegregation—excessive suburban building which draws whites out of the city, persistent shortages of decent housing in black residential areas, and a social climate in which integration is viewed with suspicion—are likely to continue unabated."[6] Those who argued otherwise were excoriated.[7]

4. *The Current Economic Status of Chicago's Black Community* (Chicago: Chicago Urban League, January 1977).

5. *The Black Housing Market in Chicago. A Reassessment of the Filtering Model* (Chicago: Chicago Urban League, Spring 1977), p. 70.

6. *The Current Economic Status of Chicago's Black Community*, p. 21.

7. Parenthetically, much of *The Black Housing Market in Chicago* was a lame attempt to debunk the analysis reported in Chapter 17. The league went to great lengths in its attempts to demonstrate that continuing shortages of decent housing have resulted from too slow a pace of transfer of properties from white to black ownership, and that, as a consequence, price differentials consistent with the race tax hypothesis persist. Unfortunately, the analysis undertaken by the Urban League staff was of doubtful validity. Regression analyses of census tract data from the 1970 census were run without controlling for property characteristics and without due care about choice of model, to list the least egregious of their many errors.

There was a continuing attachment to integration as the only means
to achieve equality:

2. . . . The only alternative to continuation of . . . racial turnover of entire
neighborhoods, is a program to ensure that adequate opportunities for
home purchase are available to blacks throughout the metropolitan area.[8]

And, to get closer to the immediate agenda of the residual clientele:

3. There is . . . a desperate need for stable neighborhoods and suitable
housing. There is a need for both low income housing, which probably
must involve some form of government subsidy, and housing for those
of middle and moderate income. . . . Actions must be taken . . . to preserve neighborhoods. . . . This would require: a) A halt to systematic
disinvestment in black neighborhoods . . . b) Government programs aimed
at strengthening the fabric of the community . . . c) Community or-
anizations should become more involved in the preservation of their
communities. . . . [9]

In Chicago the black homeownership rate was increasing rapidly,[10]
and the departure of the black middle class to newly vacated white
neighborhoods or to the suburbs produced interests in conflict with
those of the poor black community left behind. To those black
leaders who believed that they could still appeal to the wide spectrum welded into an active coalition by Rev. Dr. Martin Luther King,
Jr., the schism was a threat. The Chicago Urban League found itself
serving the poverty-stricken half of the black community and facing
rising unemployment among youth, pressures of inflation on welfare
checks, fear, crime, drug abuse, and the economic and physical
collapse of the oldest ghetto neighborhoods, and it lashed out in
frustration.

Not only in Chicago, but nationwide, the black middle class was
also in full flight: "The number of blacks living in suburbs increased
by 34 percent between 1970 and 1977. . . . Black migration to the
suburbs accelerated between 1975 and 1977 and accounts for 14 per
cent of the net increase in suburban population attributable to
migration, compared with only 7 percent in 1970-75."[11] The nation-

8. Ibid., pp. 70-71.
9. Ibid., pp. 71-72.
10. For related findings based upon a national sample, see Wilhelmina Leigh,
"An Analysis of Differential Rates of Change in Housing Consumed in the U.S.
by Race and Income Groups, 1960-1970," Discussion Paper D78-1, Department
of City and Regional Planning, Harvard University, January 1978.
11. U.S. Bureau of the Census, news release, December 1, 1978. Also Robert
W. Lake, "Racial Transition and Black Homeownership in American Suburbs,"
The Annals of the American Academy of Political and Social Science 441 (January 1979): 142-56.

wide evidence is that, since 1975, the rate of black suburbanization has come to exceed that of white suburbanization.[12] In 1977 Chicago seemed poised on the edge of a similar experience as both westside and southside ghettos spilled over the city limits. As this happened, middle class black Chicagoans had available to them an increasing array of housing opportunities, yet the Leadership Council's goal of a colorblind housing market became even more illusory, the victim of white recalcitrance and black indifference.

12. Martin T. Katzman and Harold Childs, "Black Flight: The Middle Class Black Reaction to School Integration and Metropolitan Change," *Discussion Paper* no. 17 (Richardson: The University of Texas at Dallas, February 1979).

Index

About the Author

Brian J.L. Berry is the Williams Professor of City and Regional Planning in the Graduate School of Design and in the Department of Sociology, Harvard University. He is also Director of the Laboratory for Computer Graphics and Spatial Analysis, Chairman of the Ph.D Program in Urban Planning, and a Faculty Fellow of the Harvard Institute for International Development. From 1958 to 1976 he served as Professor of Geography at The University of Chicago, and from 1974 to 1976 as Director of that university's Center for Urban Studies. It was during his tenure at Chicago that he monitored and evaluated the fair housing programs that are the subject of this book.